Implementing Halal Principles and Regulations in Business Governance

Mohammad Nabil Almunawar
Universiti Brunei Darussalam, Brunei

Achmad Ubaedillah
Universitas Islam Negeri Syarif Hidayatullah Jakarta, Indonesia

Euis Amalia
Universitas Islam Negeri Syarif Hidayatullah Jakarta, Indonesia

Anis Malik Thoha
Universiti Islam Sultan Sharif Ali, Brunei

IGI Global
Scientific Publishing
Publishing Tomorrow's Research Today

Vice President of Editorial	Melissa Wagner
Managing Editor of Acquisitions	Mikaela Felty
Managing Editor of Book Development	Jocelynn Hessler
Production Manager	Mike Brehm
Cover Design	Phillip Shickler

Published in the United States of America by
IGI Global Scientific Publishing
701 East Chocolate Avenue
Hershey, PA, 17033, USA
Tel: 717-533-8845
Fax: 717-533-7115
Website: https://www.igi-global.com E-mail: cust@igi-global.com

Library of Congress Cataloging-in-Publication Data

Names: Almunawar, Mohammad Nabil, 1960- editor | Ubaedillah, Achmad, 1967- editor | Amalia, Euis, 1971- editor | Thoha, Anis Malik editor

Title: Implementing Halal principles and regulations in business governance / [edited by] Mohammad Nabil Almunawar, Universiti Brunei Darussalam, Brunei, Achmad Ubaedillah, Universitas Islam Negeri Syarif Hidayatullah Jakarta, Indonesia, Euis Amalia, Universitas Islam Negeri Syarif Hidayatullah Jakarta, Indonesia, Anis Malik Thoha, Universiti Islam Sultan Sharif Ali, Brunei.

Description: Hershey, PA : IGI Global Scientific Publishing, [2025] | Includes bibliographical references (pages 345-402) and index. | Summary: "This book aims to explore how a Halal technopreneur ecosystem can enhance employment opportunities for graduates"-- Provided by publisher.

Identifiers: LCCN 2025016777 (print) | LCCN 2025016778 (ebook) | ISBN 9798337339177 hardcover | ISBN 9798337339184 paperback | ISBN 9798337339191 ebook

Subjects: LCSH: Business--Religious aspects--Islam

Classification: LCC HF5388 .I677 2025 (print) | LCC HF5388 (ebook) | DDC 261.8/5--dc23/eng/20250821

LC record available at https://lccn.loc.gov/2025016777

LC ebook record available at https://lccn.loc.gov/2025016778

British Cataloguing in Publication Data
A Cataloguing in Publication record for this book is available from the British Library.

Editorial Advisory Board

Nor Surilawana Sulaiman, *Universiti Islam Sultan Sharif Ali, Brunei*
Nurul Aulia Tahta, *UIN Sunan Gunung Djati Bandung, Indonesia*

Table of Contents

Detailed Table of Contents

This study explores the intersection of economic necessity, fatwa authorities, and the construction of halal awareness among producers in the context of Indonesia's mandatory halal certification. Originally voluntary, halal certification is now obligatory for all businesses, particularly in the food sector. The government has introduced two certification pathways: regular halal certification for large-scale, high-risk products and self-declare certification for small and medium enterprises (SMEs) producing low risk goods. However, the implementation of self-declare certification raises concerns about the integrity of halal standards due to insufficient audits and the profit-driven motivations of halal certification bodies. Findings suggest that while mandatory certification enhances the visibility of halal practices, it can also result in a superficial understanding of halal, where compliance is driven more by business necessity than religious commitment.

This systematic literature review reveals that food security traditionally emphasises the availability and accessibility of nutritious food to ensure consistent utilisation. The concept of Halalan Tayyiban mandates that food should be ethically sourced and produced following Shariah law and should be accessible to all. Furthermore, it highlights the importance of sharing food with those in need and considers its impact on religious and moral development. To uphold Halalan Tayyiban standards from farm to fork, active involvement from all stakeholders is essential, particularly producers, who must ensure that consumers receive lawful and high-quality food by adhering to government regulations on Halal certification. Future research should expand the study of Halalan Tayyiban principles to encompass a wider array of agricultural issues beyond food security, to further enhance understanding of this Islamic concept.

This paper examines how Islamic finance and the *halal* industry work together to create a sustainable Shariah ecosystem. It explains how the principles of Shariah-compliant finance support the goals of the *halal* industry in promoting ethical and responsible economic practices. By analyzing case studies from Southeast Asia, the paper highlights how Islamic finance helps drive sustainable economic growth, financial inclusion, and environmental protection within the *halal* industry. It also addresses the challenges and opportunities in integrating these sectors and suggests strategies for long-term sustainability through innovative financial tools, regulatory changes, and collaboration among stakeholders. The paper concludes that a well-integrated Shariah ecosystem, combining Islamic finance and the *halal* industry, can greatly support global sustainable development goals while upholding ethical standards.

The application of halal and ṭayyib principles in slaughterhouses is important to achieve SDG goals, especially the provision of safe, healthy, and sustainable food. This research examines how the concepts of halal and ṭayyib can be applied effectively in slaughtering and distributing meat in slaughterhouses, including aspects of hygiene, waste management, and physical facility standards. The integration of these two principles aims to ensure that every stage of the production and distribution process complies with Islamic law, as well as meets environmental sustainability standards. It also highlights the importance of changing work culture, implementing strict regulations, and monitoring distribution to ensure the quality of the meat products produced is maintained throughout the years. consumer's hands.

This Chapter explores how leather products can meet halal standards. It serves as a guide for industry professionals to ensure halal compliance from sourcing raw materials to final processing and certification, addressing the increasing global demand for halal products. The chapter specifically examines halal standards in Indonesia, which prohibits leather from dogs and pigs and mandates that products remain free from haram contamination. It discusses halal-compliant processing methods, focusing on permissible tanning techniques and the use of additives that do not contain haram substances. An overview of halal certification procedures is provided, detailing compliance criteria and the role of certifying bodies in verifying halal status. The chapter acknowledges challenges such as sourcing halal materials, production costs, and contamination risks, offering practical solutions for manufacturers. Ultimately, it aims to equip businesses with the knowledge needed to meet halal standards, ensuring consumer trust and enhancing market competitiveness.

Brunei Darussalam has been a Malay Muslim Monarchy for six centuries and the country follows the Sunni Shafite sect of Islam as its official religion. In 2005 the government introduced the Halal Certificate and Halal Label Order, which was amended and revised in 2017 making it compulsory for all food and beverages industry serving Muslim population to apply for the halal certificate. There is limited literature on how enterprises adopt and adapt to these new laws, seven years after it was made mandatory. This research aims to bridge this gap by exploring the state of halal certification,gauging businesses understanding and experiences with the certification process. The research uses qualitative, primary data collection, through semi-interviews with owners and managers of micro and small food enterprises. This research hopes to provide valuable data that can improve the development of a

The increasing global halal awareness also impacts the world of health. In the world of health, vaccination is one of the simplest, safest, and effective ways to protect humans from dangerous diseases. Vaccinations are still vulnerable to criticism for their halal status because the enzymes used in the past were mostly sourced from non-halal or prohibited materials. Now, through genetic engineering, enzymes sourced from non-halal or prohibited materials can be replaced. Indeed, one of the critical points of vaccine production is enzymes. As catalysts for organic chemical or biochemical reactions, enzymes are critical points in halal pharmaceuticals, including halal vaccines. Therefore, by embracing literature review and case studies, this chapter will focus on three issues as a discussion: (1) the mainstream biochemical process in vaccine production; (2) biochemical transformation of halal vaccine production through genetic engineering; (3) implications of halal vaccine production through genetic engineering for economies of scale.

This study aimed to determine the level of understanding of non-Muslim restaurant operators in one of the 1st class city in the Philippines towards halal. 30 restaurant managers of casual dining restaurants participated in the conduct of this study. Descriptive type of research was utilized to determine the level of understanding of the restaurant operators towards halal. Results showed that overall, the respondents have high understanding towards halal. This study can serve as a reference to encourage the key players of the restaurant industries and the related government agencies to work hand-in-hand to see the potential of halal market in boosting the tourism industry of the locality.

Preface

INTRODUCTION

In an era of increasing globalization and consumer awareness, the principles of Halal governance have taken center stage in various industries, particularly in food, finance, and pharmaceuticals. The concept of Halal is not merely a religious directive but a comprehensive framework that ensures ethical business practices, sustainability, and consumer trust. As economies continue to integrate and diversify, the need for standardized Halal regulations and their implementation in business governance has never been more critical. This edited volume, *Implementing Halal Principles and Regulations in Business Governance*, seeks to provide a holistic examination of halal practices across multiple sectors, offering insights into both the challenges and opportunities within this evolving field.

The research presented in this book highlights the multifaceted nature of Halal compliance, spanning from regulatory frameworks and certification processes to marketing strategies and innovative technological advancements. By bringing together scholars and practitioners from diverse backgrounds, this volume aims to bridge the gap between theoretical discourse and practical application. The chapters delve into various aspects of Halal governance, illustrating how businesses navigate regulatory landscapes while maintaining ethical integrity and consumer confidence.

This book is particularly relevant for policymakers, industry professionals, academicians, and researchers invested in the development and enhancement of Halal business governance. It serves as a resource for understanding the global impact of Halal regulations, addressing key issues such as economic necessity, sustainable development, consumer behavior, and technological innovation. Through rigorous research and case studies, the contributors provide valuable recommendations for enhancing Halal compliance and fostering a sustainable Halal ecosystem.

CHAPTER OVERVIEW

Chapter 1 explores how Indonesia's mandatory Halal certification influences producer behavior, balancing economic necessity with religious commitment. The study highlights the challenges posed by self-declared certifications and the role of fatwa authorities in ensuring compliance.

Chapter 2 presents a systematic review of *Halalan Tayyiban* principles in food security, emphasizing ethical food production and accessibility. The research calls for greater stakeholder involvement in maintaining halal integrity throughout the supply chain.

Chapter 3 examines the intersection of Islamic finance and the Halal industry, demonstrating how financial tools and regulatory frameworks contribute to a sustainable, Shariah-compliant ecosystem.

Chapter 4 discusses the application of *Halalan Tayyiban* principles in slaughterhouses, linking these practices to the United Nations Sustainable Development Goals (SDGs). The chapter highlights the importance of hygiene, waste management, and regulatory oversight in meat production.

Chapter 5 focuses on ensuring Halal compliance in the leather industry, addressing challenges such as raw material sourcing, production processes, and certification requirements. It provides insights into maintaining Halal integrity while navigating industry constraints.

Chapter 6 investigates the implementation of Halal certification in Brunei Darussalam's food and beverage sector. It presents qualitative research on how businesses adapt to evolving Halal regulations and certification mandates.

Chapter 7 explores the role of a Halal technopreneur ecosystem in promoting employment opportunities for graduates. The study proposes a framework for integrating education, policy, and industry collaboration to foster job creation in the Halal sector.

Chapter 8 examines the impact of innovative Islamic leadership on Halal SMEs in Indonesia. Through quantitative analysis, the research demonstrates how leadership practices enhance business performance and competitive advantage.

Chapter 9 delves into the application of Halal and Tayyib norms in Islamic marketing. It explores how these principles influence branding, consumer engagement, and Halal market segmentation.

Chapter 10 investigates how religiosity moderates Halal purchase decisions. The study examines consumer awareness, certification influence, and marketing strategies, revealing insights into factors shaping Halal consumer behavior.

Chapter 11 discusses the role of genetic engineering in Halal vaccine production. The chapter explores biochemical transformations, regulatory considerations, and the economic implications of Halal-compliant pharmaceuticals.

Chapter 12 assesses the understanding of Halal principles among non-Muslim restaurant operators in the Philippines. The research highlights the potential of Halal tourism and emphasizes the importance of cross-cultural awareness in the food service industry.

CONCLUSION

The contributions in this volume collectively illustrate the growing significance of Halal governance in contemporary business practices. By examining the intersection of regulation, industry dynamics, and consumer behavior, this book sheds light on the intricate processes that define Halal compliance. The research presented underscores the necessity of robust certification systems, ethical leadership, and technological innovation to ensure the continued growth and sustainability of the Halal industry.

As Halal principles extend beyond religious obligations to encompass ethical and sustainable business practices, there is a pressing need for continuous research and policy development. This book provides valuable insights that can guide future advancements in Halal governance, fostering a business environment that aligns with both regulatory standards and consumer expectations.

We hope that this volume serves as a useful resource for scholars, practitioners, and policymakers, inspiring further discussions and research on the evolving landscape of Halal business governance. We extend our gratitude to the contributing authors for their dedication and expertise in shaping this important discourse.

Mohammad Nabil Almunawar
Universiti Brunei Darussalam, Brunei

Achmad Ubaedillah
Universitas Islam Negeri Syarif Hidayatullah Jakarta, Indonesia

Euis Amalia
Universitas Islam Negeri Syarif Hidayatullah Jakarta, Indonesia

Anis Malik Thoha
Universiti Islam Sultan Sharif Ali, Brunei

Chapter 1
Economic Necessity, Fatwa Authorities, and Halal Awareness:
How Mandatory Certification Shapes Producer Practices

Nikmatul Masruroh
https://orcid.org/0000-0003-1122-0589
Universitas Islam Negeri Kiai Haji Achmad Siddiq Jember, Indonesia

Muhammad Fauzinudin Faiz
https://orcid.org/0000-0001-7076-4549
Universitas Islam Negeri Kiai Haji Achmad Siddiq Jember, Indonesia

ABSTRACT

This study explores the intersection of economic necessity, fatwa authorities, and the construction of halal awareness among producers in the context of Indonesia's mandatory halal certification. Originally voluntary, halal certification is now obligatory for all businesses, particularly in the food sector. The government has introduced two certification pathways: regular halal certification for large-scale, high-risk products and self-declare certification for small and medium enterprises (SMEs) producing low risk goods. However, the implementation of self-declare certification raises concerns about the integrity of halal standards due to insufficient audits and the profit-driven motivations of halal certification bodies. Findings suggest that while mandatory certification enhances the visibility of halal practices, it can also result in a superficial understanding of halal, where compliance is driven more by business necessity than religious commitment.

DOI: 10.4018/979-8-3373-3917-7.ch001

INTRODUCTION

In recent years, halal certification in Indonesia has undergone significant regulatory transformations following the enactment of Law number. 33 of 2014 on Halal Product Assurance (Saviera et al., 2024). This regulation marked a crucial shift from voluntary to mandatory halal certification, making it a legal requirement for all businesses, especially those in the food industry (Aziz et al., 2021). The law's introduction has not only redefined the role of halal certification but has also led to major institutional changes (Rusydiana & Mahsyar, 2024). Previously, all halal certification activities, from registration to audit and issuance of halal logos, were managed by the Indonesian Ulama Council (MUI) through its Assessment Institute for Food, Drug and Cosmetics-The Indonesian Ulama Council (AIFDC-MUI) body (Rachman, 2019). However, with the implementation of the new law, the responsibility has transitioned to the Halal Product Assurance Organizing Agency (BPJPH), under the Ministry of Religious Affairs (Nurein, 2023).

This regulatory shift has transformed the meaning of "halal" from a purely religious principle to a market-driven attribute of traded products (Indung Amalia & Nahidloh, 2023). While traditionally "halal" referred strictly to religious permissibility, under the new framework, it is increasingly associated with product safety and consumer protection (Jamil et al., 2020; Nursita et al., 2024). This evolution in meaning stems from growing consumer demands for assurance regarding the integrity of products in the marketplace. Prior to mandatory certification, several incidents revealed the presence of prohibited substances, such as pork derivatives and harmful chemicals, in food products. For instance, the Ajinomoto scandal in 2003 and the controversy surrounding carmine, a colorant derived from insects, underscored the necessity for stricter halal oversight to prevent public health risks (Masruroh, 2020b).

These incidents led to a growing mistrust among consumers, fundamentally altering purchasing behaviors. Where products were once sold with little scrutiny, market demand began to shift in response to violations of halal standards (Masruroh et al., 2024). The classical economic theory by Jean-Baptiste Say, which asserts that supply creates its own demand, proved ineffective in this context, as consumer skepticism disrupted the traditional supply-demand dynamic (Spithoven, 1996). The breakdown in market trust compelled consumers to demand greater assurances regarding product safety and compliance. In response, the Indonesian government introduced mandatory halal certification under Law No. 33 of 2014, aimed at restoring consumer confidence and regulating industry practices (Loussaief et al., 2024).

Although the implementation of this law has been gradual, on October 17, 2021, the Indonesian government, through BPJPH, introduced a comprehensive plan to ensure that all products eventually receive halal certification. This initiative aligns with Indonesia's ambition to become a global leader in the halal industry (Zuhudi

& Dolah, 2021). With halal no longer a purely national issue, many countries are competing to establish themselves as the "World Halal Center." By 2024, Indonesia aims to achieve this status by facilitating certification through cost-free programs, such as the self-declaration certification and the Free Halal Certification Program (SEHATI) initiative, especially for small and medium enterprises (SMEs). These efforts have elevated Indonesia's position in the global halal industry, moving from 5th place in 2022/2023 to 3rd place in the 2023/2024 Global Islamic Economy Indicator (SGIER). (This paragraph can be followed by data visualization or a table if necessary):

Table 1. Country rankings in the Halal industry according to the SGIER index

Number	Country	GIEI	Islamic Finance	Halal Food	Travel	Fashion	Tourism and Media	Medicine and Cosmetic
1	Malaysia	193,2	408.7	128.0	99.4	73.6	74.4	73.9
2	The Kingdom of Saudi Arabia	93.6	194.9	48.5	99.7	34.3	37.5	34.3
3	Indonesia	80.1	93.2	94.4	60.7	66.3	52.4	58.6
4	United Arab Emirates	79.8	115.7	59.2	136.2	51.3	44.5	41.3
5	Bahrain	75.0	125.1	55.0	88.1	33.4	49.6	38.5
6	Iran	74.6	159.8	41.2	65.7	20.5	24.2	33.1
7	Turkiye	74.0	46.1	85.1	161.8	86.2	46.0	52.6
8	Singapore	62.7	52.2	67.7	50.3	64.3	72.6	79.9
9	Kuwait	60.2	123.6	42.2	28.7	20.0	26.8	29.2
10	Qatar	57.1	74.4	49.7	60.4	37.4	63.3	37.2
11	Jordan	52.2	65.6	49.4	88.3	22.1	26.8	29.2
12	Oman	50.0	78.7	48.3	48.0	20.1	24.4	26.3
13	Pakistan	47.5	69.6	51.4	38.4	27.5	17.2	28.6
14	South Africa	44.7	51.1	53.8	25.3	32.4	31.9	43.2
15	England	44.7	46.0	43.7	28.1	47.7	54.4	48.2

Source: 2023/2024 GIEI Report

The data indicate a positive trend in the growth of Indonesia's halal industry, particularly in the food sector, as the implementation of halal certification has been carried out in stages. The food industry represents the first phase of the certification process, and as a result, it remains the government's primary focus (Junaidi, 2020).

The trend indicates that Indonesian producers or business actors are increasingly attentive to halal certification (Jeaheng et al., 2019a). However, this awareness is primarily driven by producers' fears of being unable to sell their products domestically or internationally. Small business owners, in particular, worry about missing out on government support if they lack certification (Bashir, 2019). Consequently, businesses of all sizes are pursuing halal certification in large numbers. This awareness is not rooted in the religious consciousness of producers or business actors but rather in compliance with legislation and a fear of losing market access without proper legal standing (Nusran et al., 2018).

As a result, even if producers or business actors do not fully understand the religious significance of "halal," they still seek certification to ensure their products can compete in both national and international markets. This means that the motivation for halal certification stems not from religious obligations as Muslim producers but from a profit-oriented drive within the business world. In this context, halal certification is crucial for enhancing product quality and achieving a competitive edge, as certified products undergo detailed audits by Assessment Institute for Food, Drug and Cosmetics-The Indonesian Ulama Council (AIFDC-MUI) or halal auditors from production to final distribution (farm to fork). This certification thereby acts as a barrier against competitors in the market (Tan et al., 2020).

In terms of religiosity, however, this is actually the primary factor; the demand for "halal" originates from consumer concerns over food standards that may not meet "halal" criteria according to Islamic law, as well as health standards. Nonetheless, for producers, religiosity is not the primary consideration, and some business actors still lack an understanding of the religious context of halal in production. Thus, from a religious perspective, when viewed from the supply side, halal certification is not given significant attention (Hew et al., 2020).

In this context, the mandatory requirement for halal certification has fostered a sense of halal awareness among producers, driven more by business concerns and the fear of potential penalties rather than by religious commitment to producing "*halalan thoyyiban*" (lawful and good) products as prescribed by faith. Amid increasingly intense business competition and rising demands for product quality and safety both nationally and internationally, this mandate plays a crucial role. Additionally, the transfer of halal certification authority from the Indonesian Ulema Council (MUI) to BPJPH (The Halal Product Assurance Organizing Agency) has influenced the development of this business-centered awareness among producers. Previously, MUI's authority over halal certification was not as authoritative as that of BPJPH, which operates under the Ministry of Religious Affairs. This shift has made halal certification a formal government mandate, compelling producers to seek certification, especially given the penalties for non-compliance (Lia Febriati et al., 2024).

This shift does not eliminate MUI's role; rather, MUI remains essential as the institution issuing fatwas on a product's halal status. BPJPH administers the certification process, while MUI provides the halal rulings. Where previously Assessment Institute for Food, Drug and Cosmetics-The Indonesian Ulama Council (AIFDC-MUI) was the sole Halal Examination Agency (LPH), BPJPH has since authorized other qualifying agencies, such as Sucofindo, Surveyor Indonesia, and others. By 2022, BPJPH had appointed 28 LPHs to expedite the halal certification process (Saidi & Sazali, 2024).

As a result, three parties are now involved in halal certification: BPJPH, responsible for organizing halal product assurance; LPH, which handles document review, audit scheduling, conducting audits, auditor meetings, issuing audit memoranda, and submitting audit reports to MUI's Fatwa Commission; and MUI, which determines the halal status of products based on the audit results and issues the MUI halal certification.

The process demonstrates that obtaining halal certification is not straightforward, as it involves several stages. However, when the government introduced free halal certification through self-declaration, especially for small businesses, it raised challenges in the field regarding the actual practices of producers seeking halal certification. Although self-declaration for MSMEs (Micro, Small, and Medium Enterprises) requires the assistance of Halal Product Companions (PPH), this often seems to be a mere formality, as the audit process is less stringent than in regular halal certification.

As a result, small business owners who have received halal certification often feel that it holds little significance for them beyond qualifying for government support. For some, having halal certification is just a matter of obtaining the label and logo, while the actual process or ingredients of their products may not fully adhere to halal standards. Additionally, there is currently no mechanism in place for monitoring or evaluating MSMEs or business owners who already hold halal certification. There is concern that these businesses may comply with halal standards only during the certification process, potentially reverting to non-compliant practices afterward (Izza et al., 2024).

Thus, this article will discuss three key areas: *first*, the obligation of halal certification for producers, particularly MSMEs; *second*, the role of fatwa authorities in fostering halal awareness among producers; and *third*, economic pressures as the primary driver for producers to pursue halal certification. In other words, the main motivation behind halal certification is economic incentive rather than religious commitment.

The theoretical gap in this study lies in the theory that the religious consciousness that Muslims have should have an impact on their behavior, both economic behavior and daily behavior. A person's faith should be able to make a producer more religious, so that he will be more compliant with the halal povisions set by religion and set by the state. Thus, the consciousness of producers is not a pseudo-consciousness, but really an awareness to become a human being oriented towards fame.

HALAL AWARENESS

Discussions on halal awareness have traditionally focused on the demand side, with little attention given to halal awareness emerging from the supply side. In this study, halal awareness is viewed through two dimensions: religious awareness and business awareness. From a religious perspective, halal awareness embodies shariah compliance—namely, a Muslim's adherence to Islamic principles. This means conducting all activities out of a commitment to follow the rules established by the faith (Usman et al., 2023).

In Islam, the concept of halal is fundamental. Halal refers to what is permissible according to Islamic law. As defined by Yusuf Al-Qaradawi (2014), halal is something that unties a harmful restriction, allowing what Allah has permitted. In contrast, haram is what Allah has explicitly forbidden, and those who defy this prohibition will face Allah's punishment in the hereafter, as well as potential sanctions in this world (Mutmainah, 2018).

According to Imam Al-Ghazali, the obligation to seek what is halal is based on a hadith of the Prophet Muhammad (peace be upon him), which states, "Seeking halal is obligatory for every Muslim." Al-Ghazali considers the pursuit of halal to be a wise priority among other religious obligations. Halal is clearly defined, as is haram, but between them lies shubhat—things that are ambiguous and difficult to distinguish (Al-Ghazali, 2001).

According to Shihab (2002), the term halal originates from a root word meaning "free" or "unbound." The permissibility of an item implies freedom from worldly and spiritual harm. Linguistically, halal means permissible, signifying religious approval and covering various categories, including recommended actions, discouraged actions (makruh), and neutral actions (mubah). Therefore, something may be halal yet not encouraged, which is considered makruh. For example, Prophet Muhammad (peace be upon him) discouraged entering a mosque after consuming garlic (Shihab, 2002).

Al-Sa'di (1992) defines halal food as food that is permissible for consumption—meaning it is not obtained without the owner's consent, is not stolen, is not produced through prohibited transactions, and is free from any inherently forbidden substances (Ahmad Taufik, 2014).This interpretation implies that halal food is more abundant than haram food. Allah has already provided for human needs according to each individual's requirements, ensuring that there should be no shortage in fulfilling those needs (Choiriyah, 2016). According to Baqr as-Sadr, what should be evaluated is the distribution process, which is often unequal and even controlled by those in power (Kusuma, 2023). This statement contrasts with Thomas R. Malthus' population theory, which argues that excessive population growth will lead to destruction (Hansen & Prescott, 2002).

In the Qur'an, halal food is also described as tayyib, meaning food that is wholesome, nutritious, and balanced, without any harmful effects on the consumer's body or mind. In essence, halal food can be defined as food that is permitted in Islam, considering its ingredients, sourcing, processing, and packaging. Additionally, it should be nutritious, healthy, and safe for consumption (Jannah & Al-Banna, 2021).

Thus, in religious terms, halal awareness can be understood as the commitment to conduct all activities in accordance with shariah law. In the context of production, this means that producers ensure halal standards at every stage—from selecting raw materials to presenting the final product—ensuring all aspects uphold halal values. There must be no elements of theft, injustice, *gharar* (uncertainty), or riba (usury). Consequently, halal awareness signifies a commitment among business actors to comply with shariah principles in their business practices (Krishnan et al., 2017).

In a business or economic context, the meaning of halal awareness is not significantly different; however, it is often interpreted with a focus on achieving greater profitability. This understanding is supported by Law No. 33 of 2014 on Halal Product Assurance (JPH), which mandates that the halal production process generally requires the separation of facilities, equipment, processing, storage, packaging, distribution, sale, and serving of halal products from those that are non-halal or contain non-halal elements. The facilities, spaces, and equipment used in the halal production process must be kept clean, hygienic, free from impurities, and free from any non-halal materials. Clear standards of assurance are essential to avoid any consumer doubt regarding the halal status of products (Kamarulzaman et al., 2018).

Riaz (2019) distinguishes between the production processes for animal-based and plant-based products. The production of animal-based products is more stringent due to the essential role of the slaughtering process in preparing animal-based foods. The Islamic criteria for slaughtering animals are strict, requiring practices such as reciting basmalah (in the name of Allah), using a sharp cutting tool, and ensuring that the animal's neck is not completely severed. In contrast, plant-based products are generally considered halal unless they are intoxicating or harmful (Riaz et al., 2018; Riaz & Riaz, 2023).

In modern processing facilities, animal and plant products may be handled in the same location and with the same equipment, leading to potential cross-contamination. For example, in some facilities, pork, peanuts, and corn are canned using shared equipment. However, with proper cleaning procedures and the separation of halal and non-halal production, contamination can be avoided. In vegetable processing, animal-derived ingredients, such as gelatin and anti-foaming agents, must be avoided.

If non-halal substances are deliberately introduced in plant-based production, the product can become non-halal. Therefore, processing equipment and production methods need careful monitoring to maintain the halal status of plant-based products (Regenstein et al., 2003).

Food ingredients, both plant-based and animal-based, require careful attention. To eliminate consumer doubts, companies must evaluate their products and apply for halal certification (Al Mazeedi et al., 2013; Kamaruddin et al., 2012). Beyond raw ingredients, other crucial aspects of halal production include labeling, packaging, and coatings.

1) *Labeling*

Batch of label are used for consumers, so labels must be descriptive, clear and meaningful. Product with halal packaging should have the product brand name, minimum matrix content information of the manufacturing material, a code representing batch information, manufacturer and expiration date, and most importantly a halal logo from a recognized certified authority (Soong, 2007)

Ingredient labels typically do not indicate the source of ingredients, such as processing aids, agents, carriers, or raw material origins (Potter & Hotchkiss, 1995). This creates challenges for Muslim consumers. For instance, in Europe, chocolate companies may use up to 5% vegetable or animal fat in products labeled simply as chocolate. To gain consumer trust, these products should obtain halal certification and display a halal label on their packaging. Proper halal certification, the correct halal marking, and logo on products are essential for consumers to confidently identify halal products. Simply reading the ingredient label is often insufficient to determine if a processed food is permissible (Talib et al., 2010).

If a company aims to attract additional consumers, such as Muslims, Jews, and vegetarians, it should include labels indicating ingredient sources, whether animal- or plant-based. This can enhance consumer interest and encourage purchases. Language is also important in making products more appealing; for example, in the U.S., bilingual labeling is required for imported products to facilitate understanding of ingredient composition (Mohammed et al., 2008). Labels serve as identifiers for products in the market; a "kosher" label indicates suitanability for Jewish consumers, while a "halal" label targets Muslim consumers. However, non-Muslims may also choose halal-labeled products, as these are often perceived to be safer than those without such labels.

According to Kotler and Keller (2016), the functions of a product label include the following: *First*, product identification, which involves tracing basic product information such as the name, brand, product type, and place of manufacture. This is essential as fundamental information for consumers. *Second*, consumer information, where the label acts as a representation to provide product details to consumers. This information includes composition, nutritional content, expiration date, and usage instructions. *Third,* safety and health, indicating that these aspects are key advantages of a product. The presence of a label helps establish a safety barrier to entry by ensuring consumers are aware of allergen content, halal certification, and other safety standards. There are various standardizations used in international trade, with health and safety standards being among the most important, both for national and international markets. *Fourth*, promotion and branding. Labels contribute to product promotion and branding through attractive designs, compelling slogans, and informative details that can capture consumers' interest. *Fifth*, legal compliance. A label serves as a form of legal compliance with government regulations, such as the Indonesian National Standards (SNI) (Kotler & Keller, 2016).

2) *Packaging*

In North America, halal food products are often manufactured in facilities that also process non-halal items. Many employees working in these environments are non-Muslims who may have limited or no understanding of halal standards, and some may even be unfamiliar with the concept altogether, as noted by Minkus-McKenna (2007). This situation has prompted business owners to engage with halal certification bodies to develop specific operational standards that ensure the integrity of halal production (Muttaqin et al., 2023).

These standards emphasize the importance of carefully organized procedures to prevent any form of cross-contamination and to uphold halal guidelines. For instance, halal products are stored separately from non-halal items, and production schedules are meticulously arranged to avoid accidental cross-contact. Specific personnel are designated to monitor halal production areas, maintaining vigilance over these critical spaces. Additionally, workers are instructed not to bring personal food into these production zones, reinforcing the importance of a contaminant-free environment. Hygiene practices, such as mandatory handwashing before entering production areas, are also emphasized to maintain the purity of the production process (Savitri & Perwita, 2020).

The care and attention required to achieve halal certification in a non-Muslim-majority country like the United States underscore a significant commitment to producing safe, high-quality food that meets halal standards. In packaging, too, there are stringent requirements: areas must be entirely free from any prohibited substances, and containers, including those made from materials such as metal or plastic, must be sterilized before use to prevent any possible contamination from non-halal substances like pork fat. Through these measures, halal certification plays a vital role in ensuring the sustainability and acceptability of these products, allowing businesses to meet both ethical and religious standards in food production (Millatina et al., 2022).

3) *Coating*

Labeling and packaging represent the final stages of halal food production, with coating also forming part of this finishing process. Coating refers to a layer applied to food to preserve or enhance its appearance. For example, in the UK, coatings help retain moisture in food (Labuza and Contrereas-Medellin, 1981). Today, coatings are used for products like sausages, chocolate coatings on nuts and fruits, and wax coatings on fruits and vegetables (Tarannum et al., 2024).

The coating materials used must also be derived from halal sources. Specifying ingredient sources is essential to educate the public on food additives. Advances in food technology mean that even plant-based foods could become non-halal, depending on added substances. Understanding the halal value chain is thus important for consumers prior to purchasing or consuming food products (Tieman et al., 2012).

Reflecting on the explanation above, halal awareness from a business perspective actually reinforces and strengthens the religious meaning of "halal" through regulatory measures. In business terms, an enterprise is considered to exhibit halal awareness if it adheres to principles of the halal value chain—specifically traceability—and implements them by obtaining halal certification. After certification, the business should display the halal logo and provide information on ingredients and nutritional content for consumers. Post-certification, the business should maintain halal production practices independently, demonstrating a commitment to halal principles not only for business compliance but also to meet Shariah standards (Tarannum et al., 2024).

These two forms of awareness—religious and business-driven—differ in their motivations: from a religious standpoint, halal practices reflect obedience to Allah SWT, whereas from a business perspective, they represent compliance with regulations and responsiveness to consumer needs. Aligning these motivations is essential to prevent the halal certification process from becoming solely business-oriented, ensuring it remains true to both regulatory and religious commitments.

The Economic Value of Halal Certification

The shift from a voluntary to a mandatory halal certification model has impacted the pattern of halal awareness among producers. As of October 17, 2024, all food products distributed in Indonesia must have halal certification, altering the dynamics of halal certification within the country. Initially, businesses could choose whether or not to obtain halal certification; now, it is required, with penalties for non-compliance (Letsoin & Riorini, 2023).

Products lacking halal certification cannot be distributed nationally or internationally, underscoring the commitment of both the government and business owners to halal certification. In theory, halal certification applications in Indonesia are divided into two types: large companies follow a standard, paid halal certification model, while small and micro-enterprises use a government-sponsored, free self-declaration process, though only with guidance from Halal Product Companions (PPH) (Margarena & Ikhwan Setiawan, 2022).

In Indonesia, the fact that there are significantly more small and micro-enterprises highlights that self-declared halal certification is more prevalent than standard halal certification. This shift has economic implications. With regulations prohibiting the sale of non-halal-certified products, business owners are compelled to certify their products, even if reluctantly, as failing to do so would prevent them from entering the market (Hidayati et al., 2023).

Using Michael E. Porter's theory, halal-certified products become differentiated products, meaning they possess advantages over other products. Differentiated products can outperform competitors in the market, with distinctions that extend beyond physical or quality attributes. From raw materials to marketing processes, halal-certified products hold unique advantages and stand out from other companies (Polo & Weber, 2010; Porter, 1997) .

Porter's (1990) concept of differentiation requires that each production unit offers a distinct advantage or uniqueness. Differentiation enables a company to deliver superior performance compared to its competitors. This concept grows out of the company's value chain, as each value activity can serve as a potential source of uniqueness. The procurement of raw materials and other inputs can influence the performance of the final product, thereby impacting differentiation (Hole et al., 2019; Weil, 1985).

Based on several studies, the relationship between trade and halal branding can be illustrated as follows:

Figure 1. Relationship of Halal branding in trade

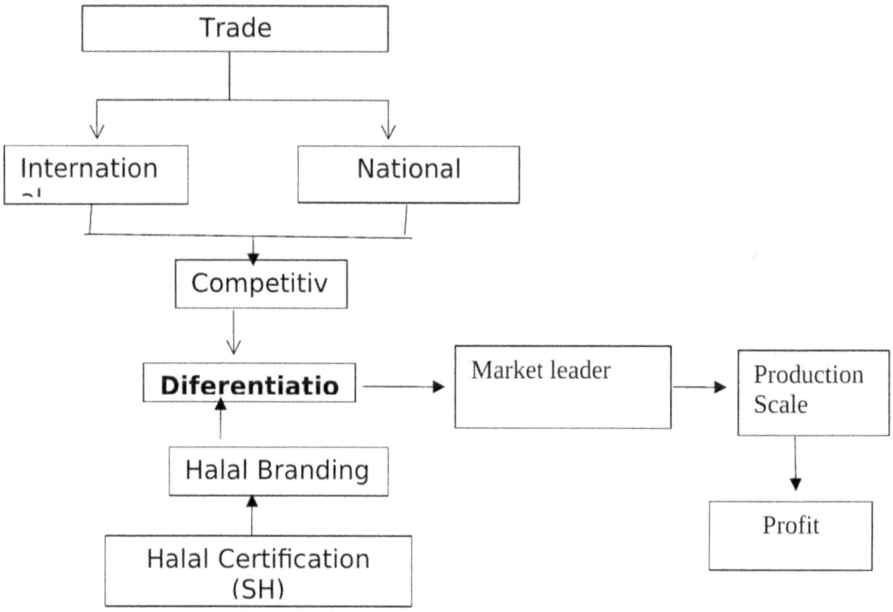

The figure illustrates that products with halal certification gain a unique branding that differentiates them from other products. This differentiation allows halal-branded products to capture the market more effectively and outperform competitors, thereby expanding market penetration. As the market grows, production scale and volume also increase. With higher production scales, certified halal products can generate larger profits (Masruroh et al., 2021)

Additionally, halal-certified products are ideally zero-waste, aligning with the goals of a green economy and the Sustainable Development Goals (SDGs). These products are projected to be sustainable, as they appeal to a broader market and support increased production scale. This expanded market share contributes to business sustainability by securing a defined market segment for halal-certified products (Vanany et al., 2019) .

The value chain in the company's products is that each process contains halal. From the raw materials to the marketing process that is carried out constain halal value chain.: *first;* special nurseries for products of natural origin. This process is carried with the Company Work Plan and Budget (CWBP). *Second;* in the process of planting (if agricultural products. *Third;* delivery from land is carried out by vehicles that are holy from uncleanness. *Fourth,* pesticide residues are minimized. *Fifth;* delivery is carried out every day, the process of receiving goods to the production process using halal standarts. *Sixth;* packaging using halal labels in accordance with the destination country of each region and finally shipping using halal standardization.

The Role of Fatwa Authorities in Halal Certification

In the halal certification process, several key stakeholders are involved, each with a specific role. These stakeholders include Business Actors (PU), BPJPH (the Halal Product Assurance Agency), LPH (Halal Examination Agencies), PPH (Halal Product Companions), Halal Supervisors, halal auditors, and MUI (the Indonesian Ulema Council). Each entity has a distinct function. The MUI's role in halal certification involves issuing religious rulings (fatwas). Thus, after the audit conducted by an LPH, the decision to grant halal certification is based on the fatwa issued by MUI.

In Indonesia, MUI is the sole fatwa-issuing authority for both regular and self-declared halal certification. When halal certification was still voluntary, MUI not only served as the fatwa authority but also acted as an auditor through Assessment Institute for Food, Drug and Cosmetics-The Indonesian Ulama Council (AIFDC-MUI). However, with halal certification now mandatory, BPJPH under the Ministry of Religious Affairs oversees the certification process, while Assessment Institute for Food, Drug and Cosmetics-The Indonesian Ulama Council (AIFDC-MUI) operates as one of the LPHs, and MUI retains its role as the fatwa-issuing authority (Muizzuddin et al., 2023).

In North America, halal food products are often manufactured in facilities that also process non-halal items. Many employees working in these environments are non-Muslims who may have limited or no understanding of halal standards, and some may even be unfamiliar with the concept altogether, as noted by Minkus-McKenna (2007). This situation has prompted business owners to engage with halal certification bodies to develop specific operational standards that ensure the integrity of halal production (Abdul Mokti et al., 2024).

These standards emphasize the importance of carefully organized procedures to prevent any form of cross-contamination and to uphold halal guidelines. For instance, halal products are stored separately from non-halal items, and production schedules are meticulously arranged to avoid accidental cross-contact. Specific personnel are designated to monitor halal production areas, maintaining vigilance over these critical spaces. Additionally, workers are instructed not to bring personal food into these production zones, reinforcing the importance of a contaminant-free environment. Hygiene practices, such as mandatory handwashing before entering production areas, are also emphasized to maintain the purity of the production process (Loussaief et al., 2024).

The care and attention required to achieve halal certification in a non-Muslim-majority country like the United States underscore a significant commitment to producing safe, high-quality food that meets halal standards. In packaging, too, there are stringent requirements: areas must be entirely free from any prohibited substances, and containers, including those made from materials such as metal or plastic, must be sterilized before use to prevent any possible contamination from non-halal substances like pork fat. Through these measures, halal certification plays a vital role in ensuring the sustainability and acceptability of these products, allowing businesses to meet both ethical and religious standards in food production (Jeaheng et al., 2019b).

DISCUSSION

Mandatory Halal Certification in Business Practices for Producers

The requirement for mandatory halal certification has significant implications for business practices among producers. This obligation ensures that all products intended for consumption, especially in Muslim-majority regions, comply with Islamic law. For producers, this means that all stages—from sourcing and handling raw materials to production, packaging, and distribution—must adhere to halal standards (Zuhudi & Dolah, 2021).

Implementing mandatory certification impacts small and large enterprises differently. Larger companies typically have established processes and resources for compliance, while smaller businesses may face challenges in meeting halal requirements due to limited resources. However, the self-declared certification option, available for small and micro-businesses, helps ease the burden by providing government assistance through Halal Product Companions (PPH) (Usman et al., 2023).

Mandatory halal certification also encourages producers to improve transparency and product traceability, fostering consumer trust and expanding market reach. This regulatory requirement not only supports religious compliance but also aligns with broader quality assurance and safety standards, promoting the competitive advantage of halal-certified products domestically and internationally (Poniman, Purchase, & Sneddon, 2015).

Halal certification has become a mandatory requirement for business operators, driven by several key principles that underscore its significance. First and foremost, this certification ensures product safety and health, providing a layer of consumer protection by guaranteeing that products meet strict safety and health standards. This aspect of certification is essential in building consumer trust, particularly among

Muslim consumers, as it assures them that the products they consume are not only permissible but also safe (Hew et al., 2020).

In addition to safety, halal certification enhances product competitiveness, offering a distinct advantage in both domestic and international markets. The certification process differentiates halal-certified products from their uncertified counterparts, making them more appealing to a global market with a growing demand for halal options. This competitive edge has led many businesses to prioritize certification to capture a broader audience (Tumiwa et al., 2023).

For Muslim producers, halal certification also reflects a deeper commitment to social and moral responsibility (Santoso & Rachman, 2023). It demonstrates a dedication to producing goods that align with the concept of *halalan thoyyiban*, or products that are lawful and wholesome according to Islamic principles (Bayumi et al., 2022). This commitment extends beyond mere compliance, embodying an ethical stance that resonates with the values of integrity and accountability (Bakhtiar et al., 2022).

Moreover, halal certification is a means of complying with Islamic law and regulatory requirements (Chan et al., 2019). It serves as formal recognition of a business's adherence to Shariah law and the standards set by relevant authorities, affirming that the products have been produced in accordance with religious and legal standards. Collectively, these principles make halal certification a crucial aspect of ethical and responsible business practices, benefiting consumers and producers alike in a marketplace that values quality, safety, and compliance (Poniman, Purchase, Sneddon, et al., 2015).

These are the ideal, normative reasons for the existence of halal-certified products. However, in practice, as research on companies and MSMEs indicates, strong economic motives, particularly the goal of maximizing profits, also play a significant role. Halal certification allows products to reach a wider market, increasing production volume. Additionally, the practice of halal certification in Indonesia is divided into two types: regular halal certification and self-declared halal certification, each with different target groups and impacts (Muharam & Asutay, 2019).

Regular halal certification is granted to large-scale companies or businesses using animal-based raw materials, such as poultry and beef (Khan & Khan, 2019). This type of certification involves a formal application and fee, valid for four years. In this model, the halal audit is conducted according to established rules, with the process managed by an LPH (Halal Examination Agency) and requiring a halal supervisor. Businesses under this model undergo closer monitoring and oversight (Suhartanto et al., 2024).

In contrast, self-declared halal certification is a much simpler process. For MSMEs, especially small and micro businesses, it only requires a declaration that the raw materials used are halal, with oversight from a Halal Product Companion

(PPH) (Ariska et al., 2024). This documentation is then submitted through the ptsp.halal.go.id platform, with no fees involved. However, PPH oversight is often less thorough due to target pressures, meaning that production sites and processes are not always closely inspected. Many MSMEs do not fully understand the meaning of halal certification; they know only that certification may increase profits and allow them to apply for government support. Once certified, many MSMEs revert to previous practices, as strict adherence to halal standards can reduce profit margins (Musataklima, 2021).

Halal certification differentiates products, making them premium due to the high-quality, certified halal ingredients involved. If the product is premium but the price remains the same, profit margins for businesses are reduced. Additionally, halal certification often raises production costs, leading to increased prices. However, MSMEs are often reluctant to raise prices for fear of losing customers, resulting in lower profits if they continue using halal ingredients and processes. Consequently, many MSMEs resume their former production methods, paying less attention to safety and health standards after certification (Mortas et al., 2022). Halal certification was particularly given the dominance of the MSME sector, as a result, the mandatory halal certification requirement impacts producer behavior differently between large corporations, small and micro business operators (Masruroh, 2023). So, the government must give different ways to halal certification for a success.

Unlike large corporations that have the resources to consistently comply with halal standards, many micro and small businesses face a dilemma between maintaining halal standards and sustaining profitability. This creates a gap in the implementation of halal certification, where ideal compliance often clashes with business realities on the ground. Moreover, the role of supervision in the halal certification system, especially under the self-declared scheme, is a crucial factor in ensuring the sustainability of halal standards. If oversight of MSMEs is not strengthened, there is a risk that halal certification will become merely an administrative formality without a tangible impact on product quality. Therefore, halal certification policies need to consider more effective monitoring mechanisms and continuous education for business operators so that awareness of halal compliance is not only driven by economic motives but also by moral and social responsibility (Masruroh, 2020a).

Thus, the sustainability of the halal industry in Indonesia does not rely solely on strict regulations but also on efforts to build an ecosystem that fully supports halal compliance. This includes providing incentives for small businesses, enhancing human resource capacity, and fostering synergy between the government, certification bodies, and business operators to uphold the integrity of halal products in both domestic and global markets (Masruroh & Fadli, 2022).

The Role of Fatwa Authorities in Shaping Halal Awareness

Fatwa authorities play a crucial role in fostering halal awareness among producers and consumers alike. By issuing religious rulings (fatwas) on halal standards, these authorities set clear guidelines on what constitutes halal practices in sourcing, production, and handling of products. This guidance builds a foundational understanding of halal principles, reinforcing that halal compliance goes beyond mere legal or regulatory obligations and aligns with deeply rooted religious values (Maulana et al., 2022).

Halal-conscious behavior in Indonesia does not emerge on its own; therefore, various efforts are undertaken to build this awareness (Aisyah et al., 2019). Regulation is a key tool for promoting halal awareness among business operators in Indonesia (Usman et al., 2022). Regulations mandate halal certification, with penalties for non-compliance, effectively enforcing halal standards. This type of awareness can be seen as "compelled awareness," but it is a necessary first step to achieve widespread halal certification targets (Luthfi & Salehudin, 2011).

Fatwa authorities hold a pivotal role in cultivating halal awareness among business operators, extending their responsibilities far beyond simple oversight (Kaptein, 2004). One of their fundamental tasks is to establish halal standards that align with Shariah principles. This step ensures that halal awareness among business operators transcends mere commercial interests, embedding a deeper commitment to Islamic law and ethical considerations in the production process (Yahya & Junaidi, 2021).

Additionally, fatwa authorities issue and define halal fatwas, which serve as essential guidelines for assessing the halal status of products. The credibility of halal products is closely tied to these rulings, underscoring the importance of precise and accurate fatwas to avoid any misunderstandings or errors regarding a product's halal status. Education also forms a core component of the role fatwa authorities play. Through various educational efforts—including training programs, seminars, and informal gatherings—they increase literacy around halal certification, helping business operators understand the nuanced standards and practices necessary for compliance. This educational approach fosters a more informed and engaged business community when it comes to halal production (Whyte, 2023).

With rapid advancements in technology and the introduction of new products, fatwa authorities also provide legal certainty, particularly for products whose halal status may be uncertain. In such cases, their expertise and rulings reassure consumers, ensuring that even novel items meet halal criteria. This assurance is essential in a globalized market where innovation frequently introduces new challenges in maintaining halal standards (Dakhoir, 2019).

Furthermore, by issuing halal fatwas, fatwa authorities encourage producers to align their practices with halal requirements, actively motivating them to adopt processes that enhance compliance. This guidance not only supports adherence to standards but also nurtures a culture of halal within the business sector. Fatwa authorities contribute to establishing a consistent commitment to halal principles, from the use of certified halal raw materials and maintaining cleanliness in production to adhering to halal packaging practices.

Through these responsibilities, fatwa authorities significantly impact not only the legal compliance of halal production but also foster a broader cultural and ethical commitment to halal values across the business landscape, reinforcing a societal dedication to integrity and adherence to Islamic principles. If these roles are carried out effectively, they will gradually foster a comprehensive halal awareness among business operators, leading to a deeper awareness that goes beyond business interests alone. So far, fatwa authorities have primarily focused on issuing fatwas, without engaging in education, outreach, or evaluation. Additionally, there has been no post-certification oversight of products for either companies or MSMEs, despite the potential for violations, such as misuse of raw materials or production processes.

While monitoring is set to begin in October 2024, this will focus only on compliance with the requirement to hold halal certification, not on evaluating the ongoing adherence to halal standards post-certification. Consequently, the evaluation process remains limited, and effective oversight of halal certification practices in Indonesia—both for companies and MSMEs—has yet to be fully established.

This lack of post-certification oversight presents a significant challenge in ensuring the long-term integrity of halal compliance. Without proper monitoring mechanisms, there is a risk that some businesses may obtain halal certification solely for market access without maintaining consistent adherence to halal standards in their daily operations. This issue is particularly concerning for MSMEs, which may struggle with the financial and logistical burdens of sustained compliance.

To address these shortcomings, fatwa authorities must expand their role beyond issuing rulings to include active involvement in education, outreach, and post-certification evaluation. This could involve collaboration with government agencies, halal certification bodies, and business associations to implement structured training programs that ensure businesses fully understand and commit to halal principles. Additionally, periodic audits and stricter enforcement measures could be introduced to verify whether certified businesses continue to meet halal standards over time.

Another crucial aspect that requires attention is consumer awareness. While fatwa authorities play a central role in shaping halal awareness among producers, they must also engage with consumers to reinforce the importance of purchasing and supporting genuinely halal-certified products. Public awareness campaigns, digital platforms, and community outreach initiatives can help educate consumers on how to verify halal products, empowering them to demand greater transparency and accountability from producers.

Furthermore, as Indonesia aims to strengthen its position in the global halal market, the effectiveness of its halal certification system will be a determining factor. To build international trust, it is essential to ensure that Indonesia's halal standards are not only aligned with domestic regulations but also recognized and accepted by global halal certification bodies. This necessitates a more rigorous and transparent monitoring system that demonstrates Indonesia's commitment to upholding halal integrity at all levels of production and distribution.

In conclusion, while fatwa authorities have played a crucial role in setting halal guidelines and issuing fatwas, their responsibilities must evolve to encompass a more comprehensive approach. By integrating education, outreach, and post-certification oversight into their framework, fatwa authorities can foster a deeper and more sustainable halal awareness among business operators. Strengthening these efforts will not only enhance compliance but also contribute to the long-term growth and credibility of Indonesia's halal industry, ensuring that halal principles are upheld as both a religious obligation and a standard of quality in the marketplace.

Motivation of Business Actors in Obtaining Halal Certification: Between Economic Pressure and Halal Awareness

The motivations driving business operators to obtain halal certification often fall between economic pressure and genuine halal awareness. On one hand, economic factors such as market expansion, competitive advantage, and eligibility for government support create strong incentives for businesses to pursue halal certification. Certified halal products have a wider consumer base, particularly in Muslim-majority regions, and can differentiate a brand, giving it a competitive edge.

On the other hand, some business operators pursue halal certification out of a sincere commitment to religious compliance and an awareness of *halalan thayyiban* principles (lawful and wholesome production). This type of halal awareness is rooted in the understanding that certification not only aligns with Islamic law but also reflects a social responsibility toward producing safe, ethical products.

As economic agents, business operators are oriented toward profit maximization. Therefore, the primary motivation for obtaining halal certification is to maximize profits by gaining access to a broader market. Additionally, mandatory regulations compel business operators to pursue halal certification, even if they do not yet fully understand its true significance. Another motivation is to gain consumer trust, as trusted products lead to repeat purchases, ultimately building a loyal customer base. Having loyal customers increases the business's economic scale, which in turn raises profits.

This economic motivation drives business operators to expand their market through halal certification. While many claim that halal certification is a responsibility to be upheld as Muslims, this is often just an initial motivation; ultimately, they seek certification to make their products more marketable. Some operators, particularly small and micro-businesses, may not display the halal logo on their products despite holding certification. In these cases, certification serves mainly as a requirement to qualify for government MSME support programs.

In the increasingly global and competitive market, economic pressures have become a primary motivation for many business operators. However, without a balance grounded in genuine halal awareness based on religious principles, this profit-driven motivation risks diluting the true spirit and intent of halal certification. The purpose of halal certification extends beyond mere compliance; it is a response to market shortcomings that have, over time, eroded consumer trust in producers. For halal certification to hold its value, economic incentives should ideally be intertwined with a moral commitment to consumer safety and health, establishing halal-certified production as a responsibility that serves both ethical and consumer-centered goals.

This approach, however, is not without its challenges. One major hurdle is the high cost associated with halal certification, especially when regular renewals are required. These expenses often push business operators to prioritize profit maximization to offset certification costs. Another significant barrier is the lengthy and complex bureaucracy involved in the certification process. This time-consuming aspect can lead to financial losses, driving operators to focus primarily on profit once certification is achieved.

Furthermore, maintaining a strong commitment to halal standards within a competitive global market is itself a formidable challenge. As operators work to balance these economic and procedural pressures, upholding the integrity of halal certification becomes even more essential. Successfully managing these factors allows businesses to honor the principles of halal certification while navigating the realities of a competitive industry landscape.

To ensure the sustainability of halal certification beyond mere economic motivations, several key strategies must be implemented. First, the government and halal certification bodies should work together to streamline the certification process, making it more accessible and affordable, especially for micro and small enterprises. Reducing bureaucratic hurdles and providing financial assistance or subsidies can help alleviate the burden on smaller businesses, encouraging them to pursue halal certification with a stronger commitment rather than mere economic compulsion.

Second, educational initiatives must be strengthened to enhance halal awareness among business operators. Many businesses still view halal certification solely as a market requirement rather than a reflection of ethical and religious values. By integrating comprehensive training programs that emphasize the holistic aspects of halal—covering sourcing, production, hygiene, and consumer trust—business operators can develop a deeper understanding of its significance beyond profitability. Educational outreach, including workshops, online courses, and collaboration with Islamic scholars, can reinforce the notion that halal compliance is not only about meeting legal obligations but also about upholding integrity and responsibility in business practices.

Another crucial aspect is the role of consumer awareness in reinforcing the true purpose of halal certification. If consumers are well-informed about the importance of halal integrity and actively seek out genuinely halal-certified products, businesses will have stronger incentives to maintain their commitment to halal compliance. Public campaigns that promote halal consumer rights and teach individuals how to verify the authenticity of halal claims can create a demand-driven push for stricter adherence to halal standards.

Additionally, post-certification monitoring and enforcement mechanisms should be strengthened to prevent businesses from treating halal certification as a mere formality. Random audits, stricter penalties for non-compliance, and transparent reporting systems can deter businesses from compromising halal standards after obtaining certification. Ensuring that halal-certified businesses maintain ongoing compliance rather than just meeting initial requirements is critical in preserving the credibility of the halal certification system.

Ultimately, balancing economic motivations with genuine halal awareness requires a multi-faceted approach that involves government support, business ethics, consumer education, and regulatory enforcement. While financial incentives will always play a role in driving halal certification, embedding a strong moral and religious foundation in halal business practices will ensure that the system remains trustworthy, sustainable, and beneficial for both producers and consumers alike. By fostering an environment where halal compliance is valued not only for its market benefits but also for its ethical and religious significance, Indonesia's halal industry can continue to grow while maintaining its integrity in an increasingly competitive global market.

CONCLUSION

The findings suggest that while mandatory certification has increased the visibility of halal practices, it has also led to a superficial understanding of halal among producers, where compliance is driven by business necessity rather than religious adherence. This raises critical questions about the efficacy of current certification processes and the need for more robust oversight and education to ensure the integrity of halal standards. The study concludes with recommendations for policy improvements and calls for a re-examination of the role of fatwa authorities to align more closely with the original religious intent of halal certification.

RECOMMENDATION

Religion should not only be a matter of worshipping Allah SWT vertically, but also to fellow humans. The company should always internalize halal awareness to all employees, so that halal compliance is not only a formality but indeed comes from the religiosity of each muslim.

REFERENCES

Abdul Mokti, H., Kamri, N. A., & Mohd Balwi, M. A. W. F. (2024). Tayyiban in halal food production: a systematic literature review. In *Journal of Islamic Marketing* (Vol. 15, Issue 2). https://doi.org/DOI: 10.1108/JIMA-03-2022-0098

Taufik, A. (2014). *TEKSTUALITAS PENAFSIRAN AL-QUR" AN (Analisis Kritis Pemahaman Nā ir al-Sa 'dī terhadap Isu Kontemporer dalam Taysīr al-Karīm al-Ra mān fī Kalām al-Mannān)* (Master's thesis, Sekolah Pascasarjana Universitas Islam Negri (UIN) Syarif Hidayatullah Jakarta). [The Textuality of the Interpretation of the Qur"an (A Critical Analysis of Nā ir al-Sa'dī's Understanding of the Contemporary Issue in Taysīr al-Karīm al-Ra mān fī Kalām al-Mannān].

Aisyah, M., Suzanawaty, L., & Said, M. (2019). The demand for halal certified restaurants in Indonesia. *International Journal of Supply Chain Management, 8*(5). Advance online publication. DOI: 10.3390/su12030820

Ariska, N., Setiawan, R. A., Setiawan, A., & Zaki, K. (2023). Implementation of the self-declare halal certification process in supporting the growth of MSMEs. Journal of Community Empowerment Learning *(JP2M), 4*(4), 807-815.

Aziz, M., Ghofur, A., & Hidayati, N. N. (2021). Regulation on the Implementation of Halal Product Assurance in Indonesia: Statute Approaches Study. *Ulul Albab: Jurnal Studi Dan Penelitian Hukum Islam, 4*(2), 209. Advance online publication. DOI: 10.30659/jua.v4i2.13649

Bakhtiar, F., Prayoga, R., & Mulya, A. (2022). Analisis Literasi Keuangan Dan Financial Technology Terhadap Inklusi Keuangan Pada Pelaku UMKM Perempuan. *Akuntabel, 19*(2), 260–268. DOI: 10.30872/jakt.v19i2.11178

Bashir, A. M. (2019). Effect Of Halal Awareness, Halal Logo And Attitude On Foreign Consumers' Purchase Intention. *British Food Journal, 121*(9), 1998–2015. DOI: 10.1108/BFJ-01-2019-0011

Bayumi, M. R., Iqbal, M., & Diem, M. J., & Muhlis. (. (2022). Rekonstruksi Konsep Bisnis Halalan Thayyiban Penguatan Integrasi-Interkoneksi Ekosistem Halal Value Chain. *Al-Mashrafiyah: Jurnal Ekonomi, Keuangan. Dan Perbankan Syariah, 6*(2). Advance online publication. DOI: 10.24252/al-mashrafiyah.v6i2.28543

Chan, C., Zulfakar, M. H., Chan, C., Jie, F., Pandiyan, V., & Sundram, K. (2019). Halal Accreditation And Certification In A Non- Muslim Country Setting : Insights From Australia Halal Meat Supply Chain Halal Accreditation And Certification In A Non- Muslim Country Setting. *Insights From Australia Halal Meat Supply Chain., 8*, 10–17.

Choiriyah, C. (2016). Pemikiran Ekonomi Muhammad Baqir Ash-Sadr. *Islamic Banking: Jurnal Pemikiran Dan Pengembangan Perbankan Syariah, 1*(2), 49–58.

Dakhoir, A. (2019). The fatwa authorities of National Syaria Council of Majelis Ulama Indonesia in supporting the principle if Syariah compliance. *Journal of Legal, Ethical and Regulatory Issues, 22*(1).

Hansen, G. D., & Prescott, E. C. (2002). Malthus to Solow. *The American Economic Review*, *92*(4), 1205–1217. Advance online publication. DOI: 10.1257/00028280260344731

Hew, J. J., Wong, L. W., Tan, G. W. H., Ooi, K. B., & Lin, B. (2020). The blockchain-based Halal traceability systems: A hype or reality? *Supply Chain Management*, *25*(6), 863–879. DOI: 10.1108/SCM-01-2020-0044

Hidayati, L., Sugiatmi, S., Aini, N., & Go, R. Y. (2023). The Role of LP3H in Increasing the economic Value through Assistance with Halal Certification. *Indonesian Journal of Islamic Economics and Business*, *8*(1), 46–54.

Hole, Y., Pawar, S., & Bhaskar, M. P. (2019). Porter's five forces model: Gives you a competitive advantage. *Journal of Advanced Research in Dynamical and Control Systems*, *11*(4).

Indung Amalia, W., & Nahidloh, S. (2023). The Indepence Of Pesantren In The Develpoment Of Halal Ecosystems Regarding The Application Of Regulations In Mta Putri Al-Amien Prenduan The Prepective Of Maslahah. *Proceeding of Annual Conference on Islamic Economy and Law, 2*(2). https://doi.org/DOI: 10.21107/aciel.v2i2.255

Izza, N. N., Fitria, L., Arsyi, M., & Nugraha, F. (2024). Twitter Data Analysis on Halal Labeling: Insights for the Food Industry in Indonesia. *Halal Tourism and Pilgrimage*, *3*(2). Advance online publication. DOI: 10.58968/htp.v3i2.391

Jamil, H., Wahab, A. Y. A., Razak, A. R. A., & Al-Saari, N. (2020). Exploring The Internationalization Strategy Of Higher Education Institutions And Halal Food Ecosystem in Malaysia. *Food Research*, *4*(S1), 145–150. Advance online publication. DOI: 10.26656/fr.2017.4(S1).S23

Jannah, S. M., & Al-Banna, H. (2021). Halal Awareness And Halal Traceability: Muslim Consumers' And Entrepreneurs' Perspectives. *Journal of Islamic Monetary Economics and Finance*, *7*(2), 285–316. Advance online publication. DOI: 10.21098/jimf.v7i2.1328

Jeaheng, Y., Al-Ansi, A., & Han, H. (2019a). Halal-friendly hotels: Impact of halal-friendly attributes on guest purchase behaviors in the Thailand hotel industry. *Journal of Travel & Tourism Marketing*, *36*(6), 729–746. DOI: 10.1080/10548408.2019.1631940

Jeaheng, Y., Al-Ansi, A., & Han, H. (2019b). Halal-Friendly Hotels: Impact Of Halal-Friendly Attributes On Guest Purchase Behaviors In The Thailand Hotel Industry. *Journal of Travel & Tourism Marketing*, *36*(6), 729–746. Advance online publication. DOI: 10.1080/10548408.2019.1631940

Junaidi, J. (2020). Halal-Friendly Tourism And Factors Influencing Halal Tourism. *Management Science Letters*, *10*(8), 1755–1762. Advance online publication. DOI: 10.5267/j.msl.2020.1.004

Kamarulzaman, N., Ruslan, A., & Sanny, M. (2018). Muslim Consumers' Awareness And Perception Of Halal Food Fraud. *International Food Research Journal*, •••, 25.

Kaptein, N. J. G. (2004). The Voice Of The "Ulam ": Fatwas And Religious Authority In Indonesia. *Archives de Sciences Sociales des Religions*, *125*(1), 115–130. Advance online publication. DOI: 10.4000/assr.1038

Khan, G., & Khan, F. (2019). "Is This Restaurant Halal?" Surrogate Indicators And Muslim Behaviour. *Journal of Islamic Marketing*, *11*(5), 1105–1123. Advance online publication. DOI: 10.1108/JIMA-01-2019-0008

Kotler, P., & Keller, K. L. (2016). *Marketing Management, 15e édition. New Jersy.* Pearson Education.

Krishnan, S., Musa, C., Omar, C., Zahran, I., Syazwan, N., & Alyaa, S. (2017). The Awareness of Gen Z's toward Halal Food Industry. *Management*, *2017*(1).

Kusuma, N. R. (2023). Analisis Keterkaitan Produksi dengan Kelangkaan Sumberdaya Pangan dalam Perspektif Baqr Al Sadr. *ANALYSIS : Accounting, Management, Economics, and Business, 1*(2).

Letsoin, B., & Riorini, S. V. (2023). The Mediating Role of Attitude Toward Product Towards Halal Cosmetic Purchase Intention in Female Consumers in Indonesia. *Journal of Social Research*, *2*(5), 1616–1633. Advance online publication. DOI: 10.55324/josr.v2i5.854

Lia Febriati, N., & Mu'in, F. M., Santoso, R., & Latua, A. (2024). Challenges of the Halal Food Industry in Era 5.0 Perspective of Science and Islamic Law. *KnE Social Sciences*. https://doi.org/DOI: 10.18502/kss.v9i2.15024

Loussaief, A., Ying-Chao Lin, J., Phuc Dang, H., Bouslama, N., & Cheng, J. M. S. (2024). Eating halal: A serial mediation model for the effect of religiosity on the intention to purchase halal-certified food. *Asia Pacific Journal of Marketing and Logistics*, *36*(1), 167–184. Advance online publication. DOI: 10.1108/APJML-10-2022-0868

Luthfi, B. A., & Salehudin, I. (2011). Marketing Impact of Halal Labeling Toward Indonesian Muslim Consumer's Behavioral Intention Based on Ajzen's Planned Behavior Theory: Policy Capturing Studies on Five Different Product Categories. *ASEAN Marketing Journal, 3*(1).

Margarena, A. N., & Ikhwan Setiawan, A. (2022). The Effect Of Perceived Value Of Economic Benefits Towards Smes Halal Certification Intention Moderated By Government Policy Regulation. *International Journal of Education and Social Science Research*, *05*(02), 308–320. Advance online publication. DOI: 10.37500/IJESSR.2022.5219

Masruroh, N. (2020a). Dynamics of Identity and Religiosity in Halal Branding in Indonesia. ISLAMICA: Journal of Islamic Studies, *14*(2).

Masruroh, N. (2020b). The Competitiveness of Indonesian Halal Food Exports in Global Market Competition Industry. *Economica: Jurnal Ekonomi Islam*, *11*(1), 25–48. Advance online publication. DOI: 10.21580/economica.2020.11.1.3709

Masruroh, N. (2023). Pemaknaan Halal Antara Simbol Dan Bentuk Implementasi Keagamaan Oleh Pemilik Umkm Pasca Pemberlakuan UU NO. 33 TAHUN 2014. *Istinbath*, *21*(2), 351–373. Advance online publication. DOI: 10.20414/ijhi.v21i2.572

Masruroh, N. (2024). European Multidisciplinary Journal of Modern Science The Development Of Halal Lifestyle In Mashlahah Mursalah Analysis: Study Of Halal Labeling Trends In Indonesia. *European Multidisciplinary Journal of Modern Science, 26*(4), 17–28. https://journal.academicjournal.id/index.php/emjmsArticle

Masruroh, N., & Fadli, A. (2022). Gerak Kuasa Negara dalam Perdagangan Komoditas Bersertifikat Halal di Indonesia. *Prooceding Annual Conference on Islam, Education and Humanitites,* 1.

Masruroh, N., Fathorrazi, M., Saleh, M., & Adenan, M. (2021). The Halal Branding in International Trade of Edamame Soybean Agricultural Products. *Annals of Agri Bio Research*, *26*(2), •••.

Maulana, D. F., Makhrus, M., & Hasanah, H. (2022). The Urgency of MUI Halal Fatwa about Food, Beverage, Medicine and Cosmetic Products for the Consumer Protection. *Volksgeist: Jurnal Ilmu Hukum Dan Konstitusi*, *5*(2), 199–214. Advance online publication. DOI: 10.24090/volksgeist.v5i2.6421

Millatina, A. N., Hakimi, F., Budiantoro, R. A., & Arifandi, M. R. (2022). The Impact of Halal Label in Halal Food Buying Decisions. *Journal of Islamic Economic Laws*, *5*(1), 159–176. Advance online publication. DOI: 10.23917/jisel.v5i1.17139

Mortas, M., Awad, N., & Ayvaz, H. (2022). Adulteration Detection Technologies Used For Halal/Kosher Food Products: An Overview. In *Discover Food* (Vol. 2, Issue 1). https://doi.org/DOI: 10.1007/s44187-022-00015-7

Muharam, I. N., & Asutay, M. (2019). Online Disclosure Practices Of Halal-Friendly Hotels. *Journal of Islamic Marketing*. Advance online publication. DOI: 10.1108/JIMA-12-2018-0239

Muizzuddin, M., Zakiyyatul, A., Universitas, F., Abdullah, K., & Gresik, F. (2023). The Islamic Moderation (A Literature Review of the Concept Islamic Moderation according to KH. Ahmad Siddiq). *Journal of Early Childhood Islamic Education, 10*.

Musataklima, M. (2021). Self-Declare Halal Products for Small and Micro Enterprises: Between Ease of Doing Business and Assurance of Consumer Spiritual Rights. *De Jure: Jurnal Hukum Dan Syar'iah*, *13*(1). Advance online publication. DOI: 10.18860/j-fsh.v13i1.11308

Mutmainah, L. (2018). The Role of Religiosity, Halal Awareness, Halal Certification, and Food Ingredients on Purchase Intention of Halal Food. *Ihtifaz: Journal of Islamic Economics, Finance, and Banking*, *1*(1), 33. Advance online publication. DOI: 10.12928/ijiefb.v1i1.284

Muttaqin, P. S., Setyawan, E. B., & Novitasari, N. (2023). Factors Influencing Readiness towards Halal Logistics among Food and Beverages Industry in the Era of E-Commerce in Indonesia. *JOIV: International Journal on Informatics Visualization*, *7*(3), 781–787. Advance online publication. DOI: 10.30630/joiv.7.3.2055

Nurein, S. A. (2023). Nexus of Halal Entrepreneurship and Islamic Finance for the Creation of a Strong Halal Ecosystem. In *Contemporary Discourse of Halal and Islamic Entrepreneurship*. https://doi.org/DOI: 10.1007/978-981-99-6427-7_9

Nursita, R. D., Adelia, D., Septiani, R., & Widyaputri, P. D. (2024). The Role of Non-State Actors in Establishing the Halal Ecosystem in Indonesia. *Hasanuddin Journal of International Affairs*, *4*(01), 44–56. Advance online publication. DOI: 10.31947/hjirs.v4i01.33028

Nusran, M., Gunawan, , Razak, M., Numba, S., & Wekke, I. S. (2018). Halal Awareness on the Socialization of Halal Certification. *IOP Conference Series. Earth and Environmental Science*, *175*(1), 012217. Advance online publication. DOI: 10.1088/1755-1315/175/1/012217

Polo, E. F., & Weber, W. (2010). Competitive Generic Strategies Evolution and the Importance of Michael E. Porter. *Revista de Gestão*, *17*(1), 99–117. Advance online publication. DOI: 10.5700/rege389

Poniman, D., Purchase, S., & Sneddon, J. (2015). Traceability systems in the Western Australia halal food supply chain. *Asia Pacific Journal of Marketing and Logistics*, *27*(2), 324–348. DOI: 10.1108/APJML-05-2014-0082

Poniman, D., Purchase, S., Sneddon, J., Purchase, S., & Sneddon, J. (2015). *Traceability systems in the Western Australia halal food supply chain*. https://doi.org/ DOI: 10.1108/APJML-05-2014-0082

Porter, M. E. (1997). Michael E. Porter replies: "What Is. *Harvard Business Review*, *75*(1).

Rachman, M. A. (2019). Halal Industry In Indonesia: Role Of Sharia Financial Institutions In Driving Industrial And Halal Ecosystem. *Al-Iqtishad: Jurnal Ilmu Ekonomi Syariah*, *11*(1). Advance online publication. DOI: 10.15408/aiq.v11i1.10221

Riaz, M. N., Chaudry, M. M., Riaz, M. N., & Chaudry, M. M. (2018). Halal Food Laws and Regulations. In *Handbook of Halal Food Production*. https://doi.org/DOI: 10.1201/9781315119564-2

Riaz, M. N., & Riaz, N. M. (2023). Requirements for Halal Food Production. In *Encyclopedia of Food Safety, Second Edition, Volume 1-4* (Vols. 1–4). https://doi.org/DOI: 10.1016/B978-0-12-822521-9.00003-4

Rusydiana, A. S., & Mahsyar, N. M. (2024). Developing Halal Industry in Indonesia using Interpretive Structural Modeling (ISM). *Halal Tourism and Pilgrimage*, *3*(2). Advance online publication. DOI: 10.58968/htp.v3i2.385

Saidi, S., & Sazali, H. (2024). Analysis of The Contention of Religious Ideology and Halal Industry in Social Media about Halal Logo Rebranding. *KOMUNIKA: Jurnal Dakwah Dan Komunikasi*, *18*(1), 1–12. Advance online publication. DOI: 10.24090/komunika.v18i1.7778

Santoso, L., & Rachman, A. (2023). Digitalising Halal Certification: The Dynamic of Regulations and Policies Concerning Halal Certification in Indonesia. *Jurisdictie: Jurnal Hukum Dan Syariah*, *14*(2), 265–293. Advance online publication. DOI: 10.18860/j.v14i2.24115

Saviera, L., R., Natasya Sirait, N., Mat Isa, N., Sulaiman, S., & Mohd Kamal, S. B. (2024). The Comparative Study of Muslim Friendly Homestay Programs in Indonesia and Malaysia: Social Legal Perspective. *KnE Social Sciences.* https://doi.org/ DOI: 10.18502/kss.v8i21.14760

Savitri, F. M., & Perwita, A. D. (2020). Mediating Role of Halal Technology Implementation on Halal Purchase Intention in Semarang. *International Journal Ihya' 'Ulum al-Din, 22*(1). https://doi.org/DOI: 10.21580/ihya.22.1.5574

Shihab, Q. (2002). Tafsir al-Misbah Jilid 6 (yunus, hud, yusuf, ar-ra'du). *Journal of Chemical Information and Modeling*, *53*(9), •••.

Spithoven, A. H. G. M. (1996). Jean-Baptiste Say (1767-1832). *International Journal of Social Economics*, *23*(7), 39–48. DOI: 10.1108/03068299610122399

Suhartanto, D., Dean, D., Amin, H., Sugiama, A. G., & Amalia, F. A. (2024). Fast, Fresh, Healthy And Halal: A Mobile Food App Recipe For Muslim Millennial Loyalty. *Journal of Islamic Accounting and Business Research.* Advance online publication. DOI: 10.1108/JIABR-08-2022-0210

Tan, A., Gligor, D., & Ngah, A. (2020). Applying Blockchain for Halal food traceability. *International Journal of Logistics Research and Applications.* https://doi.org/DOI: 10.1080/13675567.2020.1825653

Tarannum, S., Jalal, M. S., & Huda, M. N. (2024). HALALCheck: A Multi-Faceted Approach for Intelligent Halal Packaged Food Recognition and Analysis. *IEEE Access : Practical Innovations, Open Solutions*, *12*, 28462–28474. Advance online publication. DOI: 10.1109/ACCESS.2024.3367983

Tumiwa, R. A. F., Ningsih, G. M., Romarina, A., Setyadjit, S., Slamet, B., Waruwu, E., Ie, M., & Utomo, Y. T. (2023). Investigating Halal Food Supply Chain Management, Halal Certification And Traceability On Smes Performance. *Uncertain Supply Chain Management*, *11*(4), 1889–1896. Advance online publication. DOI: 10.5267/j.uscm.2023.6.003

Usman, H., Chairy, C., & Projo, N. W. K. (2022). Impact Of Muslim Decision-Making Style And Religiosity On Intention To Purchasing Certified Halal Food. *Journal of Islamic Marketing*, *13*(11), 2268–2289. Advance online publication. DOI: 10.1108/JIMA-01-2021-0027

Usman, H., Chairy, C., & Projo, N. W. K. (2023). Between Awareness Of Halal Food Products And Awareness Of Halal-Certified Food Products. *Journal of Islamic Marketing*, *14*(3), 851–870. Advance online publication. DOI: 10.1108/JIMA-07-2021-0233

Vanany, I., Soon, J. M., Maryani, A., & Wibawa, B. M. (2019). Determinants Of Halal-Food Consumption In Indonesia. *Journal of Islamic Marketing*, *11*(2), 507–521. Advance online publication. DOI: 10.1108/JIMA-09-2018-0177

Weil, K. E. (1985). PORTER, Competitive advantage, creating and sustaining superior performance. *Revista de Administração de Empresas, 25*(2). https://doi.org/ DOI: 10.1590/s0034-75901985000200009

Whyte, S. (2023). Are Fatwas Dispensable? Examining the Contemporary Relevance and Authority of Fatwas in Australia. *Oxford Journal of Law and Religion*, *11*(2–3), 314–342. Advance online publication. DOI: 10.1093/ojlr/rwac015

Yahya, I., & Junaidi, A. A. (2021). Authority of Fatwa in Digital Era: Methodology and Transmission of Nahdlatul Ulama's Bahtsul Masail in Indonesia. *Webology*, *18*(2), 654–674. Advance online publication. DOI: 10.14704/WEB/V18I2/WEB18345

Zuhudi, N. W. M., & Dolah, J. (2021). *An Experts' Perspective Based on Consumers' Perception of Halal-Related Issue*. Al-Risalah Journal.

Chapter 2
Exploring the Intersection of Halalan Tayyiban Principles and Food Security: A Systematic Review

Siti Fatimahwati Pehin Dato Musa
https://orcid.org/0000-0003-1987-4595
Universiti Brunei Darussalam, Brunei

Syahnur Farhana Haji Shahlehi
https://orcid.org/0000-0002-7664-7893
Universiti Teknologi Brunei, Brunei

ABSTRACT

This systematic literature review reveals that food security traditionally emphasises the availability and accessibility of nutritious food to ensure consistent utilisation. The concept of Halalan Tayyiban mandates that food should be ethically sourced and produced following Shariah law and should be accessible to all. Furthermore, it highlights the importance of sharing food with those in need and considers its impact on religious and moral development. To uphold Halalan Tayyiban standards from farm to fork, active involvement from all stakeholders is essential, particularly producers, who must ensure that consumers receive lawful and high-quality food by adhering to government regulations on Halal certification. Future research should expand the study of Halalan Tayyiban principles to encompass a wider array of agricultural issues beyond food security, to further enhance understanding of this Islamic concept.

DOI: 10.4018/979-8-3373-3917-7.ch002

1.0 INTRODUCTION

Strengthening the agriculture sector is important for maintaining food production, meeting increasing demand, and tackling nutrition challenges, which in turn reinforces the foundation of food security (Al-Amin, 2023; Jamaluddin & Ramli, 2022; Nordin et al., 2022; Uddin, 2021). This foundation is crucial for sustaining human populations and is directly linked to the achievement of all 17 Sustainable Development Goals (SDGs). In particular, it is pertinent to eradicating poverty (SDG 1) and achieving zero hunger (SDG 2), while also playing a significant supporting role in advancing the remaining goals (Fauzan & Syara, 2023; Idris et al., 2022; Rahim et al., 2021). The SDGs, also referred to as the Global Goals, were established by the United Nations (UN) in 2015 as a global initiative to ensure that by 2030, all individuals can experience peace and prosperity (UN, 2024).

Through the lens of Islam, the significance of food security is deeply emphasised in various verses of the Al-Quran and Hadith. This emphasis is illustrated in a study by Uddin (2021), which highlights several relevant Quranic verses and Hadiths, including:

> *"Eat and drink from the provision of Allah (SWT), and do not commit abuse on the earth, spreading corruption" [Surah Al-Baqarah, 2:60].*
>
> *"A human being fills no worse vessel than his stomach. It is sufficient for a human being to eat a few mouthfuls to keep his spine straight. But if he must (fill it), then one third of food, one third for drink and one third for air" [Hadith: Sunan Tirmidhi, 2380 and Sunan Ibn Majah, 3349].*
>
> *"A Muslim is not a believer whose stomach is filled while the neighbour to his side goes hungry" [Hadith: Sunan Al-Kubra Al-Bayhaqi, 19049].*

In this context, food security encompasses more than just providing access to Halal food as it also involves adhering to Shariah-compliant distribution practices that promote fairness and equity (Ikomatussuniah & Maler, 2021; Rahim et al., 2021). In enhancing food security, it is necessary to increase the recognition of Halal products and broaden the range of certified items. This approach not only improves food quality and availability but also aligns with Islamic principles to effectively address food insecurity (Fauzan & Syara, 2023; Ruzulan et al., 2021; Sungit et al., 2020). As such, developing a robust Halal food supply chain is pivotal for achieving sustainable Halal food security (Idris et al., 2022).

Sustainable Halal food security certainly supports the growing demand for Halal food and beverages among Muslim consumers, which is firmly rooted in Islamic guidelines on food consumption (Arif & Sidek, 2015; Nordin et al., 2022; Shafiee et al., 2017; Yahaya & Ruzulan, 2020). Nonetheless, it is also interesting to note that the demand for Halal products has expanded beyond the Muslim community to include non-Muslim consumers (Dahlal & Ahmad, 2018). Echoing this observation, Jelan et al. (2024) and Ruzulan et al. (2021) emphasise that non-Muslims are increasingly interested in Halal food, driven by their recognition of its superior quality.

Figure 1 presents the projected global market revenue for Halal food from 2018 to 2027. In 2018, the worldwide market revenue for Halal food was approximately US$715 billion, and it is anticipated to increase to US$2.04 trillion by 2027. This significant increase in market revenue underscores the growing demand for Halal food, reflecting its expanding appeal among both Muslim and non-Muslim consumers.

Figure 1. Projected global market revenue for Halal food from 2018 to 2027

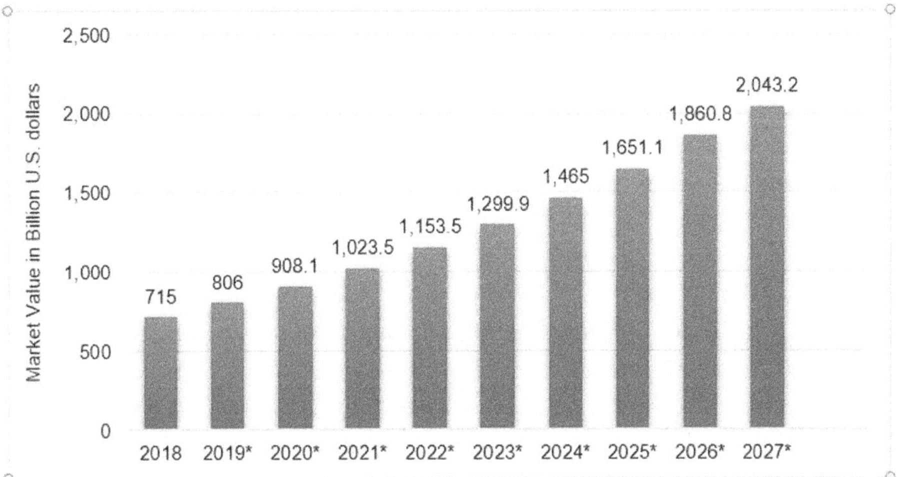

Source: Adopted from Statista (2024)

In essence, this trend highlights the growing relevance and broader appeal of Halal principles, indicating their widespread application and acceptance across diverse populations. Subsequently, ensuring the availability and accessibility of adequate Halal food is imperative not only for meeting this growing demand but also for maintaining strong Halal food security. Building on this discussion, sustainable Halal food security is explained in subsection 1.1.

1.1 Sustainable Halal Food Security

Food security ensures that individuals can consistently meet their dietary needs and preferences for a healthy life (Matnor et al., 2024; Nordin et al., 2022). It is defined as:

"Food security exists when all people, at all times, have physical and economic access to sufficient, safe and nutritious food that meets their dietary needs and food preferences for an active and healthy life" (World Food Summit, 1996 cited in Shaw, 2007).

Nevertheless, the most widely accepted definition of food security is built on four key pillars, as outlined by the Food and Agriculture Organisation (FAO, 2006) and The World Bank (2024):

- *Availability* - the supply of adequate quantities of food that meets quality standards.
- *Accessibility* - individuals' ability to obtain sufficient resources for acquiring nutritious food.
- *Utilisation* - using food, clean water, sanitation, and healthcare to achieve optimal nutritional well-being and meet all physiological needs.
- *Stability* - access to adequate food should be continuous and resilient against sudden shocks.

From an Islamic perspective, Rahim et al. (2021) suggest that food security is viewed as Allah's (SWT) provision of abundant resources to ensure that humans live healthily and can generate income from these resources. This perspective further emphasises the critical role of government in maintaining leadership trust and implementing the obligatory union kifayah (*fardhu ain*), which sets forth the political economy of sustainable development. Consequently, ensuring the availability of Halal food becomes a key priority for sustaining life. However, the authors also note that further explanation of fundamental concepts is needed for a complete understanding of Halal food security from the lens of Islamic beliefs. Echoing this view, Abdul Mokti et al. (2024) argue that the ambiguity of the indicators related to Islamic elements necessitates more explicit definitions and frameworks to grasp the integration of Islamic principles into food security fully.

This is where the importance of the Halalan Tayyiban concept is particularly evident. These principles, which are consistently affirmed in the Al-Quran and Hadith, play a fundamental role in guiding both Islamic dietary practices and broader food standards (Abdul Mokti et al., 2024; Alzeer et al., 2018; Bujang et al., 2020; Nordin et al., 2022; Salamon et al., 2021). Thus, the Halalan Tayyiban concept is explained in subsection 1.2.

1.2 Halalan Tayyiban Concept

The Al-Quran, Sunnah, and Hadith are foundational sources of Islamic law (Shariah), providing clear guidance on what is Halal (permissible) and Haram (forbidden). This divine guidance, available for over 1,400 years, continues to shape Islamic ethical and legal standards (Jelan et al., 2024). The Sunnah represents the practical application and interpretation of the Al-Quran, illustrating its teachings in daily life (Qureshi, 2020). In contrast, Hadith records the Prophet Muhammad's (PBUH) sayings and actions, validated through an examination of their chain of narrators and content. Additionally, ijtihad (legal reasoning) and fatwa (legal verdicts) issued by qualified scholars play a key role in shaping Islamic jurisprudence (Demirci et al., 2016; Khan et al., 2018; Mustaffa, 2019).

For food to be permissible in Islam, it must be Halal, while Haram foods must be avoided (Arif & Sidek, 2015). According to Ruzulan et al. (2021), The Al-Quran outlines four criteria for identifying Haram food, as detailed in verses such as Surah Al-An'am (6:145) and Surah Al-Ma'idah (5:3):

(1) Animals that die of natural causes, including those that are strangled, beaten, fall from a height, are gored, or are consumed by predators,
(2) Blood that has been spilled,
(3) The flesh of pigs, and
(4) Animals sacrificed to idols instead of to Allah (SWT).

Halal food must not only meet the basic criteria of permissibility but also adhere to the principles of "Tayyib," meaning it should be wholesome and of high quality, in line with health standards and ethical considerations (Demirci et al., 2016; Hamdan et al., 2024; Matnor et al., 2024). Chowdhury et al. (2023) highlight that classical Fiqh emphasises the importance of food safety and quality for Muslim consumers, with food needing to meet both Halal standards and Tayyib attributes such as safety, hygiene, and overall quality. Arif and Sidek (2015) reinforce this by explaining that Halalan Tayyiban integrates Halal and Tayyib, covering cleanliness, purity, and high standards. Thus, food that is nutritious but lacks guaranteed quality or clarity on its status cannot be considered Tayyib or Tayyiban (Mustaffa, 2019).

Alzeer et al. (2018) further stress that while Halal food is recognised for being free from alcohol and pork, it must also undergo thorough evaluation to ensure all ingredients are Halal and free from toxicity. This includes the removal of any Najis (ritually unclean) or harmful substances. The focus on food quality extends beyond health benefits, encompassing both product purity and the integrity of the production process (Arif & Sidek, 2015; Dahlal & Ahmad, 2018). Halalan Tayyiban principles thus apply throughout the entire food lifecycle, encompassing manufacturing, preparation, processing, storage, and serving (Arif & Sidek, 2015; Yahaya & Ruzulan, 2020). Adhering to these standards ensures food sourced from pure, high-quality materials not only meets cleanliness benchmarks but also enhances one's *Taqwa* (God-consciousness) and *Syukur* (gratefulness) towards Allah (SWT) (Ahmad & Nordin, 2023; Mohd Riza et al., 2022).

Although Tayyib appears in various forms (e.g., Thoyyiban, Toyyiban, Toyyib, Tayyab, Tayyaban) (Demirci et al., 2016), the term "Halal and Tayyiban" is consistently used throughout this study. This term is specifically mentioned in four verses of the Al-Quran: Surah Al-Baqarah (2:168), Surah Al-Mai'dah (5:88), Surah Al-Anfal (8:69), and Surah Al-Nahl (16:114) (Abdul Mokti et al., 2024; Mustaffa, 2019; Yahaya & Ruzulan, 2020).

Below are the translations of the four verses:

"O people, eat what is good and lawful from the earth, and do not follow Satan's footsteps, he is your sworn enemy" [Surah Al-Baqarah, 2:168].

"And eat of what Allah (SWT) has provided for you (which is) lawful and good. And fear Allah (SWT), in whom you are believers" [Surah Al-Mai'dah, 5: 88].

"So, eat the lawful and pure things, and fear Allah (SWT). Surely, Allah (SWT) is the Most-Forgiving and Very-Merciful" [Surah Al-Anfal, 8:69].

"So, eat of the good and lawful things Gods has provided for you and be thankful for His blessings" [Surah Al-Nahl, 16:114].

These verses underscore the necessity of conforming to Allah's (SWT) commandments regarding food consumption, emphasising that it should be both lawful and good. Subsection 1.3 outlines the research gaps that this study aims to address.

1.3 Research Gaps

Tayyiban, a fundamental principle of Shariah, underscores the sanctity and dignity of human life, highlighting its critical importance (Bujang et al., 2020). However, achieving Tayyiban is complex without a confirmed Halal status for food, suggesting that the concept involves more intricacies than initially apparent (Abdul Mokti et al., 2024). While Halalan Tayyiban is crucial for ensuring that food is both wholesome and of high quality, Demirci et al. (2016) and Jelan et al. (2024) argue that the concept still lacks a clear definition and official recognition, which are vital for global market acceptance and consumer trust. Alzeer et al. (2018) further contend that while Tayyib has been incorporated into Halal food production and has influenced the inclusion of food safety requirements in Halal certification, there is still a lack of clear practical application and rationale for Tayyib within the Halal framework. Supporting this perspective, current literature highlights that the criteria for Tayyiban remain ambiguous (Abdul Mokti et al., 2024; Dahlal & Ahmad, 2018; Islam & Wahab, 2022).

Given the pressing issue of food security, investigating how Halalan Tayyiban principles intersect with contemporary global challenges provides valuable insights. This exploration not only reveals how Islamic perspectives can address modern issues but also examines the practical applications of these principles. Islam and Wahab (2022) echo a view that a deep understanding of Halalan Tayyiban is fundamental for overcoming obstacles in the future Halal food business landscape. The authors' perspective highlights that mastering these principles is essential not only for effectively navigating the development of food businesses but also for addressing food security challenges in a meaningful way.

Indeed, there is a significant research gap in addressing Halalan Tayyiban specifically within the context of food security. While existing studies have thoroughly examined various aspects of Halalan Tayyiban, such as its impact on the overall food industry (Arif & Sidek, 2015; Hamdan et al., 2024; Hamdan & Hashim, 2022; Khan et al., 2018; Mustaffa, 2019; Yahaya & Ruzulan, 2020), its role in production and manufacturing (Abdul Mokti et al., 2024; Bujang et al., 2024; Jelan et al., 2024; Shafiee et al., 2017), food safety and quality (Ahmad & Nordin, 2023; Dahlal et al., 2024), and food law (Ikomatussuniah & Maler, 2021), there remains a need to integrate these Islamic principles into the global food security discourse. Addressing this research gap is crucial for understanding the practical implications of Halalan Tayyiban principles and their potential impact on real-world applications in food security.

Therefore, this study aims to fill this gap by first reviewing the concept of Halalan Tayyiban and then exploring how these Halalan Tayyiban principles can be applied to food security, providing a comprehensive analysis of their implications and potential integration.

The following sections detail the methodology of this study, which involves a systematic literature review (SLR) outlined in Section 2.0. Section 3.0 presents the findings and discussions, focusing on the Halalan Tayyiban concept, its intersection with food security, and the theoretical and practical contributions of this study. Finally, Section 4.0 concludes with a summary of this study, including its limitations and suggestions for future research.

2.0 METHODOLOGY

This study employs SLR to collect and critically assess existing research on the intersection of Halalan Tayyiban concepts and food security, a topic that remains notably underexplored. The effectiveness and reliability of this method are supported by its successful application in related studies, including Abdul Mokti et al. (2024) on Tayyiban in Halal food production, Hamdan et al. (2024) on meat cultivation from an Islamic perspective, Idris et al. (2022) on Halal-Tayyiban and SDGs, and Khan et al. (2018) on definitions within the Halal supply chain.

For this review, the Preferred Reporting Items for Systematic Reviews and Meta-Analyses (PRISMA) framework was specifically employed, as outlined by Page et al. (2021). PRISMA offers a rigorous, data-intensive process that enhances the quality and reliability of the review, a method also utilised by Abdul Mokti et al. (2024). PRISMA encompasses four key steps including identification, screening, eligibility, and inclusion, which are crucial for a comprehensive and structured literature review. Each of these steps will be detailed further in the following subsections, specifically from subsections 2.1 to 2.4.

2.1 Identification Stage

In the identification stage, the process involves selecting appropriate keywords and databases to initiate the review. For this study, the search strings include a combination of keywords such as “Halal”, “Tayyiban” (or “Tayyib” or “Thoyyiban”), “Food”, and “Security”, as expanded in the following:

- Search string 1: “Halal” AND “Tayyiban” AND “Food AND “Security”,
- Search string 2: “Halal” AND “Tayyib” AND “Food” AND “Security”,
- Search string 3: “Halal” AND “Thoyyiban” AND “Food” AND “Security”, and
- Search string 4: “Halalan Tayyiban Food Security”.

These specific keywords were chosen to ensure that the literature retrieved was pertinent to this study’s focus.

Unlike previous studies that typically relied on only two databases, this study utilised a broader range of sources, including Scopus, Science Direct, and Google Scholar. While focusing solely on high-quality databases like Scopus and Science Direct can provide access to a vast collection of peer-reviewed literature, their narrower coverage may limit the scope. To address this, Google Scholar was included to broaden the search and capture a wider array of relevant literature. This approach aligns with practices observed in other studies (Hamdan et al., 2024; Idris et al., 2022; Khan et al., 2018). Khan et al. (2018) justified this selection by noting that Scopus and Science Direct offer extensive peer-reviewed content, while Google Scholar was added to ensure coverage of less accessible or emerging research related to the phenomenon under investigation.

2.2 Screening Stage

During the screening stage, applying specific inclusion and exclusion criteria is essential to ensure that only relevant literature is selected. Key criteria for this process include the publication year, type, language, and scope of the publications (Abdul Mokti et al., 2024; Hamdan et al., 2024; Khan et al., 2018). Table 1 provides a summary of these inclusion and exclusion criteria for this study.

Table 1. Inclusion and Exclusion Criteria for Paper Selection

	Inclusion Criteria	**Exclusion Criteria**
Publication Year	✓ Literature published between the years 2014 and 2024	× Literature published before the year 2014
Publication Type	✓ Publications include academic journal articles, conference proceedings, and book chapters	× Publications exclude book series, note editorials, trade publications, letters, and other literature
Publication Language	✓ Publications are in English language	× Publications include sources in languages other than English
Others		× Duplicate and irrelevant studies

Source: Authors' Own

More specifically, to ensure clarity and avoid potential misinterpretations due to translation issues or inconsistencies, only publications written in English were selected (Abdul Mokti et al., 2024; Khan et al., 2018). Such approach guarantees comprehensive accessibility for researchers. This study focused on publications from the past decade (2014 to 2024), as this ten-year period represents a significant expansion in journal literature, providing a robust opportunity to assess how evolving research trends might influence various academic fields (Hamdan et al., 2024). Initially, this study aimed to include only peer-reviewed journal articles due to their thorough coverage of the study phenomena. However, given the limited availability of relevant studies, book chapters and conference proceedings were also included, as has been suggested by Abdul Mokti et al. (2024).

2.3 Eligibility Stage

Ensuring the inclusion of only eligible studies involves reviewing the titles, abstracts, and main contents of the screened publications to ensure they meet the inclusion criteria, as advised by Abdul Mokti et al. (2024). For this study, the primary focus is on the relevance of Halalan Tayyiban definitions or elements and their potential intersection with food security. However, at this stage, it has become evident that there are limited studies specifically examining Halalan Tayyiban principles in relation to food security. As a result, it is essential to apply these principles to various food-related issues to ensure that only studies addressing related and pertinent areas are included.

2.4 Inclusion Stage

Figure 2 provides a detailed overview of the article selection process for the SLR, outlining each stage from initial identification to final inclusion.

Figure 2. SLR PRISMA flowchart

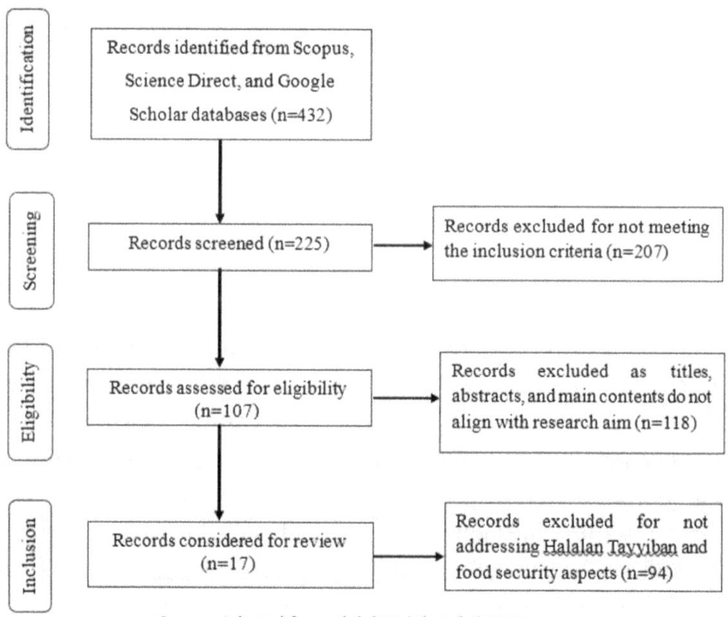

Source: Adapted from Abdul Mokti et al. (2024)

Following the three-step process outlined earlier, a total of 432 publications were initially identified. These were then screened based on the inclusion and exclusion criteria, narrowing the list to 225. After a thorough review of abstracts, titles, and full texts, 107 publications were identified as eligible. Further scrutiny, focusing on the intersection of Halalan Tayyiban and food security, narrowed this down to 12 relevant articles. To address the limited number of sources, a snowballing technique was further applied, which involved searching for additional articles that were not initially included. This approach successfully expanded the selection, leading to a final inclusion of 17 articles in the review.

While this number may appear limited, it is appropriate given the niche nature of the research topic. Similar studies have also included a small number of articles such as for instance, Khan et al. (2018) reviewed only 8 articles, while Hamdan et al. (2024) and Idris et al. (2022) included fewer than 30. As long as the selected articles offer sufficient information to address the research objectives, this scope is considered adequate.

3.0 FINDINGS AND DISCUSSIONS

Although literature specifically exploring the intersection of Halalan Tayyiban principles with food security is limited, this study integrates key publications that offer valuable insights into the nature and application of Halalan Tayyiban. These sources provide a nuanced understanding of how these principles can be applied to various aspects of food security. The findings from these publications are systematically applied to different dimensions of food security, offering a comprehensive analysis. A summary of the principal findings is presented in Table 2, encapsulating the essential insights and their implications for this study.

As such, this section will discuss the concept of Halalan Tayyiban as reviewed in the literature in subsection 3.1. It will also explore how the principles of Halalan Tayyiban can be applied to understanding food security from an Islamic perspective in subsection 3.2. In addition, subsection 3.3 will outline the theoretical contributions of this study. Since Halalan Tayyiban is especially pertinent to the food context, subsection 3.4 will examine the role of various stakeholders in implementing these principles.

Table 2. Summary of included literature

No	Authors	Scope of the Study	Halalan Tayyiban Concepts for Food or Related Aspects
1	Islam et al. (2025)	The chapter delves into concept of Ajka in Quranic teachings, with a focus on Halal-related research areas	While Tayyib must be Halal, not all Halal foods are Tayyib for everyone. Ajka represents the purest form of purity, while Tayyib means good and wholesome. Both are Halal, but Ajka holds more value as the highest form of purity. It emphasises the green, organic, and environmental aspects of Halal products.
2	Abdul Mokti et al. (2024)	The article examines and reviews Tayyiban indicators in relation to Halal food production	Tayyiban's indicators include: a) Nutrition - keeping body healthier and stronger, b) Safety - not harmful and dangerous, c) Cleanliness - hygiene and pure, d) Quality - satisfying consumers' taste buds, and e) Authenticity - meeting a) to d) points.
3	Dahlal et al. (2024)	The article investigates the integration of food safety and customer service practices in accordance with Halal and Toyyib principles	Halal and Toyyib principles include: a) Products' physical attributes to comply with Shariah law, b) Products are ethically and responsibly sourced, c) Products adhere to high standards of quality and safety, d) Acting as a servant and representative of Allah by managing responsibilities in accordance with His commands and prohibitions, e) Not excessively wasteful or extravagant, f) Positive moral and spiritual implications associated with the products, and g) Aimed at achieving prosperity in both this life and the hereafter.
4	Hamdan et al. (2024)	The article aims to systematically review the existing literature on cultivated meat from an Islamic perspective	Islamic perspectives for food cultivation include: a) Lawful food, b) Lawfully sourced, c) Meet the belief in God's creation, d) Produced in line with Halal standards, and e) Beneficial according to Islamic goals.
5	Islam et al. (2024a)	The study underlines Islamic principles to business theories and Halal marketing for practitioners	Muslims should embrace Halal and Tayyab, while avoiding Haram and Khabith (impure). Any doubt about Halal or Haram should be avoided, and Khabith should be rejected in producing, consuming, certifying, and accepting Halal and Tayyab.
6	Islam et al. (2024b)	The study emphasises on Islamic Marketing and Circular Economy to Foster Sustainability	A sustainable production approach based on Halal and Tayyib principles in Islamic marketing offers guidance to minimise waste and resource overuse, engaging both consumers and producers in sustainable practices.
7	Jelan et al. (2024)	The book chapter looks at the concepts of Halalan and Tayyiban and their application in meat production	Halalan Tayyiban food must comply with Shariah law requirements, as verified through Halal certification. Tayyib encompasses wholesomeness, nutrition, and quality, with principles that span from farming practices through production to consumption. These principles ensure that food production avoids environmental degradation and accommodates the needs of a growing population.

continued on following page

Table 2. Continued

No	Authors	Scope of the Study	Halalan Tayyiban Concepts for Food or Related Aspects
8	Ahmad & Nordin (2023)	The article links the Halalan Toyyiban concept with environmental sciences and offers a new perspective on food safety issues	Halalan Toyyiban means a comprehensive guideline for assessing the lawfulness (Halal) or unlawfulness (Haram) of food preparation from farm to fork, ensuring that the food is wholesome, clean, and hygienic. In addition, high-quality, pure Halal food nourishes both body and soul, supporting spiritual devotion and mental clarity. It embodies the principles of Ihsan (excellence) and Itqan (competence), enabling worship to be performed with greater focus and sincerity.
9	Hamdan & Hashim (2022)	The article examines Halalan Thayyiban practices currently implemented in food restaurants	Halalan Thayyiban practices include: a) Health - food quality and trust on suppliers, b) Safety - not contaminated to avoid illness and poisoning, and c) Hygiene - clean. Overall, it constitutes healthy and good quality Halal food.
10	Ikomatussuniah & Maler (2021)	The article aims to study the evolution of scholars' (ulama) roles in relation to the history of Halalan Tayyiban food law	Halalan Thayyiban's food law include: a) Producers to bear the primary responsibility for ensuring quality throughout all stages of production, b) Food regulations are evolving to meet food security needs and must align with the religious beliefs and cultural values of the community, and c) Halal product assurance is provided via Halal certification, in accordance with Halal fatwa.
11	Rahim et al. (2021)	The conference proceeding outlines fundamental criteria for understanding Halal food security from an Islamic perspective	Islamic criteria of Halal food security include: a) Allah as provider - the blessings bestowed by Allah including plants, fruits, and diverse animals, are provided abundantly to ensure that humans live in good health and well-being, b) Guaranteed income from Allah to all creatures - industrialised Halal food generates income and creates market demand within society, c) The role of government - the government must uphold the trust of its leaders and fulfill its essential duties, while also addressing the political economy of sustainable development, and d) The preservation of life - ensuring that halal food is accessible to everyone.
12	Bujang et al. (2020)	The article reviews various nanotechnology applications in the food industry and connect them with the requirements for food to be considered Halal and Tayyib	From the Halalan Tayyiban standpoint, food must not only come from Halal sources but also be of high quality, nutritious, and safe for all individuals, regardless of their religion. This ensures the highest possible standard of health for everyone.
13	Yahaya & Ruzulan (2020)	The article aims to discuss the Quranic concept of Halalan Tayyiban and its application in the food and beverage sector of the hospitality industry	Halalan Tayyiban for food and beverage cover good and pure because of the Halal status, as well as nutritious, pleasant in taste and smell, clean, fresh, and beneficial for the body, mind, and soul. Moreover, the issuance of a Halal certificate involves inspecting Halalan Tayyiban procedures and ensuring compliance with Shariah standards.

continued on following page

Table 2. Continued

No	Authors	Scope of the Study	Halalan Tayyiban Concepts for Food or Related Aspects
14	Mustaffa (2019)	The article models the concept of Halalan Tayyiban to be integrated throughout the entire food production chain	Halalan Tayyiban ensures that the food production process is both lawful and good. Accordingly, the principles are established through the implementation of Halal certification management and control systems, addressing key elements including: a) Compliance with Shariah Law, b) Unlawful elements and Syubhah prevention, c) Food hygiene and quality practices compliance, and d) Internal Halal management.
15	Khan et al. (2018)	The article offers a thorough definition of Halal Supply Chain Management by incorporating Halal and Toyyib principles	Toyyib is understood to encompass qualities such as being nourishing, safe, hygienic, and wholesome. It also includes principles like animal welfare, humane treatment of animals before slaughter, environmental protection, fair trade, and sustainable consumption practices.
16	Shafiee et al. (2017)	The paper evaluates Halalan Toiyyiban practices among food vendors to ensure the food served is safe and suitable for consumption	Halal and Toiyyib dietary factors encompass cleanliness, purity, and ethical sourcing. These principles contribute to both physical and mental well-being while fostering spiritual growth and integrity in individuals.
17	Arif & Sidek (2015)	The article develops a framework for determining Halal food based on the concept of Halalan Tayyiban	Tayyiban encompasses key elements including: a) The food must come from halal sources and not Haram, b) The food should be clean and free from impurities, c) The food should not cause any harm or discomfort to those who eat it, and d) The food must be nutritious and beneficial to those who consume it. Alternatively, The food is Halal and sourced from Halal origins, as well as of high quality (delicious, tasty, pure, hygiene, and safe) providing benefits to those who consume it. This concept applies from the initial food preparation through to its final production.

Source: Authors' Own

3.1 Understanding the Concept of Halalan Tayyiban

In a study by Islam et al. (2025), it was argued that Ajka represents the purest form of purity, making Halalan Tayyiban incomplete without it. Ajka enhances Halalan Tayyiban by incorporating spiritual elements and connecting various stakeholders in the Halal industry. However, the study did not align with existing research on Ajka in Halal food, as it was rarely discussed in the literature. Therefore, the concept of Halalan Tayyiban, as presented in this study, is understood through several indicators that, though not fully consistent, share key common points. This subsection explores these insights further.

Firstly, Halalan Tayyiban is defined by its adherence to Shariah law throughout the entire food production process, from farm to fork. This ensures that food meets Islamic requirements, verified through Halal certification and control systems. These certification processes involve inspections to confirm compliance with Shariah standards, ensuring food is free from Haram or unlawful elements (Ahmad & Nordin, 2023; Hamdan et al., 2024; Ikomatussuniah & Maler, 2021; Jelan et al., 2024; Yahaya & Ruzulan, 2020).

Secondly, food resources must be ethically and responsibly sourced, reflecting Allah's (SWT) abundant provisions and aligning with religious principles. This includes ensuring food products meet Shariah standards in their physical attributes. Mustaffa (2019) explained that Halalan Tayyiban food must adhere to Shariah law, be free from unlawful elements and Syubhah (doubtful elements), comply with hygiene and quality practices, and maintain Halal integrity through internal management (Arif & Sidek, 2015; Dahlal et al., 2024; Hamdan et al., 2024; Rahim et al., 2021).

Thirdly, Halalan Tayyiban emphasises the importance of cleanliness, which encompasses hygiene, purity, and freshness to ensure food is free from impurities (Abdul Mokti et al., 2024; Ahmad & Nordin, 2023; Arif & Sidek, 2015; Hamdan & Hashim, 2022; Yahaya & Ruzulan, 2020). Fourthly, food must be safe and should not be harmful or dangerous. Hamdan and Hashim (2022) highlighted the importance of avoiding contamination to prevent illness and poisoning, while Arif and Sidek (2015) asserted that food should not cause harm or discomfort to consumers (Abdul Mokti et al., 2024; Bujang et al., 2020; Dahlal et al., 2024).

Fifthly, food must be nutritious and beneficial, contributing positively to health and well-being. This ensures food supports the body, mind, and soul, maintaining the highest health standards (Abdul Mokti et al., 2024; Arif & Sidek, 2015; Bujang et al., 2020; Jelan et al., 2024; Yahaya & Ruzulan, 2020). When all the aforementioned criteria are met, the food is considered high-quality, which is desirable regardless of religious background. In this sense, quality refers to food that is pleasant in taste and smell, satisfying consumer preferences (Abdul Mokti et al., 2024; Ahmad & Nordin, 2023; Arif & Sidek, 2015; Bujang et al., 2020; Dahlal et al., 2024; Jelan et al., 2024; Yahaya & Ruzulan, 2020).

The ethical and spiritual dimensions of food consumption must also be considered. Food should be managed responsibly, avoiding waste, and aligning with religious and cultural values. This includes sharing food to support food security and complying with environmental considerations in line with Islamic principles (Dahlal et al., 2024; Ikomatussuniah & Maler, 2021; Jelan et al., 2024; Khan et al., 2018; Rahim et al., 2021). Food practices should also foster spiritual devotion and mental clarity, contributing to the principles of Ihsan (excellence) and Itqan (competence), enhancing both physical and spiritual well-being (Ahmad & Nordin, 2023; Dahlal et al., 2024; Shafiee et al., 2017).

Lastly, important criteria include generating economic opportunities through Halal food demand (Khan et al., 2018; Rahim et al., 2021) and ensuring that all stakeholders, including producers and government agencies, effectively apply Halalan Tayyiban principles from farm to fork (Ikomatussuniah & Maler, 2021; Islam et al., 2024a; Khan et al., 2018; Rahim et al., 2021).

3.2 Integrating Halalan Tayyiban Principles into Food Security

This subsection discusses how the Halalan Tayyiban principles identified in the reviewed literature intersect with each respective element of food security, including availability, accessibility, utilisation, and stability. Several verses from the Al-Quran will also be integrated as references where necessary, to support the application of Halalan Tayyiban principles in the context of food security.

3.2.1 Halalan Tayyiban and Food Security Availability

A key aspect of food security is availability, which includes both the quantity and quality of food supplies. Halalan Tayyiban plays a crucial role in this context. According to Rahim et al. (2021), food security, from an Islamic perspective, is linked to recognising Allah (SWT) as the ultimate provider, who has blessed humanity with a variety of plants, fruits, and animals for health and well-being. Surah 'Abasa (80:24-32) describes how Allah (SWT) provides His blessings to support sustainable consumption for humanity, as translated:

> *"Let people then consider their food: how We pour down rain in abundance and meticulously split the earth open for sprouts , causing grain to grow in it, as well as grapes and greens, olives and palm trees, dense orchards, and fruit and fodder—all as a means of sustenance for you and your animals" [Surah 'Abasa, 80:24-32].*

Yet, when it comes to consuming food, it is crucial to consider both its ethical and religious aspects. Dahlal et al. (2024) and Hamdan et al. (2024) emphasised that food should be produced following Shariah law. Mustaffa (2019) added that Halalan Tayyiban requires Shariah-compliant practices throughout production, avoiding Haram activities such as fraud, interest-based transactions, and corruption. Jelan et al. (2024) further argued that standardising these principles in food production prevents environmental degradation and ensures food availability for a growing population.

In essence, Shariah compliance ensures food meets Halal standards of quality, including wholesomeness, purity, safety, cleanliness, and nutrition. These attributes contribute to the well-being of the body, mind, and soul, regardless of religious beliefs (Abdul Mokti et al., 2024; Ahmad & Nordin, 2023; Arif & Sidek, 2015; Bujang et al., 2020; Hamdan & Hashim, 2022; Khan et al., 2018; Shafiee et al., 2017; Yahaya & Ruzulan, 2020).

3.2.2 Halalan Tayyiban and Food Security Accessibility

Food accessibility is key to achieving food security, and the Halalan Tayyiban concept offers three perspectives on making food accessible globally. Firstly, Rahim et al. (2021) emphasised that food security from an Islamic viewpoint includes both availability and accessibility. Allah (SWT) provides abundant plants, fruits, and animals, ensuring that food can be sourced, produced, and consumed in line with Shariah law. This concept is reflected in Surah Taha (20:81), which instructs humans to consume what Allah (SWT) has made permissible and avoid transgression, as translated:

> *"Eat from the good things with which We have provided you and do not transgress [or oppress others] therein, lest My anger should descend upon you. And he upon whom My anger descends has certainly fallen" [Surah Taha, 20:81].*

Secondly, Ramli et al. (2021) highlighted that individuals can lawfully convert these resources into economic opportunities, with industrialised Halal food production generating income and stimulating market demand, thus improving accessibility. Khan et al. (2018) supported this by noting that Halalan Tayyiban principles advocate for fair trade practices that benefit all parties, contributing to sustainable consumption and wider food accessibility.

The third perspective focuses on sustainable consumption, which Rahim et al. (2021) described as "the preservation of life". Here, Halal Tayyiban food should be accessible to everyone, emphasising responsible stewardship. Dahlal et al. (2024) argued that humans, as stewards of Allah (SWT), must manage resources to avoid wastefulness, and Fauzan and Syara (2023) noted that Islam provides guidance on ensuring Halal food is Shariah-compliant and equitably distributed. Those in the Halal food supply chain bear the responsibility to ensure sustainable and accessible food consumption.

Addressing these three aspects is essential for ensuring food accessibility, which is closely linked to the availability component of food security, ensuring both quantity and quality (Abdul Mokti et al., 2024; Ahmad & Nordin, 2023; Arif & Sidek, 2015; Bujang et al., 2020; Hamdan et al., 2024; Hamdan & Hashim, 2022; Jelan et al., 2024; Khan et al., 2018; Shafiee et al., 2017; Yahaya & Ruzulan, 2020).

3.2.3 Halalan Tayyiban and Food Security Utilisation

Proper utilisation of available food to meet nutritional and physiological needs is crucial for food security. Rahim et al. (2021) asserted that food resources provided by Allah (SWT) can enhance health, but they must adhere to Shariah guidelines throughout their lifecycle, including input, processing, and output (Arif & Sidek, 2015; Ahmad & Nordin, 2023; Jelan et al., 2024; Mustaffa, 2019; Shafiee et al., 2017). This ensures food is Halal, nutritious, safe, and meets both religious and health standards.

In essence, high-quality, contamination-free food benefits the body, mind, and soul, improving overall health (Abdul Mokti et al., 2024; Hamdan et al., 2024; Hamdan & Hashim, 2022; Shafiee et al., 2017; Yahaya & Ruzulan, 2020). Adherence to these standards prevents illness and foodborne poisoning (Bujang et al., 2020; Hamdan & Hashim, 2022). Arif and Sidek (2015) and Islam et al. (2024a) emphasised that food should be clean, free from impurities, and beneficial.

Ethical and responsible food use is also essential. Islam advocates avoiding waste and sharing food with those in need to ensure accessibility for all (Abdul Mokti et al., 2024; Dahlal et al., 2020). In Surah Al-A'raf (7:31) of the Al-Quran, Allah (SWT) explicitly advises against food waste, highlighting the importance of moderation and respect for the blessings provided, as translated:

> *"Children of Adam, dress well whenever you are at worship, and eat and drink [as We have permitted] but do not be extravagant: God does not like extravagant people" [Surah Al-A'raf, 7:31].*

Acting as stewards of Allah (SWT), individuals are called to manage resources responsibly, promoting moral and spiritual outcomes (Dahlal et al., 2024). Ahmad and Nordin (2023) noted that Halal food nourishes both the body and soul, enhancing spiritual devotion and mental clarity. Adhering to Ihsan (excellence) and Itqan (competence) aligns one's actions with divine guidance and strengthens worship.

3.2.4 Halalan Tayyiban and Food Security Stability

Food security depends on the consistent availability and accessibility of food, ensuring its effective use even amid global disruptions. The Halalan Tayyiban concept offers a unique perspective on sustaining food security.

Firstly, Rahim et al. (2021) emphasised that industrialising Halal food is essential for maintaining stable food supplies, generating income, and stimulating market demand. Khan et al. (2018) reinforced this view, noting that stability is strengthened when Tayyib principles, such as animal welfare, humane treatment before slaughter, environmental protection, fair trade, and sustainable consumption, are applied. This aligns with Mustaffa's (2019) perspective that food should precisely meet human needs without excess or deficiency.

Secondly, Idris et al. (2022) described Halalan Tayyiban as a holistic framework that aligns with international standards, enhancing global acceptability. This approach provides businesses with a strategic advantage in the Halal industry by ensuring comprehensive Halal certification and management systems. Rigorous inspection of Halalan Tayyiban practices ensures adherence to Shariah standards (Arif & Sidek, 2015; Mustaffa, 2019; Shafiee et al., 2017; Yahaya & Ruzulan, 2020). For example, in Malaysia, the MS1500:2009 guidelines and the Trade Description Act 2011 establish robust regulations for Halal certification and management, ensuring the integrity of Halal practices. In contrast, Indonesia's evolving food regulations, as discussed by Ikomatussuniah and Maler (2021), are being adapted to address food security needs while maintaining alignment with religious and cultural values through Halal product assurance. Therefore, Halalan Tayyiban serves as a comprehensive guideline for evaluating the lawfulness or unlawfulness of food preparation, ensuring that food is wholesome, clean, and hygienic (Ahmad & Nordin, 2023; Jelan et al., 2024).

Lastly, the stability of food supplies relies on the active involvement of all stakeholders. Food producers must maintain quality at every production stage to uphold Halalan Tayyiban standards (Ikomatussuniah & Maler, 2021). Governments play a key role in addressing the political and economic aspects of sustainable development (Rahim et al., 2021), while the food industry, including restaurants and service providers, must adhere to Halalan Tayyiban practices in compliance with Shariah law (Hamdan & Hashim, 2022).

Ultimately, stability within Halalan Tayyiban contributes to prosperity in this life and the hereafter (Dahlal et al., 2024). On Judgment Day, true benefit will be granted to those who approach Allah (SWT) with a pure and sincere heart. This profound concept is articulated in Surah Ash-Shu'ara (26:87-89), as translated:

> *"And do not disgrace me on the Day all will be resurrected - the Day when neither wealth nor children will be of any benefit. Only those who come before Allah with a pure heart will be saved" [Surah Ash-Shu'ara, 26:87-89].*

3.3 Theoretical Contributions: Halalan Tayyiban and Food Security

This study advances the body of knowledge in several significant ways. First, this study addresses the ambiguity surrounding the definition and framework of Halalan Tayyiban principles, an issue noted in the literature (Abdul Mokti et al., 2024; Dahlal & Ahmad, 2018; Demirci et al., 2016). In addition, by integrating these principles into the broader context of global food security, this study offers a structured approach that clarifies the concept and promotes its formal recognition. Such clarification has the potential to improve global market acceptance and strengthen consumer trust, thereby advancing the practical application of Halalan Tayyiban in the food industry.

Second, this study addresses a significant research gap by focusing specifically on the Halalan Tayyiban aspects of food security. While existing literature often explores various dimensions of food security, it frequently overlooks the nuanced issues related to food security from the Halalan Tayyiban perspective (Abdul Mokti et al., 2024; Ahmad & Nordin, 2023; Arif & Sidek, 2015; Bujang et al., 2024; Dahlal et al., 2024; Hamdan et al., 2024; Hamdan & Hashim, 2022; Ikomatussuniah & Maler, 2021; Jelan et al., 2024; Khan et al., 2018; Mustaffa, 2019; Shafiee et al., 2017; Yahaya & Ruzulan, 2020). By examining how Halalan Tayyiban principles can be incorporated into a comprehensive framework for food security, this study bridges this gap and aligns with SDGs.

Finally, this study significantly deepens the understanding of Halal food security from an Islamic perspective, a topic that remains underexplored in the literature (Abdul Mokti et al., 2024; Rahim et al., 2021). By integrating Halalan Tayyiban concepts, it not only enriches the existing body of knowledge but also provides a more nuanced and comprehensive perspective on Halalan Tayyiban food security. This contribution enhances the theoretical framework and practical understanding of how Islamic principles can be applied to address contemporary food security challenges.

Given the preceding discussions, Figure 3 illustrates the conceptual framework developed in this study, examining food security through the Halalan Tayyiban lens.

Figure 3. Conceptual framework of Halalan Tayyiban and food security

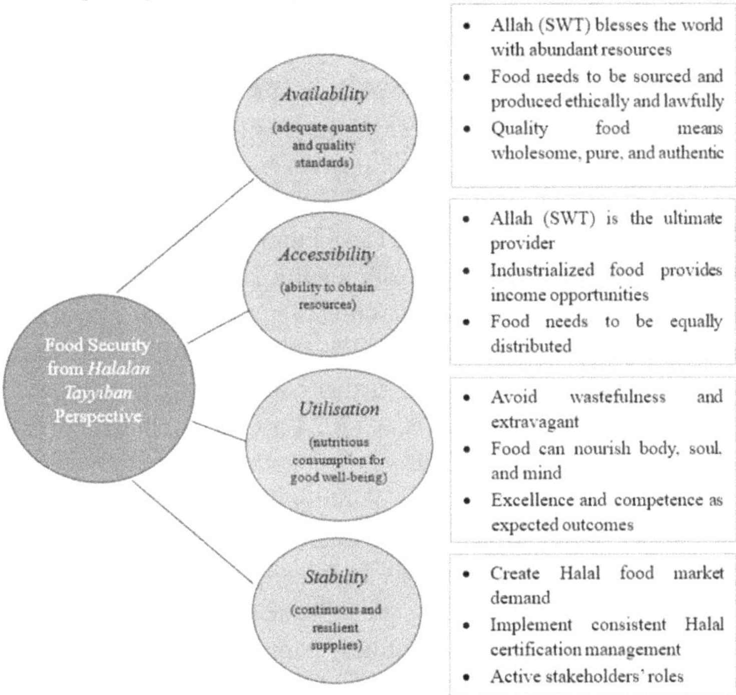

Essentially, this framework underscores that food security is fundamentally supported by Allah's (SWT) blessings, which make available a rich variety of resources, including plants, fruits, and animals. To align with Islamic teachings, these resources must be sourced and produced in a manner that is both lawful and ethical. Furthermore, these resources should be distributed responsibly to those in need, underscoring the significance of sustainable consumption practices that guarantee accessibility for all.

Utilising available and accessible food effectively contributes to the nourishment of the body, mind, and soul, thereby enhancing one's ibadah (worship) and overall well-being. For this reason, ensuring stability in food security requires adherence to consistent Halalan Tayyiban standards throughout the food supply chain, from farm to fork, and relies on the proactive involvement of all stakeholders.

3.4 Practical Contributions: The Role of Stakeholders in Halalan Tayyiban Food

This study explores how Islamic perspectives, particularly the Halalan Tayyiban view, can address contemporary challenges such as food security while examining the practical applications of these principles. Islam et al. (2023) highlighted that achieving Halalan Tayyiban is not without challenges, including inconsistent standards, varying levels of strictness, and a lack of understanding, all of which complicate compliance for Halal producers. Additionally, Halal-certified businesses often struggle with poor collaboration among scholars and a shortage of qualified Islamic experts, leading to inconsistent interpretations of Islamic principles. Moreover, certification preferences vary by country, further complicating the standardisation of Halal practices. For example, Ismail et al. (2024) found that in Brunei Darussalam, food certification may be delayed due to the lengthy approval process, despite its mandatory nature to ensure market availability. Furthermore, its Halal standard, PBD24: 2007, lacks international recognition, making its validity questionable in other countries. In contrast, Malaysia's Halal standard, MS1500:2009, adopts a broader approach, addressing not only Halal but also hygiene and food safety risks, thus demonstrating the country's commitment to implementing the Halalan Tayyiban concept in practice (Yahaya & Ruzulan, 2020).

Essentially, the Halalan Tayyiban concept provides a holistic framework for food production, encompassing health protection, food safety, animal welfare, environmental sustainability, social justice, ethical business practices, and overall well-being (Idris et al., 2022; Khan et al., 2018). A comprehensive review by Islam et al. (2024b) illustrated how the circular economy concept aligns with Islamic principles, emphasising resource efficiency while avoiding Haram and Khabith elements. Consequently, Islamic principles can play a pivotal role in optimising the product life cycle by integrating Halal and Tayyib values, yielding benefits for both individuals and society.

Given this, it is crucial for every participant in the Halal food supply chain to ensure that food meets both Halal and Tayyiban standards (Fauzan & Syara, 2023; Islam & Wahab, 2022). Rahim et al. (2021) underscored the necessity for stakeholders to guarantee food quality while ensuring it remains free from Haram elements to fulfill Halalan Tayyiban criteria. This perspective is further supported by Islam and Wahab (2022), who highlighted the significant role of stakeholders in developing effective food security solutions that align with Halalan Tayyiban standards.

Building on this, Mustaffa (2019) identified three key groups responsible for implementing Halalan Tayyiban: consumers, producers, and government agencies. Specifically, consumers have a role in reporting any breaches of Halalan Tayyiban requirements to the relevant authorities, thereby ensuring the maintenance of food safety and quality standards (Mustaffa, 2019; Rahim et al., 2021; Yahaya & Ruzulan, 2020). Producers, in turn, must adhere strictly to Halalan Tayyiban principles throughout the production process, using these principles as benchmarks to maintain quality and compliance. Fauzan and Syara (2023) asserted that food producers must ensure that any Halal food marketed to Muslims meets Halalan Tayyiban standards. Similarly, Yahaya and Ruzulan (2020) stressed the importance of food managers and operators understanding Quranic principles related to Halalan Tayyiban at every stage of food handling, from production to serving. In Brunei Darussalam, for instance, even Japanese restaurants comply with the Halalan Tayyiban concept, believing that Shariah law embedded in the system fosters a healthy, safe, and hygienic environment for food businesses (Hamdan & Hashim, 2022). Since, 2017, the country has mandated Halal certification for all local food businesses in line with the Department of Religious Affairs' requirements (Ismail et al., 2024).

In parallel, government agencies play an integral role in maintaining Halalan Tayyiban standards. Rahim et al. (2021) contended that these agencies must operate with integrity and responsibility to ensure the welfare of the population. Mustaffa (2019) elaborated that these agencies should create and enforce frameworks for traders, producers, and food manufacturers to adhere to Islamic requirements, including enforcing laws and offering ongoing training. For example, in Indonesia, religious authorities such as the ulama issue Halal fatwas and oversee compliance with certified Halal practices (Ikomatussuniah & Maler, 2021). Its government plays a critical role in protecting Muslims' rights, as seen in Indonesia's food laws and Halal product assurance acts, which institutionalise Halal standards under public law. That is, Halal agencies should be tasked with issuing valid Halal certificates and ensuring consistent adherence to Halalan Tayyiban procedures and Shariah standards (Mohd Riza et al., 2022; Yahaya & Ruzulan, 2020).

In conclusion, both producers and government authorities must uphold the integrity of the Halalan Tayyiban certification process to maintain quality and compliance throughout the food supply chain. This commitment is essential for enhancing the global Halal food market and meeting the demand for Halalan Tayyiban products among both Muslim and non-Muslim consumers (Jelan et al., 2024). Achieving food security while adhering to Halalan Tayyiban standards requires a collaborative effort from all stakeholders. Producers, regulators, and government agencies must work together to ensure the integrity of the Halal food supply chain and successfully meet these goals (Rahim et al., 2021).

4.0 CONCLUSIONS

This study explores the concept of Halalan Tayyiban and investigates how its principles align with the four key elements of food security. From an Islamic viewpoint, food should be wholesome, pure, and authentic, encompassing qualities such as nutritional value, safety, cleanliness, and hygiene. These attributes are essential for the overall well-being of individuals, irrespective of their religious beliefs. Furthermore, maintaining the stability of Halalan Tayyiban food involves rigorous adherence to ethical Halal certification standards throughout the entire food supply chain, ensuring compliance with Shariah law. This commitment is crucial for ensuring that food remains consistently high in quality and integrity.

Fundamentally, consumers need to be well-informed about Halalan Tayyiban principles and actively report any breaches or suspicious activities. This vigilance is essential for ensuring that food businesses adhere to ethical practices and comply with Shariah law, thereby maintaining high standards of food safety and quality. Food businesses, in turn, bear the responsibility of sourcing and producing food in accordance with Shariah requirements. They must rigorously apply Halalan Tayyiban principles throughout their operations to ensure transparency, high quality, and ethical conduct. In addition, government agencies play a crucial role in overseeing and enforcing Halalan Tayyiban standards. They are tasked with developing and implementing regulations, managing Halal certification processes, and providing guidance and resources to both consumers and businesses. This oversight is vital for ensuring compliance, safeguarding food security, and upholding public welfare.

This study has several limitations. Firstly, this study is constrained by the limited research specifically addressing the intersection of Halalan Tayyiban principles and food security. Most existing literature primarily concentrates on the business aspects of Halal food rather than the roles of various stakeholders in ensuring Halalan Tayyiban compliance. Secondly, while this study provides a broad overview of Halalan Tayyiban principles, it does not explore into the detailed specifics of Shariah law regarding Halal and Haram. However, this omission is considered acceptable given this study's primary focus on integrating Halalan Tayyiban principles with food security.

Future research should focus on several key areas to further build upon this study. First, a more detailed investigation into the indicators of Halalan Tayyiban and their connections to contemporary agricultural issues, industry trends, and market dynamics is needed, given the concept's application from farm to fork. Such research could deepen the understanding of how these principles influence various stages of the food supply chain. Additionally, it could explore the roles of concepts such as Haram and Khabith, highlighting how they may hinder progress in the sector and, subsequently, offer potential solutions. Furthermore, future SLR should focus on exploring how different countries implement Halalan Tayyiban principles within their food sectors. A comparative analysis of these practices would provide valuable insights into the effectiveness of different approaches and identify best practices across various contexts.

Moreover, incorporating primary data through surveys or interviews could offer a deeper understanding beyond existing literature. This approach would be particularly useful for examining how Halalan Tayyiban principles can be integrated into the Fourth Industrial Revolution (4IR) era, which is critical for advancing food security.

REFERENCES

Abdul Mokti, H., Kamri, N. A., & Mohd Balwi, M. A. W. F. (2024). Tayyiban in Halal Food Production: A Systematic Literature Review. *Journal of Islamic Marketing*, *15*(2), 397–417. DOI: 10.1108/JIMA-03-2022-0098

Ahmad, F. N., & Nordin, N. F. H. (2023). Environmental Approach for Securing Halalan Toyyiban Concept in Food Safety-A Mini Review. *Halalsphere*, *3*(1), 27–30. DOI: 10.31436/hs.v3i1.70

Al-Amin, R. A. M. (2023). Food Consumption from Islamic Perspective: Evidence from Qur'an and Sunnah. *European Journal for Philosophy of Religion*, *15*(3), 257–280.

Alzeer, J., Rieder, U., & Abou Hadeed, K. (2018). Rational and Practical Aspects of Halal and Tayyib in the Context of Food Safety. *Trends in Food Science & Technology*, *71*, 264–267. DOI: 10.1016/j.tifs.2017.10.020

Arif, S., & Sidek, S. (2015). Application of Halalan Tayyiban in the Standard Reference for Determining Malaysian Halal Food. *Asian Social Science*, *11*(17), 116. DOI: 10.5539/ass.v11n17p116

Bujang, A., Rahman, F. A., & Omar, S. R. S. (2020). Nanotechnology in the Food Processing and Packaging: An Overview of Its Halalan Tayyiban Aspect. *Malaysian J Consum Fam Econ*, *24*, 1–14.

Chowdhury, A. J. K., Hashim, N., Marsal, C. J., & Jamaludin, M. H. (2023). Water Treatment and Aquaculture Products Towards Halal Value Chain in ASEAN Countries: A Retrospective Review on Brunei Darussalam. *Desalination and Water Treatment*, *315*, 479–491. DOI: 10.5004/dwt.2023.30014

Dahlal, N. M., & Ahmad, F. A. (2018). Beyond Halal in Food Product: Present and Future of Halalan Tayyiban. *Review of Integrative Business and Economics Research*, *7*, 276–289.

Dahlal, N. M., Saniff, S. M., & Noh, C. N. C. (2024). Harmonising Food Safety and Friendly Service through Halal and Toyyib Principles. *Halalsphere*, *4*(1), 80–87. DOI: 10.31436/hs.v4i1.89

Demirci, M. N., Soon, J. M., & Wallace, C. A. (2016). Positioning Food Safety in Halal Assurance. *Food Control*, *70*, 257–270. DOI: 10.1016/j.foodcont.2016.05.059

Fauzan, T. R., & Syara, A. S. (2023). Enhancing Food Security through Halal System with a Logistic Regression Analysis. *Enrichment: Journal of Management, 13*(2), 857–867.

Food and Agriculture Organisation. (FAO, 2006). *Food Security*. Policy Brief 2. Retrieved on 07/08/24, from https://www.fao.org/fileadmin/templates/faoitaly/documents/pdf/pdf_Food_Security_Cocept_Note.pdf

Hamdan, M. N., Jalil, R. A., Ramli, M. A., Ramli, N., Ibrahim, M. N. A., Ab Rahman, M. F., & Abd Rahman, N. N. H. (2024). A Review of the Discussions on Cultivated Meat from the Islamic Perspective. *Heliyon, 10*(7), e28491. DOI: 10.1016/j.heliyon.2024.e28491 PMID: 38601623

Hamdan, N. F., & Hashim, N. (2022). The Practices of Halalan Thayyiban Aspect in Japanese Restaurants in Brunei Darussalam. *Journal of Halal Science and Technology, 1*(1), 67–73. DOI: 10.59202/jhst.v1i1.456

Idris, P. S. R. P. H., Musa, S. F. P. D., & Sumardi, W. H. H. (2022). Halal-Tayyiban and Sustainable Development Goals: A SWOT Analysis. [IJABIM]. *International Journal of Asian Business and Information Management, 13*(2), 1–16. DOI: 10.4018/IJABIM.20220701.oa9

Ikomatussuniah, M. R. B., & Maler, M. W. (2021). Transformation of Ulama's Role in Nusantara: A Case Study of Halalan Thayyiban Food Law in Indonesia. *Journal of Academic Research in Business and Social Sciences, 11*(4), 477–462.

Islam, A., & Wahab, S. A. (2022). The Concerns Associated with Future Prospects of the Food Cart Business in Chittagong, Bangladesh: Is the concept of Halalan Tayyiba Missing Link? *Rajagiri Management Journal, 16*(1), 21–35. DOI: 10.1108/RAMJ-09-2020-0052

Islam, M. M., Ab Talib, M. S., & Muhamad, N. (2023). Challenges of Halal Standards and Halal Certification for Islamic Marketing. *Muslim Business and Economics Review, 2*(1), 105–124. DOI: 10.56529/mber.v2i1.156

Islam, M. M., Ab Talib, M. S., & Muhamad, N. (2024a). Developing Theoretical Lenses for Upstream Halal businesses. *Journal of Islamic Marketing, 15*(1), 192–220. DOI: 10.1108/JIMA-05-2022-0156

Islam, M. M., Ab Talib, M. S., & Muhamad, N. (2024b). Islamic Marketing and Circular Economy to Foster Sustainability of Product Life Cycle Enhancement. In *Strategic Islamic Business and Management: Solutions for Sustainability* (pp. 125–141). Springer Nature Switzerland. DOI: 10.1007/978-3-031-61778-2_7

Islam, M. M., Ab Talib, M. S., & Muhamad, N. (2025). Could Ajka Be the Next Frontier of Halal?: Halal Food. In *Innovative Ventures and Strategies in Islamic Business* (pp. 169-194). IGI Global Scientific Publishing.

Ismail, K., Shahlehi, S. F. H., & Shaya, V. N. (2024). SMEs' Perspectives on the Benefits and Challenges of Halal Certificate Application in Brunei Darussalam. *ASEAN Journal on Science and Technology for Development, 41*(1), 3. DOI: 10.61931/2224-9028.1557

Jamaluddin, M. A., & Ramli, S. N. H. (2022). Smart Food for Future Sustainability: Halal and Tayyib Perspectives. *Journal of Halal Industry & Services, 5*(1). Advance online publication. DOI: 10.36877/jhis.a0000309

Jelan, Z. A., Pratiwi, A., & Isnaeni, P. D. (2024). Halal Meat Production in the Modern Era: Concepts and Applications. *Technological Innovations in Tropical Livestock Development for Environmental Sustainability and Food Security*, 1-6.

Khan, M. I., Haleem, A., & Khan, S. (2018, April). Defining Halal Supply Chain Management. In *Supply Chain Forum* []. Taylor & Francis.]. *International Journal (Toronto, Ont.), 19*(2), 122–131.

Matnor, R. B. H., Seri, D. H. N. B. D., & Mahalle, S. H. (2024). The Contribution of Natural Foods to the Sustainability of Halalan Toyyiban Lifestyle Based on Maqasid Shari'ah in Brunei Darussalam. *Halalsphere, 4*(2), 38–58.

Mohd Riza, N. S., Md Ariffin, M. F., Hamdan, M. N., & Ramli, N. (2022). Halal Food: A Social Responsibility on Cartel Meat Issue in Malaysia. *Food Research, 6*(3), 92–100. DOI: 10.26656/fr.2017.6(3).277

Mustaffa, K. A. (2019). Developing Halalan Tayyiban Concept in Malaysia's Food Industry. *Halal Journal, 3*(3), 97–108.

Nordin, F. N. M., Radzi, C. W. J. W. M., & Awang, M. D. (2022). Sustainability of Halal Food Industry: An Ethical Perspective. *Jurnal Al-Sirat, 22*(1), 120–126.

Page, M. J., Mckenzie, J. E., Bossuyt, P. M., Boutron, I., Hoffmann, T. C., Mulrow, C. D., & Moher, D. (2021). The PRISMA 2020 Statement: An Updated Guideline for Reporting Systematic Reviews. *BMJ (Clinical Research Ed.)*, •••, 372. PMID: 33782057

Qureshi, R. U. (2020). The Relation between Hadith and Sunnah (A Research Study). *Al-Wifaq, 3*(1), 91–102.

Rahim, S. I. A., Mansor, S. K. M., Ruzulan, Z., & Ismail, N. (2021). Developing Basic Criteria in Halal Food Security: An Overview from Islamic Perspectives. In *Enhancing Halal Sustainability: Selected Papers from the 4th International Halal Conference 2019* (Pp. 109-116). Springer Singapore.

Ruzulan, Z., Jamaludin, M. A., & Ishak, A. H. (2021, May). Meat and Meat-Based Products: Challenges and Opportunities in Halal Food Security. [). IOP Publishing.]. *IOP Conference Series. Earth and Environmental Science, 756*(1), 012017. DOI: 10.1088/1755-1315/756/1/012017

Salamon, H. B., Salbi, N. M., Rosman, A. S. B., Rosli, M. R. B., Noor, S. S. B. M., Muhamad, N. H. B. N., ... & Hussin, E. R. B. (2021). Halalan Tayyiba: An Islamic Perspective on Healthy Food. *Revista Geintec-Gestao Inovacao E Tecnologias, 11*(2), 1001-1014.

Shafiee, N. F., Karim, M., Razali, A., & Abidin, U. Z. (2017). Halalan Toiyyiban Food Handling Practices: A Review on Street Food Vendors in Malaysia. *Journal of Islamic, Social* [JISED]. *Economics and Development, 2*, 385–394.

Shaw, D. J. (2007). World Food Summit, 1996. In *World Food Security: A History Since 1945* (pp. 347–360). Palgrave Macmillan UK. DOI: 10.1057/9780230589780_35

Statista. (2024). *Forecast Market Revenue of Halal Food Worldwide from 2018 to 2027 (in Billion U.S. Dollars).* Retrieved on 23/08/24, from https://www.statista.com/statistics/785499/halal-food-market-revenue-global/

Sungit, F., Mohd Deni, M. I., Abdullah, M., & Syahwahid, F. (2020). Concepts and Practices of Halalan Tayyiban in the Islamic Manufacturing Practice (IMP): An Analysis from Syariah Perspective. *ESTEEM Journal of Social Sciences and Humanities, 4*, 214–229.

The World Bank. (2024). *What is Food Security.* Retrieved on 07/08/24, from https://www.worldbank.org/en/topic/agriculture/brief/food-security-update/what-is-food-security

Uddin, M. N. (2021). Food Controls to Build Workable Human Resource in Muslim Countries for Poverty Reduction: An Islamic View. *IIUC Studies, 18*(1), 33–46. DOI: 10.3329/iiucs.v18i1.61273

United Nations. (UN, 2024). *The SDGs in Action.* Retrieved on 23/08/24, from https://www.undp.org/sustainable-development-goals

Yahaya, A. M., & Ruzulan, Z. (2020). Quranic Concept of Halalan Tayyiban and Its Application in Food and Beverages of Hospitality Sector in Malaysia. *Journal of Contemporary Islamic Studies, 6*(1), 61–75. DOI: 10.24191/jcis.v6i1.4

Chapter 3
Islamic Finance and Halal Industry:
Building a Sustainable Shariah Ecosystem

Muhamad Yusup
https://orcid.org/0000-0002-4078-1572
State Islamic University Mataram, Indonesia

Nor Surilawana Sulaiman
https://orcid.org/0000-0002-4227-9703
Universiti Islam Sultan Sharif Ali, Brunei

ABSTRACT

This paper examines how Islamic finance and the halal industry work together to create a sustainable Shariah ecosystem. It explains how the principles of Shariah-compliant finance support the goals of the halal industry in promoting ethical and responsible economic practices. By analyzing case studies from Southeast Asia, the paper highlights how Islamic finance helps drive sustainable economic growth, financial inclusion, and environmental protection within the halal industry. It also addresses the challenges and opportunities in integrating these sectors and suggests strategies for long-term sustainability through innovative financial tools, regulatory changes, and collaboration among stakeholders. The paper concludes that a well-integrated Shariah ecosystem, combining Islamic finance and the halal industry, can greatly support global sustainable development goals while upholding ethical standards.

DOI: 10.4018/979-8-3373-3917-7.ch003

1.0 INTRODUCTION

Amidst the continuously evolving dynamics of the global economy, Islamic finance and the halal industry have emerged as two fundamental pillars of the Shariah economy. These sectors embody Islamic principles in business and financial practices and offer an inclusive, ethical, and sustainable economic model. Integrating Islamic finance with the halal industry is a strategic move to build a sustainable Shariah ecosystem. This ecosystem, supported by Islamic finance, can significantly contribute to economic growth, social welfare (Ibrahim, 2022), and environmental preservation (Talha, Faisal, & Khan, 2024).

Islamic finance operates based on Shariah principles, emphasising justice, transparency, and social responsibility (Elmelki & Ben Arab, 2009; Talha, Faisal, & Khan, 2024). These principles are reflected in the prohibition of *riba* (interest), *gharar* (uncertainty), and *maysir* (gambling) (Ibrahim, 2022), as well as encouraging investment in real and productive economic activities. Financial instruments such as *murabahah* (cost-plus financing), *mudarabah* (profit-sharing partnership), *musharakah* (joint venture), and *sukuk* (Islamic bonds) have become the foundation of Islamic finance, enabling the provision of ethical and risk-based capital (Islamic Development Bank, 2023; Radzi & Muhamed, 2019; Dewar & Hussain, 2023). Islamic finance is an alternative for the Muslim community and attracts global investors seeking stable, ethical, and sustainable financial instruments. World Bank Group (2022) stated that in Malaysia's Halal Industry Master Plan (HIMP) 2030, Islamic finance has been recognised as one of the five key enablers for implementing the strategies outlined. Nonetheless, Islamic financing to support the Halal economy varies significantly by sector and is more utilised by smaller halal-certified businesses.

On the other hand, the halal industry encompasses various economic sectors beyond traditional food and beverages, whose products comply with Islamic law, cosmetics, pharmaceuticals, fashion, and tourism (Ramadhan, Ulfah, Nurzianti, Bunkes, & Kadriyani, 2023). Global demand for halal products has increased significantly, driven by the growing Muslim population and the rising awareness of the importance of consumption in line with Islamic values (Muazu & Sjahrir, 2023). Halal standardisation and certification have become key elements in ensuring that products in the global market meet Shariah requirements. Countries such as Malaysia and Indonesia have become leaders in the halal industry (KiniHalal, 2023), the two countries are refining their halal ecosystems to strengthen their global halal industry (Nissa, 2023).

Creating a sustainable Shariah ecosystem necessitates collaboration between Islamic finance and the halal industry. The principle of sustainability in Islam highlights environmental protection, social justice, and economic responsibility, all of which are vital for establishing a balanced and sustainable financial model.

Islamic finance can offer essential funding for the halal industry's development. In contrast, the halal industry emphasises clean and ethical production, which can enhance the sustainability of the Shariah economy. Through the amalgamation of these two sectors, it is possible to cultivate an ecosystem that promotes economic growth and guarantees that such growth is advantageous to society as a whole and does not detrimentally affect the environment.

The Islamic finance and halal industries are similar in their Shariah-compliant perspectives. Islamic finance is part of financial services and the halal industry, including food, cosmetics, and pharmaceutical products, and is considered independent. This distinction arises primarily from the differing regulations that govern each market. One pertains to financial services, while the other is linked to product manufacturing and distribution. The closest intersection of these two markets lies in the availability of Shariah-compliant investment opportunities, particularly in Shariah-compliant securities, encompassing the halal manufacturing sector within the consumer goods arena.

This paper explores various concepts, challenges, and opportunities to examine how Islamic finance and the halal industry can synergise to build a sustainable Shariah ecosystem. It also aims to show how the synergy between these sectors can drive inclusive and sustainable economic growth.

2.0 FUNDAMENTALS OF ISLAMIC FINANCE AND HALAL INDUSTRY

2.1 Basics of Islamic Finance

Islamic finance operates according to Shariah principles derived from the Quran, Hadith, *ijma'* (consensus of scholars), and *qiyas* (analogy) (Yusuf, Mokoagow, Nur, & Rauf, 2023; Franzoni & Allali, 2018). These principles prohibit transactions deemed non-compliant with Islamic teachings, such as *riba*, *gharar*, and *maysir*. The primary focus is to ensure that all financial transactions are fair, transparent, and compliant with Shariah law. This encompasses applying profit-sharing principles, where profits and losses are equitably distributed among the parties involved in a transaction.

Islamic finance is a financial system that operates in accordance with Shariah principles derived from the Quran, Hadith, *ijma'*, and *qiyas*. The fundamental principles of Islamic finance prohibit practices deemed unjust or harmful, such as *riba*, *gharar*, and *maysir*. *Riba* is regarded as a form of exploitation and unfairness; therefore, Islamic finance does not impose interest charges on financial transactions. Instead, it employs mechanisms such as *mudarabah* (a partnership where one party provides capital and the other manages the business) and *musharakah* (a joint venture where all parties contribute capital and share profits and losses). Contracts such as *murabahah* (a sale with an agreed profit margin) and *ijarah* (leasing) are also utilised to ensure compliance with Shariah principles (Usmani, 2002; Visser, 2019).

Contracts in Islamic finance, such as *murabahah* and *ijarah*, must adhere to Shariah principles. Instruments like *sukuk* (Islamic bonds) are also designed to comply with these principles, generating returns from real assets and remaining free from *riba* elements. Each instrument and contract must be verified to ensure compliance with Shariah law, guaranteeing that the transactions are fair to all parties involved.

Islamic finance also emphasises social responsibility and wealth distribution. A crucial aspect of social responsibility in Islamic finance is *zakat*, the obligation to give a portion of one's wealth to assist those in need. In addition to *zakat*, there are *infaq* and *sadaqah*, which support social welfare. This system aims to reduce economic disparity and enhance social welfare, aligning with Islam's social justice principles (Hasan, 2009). Islamic finance seeks to create a fair and sustainable economic and social system by adhering to these principles.

2.2 Basics of the Halal Industry

The halal industry encompasses all economic sectors that produce goods and services that are compliant with Islamic Shariah law. In this context, 'halal' signifies 'permissible' according to Shariah, covering various products such as food, cosmetics, pharmaceuticals, and clothing. To be regarded as halal, a product or service must meet specific criteria, including the absence of haram substances like pork and alcohol, and must be produced cleanly and ethically. Halal certification plays a crucial role in this industry, with certification bodies like MUI (Majelis Ulama Indonesia) in Indonesia and JAKIM (Jabatan Kemajuan Islam Malaysia) in Malaysia conducting audits and issuing certificates to ensure that products meet Shariah standards (Poh, 2013).

Cleanliness and health are also crucial aspects of the halal industry. Halal products must be produced while upholding high standards of cleanliness and avoiding contamination with haram materials. For instance, in food production, equipment and environments must be free from non-halal substances to ensure the safety and quality of products. Furthermore, the halal industry strongly emphasises business ethics and sustainability, including fair treatment of workers and environmental protection. This reflects Shariah principles that advocate for justice, transparency, and social responsibility (Rashid, 2017).

The halal industry also emphasises the significance of business ethics and sustainability. Shariah principles underscore the necessity of transparency, justice, and social responsibility in commerce. This encompasses fair treatment of workers, environmental protection, and positive societal contributions. Sustainability within the halal industry entails efforts to minimise environmental impact and promote sustainable and ethical business practices.

3.0 THE HALAL INDUSTRY: SPECTRUM AND POTENTIAL

3.1 Spectrum of the Halal Industry

The halal industry includes various economic sectors that produce goods and services in line with Islamic Shariah principles. Initially, the main focus of the halal industry was on food and beverage products. However, as awareness and market demand have increased, the scope of the halal industry has expanded to encompass other sectors such as cosmetics, pharmaceuticals, fashion, and financial services. The definition of halal extends beyond adherence to food and beverage consumption rules to incorporate ethical principles in production and provision across various sectors, ensuring that products do not contain *haram* elements and are produced cleanly and fairly (Farouk, 2019). Some of these sectors include:

1. *Food and Beverage Sector*: The food and beverage sector is the largest segment of the halal industry. Halal food products must comply with Shariah rules, including the use of ingredients that do not contain haram substances, such as pork and alcohol, and methods of slaughtering that adhere to Islamic law. Additionally, the production process must ensure no cross-contamination with *haram* materials. The global halal food market continues to grow, driven by increasing demand from Muslim and non-Muslim consumers who are becoming more aware of the benefits of halal products (Henderson, 2021).
2. *Cosmetics and Personal Care*: Halal cosmetics are a rapidly growing sector within the halal industry. These cosmetics must be free from *haram* ingredients such as non-halal gelatin and alcohol and produced in accordance with Shariah principles. Halal personal care products also emphasise cleanliness and ethical production. Consumers concerned with halal products are increasingly seeking cosmetics that meet these standards, and many cosmetic companies are now launching halal product lines to fulfil market demand (Ali, 2020).
3. *Pharmaceuticals and Medicines*: The halal pharmaceuticals and medicines sector ensures that all active ingredients and excipients in pharmaceutical products adhere to Shariah law. This encompasses the use of halal ingredients and production methods that are free from haram elements. With the growing Muslim population and increasing awareness of the significance of halal products, there is an escalating demand for halal medicines and supplements, prompting

the pharmaceutical industry to integrate halal standards into their production processes (Sulaiman & Yusof, 2018).

4. *Fashion and Clothing:* Halal fashion encompasses clothing that complies with Shariah standards, covering the aurat and adhering to ethical production principles. Halal clothing considers compliance with Islamic law in design and material use and ensures fair and environmentally friendly production processes. This trend is followed by Muslim consumers and those seeking ethical and high-quality fashion products (Cunningham, 2022).
5. *Financial Services*: The halal financial services industry includes products and services that comply with Shariah principles, such as Islamic banking, *sukuk*, and *takaful* (Islamic insurance). These products ensure no *riba*, *gharar*, or *maysir* is involved in financial transactions. The growth of this sector is driven by increasing awareness of ethical finance and demand from the global Muslim community (Ahmed, 2021).

The halal industry, encompassing various economic sectors, produces goods and services according to Islamic Shariah principles. Initially, the focus was on food and beverage products, where halal criteria involve ingredients free from haram elements such as pork and alcohol and methods of slaughtering compliant with Islamic law. However, the scope of the halal industry has expanded far beyond food and beverages. Today, it includes sectors such as cosmetics, pharmaceuticals, fashion, and even financial services. For instance, halal cosmetics ensure that beauty products are free from prohibited ingredients and produced through clean processes. In the pharmaceutical sector, halal medicines are designed without *haram* ingredients and with production methods that comply with Shariah principles (Ariffin & Zainol, 2016).

3.2 Market Potential and Growth

The market potential for the halal industry is substantial, especially with the rapid growth of the global Muslim population and increasing awareness about halal products among non-Muslims. According to the Global Islamic Economy Report 2023, halal products' total global market value is estimated to reach USD 2.6 trillion by 2023. The food and beverage sector contributes most of this market value, but other sectors, such as halal fashion and tourism, also show significant growth. Halal fashion, which includes clothing that meets Shariah standards, has seen increased demand from consumers looking for ethical products that align with their values (Thompson, 2021). This growth is driven by the significant increase in the Muslim population, which is expected to exceed 2.2 billion by 2024, as well as the growing awareness of the benefits and quality of halal products among non-Muslim consumers (DinarStandard, 2023). The growth rates of these industry sectors are explained as follows:

1. *Growth of the Food and Beverage Sector*. The halal food and beverage sector is the most significant part of the global halal market. Demand for halal food is increasing in countries with large Muslim populations and broader international markets, including Western countries. Factors such as the increased awareness of health and food hygiene, along with the demand for products that comply with ethical standards, contribute to the expansion of this sector. According to Euromonitor International, the global halal food market is expected to grow at a CAGR (Compound Annual Growth Rate) of 6.1% from 2021 to 2026 (Euromonitor, 2021).
2. *Growth of the Cosmetics and Personal Care Sector*. The halal cosmetics sector is experiencing rapid growth as more consumers seek beauty products that align with Shariah principles. The global halal cosmetics market is estimated to reach USD 50 billion by 2024, driven by increasing consumer demand concerning ethics and product sustainability (Mintel, 2022). Halal cosmetics not only conform to Shariah standards but are also often produced with natural and environmentally friendly ingredients, which enhances their appeal in the global market.
3. *Growth of the Pharmaceuticals and Medicines Sector*. The demand for halal medicines is increasing alongside the growth of the Muslim population and the rising awareness of the significance of products that adhere to Shariah law. The halal pharmaceuticals sector produces medicines devoid of haram substances and processes them according to Shariah principles. A report from MarketsandMarkets indicates that the halal pharmaceuticals market is anticipated to grow at a CAGR of 10% from 2021 to 2026, signifying considerable potential in this sector (MarketsandMarkets, 2021).
4. *Growth of the Fashion and Apparel Sector*. Halal fashion is a rapidly growing sector, with an increasing demand for clothing that adheres to Shariah principles. The global halal fashion market is projected to reach USD 361 billion by 2024. This trend is driven by a growing awareness of ethical fashion products that align with Islamic values and an increase in non-Muslim consumers interested in more conservative and high-quality designs (Thompson, 2021).
5. *Innovation and Digitalization in the* Halal *Industry*. Innovation and digitalisation play a crucial role in the growth of the halal industry. Technologies such as blockchain track product compliance with halal standards, enhancing transparency and consumer trust. E-commerce platforms are increasingly employed to reach global consumers, facilitating access to halal products worldwide. According to

McKinsey & Company (2022), digitalisation and new technologies can improve operational efficiency and expand market reach for halal companies.

Table 1. Market potential and growth of the Halal industry

Sector	Market Value/Estimated Growth	CAGR/ Estimated Year	Sources
Food & Beverages	USD 2.6 trillion (Global)	CAGR 6,1% (2021-2026)	DinarStandard (2023); Euromonitor (2021)
Cosmetics	USD 50 million (Global)	-	Mintel (2022)
Pharmacy & Medicines	-	CAGR 10% (2021-2026)	MarketsandMarkets (2021)
Fashion & Clothing	USD 361 million (Global)	-	Thompson (2021)
Innovation and Digitalization	-	-	McKinsey & Company (2022)

4.0 TRENDS AND INNOVATIONS IN ISLAMIC FINANCE AND THE HALAL INDUSTRY

Islamic finance and the halal industry are witnessing innovations and trends shaping how halal products are produced and marketed. One of the significant trends is digitalisation, where technologies such as blockchain are employed to track and ensure compliance with halal standards. Furthermore, more companies are utilising e-commerce platforms to reach global markets, making it easier for consumers to access halal products worldwide. These innovations not only aid in expanding market reach but also enhance transparency and consumer trust in halal products (Sulaiman, 2022). Trends and innovations in Islamic finance and the halal industry include:

4.1 Digitalization and Technology in Islamic Finance

Digitalisation has become a significant trend in Islamic finance, fostering innovation and efficiency. Technologies like blockchain enhance transparency and accountability in financial transactions. Within the realm of Islamic finance, blockchain assists in tracking transactions that adhere to Shariah principles, such as *sukuk* and other financial contracts, ensuring compliance and mitigating the risk of fraud (PWC, 2022).

Shariah fintech, encompassing digital banking, investment, and insurance platforms, is also experiencing rapid growth. Shariah fintech applications enable consumers to access Shariah-compliant financial services easily via mobile devices. This innovation enhances financial inclusion by offering solutions that conform to Islamic principles for individuals who may not have previously had access to traditional financial services (KPMG, 2021).

4.2 Green and Sustainable Finance in Islamic Finance

The trend of green finance, or sustainable finance, has embraced Islamic finance, concentrating on environmentally friendly and sustainable investments. This concept aligns with Shariah principles that advocate social responsibility and sustainability. Green *Sukuk*, for instance, are Shariah-compliant financial instruments employed to finance environmentally friendly projects, such as renewable energy and the development of green infrastructure. These initiatives assist in mitigating climate change and addressing market demands for ethical and sustainable investments (Sukuk, 2023).

4.3 Innovation in Halal Products

Product innovation has experienced significant growth in the halal industry. New product developments in the food and beverage sector adhere to halal standards and integrate modern technology into production. For instance, advanced food processing technologies are used to maintain the cleanliness and quality of halal products. In the cosmetics sector, innovations in halal product formulations have increased the diversity and quality of products available (Jansen, 2022).

In the pharmaceuticals sector, there are innovations in the production of halal medicines, including using raw materials and production methods that comply with Shariah principles. Research and development in this field help ensure that pharmaceutical products are effective and adhere to Islamic ethical standards (Ali & Muda, 2021).

4.4 E-Commerce and Digital Platforms in the Halal Industry

The growth of e-commerce has transformed the sale and marketing of halal products. Digital platforms enable producers and retailers to reach global markets more efficiently. Halal e-commerce encompasses a wide range of product categories, from food to fashion, allowing consumers to purchase halal products from around the globe easily. Platforms such as Amazon and Alibaba now provide various halal products, enhancing accessibility and convenience for consumers (McKinsey & Company, 2022). Hence, the role of Islamic finance in the development of the Halal economy could be further boosted by increasing support for the adoption of digital payments, integrating halal advisory and marketplace, and enhancing current Islamic finance offerings through innovative Islamic finance solutions such as fintech, blended finance, alternative finance, and Islamic social finance (World Bank Group, 2022).

4.5 Global Collaboration and Standardization

International collaboration and standardisation are also essential trends in the halal industry. Halal certification organisations in various countries are increasingly working together to develop consistent global standards, reduce confusion in the worldwide market, and facilitate international trade in halal products. Initiatives like Halaal International are examples of efforts to unify standards and promote halal practices globally (Hassan et al., 2019).

5.0 SYNERGY BETWEEN ISLAMIC FINANCE AND THE HALAL INDUSTRY TOWARDS A GREEN ECONOMY

The integration of Islamic finance and the halal industry is becoming increasingly vital in fostering a sustainable economic ecosystem that adheres to Shariah principles. This synergy not only supports the growth of halal businesses but also enhances the overall economic landscape. Even according to (Aslam et al., 2023) the dynamic synergy that exists between Islamic finance and the halal industry is very promising for long-term growth and development. The green economy, which focuses on sustainability and environmental protection, aligns with the principles of Shariah in Islamic finance and the halal industry. This concept involves efforts to reduce negative environmental impacts, promote the use of sustainable resources, and support environmentally friendly projects. In the context of Islamic finance, this includes investments and financing that adhere to Shariah principles while also considering the environmental and social impacts of funded projects (Sulaiman & Yusof, 2020).

5.1 Green Sukuk and Sustainable Financing

Green *Sukuk* is a significant innovation in Islamic finance supporting the green economy. Green Sukuk is a Shariah-compliant bond used to finance environmentally friendly projects, such as renewable energy, energy efficiency, and green infrastructure development. Green *Sukuk* combines Shariah principles with sustainability goals, offering investment alternatives that align with Islamic ethics while promoting environmentally beneficial projects (Khan et al., 2019).

For example, governments and companies' issuance of green sukuk aims to support environmental initiatives and reduce carbon emissions. These projects often involve green technologies, improved waste management, and sustainable infrastructure development, all contributing to green economy objectives (Zulkifli et al., 2021).

5.2 Halal Investments in Environmentally Friendly Projects

The halal industry also plays a role in supporting the green economy through investments in environmentally friendly projects. For instance, halal food and cosmetics companies often adopt sustainable and eco-friendly production practices. This includes using ethically sourced raw materials, reducing waste, and implementing technologies that minimise environmental impact. Also, halal companies in the fashion and textile sectors are adopting sustainable practices, such as using organic materials and low-impact production processes (Abdullah & Rahman, 2022).

5.3 Collaboration between Islamic Finance and the Halal Industry for a Green Economy

Collaboration between Islamic financial institutions and halal industry players is crucial in achieving green economy goals. Shariah-compliant financial institutions can provide financing and investment for environmentally friendly projects, while the halal industry can implement sustainability principles. This synergy helps expand the reach of green initiatives and ensures that projects adhere to Shariah principles and contribute to environmental sustainability (Hassan et al., 2021).

For example, collaborations between Islamic banks and companies producing halal goods with strict environmental standards can accelerate the adoption of sustainable practices across the industry. Additionally, halal certification bodies can develop specific standards for environmentally friendly products, raising awareness and support for the green economy among halal consumers (Rizvi et al., 2022).

5.4 Challenges and Opportunities.

While the synergy between Islamic finance and the halal industry for a green economy offers many opportunities, some challenges must be addressed. One major challenge is the lack of consistent global standards for green sukuk and environmentally friendly investments in the context of Shariah. Furthermore, there is a need for more excellent education and awareness about the benefits of the green economy among industry players and investors. However, the growth opportunities remain strong, especially with increasing awareness of sustainability and market demand for more environmentally friendly products and investments (Mujahid et al., 2023).

6.0 SHARIAH ECOSYSTEM: INTEGRATION, COLLABORATION, AND SUSTAINABILITY

The Shariah ecosystem is a system that integrates various elements of Islamic finance and the halal industry with Shariah principles to balance legal compliance and sustainability goals. In this context, the green economy becomes a strategic objective integrating Islamic finance principles and halal industry practices to achieve environmental and social sustainability (Sulaiman & Yusof, 2020).

6.1 Fundamental Principles of Islamic Finance in the Shariah Ecosystem

Islamic finance, characterized by its adherence to Shariah principles—such as the prohibition of *Riba*, *Maysir*, and *Gharar* —is uniquely positioned to support halal enterprises. Islamic finance operates based on Shariah principles, including:

1. Prohibition of *Riba* (Interest): All interest forms are prohibited. Islamic finance uses profit-sharing contracts such as *mudharabah* (partnership) and *musharakah* (joint venture) to replace interest-based systems.
2. Prohibition of *Gharar* (Uncertainty): Transactions must be clear and free from excessive uncertainty.
3. Prohibition of *Maysir* (Gambling): Speculative transactions similar to gambling are prohibited.
4. Halal and *Haram*: Investments must comply with Shariah law, meaning they must be free from haram activities or products (e.g., alcohol, tobacco) (Ali & Muda, 2021).

6.2 Fundamental Principles of the Halal Industry in the Shariah Ecosystem

The halal industry encompasses various sectors, including food, cosmetics, pharmaceuticals, and fashion, adhering to Shariah principles. Key principles include:

1. Shariah Compliance: All products and services, including raw materials, production processes, and distribution, must comply with Islamic law.

2. Quality and Ethics: Halal products must meet high standards and be produced ethically without harming the environment or society.
3. Sustainability: Focus on environmentally and socially friendly practices that support sustainability (Jansen, 2022).

6.3 Integration of Islamic Finance and the Halal Industry Towards a Green Economy

1. Green *Sukuk* as a Financial Tool for a Green Economy. Green *Sukuk* is a Shariah-compliant financial instrument to fund environmentally friendly projects, including investments in renewable energy, energy efficiency, and waste management. Green *sukuk* supports sustainability goals by directing funds to projects that meet environmental standards and Shariah principles (Khan et al., 2019). Examples include green *sukuk* issued by governments and companies for green infrastructure projects and sustainable development.
2. Halal Investments in Environmentally Friendly Projects. The halal industry invests in environmentally friendly projects as part of its commitment to sustainability. This includes companies producing halal food with sustainable production practices, halal cosmetics using natural ingredients, and halal textiles applying eco-friendly production processes. These practices align with green economy goals and Shariah principles, emphasising social and environmental responsibility (Abdullah & Rahman, 2022).

6.4 Collaboration Between Islamic Finance and the Halal Industry

Collaboration between Shariah financial institutions and halal industry players accelerates attaining green economy goals. For instance, Islamic banks can finance environmentally friendly projects within the halal sector, while halal companies can adopt sustainable practices in their production processes. This synergy ensures that investments and production adhere to Shariah principles and promote environmental sustainability (Hassan et al., 2021).

6.5 Challenges and Opportunities in Integration

1. Lack of Global Standards: International standards for green *sukuk* and sustainable investments within the framework of Shariah are still evolving, which may cause confusion and inconsistency.
2. Education and Awareness: Industry players and Shariah investors lack an understanding of the green economy's benefits.

3. Market Growth: Increasing demand for environmentally friendly investments and products creates significant opportunities for Shariah-compliant products and services.
4. Innovation: New technologies and sustainable practices offer opportunities for innovation in Islamic finance and the halal industry (Mujahid et al., 2023).

The Shariah ecosystem that integrates Islamic finance and the halal industry towards a green economy creates synergies that support environmental sustainability while adhering to Shariah principles, as illustrated in Figure 1. By leveraging green sukuk, sustainable halal investments, and eco-friendly practices, this ecosystem contributes to achieving green economy goals. Existing challenges should be addressed through collaboration and innovation to capitalise on available opportunities.

Figure 1. Sustainable Shariah ecosystem

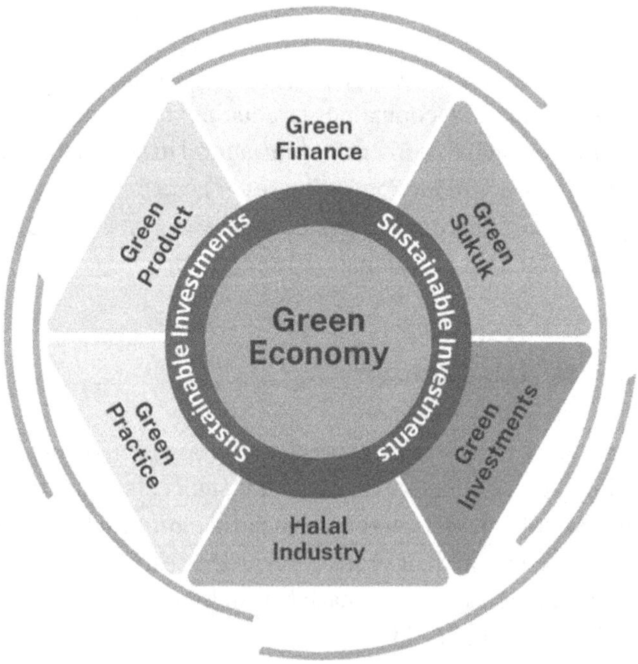

7.0 PROSPECTS OF ISLAMIC FINANCE AND THE HALAL INDUSTRY

Islamic finance has experienced considerable growth over the past few decades, with total Islamic financial assets estimated to surpass $2 trillion by 2020. This growth is driven by increased awareness among Muslims and non-Muslims about the importance of financial products adhering to Shariah principles, which prohibit *riba*, *gharar*, and *maysir*. Key markets such as the Middle East, Southeast Asia, and Africa have become centres of this development. Malaysia and the Gulf countries are leading in product innovation and Islamic financial regulation development. According to the Global Islamic Finance Report 2021, the global Islamic finance market is projected to grow at a CAGR (Compound Annual Growth Rate) of around 10-12% over the next five years, indicating an auspicious outlook for the sector (Alam & Rizvi, 2021).

The prospects of Islamic finance are driven by asset growth, ongoing diversification, and product innovation. *Sukuk*, or Islamic bonds, have become a key instrument for infrastructure financing, green projects, and public investments. Green *Sukuk*, in particular, has become vital in supporting environmentally friendly projects in Muslim and non-Muslim countries. Other financial products such as *takaful*, Shariah-compliant mutual funds, and Shariah digital banking are also rapidly growing, offering more choices for consumers and investors. This diversification enhances the appeal of Islamic finance in the global market and strengthens its position as a sustainable alternative in the international financial system (Khan et al., 2019).

Similarly, the halal industry, which encompasses food, pharmaceuticals, cosmetics, and fashion sectors, also shows extraordinary growth prospects. With the global Muslim population expected to reach 2.2 billion by 2030 (Elasrag, 2016), the demand for halal products continues to increase (Sulaiman, Abdullah, & Hashim, 2023). The Muslim population is also estimated to reach 2.6 billion by 2050 (Talib, Hamid, & Zulfakar Mohd Hafiz, 2015). According to Jamaluddin et al. (2018), the global halal industry market value is expected to reach USD 6 trillion by 2024, with the halal food sector being a major contributor. Countries such as Indonesia, Malaysia, and the United Arab Emirates have become innovation hubs in the halal industry, focusing on developing new products that adhere to strict standards. Additionally, more non-Muslim countries are recognising the potential of this market and are beginning to implement halal standards for their products (Thomson Reuters, 2020).

One of the most exciting prospects in the Shariah ecosystem is the potential integration between Islamic finance and the halal industry. Islamic finance plays a crucial role in providing funding for the halal industry's growth, whether through project financing, investments, or Shariah insurance. For instance, green sukuk can finance environmentally friendly projects within the halal industry, such as constructing sustainable production facilities or developing eco-friendly halal products. The synergy between these two sectors contributes to sustainable economic growth and ensures that the halal supply chain adheres to high ethical and sustainability standards (Obaidullah & Siti, 2022).

While the prospects for Islamic finance and the halal industry are up and coming, several challenges must be addressed to achieve sustainable growth. Significant challenges include the absence of uniform global standards for Islamic financial products and halal offerings, alongside a general lack of understanding and awareness among consumers worldwide. Nevertheless, considerable opportunities exist, particularly with the introduction of new technologies such as fintech and blockchain, which have the potential to transform transactions in both Islamic finance and the halal sector. Furthermore, focusing on the green economy and sustainability presents substantial opportunities for integrating Islamic finance and the halal industry to support sustainable development (Mujahid et al., 2023).

8.0 CONCLUSION

Islamic finance and the halal industry are vital in creating a sustainable and ethical global economy. Through Shariah principles that emphasise justice, transparency, and sustainability, both sectors not only cater to the needs of Muslims but also present an ethical alternative for the global community. Given the progressively closer integration between Islamic finance and the halal industry, one can observe the emergence of a Shariah-compliant ecosystem that promotes economic growth while ensuring equitable and sustainable development.

Building a sustainable Shariah ecosystem necessitates strong collaboration among various stakeholders, including governments, financial institutions, industry players, and the wider community. Supportive regulations, ongoing product innovation, and increasing consumer awareness are essential to reinforcing and broadening the reach of Islamic finance and the halal industry. Challenges such as non-uniform global standards and gaps in education still require attention. Still, the opportunities are considerable, particularly with the rise of new technologies and the growing emphasis on sustainability.

The synergy between Islamic finance and the halal industry will grow increasingly vital in tackling global challenges such as climate change, economic disparity, and social crises. By leveraging Shariah principles and sustainable innovation, we can develop economically advantageous solutions and align with broader sustainable development goals. A robust and sustainable Shariah ecosystem will ultimately underpin a more just, prosperous, and harmonious future for all.

REFERENCES

Abdullah, R., & Rahman, M. (2022). Sustainable Practices in the Halal Industry: Opportunities and Challenges. *Journal of Cleaner Production.*

Ahmed, H. (2021). *Islamic Finance: Principles and Practices.* Oxford University Press.

Alam, N., & Rizvi, S. (2021). *Islamic Finance: Growth and Future Prospects.* Journal of Islamic Economics.

Ali, A. (2020). Halal *Cosmetics: Trends, Opportunities, and Market Insights.* Journal of Consumer Studies.

Ali, A., & Muda, M. (2021). Pharmaceuticals and Halal Standards: Innovations and Challenges. *Asian Journal of Pharmaceutical Sciences.*

Ariffin, A., & Zainol, F. (2016). *The* Halal *Industry in Malaysia: Market Opportunities and Challenges.* Malaysian Journal of Social Sciences and Humanities.

Aslam, E., Asif, M., Sultan, A., Nasir, S., & Iqbal, A. (2023). The Synergy of Islamic Finance and the Halal Industry Development in Islamic Countries. *Tuijin Jishu/Journal of Propulsion Technology, 44*(3), 3849 - 3858.

Cunningham, C. (2022). Fashion and Halal: The Emerging Trends in Muslim Consumer Markets. *Fashion Theory.*

Dewar, J., & Hussain, M. (2023). *Islamic Finance Market.*

DinarStandard. (2023). *Global Islamic Economy Report 2023.* Retrieved from [DinarStandard] (https://www.dinarstandard.com)

Elasrag, H. (2016). Halal *Industry: Key Challenges and Opportunities.*

Elmelki, A., & Ben Arab, M. (2009). Ethical Investment and the Social Responsibilities of the Islamic Banks. *International Business Research*, *2*(2), 123–130. DOI: 10.5539/ibr.v2n2p123

Euromonitor International. (2021). *Global* Halal *Food Market Report.* Retrieved from [Euromonitor] (https://www.euromonitor.com)

Farouk, M. M. (2019). *Introduction to Halal Food: A Practical Guide.* Wiley-Blackwell.

Franzoni, S., & Allali, A. (2018). Principles of Islamic Finance and Principles of Corporate Social Responsibility: What Convergence? *Sustainability (Basel)*, *10*(3), 637. DOI: 10.3390/su10030637

Hasan, Z. (2009). *Islamic Finance: Theory and Practice*. Edward Elgar Publishing.

Hassan, S., Abdukadir, N., & Rashid, M. (2019). *Challenges and Opportunities in the* Halal *Market: A Global Perspective*. International Journal of Islamic Finance.

Hassan, S., Ahmed, F., & Rizvi, S. (2021). *Islamic Finance and Sustainable Development: A Collaborative Approach*. Journal of Islamic Finance.

Henderson, J. (2021). The Global Halal Food Market: Trends and Opportunities. *International Journal of Food Sciences*.

Ibrahim, A. (2022). *Sustainability and Sustainable Development: An Investigation on the Role of Islamic Finance and Other Determinants in the OIC Member Countries. PhD Thesis*. University of Salford., Retrieved from https://salford-repository.worktribe.com/OutputFile/1502990

Iqbal, Z., & Mirakhor, A. (2017). *Introduction to Islamic Finance: Theory and Practice*. John Wiley & Sons.

Islamic Development Bank. (2023). *Case Studies on Innovations in Islamic Finance*. United Nations Development Programme.

Jamaluddin, M., Abdullah, M., & Has-Yun, H. (2018). The Emergence of Global Halal Industry Ecosystem. *Journal of Halal Industry & Services*, *1*(1).

Jansen, L. (2022). Innovation in Halal Products: Trends and Developments. *Journal of Islamic Marketing*.

Khan, M., Ahmad, M., & Shah, M. (2019). *Green Sukuk: Innovations and Future Prospects*. International Journal of Islamic Finance.

KiniHalal. (2023, Aug 21). *Sustaining Malaysia as the Global Leader in the* Halal *Industry*. Dipetik Mar 4, 2025, dari Halal Development Corporation Berhad: https://hdcglobal.com/news/2023/08/21/sustaining-malaysia-as-the-global-leader-in-the-halal-industry/

KPMG. (2021). *Fintech and Islamic Finance: Innovations and Opportunities*. KPMG International.

MarketsandMarkets. (2021). Halal *Pharmaceuticals Market Report*. Retrieved from [MarketsandMarkets] (https://www.marketsandmarkets.com)

McKinsey & Company. (2022). *The Future of E-commerce in the* Halal *Industry*. Retrieved from [McKinsey & Company] (https://www.mckinsey.com)

McKinsey & Company. (2022). *The Impact of Digitalization on the* Halal *Industry*. Retrieved from [McKinsey & Company] (https://www.mckinsey.com)

Mintel. (2022). Halal *Cosmetics Market Overview*. Retrieved from [Mintel](https://www.mintel.com)

Muazu, M., & Sjahrir, E. (2023). *Halal Entrepreneurship and Its Impact on Sustainable Economy: Opportunities and Challenges. Dalam L. Raimi, S. Adekunle, & M. Shabbir (Penyunt.), Contemporary Discourse of Halal and Islamic Entrepreneurship*. Springer., DOI: 10.1007/978-981-99-6427-7_17

Mujahid, A., Tariq, M., & Ali, N. (2023). Opportunities and Challenges in Islamic Finance and Halal Industry for Green Economy. *Journal of Sustainable Development*.

Nissa, E. (2023). *Profesionalisation of* Halal *Industries in Indonesia And Malaysia*. Dipetik Mar 4, 2025, dari Sinofon: https://sinofon.cz/trainee-centre/profesionalisation-of-halal-industries-in-indonesia-and-malaysia/

Obaidullah, M., & Siti, H. (2022). *Integrating Islamic Finance and* Halal *Industry: Opportunities and Challenges*. Journal of Halal Studies.

Poh, M. K. (2013). *Understanding the Halal Industry: A New Approach to Consumer Protection*. Halal Research Institute.

PWC. (2022). *Blockchain in Islamic Finance: Enhancing Transparency and Efficiency*. PricewaterhouseCoopers.

Radzi, R., & Muhamed, N. (2019). Are sukuk debt or equity? A classification of sukuk by regulatory bodies and credit rating agencies. *Journal of Emerging Economies and Islamic Research*, *7*(2), 72–81. DOI: 10.24191/jeeir.v7i2.8767

Ramadhan, R., Ulfah, A. K., Nurzianti, R., Bunkes, P., & Kadriyani, E. (2023). Market Potential of Halal Products in Aceh: Case Study of Halal Industry Based on Halal Product Data 2014-2022. *Al-Falah: Journal of Islamic Economics*, *8*(2), 171–180. DOI: 10.29240/alfalah.v8i2.7083

Rashid, M. (2017). *Ethics and Compliance in the Halal Industry*. Routledge.

Rifai, M., & Thaker, M. A. M. T. (2020). *Halal Industry: Challenges and Opportunities*. International Islamic University Malaysia Press.

Rizvi, S., Ali, A., & Sulaiman, N. (2022). *Certification Standards and Green Practices in the* Halal *Industry*. Asian Journal of Business and Finance.

Sukuk, M. (2023). *Green Sukuk: Financing for Sustainable Development*. International Journal of Islamic Finance.

Sulaiman, N. (2022). Innovation in the Halal Industry: Digital Trends and Future Prospects. *Journal of Islamic Marketing*.

Sulaiman, N., Abdullah, R., & Hashim, N. (2023). Halal Industry Development in Brunei Darussalam: Realities and Challenges. *Social and Humaniora Research Symposium (SoRes), KnE Life Sciences*, 1013-1029. DOI: 10.18502/kss.v8i18.14308

Sulaiman, N., & Yusof, N. (2018). Pharmaceuticals and Halal Standards: A Review. *Asian Journal of Pharmaceutical Sciences*.

Sulaiman, N., & Yusof, N. (2020). *Green Finance and Islamic Finance: Synergies and Challenges*. Journal of Islamic Economics.

Talha, M., Faisal, S., & Khan, A. (2024). Shariah Law in Commercial Banking and Stock Market: Recent Development, Challenges and Practices. *International Journal of Religion*, *5*(6), 620–630. DOI: 10.61707/4brms430

Talib, M., & Hamid, A. (2015). Halal supply chain critical success factors: A literature review. *Journal of Islamic Marketing*, *6*(1), 44–71. DOI: 10.1108/JIMA-07-2013-0049

Thompson, G. (2021). *Global Islamic Economy Report 2023: Growth and Trends in the Halal Industry*. Dubai Islamic Economy Development Centre.

Thomson Reuters. (2020). *Global Islamic Economy Report 2020/21*.

Usmani, M. T. (2002). *An Introduction to Islamic Finance*. Idaratul Ma'ariful.

Visser, H. (2019). *Islamic Finance: Principles and Practice*. Edward Elgar Publishing. DOI: 10.4337/9781786433503

Wilson, R. (2012). *Islamic Economics: A Short History*. Brill.

World Bank Group. (2022). *Islamic Finance and the Development of Malaysia's Halal Economy*. World Bank Group.

Yusuf, S., Mokoagow, M., Nur, M., & Rauf, S. (2023). Islamic Financial Characteristics and the Sustainability of Islamic Banking in Indonesia: Challenges and Opportunities. *Scientific Journal of Unity Management, 11*(2), 363–369. DOI: 10.37641/jimkes.v11i2.2036

Zulkifli, M., Mohd, R., & Hassan, M. (2021). Sukuk Hijau dan Pembangunan Berkelanjutan: Tinjauan dan Implikasi. *Journal of Sustainable Finance & Investment*.

Chapter 4 Implementation of the Principles of Halal and Tayyib at the Slaughterhouse in Sustainable Development Goals

Hikmatul Hasanah
https://orcid.org/0009-0001-8032-6937
Universitas Islam Negeri Kiai Haji Achmad Siddiq Jember, Indonesia

ABSTRACT

The application of halal and ṭayyib principles in slaughterhouses is important to achieve SDG goals, especially the provision of safe, healthy, and sustainable food. This research examines how the concepts of halal and ṭayyib can be applied effectively in slaughtering and distributing meat in slaughterhouses, including aspects of hygiene, waste management, and physical facility standards. The integration of these two principles aims to ensure that every stage of the production and distribution process complies with Islamic law, as well as meets environmental sustainability standards. It also highlights the importance of changing work culture, implementing strict regulations, and monitoring distribution to ensure the quality of the meat products produced is maintained throughout the years. consumer's hands.

DOI: 10.4018/979-8-3373-3917-7.ch004

INTRODUCTION

Slaughterhouse (RPH) and slaughterhouse (TPH) data indicate the number of slaughters in a region. The number of slaughters also describes the level of meat consumption in the community, which is usually directly proportional to the community's population and income level. The greater the population and the higher the income, the higher the level of meat consumption in a region. (Hirmawan & Hasanah, 2023) The differences between RPH and TPH can be categorized into several types. First, on average, TPH is privately owned, while the state government owns RPH. The most significant difference is that the RPH has a laboratory in the RPH building, while the TPH has a laboratory in the pen or feedlot. Laboratory RPH to test the health of livestock and the health of meat to be distributed. While the laboratory TPH only tests the health of meat when it will be distributed. TPH itself can be classified into 2, namely modern and traditional (Gading et al., 2021).

The establishment of the RPH refers to ministerial regulations, in this case, the Ministry of Agriculture Republic of Indonesia, specifically Article 4 of the Regulation of the Minister of Agriculture of the Republic of Indonesia Number 13/Permentan/OT.140/1/2010 concerning requirements for slaughterhouses (Permentan No. 13/Permentan/OT.140/1/2010 Tahun 2010, n.d.-a). The regulation already refers to the achievement of ḥalālan ṭayyiban, but it needs to be strengthened with the obligation of halal certification because it is based on the needs of the community, who are increasingly aware of halal products.

The obligation for halal-certified products is stated in government regulations, namely Law No. 33 of 2014 concerning halal product guarantees, and has been in effect since 2017, with the implementing agency being the Halal Product Guarantee Organizing Agency (BPJPH) under the auspices of the Ministry of Religion of the Republic of Indonesia.(UU No. 33 of 2014, nd) With the enactment of the law, every producer is obliged to implement it. This halal certification obligation is also reinforced by the Decree of the Minister of Religion of the Republic of Indonesia (KMA) No. 748 of 2021 concerning the types of products that must be halal-certified. (Decree of the Minister of Religion Number 748 of 2021, 2022) So, the commands that have been emphasized in the Qur'an are also reinforced with binding regulations; of course, the main goal is for the benefit.

Data on the number of RPH/TPH/Regional apparatus that carry out government duties and functions that are still active in Indonesia is 1,690 spread across 34 provinces. Around 35% of RPH/TPH/Regional apparatus that carry out government duties and functions are in Java Island, namely 605 RPH/TPH/Regional apparatus that carry out government duties and functions. Other regions that have a distribution of RPH/TPH/Regional apparatus that carry out government duties and functions of more than 10% are Sumatra with a total of 358 (21.18%), Sulawesi 308 (18.22%), and Bali and Nusa Tenggara 184 (10.89%). The rest are in Kalimantan with 121 (7.16%), and Maluku and Papua with 114 RPH/TPH/Regional apparatus that carry out government duties and functions (6.75 RPH/TPH/Regional apparatus that carry out government duties and functions (6.75%) (Hirmawan & Hasanah, 2023).

The reality in the field of RPH throughout Indonesia, which has been certified halal, is still relatively low. This condition causes the focus of attention on the existence of RPH as a meat production unit, therefore, the existence of RPH is very much needed as a supplier of meat that is of guaranteed quality, both in terms of halalness, cleanliness, and health for consumption. Seeing this need, the government has established RPHs spread across regions throughout Indonesia. RPH is the upstream for halal products if it can be fixed, then the downstream area will be greatly assisted in realizing a product that is ready to be consumed and ready to use, which will then facilitate the halal certification process for processed meat food products that are developing in Micro, Small and Medium Enterprises (MSMEs) (Agency, nd).

Halal is currently a trending topic of discussion because it is not only in Indonesia but has become an international issue. no longer a study conducted in Islamic boarding schools or a classical study of Muslims only, but a global study that anyone can do (Masruroh, 2020).

The discussion of halal and ṭayyib in this article focuses on meat food produced from RPH based on existing problems. The emergence of several problems with the existence of RPH occur in various countries, this is because of inadequate sanitation handling and lack of attention to the standards that apply, on the other hand, the existence of RPH is very urgent related to products that move in meat processing and the nutritional needs of the community but also has an impact that can cause disease due to inadequate sanitation, therefore it is necessary to handle it that can accommodate the desires of the community around the RPH to be more comfortable and healthy and have higher economic value, so it is necessary to implement a circular economy.

Creating sustainable welfare in society is part of the proposed global agreement with targets that must be achieved regarding sustainable development. The international agreement is the Sustainable Development Goals (SDGs), which are composed of 17 points of sustainable development goals. SDGs were launched in 2015 and will be implemented until 2030. The 17 goals include: SDGs 1 no poverty, SDGs 2 zero hunger, 3 SDGs good health and well-being, SDGs 4 quality education, SDGs 5 gender equality, SDGs 6 clean water and sanitation, SDGs 7 affordable and clean energy, SDGs 8 decent work and economic growth, SDGs 9 industry, innovation and infrastructure, SDGs 10 reduced inequalities, SDGs 11 sustainable cities and communities, SDGs 12 responsible consumption and production (responsible consumption and production), SDGs 13 climate action (addressing climate change), SDGs 14 life below water (ocean ecosystem), SDGs 15 vie terrestre (land ecosystem), SDGs 16 peace, justice and strong institutions (peace, justice, and strong institutions), SDGs 17 partnership for the goals (partnership to achieve the goals) (Pujayanti, 2020).

Implementing the principles of halal and ṭayyib in RPH to create sustainable production, distribution, and provision of consumption processes to provide benefits to the wider community will greatly contribute to the goals of the SDGs. Of the seventeen SDGs, 5 (five) SDGs are relevant to efforts to implement the principles of halal and ṭayyib in RPH, including SDGs 3 good health and well-being, SDGs 6 clean water and sanitation, SDGs 8 decent work and economic growth, SDGs 11 sustainable cities and communities, SDGs 12 responsible consumption and production (Hoelman et al, 2015a).

The issue of SDGs is still hotly discussed, considering that its implementation period began in 2015 and is targeted until 2030. Minister of National Development Planning (PPN)/Head of National Development Planning Agency (Bappenas) Suharso Monoarfa said that Indonesia's achievement of SDGs indicators reached 62% of the total target that can be evaluated. From this achievement, Indonesia is considered the most progressive in achieving SDGs in the upper middle-income country category. According to Suharso, of course, there are still many challenges in several regions in Indonesia, both in terms of social, economic, environmental, and governance aspects (IPB University Raih Penghargaan Perguruan Tinggi SDGs Terbaik dari Bappenas - Tekno Tempo. Co, nd).

Suharso's statement is in line with the conditions of RPH in Indonesia in general, that RPH to achieve the SDGs goals still needs a lot of support in terms of infrastructure and resources. SDGs are also still a big challenge for many countries in the world. As quoted by the UN Secretary-General, the SDGs target that has been achieved is still 15% of the total global SDGs target. So it will take another 42 years to achieve the SDGs if there is no acceleration or innovation to speed it up (IPB University Raih Penghargaan Perguruan Tinggi SDGs Terbaik dari Bappenas - Tekno Tempo.Co, nd). Included in this discussion is the fact that RPH also needs innovation acceleration to accelerate its achievement of the SDG targets.

RPH as a meat supplier must fulfill the halalness of its products, in addition to being one of the quality standards and consumer protection, also because of the increasing consumer awareness of choosing halal products, of course, also thayyib. The choice of consumption of halal meat is not only in the Muslim majority community; non-Muslim communities also tend to choose halal products because of safety.

From the description of the research context above, this study aims to obtain information on implementing halal and ṭayyib in RPH to sustain the production and distribution process. This is important to find the ideal RPH model, namely halal, ṭayyib, and sustainable RPH, to contribute to the goals of the SDGs.

The discussion of this research is organized into several sections. The first section is the Literature Review, which covers several important concepts, such as the Concept of Halal Ṭayyib, the Legal Basis of Halal Ṭayyib, the Concept of Sustainability, and Sustainability in an Islamic Perspective. In addition, the Sustainable Development Goals (SDGs), the Principles of Halal, and Ṭayyib in Slaughterhouses (RPH) as a link in the realization of SDGs, and aspects of Sustainable Production and Distribution in RPH are also discussed. Furthermore, the Research Method section explains the approach used in this study. The Results and Discussion section outlines several key aspects, such as the conditions of RPH in Indonesia, the application of the principles of Halal and Tayyib in sustainable production in RPH, and its application in sustainable distribution in RPH. Then, the Conclusion section summarizes the main findings of this study. Finally, the References section lists the sources used in this study.

1. LITERATURE REVIEW

a. Concept of Ḥalālan Ṭayyiban

The concept halalan ṭayyiban is a combination of the elements halal and ṭayyib. Two words that underlie the concept of ḥalālan ṭayyiban are halal and haram. Halal means permitted, allowed, not prohibited, and the word haram is its antonym, which means something that must be avoided and, if done, is a sin and disobedience (Yahaya & Ruzulan, 2020).Ṭayyib means good, most important, and healthy. It can be said that food is ṭayyib if it is healthy, proportional, safe, and does not harm the body if it is eaten (Mahmudah, 2015).

Halal is an inseparable part of the lives of Muslims because halal is an obligation that must be fulfilled by Muslims in carrying out daily activities, as a form of effort to create benefits for individuals and others.

Eating haram food will also have a negative influence on human nature and behavior, including encouraging people to always do things that are forbidden or immoral and distancing people from the obligation to worship/laziness in worship. These negative effects have often been proven by penitents who provide testimonials regarding their spiritual life experiences.

In the context of halal economic activities, it is a requirement to obtain goodness that individuals and society can feel; these goodnesses are what we usually know as barokah. Barakah means ziadatul khair, namely "the increase in goodness or greatness, especially those related to the gifts and spiritual strength bestowed by Allah SWT. According to the explanation of the scholars, the meaning of barakah is everything abundant, both material and spiritual blessings, such as security, peace, health, wealth, children, and age (Mujieb et al., 2009).

Carrying out economic activities in a halal way is a measure of a Muslim's faith. A person is said to be strong in faith if he will always carry out economic activities in a halal way and vice versa if he carries out economic activities in a haram way then it is clear that the level of faith of a Muslim can be said to be low, halal alone is not enough, of course it must also be perfected with ṭayyib.

Discussion ḥalālan ṭayyiban in this context is halalan ṭayyiban on food. Halal food is food that is not forbidden or permitted to be eaten, while ṭayyib is food and drink that is acceptable to the taste, not disgusting because it is greatly influenced by the customs and progress of a nation (Amrullah & Abdulmalik, 1983).

In Islam, good and quality food products must meet the requirements of halal and ṭayyib. If a product is said to be good, but its status is doubtful, then it cannot be recognized as ṭayyib. For example, a certified food product meets quality standards, but there are doubts about its ingredients. The Qur'an generally mentions the need to implement ḥalālan ṭayyiban in all aspects, including in the food-producing industry, which can be said to meet the Halal criteria. Therefore, in the food product industry, activities can be seen from the aspects of food management, management location, equipment used, and distribution, which includes transportation operations (Mustaffa, 2019).

Ṭayyiban is mentioned in the Qur'an several times, specifically regarding the selection of halal food. The word ṭayyiban has four main elements, namely: The most important thing is that the source of the food is halal, the food is clean and free from dirt, the food is not harmful to those who consume it, and finally, the food is nutritious and physically beneficial for those who consume it. Therefore, the concept ḥalālan ṭayyiban identifies halal food as food that is high-quality, hygienic, and safe for consumption (Hasanah et al., 2021) According to the concept ḥalālan ṭayyiban, food must cover all aspects of halal, quality, and ethics throughout the value chain, starting from raw materials, processing in production activities, packaging, transportation, distribution, and the final product for consumers (Arif & Sidek, 2015). During the process, it is important to ensure that the food does not contain illegal substances or hazardous products that could endanger the health of consumers and is not contaminated with non-halal products (Idris et al., 2021).

Food can function as a means of transmitting disease, therefore, if the process is not clean and has the potential for cross-contamination or contains toxic materials, then the final product cannot be certified halal. Therefore, the issue of food safety is very much emphasized in the concept of ṭayyiban. Any food contaminated with pathogenic microbes or with potentially toxic materials that can pose a risk to human health is considered non-ṭayyib, ultimately non-halal, and cannot be used for eating purposes (Kurniadi & Frediansyah, 2017).

The concept of Ṭayyiban is clear not only in promoting clean and pure food production from farm to fork but also in ensuring ethical behavior and intentions in the process. The concept of ṭayyiban is also a process in which the behavior and intentions of the human resources involved are also under scrutiny (Wilson & Liu, 2010). Therefore, ideally, the food supply chain from upstream to downstream must be supervised to ensure its halalness and fairness.

b. Legal Basis of Ḥalālan Ṭayyiban

Consuming halal and ṭayyib food and drinks is an obligation for every Muslim. In the letter of al Baqarah verse 172 it is explained:

١٧٢ نَوُدُبْعَت ُهاَيِا ْمُتْنُك ْنِا ِهّلل اوُرُكْشاو ْمُكٰنْقَزَر ام ِتٰبِّيَط ْنِم اوُلُك اوُنَمٰا َنْيِذَّلا اهُّيَآي

"O you who believe, eat the good things that We have given you and give thanks to Allah if you truly only worship Him." (Qur'an Kemenag, n.d.-a).

The verse explicitly states that food and drink must not only be halal (permissible) but must also be of good quality, containing the nutrients and vitamins needed by the human body. The verse that mentions "being grateful to God" contains an implied meaning that halal and good quality food and drink not only guarantee physical benefits but also spiritual benefits that will increase piety and always be grateful to Allah (Yahaya & Ruzulan, 2020).

As for the term ḥalālan ṭayyiban, it is found in several verses of the Qur'an, including:

Letter Al-Baqarah verse 168.

ْمُكَل ُهَّنِاۚ ِنٰطْيَّشلا ِتٰوُطُخ اوُعِبَّتَت اَلَو اًبِّيَط اًلٰلَح ِضْرَاْلا يِف اَّمِم اوُلُك ُساَّنلا اهُّيَاٰي
ٌنْيِبُّم ٌّوُدَع

"O mankind, eat of what is lawful and good on earth and do not follow the footsteps of Satan. Indeed, he is to you an open enemy."(Qur'an Kemenag, n.d.-a).

In this verse, the command to eat halal and ṭayyib is not only directed at believers but at all humans, believers or unbelievers (Mahmudah, 2015). Because in reality, those who are responsible for protecting and creating the welfare of this earth are all humans for the sake of the sustainability of life on this planet earth.

Letter Al-Maidah verse 88

َنوُنِمْؤُم ِهِب ْمُتْنَا ْيِذَّلا َهّٰللا اوُقَّتاَّوۖ اًبِّيَط اًلٰلَح ُهّٰللا ُمُكَقَزَر اَّمِم اوُلُكَو

"Eat what Allah has bestowed upon you as lawful and good sustenance, and fear Allah in Whom alone you believe." (Qur'an Kemenag, n.d.-a).

In this verse, we are ordered to eat halal and ṭayyib food, from what Allah SWT has given us in the form of food that comes from land and sea, both vegetable protein and animal protein as halal and good sustenance to support the activities of this life, as well as commands to fear Allah and believe sincerely and istikomah.(Surah Al-Ma'idah Verse 88 Arabic, Latin, Translation and Tafsir | Read on Tafsir Web, nd).

Letter Al-Anfal verse 69

ٌمْيِحَّر ٌرْوُفَغ َهّللا َّنِا ۗ َهّللا اوُقَّتاَو ۖ اًبِّيَط اًللَح ْمُتْمِنَغ آَّمِم اوُلُكَف

"So eat what you have from the spoils of war that you have obtained as food that is halal and good and fear Allah. Indeed, Allah is Forgiving, Most Merciful."(Ministry of Religion Qur'an, nd-b).

In that verse, it is permissible to eat from the spoils of war in the form of food ingredients. It is all lawful, not a dirty job.(Surat Al-Anfal Verse 69, nd).

Letter an-Nahl verse 114

َنْوُدُبْعَت ُهاَّيِا ْمُتْنُك ْنِا ِهّللا َتَمْعِن اوُرُكْشاَّو ۖ اًبِّيَط اًللَح ُهّللا ُمُكَقَزَر اَّمِم اوُلُكَف

"Eat some of what Allah has given you as lawful and good (sustenance) and be grateful for Allah's blessings if you only worship Him."(Qur'an Kemenag, n.d.-b).

In this verse, it is ordered to eat from halal and good provisions as a form of gratitude for Allah's blessings, and to be grateful for Allah's blessings by obeying Allah alone, not others, if you truly only worship Allah (Surat An-Nahl Ayat 114, nd).

So, from the verses above, it can be understood that food and drink... ḥalālan ṭayyiban have two criteria, namely halal (permissible) and good quality (ṭayyib), which can be beneficial physically and spiritually.

c. Sustainability Concept

Sustainability is a concept that has undergone significant development in various fields, including economic, social, and environmental. The concept of sustainability can be understood as the ability of a system to survive and function in the long term, allowing future generations to meet their needs without sacrificing current needs. The definition of sustainability also varies according to the perspective used, namely:

1) From an environmental perspective, sustainability can be defined as the ability to maintain ecosystem balance and prevent environmental damage.
2) From an economic perspective, sustainability can be defined as the ability to achieve sustainable economic growth in the long term.
3) From a social perspective, sustainability can be defined as the ability to improve social welfare and correct social inequality (Simanjuntak & Lestarini, 2022).

Sustainability has become a concept widely used by organizations, governments, and academic institutions in discussions of business ethics and the impact of business activities on society and the environment. Sustainability is largely related to environmental sustainability; the concept has been developed to be broader.

The concept of sustainability is explained by Elkington, who emphasizes three main concepts that cover not only environmental aspects but also economic and social aspects. This means that social and economic aspects must be considered when dealing with environmental sustainability. Thus, sustainability can be defined as “the long-term maintenance of a system according to environmental, social, and economic considerations”. Although the concept can be and has been widely used in several different contexts, the most common use of sustainability is for sustainable development.

Sustainable development “includes the integration of environmental thinking into every aspect of social, political, and economic activities.” Sustainable development has been a leading concept in arguments about protecting our planet and has been discussed and in the process of development for decades by world political leaders. To understand the basics and development of the concept of sustainability and sustainable development, we see it necessary to propose and clarify the development of the environment and its protection (Elkington, John., 1998).

d. Sustainability in the Islamic Perspective

Sustainability in the perspective of Islam contains multidimensional and maqashid sharia as stated by Al-syatibi, namely: hifdz al-din, hifdz al-nafs, hifdz al-nasl, hifdz al-aql, and hifdz al-mal to realize human welfare. However, always being greedy and wasteful, which have become human nature, cause damage on this earth, as in the word of Allah SWT in the letter al 'Araf verse 56:

نَمّ ُبْيِرَق ِهّلل اَتَمْحَر ّنا عَمَطو افوَخ ُهوُعْداو اهِحالْصا َدْعَب ِضْرَالا ى ف اوُدِسْفُت الَو
نَيِنسْحُمْلا

“And do not do mischief on the earth after it has been set in order. Call upon Him with fear and hope. Indeed, the mercy of Allah is near to the doers of good.”(Qur’an Kemenag, n.d.-b).

Maintenance of the universe is seen as part of *Maqashid Sharia*. Thus, basic human needs no longer consist of five basic things (al-kulliyatul al-khamsah) but six (al-kulliyatul al-sittah). Without changing the structure (al-kulliyatul al-khamsah) as proposed by al-Syatibi, the rules of ushul fiqh, which say:

“ام ال ميتي بجاولا الإ هب وهف بجاو”

”(something that mediates the implementation of somethingmust then it is obligatory)”.

With this argument, it can be explained that even though the maintenance of the universe is not included in the category of al-kulliyat al-khamsah, al-kulliyat al-khamsah can't be carried out well if the maintenance of the universe is ignored. In this way, it becomes a mediator for the implementation of al-kulliyat al-khamsah (Thohari, 2013).

Islamic Sharia tells people to avoid mafsadah and attract maslahah, by the rules of fiqh,

ِحلاصمْلا ِبْلَج ىَلَع ٌمّدَقُم ِدِسافَمْلا ُءْرَد

"reject damage that takes precedence over taking away good."(Bisri, 1977).

So the implementation of sustainability is a mandate from Allah SWT, which must be carried out by humans because implementing sustainability is a manifestation of the implementation of sharia, to obtain maslahah and eliminate mafsadat (Suharti et al., 2023).

The Islamic view on a sustainable economy is based on three basic concepts, namely Tauhid, Khalifah, and adl. Tawhid is the most important thing because it is an implication that the universe created by Allah SWT each has a purpose, thus giving meaning and significance to the existence of the universe, of which humans are part of the creatures in it.

Caliph is a task entrusted by Allah SWT to humans as substitute/representative creatures on earth, who are given the mandate to maintain care for and prosper the earth/nature and not to create damage or bloodshed. In this case, Allah SWT has provided natural resources intended for humans so that humans can take action to utilize (produce) the natural resources that have been bestowed to fulfill human needs. As explained in the letter of Luqman verse 20:

ُلداجُي ْنَم ِسأنلا َنِمَو ۗةَنطابَو ْضرَألا يِف اَمَو ِتاواَمّسلا يِف اَم ْمُكَل َرّخَس َهّللا َّنَأ اوَرَت ْمَلَأ
ِريِنُم ٍباَتِك اَلَو ىًدُه اَلَو ٍمْلِع ِرْيَغِب ِهّللا يِف

"Have you not seen that Allah has to bow down for your (interest) what is in the heavens and what is on earth and perfects His blessings for you physically and spiritually? And among humans, some argue about (the oneness of) Allah without knowledge or guidance and without a book that provides enlightenment."(Qur'an Kemenag, n.d.-a).

Adl is an attitude that must be possessed when managing a government and when managing the environment, that natural resources created by Allah SWT are a means to achieve prosperity or what is called the concept of Falah (prosperity in the world and prosperity in the hereafter). Without justice, whether it is fair to humans or fair to nature, then falah will not be achieved (Mubarok & Afrizal, 2018).

e. Sustainable Development Goals(SDGs)

SDGs are a new development agreement to encourage changes towards sustainable development based on human rights and equality to encourage social, economic, and life-sustaining development. The implementation of SDGs with universal, integrated, and inclusive principles ensures that no one will be left behind (Hoelman et al., 2015b).

On September 25, 2015, precisely in New York, United States, at the UN (United Nations) general assembly, the Sustainable Development Agenda or SDGs was officially been confirmed as a global development agreement, which was followed by at least 193 heads of state. At that time, Vice President Jusuf Kalla also ratified the 2030 Sustainable Development Agenda for Indonesia (Mickael B. Hoelman et.al, 2015).

The SDGs are written in a 35-page document agreed upon by more than 190 countries containing 17 goals and 169 development targets, valid from 2015 to 2030. The 17 goals are: No Poverty, zero hunger, good health & well-being, quality education, gender equality, clean water & sanitation, affordable & clean energy, decent work & economic growth, industry, innovation and infrastructure, reduced inequalities, sustainable cities & communities, responsible consumption & production, climate action, life below water, life on land, peace, justice and strong institutions, partnerships for the goals (Hoelman et al, 2015b).

f. Halal and Ṭayyib Principles in RPH as a Link in the Realization of SDGs

As explained in the concept of ḥalālan ṭayyiban above, ṭayyiban is a process in which the behavior and intentions of those involved are also under supervision (Wilson & Liu, 2010). Thus, Ḥalālan ṭayyiban is seen as upholding sustainable practices in the halal food production process, such as economic and social justice (diversity, empowerment, transparency, equality for stakeholders [fair wages for employees, fair trade globally], and a sense of responsibility towards the environment, consumers, and society at large (Sharaai et al., 2012).

In the context of sustainable development, the implementation of halal and ṭayyib greatly contributes to increasing food security. The ultimate goal of food security is the alleviation of poverty (No Poverty SDGs 1) and ensuring zero hunger (Zero Hunger SDGs 2). However, the current challenges are environmental factors (climate change, insufficient water supply, etc.) and agricultural development policies that have an impact on the sustainable food supply chain ecosystem, which will affect the availability and accessibility of quality and safe products (Sustainable Halal Food Security, nd).

The sustainable development goals depend on the implementation of an effective food security system, which is based on a continuous food supply chain from farm to consumer. Incorporating the concepts of halal and ṭayyib into the food supply chain that upholds food safety, environmentally friendly practices, fair trade, and animal welfare is believed to provide a conducive environment for food security, which in turn facilitates the achievement of sustainable development goals.

The halal food supply chain includes farming, manufacturing, packaging, distribution, use, and disposal. For the food industry to become more sustainable, food producers need to implement sustainability initiatives in their companies upstream and downstream. Steps to fulfill the concept of halal and ṭayyib include conserving natural resources, namely animal welfare, eliminating cruelty, safe handling, housing, slaughtering, and transportation. Sustainable agricultural practices include reducing chemical fertilizers such as pesticides and eliminating the contamination of pollutant agents. This can also include health and safety features of food products, namely, food safety, traceability, and transparency (Idris et al., 2021).

Combining halal and ṭayyib standards and practices at RPH in the global food security objective provides a conducive development framework for social entrepreneurship with various opportunities created by the halal food security system. These opportunities can contribute to achieving good health, with health it will be easy to achieve prosperity (good health and well-being SDGs 3), the provision of clean water and proper sanitation (clean water and sanitation SDGs 6) poverty eradication and other sustainable development goals such as decent work and economic growth for all (SDGs 8), sustainable cities and human settlements sustainable cities and communities SDGs 11), and promoting responsible consumption and production for all (responsible consumption & production SDGs12) these opportunities can create various sizes of food-related business ventures that will grow with the system (Idris et al., 2021).

g. Sustainable Production at the RPH

The implementation of the above slaughtering standards can be recognized if the slaughterers are classified as halal slaughterers (JULEHA), which can be proven by having a halal slaughtering certificate. The requirements that must be met in determining the location of the RPH are environmental disturbances and pollution, sufficient clean water channels for animal slaughtering activities, and cleaning and disinfection processes. RPHs that meet the technical requirements by the provisions of the Minister of Agriculture must be owned by each Regency/City. To meet the provision of ASUH (Safe, Healthy, Whole, and Halal) meat, RPHs are required to implement technical requirements, including physical (buildings and equipment, human resources, and technical procedures for their implementation) (Lubis et al., 2020).

The quality of business services is determined by the final product and can also be assessed from several performance criteria. The Halal Good Manufacturing Practices (HGMP) assessment model at the RPH provides five main variables, including buildings and facilities, equipment, employees, maintenance, and halal, which also refers to aspects of animal welfare, safety, and meeting quality (Good Manufacturing Practice in Indonesian Regulation). This model has succeeded in providing a performance measurement tool and recommendations for improvement through benchmarking business services based on public service standards. Thus, the central halal certification body in Indonesia can standardize this assessment process comprehensively. the need to consider the application of critical points for raw materials, production processes, food safety, and sanitation processes at the

RPH. As a complement, it is necessary to consider the application of hygiene and sanitation requirements for the safety of animal products at the RPH, as stated in the Veterinary Control Number (NKV) certificate (Lestari et al., 2022).

RPH in Kediri Regency illustrates a tradition that is difficult to change. RPH in Kediri Regency is equipped with facilities and all utilities that function well in a magnificent building that is still not utilized. The meat-cutting process is still carried out on the ground as a place of choice to produce carcasses. The RPH building, complete with facilities worth billions of rupiah, is only a very beautiful building, and its iron is rusty. This example provides evidence that technology cannot be used for traditional practices to become professional. To achieve a green economy, it must have adequate facilities and human resources and be able to implement Krian RPH waste management for all areas that can have economic, social, and environmental value to achieve a green environment (Nuzula & Yuni K, 2022).

Less than optimal enforcement of halal certification law at RPH, thus requiring preventive law enforcement in the form of supervision from the government and the community, also requiring repressive law enforcement in the form of administrative, civil, or criminal sanctions for business actors who violate so that the implementation of halal certification at all RPH can be carried out properly (Wenovita, 2021).

All components of halal food must be from halal sources or upstream that have been processed, packaged, and stored properly by Islamic law. Therefore, this will ensure that all food ingredients and processes involved 'from farm to fork' are available halal and permissible for all Muslims (Arif & Sidek, 2015).

h. Sustainable Distribution at RPH

The sustainable development goals are driven and rooted in the halal ecosystem. However, to harness this symbiotic relationship, policymakers and the general public need to analyze the strengths, weaknesses, opportunities, and threats associated with the benefits of the linkage between halal ṭayyiban and sustainable development goals. Only by addressing these SWOT elements can the halal ecosystem serve as a platform for achieving sustainable development goals, namely ensuring quality and healthy lives and sustainable lifestyles. A vibrant and effective halal food supply chain will be a core element for sustainable halal food security (Pg Siti Rozaidah Pg Hj & et al, 2021).

Considering meat customers (retailers/consumers), meat producers (farms/slaughterhouses/processors), and SDGs goals as the foundation of an interconnected triangle, improvements in sustainable production and consumption are related to SDGs point 12 (responsible consumption and production). It is expected that producers support sustainable or environmentally friendly technologies and consumption patterns that prioritize good values, in this case maintaining nutritional value, then in parallel there will be an interconnection between producers, and consumers striving towards SDGs point 17 namely "partnerships for achieving goals" enabling deeper fulfillment of all UN SDGs to exceed the expectations of all stakeholders in the meat supply chain (Djekic, 2021).

Implementation of Halal Distribution logistics beef can be ensured that a "check-list" needs to be implemented which can be used as a standard that must be applied at the RPH (Sayuti et al., 2021).

2. METHOD

This study uses a qualitative approach to answer the questions raised in this study. The type of research used is phenomenology. This type is used to reveal the experience of RPH managers in implementing the halal ṭayyib principle in the production and distribution process so that a halal value chain is created in processed meat food products and contributes to the SDGs goals.

Data were obtained using interviews with several RPH managers and FGDs with parties related to the RPH. The speakers who attended included: Kurniawan Eko the head of the Food Security and Livestock Service-RPH, Mr. Darmaji (halal meat entrepreneur), Mr. Santoso (processed meat food entrepreneur), Mr. Adi (head of halal slaughterers in Jember), Mrs. Umi Cholifah (halal supervisor) and Mr. Tolabi (Head of the halal task force). The discussion was strengthened by observations made to see the slaughtering process, carcass cutting, and distribution.

3. RESULTS AND DISCUSSION

a. Condition of RPH in Indonesia

The origin of livestock as the main resource in the process of slaughtering animals is taken from people's farms as well as from abroad, which are raised through feedlots (fattening places for livestock that implement intensive farming). Local cattle raised by people's farmers vary greatly, namely from the breed, age, performance, and quality, and are not standard. In people's farms, the male cattle that are raised are mostly allocated for sale at the moment before Eid al-Adha (Eid al-Qurban) because there are more competitive prices in the seller when compared to regular daily slaughter to provide for the needs of people's meat consumption.

Fulfillment of meat needs for daily consumption from community farms is by utilizing culled (sorted) and productive female cows that are sold to the animal market or purchased by middlemen before entering the RPH. This trade practice has proven to be detrimental to farmers because the price of cattle is mostly determined by the middlemen. However, there are still cattle from community farms that are used to provide daily meat needs for the community, as is the case in East Java. For the practice of providing cattle in the Jakarta and West Java areas, cattle are imported from abroad. There are still many productive female cows that are slaughtered to meet the community's meat needs because farmers also need money to meet their living needs.

The common cattle trade chain in Indonesia has the following flow: starting from the breeder to the middleman, then sold to the village-level collector, then sold to the collector at the market/barn then bought by inter-city/regional traders, then to the slaughterer/meat trader (at the RPH), and to the stall meat seller. Different from TPH (Animal Slaughterhouse), if the TPH owner is allowed to buy animals directly from the breeder or already has his farm and sells his meat products directly, the trade flow is shorter (Tim Penyusun, 2022).

Figure 1. Flow of cattle and meat travel in Indonesia

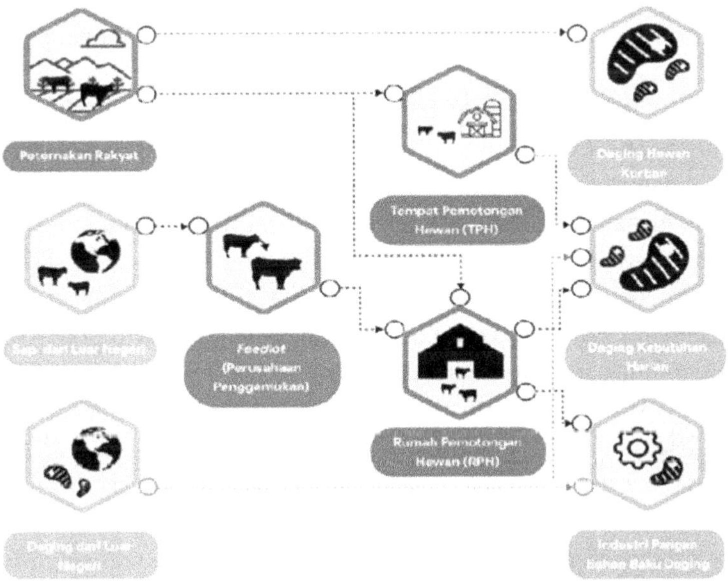

The mechanism of cattle buying and selling transactions in general from smallholder farmers is only through a system of estimating body weight or livestock performance; this model can harm farmers. The transaction mechanism between the owner of ready-to-slaughter cattle (known as a dealer) and meat traders is usually seen from the weight of the carcass produced or the meat results obtained.

The long trade flow and this method of transaction will certainly affect the price of cattle and the selling price of meat. Live cattle scales in several animal markets and carcass scales at RPH have been provided by the local government, but all of this equipment is not used because the equipment is not wanted by the actors who play a role in the trade. Unlike cattle from the fattening process in feedlots, the transaction mechanism for buying and selling to dealers is based on body weight (weighing on the spot), and the transaction mechanism between dealers and meat traders refers to the weight of the carcass produced (Tim Penyusun, 2022).

Currently, there are still many slaughterers who carry out a series of livestock slaughtering processes to produce carcasses on the floor so that the resulting product does not meet hygienic requirements and is susceptible to contamination with feces. The strong habit of slaughtering on the floor that has been going on for hundreds of years is very difficult to change in a short time. An example that can be taken from this difficult-to-change habit is the Kediri Regency RPH. The Kediri RPH is complete with facilities and tools that function well in a beautiful building, but it has not been optimally utilized. The slaughterers are still comfortable choosing the floor as a place to skin the carcasses. This condition provides evidence that the availability of technology has not been able to change traditional practices into modern and professional ones.

The results of the survey conducted by National Committee for Islamic Economics and Finance (KNEKS) at the RPH in Malang City and Padang City, present a general picture related to the management and slaughtering process at government-owned RPHs managed by both Regional Technical Implementation Unit (UPTD) and Regionally owned enterprises (BUMD) throughout Indonesia. The results of the observation obtained a picture that there are still various aspects that do not meet the criteria or standards of a modern halal RPH. This condition is a challenge in itself in the future to increase the capacity of RPH, which has a primary role as a producer of ASUH meat products with modern governance that can be achieved (Penyusun, 2022).

RPH Tunas, formerly known as RPH Gadang in Malang City, began operating on March 16, 1938, and is still operating and well-maintained. Received several national awards for meeting the criteria for the Best RPH. In realizing Malang as a "halal city", since 2021, the status of RPH has changed from a Trading Company to "Perumda RPH Tunas". In carrying out its business processes, RPH collaborates with PHRI (hotel and restaurant association) as a supplier of the frozen meat brand HABA (halal safe good blessing).

In general, the types of cattle slaughtered are local cattle and crossbred cattle. The cattle slaughtering levy fee is IDR 55,000 /head (there is a subsidy because BEP is IDR 85,000). The current human resource conditions do not have a halal supervisor, a veterinarian as the person in charge, and a halal slaughterer as a permanent employee of the RPH. Each trader has a slaughterer and his/her work team. During the visit during the RPH operating hours, there were still groups of slaughterers who did not fulfill the halal Standard Operating Procedure (SOP) (Tim Penyusun, 2022).

RPH institutions are divided into three types based on their management patterns, including:

1) Type I RPH is an RPH owned by the regional government, which is managed by the regional government as a public service.
2) Type II RPH is a privately owned RPH that is managed independently or in collaboration with other private parties.
3) Type III RPH is an RPH owned by the regional government and is managed jointly by the regional government and the private sector.

Table 1. Number of RPH/TPH by region (Annur, 2022)

No	Province	Number of RPH/TPH
1	Java	604
2	Sumatra	343
3	Sulawesi	259
4	Bali & Southeast	171
5	Kalimantan	162
6	Maluku & Papua	105

b. Implementation of Halal and Ṭayyib in Sustainable Production at RPH

The application of halal and ṭayyib in sustainable production in slaughterhouses illustrates a production approach that combines halal (according to Islamic law) and ṭayyib (clean, good quality, and beneficial) standards in sustainable animal slaughtering activities. This approach includes the application of production processes that not only comply with Islamic law but also maintain environmental sustainability, animal health and welfare, and socio-economic sustainability. By applying the principles of halal and ṭayyib in sustainable production in slaughterhouses, it is expected to produce healthy, safe, and ethical products, which contribute to the sustainability of the ecosystem and the welfare of society.

RPH is a building or building complex with a specific design and requirements that is used as a place for slaughtering animals. animal to fulfill the general public's meat consumption. Functions as a community service unit regarding the provision of safe, healthy, whole, and halal meat (Permentan No. 13/Permentan/OT.140/1/2010 of 2010, nd).

Most people's understanding assumes that food and drinks are halal only if they do not contain pork and alcohol. However, in Islam, the halal status of food and drinks is not only assessed based on their characteristics or ingredients. But food and drinks can become haram because of several external factors. For example, halal food and drinks become haram because they contain preservatives, colorings, and flavorings that are prohibited by sharia, contain dangers, and cause defects that cannot be removed.(Anas Bin Mohd Yunus et al, 2010)This is in line with the implementation of ḥalālan ṭayyiban in slaughterhouses (RPH), which must also avoid external factors that can cause halal meat to become haram.

If referring to SNI 01-6159-1999 Technical Standards for RPH(National Standardization Agency, 1999), then it must meet the building requirements, namely the separation between dirty areas (slaughter area, blood removal) and clean areas (carcass weighing area, carcass exit area, chilling room, and packaging). Ideally, there is also a laboratory and a liquid waste drainage system. Of course, all of these requirements are still a big homework to further improve the quality of production in most RPHs in Indonesia (Badan Standarisasi Nasional, 1999).

This is as has been researched by Lubis et al., that to fulfill the provision of ASUH (Safe, Healthy, Whole, and Halal) meat, RPH is required to implement technical requirements including physical (buildings and equipment, human resources, and technical procedures for implementation) (Lubis et al., 2020). However, from the research results of Nuzula and Yuni, the RPH in Kediri Regency, which is equipped with complete facilities and technology, apparently has not been utilized by the slaughterers at the RPH, who use the old habit of choosing to cut meat on the ground (Nuzula & Yuni K, 2022). This habit also occurs in this study in Jember Regency, namely the Jember City RPH has been facilitated with sophisticated equipment, although not as complete as the Kediri RPH, it is also neglected and not utilized, this shows that changing the mindset of RPH managers still cannot be directed to a more hygienic modern one and supports the fulfillment of ṭayyib.

Habits that are difficult to change require binding regulations and strict supervision, as has been researched by Wenovita, which shows the need for enforcement. Preventive law, namely in the form of supervision from the government and society, also requires repressive law enforcement, namely in the form of administrative, civil, or criminal sanctions for business actors who violate the law (Wenovita, 2021).

So the sustainability of production at the RPH, in addition to having to fulfill halal certification, must also meet hygiene and sanitation requirements for the safety of animal products at the RPH. Proof of halal certificate as the fulfillment of halal implementation, and proof of Veterinary Control Number (NKV) certificate as the fulfillment of ṭayyib implementation.

c. Implementation of Halal and Ṭayyib in Sustainable Distribution at RPH

The application of halal and ṭayyib in sustainable distribution in slaughterhouses refers to an approach that integrates the principles of halal (by Islamic law) and ṭayyib (good and clean quality) in the entire process of animal meat distribution. This distribution is intended to be sustainable, which means paying attention to environmental sustainability, animal welfare, and social and economic balance. By implementing this concept in slaughterhouses, it is hoped that the distribution of meat products will not only meet Sharia standards but also pay attention to aspects of sustainability that support the welfare of society and the environment in the long term.

Sustainable distribution that refers to the implementation of halal and ṭayyib can run if monitoring is implemented optimally. To direct this monitoring by standards, it is necessary to implement a "checklist" that can be used as a standard that must be applied to the RPH (Sayuti et al., 2021)so that control over the implementation of halal and ṭayyib in sustainable distribution can run effectively.

The reality in the field is that the distribution of meat from the RPH has very minimal monitoring. On average, when the meat leaves the RPH, it is already free from the monitoring or control of the RPH; that is where the potential for violations such as mixing with non-halal meat is very possible. Of course, this will be very detrimental to consumers, especially Muslim consumers.

The halal supply chain is essential to ensure that the entire production process, from raw material sourcing and processing to distribution, is by halal standards set out in Islamic law. This supply chain ensures that the products produced are free from contamination of non-halal ingredients, maintaining cleanliness, safety, and ethics at every stage of production and distribution. This is important not only to meet the needs of Muslim consumers but also to increase consumer confidence in the quality, cleanliness, and transparency of products. With a guaranteed halal supply chain, manufacturers can offer quality and reliable products and support sustainable and responsible business practices.

4. CONCLUSION

The concept of halal and ṭayyib in sustainable production and distribution at the Slaughterhouse (RPH) is an important step to ensure that the meat products produced not only meet the requirements of Islamic law but also hygiene and environmental sustainability standards. In addition to meeting technical standards such as physical facilities, waste management, and technology, it is important to change the work culture, strict regulations, and maximum supervision in distribution to maintain halal quality from production to the hands of consumers. With a fulfilled halal supply chain, consumer trust will increase, supporting the achievement of sustainable social, economic, and environmental welfare.

The concept of halal and ṭayyib in sustainable production and distribution in slaughterhouses supports several Sustainable Development Goals (SDGs). Through meeting hygiene standards, waste management, and the use of environmentally friendly technologies, this initiative is in line with SDGs 3 (Good Health and Well-Being), SDGs 6 (Access to Clean Water and Sanitation), and SDGs 12 (Responsible Consumption and Production). In addition, consistent changes in work culture, strict regulations, and distribution oversight contribute to SDGs 8 (Decent Work and Economic Growth) by creating a healthy and productive work environment. By prioritizing halal quality and maintaining environmental sustainability, the halal supply chain supports SDGs 2 (Ending Hunger) through the provision of safe and nutritious food and SDGs 13 (Addressing Climate Change) by reducing the environmental impact of the production process. Overall, this approach helps build sustainable social, economic, and environmental well-being, supporting the SDG targets holistically.

REFERENCES

Annur, C. M. (2022, November 16). *Ada 1.644 Rumah Pemotongan Hewan di Indonesia pada 2022, Ini Sebaran Wilayahnya.* Katadata.co.id;Databoks. https://databoks.katadata.co.id/agroindustri/statistik/402450333383476/ada-1644-rumah-pemotongan-hewan-di-indonesia-pada-2022-ini-sebaran-wilayahnya

Agency, A. N. (n.d.). *RPH dan RPU adalah hulu strategis kehalalan suatu produk.* ANTARA News Jawa Timur. Retrieved 21 October 2022, from https://jatim.antaranews.com/berita/597201/rph-dan-rpu-adalah-hulu-strategis-kehalalan-suatu-produk

Purnomo, S. H. (2022, April 25). *RPH dan RPU adalah hulu strategis kehalalan suatu produk.* ANTARA News Jawa Timur. https://jatim.antaranews.com/berita/597201/rph-dan-rpu-adalah-hulu-strategis-kehalalan-suatu-produk

Amrullah, A., & Abdulmalik, H. (1983). *Tafsir al-Azhar* (p. Juz VII). Pustaka Panjimas.

Arif, S., & Sidek, S. (2015). Application of Halalan Tayyiban in the Standard Reference for Determining Malaysian Halal Food. *Asian Social Science*, *11*(17), 116. DOI: 10.5539/ass.v11n17p116

Badan Standarisasi Nasional. (1999). *SNI 01-6159-1999 Standar Teknis RPH.* BSN.

Bisri, M. A. (1977). *Moh. Adib Bisri, 'Terjemah Al Faraidul Bahiyyah Risalah Qawa-Id Fiqh* (p. 24). Menara Kudus.

Djekic, I. V. (2021). Meat supply chain in the perspective of UN SDGs. *Theory and Practice of Meat Processing*, *6*(3), 242–247. DOI: 10.21323/2414-438X-2021-6-3-242-247

Elkington, J. (1998). *Cannibals with Forks: The Triple Bottom Line of 21st Century Business.* New Society Publishers.

Gading, B. M. W. T., Respati, A. N., & Suryanto, E. (2021). Studi Kasus: Permasalahan Limbah di Tempat Pemotongan Hewan (TPH) Amessangeng, Kota Sengkang. *JURNAL TRITON, 12*(1), 68–77. DOI: 10.47687/jt.v12i1.164

Hasanah, N. U., Safira, M. E., Kurnianingtyas Sri Agung, W., Chotib, M., Nimasari, E. P., & Lahuri, S. B. (2021). Regulation of Halal and Healthy Products for Small-Scaled Businesses as Consumer Protection. *Open Access Macedonian Journal of Medical Sciences, 9*(E), 749–753. DOI: 10.3889/oamjms.2021.6643

Hirmawan, W., & Hasanah, F. (2023). *Direktori Perusahaan Pertanian Rumah Potong Hewan (RPH) dan Tempat Pemotongan Hewan (TPH) 2023* (Vol. 9). Badan Pusat Statistik.

Hoelman., ... M. B. (2015a). *PANDUAN SDGs Untuk Pemerintah Daerah (Kota Dan Kabupaten) Dan Pemangku Kepentingan Daerah.* International NGO Forum on Indonesian Development.

Hoelman., ... M. B. (2015b). *Panduan SDGs Untuk Pemerintah Daerah (Kota dan Kabupaten) dan Pemangku Kepentingan Daerah* (pp. 1–64). International NGO Forum on Indonesian Development.

Idris, P. S. R. P. H., Musa, S. F. P. D., & Sumardi, W. H. H. (2021). Halal-Tayyiban and Sustainable Development Goals: A SWOT Analysis. *International Journal of Asian Business and Information Management, 13*(2), 1–16. DOI: 10.4018/IJABIM.20220701.oa9

IPB University Raih Penghargaan Perguruan Tinggi SDGs Terbaik dari Bappenas—Tekno Tempo.co. (n.d.). Retrieved 7 June 2024, from https://tekno.tempo.co/read/1793738/ipb-university-raih-penghargaan-perguruan-tinggi-sdgs-terbaik-dari-bappenas

Keputusan Menteri Agama Nomor 748 Tahun 2021. (2022, April 17). https://peraturanpedia.id/keputusan-menteri-agama-nomor-748-tahun-2021/

Kurniadi, M., & Frediansyah, A. (2017). Halal Perspective of Microbial Bioprocess Based-Food Products. *REAKTOR, 16*(3), 147. DOI: 10.14710/reaktor.16.3.147-160

Lestari, F., Mawardi, M., Yola, M., Muda, Y., & Abdul Hamid, A. B. (2022). A model for assessment of Halal Good Manufacturing Practice in meat industry. *Production & Manufacturing Research, 10*(1), 666–695. DOI: 10.1080/21693277.2022.2117742

Lubis, I., Soesilo, T. E. B., & Soemantojo, R. W. (2020). Pengelolaan Air Limbah Rumah Potong Hewan DI RPH X, Kota Bogor, Provinsi Jawa Barat (Wastewater Management of Slaughterhouse in Slaughterhouse X, Bogor City, West Java Province). *Jurnal Manusia Dan Lingkungan, 25*(1), 33. DOI: 10.22146/jml.35396

Masruroh, N. (2020). Dinamika Identitas dan Religiusitas pada Branding Halal di Indonesia. *ISLAMICA: Jurnal Studi Keislaman, 14*(2), 317–338. DOI: 10.15642/islamica.2020.14.2.317-338

Mickael, B. Hoelman et al. (2015). *PANDUAN SDGs Untuk Pemerintah Daerah (Kota dan Kabupaten) dan Pemangku Kepentingan Daerah.* International NGO Forum on Indonesian Development.

Mubarok, S., & Afrizal, M. (2018). ISLAM DAN. *Sustainable Development, 3*(1).

Mujieb, M. A., Ismail, A., & Syafi'ah. (2009). *Ensiklopedia Tasawuf: Imam Al-Ghazali Mudah Memahami dan Menjalankan Kehidupan Spiritual* (p. 79). Hikmah.

Mustaffa, K. A. (2019). Developing Halalan Tayyiban Concept In Malaysia's Food Industry. *Halal Journal, 3.*

Nuzula, F., & Yuni, K. K. C. (2022). Modernisasi Rumah Potong Hewan Halal RPH Krian dalam Mewujudkan Green Economy di Kabupaten Sidoarjo. *Jurnal Ilmiah Ekonomi Islam, 8*(3), 3100. DOI: 10.29040/jiei.v8i3.6796

Tim Penyusun. (2022). *Kerangka Modernisasi Rumah Potong Hewan Halal.* Komite Nasional Ekonomi dan Keuangan Syariah.

Permentan No. 13/Permentan/OT.140/1/2010 Tahun 2010. (n.d.). Database Peraturan | JDIH BPK. Retrieved 7 June 2024, from https://peraturan.bpk.go.id/Details/161577/permentan-no-13permentanot14012010-tahun-2010

Pg Siti Rozaidah Pg Hj, I.. (2021). Halal-Tayyiban and Sustainable Development Goals: A SWOT Analysis. *International Journal of Asian Business and Information Management, 13*(2), 1–16. https://doi.org/DOI. DOI: 10.4018/IJABIM.20220701.oa9

Pujayanti, D. A. (2020). Industri Halal sebagai Paradigma bagi Sustainable Development Goals di Era Revolusi Industri 4.0. *Youth & Islamic Economic Journal, 1*, 14.

Qur'an Kemenag. (n.d.-a). Retrieved 30 May 2024, from https://quran.kemenag.go.id/

Qur'an Kemenag. (n.d.-b). Retrieved 14 August 2023, from https://quran.kemenag.go.id/quran/per-ayat/surah/5?from=88&to=120

Sayuti, M., Purnamasari, A., & Pratiwi, A. I. (2021). Penerapan Halal Logistik pada Distribusi Daging Sapi di Kabupaten Karawang. *Jurnal Integrasi Sistem industri, 8*, 11.

Sharaai, A. H., Zulkifli, N. F., Mahmood, N. Z., & Sulaiman, N. M. N. (2012). *The implementation of Islamic elements in achieving best practices of sustainability concept.* DOI: 10.13140/RG.2.1.1056.7765

Simanjuntak, T., & Lestarini, R. (2022). Implementation Of The Concept Of Sustainable Development In Resolving Indigenous Law Community Conflict. *International Journal of Environmental, Sustainability, and Social Science, 3*(3). Advance online publication. DOI: 10.38142/ijesss.v3i3.342

Suharti, S., Mulyawan, S., & Ridwan, A. H. (2023). Sustainability dalam Perspektif Islam dan Pengaruhnya terhadap Firm Value dan Firm Size melalui Profitabilitas sebagai Variabel Mediasi. *Nuansa Akademik: Jurnal Pembangunan Masyarakat, 8*(1), 135–150. DOI: 10.47200/jnajpm.v8i1.1582

Surat Al-Anfal Ayat 69. (n.d.). Tafsir AlQuran Online. Retrieved 30 May 2024, from https://tafsirq.com/permalink/ayat/1229

Surat Al-Ma'idah Ayat 88 Arab, Latin, Terjemah dan Tafsir | Baca di TafsirWeb. (n.d.). Retrieved 30 May 2024, from https://tafsirweb.com/1972-surat-al-maidah-ayat-88.html

Surat An-Nahl Ayat 114. (n.d.). Tafsir AlQuran Online. Retrieved 30 May 2024, from https://tafsirq.com/permalink/ayat/2015

Sustainable Halal Food Security. (n.d.). Iofs. Retrieved 12 June 2024, from https://iofs.org.kz/post/125

Thohari, A. (2013). EpistemologiFikih Lingkungan: Revitalisasi Konsep Masalahah. *E-Journal Fakultas Syariah Dan Ilmu Hukum, 5*(2), 146–161.

UU No. 33 Tahun 2014. (n.d.). Database Peraturan | JDIH BPK. Retrieved 12 June 2024, from https://peraturan.bpk.go.id/Details/38709/uu-no-33-tahun-2014

Wenovita, C. A. A. (2021). Penegakan Hukum Sertifikasi Halal Rumah Potong Hewan. *Jurist-Diction, 4*(4), 1357. DOI: 10.20473/jd.v4i4.28452

Wilson, J. A. J., & Liu, J. (2010). Shaping the *Halal* into a brand? *Journal of Islamic Marketing, 1*(2), 107–123. DOI: 10.1108/17590831011055851

Yahaya, A. M., & Ruzulan, Z. (2020). Quranic Concept of Halalan Tayyiban and its Application in Food and Beverages of Hospitality Sector in Malaysia. *Journal of Contemporary Islamic Studies, 6*(1), 61–76. DOI: 10.24191/jcis.v6i1.4

Chapter 5
Ensuring Halal Compliance in the Leather Industry:
Standards, Practices, and Certification

Tri Cahyanto
https://orcid.org/0000-0002-5427-7959
UIN Sunan Gunung Djati Bandung, Indonesia

Yuni Kulsum
https://orcid.org/0000-0003-0102-4613
UIN Sunan Gunung Djati Bandung, Indonesia

Nurhayati Nurhayati
https://orcid.org/0000-0002-8749-6840
UIN Sunan Gunung Djati Bandung, Indonesia

Afriansyah Fadillah
https://orcid.org/0000-0003-4048-6482
UIN Sunan Gunung Djati Bandung, Indonesia

Nurul Aulia Tahta
https://orcid.org/0009-0008-6988-5878
UIN Sunan Gunung Djati Bandung, Indonesia

Neneng Windayani
https://orcid.org/0000-0002-7623-9160
UIN Sunan Gunung Djati Bandung, Indonesia

ABSTRACT

This Chapter explores how leather products can meet halal standards. It serves as a guide for industry professionals to ensure halal compliance from sourcing raw materials to final processing and certification, addressing the increasing global demand for halal products. The chapter specifically examines halal standards in Indonesia, which prohibits leather from dogs and pigs and mandates that products remain free from haram contamination. It discusses halal-compliant processing methods, focusing on permissible tanning techniques and the use of additives that

DOI: 10.4018/979-8-3373-3917-7.ch005

do not contain haram substances. An overview of halal certification procedures is provided, detailing compliance criteria and the role of certifying bodies in verifying halal status. The chapter acknowledges challenges such as sourcing halal materials, production costs, and contamination risks, offering practical solutions for manufacturers. Ultimately, it aims to equip businesses with the knowledge needed to meet halal standards, ensuring consumer trust and enhancing market competitiveness.

1. THE CONTEXT OF HALAL LEATHER: BACKGROUND AND RESEARCH OBJECTIVES

The awareness of Muslims to consume halal products continues to rise, in line with the deepening understanding of Sharia teachings, especially regarding the halal and haram status of a product. This trend is evident not only in the food and beverage sector but also in cosmetics and consumables. Over the past three decades, the halal food market has experienced significant growth, particularly in Muslim-majority countries such as Indonesia, Malaysia, Pakistan, and the Middle East region. In addition to food, consumable products such as halal fashion, pharmaceuticals, and cosmetics have also shown rapid increases. In the context of Sharia, the term halal comes from Arabic, meaning allowed or permissible according to Islamic law. When applied to pharmaceutical products, food, or beverages, this term affirms that the products are safe and suitable for consumption by Muslims in accordance with religious provisions (Kasri et al., 2023; Rafiki et al., 2023).

Islam is the second-largest religion in the world and is experiencing the fastest growth globally. In addition to being a faith that regulates worship rituals, Islam also offers a comprehensive worldview. Its teachings encompass various aspects of life, including the consumption of halal products, which is considered a form of worship to Allah and is as important as other ritual acts of devotion. The principles of Islam encourage Muslims to use products that meet halal criteria, meaning they are permissible and lawful according to Islamic law. For a Muslim, it is their duty to consume or use any products that are halal. For non-Muslim consumers, halal food or products are often viewed as those that meet the highest quality standards. The concept of halal can be examined from three main perspectives: religious and economic. From a religious standpoint, Allah commands all of humanity—both Muslims and non-Muslims—to consume food that is halal and tayyib (good and wholesome). This is explained in Surah Al-Baqarah, verse 168, which states: "O mankind, eat from that which is lawful and good from the earth, and do not follow the footsteps of Satan; indeed, he is to you a manifest enemy."

Halal is not merely a religious obligation but also involves aspects of product quality and safety (Insani et al., 2019). From an economic perspective, halal products have become one of the rapidly growing sectors globally, driven by increasing consumer demand, not only from the Muslim community but also from the general public, who appreciate high-quality standards. Global trade in halal products shows significant growth, which is in line with the rising awareness among Muslims to use products that align with sharia principles. The halal food and beverage sector is projected to experience rapid growth, with market value reaching USD 1.1 trillion in 2013 and predicted to increase to USD 1.6 trillion by 2018. According to a report from the Dubai Chamber of Commerce and Industry, the share of the global halal food and beverage market grew by 6.9 per cent, reflecting the high demand from both Muslim and non-Muslim consumers who value the quality and cleanliness of halal products (Apriliani et al., 2023; Kasri et al., 2023).

The global halal market is experiencing exponential growth, driven by a rising Muslim population and increased consumer awareness of halal certifications. This expansion transcends the traditional food and beverage sector, extending significantly into cosmetics, pharmaceuticals, fashion, and other consumer goods. The past three decades have witnessed remarkable growth, particularly in Muslim-majority countries like Indonesia, Malaysia, and Pakistan, as well as the Middle East region. This surge in demand reflects a deepening understanding of Sharia principles and a growing preference for products aligning with religious and ethical values, emphasizing not only religious compliance but also quality and safety.

The leather industry, a significant contributor to the global economy, is intricately interwoven with this expanding halal market. Leather, a longstanding material with utilitarian and aesthetic value, finds its way into numerous products, from clothing and footwear to automotive interiors and furniture. However, the leather industry faces considerable challenges in meeting halal standards. Halal standards not only guarantee compliance with Sharia but also demonstrate the producer's commitment to quality and product safety, thereby enhancing competitiveness in the increasingly demanding global market for high-quality halal products. Investment in supporting technologies and certification infrastructure is key to ensuring the sustainability of the halal industry (Hafiz Zulfakar et al., 2014; Prayuda et al., 2023). By understanding the importance of halal raw material sources, it is hoped that the industry can continue to grow and meet the needs of Muslim consumers worldwide (Prayuda et al., 2023). The challenges of halal standards arise from various sources, including the complex nature of the supply chain, concerns about environmentally damaging tanning processes often relying on chromium, and diverse interpretations of Sharia regarding the use of leather from animals that have died without slaughter.

Despite the rising demand for halal leather products and the significant economic potential of this market segment, a comprehensive and universally accepted set of halal standards for leather production remains elusive. Existing standards often vary across regions and countries, leading to inconsistencies and challenges in ensuring halal compliance throughout the complex global supply chain. This inconsistency creates obstacles for businesses seeking halal certification and generates confusion among consumers striving to make informed, ethical choices. Furthermore, the lack of halal monitoring process and potential for cross-contamination with non-halal materials throughout production adds another layer of complexity.

This chapter aims to address the critical gap in knowledge concerning comprehensive halal standards for the leather industry. Specifically, it will investigate the existing halal standards for leather, analyze the challenges in achieving halal compliance across the supply chain, and explore solutions that can bridge the gap between current practices and the ideal of comprehensive, universally accepted halal standards. By addressing these issues, this chapter will contribute to greater transparency, consumer trust, and ultimately, the sustainable growth of the halal leather industry while fostering ethical and environmentally sound practices.

2. UNDERSTANDING HALAL LEATHER THROUGH ISLAMIC LAW

Understanding halal leather necessitates a comprehensive understanding of Islamic jurisprudence and its practical applications. This chapter will delve into the Islamic legal basis for the purity of animal hides, the permissible tanning processes according to Islamic law, and the differing scholarly opinions regarding the status of carcass hides after tanning. By examining relevant hadiths, fatwas, and the opinions of various schools of thought, the chapter aims to clarify the criteria required for leather to be classified as halal and compliant with Islamic principles of permissibility.

There is unanimous agreement among Islamic scholars regarding the purity of the hides of halal animals slaughtered according to Islamic law. This includes the hides of commonly used animals such as goats, cows, and sheep, as well as other permissible animals. The consensus stems from the understanding that the entire carcass of a ritually slaughtered animal is considered pure and permissible for consumption.

This purity extends to the animal's hide, which is not only permissible to utilize for various purposes but is also considered clean enough for consumption. The permissibility of consuming the hide, while less common in practice, underscores the comprehensive purity attributed to the entire halal animal after proper slaughter, reflecting the Islamic emphasis on the utilization of resources and minimizing waste.

Tanning, known as dibagh (غابد) in Arabic, is defined by Al-Khatib Asy-Syirbini (died 977 H) in the book Mughni Al-Muhtaj as the process of removing impurities from the hide, particularly liquid and wet impurities that could damage the hide if left untreated (Asy-Syirbini, 1997). This process not only cleans the surface but fundamentally transforms the nature of the skin itself.

Tanning serves as a clear example of how an impure (najis) substance can be transformed into a pure one. This change occurs not merely due to the removal of impurities from the surface but through a fundamental transformation of the raw hide material. It converts raw hides or skins into tanned leather.

Essentially, tanning involves processing raw hides with tanning agents. Only components of the raw hide other than collagen react with these tanning agents. The end product is finished leather with organoleptic, physical, and chemical properties that are vastly different from those of the raw hide from which it originated.

Tanning leather is an important aspect in Islamic jurisprudence, particularly in discussing the cleanliness and usability of animal hides. This practice has significant implications for various aspects of daily life, from hygiene to permissible materials for clothing and tools. Understanding the Islamic perspective on this practice not only clarifies its religious significance but also reflects the broader principles of purity and utility in Islam. In the prophetic hadith, there are several narrations that discuss the subject of tanning leather, including:

1. Abdullah bin Al-Abbas radhiyallahuanhu narrated several hadiths related to the topic of tanning.

رَهُطْ دَقَفُ بَاهِإلاَ غِبُدُ اذإ

Abdullah bin Abbas said, "I heard the Messenger of Allah (SAW) say, 'When the skin has been tanned, indeed it has become pure.'" (HR. Muslim).

رَهُطْ دَقَفَ غِبُدُ بِاهِإ امَّيَأ

All skins that have been tanned are indeed pure. (HR. An-Nasai)

Abdullah bin Al-Abbas gave a goat as alms to a poor man, who was Maimunah's servant. However, not long after that, the goat died. When the Prophet Muhammad (SAW) passed by them, he suggested that they skin the goat and make use of its skin.

اهُلْكَأ مُرِحَ امَّنِإ :لَاقَف ،ٌةَتْيَم اهَّنِإ :اوُلاَقَف ؟ِهِب مُتْعَفَتْنَاف ُهوُمُتْغَبَدَف اهَباهِإ مُتْذَخَأ َّالَه

"Why don't you use the hide by tanning it so it can be utilized?" They replied, "We thought it was carrion." He (SAW) said, "What is prohibited is eating it." (Bukhari and Muslim).

Initially, they believed that the entire body of the goat had become carrion, making it impossible to use any part of it. However, the Messenger of Allah (SAW) allowed the hide of the carrion to be utilized after it was tanned. Meanwhile, the meat remains prohibited and should not be consumed.

2. Salamah bin Muhabbiq narrates that during the Battle of Tabuk, the Prophet Muhammad (SAW) requested water from a woman. The woman responded that she had no water except for what was stored in a pouch made from the skin of carrion.

The Messenger of Allah (SAW) confirmed that the skin had been tanned beforehand, and the woman affirmed this. Then he (SAW) said:

نَّإِف اَهَغاَبِد اَهُتاَكَذ

"Indeed, tanning is its purification." (An-Nasa'i).

3. In addition to the well-known hadiths that state that the hide becomes pure after tanning, there are also hadiths that question the purity of tanned carrion hide. One such hadith is narrated by Abdullah bin Ukaim.

اَناَتَأ ُباَتِك ِلوُسَر ِهّللا َلْبَق ِهِتاَفَو ٍرْهَشِب ْوَأ ِنْيَرْهَش: ّلاَأ اوُعِفَتْنَت َنِم ِةَتْيَمْلا ٍباَهِإِب
َلاَو ٍبَصَع

A letter from the Prophet Muhammad (SAW) arrived one or two months before his passing, stating: "Do not make use of carrion skin through tanning." (At-Tirmidhi).

In another narration, it is stated with different wording as follows:

ُتْنُك ُتْصَّخَر ْمُكَل يِف ِدوُلُج ِةَتْيَمْلا اَذِإَف ْمُكَءاَج يِباَتِك اَذه َلاَف اوُعِفَتْنَت َنِم ِةَتْيَمْلا
ٍباَهِإِب َلاَو ٍبَصَع

"Previously, I had permitted the purity of carrion skin. With the arrival of this letter, do not make use of tanned carrion hide." (Abu Dawood).

The two hadiths above are used by the Maliki's Mazhab, which holds that the tanning of carrion skin does not purify its impurity.

4. The Hanafi's and Hanbali's Mazhab generally contend that carrion skin will not regain its purity, even after it has been tanned.

Ibn Qudamah (died 620 AH), representing the Hanbali's mazhab, stated in his book Al-Mughni that carrion skin is considered impure, both before and after tanning (Nuryana et al., 2023)

ُّلُكَو ِدْلِج ٍةَتْيَم َغِبُد ْوَأ ْمَل ْغَبْدُي َوُهَف ٌسَجَن يِخَتْلَي ُفِلَتْخَي ُبَهْذَمْلا يِف ِةَساَجَن ِةَتْيَمْلا َلْبَق
ِغْبَّدلا، َلاَو ُمَلْعَن اًدَحَأ َفَلاَخ ِهيِف، اَّمَأَو َدْعَب ِغْبَّدلا ُروُهْشَمْلاَف يِف ِبَهْذَمْلا ُهَّنَأ ٌسَجَن اًضْيَأ

"All carrion skins, whether tanned or untanned, are considered impure. The Hanbali's mazhab unanimously agree on the impurity of carrion skin before tanning, with no known dissenting opinions among them. As for after tanning, the most well-known position is that it remains impure as well."

Syamsuddin Abul Farraj Ibn Qudamah (d. 682 AH) wrote the following in his book Asy-Syarhul Kabir:

بهذملا نم حيحصلا وه اذه غابدلاب ةتيملا دلج رهطي الو

"And carrion skin cannot be purified through tanning. This is the correct stance of the Hanbali's Mazhab."

5. Al-Kharsyi (d. 1101 AH) stated the following in his book, Syarah Mukhtashar Khalil:

ىلَع َغبُد ْولَو ٌسَجَن ِّيَحْلا ْنِم َذوُخْأَمْلا َدْلِجْلاَو ِةَتْيَمْلا َدْلِج ّنَأ يِنْعَي (ش) َغبُد ْولَو ِدْلِجَو ِروُهْشَمْلا

"And the skin, even if it has been tanned, referring to the carrion skin taken from a live animal, is considered impure, according to the widely accepted opinion."

Al-Hathab Ar-Ru'aini (d. 954 AH) wrote the following in his book Mawahibul Jalil fi Syarhi Mukhtashar Khalil:

ُغاَبِّدلا ُهُرِّهَطُي َال ِةَتْيَمْلا َدْلِج ّنَأ ِهِبَهْذَم ْنِم ُموُلْعَمْلا ٍكِلاَم ِلْوَق ْنِم ُروُهْشَمْلا

"The widely accepted opinion from Imam Malik and known from his mazhab is that tanning does not purify carrion skin."

6. Al-Mawardi (d. 450 AH), a prominent scholar in the Shafi'i's mazhab, wrote the following in his book, Al-Hawi Al-Kabir fi Fiqhi Al-Imam Asy-Syafi'i:

َتاَم ْنِإ ِةَغاَبِّدلاِبَو ،اًعاَمْجِإ ِةاَكَّذلاِب ُهُدْلِج ُرُهْطَي َفيِكلوُأْمَلا امأف

"Animals that are permissible to eat should have their skins purified through slaughter (according to consensus), and if they are already dead, they can be purified through tanning."

7. Al-Imam An-Nawawi (d. 676 H), who is an iconic figure of the Shafi'i school of thought, wrote in his book Raudhatu Ath-Thalibin wa Umdatu Al-Muftiyyin as follows:

ِبْلَكْلا َدْلِج َّالِإ ،ِهِرْيَغَو ِمَّحَلْلا ِلوُكْأَم ْنِم ِغاَبِّدلاِب ُرُهْطَي ِةَتْيَمْلا ُدْلِج َغِبُد ْنَأ :يِناَّثلاَو، اًعْطَق ُرُهْطَي َال ُهَّنِإَف ،اَمِهِعْرَفَو ِريِزْنِخْلاَو

"The skin of a dead animal that has been tanned. Animals that are permissible to eat, or those that are not (forbidden), are considered pure when tanned, except for dogs, pigs, and their descendants. This is because they cannot be purified by nature."

8. Ibn Juzai Al-Kalbi (d. 741 H) in his book, Al-Qawanin Al-Fiqhiyah, writes that some state it is impure, in accordance with the opinion of Ahmad bin Hanbal. However, others contend that it is pure, in line with the view of the Shafi'i Mazhab:

وأما جلد المْيتة فإن لم يدبغ فهُوَ نجس وإن دبغ فالمْشَهُور أنه نجس وفاقا لِابْن...
وَقِيل هُوَ طاهر وفاقا للشافعي"

"Meanwhile, the skin of a dead animal, if it has not been tanned, is considered impure. If it has been tanned, according to the prevailing opinion, it is still impure, in accordance with the view of Ahmad bin Hanbal. However, some say that the skin is pure, according to the opinion of the Shafi'i Mazhab."

3. A FIQH PERSPECTIVE ON HALAL LEATHER PRODUCTION

Halal processing is a crucial aspect of ensuring the halal status of the products produced, especially in the context of the increasing global demand for halal goods. The concept of halal encompasses not only the types of raw materials used but also the production, distribution, and storage processes. In Islamic Sharia, non-compliant processing can alter the halal status of a product, even if the raw materials are halal. Therefore, the entire production chain must be strictly monitored to meet the established halal criteria. Globalization and industrialization have increased the complexity of production processes, making the provision of halal standards more challenging. Many processed products involve multiple countries, each potentially having different halal standards. In this situation, consistent oversight and the application of updated technologies are essential to ensure that all processing stages adhere to halal principles. This responsibility lies not only with producers but also with regulators and halal certification providers.

Halal-compliant production processes include the treatment of raw materials, the use of equipment and facilities, and sanitation procedures. The equipment used must be free from contamination by najis or haram substances. Additionally, production facilities must be ensured to be clean according to sharia regulations. For instance, machinery used for halal products should not have been previously employed to process haram materials without appropriate cleaning procedures. Furthermore, the halal framework also encompasses non-material aspects, such as intention or purpose in the production process. In Islam, the principle of intention (*niyyah*) serves as one of the fundamental foundations for ensuring the halal status of a process. Thus, in addition to technical aspects, ethical and moral approaches must also be considered in the halal industry. This demands that industry players comply not only with technical standards but also uphold principles of honesty and transparency.

This comparative analysis aims to provide a more comprehensive overview and assist readers in understanding the diversity of ijtihad in determining halal standards for leather-based products.

1. **Animal Sources**: Leather must come from halal animals that are slaughtered according to Islamic law. The animal must be healthy and free from illness at the time of slaughter. A qualified person must carry out the slaughtering process in accordance with religious stipulations. There are differing opinions among schools of thought regarding the use of leather from carrion animals, which should be considered when establishing standards. The differences among schools of thought regarding the permissibility of using animal leather also extend to the types of animals allowed. Generally, the leather from halal animals that are slaughtered according to Islamic law is permissible for all schools. However, differences arise in the use of leather from animals that die without being slaughtered (carrion). For instance, the Hanafi school tends to be more permissive regarding the use of leather from carrion animals after undergoing a tanning process that eliminates impurities and unpleasant odours. They argue that a thorough tanning process can remove its najis (impurity) status, rendering the hide pure and halal for use. In contrast, the Maliki, Shafi'i, and Hanbali schools take a stricter stance. They tend to prohibit the use of leather from carrion animals, even after tanning.

The differences in opinions among the schools regarding the use of animal leather as raw material for products, particularly within the context of the halal industry, illustrate the diversity of ijtihad in understanding religious texts. In general, the majority of schools agree on the permissibility of using leather, but there are differing details regarding the conditions and requirements. Leather that meets halal standards must originate from animals that are permitted in Islam, such as cows, sheep, goats, or buffalo, and must not contain najis or haram elements, such as pig or its derivatives (Fratzl & Weinkamer, 2007; Islam et al., 2023). The slaughtering process is a central aspect in determining halal status. The animal must be slaughtered by a competent Muslim, invoking the name of Allah and cutting the windpipe, oesophagus, and blood vessels in the neck to ensure the complete outflow of blood. Animals that die without proper slaughter are considered haram, and their leather cannot be used in products intended for Muslim consumers (Riaz & Chaudry, 2003).

Several opinions regarding the halal status of animal leather as a consumer good include:

a. Leather from Halal Animals Slaughtered According to Sharia

In Sharia, the use of materials derived from halal animals that have been slaughtered according to regulations (*dhabīḥah*) is a primary requirement (Tieman, 2011; Zakaria, 2008). This includes:

1). The leather must originate from halal animals such as cows, goats, sheep, and buffalo.
2). The animals must be slaughtered by invoking the name of Allah (Bismillah) and following the prescribed sharia procedures, which include cutting the throat, esophagus, and major blood vessels. By adhering to these principles, the halal tanning process ensures the integrity of the leather and maintains the trust of consumers seeking products that meet their religious and ethical standards.
   b. Leather from Halal and Non-Halal Animals (Except Dogs and Pigs) with Purification Processes

This point represents a significant area of differing opinions. Some scholars may permit the use of leather from halal but not commonly consumed animals (such as certain reptiles or other animals that are not explicitly prohibited but are also not widely consumed), provided that the tanning and purification process eliminates odours, slime, and anything that could be considered najis or impure. However, it is important to emphasize that, even in this opinion, dogs and pigs are categorically excluded due to their explicit haram status. No leniency is granted for the leather of dogs and pigs, regardless of the tanning and purification processes performed. The requirement to "eliminate slime and odour" must be interpreted strictly, and the process must be well documented to ensure halal compliance.

c. Leather from Halal and Non-Halal Animals with Processing that Alters Basic Properties

This point is also an area of debate. Some scholars argue that if the processing alters the essential characteristics of the raw material to such an extent that it is no longer recognizable as part of a haram animal, then leniency may be applied. For instance, leather from haram animals is processed in such a way that its structure and original characteristics are entirely lost. However, this is a minority opinion, and the requirements for this leniency are pretty strict and demanding to fulfil. Most scholars uphold the principle of precaution (al-intimate) by avoiding the use of body parts from haram animals due to the difficulty in conclusively proving a comprehensive alteration of fundamental properties. This debate mainly arises in the context of rare raw materials or limitations in technology.

2. **Tanning Process**: Tanning is an art or technique that involves the process of transforming raw hides into tanned leather. In this context, tanning also refers to a series of actions or processes performed on leather using tanning agents or materials. The goal is to make the leather, which is initially vulnerable to chemical, physical, and biological influences, more stable to a certain degree (Setiawan et al., 2015; Suparno et al., 2005). Thus, tanning becomes an essential process in processing raw leather to make it more durable and suitable for human needs. Tanning is a process that converts the proteins in raw hides into stable tanned leather that is not easily decomposed and can be used for various purposes. This process is usually carried out using trivalent chrome salts. The reaction between chrome salts and the carboxyl groups in the skin proteins (collagen) imparts high hydrothermal stability to the leather, with a shrinkage temperature (Ts) exceeding 100°C, as well as resistance to microorganisms. After the chrome tanning process, the animal leather is known as wet blue or blue crust. Tanning is the most critical stage in the production of tanned leather, during which collagen binds to the tanning agents at their reactive sites (Kalangi & Kaseke, 2017; Nanda et al., 2017). Tanned leather refers to animal skin that has been processed through a tanning procedure to acquire properties suitable for the tanning agents used (Sutyasmi et al., 2016). This process involves several stages, such as soaking, liming, fleshing, and bleaching, to remove flesh and provide the desired colour and strength. The tanning of leather must utilize halal materials and not contain haram or najis substances. The materials used must be safe and not toxic to human health. The tanning process should also ensure that the leather is free from najis and unpleasant odours. These standards need to specify the types of tanning agents that are permitted and prohibited, as well as the appropriate tanning methods. The tanning of leather must be carried out using materials and methods that are free from contamination by najis. The use of enzymes, fats, or chemicals derived from haram animals will invalidate the halal status of the product. Therefore, the leather industry, adhering to halal standards, must implement strict controls throughout the supply chain and ensure cleanliness at every stage of production (Islam et al., 2023; Riaz & Chaudry, 2003). Halal standards provide technical guidance to leather producers to ensure that every stage of the tanning process complies with Islamic principles. Halal tanning opens broader export opportunities, especially to countries with high demand for halal products. By adhering to halal standards, the leather industry also adopts production practices that are often cleaner and more environmentally

friendly, as halal tanning processes frequently avoid harmful chemicals (ElTayeb et al., 2010; Hafiz Zulfakar et al., 2014; Muna & Sutopo, 2018). Overall, the commitment to halal compliance not only meets the expectations of Muslim consumers but also aligns with global trends toward sustainability and ethical production practices.

3. **Processing and Treatment:** In addition to the slaughtering process, halal standards also encompass the post-production stages. Halal standards in the leather industry are not only relevant in a religious context but also play a significant role in building consumer trust and expanding access to the global market. Halal leather products are increasingly sought after as they reflect high standards of hygiene and quality, even among non-Muslim consumers who appreciate ethical business practices and sustainability (Bonne & Verbeke, 2008; Islam et al., 2023).

All processes of leather treatment and processing, from skinning to the final product, must be conducted cleanly and hygienically. Contamination with haram or najis materials must be prevented during the processing stages. Additives such as colourants, preservatives, emulsifiers, and flavour enhancers are often necessary for processing to improve product quality, extend shelf life, or enhance the appeal. To ensure compliance with halal standards, it is crucial to examine the sources of these chemicals. For instance, stearic acid, commonly used as an emulsifier, must derive from plant fats or from animals that have been slaughtered, according to Sharia, rather than from pig fat or other non-halal animal sources. Similarly, colourants and preservatives must be free from alcohol or animal derivatives that do not conform to Sharia (Ramli et al., 2023; Sutyasmi et al., 2016). Compliance with halal standards is often associated with clean, ethical, and sustainable manufacturing practices that are valued in international markets. Thus, the use of halal additives is not only a religious obligation but also an effective business strategy for capturing the global market (Insani et al., 2019; Riaz & Chaudry, 2018; Sutyasmi et al., 2016). The stages of processes of leather treatment and processing include:

a. **Skinning**: The process of removing the skin from the animal must be conducted hygienically, avoiding contamination with faeces, blood, or other substances that may be considered najis. The tools used must be clean and sterilized.
b. **Preservation (if necessary):** If there is a preservation process for the leather before tanning, the preservatives used must be halal and safe for consumption. The preservation process must prevent the growth of bacteria and fungi that could damage the quality and safety of the leather.

c. **Tanning**: The tanning process is a crucial stage that determines the halal status of the final product. The tanning agents used must be halal and free from haram or najis substances. The tanning process should be conducted in a controlled manner and well-documented to ensure safety and quality.
d. **Washing and Cleaning:** After the tanning process, the leather must be thoroughly washed and cleaned to remove any residual tanning agents, dirt, and unwanted substances. The water used must be clean and comply with food safety standards.
e. **Drying:** The drying process must be conducted hygienically to prevent contamination and the growth of bacteria or fungi. Temperature and humidity must be well controlled.
f. **Cutting and Shaping:** The cutting and shaping of the leather into finished products must be done with clean and sterilized equipment to avoid contamination.
g. **Storage:** Finished leather products must be stored in clean, dry places, protected from contamination.

At every stage of the process, contamination with haram materials (such as pig, dog, or their derivatives) or najis substances (such as faeces, urine, blood, etc.) must be absolutely avoided. All equipment, materials, and working environments must maintain cleanliness to comply with food safety standards and Islamic law. Detailed documentation at each stage is crucial to ensure traceability and halal integrity.

Additionally, companies must maintain clean supply chains and production facilities to prevent cross-contamination with non-halal materials (Zailani et al., 2010). The halal supply chain is a systematic framework that ensures every aspect of the production process, from raw materials and processing to distribution, meets halal standards as regulated by Islamic Sharia. The primary principles of this supply chain encompass three key elements: traceability, integrity, and compliance. The halal supply chain not only governs the selection of raw materials from halal sources but also prevents cross-contamination with non-halal elements during the production and distribution processes (Muna & Sutopo, 2018; Wulandari et al., 2023). Raw materials must originate from permitted (halal) sources according to Islamic Sharia, such as animals that have been slaughtered according to Sharia procedures or non-animal ingredients that do not contain haram substances. Soon et al. (2017) note that consumers are increasingly demanding halal assurance in the distribution of products, including logistics facilities.

4. INTERNATIONAL AND NATIONAL REGULATIONS GOVERNING HALAL LEATHER

It is important to understand how global laws and regulations govern the production and distribution of halal leather, as well as the challenges faced by countries in meeting these standards (Nurainun et al., 2023; Roswandi, 2023). Globalization of markets and the increasing demand for halal leather products have driven the adoption of international standards that accommodate the principles of Islamic law. In this regard, the Organization of Islamic Cooperation (OIC) plays a central role in formulating policies that regulate halal products, including leather goods (Akbar et al., 2022). One of the main criteria for determining whether a product is halal is the slaughtering process of the animal, which must follow the "zabihah" procedure in accordance with Islamic law. As such, countries with large Muslim populations, such as Indonesia, Malaysia, and the Middle Eastern countries, have started developing halal regulations and certifications for leather products that align with international standards (Chen et al., 2023; Salam et al., 2023).

Halal certification is a crucial step in ensuring that leather products in the market meet religious requirements. This certification process involves verifying that all raw materials and production methods comply with the standards set by recognized halal certification bodies. For example, Malaysia, with the Halal Management Division of the Department of Islamic Development Malaysia (JAKIM), has pioneered halal certification for leather products, aiming to build consumer confidence in the halal compliance of products available in the global market (Chen et al., 2023; Roswandi, 2023; Salam et al., 2023). Halal certification not only covers raw materials but also ensures that the production, processing, and distribution of leather goods do not involve any chemicals or additives prohibited by Islamic law. Global law also faces significant challenges in aligning halal standards with principles of sustainability and animal welfare. Leather production often involves the use of natural resources and industrial processes that are not always environmentally friendly or ethical. Therefore, the main challenge faced by leather-producing countries is how to integrate sustainability principles with the requirements of halal. Some countries have begun adopting green economic principles in halal leather production, which involves using eco-friendly raw materials and methods that reduce environmental impact (Djunaidi et al., 2021).

Furthermore, the role of international law in regulating the trade of halal leather products is crucial. The World Trade Organization (WTO) plays a role in facilitating international trade, including halal products, by ensuring that existing rules and regulations do not hinder trade between nations. However, in practice, differences in halal standards between countries often present obstacles in the trade of halal leather goods. Some countries that produce halal leather have stricter requirements than others, which leads to differences in certification and the validity of products that can be marketed in international markets. In response to these challenges, several international organizations have started developing global standards that can be adopted by countries worldwide. One notable initiative is the establishment of international standards for halal products by the International Organization for Standardization (ISO). ISO 22000, which governs food safety management systems, has become an important reference in the development of halal standards that integrate Islamic law with modern industrial practices. With the increasing global demand for halal products, particularly in Southeast Asia, the Middle East, and Europe, the halal leather industry is expected to continue growing. However, to ensure the continued growth of this sector, consistent halal certification and harmonized global standards are vital. As such, countries and international organizations need to collaborate to develop policies and regulations that support the growth of the halal leather industry, while upholding ethical principles, sustainability, and social justice (Al-Mahmood & Fraser, 2023; Suhaimi et al., 2023; Syed Fazal ur Rahim & Muhammad Abdullah Bin Masood, 2022).

The application of halal principles to leather products extends beyond the selection of raw materials and the production processes. It also includes other aspects such as distribution, storage, and finishing. This makes the halal leather industry a complex sector that requires serious attention from policymakers and related parties. Although there are some similarities in halal regulations across different countries, the interpretation and implementation of Islamic law in this industry can vary according to local contexts and the level of awareness in society regarding halal products (Ahmada et al., 2023). Countries like Indonesia, with the largest Muslim population in the world, have implemented stringent halal certification systems, while in Western countries, the adoption of these regulations has been slower and is often limited to niche markets. On the other hand, sustainability has become an increasingly urgent issue in the halal leather industry. Sustainability in leather production not only refers to ecological aspects but also to social and economic dimensions. In this regard, production approaches that are more environmentally friendly, such as using natural materials and processes that reduce carbon footprints, are becoming more important. Halal certification, which has become a primary requirement for ensuring the halalness of leather products, now needs to adapt to the demand for sustainability. This calls for collaboration between halal authorities, certification bodies, and the industry to create standards that accommodate both halal principles and sustainability (Jahangir et al., 2016; Zakaria, 2008).

Several countries have begun integrating sustainability principles into their halal certification processes, as seen in the Middle Eastern nations, where halal certification bodies like the Emirates Authority for Standardization and Metrology (ESMA) strive to ensure that halal products meet not only the requirements of Islamic law but also environmental and social standards. Through the implementation of a more holistic halal certification system, these countries aim to improve the competitiveness of their leather industries in the global market, which is increasingly concerned with sustainability (Jahangir et al., 2016; Suwanan et al., 2021). In addition, modern technology plays an important role in ensuring that leather products can be produced in accordance with halal principles and sustainability. Innovations in bioengineering and more efficient leather processing methods have made it possible to produce leather that is more environmentally friendly and meets stricter halal standards. Some companies have started developing synthetic leather that is environmentally friendly and halal-compliant, which could serve as an alternative to animal-based leather. However, the use of these new technologies also presents challenges, as not all technologies and materials used in the process can be guaranteed to be halal in accordance with Islamic law. Given these challenges, it is crucial for countries and international organizations to strengthen collaboration in formulating policies that can support the global halal leather industry. This includes formulating international standards that are clear and acceptable to all countries, both Muslim-majority and non-Muslim countries. One important effort in this regard is the development of a mutual recognition agreement for halal certifications, which would simplify international trade in halal leather products. Currently, many countries recognize halal certifications from other countries, but there is no binding international standard that ensures uniformity and validity of certifications worldwide (Akbar et al., 2022; Syed Fazal ur Rahim & Muhammad Abdullah Bin Masood, 2022).

International bodies such as ISO and Codex Alimentarius have started developing global standards that are more inclusive of halal products, which not only cover food safety but also broader halal aspects, including leather products. The development of these international standards is expected to help reconcile the different halal regulations across countries, making it easier for halal leather producers to meet global market requirements. Therefore, the development of transparent certification systems that can be accepted globally is critical to ensuring that halal leather products traded around the world meet high standards. However, the main challenge in global trade of halal leather products lies in the differences in the understanding of what constitutes "halal." Each country may have a different interpretation regarding slaughter procedures, the additives used, and other processes involved in the production of leather products (Jahangir et al., 2016; Suhaimi et al., 2023; Zakaria, 2008). In some cases, this has led to tensions between leather-producing countries and importing countries, particularly when there are disagreements regarding the halal standards applied. Furthermore, advancements in microbiology and chemistry can also make significant contributions in addressing the issues faced by the halal leather industry. For instance, regarding the use of preservatives and dyes in leather production, the latest technologies can help produce materials that are safer, more environmentally friendly, and in compliance with halal principles. Thus, it is important for the leather industry to continue innovating, both technically and in adhering to the laws and ethics that apply (Nurainun et al., 2023; Prayuda et al., 2023).

The marketing of halal leather products requires a more strategic approach, particularly in introducing these products to consumers in international markets. Global awareness of ethical consumption and environmental friendliness is growing, and this includes leather products (Suwanan et al., 2021). This provides an opportunity for the halal leather industry to develop a broader market, emphasizing that halal leather products not only meet religious requirements but also adhere to sustainability and social responsibility standards. The awareness of Muslim consumers regarding the importance of halal products is also increasing, as reflected in the growing demand for halal leather products. However, the greatest challenge for the halal leather industry is maintaining a balance between meeting market demand while still adhering to the strict principles of Islamic law (Suhaimi et al., 2023; Syed Fazal ur Rahim & Muhammad Abdullah Bin Masood, 2022). This requires a deep understanding of Islamic law, as well as a commitment to producing leather that not only meets halal standards but is also sustainable and ethical. In conclusion, while the halal leather industry faces many challenges, whether in terms of regulations, sustainability, or technology, its potential for growth remains significant. Through close collaboration between governments, industries, and certification bodies, and by continuously considering market and technological developments, the halal leather industry can evolve into a sector that is not only economically viable but also upholds broader moral and ethical demands (Akbar et al., 2022; Nurainun et al., 2023; Prayuda et al., 2023).

Certification Regulations in Indonesia

Indonesia, as the country with the largest Muslim population in the world, has a strong commitment to applying halal principles in all aspects of life, including the leather products industry. The halal certification regulations in Indonesia are designed to ensure that all products circulating in the market, particularly those pertaining to consumption and use, meet halal standards according to Islamic sharia. The formulation of these regulations aims not only to protect consumers but also to support the industry in capitalizing on the continuously growing halal market potential. One significant step taken by the Indonesian government is the establishment of the BPJPH. BPJPH serves as the agency responsible for managing halal certification, implementing policies, and making decisions regarding products deemed halal. This certification process involves comprehensive testing and evaluation of products, from the ingredients used to their production processes, to ensure that no haram elements are involved.

The regulations governing halal certification in Indonesia are outlined in various laws and regulations, including:

1. **Law No. 33 of 2014 on Halal Product Assurance**

This law serves as the legal basis for the regulation of halal products in Indonesia, stipulating the obligation for halal certification for products that are produced, imported, and traded within the country. The law emphasizes that every product intended for sale must possess a halal certificate.

2. **Government Regulation No. 39 of 2021 on Halal Product Assurance**

This regulation provides further details regarding the implementation of the Halal Product Assurance Law, including the certification process, the execution of audits, and the role of the BPJPH in monitoring halal products. It also outlines the steps that business operators must take to obtain halal certification.

3. **Minister of Religious Affairs Regulation No. 26 of 2019 on Halal Certification**

This regulation establishes the technical procedures required in the halal certification process, which includes application submission, product evaluation, and the issuance of halal certificates. In addition, this regulation governs the implementation of these processes at both the national and regional levels.

4. **Halal Product Assurance Agency (BPJPH)**

The BPJPH issues various rules and operational guidelines to support the implementation of halal certification in Indonesia. One of the key regulations is the Halal Certification Process Standards, which outlines the steps and stages to be followed during the certification process, from application submission to product evaluation, the audit by halal auditors, and the issuance of halal certificates. Furthermore, BPJPH offers Halal Auditor Guidelines that specify the criteria and procedures for auditors conducting audits to ensure compliance with halal standards. To ensure that halal certification bodies operate effectively, BPJPH also issues Guidelines for the Utilization of Halal Inspection Agency (LPH), which cover the accreditation and oversight of these institutions.

As part of the effort to ensure compliance, the Halal Management System Implementation Guidelines have also been introduced, providing direction to business operators on the application of halal management systems during the production process. Furthermore, there is a Halal Certification Application Procedure that outlines the details of how business operators can submit their applications, including the necessary documents and the estimated time for the certification process. To strengthen consumer confidence, the BPJPH has established regulations concerning the Renewal of Halal Certificates, which include the procedures and requirements for renewing certificates once they have expired.

BPJPH also emphasizes the importance of socialization and education by designing Halal Socialization and Education Guidelines to raise awareness among the public and business operators regarding the significance of halal certification. Lastly, there are regulations on the Procedures for Handling Complaints and Halal Disputes, which govern the procedures for addressing complaints related to violations or dissatisfaction with the certification process. With all these rules and guidelines in place, BPJPH strives to ensure that products circulating in Indonesia meet halal standards and protect consumers while also assisting business operators in understanding and fulfilling the requirements for obtaining halal certification.

The existence of this regulation requires business operators to submit applications for halal certification before introducing their products to the market. In this process, various documents must be prepared, including proof of the source of raw materials, production processes, and statements from suppliers. This aims to create a transparent and accountable system whereby the origins of each product can be traced. The involvement of modern technology, such as halal management information systems, also plays an integral role in this regulatory process. This technology helps industry players manage and monitor the certification process more efficiently. Overall, halal certification regulations in Indonesia aim to create an ecosystem that supports the industry and protects consumers. With a strong and systematic regulatory framework, Indonesia is committed to becoming a leader in the global halal industry, making its products increasingly recognized and accepted in international markets.

Halal Product Assurance System

The essence of halal certification lies in the implementation of the Halal Product Assurance System (SJPH). SPJPH is an integrated system that is developed, applied, and maintained to regulate materials, production processes, products, resources, and procedures in order to ensure the continuity of halal product processes.

a. Commitment and Responsibility

Business operators must be committed to fulfilling the requirements of the Halal Product Assurance System, creating halal policies, and applying them.

b. Materials

Business operators must consistently use materials that comply with the requirements of SPJPH, including materials whose halal status is clear or has halal certification and can be traced for their halal status.

c. Halal Product Processes

Business operators commit to meeting the requirements of SPJPH related to location, premises, equipment, procedures, facility purification, incoming materials inspection, production processes, transportation, and distribution of products and materials, halal traceability, handling of non-halal compliant products, product sales, and product development.

d. Products

Business operators are committed to meeting the requirements of SPJPH related to products, as well as their identification and traceability.

e. Monitoring and Evaluation

Business operators commit to fulfilling the requirements of SPJPH related to monitoring and evaluation, such as conducting internal audits and reporting them to BPJPH and LPH.

Halal Certification Process for Leather-Based Products

The halal certification process for leather-based consumer goods in Indonesia begins with a certification application by the producer to a LPH accredited by the BPJPH. Producers must complete the required documentation, including detailed information about raw materials, production processes, and supply chain management. These documents must demonstrate compliance with all applicable halal requirements in Indonesia.

Once the application is received, the LPH will conduct an audit of the producer's production facility and processes. This audit includes an examination of raw materials, processing methods, and the halal management system in place. Auditors will review all stages of production, from the procurement of raw leather to the finished product, ensuring that all materials and processes align with halal standards. Special attention is given to the tanning process, which includes the selection of tanning agents, tanning methods, and prevention of contamination. A well-documented traceability system becomes a crucial aspect of the audit. The audit results will then be reviewed by the LPH audit team and reported to the fatwa commission Indonesian Ulema Council. The halal determination given by the fatwa commission is a reference for BPJPH in issuing halal certificates. The stages of the halal certification application process for leather businesses are illustrated in Figure 1.

Figure 1. Regular Halal certification process flow

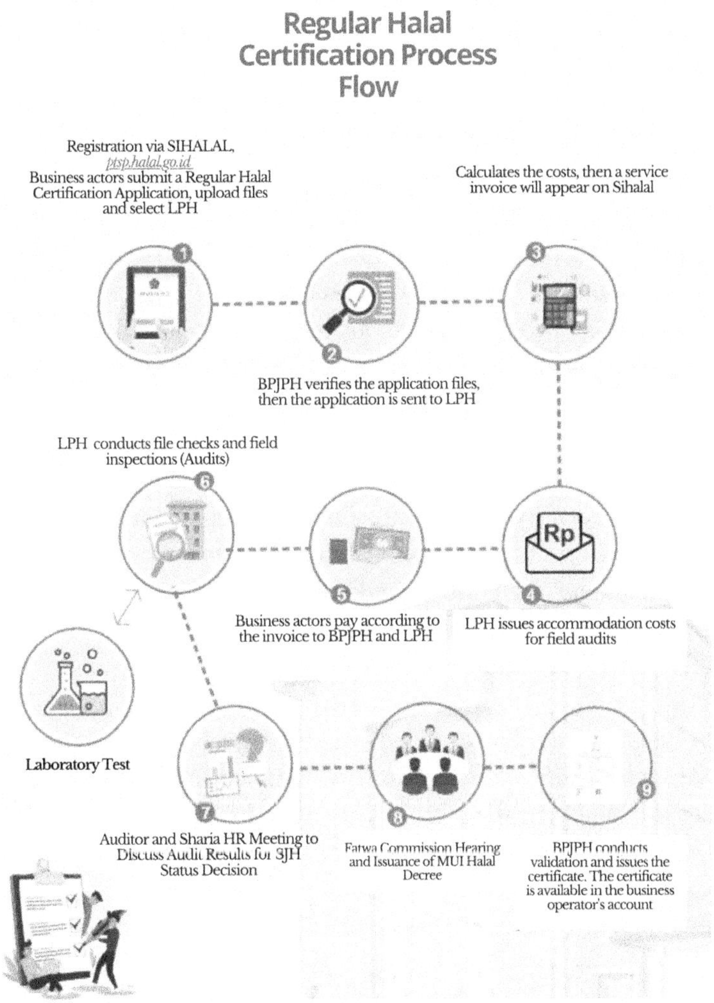

Case Study: Identifying the Halal Industry of "Agisna Leather" Store in the Sukaregang Leather Tanning Industry Center, Garut, West Java

One of the most renowned leather tanning industry centers in Indonesia is the Sukaregang Leather Tanning Industry Center, located in Garut City District, Garut Regency, West Java. Sukaregang has been a key hub for leather production and processing for several decades. The products manufactured in this area not only meet domestic market demands but are also exported to various countries. However, despite its strong reputation in the leather industry, the halal aspect of Sukaregang's production process remains a primary concern for Muslim consumers who prioritize halal assurance in the products they purchase. The concept of halal in the leather industry extends beyond raw materials and involves the entire production process. A crucial aspect that must be considered is the source of leather. If the leather originates from animals that were not slaughtered according to Islamic guidelines, it raises concerns regarding the final product's halal status. Additionally, the tanning process often involves the use of various chemicals, which must be carefully examined to ensure the absence of prohibited substances under Islamic law.

In this context, identifying halal industry standards is an essential step to ensure that leather products available in the market comply with established halal regulations. This identification process includes verifying raw material sources, analyzing tanning methods, and ensuring compliance with halal certification standards set by authorized institutions. A clear identification process enables the leather industry to provide assurance to consumers that the products they use adhere to halal principles. Agisna Leather is one of the businesses committed to maintaining the halal integrity of its leather products. By implementing halal standards throughout its production chain, the store ensures that its products align with Islamic principles and national and international halal regulatory standards.

1. Halal Raw Material Sourcing from Local Livestock Farmers

Agisna Leather exclusively utilizes leather sourced from animals slaughtered in accordance with Islamic law. All leather comes from local livestock farmers who collaborate with halal-certified slaughterhouses (RPH), verified by relevant authorities. This practice minimizes the risk of contamination with non-halal materials.

2. Halal-Compliant Tanning Process and Certified Material Usage

The tanning process at Agisna Leather employs chemicals that have been certified as halal. No non-halal substances, such as enzymes derived from pigs or non-food-grade alcohol, are used, ensuring the halal integrity of the final product. The company also implements a clean production system by ensuring that all equipment and production areas are free from impurities (najis). Additional materials such as tanning agents, lubricants, and dyes undergo rigorous testing to confirm their halal compliance and safety for consumers.

3. Halal Certification and Stringent Monitoring

Agisna Leather has obtained halal certification from authorized institutions is BPJPH. The company also enforces stringent monitoring systems, including regular inspections and periodic halal audits, to maintain compliance with established halal standards.

4. Transparency and Consumer Education

As part of its commitment to consumers, Agisna Leather provides transparent information regarding the halal status of its products. Halal labels and documentation are prominently displayed on all products, allowing consumers to easily verify that their purchases meet halal standards.

5. CHALLENGES AND SOLUTIONS IN NAVIGATING HALAL STANDARDS

Identifying Challenges

The global halal industry faces significant challenges due to both external and internal factors, especially in aligning halal standards across different countries. Predominantly Muslim countries tend to have stricter regulations compared to non-Muslim countries, leading to a demand for global standard harmonization. Competition among halal exporting countries is intense and can affect market access, potentially creating barriers for new entrants. Additionally, the lack of international standardization in halal certification remains a significant obstacle. Internally, there is often low awareness about halal standards even in Muslim-majority regions, where religiosity influences consumption more than knowledge. Challenges also include technical barriers in certification processes and insufficient understanding among industry stakeholders.

Strategies and Solutions

To address these challenges, the halal industry must adopt comprehensive strategies, such as harmonizing international halal standards and leveraging modern technologies like blockchain for transparency in the supply chain. These innovations facilitate real-time tracking of materials, enhancing trust in halal product claims. Additionally, educating industry players through training on certification procedures and compliance guidelines is essential. Collaborating between halal certification bodies and government agencies can provide clear information and reduce uncertainties. Research into practical solutions, such as innovative halal additives, can also play a crucial role. These strategies aim to overcome challenges, increase competitiveness, and expand consumer access to halal products globally.

Innovations and Technology in Supporting Halal Compliance

In the leather industry, technological innovations are pivotal for maintaining halal compliance throughout production. Blockchain technology enhances supply chain transparency, enabling tracking from raw materials to finished products, ensuring authenticity. Furthermore, IoT devices like smart sensors can improve quality control by monitoring production conditions. Eco-friendly additives aligning with halal standards help improve product quality without harmful chemicals, meeting consumer demands for sustainability. Enhanced communication technologies, such as e-learning platforms, further facilitate understanding of halal standards among industry players. These innovations not only help meet halal standards but also enhance competitiveness and foster consumer trust, promoting sustainable industry growth.

REFERENCES

Ahmada, Z., Rahman, M. M., & Hidthiira, M. H. (2022). Corporate Social Responsibility: A Critical Analysis of Discloser and Malaysian Halal Food Industry. *Islamic Business and Covid 19 Recovery: Towards Attaining Financial And Social Wellbeing*, 11.

Akbar, J., Raza, A., Gul, M., & Ikramullah, M. (2022). International Halal Industry And Its Impact On Global Halal Market (A Historical Review And Future Business Prospect). *Journal of Positive School Psychology*, *6*(7), 5890–5907. http://journalppw.com

Al-Mahmood, O. A., & Fraser, A. M. (2023). Perceived challenges in implementing halal standards by halal certifying bodies in the United States. PLoS ONE, *18*(8 August), 1–11. DOI: 10.1371/journal.pone.0290774

Apriliani, F. D., Widihastuti, , Daryono, R. W., Jaya, D. J., & Rizbudiani, A. D. (2023). The Influence of Fashion Knowledge, Fashion Selection Factor, and Dress Etiquette on Dress Look. *Jurnal Pendidikan Dan Pengajaran*, *56*(1), 194–207. DOI: 10.23887/jpp.v56i1.53677

Ary, O., & Of, N. (2018). *A series published with the Society for the Anthropology of Religion.*

Asy-Syirbini, S. M. bin A. (1997). *Mughni Al-Muhtaj* (1 ed.). Dar Al-Ma'rifah.

Bonne, K., & Verbeke, W. (2008). Religious values informing halal meat production and the control and delivery of halal credence quality. *Agriculture and Human Values*, *25*(1), 35–47. DOI: 10.1007/s10460-007-9076-y

Chen, X., Xu, L., Ren, Z., Jia, F., & Yu, Y. (2023). Sustainable supply chain management in the leather industry: A systematic literature review. *International Journal of Logistics*, *26*(12), 1663–1703. DOI: 10.1080/13675567.2022.2104233

Djunaidi, M., Oktavia, C. B. A., Fitriadi, R., & Setiawan, E. (2021). Perception and Consumer Behavior of Halal Product Toward Purchase Decision in Indonesia. *Jurnal Teknik Industri*, *22*(2), 171–184. DOI: 10.22219/JTIUMM.Vol22.No2.171-184

ElTayeb, T. K., Zailani, S., & Jayaraman, K. (2010). The examination on the drivers for green purchasing adoption among EMS 14001 certified companies in Malaysia. *Journal of Manufacturing Technology Management*, *21*(2), 206–225. DOI: 10.1108/17410381011014378

Fratzl, P., & Weinkamer, R. (2007). Nature's hierarchical materials. *Progress in Materials Science*, *52*(8), 1263–1334. DOI: 10.1016/j.pmatsci.2007.06.001

Hafiz Zulfakar, M., Chan, C., & Jie, F. (2014). *Factors Influencing the Operations of the Halal Meat Supply Chain in Australia. March 2016*, 1–8.

Insani, T. D., Al-Faizin, A. W., & Ryandono, M. N. H. (2019). the Impact of Halal At Thayyib and Consumption Ethics on Economic Growth: An Economic Tafsir of Al-Baqarah 168. *Journal of Islamic Monetary Economics and Finance*, *5*(2), 459–474. DOI: 10.21098/jimf.v5i2.1071

Islam, M. M., Ab Talib, M. S., & Muhamad, N. (2023). Challenges of Halal Standards and Halal Certification for Islamic Marketing. *Muslim Business and Economic Review*, *2*(1), 105–124. DOI: 10.56529/mber.v2i1.156

Jahangir, M., Mehmood, Z., Saifullah, , Bashir, Q., Mehboob, F., & Ali, K. (2016). Halal status of ingredients after physicochemical alteration (Istihalah). *Trends in Food Science & Technology*, *47*, 78–81. DOI: 10.1016/j.tifs.2015.10.011

Kalangi, S. J. R., & Kaseke, M. M. (2017). *Macroscopic and microscopic images of the bladder in postmortem experimental animals, 5*, 3–9.

Kasri, R. A., Ahsan, A., Widiatmoko, D., & Hati, S. R. H. (2023). Intention to consume halal pharmaceutical products: Evidence from Indonesia. *Journal of Islamic Marketing*, *14*(3), 735–756. DOI: 10.1108/JIMA-06-2021-0192

Muna, N., & Sutopo, W. (2018). Perkembangan Penelitian Halal Food Supply Chain: Studi Kasus Database Scopus. *Prosiding SNST*, *9*(1), 131–139. DOI: 10.36499/psnst.v1i1.2339

Nanda, Y., Salim, M. N., & Iskandar, C. D. (2017). *Yunita Nanda 1, M. Nur Salim 2, Cut Dahlia Iskandar 3 1. 01*(4), 780–787.

Nurainun, T., Talib, H. H. A., Jamaludin, K. R., Yusof, S. M., Putri, N. T., & Lestari, F. (2023). Identifying Factors for the Success of Halal Management Practices in Leather Industry. *Journal of Applied Engineering and Technological Science*, *4*(2), 808–824. DOI: 10.37385/jaets.v4i2.1989

Nuryana, S., Isa, L., & Fikri, I. (2023). Studi Komparatif Terhadap Hukum Penyucian Kulit Bangkai Dengan Cara Disamak Menurut Ibnu Qudamah Al-Maqdisi dan Imam Asy-Syaukani. *Muqaranah*, *7*(1), 45–54. DOI: 10.19109/muqaranah.v7i1.17199

Prayuda, D., Arby, S., Adli, I., & Al-Ayubi, S. (2023). Halal Industry: Opportunities and Challenge in the Global Market. *Jurnal Ekonomi Islam*, *14*(2), 2579–6453. DOI: 10.32507/ajei.v14i2.2376

Rafiki, A., Hidayat, S. E., & Nasution, M. D. T. P. (2023). *An extensive effect of religiosity on the purchasing decisions of halal products*. PSU Research Review., DOI: 10.1108/PRR-07-2022-0093

Ramli, M. A., Abd Razak, M. A., & Jaafar, M. H. (2023). Understanding non-Muslims' reluctance to halal food: A systematic review. *Journal of Islamic Marketing*, *14*(2), 544–561. DOI: 10.1108/JIMA-05-2021-0134

Riaz, M. N., & Chaudry, M. M. (2003). Halal food production. *Halal Food Production*, 1–380. DOI: 10.1201/9780203490082

Riaz, M. N., & Chaudry, M. M. (2018). General Guidelines for Halal Food Production. *Handbook of Halal Food Production*, 17–28. DOI: 10.1201/9781315119564-3

Salam, S., Mohd, H., Muflih, B., & Jaiyeoba, H. (2023). Halal industry and standardization. *Ekonomski Izazovi*, *12*(24), 20–30. DOI: 10.5937/EkoIzazov2324020S

Setiawan, A., Riyadi, P., & Sumardianto, S. (2015). The Effect of Gambir (Uncaria Gambier) as a Tanning Agent in the Leather Tanning Process on the Physical Quality of Tilapia Fish Skin (Oreochromis Niloticus). *Journal of Fishery Products Processing and Biotechnology*, *4*(2), 124–132. https://ejournal3.undip.ac.id/index.php/jpbhp/article/view/9202/8933

Soon, J. M., Chandia, M., & Mac Regenstein, J. (2017). Halal integrity in the food supply chain. *British Food Journal*, *119*(1), 39–51. DOI: 10.1108/BFJ-04-2016-0150

Suhaimi, A. R., Nur Izyana, A. R., & Nusran, M. (2023). Halal Standards and Their Contributions To the Growth of Halal Economy in Malaysia and Indonesia. [InJHSS]. *International Journal of Halal System and Sustainability*, *3*(2), 2808–9154. DOI: 10.33096/injhss.v3i2.278

Suparno, O., Covington, A. D., & Evans, C. S. (2005). New Environmentally Benign Leather Technology: Combination Tanning Using Vegetable Tannin, Naphthol and Oxazolidine. *J. Tek. Ind. Pert*, *18*(2), 79–84.

Sutyasmi, S., Widowati, T. P., & Setyadewi, N. M. (2016). The effect of mimosa on tanning vegetable tanned sheepskin jacket using the C-RFP system, reviewed from the organoleptic, physical, and morphological properties of the leather. *Leather, Rubber, and Plastic Magazine.*, *32*(1), 31. DOI: 10.20543/mkkp.v32i1.932

Suwanan, A. F., Putro, A. C., Triyanto, A., Munir, S., & Merlinda, S. (2021). Analysis of the impacts and challenges of Covid-19 on green sukuk in Indonesia. In *Halal Development*. Trends, Opportunities and Challenges., DOI: 10.1201/9781003189282-6 ur Rahim, S. F., & Masood, M. A. B. (2023). Global view of animal feed in halal perspective. *International Journal of Halal Research, 5*(1), 45-57.

Tieman, M. (2011). The application of Halal in supply chain management: In-depth interviews. *Journal of Islamic Marketing*, *2*(2), 186–195. DOI: 10.1108/17590831111139893

Wulandari, S. A., Sari, R. P., & Hadining, A. F. (2023). Analysis of Customer Behavior and Attitudes (General Risk) on Satisfaction, Trust and Halal Awareness of Purchase Intentions in Food Delivery Applications. *Jurnal Dinamika Manajemen, 14*(1), 99–110. DOI: 10.15294/jdm.v14i1.38386

Zailani, S., Arrifin, Z., Wahid, N. A., Othman, R., & Fernando, Y. (2010). Halal Traceability and Halal Tracking Systems in Strengthening Halal Food Supply Chain for Food Industry in Malaysia (A Review). *Journal of Food Technology*, *8*(3), 74–81. DOI: 10.3923/jftech.2010.74.81

Zakaria, Z. (2008). Tapping Into the World Halal Market : Some Discussions on Malaysian Laws and. *Shariah Journal*, *16*, 603–616.

Zulfakar, M. H., Anuar, M. M., & Talib, M. S. A. (2014). Conceptual Framework on Halal Food Supply Chain Integrity Enhancement. *Procedia: Social and Behavioral Sciences*, *121*(April), 58–67. DOI: 10.1016/j.sbspro.2014.01.1108

Chapter 6
Implementation of Halal Certification in Brunei Darussalam's Food and Beverages Enterprises

Pang Li Li
https://orcid.org/0000-0002-9453-0496
Universiti Brunei Darussalam, Brunei

Afiqah Amin
https://orcid.org/0000-0002-1747-1250
Universiti Brunei Darussalam, Brunei

Mohamed Syazwan Ab Talib
https://orcid.org/0000-0001-8190-9096
Universiti Brunei Darussalam, Brunei

ABSTRACT

Brunei Darussalam has been a Malay Muslim Monarchy for six centuries and the country follows the Sunni Shafite sect of Islam as its official religion. In 2005 the government introduced the Halal Certificate and Halal Label Order, which was amended and revised in 2017 making it compulsory for all food and beverages industry serving Muslim population to apply for the halal certificate. There is limited literature on how enterprises adopt and adapt to these new laws, seven years after it was made mandatory. This research aims to bridge this gap by exploring the state of halal certification,gauging businesses understanding and experiences with the certification process. The research uses qualitative, primary data collection, through semi-interviews with owners and managers of micro and small food enterprises.

DOI: 10.4018/979-8-3373-3917-7.ch006

This research hopes to provide valuable data that can improve the development of a more streamlined and accessible halal certification process and ensure the industry continues to meet the highest standards of halal compliance in Brunei Darussalam

1. INTRODUCTION

The global halal industry has experienced substantial growth in recent years, driven by the increasing demand for halal-certified food and beverages among Muslim and non-Muslim consumers alike. Valued at over USD 2 trillion, the halal economy extends beyond religious observance to include concerns over food safety, hygiene, ethical sourcing, and quality assurance (Calder, 2020; Lever & Miele, 2012; Mukherjee, 2014). Halal has become paramount for ensuring consumer trust in majority-Muslim countries and in regions with growing Muslim populations (Aziz & Chok, 2013; Bonne & Verbeke, 2008). Consequently, governments, businesses, and certification bodies worldwide have intensified efforts to develop robust halal certification systems to meet these expectations and tap into the expanding halal market (Izberk-Bilgin & Nakata, 2016; Latif et al., 2014).

At the heart of this global expansion lies the halal certification, which stems from Islamic dietary laws and has evolved into a formalized system governed by religious authorities and national regulations. While international efforts have sought to harmonize halal standards, implementation at the national level remains varied, often shaped by local governance, market maturity, and business structures (Latif et al., 2014; Othman et al., 2016). Studies from Malaysia, Indonesia, and other Muslim-majority countries have highlighted recurring barriers such as administrative complexity, cost burdens, limited awareness, and inadequate support for micro, small, and medium enterprises (MSMEs) (Haleem et al., 2019; Islam et al., 2023). Despite shared Islamic values, each country presents a distinct regulatory and socio-economic landscape. Against this backdrop, Brunei Darussalam, henceforth, Brunei, offers a unique case. The Sultanate is a wealthy Islamic state with a strong policy commitment to halal development yet facing a declining rate of halal certification uptake among its food and beverage enterprises.

Brunei is a constitutional Muslim Sultanate in Southeast Asia with a population of 450,000. Despite its small population, Brunei's gross domestic product, GDP, per capita is among the highest in the region (Department of Economic Planning and Statistics, 2024a), due to the country's primary source of revenue – the production and export of oil and natural gas (Hamdan & Hoon, 2019; Musa, 2019; Tahir et al., 2023). However, its heavy dependence on the non-renewable petroleum sector leaves the country vulnerable to unsustainable income and volatile global crude oil prices (Slesman & Hoon, 2023; Tahir et al., 2023). Therefore, the Brunei government is driving economic diversification to reduce this reliance on non-sustainable revenues (Arifin et al., 2024).

Brunei has attempted economic diversification for over six decades since its second National Development Plan (1962-1966) was published. Additionally, the country's long-term development plan, the *Wawasan Brunei 2035* (Brunei Vision 2035), unveiled in 2004, aims to create a dynamic and sustainable economy through local business development and promoting foreign and domestic investment (Hoon & Zhao, 2024; Slesman & Hoon, 2023). One of the critical areas Brunei continues to explore is the halal industry (Khalid et al., 2018; Muhamad et al., 2019; Shahlehi et al., 2024; Sulaiman et al., 2023). Similar to other Muslim nations, the Brunei government sees the vast and profitable global halal industry as an avenue to generate new jobs and enhance local businesses with a worldwide presence (Ab Talib & Zulfakar, 2024; Sufri et al., 2023; Sulaiman et al., 2023). Moreover, the country actively supports micro, small, and medium enterprises (MSMEs) and provides resources and facilities to foster the development of the halal industry and its national agenda (Basir, 2022; Heilmaier & Ling, 2021).

Although Brunei has actively supported MSMEs and implemented initiatives to promote halal industry development, the number of halal food certificate applications has sharply decreased in recent years. Table 1 illustrates this trend, showing a significant drop in total applications from 362 in 2017 to 22 in 2024. This decline is evident across various businesses, especially food MSMEs, which experienced a drastic reduction in successful applications, from 86 companies in 2017 to a mere three in September 2024. Note that the food and beverages industry accounts for about 11% out of 6,500 businesses in the country, employing about 9% of the workforce and generating about 2% of the private sector revenue in 2019 (Department of Economic Planning and Statistics, 2024b).

Table 1. Applied and awarded Halal food certification by category (2017-September 2024)

Year	Applied	Business Category					Awarded
		Micro	Small	Medium	Macro	Multinational	
2017	362	79	6	1	-	-	86
2018	134	33	6	1	-	1	41
2019	48	21	8	1	-	1	31
2020	42	11	4	-	-	-	15
2021	22	5	4	-	1	-	10
2022	20	5	2	3	1	-	11

continued on following page

Table 1. Continued

Year	Applied	Business Category					Awarded
		Micro	Small	Medium	Macro	Multinational	
2023	36	3	2	2	-	1	8
2024	22	2	1	-	-	-	3

Source: Halal Food Control Division, Ministry of Religious Affairs

This downward trend raises concerns; the persistent decline in certification applications suggests potential obstacles hindering businesses from fully engaging with the halal sector. It also underscores the need to critically examine existing policies and resources to understand why businesses, particularly MSMEs, face challenges in obtaining halal certification.

Building on the diverging outlook, this explorative primary research explores the underlying factors contributing to the issue. By examining various economic, regulatory, and operational challenges businesses face, particularly MSMEs, the paper seeks to uncover the barriers that may prevent them from fully participating in Brunei's halal industry. The objective is to identify the obstacles, evaluate their impact on halal certification processes, and provide recommendations that could assist in revitalizing the sector, ensuring alignment with the broader goals of Brunei Vision 2035. Therefore, this chapter provides new insights that could be crucial for recalibrating future strategies to revitalize Brunei's ambitions in the global halal market and possibly realign its halal sector with the long-range 2035 vision.

2. LITERATURE REVIEW

The adoption and implementation of halal certification present significant challenges across various stages of the halal supply chain. Despite the increasing demand for halal-certified products, numerous barriers deter businesses, particularly MSMEs (Ardiantono et al., 2024), from engaging in halal certification. These barriers encompass administrative requirements (M. I. Khan et al., 2022), financial limitations (Susanty et al., 2020), technical issues (S. Khan et al., 2019), and operational dimensions (Amer, 2024), therefore affecting businesses and constraining the growth of the halal industry.

Extant research frequently highlights the complexity and lengthiness of the halal certification process, which is often criticized for being time-consuming and bureaucratic (Darmalaksana, 2023; Fauzi et al., 2024; Suryawan et al., 2022). A typical halal certification process requires extensive documentation and multiple audits, which can be particularly challenging for smaller businesses with limited resources and expertise (Fard & Amiri, 2018; Ismail et al., 2013). Additionally, ambiguities in halal guidelines further complicate the certification process (Ali & Suleiman, 2018). According to Ali & Suleiman (2018), companies often experience confusion, and inconsistencies may arise in how these standards are applied. Besides, the lack of universally accepted standards exacerbates this complexity, making compliance more difficult for companies, particularly MSMEs, to achieve (Islam et al., 2023).

Furthermore, the financial implications associated with halal certification represent a considerable barrier. Studies have shown that the costs required to obtain and maintain halal certification, which may include application fees, auditor expenses, transportation, and adopting halal-compliant practices, are often exorbitant, especially for smaller businesses (Ab Talib, 2017; Al-shami & Abdullah, 2023; Haleem et al., 2019). Hence, these expenses substantially strain the already limited finances and may eventually discourage MSMEs from pursuing and maintaining halal certification. Undoubtedly, many companies experience inadequate financial support that could help cover these certification costs (Haleem et al., 2019). Husin and Haron (2019) argue that companies may need more funding to afford the financial requirements necessary to sustain business.

It has also been widely reported that a lack of awareness and expertise in halal principles presents another significant challenge, particularly prevalent in regions with limited exposure to halal practices and non-Muslim majority markets (Bux et al., 2022). Research indicates that many non-Muslim businesses lack a comprehensive understanding of halal requirements, making implementing compliant practices challenging (Bux et al., 2022; Koeswinarno et al., 2023; Ziegler et al., 2022). Compounding this issue is the need for more skilled personnel within the industry, including auditors and halal-trained staff (Abdul Rahim et al., 2022; Hashmi & Ali, 2021). As a result, the limited pool of qualified professionals restricts the industry's ability to meet rising demands for certification (Abdul Rahim et al., 2022), thus impacting the efficiency and effectiveness of the certification process.

Government support and regulatory frameworks also play an essential role in shaping the adoption of halal certification (Haleem et al., 2019). Evidence suggests that in some regions, the absence of government initiatives and incentives creates additional hurdles for businesses, particularly smaller enterprises, seeking halal certification (Darmalaksana, 2023; Silalahi et al., 2022). Also, the need for consistent halal standards and regulations across countries complicates the process for international companies, as they must abide by varying requirements depending on the market (Latif et al., 2014). Such regulatory fragmentation poses a considerable obstacle for companies aiming to maintain halal certification on a global scale (Haleem et al., 2019; S. Khan et al., 2019).

Technological and infrastructural constraints further impede the adoption of halal certification. Several studies (Ali et al., 2023; Fernando et al., 2023; Tan et al., 2022) have pointed out that the halal industry has slowly embraced technology that could enhance traceability and transparency in the supply chain. Along the same line, Ali et al. (2023) point out that limited adoption of digital solutions affects businesses' ability to ensure compliance efficiently. Additionally, inadequate halal-specific infrastructure, such as dedicated halal warehouses and transportation, in certain regions raises logistical challenges and costs for businesses attempting to maintain halal integrity across the supply chain (Ab Talib, 2021).

Moreover, concerns about trust and credibility in the varying halal certifications add another layer of complexity. In the same vein, scholars observe that the presence of multiple halal standards and certification bodies worldwide can lead to confusion and doubts regarding the authenticity of halal certification (Abdallah et al., 2021; Akbar et al., 2023). Instances of fraudulent certification practices, such as using fake halal logos and mislabelling (Fuseini et al., 2017; Jaya & Darul Ehsan, 2015), have further eroded consumer trust and raised concerns about some certification bodies' reliability (Jaya & Darul Ehsan, 2015).

Internal resistance to change within businesses is often a barrier to adopting halal certification (S. Khan et al., 2019). Many companies perceive halal certification as an added burden, primarily due to the perceived complexity and costs involved (Prabowo et al., 2015). This perception is particularly pronounced among businesses within Muslim-minority markets, where halal standards are seen as disruptive (Al-Mahmood & Fraser, 2023; Ziegler et al., 2022). As a result, companies may be reluctant to integrate halal practices and certification into their operations, further complicating efforts to expand the halal sector (Ziegler et al., 2022).

Overall, the barriers to halal certification adoption and implementation involve many factors and dimensions and are particularly challenging for smaller businesses, which may need more resources, knowledge, and support to engage fully in the halal certification process. Addressing these barriers will likely require collaborative efforts among policymakers, certification bodies, and industry stakeholders in Brunei to create a more accessible and efficient halal certification system that meets the needs of diverse businesses; especially when the government made it compulsory in 2017 for all food and beverages industry serving Muslim population in the country to apply for halal certification.

3. METHODOLOGY

The research aims to find out the challenges faced by the food and beverages businesses in the country when applying for the halal certification, therefore the research uses primary data collection, in the form of qualitative semi-structured interviews from business owners who are impacted and involved in the actual process. Many aspects of the halal industry in Brunei are still relatively unexplored, and qualitative approaches can provide rich, in-depth insights into the challenges of this context (Haji Shahlehi et al., 2024). This methodological choice is particularly suitable for investigating areas with limited prior research (Bryman & Bell, 2011). The research gap highlights the unique value of qualitative approaches in capturing the complexities inherent to halal certification implementation.

Semi-structured interviews took place in Brunei-Muara District with business owners and the interviews were conducted in three months, from September to November 2024. Since the Halal Certificate and Label Order Amendment 2017 made it mandatory for all food and beverage businesses serving Muslims to apply for certification, businesses even whether it's at a small stall, in shop houses, or home-based are included in the law. All the respondents were Malay Muslim business owners and Brunei Malay language was predominantly used in interviews, with English language being used mainly by those business owners who have graduated from universities.

The interviews were prompted to discuss the issues relating to halal certification; the interview protocol includes critical inquiries:

1. Are you aware that applying for halal certification is mandatory for your business?
2. What challenges or barriers have you encountered during the halal certification process?
3. How do you think the process can be improved?

All interviews were recorded with consent, and interviewees were given the code R, in the final writeup. The interviews were transcribed verbatim to ensure the accuracy of the data portrayed. Ethical considerations were paramount throughout the study, with guarantees of confidentiality and the option for participants to withdraw at any stage. The analytical process involved transcribing, coding, cataloging, and initial analysis of the interview data in the Malay language, which was subsequently translated into the English language. CAQDAS software is used to help researchers use qualitative methods to organize, annotate, collaborate on, analyze, and visualize their work (Rampin & Rampin, 2021). Descriptive analysis techniques typical of qualitative research were applied to the interview transcripts, which underwent thematic and directed content analysis. Emerging themes were identified, coded, and integrated into the findings, with selected quotations from the interviews included to enrich the discussion of the research outcomes.

4. FINDINGS

4.1 Socio-Economic Profiles of Interviewees

Fifteen interviews were conducted from September to November 2024 with 14 MSMEs and one SME as defined by Brunei's standard on MSME definition (BusinessBN, 2024). The only SME, R15, operated three branches, employed 28 employees, and had assets over B$60,000, therefore is qualified as an SME under Brunei MSME standards. Ten, or 66.7% were conducted with business owners, while two were with managers and three with staff of the food and beverage business (Table 2). Eight men and seven women were interviewed for the research. All except two of the interviews were conducted with Bruneians and the other two with permanent residency status in Brunei. The majority of the respondents, 33.3% of them were between the ages of 20 to 29 years of age, 20% of them were between 30 to 39 years old and the rest constituted 13.3% respectively. Two retirees, those over the age of 60 were also interviewed in the research. Nine of the respondents were single, five of the respondents were married, and one was widowed.

Of the fifteen respondents, one did not have any formal education, while six individuals completed their secondary school. Five respondents had bachelor's degrees while two had master's degrees. One of the respondents had a business diploma. Of the fifteen respondents, five respondents were not comfortable revealing their household income, while five of the respondents declared their household income was less than B$3,000, three were between B$3,001 to B$5,000, and two were less than B$1,000.

Table 2. Socio-demographic profile of interviewees

Variables	Frequency	%	Variables	Frequency	%
Gender Male Female	8 7	53.3 46.6	Position in Business Business Owners Manager Staff	10 2 3	66.6 13.3 20.0
Age Range Under 19 20-29 30-39 40-49 50-59 60 and above	1 5 3 2 2 2	6.6 33.3 20.0 13.3 13.3 13.3	Food and Beverage Experience 1-3 years 4-6 years 7-9 years Over 10 years	4 4 2 5	26.6 26.6 13.3 33.3
Education Level No formal education Secondary education Diploma Bachelor Degree Masters	1 6 1 5 2	6.6 40.0 6.6 33.3 13.3	Types of Food and Beverages Shophouse Food Stalls Homebase	5 4 6	33.3 26.6 40.0

Four of the respondents were operating at a roadside stall, while six operated home-based businesses, and five were operating in shophouses. In terms of food and beverages experience, the majority, 33.3%, had 1 to 3 years of experience while four respondents had over 10 years of experience in operating a food and beverages business. All the businesses interviewed, except one, had been registered with the Registry of Companies and Business (ROCBN). The only one who seemed unsure, was a 19-year-old roadside stall owner, R4, whose household income was claimed between the range of B$3,00 to B$5,000.

All respondents except one, R6, pay rent for their business premises, even though the house belongs to their family. The highest amount of rental paid by a business owner in a shop is B$2,500 while the lowest was B$500.

4.2 Awareness of Halal Certification Being Mandatory

All respondents are aware that Halal Certification for their food and beverages **is** mandatory; however, of the fifteen respondents, six have yet to apply for it. According to the interviewees, the reason why they have not applied for the certification is due to,

... it is only mandatory for big restaurants. For small stalls, there is no need" – R1

... Because people already know I am a Muslim. So people/customers will buy from us because we are Muslim. For example, when we sell at the gerai, customers will see that we use hijab, so that's an indication that we sell halal food" – R11

Well, basically what we think, since all of our ingredients are bought locally, and it's just coffee beans, it's not luwak coffee, so we don't see the urgency to apply halal certs.– R12

... When I only sold the food online, I knew that I should apply, but I was hesitating because there were many processes. I know it's going to be tough. They said that even though the case that they're not going to approve it, at least they will give me a certificate indicating that I did apply for it." – R13

I haven't applied. Not yet. Because this is home-based, we are sharing a kitchen, we know for a fact that that is one condition to get halal certified, to have a dedicated kitchen for the cafe."- R14

Based on the responses gathered, it is evident that confusion persists regarding the extent of halal certification implementation within the food and beverage industry. While some business owners are well-informed about the certification's rules and regulations and choose not to apply—anticipating rejection for not meeting specific criteria like R13 and R14—others, particularly micro-businesses such as R1 and R11, operate under the misconception that halal certification is unnecessary for their food stall business. This indicates a significant disparity in understanding the requirements and implications of halal certification across different segments of the industry. According to the government's rules and regulations, there are no exceptions to the rule, all food and drinks that are to be sold and consumed by Muslim customers must be halal certified. However, how these rules are enforced has yet to be scrutinized, which explains why not all food and beverage businesses that cater to Muslim consumers are Halal-certified in the country.

This misperception echoes broader challenges identified in the literature where internal resistance to change poses a significant barrier to adopting Halal certification practices (S. Khan et al., 2019). The inconsistent enforcement of these rules, as yet unscrutinized, further contributes to the reluctance among businesses to integrate Halal practices into their operations, complicating efforts to expand the Halal sector (Ziegler et al., 2022). Therefore, understanding and addressing these perceptual barriers is crucial for enhancing compliance and facilitating broader acceptance of Halal certification standards

4.3 Challenges of Applying for Halal Certification

There were several challenges reported by interviewees in applying the halal certification as highlighted during the interviews with the respondents.

4.3.1 Tedious and Long Process, Even for Renewal

Respondents in the study highlighted the burdensome paperwork and the tedious nature of obtaining halal certification for their businesses, as found by Darmalaksana (2023); Fauzi et al., (2024), and Suryawan et al., (2022) earlier on. Similarly, smaller businesses that lack the necessary resources and expertise, as noted by Fard

& Amiri (2018) and Ismail et al. (2013), who emphasized the multiple audits and extensive documentation required were also reported in the interviews.

R3 from the study reported that the process took a long time, and R6 expressed concerns about the unpredictability of what officials might inquire about during inspections. Furthermore, in R8's experience, where there was a need to modify the forms and restart the certification process due to items not being listed in the department's registry.

According to R9,

So the halal certification itself, once you apply, it takes two to three months to process. Now, it doesn't make sense to us because you tell us within the six months, we have to... Close the business, right? Yes, we need to apply for the halal certification. But we don't know that there is a halal certification or how to apply for it, but we just know it's mandatory. Then the next step is, yes, after you've applied, now they've approved it, the approval itself takes two to three months. And after the approval, we need to have two supervisors coming here daily just to see how we run our business. Is it conducted in a halal manner? See how we cook? And that's going to be about a month or two months, and then only afterwards you get your halal permit.

R15 also raised her concerns on the process,

It is just too much work to do the paperwork for the ingredients, its 'malas' to do it. Its so tough to apply and tedious. .... The difficult part was that every new drinks or food that we have, by right we have to apply for halal certification, however this is quite tedious. Sometimes ideas can come very fast and if we have to apply for halal certification, which we don't know how fast the process will be, it is quite tedious for us. We are in the business and we have competitors; and we always have to stay ahead from our competitors by offering new menus and if we want to follow the rules, we have to apply first before we can display and sell to our customers. However, thinking about the process, it is tiring for us to do the paperwork.

Together, this study suggests that while the halal certification process is critical, its implementation could be significantly improved to reduce the burden on businesses, particularly smaller ones, thereby enhancing compliance and the expansion of the halal market. Processes can be streamlined to make sure it is easy for business owners to fill in the necessary information for the certification process and to ensure business owners can check the stage of their submission process easily (online, preferably) so they can check it anytime. If it is available online, then business owners can show their certification progress to their customers should they inquire about their certification. If approval can be made, a temporary digital approval can be provided to businesses, to ease their worries, to get the physical approval, and to show to their customers, again if it is inquired.

4.3.2 Product and Price Disclosure Uneasiness

Ingredient disclosure emerged as a key concern for business owners applying for halal certification. Business owners expressed hesitation about revealing recipes and ingredient details due to the potential risk of intellectual property being misused. This sentiment reflects the tension between regulatory compliance and protecting a business's competitive advantage, especially for enterprises that rely on unique, homemade recipes. Furthermore, this highlights a broader trust issue within the system, where businesses fear potential misuse of sensitive information.

As highlighted by R10,

> *Currently, we do have to get physical documentation. And it's difficult because not only the physical documentation, for every item on the menu, you have to list down your ingredients. And for some businesses, maybe like ours to some extent, we would like to keep those ingredients secret because it's homemade and what not, and they ask us to list down those things. But how can we keep those ingredients secret?*
>
> *Then the other step is, after we've passed that, down with the prices of those things, you're going to be charged by each and every one of those items. For example, yes, you might have for that one, let's say, nasi katok. That one nasi katok has various different ingredients. So you have to list down those ingredients, and that's considered one meal. Now the next meal, let's say a drink. Now you have to list down all of those drink items or drink ingredients and that becomes the second item. Then they charge you for those two items. But there's only like two items from the whole menu.*

R10 is also concerned as since her business does not produce the cake sold in her business premises, her cake supplier had to provide her halal certificate, which can be difficult, as they have not applied for halal certification as well. According to R10,

> *Since our cakes are outsourced, we have to get their halal certification. When we asked our supplier to do so, they had problems as their extension was not approved and the authorities asked them to set up their baking in a commercial area which is adding cost to their product. If that is the case, then, wouldn't the price increase again?*

These concerns highlight the need for clear assurances from halal certification authorities about data confidentiality and intellectual property protection. Without such measures, small businesses, particularly those dependent on unique recipes, may hesitate to pursue certification despite its potential benefits. Furthermore, the requirement to disclose proprietary information could inadvertently discourage innovation and competition in the food and beverage industry, and a solution is required to appease business owners concerns.

4.3.3 Buying for Local Market Should Already Ensure its Halalness?

Businesses highlighted their uneasiness of the product they bought for their food and drink items to be halal certified, despite the product being bought at supermarkets and wholesalers in the country. If the product is sold openly, then the product should be assumed to be halal, as in Brunei, halal and haram products sold in the country must be separated. Hence interviewees were concerned why, even if they bought the items in Brunei, which is not inside a non-halal product section, should they be questioned on the halalness of the product or items they used. For example,

Where do we buy our chicken, if I bought it at Soon Lee and if that is not halal, I don't know what is it anymore....If I buy from Hua Ho, and Hua Ho already has its certificate, that means Hua Ho chicken should be halal already... - R5

So many forms, so many. Every food they want to check. Whatever I buy from the supermarket should be halal, if you want to ask if its halal, they can check with the supermarket suppliers. We a small business, and we only buy things wholesale, so the wholesaler must be using halal products. As long as the wholesaler is halal, we are halal already. This is the right way... - R14

During the inspection, they took our brush, salt, and one of the food coloring as the halalness of it was not verified; sometimes I don't understand as I bought my product from a bakery shop here in the country, and were they not told that their brush or coloring was not halal, that's why it continued to be sold? Shouldn't they be inspected too? – R15

There is a need to ensure that if food and beverage business owners bought items in the country that have been halal certified, it is only fair that wholesalers or big supermarkets that sold the items should provide the certificate and give it to food and beverage business owners if they required it for halal certification submission. This will make the process easier for the food and beverage business owners as they do not have to worry about where to get the certification from when required. Bigger supermarkets and wholesalers should have this information ready as long as business owners show proof of their receipts of where they bought the food and drink items from that particular place.

4.3.4 Confusion on the Cost of Halal Certification

Confusion was apparent regarding the cost of obtaining halal certification, based on the interviews conducted. Several business owners expressed uncertainty about both the certification process and the associated costs of the food and beverages permit. For example,

Expenses to start up the halal cert is expensive for an MSME. Every, each one of your ingredients, again, the items on the menu, you have to pay for them. Not to mention, I think it's only a year if I'm not mistaken. So a year, then you have to reapply. Three years, then you have to reapply. Yeah, so that's where it is. Plus, not to mention, this is another thing that makes it difficult. You have to have two supervisors on the Halal Certification itself. If you don't have two supervisors, you won't be approved for the Halal Certification. They have to be Muslim, they fulfill all the criteria. – R10

For R15, who has received her halal certification,

We only paid $90 for the halal certification, which will be renewed in 3 years. I don't think we were required to pay for the $5 per ingredient matter, as I only pay $90 for it. – R15

The confusion about the costs of halal certification noted in our interviews reflects a significant information gap among business owners. The business owner, R15, who received her certification, pays only B$90 for her business halal certification, while R10 who has yet to apply for it believes that he has to pay for every product he produces. However, in an explanation from the Halal Food Control Division's leaflet on the Halal Certificate and Permit, it is clear that certification is only B$90, and for those who applied for a permit, then the cost of the permit increases based on the categorization of the business, either its micro, small, medium, macro or multinational. Depending on the number of employees of the said businesses, the halal permit costs are listed in Table 3 below.

Table 3. Cost of Halal permit

Classification	Employees	Rate B$
Micro	1-4 people	**$5/product**
Small	5-19 people	**$150/1-20 product**
Medium	20-99 people	**$300 / 1-20 product**
Macro	More than 99 People	**$700/1-20 product**
Multinational		**$1000 / 1-20 product**

Source: Halal Food Control Division, Ministry of Religious Affairs

The difference between halal certification and a permit is also defined. The certificate is for those who have food and beverages businesses such as restaurants, food stalls or canteen, at home or shops; while the permit is for those business that produces a product and requires a halal label and sticker approved by the Brunei Islamic Religious Affairs (MUIB). This permit is not for food and drinks operators which does not require the MUIB label on the food and drink items but the halal certificate for the whole business premises.

The Halal Food Control Division has been lenient to those businesses that could not yet obtain or start their halal certification processes due to certain limitations as highlighted in sections 4.2 and 4.3 respectively, and these businesses are allowed only to get halal permits hence the cost of the product for the items they produced can be more expensive if they are issued a permit. Although high costs have been highlighted in the literature by Ab Talib, (2017); Al-shami & Abdullah, (2023); Haleem et al., (2019), there is a need to be more research in Brunei on the nature of the costs and if those are a huge issue or is it a misinformation which has been passed from words of mouth rather than the actual fees of the certification and permits. What is clear is that, from the interviews, the paperwork and actual approval once given, seemed more of a concern rather than the cost of obtaining halal certification for food and beverage businesses in Brunei.

4.3.5 Not all are Halal Certified and Still In Operation

While the Halal Certificate and Halal Label Order Amendment 2017 has been in place for several years, not all food and beverage businesses in the country are certified. The Ministry had allowed businesses to operate leniently, especially during the Covid-19 pandemic which affected not only movements in the country but also businesses (Pang, 2021). Therefore,

> *You see, there are so many stalls around, if the Government really wants to control, then they have to enforce it properly. Why do some other stall owners don't have to pay for their certification? -R5*
>
> *The thing is I think most competitors, let's say smaller cafes and home-based cafes don't even have halal certification. So they don't get checked. And therefore, why do we get checked? And also nasi katok places, they don't get checked, which begs the question, why aren't they getting forcibly asked to get the halal certification but everyone else needs to get it? – R10*

It is commonly recognized that businesses can identify whether food and beverage establishments are halal certified based on the certification displayed on their premises. Despite this, it is widely acknowledged that not all establishments are certified. Additionally, food products made at home and sold in small supermarkets often lack halal certification. However, even with this apparent leniency towards micro businesses, they still face scrutiny from other business owners. This scrutiny underscores the vital role that government support and regulatory frameworks play in the adoption of halal certification, as outlined by Haleem et al. (2019). In certain regions, the absence of government initiatives and incentives, as discussed by Darmalaksana (2023) and Silalahi et al. (2022), presents significant challenges for businesses, particularly smaller enterprises, seeking halal certification. Should micro-businesses be exempted from the certification, should they be given a timeline to comply to apply for the halal certification, and the consequences if they do not cease their business if do not comply? If they are fined, as stipulated in the law, would their names be published in the newspapers to deter others from doing the same, hence having to comply with the certification process as mandated? If it is not publicized, the public would not know about the consequences of non-compliance therefore, the regulations need to be uniform for all food and beverage industries serving the Muslim population.

5.0 RECOMMENDATIONS

Despite the widespread news on the implementation of the Halal Certificate and Halal Label Order Amendment 2017, there is still confusion among business owners if they should apply for the Halal certificate or not. It is clear from the pamphlet that has been distributed by the Halal Food Control Division, Ministry of Religious Affairs, which stated that a halal certificate must be applied for all food and beverages businesses be it restaurants, food stalls, or canteens as well as those selling from home. However, since enforcement of the Order has not reached out to all businesses that serve the Muslim population, perhaps there is a need to review or re-educate the public on which businesses need to have this halal certification and permits.

However, if compliance is required, based on the interviews, while business owners are keen and want to comply with the regulation, the said process is seen as tedious and difficult. If the processes can be streamlined and made easier for business owners, there can be less fear among business owners to apply for halal certification. Inspections of business properties can be made to educate business owners and not for business owners to fear them. Under Brunei's Digital Economy Masterplan 2025, the Halal Certification System was supposed to be implemented between 2022 and 2023 (Ministry of Transport and Infocommunications (MTIC), 2020) however, from the interviews it is clear that this is yet to be fully implemented by the government.

Most respondents hope that the application process can be made online for easier monitoring and when faced with complications, it can be dealt swiftly. Business owners also want the process of certification to be fast as it affects how fast they can open their business. Those businesses that need to pay rent and pay for their employees would need the process to be faster as the extra costs are not favorable to them. As reported by R10,

> *I think for us MSMEs, yes make all the information readily available online. Another thing is, when officers do check, they straight away come with consequences rather than education. The first time we run over the limit, let's say,*

I would rather have them educate me that I need the halal certification and therefore I will apply. Now the second barrier I feel like they need to have, is a short application, for example, instead of two to three months of approval, maybe one month.

We understand that the process is long, but you need to quicken up the pace because, for us, it's lagging our business. Sometimes businesses get closure, closed down because they don't have the cert. it will take us three months for us to get approval, then we can open again to run our business. It doesn't make sense. At the very most, one month should be the maximum. Finally, what I do think, it shouldn't be mandatory for everyone, rather it should be mandatory for only those who can afford it. I would much prefer it that way because there are up-and-coming businesses that can't afford it. And you have to, there should be regulators that can judge the income of, let's say a cafe, and dictate whether they should have the halal cert or shouldn't.

Business owners hope for a better tracking system, for transparency, where they can see where their application has gone through and what are they steps they must check and resubmit should they need to do so. The process they also hope can be reduced to ensure their business can run smoothly without the concern of not complying with government regulations. There is also a need to show which businesses had the halal certification to ensure those claimed by businesses are backed up by authorities, as shown by the recent issues in Malaysia where the public questioned if several popular businesses had the halal certification and sought the government agency response on this (Chong, 2024; Shadiqe, 2024). If the matter is available on their website, then the public can easily check it and verify the matter easily.

Enforcement of halal certification on food and beverages is perhaps difficult for government agencies due to lack of manpower however, there are other avenues where practice from other countries can be used in Brunei. For example, in Indonesia, under the Halal Product Assurance Organizing Body, the government allows universities to perform the task of halal certification at a specific fee from businesses (Hidayat et al., 2024). There is a demand for food and beverage products to be halal certified therefore since the authorities would not be able to cope with the demand, other agencies to help with the certification process. Since university academics are also sought for their expertise in the halal certification process in Indonesia, therefore, Brunei can have such an arrangement as well. The Halalan Thayyiban Research Centre at Universiti Islam Sultan Sharif Ali (UNISSA), or Kolej Universiti Perguruan Ugama Seri Begawan (KUPUSB) can provide such service to businesses, with cooperation with the Halal Food Control Division, before the certification is issued.

The issue of ingredient and product disclosure seemed unique in Brunei as businesses are not keen to give their secrets away from their best-selling items, perhaps there is a way where to ensure that the items used are not only halal but the specifics of how its it not made, are not revealed since confidentiality are a main concern for business owners. Copycats on popular food and drink items are a norm, for example, the recent Dubai kunafa chocolates saw many imitations and copies being sold by various businesses (Cairns, 2024; Yi, 2024), therefore, businesses' concern about copycats is not without merit.

Clear, equal, and fair enforcement of all food and beverage businesses that serve the Muslim populations is important since comparisons will be made by businesses which has halal certificates or permits and which do not and yet are still in operation and not fined. If non-compliance is also allowed, therefore businesses are not encouraged to apply for the certification since others who do not apply are not sanctioned. Therefore to ensure more compliance, and equal application of the law as well as ensuring the certification process is easy to do, can encourage businesses to apply for the certification and renew it easily when their expiration is near for re-application.

6.0 CONCLUSION

The issue of halal certification is an important issue in Brunei and business owners are keen to be halal certified however, the processes are seen as difficult and tedious. Interviews from the respondents revealed that information seemed to be unclear to some, especially for micro businesses where they believed that they were exempted from the process. As the government is keen not only to make Brunei an important niche in the halal global market as well as forwarding the digital and smart governance system in place, once the online halal certification system is up and running, businesses will be able to apply the certification with ease in compliance with the government's directive. Halal certification not only ensures that food is clean for Muslim consumption, but the ingredients are safe and hygienic and also clean from non-halal products, the halal certification process is a step towards Brunei revitalizing its global halal niche market aspiration.

This study identifies several interrelated gaps. From a knowledge perspective, many business owners remain unclear about the certification process, costs, and requirements. Contextually, there is limited research on how Brunei's specific administrative and socio-cultural environment influences halal certification uptake, particularly among MSMEs. The practical challenges include procedural burdens, limited support mechanisms, concerns over the confidentiality of recipes, and cost-related misinformation. Moreover, policy-level gaps emerge from inconsistent enforcement and a lack of tailored support systems for smaller businesses.

By conducting in-depth interviews with business owners, this study addresses these gaps and contributes empirical evidence that has been missing from the literature. It offers a grounded understanding of how policies are perceived and experienced on the ground, thereby informing a more nuanced view of halal certification in Brunei. These findings are relevant not only for local policymakers seeking to improve compliance and support mechanisms but also for researchers interested in halal governance, certification practices, and MSME development. Therefore, future research could explore comparative models from other countries that have successfully integrated support systems into halal certification processes. Policymakers may also consider decentralized approaches, partnerships with academic institutions, or digital platforms to streamline applications and strengthen enforcement.

REFERENCES

Ab Talib, M. S. (2017). Motivations and benefits of halal food safety certification. *Journal of Islamic Marketing*, *8*(4), 605–624. DOI: 10.1108/JIMA-08-2015-0063

Ab Talib, M. S. (2021). Identifying halal logistics constraints in Brunei Darussalam. *Journal of Islamic Marketing*, *12*(6), 1145–1158. DOI: 10.1108/JIMA-09-2019-0189

Ab Talib, M. S., & Zulfakar, M. H. (2024). Sustainable halal food supply chain management in a small rentier halal market. *Arab Gulf Journal of Scientific Research*, *42*(3), 449–463. DOI: 10.1108/AGJSR-11-2022-0251

Abdallah, A., Rahem, M. A., & Pasqualone, A. (2021). The multiplicity of halal standards: a case study of application to slaughterhouses. In *Journal of Ethnic Foods* (Vol. 8, Issue 1). BioMed Central Ltd. DOI: 10.1186/s42779-021-00084-6

Abdul Rahim, N. R., Abdullah, I., Yahya, N. A., Awang, M. N., Muhammad, S. Z., Ahmad Sabri, S., & Ahmad, N. N. (2022). Negotiation of needs towards halal talents sustainability. *Journal of Islamic Marketing*, *13*(1), 20–44. DOI: 10.1108/JIMA-11-2019-0245

Akbar, J., Gul, M., Jahangir, M., Adnan, M., Saud, S., Hassan, S., Nawaz, T., & Fahad, S. (2023). Global Trends in Halal Food Standards: A Review. *Foods*, *12*(23), 4200. DOI: 10.3390/foods12234200 PMID: 38231601

Al-Mahmood, O. A., & Fraser, A. M. (2023). Perceived challenges in implementing halal standards by halal certifying bodies in the United States. *PLoS One*, *18*(8), e0290774. DOI: 10.1371/journal.pone.0290774 PMID: 37651404

Al-shami, H. A., & Abdullah, S. (2023). Halal food industry certification and operation challenges and manufacturing execution system opportunities. A review study from Malaysia. *Materials Today: Proceedings*, *80*, 3607–3614. DOI: 10.1016/j.matpr.2021.07.331

Ali, M. H., Chung, L., Tan, K. H., Makhbul, Z. M., Zhan, Y., & Tseng, M.-L. (2023). Investigating blockchain technology adoption intention model in halal food small and medium enterprises: moderating role of supply chain integration. *International Journal of Logistics Research and Applications*, 1–25. DOI: 10.1080/13675567.2023.2217772

Ali, M. H., & Suleiman, N. (2018). Eleven shades of food integrity: A halal supply chain perspective. *Trends in Food Science & Technology*, *71*, 216–224. DOI: 10.1016/j.tifs.2017.11.016

Amer, M. (2024). Linkage among halal quality standard certification and SME's performance: Palestinian food halal certified SME's context. *Arab Gulf Journal of Scientific Research*, *42*(4), 1414–1425. DOI: 10.1108/AGJSR-03-2023-0109

Ardiantono, D. S., Ardyansyah, G. D., Sugihartanto, M. F., Al Mustofa, M. U., & Lisdiantini, N. (2024). Mapping the barrier and strategic solutions of halal supply chain implementation in small and medium enterprises. *Journal of Islamic Marketing*, *15*(7), 1673–1705. Advance online publication. DOI: 10.1108/JIMA-08-2022-0229

Arifin, E. N., Ananta, A., Musa, S. F. P. D., & Hoon, C. Y. (2024). A pioneering study on measuring poverty in the hydrocarbon-rich state of Brunei Darussalam. *Asian Population Studies*, *20*(2), 222–240. DOI: 10.1080/17441730.2023.2240108

Aziz, Y. A., & Chok, N. V. (2013). The role of Halal awareness, Halal certification, and marketing components in determining Halal purchase intention among non-Muslims in Malaysia: A structural equation modeling approach. *Journal of International Food & Agribusiness Marketing*, *25*(1), 1–23. DOI: 10.1080/08974438.2013.723997

Basir, K. H. (2022). Business Innovation Amid the COVID-19 Crisis in Brunei Darussalam: A Viewpoint. In Ratten, V. (Ed.), *Strategic Entrepreneurial Ecosystems and Business Model Innovation* (pp. 31–40). Emerald Publishing Limited., DOI: 10.1108/978-1-80382-137-520221003

Bonne, K., & Verbeke, W. (2008). Muslim consumer trust in halal meat status and control in Belgium. *Meat Science*, *79*(1), 113–123. DOI: 10.1016/j.meatsci.2007.08.007 PMID: 22062604

Bryman, A., & Bell, E. (2011). *Business Research Methods*. Oxford University Press.

Business, B. N. (2024). *National Definitons for Business Categories in Brunei Darusaalam*. Ministry of Finance and Economy. https://business.mofe.gov.bn/SitePages/Brunei Darussalam Micro Small & Medium Enterprise Definition.aspx

Bux, C., Varese, E., Amicarelli, V., & Lombardi, M. (2022). Halal Food Sustainability between Certification and Blockchain: A Review. *Sustainability (Basel)*, *14*(4), 2152. DOI: 10.3390/su14042152

Cairns, R. (2024). *Meet the woman behind Dubai's viral super-chunky chocolate bar*. CNN Travel. https://edition.cnn.com/travel/dubai-viral-chocolate-bar-fix-hnk-spc/index.html

Calder, R. (2020). Halalization: Religious Product Certification in Secular Markets. *Sociological Theory*, *38*(4), 334–361. DOI: 10.1177/0735275120973248

Chong, D. (2024). *Halal or not? Jakim clarifies certification issue for six popular F&B chains amid online queries*. The Malay Mail.

Darmalaksana, W. (2023). How is the halal certification policy implemented? Perspective analysis of small and medium enterprises (SMEs) in Indonesia. *Journal of Islamic Accounting and Business Research*. Advance online publication. DOI: 10.1108/JIABR-12-2022-0342

Department of Economic Planning and Statistics. (2024a). Brunei Darussalam. *Statistical Yearbook. Annuaire Statistique, 2023*, •••. https://deps.mofe.gov.bn/DEPD%20Documents%20Library/DOS/BDSYB/2023/RPT.pdf

Department of Economic Planning and Statistics. (2024b). *Food and Beverages Services Index: 3rd Quarter 2024*.

Fard, M. H., & Amiri, N. S. (2018). The effect of entrepreneurial marketing on halal food SMEs performance. *Journal of Islamic Marketing*, *9*(3), 598–620. DOI: 10.1108/JIMA-12-2016-0097

Fauzi, M. A., Mohd Ali, N. S., Mat Russ, N., Mohamad, F., Battour, M., & Mohd Zaki, N. N. (2024). Halal certification in food products: Science mapping of present and future trends. *Journal of Islamic Marketing*, *15*(12), 3564–3580. DOI: 10.1108/JIMA-12-2023-0407

Fernando, Y., Wahyuni-TD, I. S., Zainul Abideen, A., & Mergeresa, F. (2023). Traceability technology, halal logistics brand and logistics performance: Religious beliefs and beyond. *Journal of Islamic Marketing*, *14*(4), 1007–1031. DOI: 10.1108/JIMA-06-2020-0183

Fuseini, A., Wotton, S. B., Knowles, T. G., & Hadley, P. J. (2017). Halal Meat Fraud and Safety Issues in the UK: A Review in the Context of the European Union. *Food Ethics*, *1*(2), 127–142. DOI: 10.1007/s41055-017-0009-1

Haji Shahlehi, S. F., Shaya, V. N., Ismail, K., & Kawi, F. (2024). Bruneian SMEs amid the COVID-19 pandemic: Challenges for the Halal food processing industry. *Journal of Islamic Marketing*, *15*(1), 142–158. DOI: 10.1108/JIMA-11-2021-0364

Haleem, A., Khan, M. I., & Khan, S. (2019). Halal certification, the inadequacy of its adoption, modelling and strategising the efforts. *Journal of Islamic Marketing*, *11*(2), 384–404. DOI: 10.1108/JIMA-05-2017-0062

Hamdan, M., & Hoon, C.-Y. (2019). Brunei Darussalam: Making Strides with a Renewed Focus on the Future. In D. Singh & M. Cook (Eds.), *Southeast Asian Affairs 2019* (Vol. 2019, pp. 85–102). ISEAS–Yusof Ishak Institute Singapore. DOI: 10.1355/9789814843164-008

Hashmi, H. S., & Ali, H. (2021). Education for young generations on halal food audit and certification. In Qadri. Hussain Mohi-ud-Din & M. I. Bhatti (Eds.), *Contemporary Issues in Islamic Social Finance* (1st ed., pp. 273–292). Routledge. DOI: 10.4324/9781003050209-19

Heilmaier, J., & Ling, M. (2021). SMEs and HEIs: Observations from Brunei Darussalam and Germany. *Industry and Higher Education, 35*(3), 244–251. DOI: 10.1177/0950422220944749

Hidayat, R., Zulham, Z., & Ramadi, B. (2024). DEVELOPMENT STRATEGY FOR HALAL CENTER IN UNIVERSITY: A TECHNICAL RECOMMENDATION. *UMAN FALAH: Jurnal Ekonomi Dan Bisnis Islam, 11*(1), 17–35.

Hoon, C.-Y., & Zhao, K. (2024). Emerging Chinese Foreign Direct Investment in Brunei. *East Asian Policy, 16*(03), 100–114. DOI: 10.1142/S1793930524000230

Husin, M. M., & Haron, R. (2019). Financial Sustainability of SMEs Through Islamic Crowdfunding. In Rafay, A. (Ed.), *Handbook of Research on Theory and Practice of Global Islamic Finance* (Vol. 1, pp. 321–337). IGI Global., DOI: 10.4018/978-1-7998-0218-1.ch018

Islam, M. M., Ab Talib, M. S., & Muhamad, N. (2023). Challenges of Halal Standards and Halal Certification for Islamic Marketing. *Muslim Business and Economic Review, 2*(1), 105–124. DOI: 10.56529/mber.v2i1.156

Ismail, M. M., & Islam, Md. S., & Wan Bakar, W. M. M. (2013). Export Barriers to Halal Food Processing Small and Medium Enterprises (SMEs) in Malaysia. *Pertanika Journal of Social Science and Humanities, 21*(S), 31–46. http://www.pertanika.upm.edu.my/pjssh/browse/regular-issue?article=JSSH-0826-2013

Izberk-Bilgin, E., & Nakata, C. C. (2016). A new look at faith-based marketing: The global halal market. *Business Horizons, 59*(3), 285–292. DOI: 10.1016/j.bushor.2016.01.005

Jaya, S., & Darul Ehsan, S. (2015). Multiple halal logos and Malays' beliefs: A case of mixed signals. *International Food Research Journal, 22*(4), 1727–1735.

Khalid, A. M., Haji Masi, M., Muhammad, N., & Pang, W. L. (2018). Brunei Darussalam: Halal Meat and Meat Products Processing. In J. Gross & P. S. Intal (Eds.), *Reducing Unnecessary Regulatory Burdens in ASEAN: Country Studies* (pp. 89–117). Economic Research Institute for ASEAN and East Asia. https://www.eria.org/uploads/media/RURB_2018_Chapter_4_Halal_meat_Brunei.pdf

Khan, M. I., Khan, S., & Haleem, A. (2022). Analysing barriers towards management of Halal supply chain: A BWM approach. *Journal of Islamic Marketing*, *13*(1), 66–80. DOI: 10.1108/JIMA-09-2018-0178

Khan, S., Khan, M. I., & Haleem, A. (2019). Evaluation of barriers in the adoption of halal certification: A fuzzy DEMATEL approach. *Journal of Modelling in Management*, *14*(1), 153–174. DOI: 10.1108/JM2-03-2018-0031

Koeswinarno, S. B. J., Fakhruddin, M., & Atieqoh, S. (2023). Non-Muslim Acceptance of Halal Products in the Context of Business Development. In A. Rafiki (Ed.), *Digitalization in Halal Management* (pp. 193–207). Springer. DOI: 10.1007/978-981-99-5146-8_13

Latif, I. A., Mohamed, Z., Sharifuddin, J., Abdullah, A. M., & Ismail, M. M. (2014). A comparative analysis of global Halal certification requirements. *Journal of Food Products Marketing, 20*(sup1), 85–101. DOI: 10.1080/10454446.2014.921869

Lever, J., & Miele, M. (2012). The growth of halal meat markets in Europe: An exploration of the supply side theory of religion. *Journal of Rural Studies*, *28*(4), 528–537. DOI: 10.1016/j.jrurstud.2012.06.004

Ministry of Transport and Infocommunications (MTIC). (2020). *Digital Economy Masterplan 2025*.

Muhamad, N., Leong, V. S., & Masri, M. (2019). Brunei Halal Tourism Outlook. In Hall, M. C., & Prayag, G. (Eds.), *The Routledge Handbook of Halal Hospitality and Islamic Tourism* (pp. 180–190). Routledge., DOI: 10.4324/9781315150604-13

Mukherjee, S. R. (2014). Global Halal: Meat, money, and religion. *Religions*, *5*(1), 22–75. DOI: 10.3390/rel5010022

Musa, S. F. P. D. (2019). Brunei Darussalam, a Country Profile. In R. Macdonald (Ed.), *Southeast Asia and the ASEAN Economic Community* (pp. 295–311). Springer International Publishing. DOI: 10.1007/978-3-030-19722-3_8

Othman, B., Shaarani, S. M., & Bahron, A. (2016). The Potential of ASEAN in Halal Certification Implementation: A Review. *Pertanika Journal of Social Science & Humanities*, *24*(1), 1–24.

Pang, L. L. (2021). Leadership and Crisis Communication During Covid-19: The Case of Brunei Darussalam. *Policy & Governance Review*, *5*(2), 97. DOI: 10.30589/pgr.v5i2.388

Prabowo, S., Rahman, A. A., Rahman, S. A., & Samah, A. A. (2015). Revealing factors hindering halal certification in East Kalimantan Indonesia. *Journal of Islamic Marketing*, *6*(2), 268–291. DOI: 10.1108/JIMA-05-2014-0040

Rampin, R., & Rampin, V. (2021). taguette: open source qualitative data analysis. *The Journal of Open Source Software*. https://joss.theoj.org/papers/10.21105/joss.03522.pdf

Shadiqe, J. (2024). *Several popular restaurant chains not halal-certified, says Jakim*. New Straits Times.

Shahlehi, S. F. H., Shaya, V. N., Ismail, K., & Kawi, F. (2024). Bruneian SMEs amid the COVID-19 pandemic: Challenges for the Halal food processing industry. *Journal of Islamic Marketing*, *15*(1), 142–158. DOI: 10.1108/JIMA-11-2021-0364

Silalahi, S. A. F., Fachrurazi, F., & Fahham, A. M. (2022). Factors affecting intention to adopt halal practices: Case study of Indonesian small and medium enterprises. *Journal of Islamic Marketing*, *13*(6), 1244–1263. DOI: 10.1108/JIMA-05-2020-0152

Slesman, L., & Hoon, C.-Y. (2023). Brunei Darussalam in 2022: Towards Post-COVID-19 Economic Recovery, Diversification and Sustainability. *Southeast Asian Affairs*, *2023*(1), 52–68.

Sufri, N. M. H. M., Abubakar, Y. A., Masri, M. B. H., & Ab Talib, M. S. (2023). Traditional Versus Born-Global Theories and the Internationalisation of Halal Food SMEs from an SSMC: Conceptual Framework and New Propositions. *Journal of Entrepreneurship and Innovation in Emerging Economies*, *9*(2), 222–237. DOI: 10.1177/23939575231186487

Sulaiman, N. S., Abdullah, R., & Hashim, N. (2023). Halal Industry Development in Brunei Darussalam: Realities and Challenges. *Social and Humaniora Research Symposium*, 1013–1029. DOI: 10.18502/kss.v8i18.14308

Suryawan, A. S., Hisano, S., & Jongerden, J. (2022). Negotiating halal: The role of non-religious concerns in shaping halal standards in Indonesia. *Journal of Rural Studies*, *92*, 482–491. DOI: 10.1016/j.jrurstud.2019.09.013

Susanty, A., Puspitasari, N. B., Caterina, A. D., & Jati, S. (2020). Mapping the barriers for implementing halal logistics in Indonesian food, beverage and ingredient companies. *Journal of Islamic Marketing, ahead-of-p*(ahead-of-print). DOI: 10.1108/JIMA-11-2019-0244

Tahir, M., Burki, U., & Hayat, A. (2023). Natural resources and economic growth: Evidence from Brunei Darussalam. *International Journal of Emerging Markets*, *18*(10), 4252–4269. DOI: 10.1108/IJOEM-05-2021-0762

Tan, A., Gligor, D., & Ngah, A. (2022). Applying Blockchain for Halal food traceability. *International Journal of Logistics*, *25*(6), 947–964. DOI: 10.1080/13675567.2020.1825653

Yi, L. K. (2024). *Trendspotting: Catch the chocolate pistachio 'kunafa' fever in KL with chocolate bars, croissants and even cookies*. The Malay Mail. https://www.malaymail.com/news/eat-drink/2024/11/04/trendspotting-catch-the-chocolate-pistachio-kunafa-fever-in-kl-with-chocolate-bars-croissants-and-even-cookies/155736#google_vignette

Ziegler, Y., Uli, V., & Tatari, M. (2022). Implementing halal logistics in a non-Muslim-dominant environment: A proposal for reengineering the business processes in two stages. *Business Process Management Journal*, *28*(8), 48–65. DOI: 10.1108/BPMJ-12-2020-0593

Chapter 7
Promoting Employment Opportunities Through a Halal Technopreneur Ecosystem for Graduates

Nor Surilawana Sulaiman
https://orcid.org/0000-0002-4227-9703
Universiti Islam Sultan Sharif Ali, Brunei

Mohamed Syazwan Ab Talib
https://orcid.org/0000-0001-8190-9096
Universiti Brunei Darussalam, Brunei

Norkhairiah Hashim
https://orcid.org/0000-0001-9631-3789
Universiti Islam Sultan Sharif Ali, Brunei

ABSTRACT

This study explores the potential of a halal technopreneurial ecosystem in addressing the challenge of graduate unemployment. Utilizing a qualitative research methodology, the study employs content analysis and interviews with key stakeholders, including graduates, academician, and technopreneurs, to gain insights into the current landscape and opportunities within the halal sector. The research aims to identify the components and dynamics of a robust halal technopreneur ecosystem that can facilitate employment opportunities for graduates. The study will develop a comprehensive framework for a halal technopreneurial ecosystem by synthesising findings from stakeholder perspectives and existing literature. This framework is intended to guide policymakers, educational institutions, and industry players in

DOI: 10.4018/979-8-3373-3917-7.ch007

creating an environment conducive to job creation and sustainable economic growth within the halal sector. The ultimate goal is to propose actionable strategies for leveraging halal technopreneurship as a viable solution to reduce unemployment rates among graduates.

INTRODUCTION

The advent of Industry 4.0 has increased the number of technology-based firms that contribute to boosting GDP and creating job opportunities (Barbe et al., 2003). Vojtovič et al. (2016) stated that the Industrial Revolution 4.0 (IR 4.0) is progressing towards a socio-technology-digital era, where everything becomes limitless through the use of unlimited computing and data. This evolution is driven by the advancement of the internet and digital technology, which serve as the backbone for connectivity among humans, machines, and digital technologies. As technology advances, businesses must adopt trends and incorporate them into their operations (Lukita et al., 2023). The use of advanced technology in business, including automation, the Internet of Things, and innovative technological practices, is emphasised by Industry 4.0, and traditional entrepreneurs must transition to technopreneurship (Koe et al., 2020). Technopreneurship is a type of entrepreneurship that is straightforward and set in a technology-driven context, involving the integration of technological expertise, entrepreneurial talent, and the skills necessary to transform goods and services (Hoque et al., 2017). Technopreneurship has recently been considered a critical driver of increased economic growth in both industrialised and developing nations (Darajah & Kassim, 2019). Furthermore, technopreneurship can be viewed as a crucial catalyst for economic growth, competitiveness, job creation, and the advancement of social interests within the context of social development. Technopreneurship is emerging as a key driver of lasting competitive advantage (Darajah & Kassim, 2019).

Furthermore, the COVID-19 pandemic has necessitated the integration of technology and innovation into business practices, preparing companies for the post-pandemic future (Sallomi, 2020). In this crucial period, the role of technopreneurship becomes even more significant, offering hope for recovery. The swift advancement of information and communication technology fuels the expansion of tech-driven businesses, generating new opportunities for jobs and financial success (Aryanti et al., 2022). Technopreneurs play a crucial role in developing and promoting innovative information and communication technology (ICT) products and services for both local and global markets, effectively addressing the demands of the digital economy (Soomro & Shah, 2021). Combining business acumen with technology makes technopreneurship a crucial contributor to economic growth and job creation (Wijayanto et al., 2023).

Although technopreneurship, or technology-based entrepreneurship, is significant in the future competitive landscape, many people still view it as a new breed of business. As a result, numerous obstacles remain, particularly in the areas of entrepreneurial education and development (Jusoh & Halim; Tan et al., 2010). This gap is also faced by students in higher education. Some obstacles to technopreneurship include the lack of knowledge, digital literacy, and the low quality of students' products and skills (Winarni et al., 2021; Salman et al., 2020). Many students at higher institutions lack enthusiasm for entrepreneurial careers, which can lead to new intellectual unemployment due to students' inability to innovate new products and services that create jobs.

Halal technopreneurship is deeply rooted in Shariah-compliant principles, ensuring that all business practices, products, and services align with Islamic values and ethics. This includes ethical financing, adherence to halal certification standards, and compliance with Islamic rules in areas such as marketing, sales, and product development (Nurein, 2023; Ahmed, 2025). Thus, the halal technopreneurship ecosystems are believed to operate within the framework of Islamic values and principles. These values influence decision-making, business models, and ethical standards. The businesses are not only focused on profitability but also on ensuring that their activities comply with Islamic law.

Hence, this study seeks to enhance employment opportunities for graduates by establishing halal technopreneur ecosystems. It strives to create a supportive platform that nurtures entrepreneurship in accordance with halal principles while leveraging technology.

Based on previous studies, there are gaps in the literature that have not been addressed or discussed, particularly regarding how halal technopreneurs can enhance employability. Most prior research has empirically demonstrated that academic support and educational backgrounds in study can influence students' interest in starting a technology-based entrepreneurship. On the other hand, higher education plays a key role in encouraging students to translate their interests into tangible actions by choosing technopreneurship as a career through entrepreneurship education. Therefore, this research is vital in responding to previous research also conducted by Jangcik et al. (2022), which aimed to formulate strategies for developing technopreneurship in higher education to expand career options in entrepreneurship for students.

METHODOLOGY

This research aims to explore how a Halal technopreneur ecosystem can enhance employment opportunities for graduates. A qualitative approach is chosen to gain in-depth insights into the experiences and perceptions of stakeholders involved in this ecosystem, including graduates, technopreneurs, and academicians. The methodology employed will be qualitative content analysis, which enables an in-depth understanding of the textual data related to the topic. The study used qualitative content analysis as its primary method for data collection and analysis. This approach is suitable for examining the nuances and underlying meanings within textual data, which is crucial for understanding the complexities of the Halal technopreneur ecosystem.

Data was collected from various sources, as shown in Figure 1. The selection criteria for these sources focused on relevance, credibility, and the richness of information provided regarding the Halal technopreneur ecosystem.

Figure 1. Data Collection

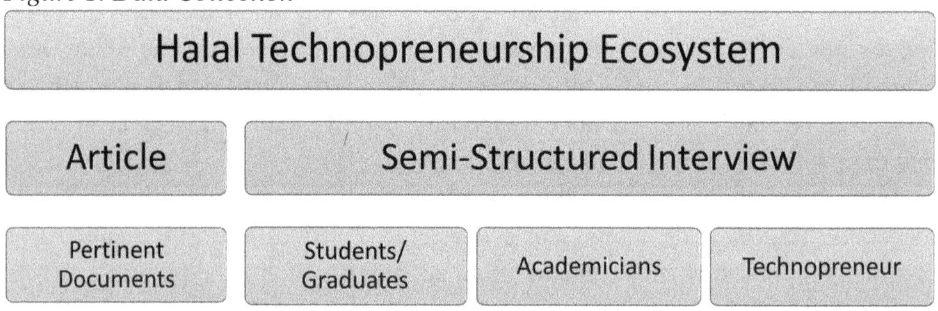

Table 1 provides an overview of the backgrounds of the informants, including students, academicians, and technopreneurs. The study has also contacted government officials; however, no response has been received to date.

Table 1. Informants Background

<table>
<tr><th colspan="6">Students / Graduates</th></tr>
<tr><th>No</th><th>Informant</th><th>Gender</th><th>Age Group</th><th>Level of Study</th><th>University</th></tr>
<tr><td>1.</td><td>S1</td><td>Female</td><td>18-24</td><td>Bachelor's Degree</td><td rowspan="5">Universiti Islam Sultan Sharif Ali</td></tr>
<tr><td>2.</td><td>S2</td><td>Male</td><td>18-24</td><td>Bachelor's Degree</td></tr>
<tr><td>3.</td><td>S3</td><td>Male</td><td>18-24</td><td>Bachelor's Degree</td></tr>
<tr><td>4.</td><td>S4</td><td>Female</td><td>25-34</td><td>Ph.D.</td></tr>
<tr><td>5.</td><td>S5</td><td>Female</td><td>18-24</td><td>Bachelor's Degree</td></tr>
<tr><th colspan="6">Academician</th></tr>
<tr><th>No</th><th>Informant</th><th>Gender</th><th>Year of Expertise</th><th>Teaching</th><th>Institution</th></tr>
<tr><td>6</td><td>A1</td><td>Male</td><td>9</td><td>Entrepreneurs</td><td>Universiti Islam Sultan Sharif Ali</td></tr>
<tr><th colspan="6">Technopreneur</th></tr>
<tr><th>No</th><th>Informant</th><th>Gender</th><th>Foundation Year</th><th>Product</th><th>Platform of Business</th></tr>
<tr><td>7</td><td>T1</td><td>Female</td><td>2024</td><td>Scarf, Modest fashion</td><td>Instagram, TikTok Live</td></tr>
</table>

Source: Authors

The informants were interviewed using a different set of questions tailored to their respective categories. Table 2 shows the semi-structured questions constructed for the interview session.

Table 2. Interview Questions for Informants

	Students
1.	**Are you familiar with the concept of halal technopreneurship?**
2.	Have you taken any entrepreneurship courses?
3.	Where did you learn about halal technopreneurship?
4.	Rate the effectiveness of these courses in promoting knowledge of halal technopreneurship.
5.	Would you participate in training programs or workshops focused on halal technology entrepreneurship?
6.	Are you interested in pursuing a career in halal technopreneurship after graduation?
7.	If yes, what motivates you to consider halal technopreneurship as a career?
8.	What challenges do you perceive in pursuing halal technopreneurship?
9.	Do you believe a halal technopreneur ecosystem can provide better employment opportunities for graduates? Why?
10.	What features do you think should be included in a halal technopreneur ecosystem?
11.	What role can universities play in developing a halal technopreneur ecosystem?
12.	What recommendations do you have to promote halal technopreneurship among students and graduates?

continued on following page

Table 2. Continued

	Students
1.	**Are you familiar with the concept of halal technopreneurship?**
	Academician
1	How are educational institutions currently preparing graduates to enter the Halal technopreneur ecosystem?
2	What specific training or curriculum does your institution offer to help students understand the principles of halal business practices and entrepreneurship?
3	How do you collaborate with industry leaders to provide graduates with relevant knowledge and experience in the halal tech sector?
4	In your opinion, how can educational institutions strengthen their role in promoting halal technopreneurship among students and graduates?
5	How do you engage with potential technopreneurs to help them understand the value of combining technology with halal principles?
	Technopreneur
1	Can you tell us about your journey into halal technopreneurship? What inspired you to start your venture?
2	What challenges have you encountered in ensuring that your business adheres to halal principles, particularly in technology-driven industries?
3	In what ways does your business create employment opportunities, particularly for fresh graduates?
4	What advice would you give graduates aspiring to become halal technopreneurs?
5	How can governments, universities, and other organisations support the growth of halal technology entrepreneurs and create jobs for graduates?

Source: Authors

The analysis begins by familiarising oneself with the data by reading through all the collected texts to gain a comprehensive understanding of the content. Then, follow up with coding by developing a coding scheme based on key themes and concepts that emerge from the data. This may include categories such as 'halal technopreneur', 'employability', and 'support systems'. Lastly, the categorised data will be analysed to extract meaningful insights regarding how the halal technopreneur ecosystem can promote employment opportunities. This process involves iterative refinement of categories as new insights emerge.

The analysis primarily adopts an inductive approach, allowing themes to emerge organically from the data rather than imposing predefined categories. This flexibility is essential for exploring new dimensions of the Halal technopreneur ecosystem that may not have been previously studied

To ensure the validity and reliability of the data, the study employs triangulation, utilizing multiple data sources (academic literature, industry reports, and interviews) to corroborate the findings. Moreover, maintain a reflexive journal throughout the research process to reflect on personal biases and assumptions that may influence data interpretation

This qualitative content analysis methodology will provide a robust framework for exploring how a Halal technopreneur ecosystem can create employment opportunities for graduates. By focusing on rich qualitative data, this research aims to contribute valuable insights into the intersection of entrepreneurship and employment within the context of Halal practices.

THE HALAL INDUSTRY

The halal industry has experienced substantial global growth, propelled by the rising demand for halal products and services among Muslim consumers (Bagundang & Gallo, 2024). The halal industry encompasses various sectors, including food, pharmaceuticals, cosmetics, and finance (Utomo et al., 2021), in accordance with Islamic principles (Laldin, 2006; Bagundang & Gallo, 2024). According to the State of the Global Islamic Economy Report, the halal economy is projected to reach $4.9 trillion by 2025. In 2019, Muslim consumers spent over $2 trillion globally, as indicated by the State of the Global Islamic Economy Report 2020/2021. This data highlights the increasing prominence of the halal economy. Thus, halalpreneurs are tapping into the halal industry due to strong market demand (Elias et al., 2016; Puspaningtyas, 2021).

The global halal market is estimated to be worth USD 2.3 trillion, encompassing both the food and non-food sectors (Baharuddin et al., 2015). It is also anticipated to grow due to the increasing Muslim population worldwide (Elias et al., 2016), projected to reach 8.2 billion by 2030 (Ngui, 2015). With the global halal market, halal technopreneurs could tap into a vast market comprising over a billion Muslims worldwide. This market potential drives the need for scalable businesses that cater to the unique demands of consumers while adhering to Islamic values.

TECHNOPRENEURSHIP

The era of IR 4.0 has led to the development of entrepreneurship into a technology-based approach known as technopreneurship (Sakti et al., 2020). Technopreneurship is a subset of entrepreneurship that incorporates fundamental technological innovations and advancements. The tools employed in technopreneurship are grounded in technology (Harsono, 2013). In essence, technopreneurship merges entrepreneurship with technology (Kosasih et al., 2016).

Technopreneurs are entrepreneurs who use technology as a driving force to transform resources into goods and services. They employ technology to develop new or innovative products through a process called commercialisation. Technology is like any other tool, which can be used for good or evil (Kamdar, 2011). So, it is up to the user to fear Allah and use His gifts to please Him. However, completely cutting Muslims off from technology would stifle the growth of Islam (Kamdar, 2011). Thus, Muslims should adopt and master technology and then go on to develop more beneficial ways to utilize it. Hence, businesses' use of technology is crucial to their development and growth. Khaeriyah (2022) also asserted that for Muslims, the use of digital technology is considered a medium, not the purpose of life. Therefore, Rahmayanti et al. (2023) emphasise the importance of using digital technology for personal and societal purposes.

Technopreneurs are innovative, creative, and passionate entrepreneurs who combine technology and entrepreneurial skills to create technology-based businesses (Selladurai, 2016; Nasution et al., 2007; Suradi et al., 2017). They recognize opportunities and organize resources, transforming technology into a business model that has a significant impact on entrepreneurship (Ibrahim et al., 2015; Yudha, 2010). Whereas technopreneurship, inspired by future synthesis and re-engineering, combines technology and entrepreneurship to build new and flexible business models.

For centuries, economic growth has been driven by innovation and technology (Salman et al., 2020). Recently, advancements in information technology (IT) have offered promising solutions to drive market growth, enabling stakeholders better to meet the needs and expectations of Halal consumers (Bagundang & Gallo, 2024). Technopreneurship is a new concept in entrepreneurship that involves a combination of individuals who are intelligent, driven, creative, tech-savvy, and eager to take calculated risks. The success of technopreneurship hinges on how well everyone functions together as a team. Technopreneurship merges technology prowess, entrepreneurial talent, and skills.

In other words, technopreneurship refers to the intersection of technology and entrepreneurship, where individuals leverage technological innovations to create new business ventures. This concept emphasises the importance of technology as a core component for developing products or services that meet market demands. Technopreneurs often harness cutting-edge technologies to solve problems, improve efficiencies, or create new markets.

In the era of technological globalisation, technopreneurs have had to become authoritative in shifting societies and economies worldwide (Hoque et al., 2017). The digital era creates vast open market opportunities, enabling Muslim entrepreneur to expand their merchandise distribution channels across multiple countries rather than being limited to a single location (Rahmayanti et al., 2023). Hence, the number of students enrolled in business courses in Malaysian universities has been increasing due to the growing interest in becoming technopreneurs (Lukita et al., 2023; Abu et al., 2017). Even Star2.com stressed that technopreneurs are essential in transforming Malaysia into a knowledge-based economy. MDec, the Malaysian

Global Innovation and Creativity Centre (Magic), and Cradle Sdn. Bhd. are among the government and government-related agencies that have contributed to the start-ups of many technopreneurs by offering funding opportunities, business advisory services, and physical infrastructure (Sharon, 2018).

The internet enables technopreneurs to transcend geographical limitations and tap into international markets. This global reach increases potential sales and fosters diverse customer interactions that can inform product development. The process of digital transformation changes the traditional business world dramatically by globalising competition between organisations and enhancing customer expectations standards (Wibowo, 2021).

Technopreneurship refers to the integration of technology and entrepreneurship to create innovative solutions and business models. This approach is particularly relevant in the halal industry, where technological advancements can drive efficiency, transparency, and market reach.

TECHNOPRENEUR AND DIGITAL ERA

Technopreneurship, a fusion of technology and entrepreneurship, is pivotal in shaping the modern online business environment. This relationship is characterised by the innovative use of technology to create and expand business opportunities, particularly in the digital domain. Digital technology is a phenomenon in the 4.0 era, and its development is so rapid that everyone must adapt (Akmal & Effendi, 2023). Technopreneurship in the digital era represents a dynamic fusion of technology and entrepreneurship, driving innovation and reshaping industries.

Online business encompasses any commercial transaction conducted over the internet, including e-commerce platforms, digital services, and online marketplaces. The rise of the internet has transformed traditional business models, enabling entrepreneurs to reach global audiences with minimal overhead costs compared to brick-and-mortar establishments. Technopreneurs use technological advancements to develop products and services that can be marketed online. The internet offers a vast platform for these innovations, enabling technopreneurs to quickly and efficiently reach a global customer base.

In addition, the rise of e-commerce has revolutionised technopreneurs' operations. Online platforms allow for broader market reach, enabling businesses to connect efficiently with global customers. This shift has led to new business models that prioritise digital transactions and customer engagement through websites and mobile applications (Olusegun et al., 2019).

Technopreneurs use digital tools—such as cloud computing, social media marketing, and data analytics—to enhance operational efficiency and customer outreach. These technologies facilitate real-time inventory management, automated marketing campaigns, and personalised customer experiences, all of which are crucial for staying competitive online (Olusegun et al., 2019).

Basir et al. (2022) stated that social media, be it online or offline, is undoubtedly the most powerful source of marketing. Social media is also utilized for marketing and customer engagement by leveraging networks to increase brand awareness (Tarmizi et al., 2023). Social proofing is immensely necessary for engagement, as a majority of interested audiences are committed to digital platforms for the business. Social media can also persuade consumers to purchase goods by communicating directly and disseminating advertisements and brochures digitally through platforms like Instagram, Facebook, TikTok, and others. Digital mainstream lies in the fact that where there are more people, the business works better.

Akmal and Effendi (2023) mention that the benefits of digital ecosystems for businesses are exciting and can be a step in the right direction for business owners. Not only as a way to keep up with and adapt to the business development trends of the times but also to understand how business types are interconnected through the presence of a digital ecosystem. Unquestionably, the advancement of sophisticated technology has expanded the reach of product and service promotion. Institute of Data (2023) stated that modern digital entrepreneurs frequently utilize multiple social media platforms and e-commerce tools to market their brands, generate leads, and close sales. The most common ones include Facebook, WhatsApp, WooCommerce, Wix Ecommerce, Shopify, Amazon, WhatsApp and Instagram (Institute of Data 2023).

ISLAMIC PERSPECTIVE OF TECHNOPRENEUR

Technology is permissible, and technological advancement is desirable for Muslims (Kamdar, 2011). However, a gadget's use can render it *haram* (prohibited/forbidden) (Kamdar, 2011). Hence, the *hukm* (Islamic ruling) concerning technopreneurs involves several considerations, primarily focused on the ethical, legal, and economic implications of entrepreneurship within the framework of Islamic law. The concept of Islamic entrepreneurship, particularly in the context of technopreneurs, is grounded in the principles outlined in the Qur'an and Hadith, emphasising ethical conduct, social responsibility, and adherence to Islamic law (Shariah).

Online shopping has become prevalent due to its convenience and accessibility, allowing people to purchase goods without visiting physical stores. However, the increasing popularity of online transactions raises questions about their compatibility with Islamic principles, prompting a detailed examination. Besides, online business transactions are conducted between parties without direct interaction, which emphasises that these transactions often involve non-cash payments, which can lead to complications if not properly structured according to Islamic principles (Isnawati, 2018).

In Islam, business and entrepreneurship are generally permissible (*halal*) as long as they comply with Islamic principles. Technopreneurs must ensure that their business practices do not involve *haram* elements, such as dealing in alcohol, gambling, or usury (*riba*). Focusing on halal products and services is essential for technopreneurs operating within a halal ecosystem. Moreover, Isnawati (2018) emphasises the legal aspects of online transactions under Islamic law, highlighting that online sales can be permissible if they adhere to principles such as clarity in payment terms and the nature of the goods involved. Several conditions must be met for online sales to be considered valid: clear and immediate payment, specification of the goods being sold, defined timeframes for delivery, and availability of goods at the time of delivery. Isnawati (2018) outlines elements that render a transaction *haram*, such as ambiguity in payment or product specifications, which can lead to disputes.

Therefore, Islam emphasises ethical behaviour in all business dealings. Technopreneurs are expected to adhere to principles of honesty, transparency, and fairness. This includes ensuring their products are safe, ethically sourced, and beneficial to society. As asserted by Bakar et al. (2020), Islam views entrepreneurship, including technopreneurship, as a form of worship when conducted ethically and aligned with Shariah principles. The concept of *maslahah* (public interest) plays a crucial role in guiding technopreneurs to consider the broader impact of their businesses on the community. Hence, the integration of technology into entrepreneurship is considered a communal obligation (fardh kifayah), emphasizing the necessity for Muslims to acquire technological knowledge for the benefit of society (Bakar et al., 2020).

Islam encourages innovation and creativity as long as they align with Shariah principles. Technopreneurs are motivated to develop new technologies and solutions that improve the quality of life while adhering to Islamic guidelines. This innovation can benefit society by promoting economic growth and generating employment opportunities.

Compliance with Shariah law is paramount for technopreneurs operating in Muslim-majority countries or targeting Muslim consumers. To maintain compliance, technopreneurs may obtain certifications for halal products or services and ensure that business practices are regularly reviewed by Shariah boards or advisors.

In summary, technopreneurs' *hukm* revolves around engaging in permissible business activities while adhering to ethical standards, contributing positively to society, and ensuring compliance with Islamic law. By aligning their ventures with these principles, technopreneurs can foster sustainable economic growth while upholding Islamic values.

Despite the potential benefits, comprehensive research is lacking on the application of technology to halal entrepreneurs. Understanding the current landscape, challenges, and opportunities for leveraging technology among halal entrepreneurs is crucial for developing and implementing effective halal technopreneurship strategies.

HALAL TECHNOPRENEURSHIP ECOSYSTEM

Halal technopreneurship refers to the integration of technology, innovation, and entrepreneurship within the halal industry, ensuring that products and services comply with Islamic principles and values. Over the past few decades, this sector has experienced significant growth, driven by increasing demand from Muslim consumers, technological advancements, and the expansion of the global halal market.

In its early development, the concept of halal entrepreneurship primarily centred on traditional sectors, including food and beverages, pharmaceuticals, and modest fashion. Businesses focused on meeting basic halal compliance without significant technological integration. Certification bodies and regulatory frameworks began to emerge, laying the groundwork for the future development of the halal industry.

Then, with globalisation and digital transformations, halal businesses started leveraging technology to improve certification, traceability, and consumer engagement. Innovations such as blockchain for halal supply chain transparency, digital halal authentication, and online halal marketplaces have emerged (Bagundang & Gallo, 2024). The growth of e-commerce platforms has enabled halal products to reach a wider audience, extending beyond Muslim-majority countries. The application of social media platforms, such as Instagram, TikTok, Facebook, and WeChat, as e-commerce tools has become a trend.

Value co-creation within the marketing technology ecosystem occurs through complex interactions among organisations, customers, and technology providers. This process is facilitated by digital platforms that enable real-time engagement and personalisation (Buhalis & Sinarta, 2019). The ecosystem approach emphasises how value is created through individual technologies as well as the interactions and relationships between different components and stakeholders (Mačiulienė & Skaržauskienė, 2021). The customer experience has become increasingly sophisticated, with organisations leveraging technology to create seamless, personalised interactions across multiple touchpoints (Buhalis & Sinarta, 2019).

As time passes, halal technopreneurship is likely to become increasingly intertwined with IR 4.0 technologies. This will enhance automation, tracking, and halal compliance, making them more efficient and effective. Sustainable and ethical halal business models, driven by environmental concerns and consumer awareness, will shape the next phase of the industry. Global investment in halal startups and cross-border collaborations is expected to continue expanding, making halal technopreneurship a key player in the global digital economy.

Therefore, the halal technopreneurship ecosystem is a dynamic environment where technology, entrepreneurship, and halal principles intersect to create innovative and ethical business solutions. As the global halal economy continues to grow, encompassing industries such as food, pharmaceuticals, cosmetics, tourism, and fintech, entrepreneurs must leverage technology, government support, finance, human capital, and cultural factors to thrive. According to Isenberg's (2016) model, entrepreneurship has six domains: policy, finance, culture, support, human capital, and markets. These six domains of the entrepreneurial ecosystem are proposed to interact in ways that make entrepreneurship more likely, prevalent, and self-sustaining (Isenberg, 2016). Hence, in this study, a strong halal technopreneurship ecosystem comprises seven key components, each playing a vital role in supporting and sustaining businesses that comply with Islamic principles: government, halal certifying bodies, finance, human capital, support, technology, and culture. This ecosystem aims to foster innovation and entrepreneurship while adhering to Islamic principles.

Before proceeding with the discussion, Figure 2 illustrates the detailed analysis of key findings among the students. The majority of participants belong to the 18-24 age group, indicating a younger demographic interested in halal technopreneurship, in which the participants are more female than male. Most respondents are familiar with the concept of halal technopreneurship, indicating moderate awareness. All five participants among students have a strong belief that halal technopreneurship can create job opportunities. Although the largest segment remains uncertain, there is notable interest in pursuing a career in this field. There is also a significant number of participants who expressed willingness to participate in training programmes related to halal technopreneurship.

Figure 2. Key Findings of Responses among Students

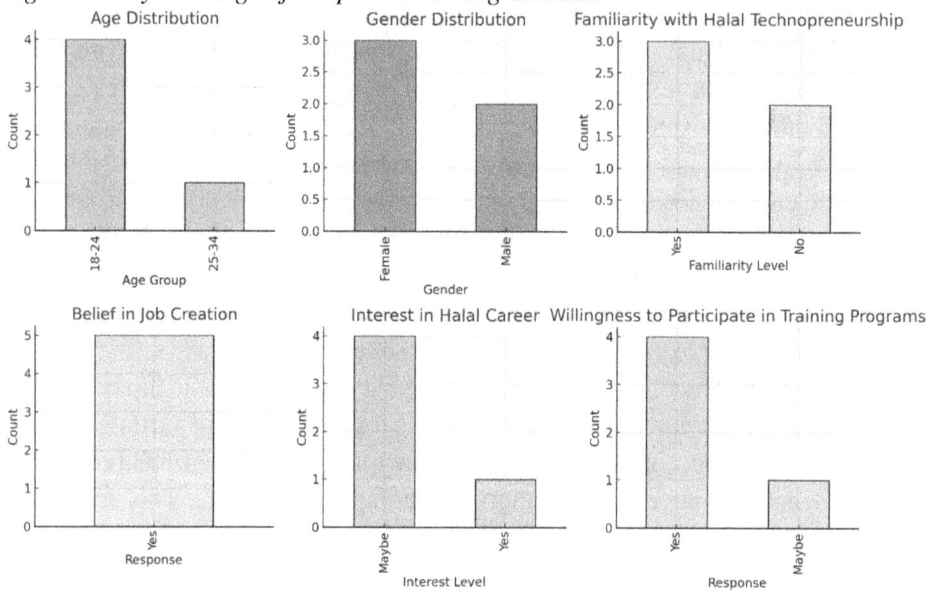

Figure 3 illustrates the word clouds, which highlight the most frequently mentioned themes in the responses. The common motivators for the responses among students include alignment with personal values, financial opportunities, societal development and innovation. The respondents also highlighted a lack of mentorship, insufficient funding, and limited job opportunities as key challenges. Then, provide suggestions focusing on awareness campaigns for halal technopreneurship through social media, workshops and seminars, specialised courses, mentorship programs, and industry collaboration, partnering with both established industries and aspiring entrepreneurs.

Figure 3. Word Clouds of Data Analysis

The data analysis presented in Figures 2 and 3 suggests that it is essential for the government to establish a halal technopreneurship ecosystem to encourage the young generation to venture into halal technopreneurship. Figure 4 illustrates the ecosystem of halal technopreneurs. A robust Halal technopreneurship ecosystem necessitates a synergistic relationship among government, halal certifying bodies, financial institutions, educational institutions, business accelerators, technology providers, and the cultural sector. With the right support, halal technopreneurs can thrive locally and expand globally.

Figure 4. Halal Technopreneur Ecosystem

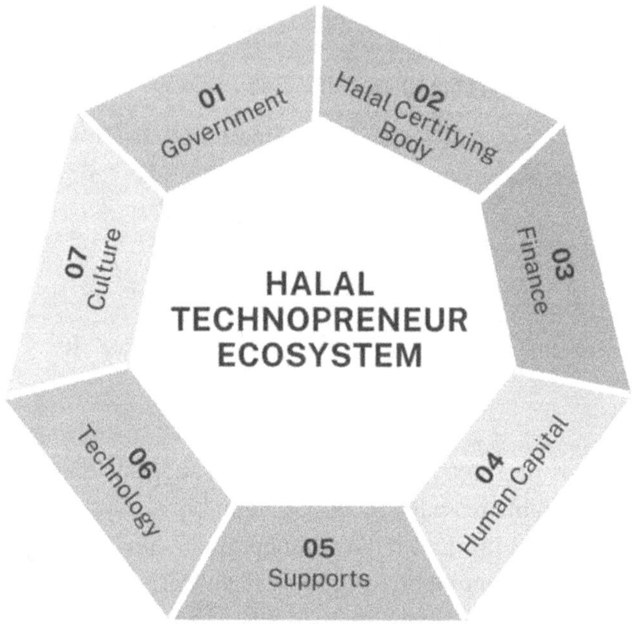

Government

The role of government in fostering a halal technopreneurship ecosystem is crucial through regulations, funding, policy support, and public-private collaborations. The government plays a crucial role in establishing a supportive regulatory environment. This includes developing policies that encourage halal technopreneurship and setting standards to ensure products and services meet halal requirements. Such an effort could involve creating specific support and incentives for halal tech startups by providing grants and regulatory support to encourage entrepreneurs in the halal sector. Perhaps the government can also streamline the certification process for halal products and invest in infrastructure that supports the growth of the halal industry in both local and international markets. The government should also establish frameworks to support halal businesses, ensuring compliance with Shariah laws and international standards.

Venkataraman (2004) stated that one of the important roles of the government was to create the intangible infrastructure needed to enhance the culture of technology entrepreneurship. Svirina et al. (2017) stated that the entrepreneurial ecosystem has a positive influence on the growth of technopreneurial startups in all types of environments. The term "technopreneurial infrastructure" used in this study is part of a broader concept of technopreneurial activity. Therefore, technopreneurial infrastructure refers to the existing facilities and services in a specific geographic area that facilitate the establishment of new businesses. They also promote the growth and development of small enterprises.

Infrastructure development is a sector that should be the focus of creating technopreneurs in the future. Entrepreneurial infrastructure helps people who want to start their own digital businesses, small and medium-sized businesses that are growing, and small businesses that are already in existence in four ways: (1) by helping them with tasks that they need to do; (2) by giving them physical or financial resources; (3) by providing them information; and finally, by giving them knowledge. Infrastructure is crucial for the community's economic growth and development because it can influence the value of technopreneurship activities in its area by modifying specific aspects of the technopreneurship infrastructure (Bull & Winter, 1991).

T1 reveals a lack of awareness about specific government policies or incentives that support halal technopreneurship. The finding suggests a potential gap in government support that could be filled to foster growth in this sector. Therefore, the government should modify policies to facilitate closer collaboration between universities, businesses, and halal regulatory bodies. Such collaboration will help bridge the gap between what is taught in schools and what is needed in the business world. Both governments and policymakers can also utilise the findings from research to develop policies and programs to improve the country's halal markets (Sulaiman et al., 2023).

Halal Certifying Body

Halal certifying bodies (HCBs) in the halal technopreneur ecosystem play a crucial role in ensuring that products, services, and technologies developed within the ecosystem comply with Shariah. The HCB is an organisation authorised to assess and verify that products, services, and processes comply with Islamic dietary and ethical standards (Al-Mahmood & Fraser, 2023). The HCB also serves as an authority to verify and authenticate that business practices, technologies, and innovations comply with the principles of Halal, which means "permissible" or "lawful" in Islam. These bodies ensure that all types of businesses adhere to halal guidelines, encompassing aspects such as ingredient sourcing, production, hygiene, and logistics.

The HCB should ensure that the products or services (e.g., food, software, healthcare, fintech solutions) align with Islamic principles. This includes ensuring there is no involvement in *haram* activities, such as consuming alcohol, participating in gambling, or engaging in unethical practices. For tech products, namely apps, software, and platforms, the HCB should assess whether the product adheres to

Islamic ethical standards. For instance, in e-commerce, the platform must refrain from selling haram products, and for financial services, the business must adhere to Islamic finance principles, such as avoiding *riba*.

To date, there are no comprehensive halal standards or guidelines, particularly for halal technopreneurs or online-based businesses. Therefore, the HCB should set clear guidelines for businesses to follow. These could involve procedures for obtaining Halal certification, audits, and maintaining compliance with Shariah principles in all operations. Regular audits ensure ongoing compliance. This may involve reviewing financial practices, product sourcing, supply chains, or services to ensure they meet Halal standards.

Halal assurance refers to the systematic approach adopted by businesses to maintain halal integrity throughout the supply chain. It involves compliance with halal certification standards, regular audits, staff training, and halal traceability systems. In the halal technopreneur ecosystem, halal assurance plays a vital role in building consumer trust, ensuring product credibility, and facilitating market expansion, especially in the global halal economy. By integrating digital solutions such as blockchain, AI, and IoT, halal technopreneurs enhance transparency and efficiency in halal certification and monitoring.

Table 3 tabulated the key halal standards that halal technopreneurs must comply with to ensure their products, services and business models align with Shariah. By integrating these key halal standards, halal technopreneurs can enhance credibility, expand into the global halal market, and gain consumer trust.

Table 3. Key Halal Standard for Halal Technopreneurs

No	Key Components	Detail
1	Halal Certification and Standards	• Must comply with the halal standards, guidelines, and halal assurance systems employed by respected countries. For instance, in Brunei, halal technopreneurs should comply with the PBD24:2007 Halal Food Standards. • Products and services must be free from *haram* elements
2	Shariah-Compliant Business Practices	• Business transactions must avoid *riba*, *gharar* (uncertainty), and *maysir* (gambling). • Should adopt Islamic fintech solutions, such as Shariah-compliant payment gateways and blockchain-based halal traceability. • Follow transparent and fair business practices, ensuring ethical advertising and marketing.
3	Halal Digital and E-Commerce Standards	• Utilize blockchain to maintain the integrity of halal supply chains, facilitate halal authentication, and prevent fraud. • Implement AI-driven halal verification and monitoring systems. • Ensure Shariah-compliant online platforms in online transactions and marketplace models. • Ensure advertising and digital marketing do not include deceptive or unethical content.
4	Halal Supply Chain & Logistics	• Adhere to halal logistics standards for transportation, warehousing, and retail operations to prevent any form of contamination. • Ensure proper halal certification of suppliers, manufacturers, and distributors. • Implement a halal cold chain management system to prevent contamination, particularly in food products. • Utilize traceability systems for tracking halal authenticity.

Finance

Financial access remains a key challenge for aspiring halal technopreneurs. Past studies have revealed that financial barriers have an advanced impact on innovation for young firms, as well as SMEs (Medina & Rufín, 2009). Huge organisations or companies that are divisions of a business group are less likely to experience these issues, and due to their size, it is not difficult to set up collateral funds within the group. Financial barriers are primarily crucial for technopreneurship involving narrative technologies and products (Hernández-Espallardo & Delgado-Ballester, 2009).

T1 believes that graduates transitioning into halal technopreneurship require financial resources, such as funding, to establish and grow their ventures successfully. Basir et al. (2022) also emphasized that access to financial and business funds plays a crucial role in launching a new business. Access to funding is essential for any entrepreneur. In the halal tech space, this includes Islamic finance options. There is an emphasis on maintaining halal integrity in business practices. Hence, institutions need to guide the students on how to attract halal investors and ethical funding sources. A1 mentions that *'UNISSA offers dedicated halal entrepreneurship courses that cover Islamic business ethics, focusing on maintaining halal integrity throughout the value chain – from production to marketing – while avoiding unethical practices, such as deceit for profit.'* This curriculum highlights the significance of halal technopreneurship not only as a religious obligation but also as a sustainable business practice aligned with Islamic principles. As a result of operationalising these principles, the halal technopreneurship ecosystem should have Islamic funding options available from local banks, such as partnership-based financing models (e.g., *Mudarabah* and *Musharakah*) rather than debt-based financing.

In Brunei, numerous financial support mechanisms are available to assist businesses, particularly micro, small, and medium-sized enterprises (MSMEs). These initiatives are designed to foster entrepreneurship, encourage innovation, and support economic diversification. Table 4 shows some key financial support options available in Brunei. By leveraging this financial support mechanism, businesses in Brunei can access the necessary resources to grow, innovate, and contribute to the nation's economic development.

Table 4. List of Financial Support in Brunei

No	Type	Funding Assistance	Amount Offered (BND)	Organisation
1	Grants	Co-Matching Scheme		DARe
2		Starting up Category	Up to BND10,000	
3		Expansion Category	Up to BND20,000	
4		Small Grants Programme	Rolling basis of up to BND30,000	U.S. Embassy
5		*Skim Pembiayaan Kebajikan* (Welfare Financing Scheme)	Disclosed upon engagement	Yayasan Sultan Haji Hassanal Bolkiah
6		*Geran Belia Membangun* (Youth Development Grant)	Up to BND2,000	Ministry of Home Affairs
7		"Penjana" Productivity and Efficiency Joint-Funding for Digital Adoption	Up to BND5,000	Authority for Info-Communications Technology Industry (AiTi)
8		*Agihan Zakat Modal Berusaha & Peralatan Berniaga*	Amount varies by the cost of the item	Ministry of Religious Affairs
9		Financial Support	Disclosed upon engagement	Ministry of Culture Youth and Sports

continued on following page

Table 4. Continued

No	Type	Funding Assistance	Amount Offered (BND)	Organisation
10	Cash Prize Competitions	Business Awards	First Place: BND5,000 Second Place: BND2,000	Shell LiveWIRE Brunei
11		Hackhathon	First Place: BND2,000 Second Place: BND1,500 Third Place: BND1,000	
12		Brunei ICT Awards (BICTA)	Between BND1,000 - BND10,000 (depending on the category	Ministry of Transport and Infocommunications (MTIC), AITI and InfoCom Federation of Brunei (IFB)
13	Banking Facilities	Financing	To be disclosed upon engagement	Baiduri Bank
14		SME Working Capital		
15		SME Installment Loan		
16		SME Indent Financing		
17		SME Account Receivables Financing		
18		SME Property Financing		
19		SME Fully Cash Secured Facility		
20		Naqad Financing	To be disclosed upon engagement	Bank Islam Brunei Darussalam (BIBD)
21		Business Instalment Loan	To be disclosed upon engagement	Standard Chartered Bank (SCB)
22		Asset Financing – Murabaha	Up to BND750,000	Bank Usahawan
23		Working Capital Financing – Tawarruq	Up to BND500,000	

Source: Ministry of Finance and Economy (n.d.); Darussalam Enterprise (n.d.)

Human Capital

Thus, educational institutions, from primary to tertiary levels, should emphasise developing these skills in preparation for IR 4.0. In facing IR4.0, the lack of the aforementioned necessary skilled labour would hinder the development of Industry 4.0 within the country. Educational institutions at all levels should shift their focus to producing a new type of workforce that has an innovative creative mindset and respectable digital literacy, i.e., obtaining an extensive understanding of ICT and computing and being equipped with soft skills to cater to the demand for highly skilled labour in IR4.0 (Manda & Backhouse, 2017).

A1 also mentioned that *educational institutions are leveraging existing infrastructure and technology to prepare graduates while acknowledging inherent limitations. For example, they use free software and social media tools responsibly, ensuring alignment with halal principles. However, technopreneurship as a concept remains relatively new, requiring academic staff to be well-versed in both entrepreneurship and technology — an area where capacity building is often needed.*

Therefore, the academic curriculum must be redesigned to emphasise the instigation of soft skills, i.e., leadership skills, social skills, and intercultural skills, as well as broad and better-structured knowledge that captures the basic knowledge of the new industrial revolution, as these are believed to be necessary in the advancement of Industry 4.0 (Baygin et al., 2016; Motyl et al., 2017). T1 suggests that graduates need a combination of business management, digital marketing, knowledge of the halal industry, financial literacy, and innovation skills to succeed in this ecosystem. Therefore, educational institutions and training programs can focus on developing these skills to prepare graduates for careers in halal technology entrepreneurship.

Brunei's universities, Universiti Brunei Darussalam (UBD), Universiti Islam Sultan Sharif Ali (UNISSA), and Universiti Teknologi Brunei (UTB), have established dedicated hubs and programs to foster entrepreneurship among students and alumni. The hubs and programs are tabulated in Table 5. These hubs collectively contribute to Brunei's entrepreneurial ecosystem by providing training, mentorship, resources, and industry collaborations tailored to foster innovation and economic growth.

Table 5. Entrepreneurs Hubs and Programs in Brunei Universities

No	University	Hubs/Programs	Details	Source
1	UBD	Industry Engagement and Enterprise Development (IEED)	fosters collaboration between academia and industry. It provides resources such as guidebooks for incubation and venture labs to cultivate entrepreneurial skills among students	Ihsan (2024)
2		UBD Startup Centre (USC)	Serves as a hub for innovation and entrepreneurship, supported by partnerships like the Memorandum of Understanding with BruIPO to enhance intellectual property development and entrepreneurship education	Ihsan (2023)
3		Entrepreneurship Major	Offered by the UBD School of Business and Economics (UBDSBE), this four-year degree program is designed to equip students with the skills to create innovative ventures and manage growth in existing organizations. It emphasizes practical skills and entrepreneurial thinking to prepare graduates for dynamic economic environments.	UBDSBE (n.d.)
4	UNISSA	Entrepreneurship Hub (eHub)	Operating under the Assistant Rector's Office (Student and Alumni Affairs), eHub aims to instill entrepreneurial mindsets and competencies among students and alumni. It offers various support mechanisms, including activities, programs, workshops, and training focused on cultivating business skills and fostering an entrepreneurial environment	UNISSA (n.d.)
5	UTB	UTB Experiences PLUS	UTB focuses on hands-on learning and industry-based programs through initiatives like ExperiencePLUS, which includes industrial training and incubation projects embedded in academic curricula	UTB (n.d.)

In the development of the digital era, many innovative young technopreneurs have emerged (Wibowo et al., 2022). It is anticipated that technology and digitalization-driven industries will emerge as significant growth engines, necessitating the recruitment of skilled human resources and competitive technopreneurs. This opportunity can be leveraged by Generation Z to optimise creativity and innovation, serve as an inspiration, and explore their potential to enhance knowledge and skills. There are numerous promising digital businesses due to the demographic advantages.

Additionally, Halal science programs produce human capital and skilled workers to help drive economic growth (Valero & Reenen, 2019). Yet, education should shift from content-driven and knowledge-orientated to future-driven, employability-orientated, and growth-focused. The education ecosystem needs to become more outcome-focused and offer experiential learning opportunities.

Support

Small enterprises and businesspeople require facilitative resources to run their business activities effectively. Wibowo et al. (2022) stated that infrastructure support networks can be effective if there are sufficient physical facilities and installations, as well as ample space for potential business actors (such as incubators) and growth-oriented businesses (like those in industrial estates), or sufficient sources of capital (like venture capital firms). Technopreneurial infrastructure is also considered one of the most important things that can help digital businesses start up and small businesses grow in the region.

As stated by A1, *'there is a clear divide that often exists between academic learning and industry practices, making collaboration essential. Stakeholders across academia, industry, and government must actively contribute to bridging the gap. For instance, during my time in Australia, we implemented Work-Integrated Learning (WIL), where students worked on real industry projects as consultants. Such initiatives enable students to gain firsthand exposure to industry expectations, particularly in the halal tech sector, while understanding practical applications of their knowledge.*

The statement highlights a weak link between industry and universities, leading to a shortage of hands-on experience for graduates. Therefore, schools need to employ the same methods to ensure that their graduates are prepared for the workforce and can easily integrate into the Halal technopreneur ecosystem. Such an approach will help solve the common problem of skill gaps between academia and the workplace. Institutions should strive to bridge the academic and industry gaps through guest lecturers and industry talks, and these efforts should translate into actionable skills. T1 also believes that mentorship, business training, and networking opportunities are crucial for graduates entering the halal technopreneur space.

As a recommendation, stakeholders related to this issue should develop incubation programs, such as entrepreneurship hubs and mentorship programs, to help students transition into halal technopreneurship. There are several key programmes and initiatives designed to foster innovation and economic growth in Brunei, including the Industry Business Academy (IBA), the DARe Business Bootcamp Programme, the Brunei Mentors for Entrepreneurs Network (BMEN), the iCentre Incubation Programme, and the energy incubation Programme (DARe, n.d.).

Technology

Leveraging technology to enhance product verification, supply chain transparency, and customer engagement can drive growth in halal technopreneurship. Developing and emerging countries, such as China, that heavily rely on manufacturing industries, are shifting towards investing more in technologies that will catalyse their production development level for Industry 4.0 (Bahrin et al., 2016; Berawi, 2018).

The advancement of technologies in IR4.0 will create new business models, resulting in a shift in job patterns and the emergence of new employment opportunities (Rajnai & Kocsis, 2017). However, the processes and results of the developed business units can be optimised by utilising the latest appropriate technology in business development based on an established entrepreneurial spirit. It is undeniable that technopreneurs play a crucial role in generating the growth of the national economy, as they accelerate the spread and adoption of innovative ideas of the younger generation (Naudé, 2010).

The marketing technology ecosystem is a critical and rapidly evolving field that reflects the profound impact of digital transformations on marketing practices and consumer behaviour. Masrianto et al. (2022) highlight the fact that the convergence of information technology, media, and telecommunications has significantly altered consumer behaviour regarding the search for, acquisition, processing, and response to company information and services. The significance of this ecosystem lies in its ability to enhance a company's digital marketing capabilities, which are crucial for maintaining competitiveness. Masrianto et al. (2024) emphasize the inevitability of marketing transformations to enhance companies' performance in the digital era.

Culture

Isenberg (2016) asserts that social media, published case studies, and university classes might directly stimulate entrepreneurship. Thus, a paradigm shift in social mindset is needed to provide equal access to opportunities for both males and females in technological education and technical training. Parents and educators need to be guided to value technopreneurship as a viable career choice for the young generation, on par with other professions, and encourage children to pursue entrepreneurial endeavours. Proactive approaches, such as special upskilling and reskilling programmes, are to be held targeting young females, to support the acquiring of modern technical know-how.

In the economic sector, the number of unemployed people continues to increase year over year due to a lack of jobs, while the number of secondary and tertiary education graduates is ever-growing (Permana et al., 2020). Layoffs and the bankruptcy of several companies have exacerbated this situation. The problem of unemployment can be addressed if the state can provide as many jobs as possible. However, it appears unlikely that this goal will be realised quickly, given the numerous constraints in both the economy and human resources. In light of this situation, an immediate solution is necessary to enhance education and foster an entrepreneurial spirit among people. Such goals can be achieved through an educational model that emphasises knowledge and takes emotional intelligence into account.

Students should understand the role of entrepreneurship as the foundation for their nation's future. So, through the education they control, they can create jobs rather than increasing the number of job seekers or even contributing to unemployment after graduation from a university. To the greatest extent possible, students are encouraged to think creatively about business opportunities in society and dare to start their own businesses. Do not be apathetic because it is difficult to find a job after applying everywhere, and the results are always nil. They forget they are entrepreneurs as well as coworkers and civil servants.

IMPACT OF EMPLOYMENT OPPORTUNITIES

The global unemployment crisis, particularly among recent graduates, represents a critical economic and social challenge. In many countries, the youth unemployment rate remains stubbornly high, exacerbating economic instability and social discontent. However, unemployment is not a new issue, as already discussed in Teichler's (1996) study. Teichler (1996) emphasises that there are three primary issues related to overeducation and the mismatch between demand and supply: the broad spectrum of higher education and employment opportunities, the rise in graduate unemployment, and the associated risks of employment. Cheong and Lawrey's (2009) study on unemployment issues among registered job seekers, both graduates and non-graduates, showed that skills and job goals were not always compatible. There was also a big gap between what people expected from their jobs and what they actually had to do.

Brunei has not escaped this issue (Musa & Idris, 2020). In Brunei, one of the greatest challenges is ensuring stable employment opportunities for university graduates upon completion of their studies (Deuraseh et al., 2022). According to JobCentre Brunei, in 2021, the unemployment rate among university graduates remained high, and Universiti Islam Sultan Sharif Ali (UNISSA) achieved a ranking of third, with a total of 237 graduates. (Raffi et al. 2023). The Department of Statistics (2024) reported that the unemployment rate in 2023 was 5.1 percent. Of the total population aged 18 and over, approximately 11,700 individuals were unemployed and actively seeking work, comprising 7,000 males (59.6%) and 4,700 females (40.4%) (Department of Statistics, 2024).

Furthermore, with the advent of the Industrial Revolution 4.0, a shift in the job market is anticipated (Sait & Anshari, 2021). This paradigm shift results in employees losing their jobs, leading to an increase in unemployment. Only a particular pool of human capital is able to retain its position because it possesses the necessary skills to remain relevant in the digital age (de Pablos, 2003). Furthermore, given the ongoing unemployment challenges in Brunei, academia has raised a significant question: how will developing countries remain relevant in the near future and will IR4.0 further exacerbate unemployment among their labour force? (Sait & Anshari, 2021). Brunei's long-term national development plan, "Wawasan 2035", aims to ensure the nation's relevance in the future, with three key outcomes: for the population to be highly educated, skilled, and accomplished; to enjoy a high quality of life; and for the country to achieve a dynamic and sustainable economy. Thus, related stakeholders, such as universities, should provide relevant technology and entrepreneurship courses to prepare young people for the digital era and support the development of halal technopreneurs.

Furthermore, the Ministry of Higher Education Malaysia, under the Malaysian Higher Education Development Plan 2015-2025, has implemented a few strategies targeted to ensure that 15% of students become entrepreneurs during their studies by the year 2020 and 5% choose entrepreneurship as their career when they graduate (Salman et al., 2020). Entrepreneurship education for students at higher education institutions may instil interest and enhance the likelihood of students pursuing entrepreneurship. Entrepreneurship education is a planned model that changes knowledge, skills, and attitudes through learning experiences (Othman & Ishak, 2011). Entrepreneurship education can instil in individuals the tendency to pursue a business career.

Siyanbola et al. (2011) identified two key features of technopreneurship: high-potential opportunity and technology-intensive opportunity. According to a study by Alvarez and Barney (2007), entrepreneurs who base their businesses on technology are able to identify and create new business opportunities and are willing to pursue them even when the market is uncertain or facing other challenges. The abilities and willingness of these entrepreneurs to take action significantly impact business activities not only within their own business units and industries but also across the entire economy. Furthermore, Jangcik et al. (2022) asserted that educators must enhance students' cognitive, affective, and psychomotor skills to foster greater student interest in becoming technopreneurs and help reduce a country's unemployment rate.

Clearly, numerous factors drive unemployment among graduates, including a mismatch between academic qualifications and job market demands, insufficient practical experience, and a lack of entrepreneurial opportunities. The traditional employment model often fails to absorb the influx of new graduates, necessitating innovative solutions to bridge the gap between education and employment. Thus, the ecosystem is expected to create new job opportunities for graduates by encouraging the establishment of halal tech start-ups and expanding existing businesses. Furthermore, by creating new markets and generating job opportunities, technopreneurs make a significant contribution to economic growth. Their ventures often stimulate demand for innovative solutions, driving consumption and enhancing overall economic activity (Wisdom, 2023).

Thus, IR 4.0 opens the flow of trade in goods and services, as well as professional human resources. This situation presents a challenge for vocational education institutions to produce students who are ready to compete (Rojko, 2017). Hence, institutions must be able to create graduates with an entrepreneurial and technopreneur spirit (Sakti et al., 2020). Institutions play a crucial role in preparing their graduates to succeed in the digital era.

In Indonesia, to prepare graduates for IR4.0, Indonesian vocational education—even vocational high schools, universities, and other vocational institutions—must focus on preparing quality human resources to compete in this era of Industrial Revolution 4.0. Indonesia can prepare quality human resources through vocational education, as the philosophy of vocational education is designed to meet the needs of the community and industry in the locations where vocational education is offered (Usman & Raharjo, 2012). The orientation of vocational education should be aimed at achieving success in terms of output or graduation, which can meet the needs of the labour market (Sakti et al., 2020). Furthermore, the education program's success is completely orientated towards the quality of its graduates in the business and industrial worlds (Ganefri, 2013).

However, many respondents are either unfamiliar or moderately familiar with halal technopreneurship, suggesting a gap in awareness and education. Additionally, a significant portion of informants are both familiar (3 participants) and unfamiliar (2 participants) with halal technopreneurship, and they believe it can create job opportunities. Hence, universities should offer structured programs focusing on halal entrepreneurship, as Wibowo et al. (2022) suggest that the success of technopreneurs in running their businesses can be achieved when they possess adequate knowledge. Entrepreneurial skills serve as a pathway for technopreneurs to achieve success and foster innovative thinking, thereby enhancing an organisation's ability to acquire the necessary skills and understand future business outcomes (Sweeny, 2019).

Training in concepts and skills directly applicable to business ventures is another way to acquire this technopreneurial knowledge (Hidayat et al., 2019). Training and courses for students are important organisational activities because of their impact on productivity when they enter the workforce. A facility becomes a component of the technopreneurial infrastructure when it facilitates the transfer of knowledge and expertise. Training programs and courses provide students with the opportunity to grow and advance in their future careers, whether within or outside the organisation. The implementation of this training aims to enhance the current and future performance of students by improving their ability to perform their duties effectively, thereby enabling the organization to achieve its objectives.

Not all participants (S1-S5) have taken specific courses on halal technopreneurship, suggesting a gap in educational offerings. Therefore, universities need to integrate the halal technopreneurship concepts into broader educational curricula to enhance knowledge and skills among students. The establishment of the Halalan Thayyiban Research Centre (HTRC) in 2017 was a response to an excerpt from His Majesty's 2016 convocation speech at UNISSA. The HTRC has offered several courses for undergraduate and postgraduate students, yet not one module teaches technopreneurship. The courses are available in halal science, in which the students are expected to understand that halal discipline comprises many aspects of Muslims' daily lives, including halal food, halal education, halal tourism, halal finance, halal logistics, halal cosmetics, halal pharmaceuticals, and many more that are associated with the application of science and technology in this contemporary era.

CONCLUSION

The rise of IR 4.0 and the growing importance of the halal industry offer unique opportunities for halal technopreneurs. While technopreneurship offers a promising path for economic growth, job creation, and technological advancement, various challenges must be addressed to nurture a successful halal technopreneurship ecosystem.

One of the major problems is the inconsistency in Halal certification standards, which creates obstacles for businesses trying to expand internationally. Furthermore, many Halal technopreneurs face financial constraints due to limited funding options and low investor confidence. The slow adoption of emerging technologies, like blockchain and artificial intelligence, further hinders innovation and efficiency within the ecosystem. Additionally, the quality of products and skills developed by students in higher education often falls short of industry standards, reducing their competitiveness and employability.

To address these problems, several strategic recommendations are proposed. Firstly, harmonising Halal certification standards across regions will facilitate easier market entry and expansion. Governments and regulatory bodies should collaborate to create unified guidelines that ensure compliance and build consumer trust. Secondly, financial institutions and investors should be encouraged to develop specialised funding programs tailored for Halal technopreneurs. This could include venture capital initiatives, grants, and Islamic financing options. Lastly, fostering digital transformation through training programs and incentives for technology adoption can significantly enhance operational efficiency and global competitiveness.

Hence, developing a Halal Technopreneur Ecosystem Framework represents a strategic and innovative strategy to address the high unemployment rates among graduates. This framework aims to create meaningful jobs, enhance economic growth, and cultivate an environment that supports entrepreneurs by leveraging the expanding halal industry and the potential of technopreneurs. Through careful research, stakeholder engagement, and iterative refinement, this study has the potential to significantly impact both the halal industry and the broader economic landscape.

The Halal Technopreneur Ecosystem distinguishes itself through the integration of specific components that ensure adherence to Shariah, influencing the interactions within the ecosystem. Unlike conventional ecosystems, this framework requires a strong interplay among the Government (01), Halal Certifying Body (02), Finance (03), Human Capital (04), Support (05), Technology (06), and Culture (07). This halal technopreneur ecosystem emphasizes compliance with Shariah, which governs not only the production and consumption of goods but also the processes involved in logistics, finance, and certification. The HCB plays a crucial role in ensuring products, services, and processes align with halal standards, which subsequently impacts financing decisions, technological development, and cultural considerations. Government regulations and support mechanisms must also be tailored to facilitate compliance with halal standards. This ecosystem promotes ethical and Shariah-compliant innovation and entrepreneurship, distinguishing it from conventional systems that prioritize profit maximization without necessarily considering ethical or religious principles.

Acknowledgements

The authors extend their utmost gratitude to all participants for their time and invaluable insights, which contributed to this study.

REFERENCES

Ahmed, H. M. (2025). Halal-Preneurship: Halal Tech Building a Digital Halal Ecosystem. Retrieved Mar 30, 2025, from The Halal Times: https://www.halaltimes.com/halal-preneurship-halal-tech-building-a-digital-halal-ecosystem/

Akmal, & Effendi, A. (2023). Business Strategy in the Halal Industry (The Use of Digital Ecosystems in Introducing Indonesia as The World's Halal Industry). *International Journal of Economics, Business and Innovation Research, 2*(4), 14-30.

Al-Mahmood, O. A., & Fraser, A. M. (2023). Perceived Challenges in Implementing Halal Standards by Halal Certifying Bodies in the United States. *PLoS One, 18*(8), e0290774. DOI: 10.1371/journal.pone.0290774 PMID: 37651404

Alvarez, S., & Barney, J. (2007). Discovery and Creation: Alternative Theories of Entrepreneurial Action. *Strategic Entrepreneurship Journal, 1*(1-2), 11–26. DOI: 10.1002/sej.4

Aryanti, L., Rachmat, S. R., Nurniwati, E., & Kristiadi, D. (2022). Knowledge Management Strengthening Character of Entrepreneurs Students Department of Technopreneur at School of Technopreneur Nusantara. *International Journal of Information System and Technology, 6*(4), 462–468. DOI: 10.30645/ijistech.v6i4.262

Bagundang, E., & Gallo, M. (2024). Technological Advancements in Halal Ecosystem: Harnessing Information Technology for Certification and Traceability. *International Journal for Multidisciplinary Research, 6*(2), 1–8.

Baharuddin, K., Kassim, N. A., Nordin, S., & Buyong, S. (2015). Understanding the Halal Concept and the Importance of Information on Halal Food Business Needed by Potential Malaysian Entrepreneurs. *International Journal of Academic Research in Business & Social Sciences, 5*(2), 170–180. DOI: 10.6007/IJARBSS/v5-i2/1476

Bahrin, M. A. K., Othman, M. F., Azli, N. H. N., & Talib, M. F. (2016). Industry 4.0: A review on industrial automation and robotic. Jurnal Teknologi, 78(6–13), 137–143.

Bakar, M.A., Bakar, A.A., Noor, A.M., & Mohamad, N.M. (2020). Islamic Technopreneurship in the Midst of Covid-19 Pandemic: A Malaysia Review, *Palarch's Journal of Archaeology of Egypt/Egyptology, 17*(9): 3005 – 3024.

Barbe, D., Magids, S., & Thornton, K. (2003). Holistic Approach for Technology Entrepreneurship Education in Engineering. *Proceedings - Frontiers in Education Conference, FIE* (pp. T2D1 - T2D6). Institute of Electrical and Electronics Engineers Inc. DOI: 10.1109/FIE.2003.1263299

Basir, K., Raffi, R., & Marmaya, N. (2022). Enhancing Young Graduates' Intention towards Halal Entrepreneurship Development in Brunei Darussalam: A Case of Universiti Islam Sultan Sharif Ali. *Proceedings Borneo Islamic International Conference*, 168-179.

Berawi, M. A. (2018). Utilizing Big Data in Industry 4.0: Managing Competitive Advantages and Business Ethics. *International Journal of Technology*, *3*(1), 430–433. DOI: 10.14716/ijtech.v9i3.1948

Buhalis, D., & Sinarta, Y. (2019). Real-time co-creation and nowness service: lessons from tourism and hospitality. *Real-time co-creation and nowness service: lessons from tourism and hospitality*, *36*(5), 563-582. DOI: 10.1080/10548408.2019.1592059

Cheong, D., & Lawrey, R. (2009). *A Study of Unemployment Issues among Registered Job Seekers in Brunei Darussalam*. The Centre for Strategic and Policy Studies.

Darajah, M., & Kassim, U. (2019). The Factors Influence University Students Decision in Selecting Their Career as A Technopreneur in Malaysia. *International Journal of Social Science Research*, *1*(2), 76–86.

Darussalam Enterprise. (n.d.). Available Funding Options in Brunei. Retrieved on Mar 30, 2025 from DARe: https://www.dare.gov.bn/_files/ugd/06a3d1_456883dabef7 4dfa830dbf1d44100710.pdf

de Pablos, P. (2003). Intellectual Capital Reporting in Spain: A Comparative View. *Journal of Intellectual Capital*, *4*(1), 61–81. DOI: 10.1108/14691930310455397

Department of Statistics. (2024). *Labour Force Survey 2023*. Ministry of Finance and Economy.

Deuraseh, N., Hashim, N., Raffi, R., & Rosli, N. (2022). Halal Food Producer as an Alternative Employment Job for Halal Science Graduates in Brunei Darussalam. *Journal of Halal Science and Technology*, *1*(1), 55–66. DOI: 10.59202/jhst.v1i1.455

Elias, E. M., Othman, S., Yaacob, N., & Saifudin, A. (2016). A Study of Halal Awareness and Knowledge among Entrepreneur Undergraduates. *International Journal of Supply Chain Management*, *5*(3), 147–152.

Ganefri, G. (2013). The Development of Production-Based Learning Approach to Entrepreneurial Spirit for Engineering Students. *Asian Social Science*, *9*(12), 162–167. DOI: 10.5539/ass.v9n12p162

Harsono, A. (2013). Building Technopreneurship For Next Generation: How The Benefits Of Techno- Entrepreneurship Education Affect Career Intentions of College Students. *Jurnal Ilmiah Sistem Informasi dan Teknik Informatika, 3*(1), 31-40.

Hernández-Espallardo, M., & Delgado-Ballester, E. (2009). Product Innovation in Small Manufacturers, Market Orientation and the Industry's Five Competitive Forces: Empirical Evidence from Spain. *European Journal of Innovation Management*, *12*(4), 470–491. DOI: 10.1108/14601060910996927

Hidayat, H., Tamin, B., Herawati, S., Khairul, K., & Syahmaidi, E. (2019). The contribution of technopreneurship scientific learning and learning readiness towards the entrepreneurship learning outcomes in higher vocational education. *Jurnal Pendidikan Vokasi*, *9*(1), 21–32. DOI: 10.21831/jpv.v9i1.20466

Hoque, A., Awang, Z., & Siddiqui, B. (2017). Technopreneurial Intention among University Students of Business Courses in Malaysia: A Structural Equation Modeling. *International Journal of Entrepreneurship and Small & Medium Enterprise*, *4*, 1–16.

Ibrahim, M. A., Malek, J. A., & Salman, A. (2015). Evaluating the Development of Technopreneurs: A Case Study of PPR Telecenter Jalan Jelatek. *Journal of Social Sciences and Humanities*, *2*, 157–161.

Ihsan. (2023). UBD, BruIPO Sign MoU. Retrieved on 30 Mar, 2025, from UBD: https://ubd.edu.bn/2023/03/08/ubd-bruipo-sign-mou/

Ihsan. (2024). UBD Forges Stronger Industry Ties, Unveils New Entrepreneurial Initiatives at the IEED Exchange. Retrieved on Mar 30, 2025, from UBD: https://ubd.edu.bn/2024/09/05/ubd-forges-stronger-industry-ties-unveils-new-entrepreneurial-initiatives-at-the-ieed-exchange/

Institute of Data. (2023). Digital Entrepreneurship: Navigating Business with Digital Platforms. Retrieved on Mar 30, 2025, from Institute of Data: https://www.institutedata.com/blog/digital-entrepreneurship-navigating-business-with-digital-platforms/

Isenberg, D. J. (2016). Applying the Ecosystem Metaphor to Entrepreneurship: Uses and Abuses. *Antitrust Bulletin*, *61*(4), 564–573. DOI: 10.1177/0003603X16676162

Isnawati, L. (2018). *Jual-beli Online Sesuai Syariah*. Rumah Fiqih Publishing.

Jangcik, I., Jama, J., Rizal, F., & Rahmayati, D., & Sasmita. (2022). Categorization of Problems and Solutions in Technopreneurship Course: A Literature Study. *Journal of Positive School Psychology*, *6*(6), 6712–6711.

Jusoh, M., & Halim, H. (n.d.). *Role of Technopreneurs in Malaysian Economic.* Retrieved November 21, 2024, from Academia.edu: https://www.academia.edu/33238691/Role_of_Technopreneurs_in_Malaysian_Economic

Kamdar, A. (2011). *Having Fun the Halal Way - Entertainment in Islam.* International Islamic Publishing House.

Khaeriyah, H. (2022). *Islam dan Transformasi Paradigma di Era Digitalisasi.* Retrieved December 2, 2024, from Kitorang News: https://kitorangnews.com/2351/islam-dan-transformasi-paradigma-di-era-digitalisasi/

Koe, W.-L., Alias, N., Marmaya, N., Majid, I., Mohamad, M., & Mohamad, M. (2020). Likelihood in Choosing Technopreneurship as Career among Undergraduate Students. *International Journal of Academic Research in Business & Social Sciences*, *10*(4), 686–696. DOI: 10.6007/IJARBSS/v10-i5/7241

Kosasih, W., Ahmad, A., Salomon, L., & Utama, D. (2016). Peranan Pendidikan Technopreneurship Untuk Pembangunan Berkelanjutan: Studi Konseptual. *Jurnal Rekayasa Sistem Industri*, *5*(2), 79–88. DOI: 10.26593/jrsi.v5i2.2215.79-88

Laldin, M. (2006). *Introduction to Shariah and Islamic Jurisprudence.* CERT Publisher.

Lukita, C., Chakim, M., Supriati, R., Santoso, N., & Kamil, M. (2023). Exploration of Perceived Use of Technology Using A Digital Business Perspective. *ADI Journal on Recent Innovation*, *5*(1Sp, 1SP), 87–96. DOI: 10.34306/ajri.v5i1Sp.984

Mačiulienė, M., & Skaržauskienė, A. (2021). Conceptualizing blockchain-based value co-creation: A service science perspective. *Systems Research and Behavioral Science*, *38*(3), 330–341. DOI: 10.1002/sres.2786

Marti'ah, S. (2017). Kewirausahaan Berbasis Teknologi (Technopreneurship) dalam Perspektif Ilmu Pendidikan. *Jurnal Ilmiah Edutic*, *3*(2), 75–82. DOI: 10.21107/edutic.v3i2.2927

Masrianto, A., Hartoyo, H., Hubeis, A., & Hasanah, N. (2022). Digital Marketing Utilization Index for Evaluating and Improving Company Digital Marketing Capability. *Journal of Open Innovation*, *8*(3), 153. DOI: 10.3390/joitmc8030153

Masrianto, A., Hartoyo, H., Hubeis, A., & Hasanah, N. (2024). How to Boost Your Firm's Digital Marketing Capability? *International Journal of Technology*, *15*(3), 677–686. DOI: 10.14716/ijtech.v15i3.5691

Medina, C., & Rufín, R. (2009). The Mediating Effect of Innovation in the Relationship between Retailers, Strategic Orientations and Performance. *International Journal of Retail & Distribution Management*, *37*(7), 629–655. DOI: 10.1108/09590550910964639

Ministry of Finance and Economy. (n.d.). List of fundings and financing available for businesses in Brunei Darussalam. Retrieved on Mar 30, 2025, on businessBN Portal: https://business.mofe.gov.bn/SitePages/Business%20Fundings.aspx?utm

Musa, S. P., & Idris, D. P. (2020). Addressing Issues of Unemployment in Brunei: The Mismatch between Employers Expectations and Employees Aspirations. *International Journal of Asian Business and Information Management*, *11*(2), 88–101. DOI: 10.4018/IJABIM.2020040106

Nasution, A. H., Noer, B. A., & Suef, M. (2007). *Entrepreneurship: membangun spirit teknopreneurship*. ANDI.

Naudé, W. (2010). Entrepreneurship, developing countries and development economics: New approaches and insights. *Small Business Economics*, *34*(1), 1–12. DOI: 10.1007/s11187-009-9198-2

Ngui, N. (2015, Aug 19). *M'sia halal exports hit US$2.44b*. Retrieved Jan 30, 2025, from The Jakarta Post: https://www.thejakartapost.com/news/2015/08/19/msias-halal-exports-hit-us244b.html

Nurein, S. A. (2023). Nexus of Halal Entrepreneurship and Islamic Finance for the Creation of a Strong Halal Ecosystem. In Raimi, L., Adekunle, S. M., & Shabbir, M. S. (Eds.), *Contemporary Discourse of Halal and Islamic Entrepreneurship*. Springer., DOI: 10.1007/978-981-99-6427-7_9

Olusegun, O., Akpoviroro, K., & Adebowale, O. (2019). Impact of Technopreneurship on Business Performance. *Journal of Economics and Management Research*, *8*, 55–71. DOI: 10.22364/jemr.8.03

Othman, N., & Ishak, S. (2011). Kecenderungan Terhadap Pemilihan Kerjaya Keusahawanan Mengikut Persepsi Peserta Skim Usahawan Siswa. *Jurnal Teknologi (Sciences & Engineering)*, *56*(1), 47-63. DOI: 10.11113/jt.v56.59

Permana, A., Srihartati, R., Akbardin, J., Setiawan, A., Jatnika, D., & Rustandi, W. (2020). Technopreneur Training Model in Building an Entrepreneurship. *Journal of Architectural Research and Education*, *2*(2), 190–197. DOI: 10.17509/jare.v2i2.29258

Puspaningtyas, M. (2021). Is halal certificate socialization effective in increasing the number of MSMEs in the food sector to register for halal certificates? In H. Pratikto, A. Taufiq, A. Voak, N. Deuraseh, H. Nur, W. Dahlan, & A. Purnomo (Eds.), *Halal Development: Trends, Opportunities and Challenges* (pp. 69-74). CRC Press. DOI: 10.1201/9781003189282-12

Raffi, R., Deuraseh, N., Hashim, N., & Yunus, N. (2023). Determinant of Employment and Employability Attributes in the Halal Sector for Halal Science Graduates in Brunei Darussalam. *Journal of Halal Industry & Services*, *6*(1), a0000311. DOI: 10.36877/jhis.a0000311

Rahmayanti, I., Wardiyanta, W., & Ikawati, R. (2023). Does Islamic Entrepreneurship Aligned with Digitalization Era? *Jurnal Doktor Managemen*, *6*(2), 204–216. DOI: 10.22441/jdm.v6i2.22475

Rajnai, Z., & Kocsis, I. (2017). Labor Market Risks of Industry 4.0, Digitization, Robots and AI. 2017 IEEE 15th International Symposium on Intelligent Systems and Informatics (SISY), 343–346.

Rojko, A. (2017). Industry 4.0 Concept: Background and Overview. *International Journal of Interactive Mobile Technologies*, *11*(5), 77–90. DOI: 10.3991/ijim.v11i5.7072

Sait, M., & Anshari, M. (2021). Industrial Revolution 4.0: A New Challenge to Brunei Darussalam's Unemployment Issue. *International Journal of Asian Business and Information Management*, *12*(4), 33–44. DOI: 10.4018/IJABIM.20211001.oa3

Sakti, R. H., Yetti, W., & Wulansari, R. E. (2020). Technopreneurship and IT-Preneurship in Vocational Education Perspective: Perspective Theory. *Jurnal Pendidikan Teknologi Kejuruan*, *3*(4), 194–198. DOI: 10.24036/jptk.v3i3.10423

Sallomi, P. (2020, March 25). *Understanding the Sector Impact of COVID-19 Technology Sector*. Retrieved November 21, 2024, from Deloitte: file:///C:/Users/offic/Downloads/COVID-19-Impact-Technology-Sector.pdf

Salman, A., Rahman, A., Sitorus, M., Wok, R., Mustapha, S., & Ghani, N. (2020). The Impact of Knowledge and Skills Acquired on Business Performance of Malaysia and Indonesia TVET Graduates. *International Journal of Technical Vocational and Engineering Technology*, *2*(1), 1–14.

Selladurai, M. (2016). Conceptual Framework on Technopreneurship. *SELP Journal of Social Science*, *7*(27), 92–97.

Sharon, A. (2018). Future-ready 'technopreneurs' important to Malaysia's transformation. Retrieved January 30, 2025 from Open Gov: https://opengovasia.com/2018/10/08/future-ready-technopreneurs-important-to-malaysias-transformation/

Siyanbola, W., Aderemi, H., Egbetokun, A., & Sanni, M. (2011). Framework for Technological Entrepreneurship Development: Key Issues and Policy Directions. *Gongshang Guanli Xuekan, 1*(1), 10–19. DOI: 10.4236/ajibm.2011.11002

Soomro, B., & Shah, N. (2021). Technopreneurship Intention Among Nonbusiness Students: A Quantitative Assessment. *World Journal of Entrepreneurship, Management and Sustainable Development, 17*(3), 502–514. DOI: 10.1108/WJEMSD-10-2020-0129

Sulaiman, N. S., Abdullah, R., & Hashim, N. (2023). Halal Industry Development in Brunei Darussalam: Realities and Challenges, *KnE Social Sciences 5th Social and Humaniora Research Symposium,* 8(18): 1013 – 1029. DOI: DOI: 10.18502/kss/v8.18.14308

Suradi, S., Yasin, M., & Rasul, M. S. (2017). Increasing Technopreneurs for a Developing a Nation: The Majlis Amanah Rakyat (MARA) Experience. *Journal of Technical Education and Training*, *9*(1), 73–86.

Svirina, A., Syurkova, S., Laizans, T., Appalonova, N., & Bazarov, R. (2017). Technopreneurial Development: Why Ecosystem Approach is Unsustainable in Case of Low Competition. *Proceedings of the 21st World Multi-Conference on Systematics, Cybernetics, and Informatics (WMSCI 2017), pp.* 31-36.

Sweeny, P. (2019). Entrepreneurial inference in the high-technology start-up: A model for optimised decision making and principled praxis. *PhD Thesis*. University of Sheffield.

Tan, W., Egge, K., & Mohamed, O. (2010). National Venture Competition and Technopreneurship Development in Malaysia. *Journal for International Business and Entrepreneurship, 11*(2), 69–81. https://ink.library.smu.edu.sg/lkcsb_research/2682

Tarmizi, R., Septiani, N., Sunarya, P. A., & Ayu Sanjaya, Y. P. (2023). Harnessing Digital Platforms for Entrepreneurial Success: A Study of Technopreneurship Trends and Practices. [ATT]. *Aptisi Transactions on Technopreneurship*, *5*(3), 278–290. DOI: 10.34306/att.v5i3.360

Teichler, U. (1996). Research on Academic Mobility and International Cooperation in Higher Education: An agenda for the future. In Peggy, B., Goodwin, C., Smith, A., & Teichler, U. (Eds.), *Academic Mobility in a Changing World*. Jessica Kingsley Publishers.

UBDSBE. (n.d.) Entrepreneurship Major. Retrieved on Mar 30, 2025 from UBD School of Business and Economics: https://sbe.ubd.edu.bn/new_major_entrepreneurship.aspx?val=ProStud&val2=Prospective+Students+%3E+Bachelor+of+Business+%3E+Entrepreneurship+Major&utm

UNISSA. (n.d.) Entrepreneurship Hub. Retrieved on Mar, 30 2025. From UNISSA: https://unissa.edu.bn/offices/entrepreneurship-hub-unissa/?utm

Usman, H., & Raharjo, N. (2012). Model Pendidikan Karakter Kewirausahaan di Sekolah Menengah Kejuruan. *Jurnal Pendidikan Teknologi Dan Kejuruan, 21*(2), 140–147.

UTB. (n.d.) UTB Experiences PLUS. Retrieved on Mar 30, 2025 from UTB: https://www.utb.edu.bn/students/life-skills-development/utb-experience-plus/

Utomo, S., Sekaryuni, R., Widarjono, A., Tohirin, A., & Sudarsono, H. (2021). Promoting Islamic financial ecosystem to improve halal industry performance in Indonesia: A demand and supply analysis. *Journal of Islamic Marketing*, *12*(5), 992–1011. DOI: 10.1108/JIMA-12-2019-0259

Valero, A., & Reenen, J. (2019). The economic impact of universities: Evidence from across the globe. *Economics of Education Review*, *68*, 53–67. DOI: 10.1016/j.econedurev.2018.09.001

Venkataraman, S. (2004). Regional transformation through technological entrepreneurship. *Journal of Business Venturing*, *19*(1), 153–167. DOI: 10.1016/j.jbusvent.2003.04.001

Vojtovič, S., Navickas, V., & Gruzauskas, V. (2016). Strategy of Sustainable Competitiveness: Methodology of Real-Time Customers' Segmentation for Retail Shops. *Journal of Security and Sustainability Issues*, *5*(4), 489–499. DOI: 10.9770/jssi.2016.5.4(4)

Wibowo, A. (2021). *Bisnis digital (Algoritma Bisnis, Komputasi Awan dan Data Teknik)*. Prima Agus Teknik.

Wibowo, A. (2022). Technopreneurship Development in Indonesia: Digital Business Development. *Journal of System and Management Sciences*, *12*, 87–103. DOI: 10.33168/JSMS.2022.0305

Wijayanto, G., Ayesha, I., Wibowo, T., Suparwata, D., Suroso, A., & Fathurohman, A. (2023). The Influence of Digital Literacy Mediation on the Effect of Entrepreneurship Knowledge on Technopreneurship. *International Journal of Economics. Business and Accounting Research*, *7*(1), 1–10.

Winarni, D., Susilo, S., & Widiyatmoko, A. (2021). Penerapan pendekatan Socio-Scientific Issue (SSI) Menggunakan Desain Project untuk Meningkatkan Penguasaan Technopreneurship Mahasiswa. *Prosiding Seminar Nasional Pascasarjana*, *4*(1), 180–184.

Wisdom, A. (2023, August 21). *Technopreneurship: Empowering Innovation and Business in the Digital Age*. Retrieved December 5, 2024, from LinkedIn: https://www.linkedin.com/pulse/technopreneurship-empowering-innovation-business-age-anthony

Yudha, P. (2010). Utilization of Human Virtual Intelligence Framework in Managing Technopreneur Knowledge. *Jurnal Generic*, *5*(1), 31–34.

KEY TERMS AND DEFINITIONS

Ecosystem: A network of interconnected stakeholders, including businesses, institutions, and policymakers, that supports the growth and sustainability of a specific industry or sector.

Employment Opportunities: Available job positions or entrepreneurial ventures that individuals can pursue to earn a livelihood, particularly within the halal and technology sectors.

Entrepreneurial Mindset: A set of attitudes and behaviours that enable individuals to identify opportunities, take risks, and innovate in business.

Graduates: Individuals who have completed a higher education program and are seeking career or entrepreneurial opportunities.

Halal Technopreneur: An entrepreneur who integrates halal principles into technology-driven business models, ensuring compliance with Islamic ethical and legal guidelines.

Halal: Anything that is permissible or lawful according to Islamic principles, particularly in relation to products and services.

Shariah Compliance: Adherence to Islamic legal principles in business, finance, and daily life, ensuring ethical and lawful practices.

Technopreneur: An entrepreneur who creates and manages businesses based on technological innovations and advancements.

Technopreneurship: The combination of technology and entrepreneurship, where innovative technological solutions are leveraged to create and sustain business ventures.

Chapter 8
The Effects of Innovative Islamic Leadership on Business Performance Halal Food SMEs:
The Role of Moderation in Competitive Advantage

Muafi Muafi
https://orcid.org/0000-0002-5078-4670
Universitas Islam Indonesia, Indonesia

Ali Jufri
https://orcid.org/0000-0001-7962-0066
Universitas Muhammadiyah Cirebon, Indonesia

ABSTRACT

This study aims to examine the relationship between innovative Islamic leadership, competitive advantage, and the performance of small and medium-sized enterprises (SMEs) in Indonesia. The study focuses on the SMEs that produce food products in Cirebon, West Java. The study used a quantitative approach with a survey method to gather data from 110 Cirebon-typical culinary halal SMEs. The results of the research showed that there was a significant positive relationship between the innovation of Islamic leadership and the performance of SMEs, as well as the superiority of their resources and products. The findings imply that SME owners must apply innovative Islamist leadership models as a source of competitiveness in their business operations. Based on the moral values of honesty, the owners are expected to foster an innovative culture, thereby enhancing the company's competitiveness and

DOI: 10.4018/979-8-3373-3917-7.ch008

sustainable growth. The research also suggests the importance of genuine, inspiring, and enthusiastic leaders to foster innovative behavior that becomes a competitive advantage among SME employees.

INTRODUCTION

Small and medium-sized enterprises (SMEs) in a country are better at dealing with a crisis than large ones. However, there are a few SMEs experiencing difficulties during the crisis. These enterprises are known to be able to adapt faster and more flexibly than large corporations to environmental factors or external changes. The presence of SMEs in Indonesia can significantly contribute to the Indonesian economy's growth, particularly in the aftermath of the 2017 and current economic crises (Munandar, 2016). This study is based on the resource advantage theory (RAT) of competition. According to the RAT hypothesis, a company's resources will determine its market position in the form of a competitive advantage, a competitive disadvantage, or a competitive average (Hunt & Morgan, 1997). Resource Advantage Theory (RAT) emphasizes the management of unique resources, such as innovative Islamic leadership and halal standards, by accommodating innovation and Islamic values as strategic elements and explaining how competitive advantage mediates the relationship between leadership and business performance. This approach is not only academically relevant but also provides practical insights for halal food SMEs to enhance their competitiveness and performance in both local and global markets.

The halal industry in Indonesia and the world is rapidly growing along with the increasing awareness of the importance of high-quality halal products. The interaction between digitization, the blue economy, and the global halal industry is key to the transformation of the modern economy. Digitization strengthens the blue economy by optimizing supply chains, mapping resources, and enhancing the transparency of halal products. (Asna Annisa & Indriyani, 2024). In this ecosystem, halal SMEs play a significant role as providers of quality products and drivers of local and global economies. The contribution of SMEs, especially in the halal food sector, is very significant to the national economy. However, the optimization of the halal industry still faces unique challenges that require strategic solutions to achieve sustainable economic and Sharia financial growth. (Amalia et al., 2023).

SMEs in the halal food industry confront significant obstacles in sustaining and enhancing their performance in the age of globalization and heightened competition. Halal food SMEs must use creative leadership techniques that promote efficiency and creativity while upholding moral principles if they hope to prevail in the marketplace. Fairness, integrity, and service are just a few characteristics underpinning Islamic values-based leadership, which provides a distinctive strategy for improving corporate performance while upholding moral standards. (Salaheldeen & Battour, 2024)

However, the reality on the ground shows that the failure of leadership patterns has become one of the main obstacles in the development of halal MSMEs, affecting business performance and sustainability. Many halal MSME leaders fail to identify and leverage competitive advantages such as the quality of halal products, understanding of niche market segments, and services based on Islamic values (Wekke et al., 2024). SMEs often find themselves in intense competition, lacking clear differentiation, which hinders their ability to compete in the global market. The inability to implement visionary and value-oriented innovative Islamic leadership hinders innovation and long-term growth. Leadership that does not support change causes SMEs to stagnate and be unable to create sustainable competitive advantages. (Amalia et al., 2023). Therefore, a conducive business ecosystem supports innovative leadership that focuses on developing unique potential. Apart from internal failures, the absence of support from the business ecosystem exacerbates the situation. The government and supporting institutions frequently fail to provide adequate policies, simple access to financing, or incentives for innovation (Santoso et al., 2024); (Hidayat et al., 2024). Some of the problems that happen when trying to help small businesses that make halal food are the high cost of getting certified, the time-consuming paperwork needed to get certified, the lack of facilities (like halal labs), the lack of knowledge about how to meet halal standards, the lack of training or mentoring, and the difficulty in getting funding. With strengthened leadership patterns and a supportive environment, halal SMEs have enormous potential to enhance their competitiveness in the global market and drive Sharia-based economic growth.

Adopting new technologies and fostering innovation in procedures, products, and services is vital for enhancing SMEs' performance and gaining a competitive advantage (Febriani & Sa'diyah, 2021). Integrating fintech and Islamically compliant creative approaches can improve operational efficiency, particularly in the halal food sector (Novitasari et al., 2022; Kumalasari et al., 2024). Competitive advantage, driven by ethical and innovative leadership, is essential for SMEs to thrive in competitive markets, as it encourages creativity, innovation, and applying best practices in technology and management (Jaaffar et al., 2024). However, many halal SMEs struggle to integrate Islamic values with business innovation due to a limited understanding of how Sharia principles can enhance competitive advantages, such as ethical human resource management, sustainable production, and high-quality product development. A cautious leadership style often stifles the risk-taking needed for innovation and market expansion, leaving many halal SMEs unable to adopt critical digital technologies like e-commerce, hindering their competitiveness in global markets (Raimi et al., 2023). So, the government, the private sector, and society need to work together to support and change how small halal food businesses get simple digital platforms for customers. This will improve their efficiency, competitiveness, and market penetration locally and globally.

Halal SMEs face challenges in competing in dynamic markets due to inadequate human resource management, which includes a lack of investment in training, motivation, and empowerment, and an organizational culture that disregards Islamic values such as justice, transparency, and honesty (Nur'Aini Ihsan et al., 2022). A bold, innovative leadership model, rooted in Islamic values, and strategic human resource management are essential to address this. There is evidence that creative leadership can improve business performance, but there isn't a lot of research on this topic in halal small businesses. Not many studies also examine how outside factors like government policies, market support, digital infrastructure, and consumer awareness affect these businesses' ability to compete (Sutono et al., 2022).

The halal MSME ecosystem has become a major focus in the global economy, especially with the rapid growth of the Muslim population and the increasing demand for products and services that comply with Sharia principles. Indonesia, as the country with the largest Muslim population in the world, has enormous potential to lead the global halal market. However, the halal MSME ecosystem in Indonesia and the world faces various debates that encompass strategic issues, regulations, technology, and sustainability (Amalia et al., 2023).

The potential of the Halal MSME ecosystem is that the global halal market has developed into a significant economic sector, encompassing food, beverages, pharmaceuticals, cosmetics, fashion, and halal tourism. Halal SMEs have become the backbone of the halal supply chain, both at the local and international levels. In Indonesia, halal SMEs contribute significantly to the national GDP and create jobs for millions of people. Despite its great potential, the halal MSME ecosystem in Indonesia and around the world continues to face various debates. One such issue is the lack of uniform halal standards across different countries, which complicates international trade and creates challenges for SMEs seeking to export their products. The second difficulty lies in halal certification, which is often considered a complex, time-consuming, and expensive process, especially for SMEs. This prompts discussions on enhancing the accessibility of halal certification while maintaining its credibility. The third challenge is the uneven adoption of technology, such as blockchain, to ensure transparency in the halal supply chain, particularly among SMEs (Akmal & Effendi, 2023). This sparks discussions about the technological gap between developed and developing countries. The final difficulty is the opportunities and competition in non-Muslim markets; while halal products have universal appeal, many SMEs are still limited in reaching non-Muslim consumers, raising debates about how halal brands can be positioned for a broader market.

As the country with the largest Muslim population, Indonesia has ambitions to become the center of the global halal industry. The government has launched various initiatives, including halal industrial zones and halal certification incentives for SMEs. However, Indonesia also faces challenges in the form of competition with other countries such as Malaysia, the United Arab Emirates, and Turkey, which have already developed their halal ecosystems. In-depth research is necessary to identify the potential, challenges, and strategies in developing a sustainable halal ecosystem, given the significance of the halal SME ecosystem as a pillar of the Sharia economy and its contribution to global economic inclusivity. To address this gap, it is important to develop a deeper understanding of innovative Islamic leadership and its role in strengthening the performance of halal SMEs. Additionally, research needs to highlight the role of competitive advantages as a moderating factor that influences the relationship between innovative leadership and business performance, as well as how the business ecosystem can support or hinder the sustainability of halal SMEs' competitiveness.

This research aims to explore innovative Islamic leadership's role in improving halal SMEs' performance, analyze the moderation of competitive advantages, and examine the influence of the business ecosystem in creating sustainable competitiveness for halal SMEs in Indonesia and the world. The findings of this research are expected to bridge the gap between theory and practice, while also providing strategic insights for entrepreneurs and policymakers to optimize the potential of halal SMEs in the global market.

RESEARCH METHOD

We conducted research in Cirebon, West Java, involving 110 halal culinary SMEs that have integrated digital marketing into their strategies. This research focuses on halal-food SMEs in Cirebon because the city has a majority Muslim population, creating a high demand for halal products. Focusing on halal food SMEs in Cirebon is relevant as it reflects significant local needs for sharia-compliant products and provides valid data within the halal industry context. Cirebon is experiencing rapid development of food SMEs, with high adoption of digital marketing through social media and e-commerce to expand markets and enhance competitiveness. As a crossroads of culture and economy, Cirebon offers a diverse consumer base from various social strata, making it an ideal context for analyzing the relationship between innovation, digitalization, and the performance of halal SMEs.

This research uses a quantitative approach with the Partial Least Squares-Structural Equation Modeling (PLS-SEM) method. We selected SmartPLS to analyze complex relationships between latent variables, particularly in the presence of moderation effects, and to manage non-normally distributed data. The point of this study is to look into how innovative Islamic leadership affects the business performance of small and medium-sized halal food stores and how competitive advantage affects that relationship. The Partial Least Squares Structural Equation Modeling (PLS-SEM) method will guide us through the following stages (Hair *et al.*, 2014):

1. Measurement Model testing is comprised of two tests:
   a. Validity Test: Convergent validity occurs when the Average Variance Extracted (AVE) value is greater than 0.5 and Discriminant Validity (cross-loading and Fornell-Larcker criterion).
   b. Reliability Test: Composite Reliability (CR) has a value > 0.7 and Cronbach's alpha has a value > 0.7.
2. Structural Model Testing:
   a. Path Coefficients:
      We are testing the relationship between innovative Islamic leadership and business performance.
   b. R-Square (R^2):
      The process involves measuring the contribution of independent variables to the dependent variable.
   c. Effect Size (f2):
      We are assessing the relative impact of each variable on the model.
   d. Significance Test:
      Using the t-statistic value (> 1.96) and p-value (< 0.05) through bootstrapping.
3. We use moderation testing and interaction analysis to determine whether competitive advantage strengthens or weakens the relationship between innovative Islamic leadership and business performance.

LITERATURE REVIEW

Resource Advantage Theory (RAT)

Resource Advantage Theory (RAT), proposed by Shelby D. Hunt and Robert M. Morgan, offers a comprehensive framework to understand competition in dynamic markets. RAT integrates insights from various theories, including resource-based view (RBV), evolutionary economics, and institutional theory. It emphasizes the role of resources and their heterogeneity as key drivers of competitive advantage and market performance. Unlike neoclassical models that assume perfect competition,

RAT acknowledges market imperfections and highlights the dynamic interplay between firms and their environments. (Hunt & Morgan, 1997)

RAT argues that firms possess unique bundles of resources, which can lead to competitive advantages. These resources include tangible (e.g., infrastructure, capital) and intangible (e.g., knowledge, brand equity, organizational culture). RAT also focuses on competition as an evolutionary process where firms seek to enhance their resource bundles. Success depends on the ability to innovate and adapt to market changes. Positioning and Comparative Advantage: Firms gain a comparative advantage in resource bundles when they are rare, valuable, inimitable, and non-substitutable (VRIN framework). This advantage translates into a competitive advantage, leading to superior performance in the marketplace. RAT highlights variations in consumer preferences and needs, continuously driving firms to align their resources with market demands. The theory recognizes the role of legal, political, and social institutions in shaping resource utilization and competitive strategies.

Resource Advantage Theory provides a robust lens for analyzing competitive dynamics in diverse contexts. By emphasizing resource heterogeneity, market imperfections, and adaptive strategies, RAT offers valuable insights for both academic research and practical applications. However, future research should address its limitations, particularly in measuring resources and extending its applicability to dynamic, digital, and collaborative environments. The Resource-Advantage Theory posits that halal MSMEs can achieve their competitive advantage by strategically managing their unique resources. Innovative leadership oriented toward Islamic values is the key to creating sustainable competitive advantages that positively impact business performance. Halal MSMEs can leverage their unique resources, such as halal certification as a primary competitive advantage, cultural knowledge, and the Muslim market. A halal MSME leader must support this by creating an innovative and flexible work environment that can adapt to market changes. Additionally, leaders also need to formulate performance improvement strategies by enhancing the quality of halal products to meet global standards and adopting technology to increase efficiency and transparency in the halal supply chain (Ho, 2018).

Innovative Islamic Leadership

The Islamic concept of leadership is comparable to that of conventional leadership, except for its religious, moral, and human values. During the rule of the Prophet Muhammad (SAW) and the Four Caliphs, religious and moral spirit, often known as fear of God, was the dominant force in leadership. In general, the Islamic origins of leadership may be found in the fundamental sources of Shariah, which are the Qur'an and Sunnah, in addition to the behaviors of the early Muslims. This is the perspective brought from the Islamic perspective. Additionally, there is a school of thinking within traditional leadership that emphasizes the significance of spirituality, religious values, and human relationships. This school of thought is complementary to the other. Offering oneself and one's spirit is the essence of what it means to be a powerful leader. People are said to have failed in their leadership roles when they have placed an excessive amount of importance on bureaucratic, psychological, and technical-rational authority while neglecting professional, moral, and spiritual authority: Since individualism has been so prevalent throughout our existence, it is possible that we have not yet had the opportunity to contemplate the concept of a life that is truly shared by all. Thinking of a business as an entity that serves the needs of families and communities is not a difficult concept to conceptualize. The ability to integrate one's work with one's particular calling and to be oriented toward the actual needs of a community would not require a great deal of imagination. If this is the case, we might be surprised to learn that finance, business, commerce, and industry can all be considered to be a component of our activity related to the soul (Husti & Mahyarni, 2019).

In the Islamic view, spiritual awareness (as a servant of God) and cognitive awareness (as a representative of God) are necessary components for a capable Islamic leader. As a result of their role as servants of God, humans develop into loyal beings who always behave or refrain from acting according to God's guidance. The accumulation of knowledge is how humans, in their capacity as representatives of God, become successful beings in this existence (Febriani, rizki & Sa, 2022). When rational perfection, akin to God, and emotional and spiritual balance, akin to God's servant, unite, they create a soul and conviction that lead to actions favored by God. Divine consciousness, known as al-Rabbani, and rational consciousness, known as al-ilmiy, must be integrated by Islamic leaders. Intelligent individuals, who can read, understand, and effectively use the facts of life for their benefit, as well as those who feel fear (al-khasyyah) of God, are considered capable and qualified leaders in the Qur'an to achieve their goals. Islamic leaders, essentially, possess knowledge that is integral to their calling and a constant fear of God.

Innovative leadership is defined as the ability to inspire and drive change through creative and effective methods. Innovative leadership focuses on adaptable, visionary leaders who can encourage innovation among their followers. Innovative leadership creates peacebuilding, described as an effort to build lasting peace by addressing the root causes of conflict and promoting reconciliation. In the Islamic perspective, innovative leadership emphasizes values such as justice, compassion, and collective well-being. The Islamic perspective draws from the Quran, Hadith, and examples from the lives of Prophet Muhammad and early Islamic leaders. (Aziz, Badshah & Khan, 2021).

This leadership style is based on religious values that guide decision-making, resource management, and innovation development in the business environment. These values include honesty, justice, responsibility, and empathy toward employees and customers. The aspect of innovation is also an important focus. Innovative Islamic leadership supports the development of new products and services that align with Sharia principles while also meeting the needs of the modern market. This innovation, based on Islamic values, creates product differentiation, which helps SMEs compete in an increasingly competitive market. Innovative Islamic leadership encourages creativity. Islamic leaders promote an environment that values creativity and new ideas. Innovative behavior also requires adherence to ethical and moral principles to ensure that the development of new ideas is beneficial and does not harm society (Elias, Yaacob & Othman, 2018).

The following are the core principles of innovative leadership in the Islamic context: the first is justice, which is central to Islam's teachings and essential to building peace. The leader is expected to uphold justice in all actions and decisions, ensuring fairness. The second is compassion (Rahmah), where a leader must show empathy and kindness and promote a culture of care and support. Compassionate leadership helps heal disputes and build trust in the community. The third is consultation (Shura), where leaders encourage collective decision-making and inclusion. Leaders must seek and appreciate others' opinions, as well as promote transparency and shared responsibility. The fourth is trustworthiness (Amanah), where leaders must be reliable and maintain integrity. Trust is fundamental to building and maintaining peace, as it strengthens relationships and promotes cooperation. Finally, Islam places a high value on the pursuit of knowledge, known as Ilm. Leaders should be well-informed and encourage continuous learning and innovation. (Aziz, Badshah & Khan, 2021)

Business Performance

The performance of MSME businesses is understood as the organization's ability to achieve its strategic goals, including revenue growth (sales and profit), business sustainability (the ability to survive in a dynamic market), meeting customer needs with innovative products or services, and operational efficiency (Othumary Mgeni, 2015). Another perspective states that business performance is the result measured from the organization's activities to achieve its strategic goals. Performance measurement in SMEs involves the assessment of various dimensions, namely financial dimensions (Profit, revenue, cost efficiency), non-financial dimensions (Customer satisfaction, innovation, sustainability, and internal process performance), and temporal dimensions (operational efficiency, growth, and adaptation) (Rojas-Lema et al., 2021)

As business performance becomes increasingly competitive, SMEs face a variety of challenges that impact their ability to measure performance. These challenges include resource limitations (time, finance, and technology), a lack of technical expertise in performance measurement, rapidly changing markets that demand flexibility in performance metrics, and the fact that many SMEs only measure performance based on financial indicators without considering other strategic dimensions. Therefore, to enhance performance measurement in SMEs, it is essential to adopt a holistic approach that integrates both financial and non-financial metrics, thereby providing a more comprehensive picture of performance. The next step is to digitalize and utilize modern technologies like data analytics to improve performance-based decision-making. Next, engage in external collaboration by involving external partners, such as consultants and research institutions, to address internal resource limitations. Make sure the indicators are adaptable to the context and market dynamics. (Rojas-Lema et al., 2021)

Several studies have investigated the correlation between religiosity in leadership and performance metrics. (Elias, Yaacob & Othman, 2018). The performance of SMEs depends heavily on characteristics and competencies, such as leadership, managerial and networking skills, technological capabilities, and the level of entrepreneurial education (Muklis Lateh and Hussain, 2018). Key indicators in measuring the performance of small and medium-sized enterprises are financial performance (growth of revenue and efficiency), innovation performance (new halal product innovation and adaptation of new technologies that support halal compliance), knowledge performance (knowledge and implementation of halal-related best practices in management), market performance (expansion and enhancement of halal product market share), compliance performance (halal compliance and certification), and customer performance (customer confidence and loyalty to halal products) (Suhartanto et al., 2021). In sum, financial metrics, market share, customer satisfaction, employee engagement, operational efficiency, and overall organizational effectiveness are measures of business performance. (Husti & Mahyarni, 2019).

Competitive Advantages

SMEs need an innovation strategy to create a competitive advantage in a dynamic environment. To achieve this, organizations must be able to continuously see and exploit opportunities, as well as periodically change the organizational and cultural aspects so that they can proactively rebuild to address new threats and opportunities. One way to achieve this is through innovation. To attract new markets and consumers in Indonesia, small and medium-sized enterprises (SMEs) are expected to acquire new knowledge and create new products because innovation is the basis for organizations to survive (Hurley & Hult, 1998).

A business can outperform its rivals by obtaining a competitive advantage through cost leadership, differentiation, or niche market tactics (Jaaffar et al., 2024). An organization's attempt to establish a defendable position over its rivals is known as its competitive advantage. The organization's ability to differentiate itself from its rivals and key management tactics make up its competitive advantage (Javid & Amini, 2023). The competitive advantage is composed of three elements: the first is ethical principles, which encompass ethical practices, practice differentiation, and Islamic values-based differentiations that uphold moral principles and social responsibility. The second is to lower costs and improve reputation by using ethical business methods. The third is customer trust, which means building reliable and trustworthy relationships with customers, resulting in consumer loyalty and business sustainability. (Husti & Mahyarni, 2019)

Halal food SMEs can pay attention to key principles when building competitive advantages to ensure their sustainability:

1. Vision and Long-Term Strategy

   SMEs need to formulate a clear vision and a long-term strategy focused on the global market. This strategy must include product innovation, differentiation, and adaptation to international market needs.
2. Sustainable Innovation

   Innovation is mentioned as one of the keys to competing globally. SMEs must build an innovation culture by investing resources in research and development (R&D) as well as implementing the latest technology.
3. Strategic Partnerships

   Organizations are building strategic partnerships with various parties. SMEs can also do the same by collaborating with global companies, research institutions, or educational institutions to enhance knowledge and networks.
4. Improvement of Human Resource Competence (HR)

   SMEs must focus on developing their HR capacity through training, skill development, and employee mentoring to be ready to face the challenges of the global market.
5. Global Image

   Organizations rely on their reputation to compete globally. SMEs need to establish a robust brand that prioritizes quality, uniqueness, and local values, ensuring global acceptance.
6. The use of digital technology

Digital transformation has become one of the focuses in enhancing global competitiveness. SMEs must leverage digital technology to improve their operational efficiency, marketing, and product distribution.

7. Focus on sustainability.

   The importance of sustainability in competitive strategies. SMEs can integrate environmentally friendly and sustainable business practices to attract the global market that cares about this issue.

8. Risk Management

   SMEs must have a well-developed risk management strategy to face the challenges that arise in the global market, such as regulatory changes, currency fluctuations, and international competition.

Innovative Islamic Leadership and Business Performance

To manage a business and have an individual entrepreneurial orientation, one must possess good managerial skills. Leadership as entrepreneurial behavior is significant because it has the potential to recognize values and various aspects related to organizational sustainability, such as fostering innovation and adapting to environmental changes (Renko et al., 2015). Research studies related to entrepreneurial leadership show results where entrepreneurial leadership is measured through several indicators, consisting of vision, innovation capability, risk-taking, and a proactive attitude, which positively influence business performance (Othumary Mgeni, 2015); (Mgeni & Nayak, 2015). Thus, innovative Islamic leadership is expected to enhance business performance through the application of ethical values, justice, and innovation that align with Islamic principles. (Aziz, Badshah & Khan, 2021).

SME leaders adopt a religiosity-based approach in their managerial strategies. By integrating Islamic values, SMEs can enhance organizational efficiency, strengthen work culture, and generate relevant innovations to improve business performance (Elias, Yaacob & Othman, 2018). Innovation is considered a key element that connects Islamic leadership with SME performance. Islamic leaders encourage the development of new products, processes, or business models under Sharia principles. This innovation not only helps SMEs remain relevant in the market but also adds value for customers. In the RAT framework, innovation is considered a strategic resource that can provide a competitive advantage if managed well by competent leaders (Husti & Mahyarni, 2019).

Aziz, Badshah and Khan (2021) say that innovative Islamic leadership based on Islamic values like justice, innovation, consultation, and universal blessings has a big positive effect on business performance by boosting productivity, innovation, reputation, and the long-term success of the business. This approach reflects the relevance of innovative Islamic-based leadership as a strategic solution for managing performance-oriented and sustainable businesses. Values such as justice and deliberation encourage the creation of a harmonious and collaborative work environment that enhances employee motivation and productivity, which directly contribute to business performance. The application of the principle of ijtihad helps leaders to continuously drive innovation in products, processes, or services, which provides a competitive advantage in the market. Islamic leadership emphasizes trust and blessings, strengthening the company's image as an entity that not only seeks profit but also provides benefits to society, enhancing customer and business partner loyalty. The final focus is the principle of the value of blessings for all of nature, ensuring that the business operates sustainably, both socially and ecologically, providing a long-term positive impact on business stability.

Innovative Islamic leadership is capable of improving SME performance by encouraging creative work behavior among employees and utilizing financial technology to expand efficiency and market access. Islamic leadership oriented towards innovation is based on Islamic values such as responsibility, consultation, and ijtihad (innovation). An Islamic leader not only acts as a moral guide but also encourages creativity, technology adoption, and process innovation. Islamic leaders inspire their teams to try new solutions that align with Islamic ethical principles, thereby enhancing productivity and work quality. With its role as both a moral leader and an innovator, Islamic leadership creates an ecosystem that supports the renewal of work behavior and the adoption of technology, ultimately resulting in better business performance, particularly in the context of SMEs. (Febriani & Sa'diyah, 2021).

H_1: Innovative Islamic leadership has an impact on business performance.

The Role Moderation of Competitive Advantage in the Influence of Innovative Islamic Leadership on Business Performance

A strong competitive advantage is expected to enhance the positive impact of innovative Islamic leadership on business performance by creating a conducive environment for innovation and efficiency. SMEs with high competitive advantages are better able to translate innovative leadership into improved business performance because they possess better resources and capabilities (Husti and Mahyarni, 2019). The synergy between innovative Islamic leadership and competitive excellence can create a greater impact on business performance through the optimization of strategies and implementation (Aziz, Badshah & Khan, 2021). Islamic leadership can drive innovation, create competitive advantages, and enhance the performance of SMEs in Indonesia. By integrating moral integrity, social justice, and a welfare orientation with innovative practices, Islamic leadership offers a sustainable and ethical approach to business success. The main thing is to align business strategies with Islamic values to achieve long-term growth and prosperity. (Husti & Mahyarni, 2019)

Innovative Islamic leadership combines Islamic values (such as justice, honesty, and responsibility) with innovation to create a creative, effective, and efficient business environment. This leadership directly contributes to improving business performance through increased employee motivation and satisfaction, the creation of a work environment that encourages innovation, and a positive reputation in the halal market. Innovative Islamic leadership creates a unique management approach that enhances the quality of business decisions and outcomes. According to the Resource-Based View (RBV) and Resource-Advantage Theory, innovative leadership is capable of managing strategic resources to create product and service differentiation (Hunt & Morgan, 1997). Furthermore, leaders can leverage market knowledge to develop innovation-based competitive strategies. Leaders also play a role in improving operational efficiency through approaches that align with Islamic values. Innovative Islamic leadership also encourages organizations to develop sustainable competitive advantages, such as halal product differentiation, supply chain efficiency, and a reputation based on Islamic values (Javid & Amini, 2023).

The competitive advantages held by the company have a direct impact on business performance through the increased appeal of halal products in domestic and international markets. Higher profit margins, resulting from cost efficiency and product differentiation, also contribute to achieving competitive advantages. Mastery of a larger market share through the uniqueness of halal products also becomes a source of strength for halal SMEs. Therefore, competitive advantage plays a crucial role in guaranteeing business success by employing strategies that are difficult for competitors to replicate. Competitive advantage theoretically can mediate the relationship between innovative Islamic leadership and business performance by transforming innovation and Islamic values into strategic advantages relevant to the market. The next step involves utilizing innovative leadership to establish the distinctiveness of halal products, making them hard to replicate, and enhancing the influence of innovative leadership on business performance through strategic resource management. In conclusion, we can assert that innovative Islamic leadership fosters the development of competitive advantage, thereby boosting business performance. Thus, competitive advantage serves as a mediating variable between innovative Islamic leadership and business performance (Jaaffar *et al.*, 2024).

H_2: The Influence of Innovative Islamic Leadership on Business Performance, moderated by Competitive Advantage

RESULT AND DISCUSSION

Outer Model Evaluation Validity

Table 1. Construct reliability and validity

	Cronbach's Alpha	rho_A	Composite Reliability	Average Variance Extracted (AVE)
Business Performance (Y)	0,994	0,994	0,995	0,975
Competitive Advantage (M)	0,993	0,993	0,995	0,974
Innovative Islamic Leadership (X_1)	0,913	0,948	0,937	0,790
Moderating Effect 1	0,990	1.000	0,979	0,701

The reliability measure indicates whether a variable can be continued in a research model. The present study also included reliability analysis, specifically the composite reliability value. The composite reliability value for all variables was above 0.7, and the Cronbach alpha value was > 0.6, indicating that the variables in this study were trustworthy. Meanwhile, AVE measures the proportion of variance explained by the construct compared to the total variance of the measured items. A favorable AVE value is typically above 0.5, indicating that the construct explains more than half of the variance of the measured items. When the items fail to fully reflect the concept under measurement, a low AVE may suggest problems with construct validity. According to the calculated AVE, all variables obtained an AVE value greater than 0.5, indicating that the measured items are sufficient in explaining construct validity (Hair *et al.*, 2014).

Table 2. Discriminant validity

	Business Performance (Y)	Competitive Advantage (M)	Innovative Islamic Leadership (X_1)	Moderating Effect 1
Business Performance (Y)	0.988			
Competitive Advantage (M)	0.645	0.987		
Innovative Islamic Leadership (X_1)	0.435	0.374	0.889	
Moderating Effect 1	-0.086	0.033	0.094	0.837

The measurement model validation (outer model) in Partial Least Squares (PLS) includes discriminant validity, which guarantees the distinction of latent constructs from one another. The Fornell-Larcker criterion examines discriminant validity, requiring each latent construct's square root of the extracted average variance (AVE) to exceed its correlation with other constructs. Here is the interpretation of the table:

1. AVE (Main Diagonal)

The values on the main diagonal of the table are the square roots of the AVE for each latent construct: Business Performance (Y): 0.988; Competitive Advantage (M): 0.987; Innovative Islamic Leadership (X1): 0.889; Moderating Effect 1: 0.837. These values indicate that each construct has strong discriminant validity because the square root of the AVE for each construct is greater than the correlation values between the other constructs. (non-diagonal value).

2. Correlation Between Constructs (Non-Diagonal Value)

The values in the non-diagonal section indicate the correlation between latent constructs:

a. The correlation between Business Performance (Y) and Competitive Advantage (M) is 0.645, indicating a moderate relationship between the two.
b. The correlation between Business Performance (Y) and Innovative Islamic Leadership (X1) is 0.435, indicating a weak relationship between the two.
c. The correlation between Competitive Advantage (M) and Innovative Islamic Leadership (X1) is 0.374, indicating a weak relationship between these two factors.
d. The correlation between Moderating Effect 1 and Other Constructs is low or negative, ranging from -0.086 to 0.094, suggesting a weak relationship between the moderating effect and the main construct.

3. Evaluation of Discriminant Validity

By comparing the AVE root values (main diagonal) against the correlation values (non-diagonal), it appears that all AVE roots are greater than the correlation values with other constructs. Each construct exhibits good discriminant validity, signifying its unique measurement and lack of significant overlap with other constructs.

Thus, it can be concluded that discriminant validity is met: all constructs have AVE roots greater than the correlation values with other constructs. Also, there is a moderate relationship between the constructs, specifically between business performance (Y) and competitive advantage (M). This supports the direct relationship hypothesis. However, there is a weak relationship between Innovative Islamic Leadership (X1) and Moderating Effect 1, which means that the moderating effects and the direct effect of innovative Islamic leadership need more research. Thus, this analysis shows that the research model meets the necessary discriminant validity to proceed to the inner model evaluation.

Table 3. Output bootstrapping

	Original Sample (O)	Sample Mean (M)	Standard Deviasi (STDEV)	T Statistic (|O/STDEV|)	P Values
Competitive Advantage (M) → Business Performance (Y)	0.560	0.562	0.077	7.257	0.000
Innovative Islamic Leadership (X_1) → Business Performance (Y)	0.238	0.236	0.072	3.299	0.001

Table 3 presents the bootstrapping results to evaluate the significance of paths in the structural model (inner model). Here is a descriptive analysis of the provided results:

1. Competitive Advantage (M) → Business Performance (Y)
    a. Original Sample (O): 0.560, this value indicates that Competitive Advantage has a positive and significant impact on Business Performance with a coefficient of 0.560. This means that a 1 unit increase in Competitive Advantage will increase Business Performance by 56%. This value indicates that competitive advantage plays a significant role in determining business performance. The greater the ability of SMEs to build competitive advantages (for example, through product innovation, efficiency, or marketing strategies), the higher their chances of improving business performance.
    b. Sample Mean (M): 0.562, the average value of this bootstrapping result is consistent with the Original Sample, indicating estimation stability.
    c. Standard Deviation (STDEV): 0.077, this value indicates the level of dispersion of the path coefficient estimates. A small value like this indicates a reliable estimate.
    d. T Statistic (|O/STDEV|): 7.257, this T value is far above the 1.96 threshold for a 5% significance level. This means the relationship is highly significant.
    e. P Values: 0.000, a p-value < 0.05 indicates that this relationship is statistically significant at a 95% confidence level. The relationship between competitive advantage and business performance in this study is statistically significant, providing strong evidence that competitive advantage plays a real role in

influencing business performance. Researchers can be confident that the results are not due to chance but rather reflect a relationship that can be applied in real-world contexts.

Therefore, it can be said that Competitive Advantage has a strong and significant positive relationship with Business Performance.

2. Innovative Islamic Leadership (X1) → Business Performance (Y)
   a. Original Sample (O): 0.238, this path coefficient indicates that Innovative Islamic Leadership has a positive and significant impact on Business Performance with a contribution of 23.8%. This shows how important innovative Islamic leadership is for the success of small and medium-sized businesses, especially in the halal food industry. This is because innovative Islamic leadership combines Islamic principles with new ideas to make businesses that are competitive, flexible, and long-lasting.
   b. Sample Mean (M): 0.236, the average of the bootstrapping estimation results is consistent with the Original Sample, indicating result stability.
   c. Standard Deviation (STDEV): 0.072, the small standard deviation indicates that this coefficient estimate is reliable.
   d. T Statistic (|O/STDEV|): 3.299, this T-value is above 1.96, indicating a significant relationship.
   e. P Values: 0.001, the p-value < 0.05 indicates that this relationship is significant at the 95% confidence level. Competitive advantages play an important role in driving the performance of MSME businesses, and these results can serve as a foundation for more competitive and long-term excellence-oriented business development strategies.

Thus, it can be said that Innovative Islamic Leadership has a significant positive relationship with Business Performance, although with a weaker strength compared to Competitive Advantage.

3. Thus, it can be concluded that both paths (Competitive Advantage → Business Performance and Innovative Islamic Leadership → Business Performance) have a significant positive impact on Business Performance. Furthermore, Competitive Advantage has a greater influence (56%) compared to Innovative Islamic Leadership (23.8%). Meanwhile, the T-value and P-value indicate that the estimation results for both paths are highly significant, thereby supporting the research hypothesis. This analysis shows that in the context of the study, Competitive Advantage plays a more dominant role compared to Innovative

Islamic Leadership in enhancing Business Performance. However, both variables remain significant and relevant to consider in the management of SMEs.

Inner Model Evaluation

The inner model test includes numerous experiments, including coefficient of determination, goodness of fit, and hypothesis testing. Figure 1 displays the results of hypothesis testing with PLS bootstrapping.

Figure 1. Inner model evaluation

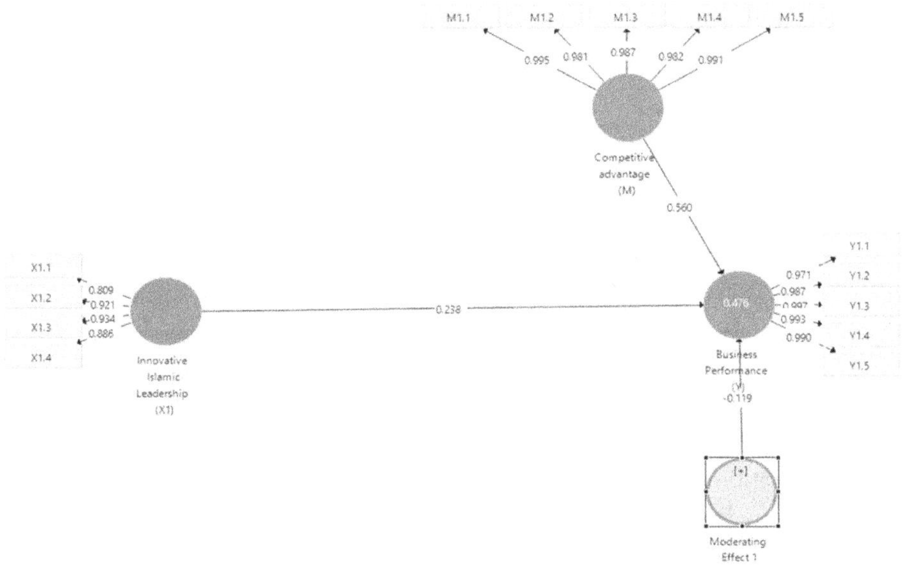

Hypothesis Testing

The measurement is considered significant if the T-statistical value exceeds 1.96 and the p-value is less than 0.05 at a critical value of 5%. The parameter coefficient, on the other hand, displays the propensity for influence, as evidenced by the actual specimen's positive or negative value. Table 4 summarizes the hypothesis testing outcomes.

Table 4. The hypothesis testing outcomes

	Original Sample	T-statistic	P-value	Description
Innovative Islamic Leadership -> Business Performance	0.238	7.257	0.000	H1 is Supported
Innovative Islamic Leadership -> Business Performance Moderating Competitive Advantages	0.560	3.299	0.001	H2 is Supported

Table 4 displays the outcomes of the pathway analysis, including the following details:

1. Influence of Innovative Islamic Leadership Toward Business Performance

The magnitude of influence is 0.238; the coefficient of 0.238 indicates that innovative Islamic leadership positively influences business performance. In other words, we expect an increase of one unit in Innovative Islamic Leadership to improve business performance by 0.238 units. (dalam skala yang digunakan dalam model). This indicates that innovative Islamic leadership drives business performance improvement through a creative, ethical, and value-based approach rooted in Islamic principles. Furthermore, the coefficient has a positive value, indicating a direct relationship. Enhancing innovative Islamic leadership also leads to improvements in business performance. The T-statistic value of 7.257 suggests that it exceeds the critical value at the 5% significance level. The bias is approximately 1.96 for both categories. This indicates that the influence of innovative Islamic leadership on business performance is statistically very significant. These results indicate that the observed effect (0.238) is not the result of coincidence or random variation. In other words, there is strong evidence to support that innovative Islamic leadership truly affects business performance. The P-value of 0.000 indicates that the probability of this result occurring by chance is very small, less than 0.001 or 0.1%. In this context, the P value supports the hypothesis test that innovative Islamic leadership significantly affects business performance. Therefore, because the P-value is less than 0.05 (the standard significance level), we reject the null hypothesis (no influence). This confirms that innovative Islamic leadership significantly contributes to the improvement of business performance. Accordingly, H_1 was supported. The research findings align with the understanding developed about innovative Islamic leadership, indicating that leaders who are ethical in Islam and innovative can drive higher productivity and efficiency, thereby enhancing profitability and business growth (Husti and Mahyarni, 2019). Islamic values, such as honesty and justice, create a positive image for SMEs and improve customer loyalty, ultimately providing a competitive advantage in the market (Manzoor, 2023). Conceptually, innovative Islamic leadership can find new solutions and develop technology to enhance business performance (Manzoor, 2023). However, the potential for applying Islamic values and innovation in improving the performance of halal-based SMEs faces various structural, operational, and cultural challenges that remain the main obstacles (Supplements and Care, 2025). Therefore, halal SMEs need to receive more support in terms of education, training, and policies to overcome these limitations. Furthermore, increasing access to technology and resources is critical to encouraging innovation and strengthening market competitiveness. (Febriani and Sa'diyah, 2021)

Some intriguing findings at the research site are that many halal culinary SME leaders in Cirebon explicitly integrate Islamic principles, such as justice, trustworthiness, and excellence, in running their businesses. An example of applying these principles is transparent financial management and fair policies toward employees, which contribute to increased team loyalty and productivity. Regarding innovation, MSME leaders in Cirebon exhibit creativity by developing halal products. For instance, they present traditional Cirebon dishes with a modern twist, such as halal frozen empal gentong, targeted at the out-of-town market. In addition, sharia-based innovations are also applied in customer service, such as offering special discounts during Ramadan or organizing food-sharing programs for the underprivileged.

Most halal culinary SMEs in Cirebon are also starting to utilize digital platforms to expand their market reach. Innovative leaders use social media to promote Islamic values in their businesses, such as showcasing the halal certification process and kitchen cleanliness. However, due to a lack of digital literacy, some MSMEs have not yet optimized their use of digital technology. UMKM, led by the Innovative Islamic Leadership style, experienced an increase in revenue over the past year. The adoption of innovations in the production process, such as the use of vacuum machines for product packaging, has proven to help increase the competitiveness of their halal products in the market. Additionally, MSME leaders actively use Islamic communication approaches, such as dialoguing with employees using the principle of consultation, to solve problems or make innovative decisions.

Behind these ideal findings, there are several challenges faced. Many SMEs find it difficult to innovate due to limited funds, especially among small businesses that are just starting. Another challenge is the lack of education about halal and innovation; leaders still do not fully understand the comprehensive concept of halal, resulting in their product innovations often being suboptimal. Additionally, the increasing number of halal culinary SMEs in the Cirebon area has led to intense competition, especially in attracting loyal customers.

Cooperation with Halal Certification Institutions is necessary to address these challenges, expedite the halal certification process, and support product innovation. In addition, it is essential to hold Islamic-based leadership and digital technology training organized by local business communities. The development of a mutually supportive halal business ecosystem is also key, for example, through collaboration among MSMEs in the provision of halal raw materials. Halal culinary SMEs managed with the principles of innovative Islamic leadership also make a tangible contribution to the empowerment of the local community, such as creating job opportunities for housewives and young people. The regular food donation program conducted by several halal culinary SMEs also positively impacts their business image in the community. Thus, the implementation of innovative Islamic leadership has proven to have a positive impact on the performance of halal culinary SMEs in the Cirebon area, both in terms of product innovation and services and strengthening market competitiveness. However, to overcome the various existing challenges, we need further support from the government, financial institutions, and the business community.

2. The Role of Moderation of Competitive Advantage in the Influence of Innovative Islamic Leadership on Business Performance

The coefficient value of 0.560 indicates that competitive advantage strengthens the relationship between innovative Islamic leadership and business performance. As competitive advantage increases, the positive influence of innovative Islamic leadership on business performance becomes greater. In practical terms, organizations with strong competitive advantages can leverage innovative Islamic leadership more effectively to drive business performance. The positive coefficient (0.560) indicates that competitive advantage is not only present as an additional variable but also strengthens the core relationship in the research model. The T-statistic of 3.299 is extremely high and significantly surpasses the critical value at the 5% significance level. The bias is approximately 1.96 for each of the two variables. This suggests that the influence of competitive advantage on the relationship between innovative Islamic leadership and business performance is statistically significant. The high T-statistic indicates substantial evidence that this moderating effect is real and not coincidental. This means that competitive advantage plays an important role in strengthening the impact of innovative Islamic leadership on business performance. Meanwhile, we reject the null hypothesis (that there is no moderating effect) because the P-value of 0.001 is smaller than the commonly used significance level (0.05). This result indicates that competitive advantage as a moderating variable is statistically significant in the model. With a very low P-value, there is a high level of confidence that the moderating role of competitive advantage is not coincidental. Companies with a competitive advantage tend to gain greater benefits from innovative Islamic leadership compared to those without one.

The research findings align with the understanding developed about innovative Islamic leadership, indicating that leaders who are ethical in Islam and innovative can drive higher productivity and efficiency, thereby enhancing profitability and business growth. Islamic values, such as honesty and justice, create a positive image for SMEs and enhance customer loyalty, ultimately providing a competitive advantage in the market. Innovative Islamic leadership can improve SMEs' competitive advantage and performance in Indonesia. However, success in implementing this concept greatly depends on how leaders can integrate Islamic values with innovative and adaptive business practices (Husti and Mahyarni, 2019). Jaaffar et al. (2024) measure the performance of SMEs not only in financial terms but also in their ability to create a positive impact on society and meet market needs sustainably. SMEs face several obstacles and shortcomings in their development, including limited resources, limited access to technology, and inadequate policy support. Therefore, building trust, enhancing loyalty, and inspiring employees to work with integrity requires innovative Islamic leadership. Then, leaders facilitate a culture of innovation by encouraging employees to think creatively, find new solutions, and adapt to market changes while also advocating for fairness in trade, resulting in an overall improvement in business performance. (Husti and Mahyarni, 2019)

To create a competitive advantage, halal culinary SMEs need to implement various holistic strategies that involve the integration of Sharia-based added value, such as ensuring transparency in the halal production process and obtaining official halal certification as a form of commitment to consumer trust. In addition, the development of unique and innovative products, by combining elements of local culture with a modern touch, becomes a key element, such as packaging Cirebon's traditional foods, like "jamblang" rice and "empal gentong", to meet the preferences of urban consumers and reach markets outside the region. The improvement of service quality based on Islamic values is also an important factor, which can be realized through the application of friendliness in customer interactions and a strong commitment to service promises. SMEs that can build competitive advantages through a combination of product innovation, operational efficiency, and consistently applied Sharia-based marketing strategies show significant improvements in business performance. The halal guarantee integrated with product quality indirectly strengthens customer trust and loyalty towards a particular brand, thereby providing a sustainable advantage.

Furthermore, the implementation of Innovative Islamic Leadership directly influences the performance of halal culinary SMEs through an approach that integrates Islamic values with strategic innovation. In this context, competitive advantage plays a crucial mediating role, where the competitive edge created from product innovation, operational efficiency, and marketing strategies aligned with Sharia values can strengthen the positive impact of Islamic leadership on overall business performance. To ensure the optimization of the relationship between innovative Islamic leadership and competitive advantage on business performance, additional strategic support is needed, such as training to encourage innovation, increased access to business capital, and strengthening collaboration within the mutually supportive halal business ecosystem. This support not only helps SMEs face increasingly fierce market competition but also strengthens their contribution to building a sustainable and highly competitive halal business ecosystem.

CONCLUSION

This research aims to analyze innovative Islamic leadership's impact on halal food SMEs' performance, taking into account the moderating role of competitive advantage. Based on the research findings, firstly, leadership grounded in Islamic values and oriented towards innovation has a significant positive impact on the business performance of halal food SMEs. Leaders who apply Islamic principles and encourage innovation tend to enhance business competitiveness and performance. Secondly, researchers discovered that a competitive advantage moderates the relationship between innovative Islamic leadership and business performance. Small and medium-sized enterprises (SMEs) need to gain a competitive edge by leveraging their human resources and technology, which they currently possess in minimal amounts. Therefore, innovative leadership is necessary to facilitate knowledge transfer and improve business performance. Innovative Islamic leadership must identify competitive advantages that can foster the growth of small-scale halal food businesses. These advantages should be in the area of new products and hiring people who are proficient at digital marketing. This way, small halal food businesses in Cirebon can improve their business performance in terms of how well they run, how flexible they are, and how competitive they are on a national and global level.

This finding underscores the importance of innovative Islamic leadership in driving the success of halal food SMEs in Cirebon. Innovative Islamic leadership enables business owners to combine ethical principles with creativity and high adaptability to market changes. Leaders who focus on developing halal product quality and empowering business teams are more effective in building positive relationships with consumers and suppliers.

Digital marketing is the main catalyst in expanding market access for halal food SMEs in Cirebon. In the digital era, consumers increasingly rely on online platforms to search for and purchase halal products. Therefore, digital marketing enables SMEs to more easily interact with consumers, strengthen their brand, and increase sales. Additionally, digital marketing enhances SMEs' competitive advantage, as they can more effectively promote quality and halal certification, as well as differentiate their products from competitors.

By leveraging competitive advantages, SMEs can strengthen business performance and gain consumer trust, which is increasingly important in the competitive halal market. For halal food SMEs in Cirebon, this means continuously developing innovations in digital marketing and maintaining Islamic integrity in every aspect of the business to enhance competitiveness and growth. A strong business ecosystem acts as a catalyst in creating sustainable competitiveness for halal SMEs in Indonesia and the world. The research findings highlight several key elements of the business ecosystem, including government policies that support halal SMEs, such as fiscal incentives, sharia financing, and the simplification of the halal certification process, all of which have a positive impact. Furthermore, developing digital platforms for the halal ecosystem enables MSMEs to access the global market more easily. Finally, SMEs should collaborate with research institutions, universities, and business incubators to encourage the need for halal product innovation. We anticipate that this research will offer valuable insights to MSME actors and stakeholders, emphasizing the importance of innovation in Islamic leadership and digital marketing as crucial strategies for enhancing the performance of halal MSMEs in Cirebon.

IMPLICATION

The contribution of the research from the Islamic Leadership Theory and Innovation perspective is to enrich the literature on Islamic leadership by highlighting the element of innovation as an important factor influencing business performance. This study also emphasizes the relationship between Islamic leadership innovation, competitive advantage, and business performance in halal SMEs. Furthermore, from the perspective of moderating competitive advantage, it contributes to understanding the role of moderating competitive advantage in expanding the theoretical understanding of how internal elements of the company, such as innovation, can be strengthened through strategies focused on differentiation and efficiency. Finally, in Contribution to the Theory of Halal Economy, this research supports the literature on the halal economy by demonstrating how innovative Islamic leadership can positively impact the performance of halal SMEs' performance while supporting the halal ecosystem's development. The implications that arise from the implementation of innovative Islamic leadership strategies involve integrating Islamic principles with innovation to create strategies that are adaptive to market dynamics. They can implement innovations in products, processes, and management to improve business performance. The way to optimize competitive advantage is for managers to leverage competitive advantages, such as halal product differentiation and quality, to enhance competitiveness. Managers can implement strategies such as digital technology usage, halal brand management, or collaboration with halal certification bodies. Next, the organization supporting halal SMEs can enhance their capacity to offer innovative leadership training based on Islamic values, as well as provide financial and technological support to accelerate the adoption of innovative strategies.

SUGGESTIONS FOR FUTURE RESEARCH

Future research could examine the effects of innovative Islamic leadership in sectors beyond the halal food industry, such as halal tourism or halal fashion, to broaden the relevance of the findings. This study can be conducted longitudinally to measure the long-term impact of innovative Islamic leadership on business performance and competitive advantage. Additionally, the exploration of moderating factors, such as the adoption of digital technology, halal regulations, and market dynamics, can also be studied to deepen the understanding of the relationships between variables. Research in various geographical contexts, especially in countries with developing halal ecosystems, can provide broader comparative insights into the generalization of these findings across cultural and economic diversity. The latter can conduct Consumer Perspective Integration by integrating consumer perspectives to understand how their perceptions of Islamic leadership and innovation influence their loyalty and preferences for halal products.

REFERENCES

Akmal, A., & Effendi, A. (2023). Business strategy in the halal industry the use of digital ecosystems in introducing Indonesia as the world's halal industry. *International Journal of Economics, Business and Innovation Research, 02*(04), pp. 14–30. Available at: https://www.e-journal.citakonsultindo.or.id/index.php/IJEBIR/article/view/320%0Ahttps://www.e-journal.citakonsultindo.or.id/index.php/IJEBIR/article/download/320/255

Amalia, E., Rahmatullah, I., Muslim, M. B., & Fathoni, M. (2023). Enhacing halal economy ecosystem for strengthening halal business smes sector in Indonesia. *Journal of Namibian Studies, 34*, 2197–5523.

Asna Annisa, A., & Indriyani, F. (2024). Understanding the digitalization of the blue economy in a global halal-hub. *Research Journal on Islamic Economics, 10*(1), 1–14.

Aziz, F., Badshah, S. N., & Khan, B. ullah. (2021). Innovative leadership principles for peace building in society an analysis in Islamic perspective, *Acta-Islamica*, pp. 1–17. Available at: http://www.aisbbu.com/index.php/ai/article/view/43%0Ahttp://www.aisbbu.com/index.php/ai/article/download/43/39

Elias, E. M., Yaacob, N. S. A., & Othman, S. N. (2018). Enhancing business performance through religiosity leaderships style among the small and medium enterprises. *International Journal of Supply Chain Management, 7*(2), 95–102.

Febriani, R., & Sa'diyah, C. (2021, September). Febriani, rizki & Sa, C. (2021). Exploring Islamic leadership on sme performance: mediated by exploring islamic leadership on SME performance: mediated by innovative work behavior and financial technology. [JAM]. *Journal of AppliedManagement, 19*(3), 495–506. Advance online publication. DOI: 10.21776/ub.jam.2021.019.03.04

Febriani, R., & Sa'diyah, C. (2021). Exploring Islamic leadership on SME performance: Mediated by innovative work behavior and financial technology'. *Jurnal Aplikasi Manajemen, 19*(3), 495–506. DOI: 10.21776/ub.jam.2021.019.03.04

Hair, J.F.Jr., Sarstedt, M., Hopkins, L., & Kuppelwieser, Volker G. (. (2014). Partial least squares structural equation modeling (PLS-SEM): An emerging tool in business research. *European Business Review, 26*(2), 106–121. DOI: 10.1108/EBR-10-2013-0128

Ho, K. L. P. (2018). A resource-advantage theory approach on competitive advantage and financial performance of beef cattle value chain in Vietnam Central Highlands, *Dissertation*, August, *University Of Tasmania.*

Hunt, S. D., & Morgan, R. M. (1997). Resource-advantage theory: A snake swallowing its tail or a general theory of competition? *Journal of Marketing*, *61*(4), 74–82. DOI: 10.1177/002224299706100406

Hurley, R. F., & Hult, G. T. M. (1998). Innovation, market orientation, and organizational learning: An integration and empirical examination. *Journal of Marketing*, *62*(3), 42–54. DOI: 10.1177/002224299806200303

Husti, I., & Mahyarni, M. (2019). Islamic leadership, innovation, competitive advantages, and performance of SMEs in Indonesia. *East Asia (Piscataway, N.J.)*, *36*(4), 369–383. DOI: 10.1007/s12140-019-09325-7

Jaaffar, A. H., Abd Majid, N., Kasavan, S., Isa, A., Alwi, M.N.R., & Zahari, A.R. (2024). The effect of innovative mindset and behavior on innovation performance and competitive advantage: a case of halal SMEs owner-managers from Malaysian energy-intensive industry. Journal of Innovation and Entrepreneurship, Springer, vol. 13(1), pages 1-19, December. Available at: .DOI: 10.1186/s13731-023-00359-z

Javid, N. J., & Amini, M. (2023). Evaluating the effect of supply chain management practice on implementation of halal agroindustry and competitive advantage for small and medium enterprises. *International Journal of Computer Science and Information Technologies*, *15*(6), 8997–9008. https://ssrn.com/abstract=4348136

Manzoor, S. (2023). The Model of visionary and innovative Islamic leadership. *Society*, *11*(1), 41–51. DOI: 10.33019/society.v11i1.539

Mgeni, T. O., & Nayak, P. (2015). Impact of different leadership styles of CEOs on business performance of SMEs in East Africa: A systematic review of literature. *Journal of Entrepreneurship & Management*, *4*(3). Advance online publication. DOI: 10.21863/jem/2015.4.3.012

Lateh, M. (2018). Social entrepreneurship development and poverty alleviation-A Literature review. *MAYFEB Journal of Business and Management, 2.*

Munandar, A. (2016). The strategy development and competitive advantages of micro small medium entreprise business institution toward regional development. *AdBispreneur*, *1*(2), 103–112. DOI: 10.24198/adbispreneur.v1i2.10233

Othumary Mgeni, T. (2015). Impact of entrepreneurial leadership style on business performance of SMEs in Tanzania'. *Journal of Entrepreneurship & Organization Management*, *04*(02). Advance online publication. DOI: 10.4172/2169-026X.1000142

Renko, M., El Tarabishy, A., Carsrud, A. L., & Brännback, M. (2013). Understanding and Measuring Entrepreneurial Leadership Style. *Journal of Small Business Management*, *53*(1), 54–74. DOI: 10.1111/jsbm.12086

Rojas-Lema, X., Alfaro-Saiz, J.-J., Rodríguez-Rodríguez, R., & Verdecho, M.-J. (2020). Performance measurement in SMEs: Systematic literature review and research directions. *Total Quality Management & Business Excellence*, •••, 1–26. DOI: 10.1080/14783363.2020.1774357

Salaheldeen, M., & Battour, M. (2024). Fostering innovation capability and sustainable innovation in halal industry: The role of halal entrepreneurs' success'. *Journal of Islamic Marketing*, *15*(3), 777–799. DOI: 10.1108/JIMA-12-2022-0323

Santoso, S., Dewandaru, G., Nugroho, L., Hidayat, S. E., Isa, S. M., Hidayat, R. N., & Marfatah, M. R. (2024). Developing an integrated innovation ecosystem to strengthen Islamic economy in Indonesia. *IQTISHODUNA: Jurnal Ekonomi Islam*, *13*(2), 681–706.

Suhartanto, D., Dean, D., Sarah, I. S., Hapsari, R., Amalia, F. A., & Suhaeni, T. (2021). Does religiosity matter for customer loyalty? Evidence from halal cosmetics. *Journal of Islamic Marketing*, *12*(8), 1521–1534. DOI: 10.1108/JIMA-03-2020-0069

Wekke, I. S., Nusran, M., Henny, A., & Azis, St. N. (2024). Indonesia's Halal Future: Charting a Path to Global Leadership. *SSRN*: https://ssrn.com/abstract=4737469 or http://dx.doi.org/DOI: 10.2139/ssrn.4737469

Chapter 9

Applying the "Halal" and "Tayyib" Norms in Marketing:
Islamic Marketing

Mohammad Mominul Islam
IUBAT, Bangladesh

ABSTRACT

"Halal" (ÍáÇá) and "Tayyib" (ØíÈ) are two Islamic terms mentioned in the Noble Quran. Halal refers to what is permissible, allowed, and legal, while Tayyib signifies what is good, pure, and wholesome. Halal is closely linked with the fundamental principles of Islam, whereas Tayyib emphasizes ensuring that something is good, pure, and wholesome. The distinction between Halal and Tayyib in Islamic marketing is intentional, not random. This chapter expands on the norms of Halal and Tayyib, guided by a qualitative approach. Applying Halal and Tayyib in marketing involves engaging in Islamic marketing, where Halal establishes the foundation, and Tayyib outlines the process. The norms of Halal and Tayyib can foster various halal disciplines, including Islamic marketing, the Halal supply chain, tourism, finance and banking, research methodology, and more. Consequently, the halal marketing mix can leverage all halal disciplines, catering to different market segments and involving Muslim and non-Muslim marketers within the halal industry.

DOI: 10.4018/979-8-3373-3917-7.ch009

INTRODUCTION

Halal, an Arabic word, refers to permissible for humanity documented in the Noble Quran. The Noble Quran welcomes people of faith in Christianity, Judaism, and Muslims to consume halal (Islam et al., 2025). Halal consumption surpasses food, beverage, cosmetics, entertainment, pharmaceuticals, tourism, fashion, and alike in the halal industry (Islam et al., 2024a).

The halal industry is a growing sector within the Islamic economy (Ab Talib & Zulfakar, 2023), fueled by Muslim markets, which represent the fastest-expanding consumer base worldwide (Ab Talib et al., 2020). This industry is rapidly expanding and has already reached 1.8 billion consumers globally. It has an estimated value of USD 2.1 trillion and has become a significant focus within the global market (Darmawati et al., 2023). Opportunities remain open to participate in various sectors and marketers compete for a share of the global halal market (Prakoso & Tiurma, 2023). Sectoral focus on halal research includes consumer behavior, Islamic branding, halal supply chains, halal certification, halal tourism of Islamic marketing (Putera & Rakhel, 2023). Islamic marketing is embedded within all the subsectors of halal research. Halal and Tayyiban norms denote the guiding principles of Islamic marketing (Islam & Hasan, 2024).

"Halal" means permissibility, and its opposite is "Haram" (Prohibited). "Tayyiban" outlines wholesomeness, cleanliness, goodness, and purity, involving a rigorous process to differentiate halal from impure (Islam et al., 2025). As such, Tayyiban involves an integrated mechanism to ensure halal integrity. This indicates that halal is incomplete without tayyiban, as each complements the other. Tayyiban is impossible to achieve if the halal status of the product is in question. Therefore, the halal status must be confirmed before determining tayyiban state.

The concept of tayyiban is highly significant in the context of halal production, as it preserves human well-being. Many Quranic verses including 2:168, 187, 228-230, 275; 3:50, 93; 4:19, 24, 160; 5:1-5, 7-8, 88, 96; 7:157; 8:69; 9:37; 10:59; 11:39, outline the concept of halal and tayyib. Allah has instructed halal and tayyib-oriented consumption for the public, faithful Muslims, and all prophets. This instruction indicates that halal consumption is rooted in broad segments of society.

Problem Statement

Secular theoretical frameworks cannot fully enable Islamic and halal marketing (Ali et al., 2013; Bouzenita & Boulanouar, 2016; Zakaria & Abdul-Talib, 2010). Ontological theoretical frameworks cannot elucidate the spirituality of halal, tayyib and haram (Islam, 2021a, 2018). Eventually, simplification of the halal marketing mix enlightened with Islamic principles remains vacant.

Given the context of halal marketing, numerous studies (Ali & Suleiman, 2018; Fujiwara & Ismail, 2018) have centered on the role of halal in product development, certification, and standards. Research has also explored facets such as Halal logistics, consumer awareness, and transportation (Haleem et al., 2021; Karim et al., 2021). Nonetheless, tayyibat approach linked with the halal paradigm of the supply chain seems underdeveloped.

Developing models in the halal supply chain received attention in several studies (Ab Rashid & Bojei, 2020; Hashim et al., 2020). Certain studies have delved into the intersections of halal integrity, sustainability, traceability, religious beliefs, and management commitment (EI Daouk, 2022; Khan et al., 2022). Yet, crucial Islamic norms and issues about Shariah have not drown enough consideration in the contemporary research.

Contemporary research highlights halal and *tayyiban* illustrating five themes. Five main themes: safety, nutrition, cleanliness, quality, and authenticity are built to comprehend *tayyiban* concept (Abdul Mokti et al., 2024). Halal is also explained within the traditional permissibility norms (Salam and Hasan, 2024). Nevertheless, simplifying basic Islamic norms and applying the "Halal" and "Tayyib" norms in Marketing remain unexplored. Moreover, scholarly works to advance current body of Islamic marketing linger shallow.

Aim, Objective, and Research Question

This chapter aims to simplify the application of the halal and tayyib approach to marketing under qualitative Islamic principles. The Islamic principles can help attain the practicality of the ongoing marketing activities in halal and Islamic marketing. To be specific, the sole objective of this chapter is to outline halal and tayyib norms to design the four Ps in marketing. The aim and objective result in a research question: what are the specific halal and tayyib issues pertaining four Ps of the Islamic marketing mix?

2. LITERATURE REVIEW

Islamic marketing can mitigate social criticisms of conventional marketing (Islam, 2018), thereby extending the halal industry and its prospects (Islam, 2021a, b). Theoretical premises of Islamic marketing are emerging (Islam et al., 2024a, b). Integrating Islamic principles into marketing is a strategic tool in the halal industry, where halal standards and certifications are prerequisites for sustainability (Islam,

2022a, b, c). Unique halal standards and certifications are qualitative phenomena and necessary for marketing but challenging to implement (Islam et al., 2023; Islam, 2023). The latest systemic literature review shows that most studies in Islamic marketing use a qualitative approach, focusing on 'halal' and 'Islamic' content (Aziz et al., 2025). Still, the content depicts limited Islamic marketing studies outlining prescriptive Quranic verses and Prophetic traditions or hadiths to steady the theoretical premises.

Islamic marketing still lacks consensus, as marketers and consumers interpret Islamic and Halal terms differently (Islam & Hasan, 2024). Non-Muslim marketers are primarily motivated by capturing a share of the Halal industry, while Muslim marketers have both economic and religious interests. Similarly, non-Muslim consumers choose Halal products due to subjective norms like value, safety, ingredients, cleanliness, and other extrinsic factors. In contrast, Muslim consumers are driven by religious obligations to consume Halal, in addition to considerations of safety, ingredients, cleanliness, and other aspects. Halal certification serves as a bridge between marketers and consumers regarding halal production. As such, emerging trends in Islamic marketing suggest a growing concentration on consumer behavior, branding, halal certification, and ethical marketing practices (Ali et al., 2025). Nonetheless, the baselines of certification and ethics of Islamic marketing for halal production refer to halal and tayyib norms remain unexplained.

Halal production emphasizes safety, nutrition, cleanliness, quality, and authenticity, which are essential in shaping the holistic concept of Tayyiba in Halal (Abdul Mokti et al., 2024). The performance of Halal production also contributes to its financial success (Deku et al., 2023). Halal Good Manufacturing Practices (HGMP) positively impact Halal production, with significant differences observed in aspects such as building, employees, storage, and maintenance when manufacturing is guided by Islamic principles (Lestari et al., 2023). Religious environment and practicing religious culture affect halal product choices. Intrareligious notion depicts more significance than interreligious issues (Osanlou and Rezae, 2025). Yet, religious dimensions like halal and tayyib have not received proper attention in Islami marketing.

Islamic marketing promotes safety and environmentally friendly practices (Rezai et al., 2012), while religiosity influences mediating factors like awareness, trust, subjective norms, and perceived behavioral control, which shape attitudes toward Halal products (Ali et al., 2018). These mediating factors lead to a stronger intention to purchase Halal-certified products (Loussaief et al., 2023). Moreover, exposure and religious commitment enhance knowledge and awareness of Halal-certified goods (Usman et al., 2023). For consumers with high Islamic religiosity (Elseidi, 2018), positive personal attitudes, personal convictions, and perceived control are key drivers of Halal consumption (Ali et al., 2017). A positive attitude, motivation to comply, and perceived control also predict Muslims' intention to consume Halal (Sherwani et al., 2018). Overall, halal integrity signifies the key issue in many studies (Mustapha et al., 2024; Rajendran et al., 2024; Susiang et al., 2024;). But analyses of halal and tayyib dente the key components of halal integrity in Islamic marketing remain undocumented.

In addition to integrity, labeling products as Halal has a psychological impact (Anam et al., 2018). Attitude and religious self-identity influence the willingness to pay for certified Halal products (Iranmanesh et al., 2020), while primary personal values such as personal security, benevolence, and achievement are linked to trying Halal products (Arsil et al., 2018). The level of knowledge, Halal quality assurance practices, commitment (Othman et al., 2016), subjective norms, and perceived behavioral control influence consumers' intention to purchase Halal items (Marmaya et al., 2019). Notably, image, trust, and satisfaction play roles in shaping consumer shopping behavior for Halal-labeled products (Muflih & Juliana, 2021). Yet, haram (prohibition) and other negative and avoidable issues for satisfying consumers did not receive enough concentration.

Given the content of prohibited issues, consciousness impacts the intention to purchase Halal-certified goods (Usman et al., 2022), and consumers often believe they possess above-average competence regarding Halal concepts, sources, ingredients, processing, and production (Ahmad et al., 2015). Consumer engagement with Halal products is shaped by the interaction of identities and value sources (Hassan & Pandey, 2020), and factors like consumer pressure, industry competition, marketing functions, operational improvements, and organizational commitment all influence Halal and Tayyiban (Najmi et al., 2023). The interplay between firms and consumers further impacts consumer engagement with Halal products (Hassan & Pandey, 2020). Customer attitude, comparison studies, digital products, customer loyalty, customer trust, consumer determinants, and service quality have been recent focus (Bonang et al., 2025). However, halal and tayyib denote the key determinants that remain insufficient in Islamic marketing.

Halal products, supported by proper implementation and certification, positively affect operational, financial, and marketing performance (Amer, 2023). Additionally, Halal labeling and safety concerns drive positive performance, with brand origin, religiosity, and price influencing preferences (Khan et al., 2020). Despite these benefits, challenges in obtaining Halal certification include the complex certification process, lack of owner commitment, and high certification fees (Wannasupchue et al., 2023). These challenges are further compounded by the institutional context and limited awareness of Halal principles. Given the growing demand for Halal products, a new paradigm is needed to organize their production and trade (De Boni & Forleo, 2019). Nonetheless, qualitative works with prescriptive shariah principles are deemed inadequate to shape the proposed paradigm.

Figure 1. Content analysis of the literature review

Figure 1 shows 81 articles from different journals exploring Islamic marketing, halal supply chain management, halal food consumption, Islamic advertising, and the impact of Islamic principles on purchasing behavior. They discuss issues like sustainability, traceability, consumer perceptions, and the role of government in promoting Halal industries. Authors explored themes like halal tourism, ethical considerations in advertising, consumer knowledge of halal products, and the integration of Islamic principles in marketing and business practices.

Further, they provided insights into the halal market, addressed challenges faced by businesses, and understood consumer preferences within the context of Islamic principles. Several studies explored halal food consumption, including religiosity's influence on purchasing intentions, gen Y consumers' behavior, ethical issues in the supply chain, and readiness for halal food standard adoption among firms. Others focused on halal transportation adoption, halal quality assurance practices among food industries, and challenges in obtaining halal certification among restaurants. The research also delved into topics like Islamic marketing ethics, halal meat consumption determinants, and the impact of decision-making style and religiosity on purchasing halal food.

Previous literature identifies a connection between Halal and Tayyiban, with Halal certification being used as a tool of Islamic marketing. While Halal represents the basic requirements, Tayyibat defines the Halal status. Furthermore, Tayyibat becomes central in adding value to Halal. However, how Tayyibat can be a rigorous process encompassing cleanliness, purity, safety, and wholesomeness has not received adequate attention in previous studies. Applying the "Halal" and "Tayyib" norms in marketing by emphasizing the mechanisms and processes of Tayyib can enhance

Halal integrity and Halal certification. Halal integrity and Halal certification signify the core of Islamic marketing.

3. THEORETICAL FRAMEWORK

Quranic verses guide Islamic marketing, as illustrated in chapter Al-Baqara (2:275). Beyond this, other verses offer insights into halal business as theoretical foundations. Theoretically, prohibited (haram) practices are considered dangerous. Haram (مارح), which means forbidden, prohibited, or banned, is referenced in the Noble Quran (2:144, 149, 150, 173, 191, 196, 275; 3:50, 93; 4:23, 160; 5:1-3, 72, 87, 95-97; 6:119, 138, 140, 144-146, 150-151). These verses outline the fundamental Islamic rulings that invalidate halal and tayyib. Khabith (ثيبخ) also renders halal and tayyib invalid, as mentioned in the Glorious Quran (2:267; 3:189; 4:2; 5:100; 7:58, 157; 8:37; 14:26; 21:74; 24:26), where it is described as evil, bad, wicked, or impure. Najas (إسَجَن), translated as unclean and impure, is directly haram according to the Noble Quran (9:28). Furthermore, Shubuhat (ةهبش) in the Quran (2:25, 70, 118; 3:7; 4:157; 13:16) means obscurity, uncertainty, conceit, conflict, mixing, or similarity, and Makruh (أهوُرْكَم), depicted in the Quran (17:38; 7:28; 8:5; 9:48, 54; 11:28; 43:78), means hateful and disliked, which can also be part of haram and khabith.

On the contrary, halal and tayyib are the opposites of haram and khabith. Halal and tayyib must be fostered through micro and macro processes embedded in product purification. Halal (للاح) is a fundamental Islamic ruling that supports tayyib, and tayyib (بيط) is supported by zakka (اكَز), tajakka (ىكّزَت), and ajka (ىكزا). Zakka, a verbal form (Fei’l in Arabic), mentioned in the Quran (2:43, 83, 110, 177, 277, 232; 4:162; 9:11, 18, 71), means “purify frequently.” This represents stakeholders’ tasks, frequent activities, and the second form of the Arabic verb, emphasizing the processor’s actions to maintain the integrity of tayyib. Tajakka, another verbal form in the Quran (20:76; 24:28, 30; 35:18; 79:18; 80:3, 7; 87:14; 92:18), translates to “purify yourselves.” This implies stakeholders' joint action, involvement of actors, dependent functions, and the fifth form of the Arabic verb, highlighting processors' collaboration to maintain the integrity of tayyib. Ajka, a noun (Ism in Arabic) in the Quran (18:19), means “the purest.” It refers to producing the purest food and products, improving product quality, and achieving the superlative form of a product. It signifies the process of refining tayyib products to their best state.

Figure 2. Theoretical aspects of halal and tayyib for Islamic marketing

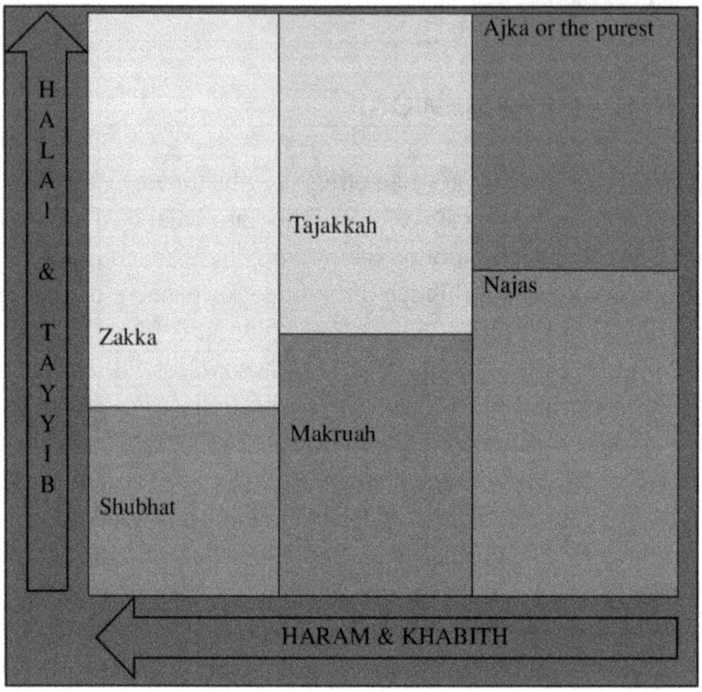

To apply halal and tayyib principles in marketing, elements of haram and khabith must be avoided. Najas, makruh, and shubhat can be part of haram and khabith. Najas, being impure, is considered haram and marked in red. The red zone can nullify the halal integrity of a product. The makruh zone is close to the red zone because makruh is in proximity to haram, known as makruh-at-tahrimi. Furthermore, shubhat sometimes resembles haram and must, therefore, be avoided in halal operations. Thus, the haram and khabith elements, consisting of najas, makruh, and shubhat, must be avoided to foster halal and tayyib practices illustrated in Figure 2.

Beyond shubhat, halal and tayyib-based operations should be pursued. Zakka denotes the activities marketers engage in to safeguard purity or tayyib. Tajakka outlines the marketing and supporting activities within the ecosystem that uphold tayyib. Ultimately, the purest state of the product will be achieved through ajka. Therefore, halal and tayyib are the opposites of haram and khabith. To apply halal and tayyib principles, one must eliminate najas, makruh, and shubhat, while incorporating zakka, tajakka, and ajka. The elements to be removed are value-destructing, while the elements to be added are value-enhancing in marketing.

4. METHODOLOGY

4.1 Research Approach

This chapter adopted a qualitative research approach, concentrating on delving deeply into the subject matter. Using qualitative methodology provides researchers with the flexibility to grasp the underlying context of the research issue (Bryman, 2016; Robson, 2011). Notably, qualitative research employs an inductive method to explore novel theoretical elements (Eisenhardt et al., 2016). The primary aim of this chapter is to contribute to the existing knowledge about halal and tayyib to lead zakka, tajakkah, and ajka. Given the nature of this research question, an inductive notion guided by a qualitative approach is well-suited. Moreover, qualitative research allows researchers to offer insights that bridge gaps in understanding the current body of knowledge. Accordingly, this chapter inducted the prescriptive Qur'anic verses to advance Islamic marketing.

Furthermore, an inductive approach plays a pivotal role in advancing knowledge (Eisenhardt et al., 2016). The inductive approach involves moving from specific observations to general concepts and theories (Woiceshyn & Daellenbach, 2018). Advancing the Islamic marketing theories remains the prime concentration of this study. This study aims to enhance the understanding of Halal, it has adopted a qualitative approach with inductive reasoning, drawing from Quranic textual and contextual themes. These themes primarily revolve around the concepts of Halal, and Tayyib with the marketing mix, qualitative approach, and inductive notion.

4.2 Data Collection

Quranic verses are rich sources of qualitative and authoritative information, and researchers can extract relevant guidelines from the Quran (Saeed et al., 2001). The author sourced the pertinent verses from the Noble Quran about halal and tayyib. Additionally, the study examined secondary data from previous literature on halal research. As such, the author gathered all the data from secondary sources to meet the study requirements from spiritual and materialistic origins.

4.3 Data Analysis

The content of halal and tayyib affiliated with haram and khabith received priority to delve into marketing. The Islamic principles supplied the inputs to showcase the conventional marketing mix to result in Islamic marketing mix. The content has been understood to align with the halal domain focus, such as supply chain, tourism, certification, and finance. The halal domain focus also outlines processed food, meat, cosmetics, pharmaceuticals, hotels, restaurants, and intangible services. The disciplines and domains have been galvanized with the themes of halal and tayyib. Atlas.ti helped to accomplish the content, concepts, and thematic analysis to reach the results.

5. RESULTS AND DISCUSSION

5.1 Halal and tayyib Issues Pertaining Four Ps of the Islamic Marketing Mix

5.1.1 Halal Product

Islamic principles are based on the Holy Quran, the final revelation from Allah, which is a comprehensive guideline for believers and humankind (The Noble Quran, 2:185). The guideline is easy to follow (The Noble Quran, 54:32). Then, the last messenger was authorized to explain the guideline, and the believers must accept the prophetic traditions for better clarification of Islamic knowledge (The Noble Quran, 59:7). Shariah and the prophetic traditions are the rules of thumb (The Noble Quran, 4:59, 65; 33:21) associated with halal products.

Arguably, halal products illustrate the primary variable for marketing. Allah orderes Muslims and others to consume halal and tayyib, referring to the basic rules for consumption by Muslims. The market coverage of halal is the key to Islamic marketing aligned with halal certification while the market coverage of halal products is wide and comprehensive, catering to both Muslim and non-Muslim consumers. The Noble Quran outlines clearly on halal products:

ِةّضِفـلْٱوِ بَهّذلٱ نَمِ ةِرَطَنقَمُلۡٱ رِيطانَقَلۡٱوَ نَينِبَلۡٱوَ ءِاسَنّلٱ نَمِ تِاوَهّشَلٱ ُبُّحِ سِانّللِ نَيّزُ
ايَنۡدّلٱ ِةاَيحَلۡٱ ُعاَتَمَ كَلِذَ ِثۡرحَلۡٱوَ ِمۡاعَنَأۡلٱوَ ِةَمّوَسُمُلۡٱ ِلۡيَخلۡٱوَ

"The enjoyment of worldly desires—women, children, treasures of gold and silver, fine horses, cattle, and fertile land—has been made appealing to people. These are the pleasures of this worldly life...." The Noble Quran, quran.com/3:14).

ْمُكَل ُهّنِإ ِنَاطَيّشّلٱ ِتاوَطُخ ْاوُعِبّتَت َالَو اًبّيَِط ًالَٰلَح ِضرَۡأۡلٱ ىِف اّمِم ْاوُلُك ُسانّلٱ اَهّيَأٰي
نيِبُّم ّوُدَع

"O humanity! Eat from what is lawful and good on the earth and do not follow Satan's footsteps. He is truly your sworn enemy" (The Noble Quran, quran.com/2:168). It also says:

نوُدُبۡعَت ُهاّيِإ ۡمُتنُك نِإ ِهّلِل ْاوُرُكۡشٱوَ ۡمُكاَنۡقَزَر اَم ِتاَبّيِطَ نمِ ْاوُلُك ْاوُنَماَ نَيذِّلٱ اَهّيَأٰي

"O believers! Eat from the good things We have provided for you. And give thanks to Allah if you truly worship Him alone" (The Noble Quran, quran.com/2:172).

As per the verses, a product can only be considered halal when it has been certified, a process that requires trust, responsibility, and authority from various stakeholders. The halal certification process starts when producers apply to certifiers. Certifiers then visit the production process and plants to ensure Shariah compliance. They report their findings to Islamic scholars who evaluate the certification process using their knowledge of Islamic principles. Upon a satisfactory investigation, the certification is issued, and consumers trust the Islamic scholars and certifiers. Finally, the certifiers, producers, and Islamic scholars work together to ensure a seamless halal certification process. The authorized people must take a lesson from the verse that says:

لْدَعْلٱِب اوُمُكْحَت نَأ ِسانلٱ نَيْب مُتْمَكَح اَذِإَو اهِلْهَأ ىَلِإ ِتاَنَامَ ٱلْأ اوُدَؤُت نَأ مُكُرُمْأَي َهللٱ َّنِإ

"Indeed, Allah commands you to return trusts to their rightful owners; and when you judge between people, judge with fairness" (The Noble Quran, quran.com/4: 58). Accordingly, certifiers and auditors must show fairness to the certification applicant and properly return the certification. Then, the producers must be submissive toward the authoritative entities of halal certification according to the teaching of the verse saying:

مُكنِم ِرْمَأْلٱ ىلْوُأَو َلوُسَّرلٱ اوُعيِطَأَو َهّللٱ اوُعيِطَأ اوُنَمآ َنيِذَّلٱ اَهُّيَأ اَي

"O believers! Obey Allah and obey the Messenger and those in authority among you" (The Noble Quran, quran.com/4:59). Thus, halal producers must be obedient toward the government, halal certification board, Islamic scholars, and other experts associated with halal certification. Then, inspection must be in an authentic way considering the verse depicting:

ٍةَلاَهَجِب اًمْوَق اوُبيِصُت نَأ اوُنَّيَبَتَف ٍإَبَنِب ٌقِساَف ْمُكَءاَج نِإ اوُنَمآ َنيِذَّلٱ اَهُّيَأَاي
نيِمِداَن ْمُتْلَعَف اَم ىَلَع اوُحِبْصُتَف

"O believers, if an evildoer brings you any news, verify it so you do not harm people unknowingly, becoming regretful for what you have done" (The Noble Quran, quran.com/49:06). As Islamic knowledge is the key to halal certification and its verification, producers, auditors, and certifiers must ask Islamic scholars about Islamic rulings followed by the Holy verse:

نوُمَلْعَت َال ْمُتنُك نِإ ِرْكِّذلٱ َلْهَأ اوُلَئْسٱَف

"Then ask those who have knowledge if you do not know" (The Noble Qur'an quran.com/16: 43; 21: 7).

All stakeholders, namely the applicant or marketers, auditors, authorities, and Islamic scholars of halal certification, are responsible for the entire halal certification process. It is an *Amanah* (ٱلْأَمَانَات) and Allah will ask the individual involved in the halal certification process. The prophetic tradition says:

هِتَّيِعَر ْنَع ٌلوُئْسَم ْمُكُّلُكَو ٍعاَر ْمُكُّلُك َالَأ

"Every one of you is a shepherd and is responsible for his flock" (Ṣaḥīḥ al-Bukhārī, 7138, Ṣaḥīḥ Muslim, 1829).

The sense of seriousness that all the halal certification stakeholders will be asked on the day of judgment can make the halal certification process smooth, authentic, and integral. In essence, halal certifications and logos symbolize a trusting place for consumers who depend on the certifiers. Certifiers and the Shariah board act as agents that consumers can rely on. So, most people need to depend on knowledgeable Shariah boards.

The Shariah board includes Islamic experts and governments. Then, general people can ask the board for further clarification by putting their trust. Under Islamic principles, members of the Shariah board must verify the halal production process, and the mass people can rely on the halal certification. Regarding *halal* and *haram* concerns, the certification board must avoid suspicion. Allah says:

نيرَتْمُمْلٱ نَم ّنَنوُكَت َالَف َكِّبَّر نم ُقَحْلٱ

"This is the truth from your Lord, so do not ever be one of those who doubt" (The Noble Quran, quran.com/2:147). Notably, Islam outlines guidelines to form the board by Shura to discuss the issues to certify halal. Shura'means consultation and the stakeholders can form a Shariah board. The halal certification counseling board may comprise government representatives, product experts, and academicians of Islamic marketing. So, halal certification, the source of resources, trust, and spirit, emerges from the Shariah knowledge, the board, and Shariah followers. Under Islamic principles, members of the Shariah board must verify the halal production process.

Allah says:

نيلّكَوَتُمْلٱ ُّبِحُي َهّللٱ ّنِإ ِهّللٱ ىَلَع ْلّكَوَتَف َتْمَزَع اَذِإَف ِرْمَأْلٱ ىِف ْمُهْرِواَشَو

"And consult with them in conducting matters. Once you make a decision, put your trust in Allah. Surely Allah loves those who trust in Him" Notably, Islam outlines guidelines to form a halal certification board" (The Noble Quran, quran.com/3:159). And

مُهَنْيَب ٰىَروُش ْمُهُرْمَأَو

"Conduct their affairs by mutual consultation" (The Noble Quran, quran.com/42:38).

As per the ruling of the verse, mutual consultation among the certification stakeholders can help mitigate communication gaps and enhance the credibility of halal certification. Spirituality and religious sensitivity are the cornerstones of halal certification sustainability. As such, halal certification is merely not a means of bread and butter, not a tool for economic gain, it is the ticket to the afterlife success for the Muslim stakeholders. This spiritual and religious sentiment can help to boost the credibility and sustainability of halal certification. Eventually, a competitive advantage will be the product of halal certification.

However, the Holy Quran says to compete in good deeds and not help in sinful acts. While competition for money, market share, and profit may generate hostility among the firms in the industry, cooperation from the industry, suppliers, consumers, and individual firms can create a congenial business environment and advantageous position for all. Obeying halal norms and encouraging other firms to follow need to be the norms of cooperation. Islam suggests cooperation instead of competition in business. Allah says:

َّللٱ َّنإ َّللٱ ْاوُقَّتٱَو ِنَٰوۡدُعۡلٱَو ِمۡثِإۡلٱ ىَلَع ْاوُنَواَعَت اَلَو ٰىَوۡقَّتلٱَو ِّرِبۡلٱ ىَلَع ْاوُنَواَعَتَو
ِباَقِعۡلٱ ُديِدَش

"Cooperate in goodness and righteousness, and do not cooperate in sin and transgression. And be mindful of Allah. Surely Allah is severe in punishment" (The Noble Quran, quran.com/5:2).

The basis of cooperation among the industry players may consist of halal pricing, halal distribution channels, and halal promotional activities to boost the sales of halal products. Alternatively, involvement with haram business activities must be avoided as Allah banned haram activities. Surely, haram harms that cannot result in favor or advantageous to Allah. As such, practicing halal and refraining from haram must guard the welfare of the individual business and society. This requires submission of will to Allah. Allah says:

ٞوُدَع ۡمُكَل ۥُهَّنِإ ِنَٰطۡيَّشلٱ ِتَٰوُطُخ ْاوُعِبَّتَت اَلَو ٗةَّفٓاَك ِمۡلِّسلٱ يِف ْاوُلُخۡدٱ ْاوُنَماَء َنيِذَّلٱ اَهُّيَأٰٓي
ٞنيِبُّم

"O believers! Enter into Islam wholeheartedly and do not follow Satan's footsteps. Surely, he is your sworn enemy" (The Noble Quran, quran.com/2:208). Arguably, halal business affairs must be conducted in a manner that is pure and free from any suspicion of impurity as the principles of Islamic law dictate to avoid impure and prohibited practices. Therefore, the key to success in the halal business is to accept only halal and pure (tayyib) products, while rejecting anything that is haram (prohibited), impure (khabith), suspicious (mushabbah), and disliking affairs (makruh) in Islam.

5.1.2 Halal Price

According to Islamic teachings, halal products, pricing, place, promotion, process, physical evidence, and people are all essential components for achieving a competitive advantage in the halal market. First, halal pricing means setting prices for halal products without any interest or riba. Interest can increase product prices many times over, leading to inconvenience for consumers and reduced value and welfare. Instead, lowering costs can increase the value for consumers. Allah has forbidden interest in any form or amount. Allah says:

اَبِّرلٱ َمَّرَحَو َعۡيَبۡلٱ ُهَّللٱ َّلَحَأَو

"But Allah has permitted trading and forbidden interest" (The Noble Quran, quran.com/2:275). Then it says:

ميثأ رافك لك بحي ال هللاو تاقدصلا ىبريو ابرلا هللا قحمي

"Allah has made interest fruitless and charity fruitful. And Allah does not like any ungrateful evildoer" (The Noble Quran, quran.com/2: 276). Next it further depicts:

نوحلفت مكلعل هللا اوقتاو ةفعاضم افاعضأ ابرلا اولكأت ال اونمآ نيذلا اهيأ اي

"O believers! Do not consume interest, multiplying it many times over. And be mindful of Allah, so you may prosper" (The Noble Quran, quran.com/3: 130). Though valued consumers bear the ultimate burden of interest (usury), contributing to increasing customer costs and suffering, marketers adopting interest-based businesses become economically benefitted, which the Quran has prohibited. Allah says:

ال مكلاوما سوؤر مكلف متبت نإو هلوسرو هللا نم برحب اونذأف اولعفت مل نإف
نوملظت الو نوملظت

"If you do not, then beware of a war with Allah and His Messenger! But if you repent, you may retain your principle- neither inflicting nor suffering harm" (The Noble Quran, quran.com/2:279). Therefore, riba-free (interest) pricing will be halal pricing and a win-win situation for the producers and consumers of society. As such, riba-free pricing indicates a vital variable for competitive advantage. Similarly, halal pricing covers fair price, no unjustified price manipulation, no predatory pricing, no hoarding, no switch and bait, and no restriction in trade other unfairness. Overall, businesspeople must not eat the resources of other people in an invalid way. In this regard, Allah says:

ضارت نع ةراجت نوكت نأ الإ لطابلاب مكنيب مكلاوما اولكأت ال اونمآ نيذلا اهيأ اي
مكنم

"O believers! Do not devour one another's wealth illegally, but rather trade by mutual consent. And do not kill each other or yourselves. Surely Allah is ever Merciful to you." (The Noble Quran, quran.com/4:29). Logically, if any party does an unfair act, it will affect the individual and others. This is called golden rule said by the Noble Quran:

نوملظت الو نوملظت ال

"Do not do unjust, you will not be unjustified" (The Noble Quran, quran.com/2: 279). About injustice, unfairness, and harming others, the prophetic traditions say that:

رارض الو ررض ال

"Do not cause harm or return harm" (Sunan Ibn Mājah, 2340).

In essence, no-harm principles, unfairness, and averting interest (riba) can result in halal pricing. This halal pricing can ensure the welfare, and protection of self, resources, and society. Eventually, halal competitive advantage (HCA) can be gained among the halal business stakeholders through halal pricing.

5.1.3 Halal Place

Besides, halal marketers must source raw materials, produce finished products, and channel the product to the consumers' hands halal way. The combination of all networks is a halal distribution in Islamic marketing. The Noble Quran has outlined the process by saying it is tayyib (The Noble Quran, quran.com/2:275). The Noble Quran also has an Ayat or sign on the halal distribution in chapter 18:19, depicting empirical evidence.

اماعَط ىٰكۡزَأ آهُّيَأ ۡرُظنَيۡلَف ِةَنيِدَمۡلٱ ىَلِإ ِٓۦهِذَٰه ۡمُكِقِرَوِب ۡمُكَدَحَأ ْاوُثَعۡبٱَف

"So, send one of you with these silver coins of yours to the city, and let him find which food is the purest, and then bring you provisions from it" (The Noble Quran, quran.com/18:19). The verse signals consumers-based halal distribution focusing on halal retailing, halal products, and halal integrity. Therefore, suppliers' functions like handling raw materials, production processes, shipment, and transportation must be halal. Such halal distribution can give halal marketers a competitive advantage. Largely, wholesomeness, halal retailing, halal products, and halal integrity are the key variables of distribution to receive a competitive advantage.

5.1.4 Halal Promotion

While halal distribution creates place utility, competitive advantage can result from halal promotion meaning advertising halal products following Islamic principles to increase sales and profit. Halal promotion helps to create knowledge utility. In halal advertising, messages, models, and media are crucial to show the consumers that non-halal does not exist in advertisements. Importantly, the halal products' message in promotion should be authentic. Allah says:

اديِدَس ًالۡوَق ْاوُلوُقَو َهَّللٱ ْاوُقَّتٱ ْاوُنَمآ َنيِذَّلٱ اَهُّيَأٰٓي

"O believers! Be mindful of Allah and say what is right" (The Noble Quran, quran.com/33: 70).

The promotional message must be free from falsehood and exaggeration. Allah also says:

نوُمَلۡعَت ۡمُتنَأَو َّقَحۡلٱ ْاوُمُتۡكَتَو ِلِطَٰبۡلٱِب َّقَحۡلٱ ْاوُسِبۡلَت َالَو

"Do not mix truth with falsehood or hide the truth knowingly" (The Noble Quran, quran.com/2:42). Moreover, the message in promotion must be effective. Allah further says:

انْسُحِ سانلل اولُوقَو

"Speak kindly to people" (The Noble Quran, quran.com/2: 83).

Subsequently, halal marketers must design advertisement messages according to The Quranic guidelines. The guidelines imply communicating right, avoiding falsehood, and following kindness for advertisement. The designed advertisement and the models used in the advertisement must be Islamic. Later, halal marketers must select advertising models considering the Quranic guidelines. As Allah guides:

امّ ال إ نُهَتَنيز نَيدبُي َالَو نُهَجورُف نَظفحيَو نهِراصبأ نم نَضضغي ِتانموُملّ لُقَو
اهنم رَهَظ

"And tell the believing women to lower their gaze and guard their chastity, and not to reveal their adornments except what normally appears" (The Noble Quran, quran.com/24:31). Again, Allah says:

كَلِذ نهِبيبَالَج نم نهيلَع نينْدُي نَينمؤُملٱ ِءآسنَو كِتانَبَو كِجاوزَأل لُق ىبنَّلٱ اهُيَأي
نْيَذؤُي َالَف نَفرْعُي نَأ ىنْدَأ

"O Prophet! Ask your wives, daughters, and believing women to draw their cloaks over their bodies. In this way it is more likely that they will be recognized as virtuous and not be harassed" (The Noble Quran, quran.com/33:59).

Moving forward, Shariah's compliant promotional activities with modest and cost-saving halal product-focused advertisements will be another issue for producers' competitive advantage. Other issues namely avoidance of falsehood and questionable presentation of the female in the promotion are the crucial variables of halal promotion resulting in competitive advantage. So, Islamic advertisements will leverage halal certification and halal products.

Halal and tayyib are the only principles that guide cooperation and competitive advantages in comparison to non-halal certification. While halal involves ensuring that products are compliant with Islamic dietary laws, tayyib principle refers to the purification process that ensures products' good and wholesome status or halal integrity. For halal integrity, resources such as physical evidence, transportation, logistics, warehousing, and working environment, among other tangible environmental issues, are required. In essence, halal certification and competitive advantage are followed by the 7Ps namely halal product, price, place, promotion, physical evidence, process, and people. Physical evidence is linked with place or distribution. Further, processes cemented with people are integral to all Ps. Hence, 4 Ps are the fundamentals, and the other 3 Ps are additional in Islamic marketing.

Figure 3. Islamic marketing mix with Shariah principles

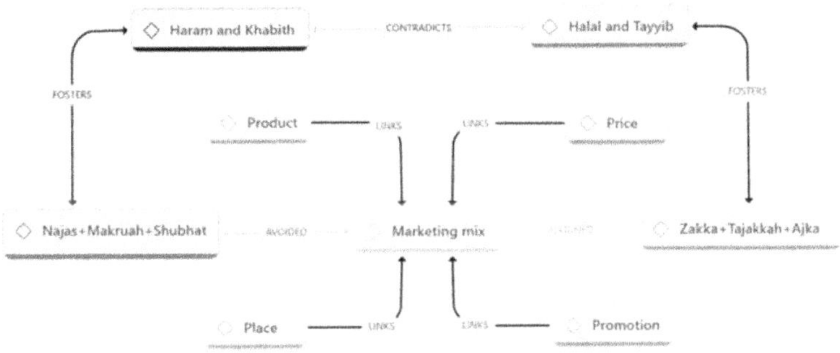

Figure 3 illustrates that the marketing mix consists of 4Ps. Shariah principles, Zakka, Tajakkah, and Ajka fostered by halal and tayyib norms, shed light on the product, price, place, and promotion to accelerate the purity state. On the other hand, haram and khabith resulting from najas, makruah, and shubhat make the halal and tayyib status null and void. So, haram and khabith must be avoided while halal and tayyib must be aligned with the marketing mix. Taken together, halal and tayyib cannot stay with haram and khabith to operate a marketing mix for Islamic marketing.

5.2 Applying the "Halal" and "Tayyib" Norms With Different Halal Disciplines

One of the core challenges of Islamic marketing faced by the B2B model is compliance (Hindolia et al., 2024). Shariah compliance is subject to variations in Islamic jurisprudence and different schools of thought in Islamic literature (Islam et al., 2024a). The theoretical framework captured in Figure 2 can help overcome these challenges. Acknowledging halal and tayyib while avoiding shubhat can help B2B stakeholders resolve the challenges of compliance and disparities in Islamic thought. Stakeholders' contributions (Tajakkah), marketers' actions (Zakka), and efforts to ensure the purest state (Ajka) must enhance compliance. Islamic thought is fully unanimous in safeguarding purity. Thus, Islamic marketing stakeholders can simplify halal and tayyib approaches to Islamic jurisprudence for better functioning of the marketing mix.

The marketing mix for Muslim and non-Muslim marketers can vary. Non-Muslim marketers are not bound to adhere to Islamic norms as a code of life; therefore, a product with halal certification often suffices for their marketing strategy. However, Muslim marketers have a moral obligation to comply with Islamic norms, and the full marketing mix becomes the code of their halal business. Importantly, Muslim marketers gain a competitive advantage due to ethnicity, country of origin, and “taken-for-granted” norms that non-Muslim marketers do not enjoy. This further helps both Muslim and non-Muslim marketers extend their market segmentation and target markets.

After marketing, the halal supply chain faces ethical challenges that manufacturers encounter in ensuring authenticity, compliance with Shariah law, and the avoidance of contamination with non-halal ingredients in halal products (Mustapha et al., 2024). Issues such as process, packaging, storage, transportation, supporting policy, and technology disrupt the halal supply chain (Ardiantono et al., 2024). Avoidance of haram and khabith is fundamental to resolving these ethical and authenticity issues. Furthermore, the marketing mix enlightened with Quranic verses, depicted in Figure 3, offers remedies for process, packaging, storage, transportation, and supporting policies embedded within the halal supply chain.

Halal certification is inseparable from supply chain management and other disciplines. The core challenges of halal certification include a lack of Islamic knowledge to govern the certification process the stakeholders possess (Fauzi et al., 2024). Communication gaps among halal certification stakeholders and their varied perceptions also present challenges (Wannasupchue et al., 2024). Prescriptive Quranic verses linked with the Islamic marketing mix can help fill in the gaps in Islamic knowledge needed for halal certification. Additionally, the Tajakkah principle can overcome the problems of negative perceptions and communication breaches among stakeholders. Thus, Figures 2 and 3 are helpful guides for the halal certification process.

Halal certification is linked with hospitality and tourism discipline. The absence of sustainable consumption is a significant issue in halal hospitality and tourism (Al-Ansi et al., 2023). Unsustainable consumption accelerates haram consumption, leading to numerous Shariah problems, compliance issues, and challenges in adherence to Islamic norms. Religion, alcohol, tourism, and hospitality within the context of an Islamic tourist destination are pressing issues (Afifi et al., 2021). Islamic principles are straightforward in banning any form of haram consumption, its production, and its association. The haram and khabith framework can help resolve the problems of unsustainable consumption in halal hospitality and tourism.

5.3 “Halal” and “Tayyib” Norms and Product Categories

Increasing scandals involving non-halal foods, contamination, and fraudulent practices within halal food are grave concerns (Dashti et al., 2024). As such, the challenge of sustainable traceability in halal food threatens the halal ecosystem (Bachtiar et al., 2024). Halal and tayyib norms can resolve non-halal contamination. Additionally, an uncompromising chain to avoid shubhat and makruh can strengthen the halal ecosystem, leading to sustainable traceability. A robust halal marketing mix is a prerequisite for a thriving halal ecosystem. If only the product is halal while the distribution (place), price, and promotion are neglected, it becomes difficult to prevent the involvement of haram with halal.

Apart from halal food issues, halal meat faces challenges related to the stunning and slaughtering process (Badu et al., 2023). Consumers of halal meat often lack awareness and Islamic knowledge about the slaughtering process (Hanifasari et al., 2024). Integration of halal distribution (place) and avoidance of shubhat are remedies for the issue of stunning. Furthermore, knowledge about haram, khabith, najas, and makruh can help consumers become more informed about halal slaughtering. Marketers can disseminate halal knowledge through the packaging of halal meat, and halal promotion can help fill the knowledge gaps that consumers possess.

Halal cosmetics and pharmaceuticals face various problems, including contamination from animals and plants, as well as issues with transportation (Ngah et al., 2020, 2021). Conflicting viewpoints and limited replication studies pose challenges for producers of halal cosmetics (Liew & Karia, 2024). Particularly, the promotion of beautiful women in halal cosmetics advertisements has been criticized (Arbak et al., 2019 a, b). Common issues in halal cosmetics and pharmaceuticals include the risk of mixing haram ingredients in processed raw materials. Avoidance of shubhat and makruh can mitigate these problems from the outset. Moreover, halal promotion in the marketing mix can address advertising concerns. Therefore, a comprehensive halal marketing mix is the solution to the challenges faced by halal cosmetics and pharmaceutical products.

Nowadays, the attractive presentation of female models in advertisements for halal cosmetics is very common. However, showcasing an appealing look with halal cosmetics is not permissible in Islam. Additionally, providing false information about the product or mixing truth with falsehood in advertisement messages is prohibited in Islam. If such haram activities are not checked, cosmetics bearing Arabic halal logos could lead to sinful actions.

Besides, retailers often stock non-halal cosmetics alongside halal ones. When products are displayed or tested by consumers, there is a high risk of halal-haram contamination. Therefore, the lack of dedicated halal retailers may render the halal status of these cosmetics questionable. Further, cosmetic producers may borrow money from conventional banks that deal with usury or interest. Producing halal-branded cosmetics with haram funding is not permissible. Consequently, haram pricing can make halal-certified cosmetics non-compliant with Shariah law.

Shariah law and halal certification are inseparable. Halal certification must encompass the product, price, place, and promotion. Certifying only the product addresses just one-fourth of the process. Failing to ensure the other three aspects comply with halal standards calls into question the validity of the certification. Although halal product certification may suffice for non-Muslim producers, Muslim producers have a moral obligation to adhere to the complete halal certification norms.

Hospitality and tourism products also pose challenges, including compliance with Islamic principles (Aysan & Syarif, 2024). Halal certification and its application to hospitality and tourism products are still in their infancy (Hariani & Hanafiah, 2024). Serving alcohol and playing music are non-Islamic practices commonly associated with hospitality and tourism issues. Islamic marketing, incorporating the four halal Ps, is the solution to these problems. Furthermore, halal and tayyib principles can guide the halal certification of the hospitality and tourism sectors, provided that all forms of haram and khabith are eliminated from the business ecosystem.

In the realm of halal banking and finance, the mixing of halal and haram in the modaraba business model is a debatable issue (Rahman & Chowdhury, 2024). Questions also arise when traditional banks engage with Islamic banking by opening Islamic windows and promoting Islamic marketing (Islam & Hasan, 2024). Avoiding shubhat and makruh can resolve the debate over halal and haram contamination. Additionally, a full Islamic marketing mix can mitigate issues related to the promotion of haram and halal. Halal distribution (place) can also address the challenges of halal integrity by focusing exclusively on delivering halal products and services to customers.

5.4 Exploring the Halal Industry and Its Business Ecosystem Prospects

Apart from the ongoing disciplines and product categories associated with halal issues, new areas need to be explored within the halal industry to better align with its business ecosystem. The development of a dedicated halal research domain and methodologies is imperative. Traditional methodologies, being ontological, cannot adequately serve the needs of halal research. Particularly, qualitative approaches guided by prescriptive Shariah principles, authentic prophetic traditions, and the integration of mainstream Islamic scholars are urgently required. Specifically, halal research methodology should be established as a distinct academic discipline. Furthermore, it is essential to comprehend Islamic resources within their Arabic context and text and to simplify these in various languages. As a result, halal research methodologies can give rise to many other subdisciplines linked to the halal industry.

In addition, the halal industry must continuously work to develop its ecosystem. This ecosystem should be strengthened by adhering to halal and tayyib principles, governed by the concepts of zakka, tajakka, and ajka, to foster collaboration among halal industry stakeholders. Conversely, elements of haram and khabith, compounded by shubha, makruh, and najas, could threaten the sustainability of the halal ecosystem. In other words, a sustainable halal ecosystem depends on globally accepted halal standards, leading to globally recognized halal certification. A unanimous halal certification can facilitate the exploration of more halal products and academic issues.

5.5 Chapter Implications

5.5.1 Managerial Implications

From a halal management perspective, this chapter entails Islamic principles related to product, price, place, and promotion, offering strategic tools for creating and operating halal certification. This can enhance the spiritual attachment involved in making crucial management decisions for both employees and employers. Overall, the current body of knowledge in halal marketing management can benefit from the extension of halal and tayyib norms linked to marketing theories leading the managerial applications.

The applications of these theories will have significant managerial implications. Conventional managers can gain insights into navigating halal certification and the marketing mix. They can also learn how to manage change for competitive advantage within the halal marketing mix by integrating Islamic principles. Halal managers can apply essential Islamic principles to ensure that the entire certification process is halal, to foster its development, and to address potential non-halal threats. Ideally, the halal industry will benefit from the privilege of creating and managing halal certification from the upstream side.

5.5.2 Policy-Making Implications

Policymakers are powerful change agents within the halal ecosystem, acting as coercive forces to manage halal stakeholders and bridge communication gaps. This chapter is valuable in providing qualitative and prescriptive inputs to policymakers, enabling them to motivate and steer other forces toward any necessary changes in the halal industry. In particular, halal certification boards and government bodies will gain valuable insights that will benefit the industry.

Figure 4. Simplification of Halal and Tayyib in marketing across products

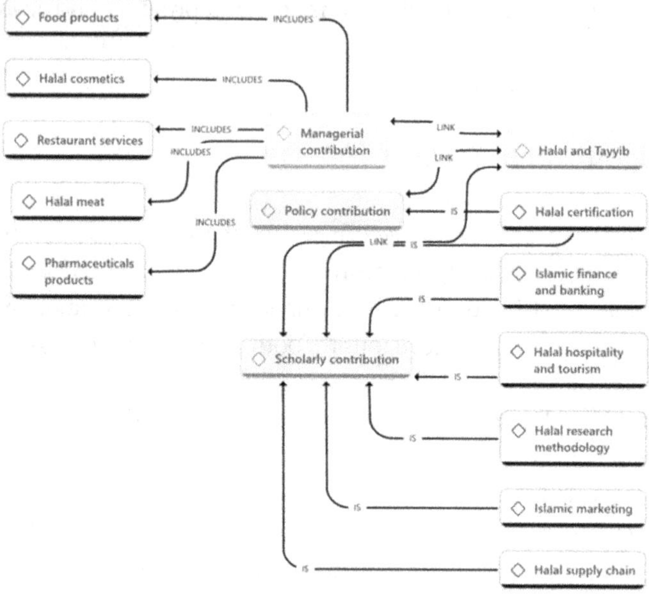

Figure 4 summarizes the chapter's implications of halal and tayyib norms in the marketing mix. Halal and tayyib serve as guiding principles for constructing the 4Ps of marketing. The scholarly contribution highlights how the 4Ps connect with Islamic marketing. For instance, one of the Ps, like distribution, is closely linked to the halal supply chain. Other disciplines, including hospitality, tourism, and halal research methodology, also relate to halal and tayyib principles for halal certification.

Halal certification, when applied across these disciplines, underscores the academic implications. Halal certification outlines policy issues, as state certifiers, stakeholders of halal standards, and halal research practitioners must closely adhere to halal and tayyib principles. Global accredited halal standards and certifications, along with regional certifiers, have strong connections to these norms.

Furthermore, Islamic finance and banking have dual implications. First, halal and tayyib-based business activities play crucial roles in differentiating from haram and suspicious practices in their internal operations. Second, other disciplines that aim to adopt halal pricing (riba-free pricing) can collaborate to enhance the entire halal marketing mix. As such, policymakers in Islamic finance can individually and collaboratively uphold the marketing mix.

5.5.3 Theoretical Contribution

This chapter helps advance the current body of halal marketing mix adding halal, tayyib, haram and khabith. The halal marketing mix directly impacts various products, including food, meat, pharmaceuticals, cosmetics, restaurant services, and more. These represent the managerial implications of halal and tayyib. While managers use halal certification as an application of halal and tayyib principles, they can also understand Shariah principles and assess halal certification comprehensively. The comprehensive exploration of Islamic principles on halal and tayyib norms signifies the theoretical contribution. Moreover, halal branding, an integral part of Islamic marketing, faces challenges when any of the 4Ps risks mixing with haram elements. The elementary inclusion refers to the scholarly contribution and novelty of this chapter. Therefore, academic researchers can protect marketers and halal brand equity by emphasizing halal practices and avoiding haram by these scholarly and thetical contributions.

6. CONCLUSION

The core challenge in Islamic marketing for B2B models is compliance with Shariah law, which varies across different Islamic schools of thought. Acknowledging halal and tayyib principles in the marketing mix and avoiding shubhat can help overcome these challenges. However, the marketing mix differs for Muslim and non-Muslim marketers. Muslim marketers have a moral obligation to adhere to Islamic norms, gaining a competitive advantage by maintaining a halal supply chain.

Halal supply chains face ethical challenges such as ensuring authenticity, compliance, and avoiding contamination. The marketing mix can help address these challenges in processing, packaging, storage, transportation, and supporting policies aligned with halal certification. Halal certification faces knowledge gaps and communication issues among stakeholders, which Quranic and Tajakkah principles can help resolve, leading to sustainable consumption.

Sustainable consumption is a significant issue in halal hospitality and tourism due to unethical practices. Halal and tayyib principles can guide the industry in eliminating haram practices. Other haram practices and challenges in halal food, meat, cosmetics, and pharmaceuticals can be addressed by adhering to halal and tayyib principles.

Importantly, in the halal industry, developing a robust research domain and methodology aligned with Islamic principles is crucial. Collaborative efforts among stakeholders, based on zakka, tajakka, and ajka principles, can strengthen the halal ecosystem. As policymakers play a significant role in managing halal stakeholders and bridging communication gaps, adhering to Islamic principles in price, place, and promotion is essential for halal management and certification processes. The application of these principles can benefit both conventional and halal managers by helping them navigate halal marketing challenges within the halal industry.

Since the halal industry is currently focusing on halal products, the other three halal Ps—price, place, and promotion—have yet to be fully integrated. As a result, a complete halal certification process is currently absent in the industry. This empirical relevance is missing in this chapter and could be noted as a limitation. Future research could explore the halal marketing mix and complete halal certification, as well as further prospects aligned with the halal ecosystem.

7. REFERENCES

Ab Rashid, N., & Bojei, J. (2020). The relationship between halal traceability system adoption and environmental factors on halal food supply chain integrity in Malaysia. *Journal of Islamic Marketing*, *11*(1), 117–142. DOI: 10.1108/JIMA-01-2018-0016

Ab Talib, M. S., Pang, L. L., & Ngah, A. H. (2020). The role of government in promoting Halal logistics: A systematic literature review. *Journal of Islamic Marketing*, *12*(9), 1682–1708. DOI: 10.1108/JIMA-05-2020-0124

Ab Talib, M. S., & Zulfakar, M. H. (2023). Sustainable halal food supply chain management in a small rentier halal market. *Arab Gulf Journal of Scientific Research*. Advance online publication. DOI: 10.1108/AGJSR-11-2022-0251

Abdul Mokti, H., Kamri, N. A., & Mohd Balwi, M. A. W. F. (2024). Tayyiban in halal food production: A systematic literature review. *Journal of Islamic Marketing*, *15*(2), 397–417. DOI: 10.1108/JIMA-03-2022-0098

Afifi, M. F., Mohsin, A., & Farouk, M. (2021). Halal hospitality goes global: Challenges of (not) serving alcohol in an Islamic tourist destination: A case study of Egypt. *Tourism Critiques*, *2*(2), 134–152. DOI: 10.1108/TRC-12-2020-0022

Ahmad, A. N., Yang, T. A., & Wan Abdullah, W. N. (2015). Perceived versus actual knowledge of alcohol and halal food among food technology undergraduate students in a Malaysian university. *Journal of Islamic Marketing*, *6*(3), 294–313. DOI: 10.1108/JIMA-10-2013-0069

Al-Ansi, A., Olya, H., & Han, H. (2023). Two decades of research on halal hospitality and tourism: A review and research agenda. *International Journal of Contemporary Hospitality Management*, *35*(6), 2017–2055. DOI: 10.1108/IJCHM-12-2021-1515

Ali, A., Ali, A., Xiaoling, G., Sherwani, M., & Hussain, S. (2018). Expanding the theory of planned behaviour to predict Chinese Muslims' halal meat purchase intention. *British Food Journal*, *120*(1), 2–17. DOI: 10.1108/BFJ-05-2017-0278

Ali, A., Xiaoling, G., Sherwani, M., & Ali, A. (2017). Factors affecting halal meat purchase intention: Evidence from international Muslim students in China. *British Food Journal*, *119*(3), 527–541. DOI: 10.1108/BFJ-10-2016-0455

Ali, A. J., Al-Aali, A., & Al-Owaihan, A. (2013). Islamic perspectives on profit maximization. *Journal of Business Ethics*, *117*(3), 467–475. https://www.jstor.org/stable/42001863. DOI: 10.1007/s10551-012-1530-0

Ali, H., Qazi, H. S., Hashmi, H. S., Yasin, T., & Abbas, M. H. (2025). Mapping the two decades of Islamic marketing research using bibliometric analysis and novel machine learning topic modeling. *Journal of Islamic Marketing*. Advance online publication. DOI: 10.1108/JIMA-03-2024-0127

Ali, M. H., & Suleiman, N. (2018). Eleven shades of food integrity: A halal supply chain perspective. *Trends in Food Science & Technology*, *71*, 216–224. DOI: 10.1016/j.tifs.2017.11.016

Amer, M. (2023). Halal standards' implementation in Palestinian food sector: Its drivers and impact on performance. *Arab Gulf Journal of Scientific Research*. Advance online publication. DOI: 10.1108/AGJSR-09-2022-0168

Anam, J., Sany Sanuri, B. M. M., & Ismail, B. L. O. (2018). Conceptualizing the relation between halal logo, perceived product quality and the role of consumer knowledge. *Journal of Islamic Marketing*, *9*(4), 727–746. DOI: 10.1108/JIMA-02-2017-0019

Arbak, S., Islam, R., & Al Rasyid, H. (2019a). Influence of Islamic advertising: Ethic violation on customer purchase intention of halal cosmetic products in Malaysia. *Humanities and Social Sciences Reviews*, *7*(3), 671–682. DOI: 10.18510/hssr.2019.7398

Arbak, S., Islam, R., & Al Rasyid, H. (2019b). Relationship between advertisement and purchase intention on halal cosmetic products in Malaysia. *Humanities and Social Sciences Reviews*, *7*(3), 683–694. DOI: 10.18510/hssr.2019.7399

Ardiantono, D. S., Ardyansyah, G. D., Sugihartanto, M. F., Al Mustofa, M. U., & Lisdiantini, N. (2024). Mapping the barrier and strategic solutions of halal supply chain implementation in small and medium enterprises. *Journal of Islamic Marketing*, *15*(7), 1673–1705. DOI: 10.1108/JIMA-08-2022-0229

Arsil, P., Tey, Y. S., Brindal, M., Phua, C. U., & Liana, D. (2018). Personal values underlying halal food consumption: Evidence from Indonesia and Malaysia. *British Food Journal*, *120*(11), 2524–2538. DOI: 10.1108/BFJ-09-2017-0519

Aysan, A. F., & Syarif, M. F. (2024). Shaping the halal tourism industry landscape through NFT and metaverse: New horizons for halal brand and halal booking hotel. *Journal of Islamic Marketing*. Advance online publication. DOI: 10.1108/JIMA-07-2023-0206

Aziz, S., Md Husin, M., Gazali, S., Zameer Rahman, E., & Afaq, Z. (2025). Trends and directions of Islamic marketing: A bibliometric and scientometric analysis (2001–2023). *Journal of Islamic Marketing*. Advance online publication. DOI: 10.1108/JIMA-12-2023-0399

Bachtiar, W. F., Masruroh, N. A., Asih, A. M. S., & Sari, D. P. (2024). Halal food sustainable traceability framework for the meat processing industry. *Journal of Islamic Marketing*, *15*(11), 2759–2784. Advance online publication. DOI: 10.1108/JIMA-12-2023-0412

Badu, R., Teye, M., Bannor, R., & Awal, F. (2023). Meat consumers and Islamic scholars' understanding of humane slaughter, and effects of pre-slaughter stunning on meat purchasing decisions in Ghana. *Journal of Islamic Marketing*, *14*(2), 504–522. DOI: 10.1108/JIMA-02-2021-0041

Bonang, D., Fianto, B. A., & Sukmana, R. (2025). Bibliometric analysis of service quality and customer satisfaction in Islamic banking: A roadmap for future research. *Journal of Islamic Marketing*, *16*(2), 462–483. DOI: 10.1108/JIMA-06-2023-0177

Bouzenita, A., & Boulanouar, A. (2016). Maslow's hierarchy of needs: An Islamic critique. *Intellectual Discourse, 24*(1), 59–81. https://squ.elsevierpure.com/en

Bryman, A. (2016). *Social research methods*. Oxford University Press.

Darmawati, H., Hardiana, D., Mainata, D., & Nuryadin, M. B. (2023). Halal industry: A literature bibliometric analysis on halal studies. *Mazahib Jurnal Pemikiran Hukum Islam*, *22*(1), 175–211. DOI: 10.21093/mj.v22i1.5477

Dashti, L. A. H. F., Jackson, T., West, A., & Jackson, L. (2024). Enhancing halal food traceability: A model for rebuilding trust and integrity in Muslim countries. *Journal of Islamic Marketing*, *15*(12), 3382–3408. Advance online publication. DOI: 10.1108/JIMA-06-2023-0167

De Boni, A., & Forleo, M. B. (2019). Italian halal food market development: Drivers and obstacles from experts' opinions. *Journal of Islamic Marketing*, *10*(4), 1245–1271. DOI: 10.1108/JIMA-05-2018-0087

Deku, W. A., Wang, J., & Das, N. (2023). Innovations in entrepreneurial marketing dimensions: Evidence of Halal food SMEs in Ghana. *Journal of Islamic Marketing*, *14*(3), 680–713. DOI: 10.1108/JIMA-03-2021-0098

Eisenhardt, K. M., Graebner, M. E., & Sonenshein, S. (2016). From the editors: Grand challenges and inductive methods: Rigor without rigor mortis. *Academy of Management Journal, 59*(4), 1113–1123. https://doi.org/DOI: 10.5465/amj.2016.4004

El Daouk, M. (2022). Introducing ḥalāl to construction supply chains in the UK's construction sector. *Journal of Islamic Marketing*. Advance online publication. DOI: 10.1108/JIMA-01-2022-0016

Elseidi, R. I. (2018). Determinants of halal purchasing intentions: Evidences from the UK. *Journal of Islamic Marketing*, *9*(1), 167–190. DOI: 10.1108/JIMA-02-2016-0013

Fauzi, M. A., Mohd Ali, N. S., Mat Russ, N., Mohamad, F., Battour, M., & Mohd Zaki, N. N. (2024). Halal certification in food products: Science mapping of present and future trends. *Journal of Islamic Marketing*, *15*(12), 3564–3580. Advance online publication. DOI: 10.1108/JIMA-12-2023-0407

Fujiwara, T., & Ismail, R. M. (2018). Supplier management system in halal food supply chain: A case study approach. *International Journal of Supply Chain Management*, *7*(3), 216–220. http://dsgate.uum.edu.my/jspui/handle/123456789/4509

Haleem, A., Khan, M. I., & Khan, S. (2021). Conceptualising a framework linking halal supply chain management with sustainability: An India centric study. *Journal of Islamic Marketing*, *12*(8), 1535–1552. DOI: 10.1108/JIMA-07-2019-0149

Hanifasari, D., Masudin, I., Zulfikarijah, F., Rumijati, A., & Restuputri, D. P. (2024). Millennial generation awareness of halal supply chain knowledge toward purchase intention for halal meat products: Empirical evidence in Indonesia. *Journal of Islamic Marketing*, *15*(7), 1847–1885. DOI: 10.1108/JIMA-01-2023-0012

Hariani, D., & Hanafiah, M. H. (2024). The competitiveness, challenges, and opportunities to accommodate the halal tourism market: A Sharia-law tourism destination perspectives. *Journal of Islamic Marketing*, *15*(3), 919–942. DOI: 10.1108/JIMA-05-2023-0147

Hashim, N. A. M. K., Aziz, R. C., & Yusoof, A. M. (2020). The success of halal supply chain management practices in Malaysia. *Journal of Advanced Research in Dynamical and Control Systems*, *12*(8), 232–236. DOI: 10.5373/JARDCS/V12I8/20202469

Hassan, Y., & Pandey, J. (2020). Examining the engagement of young consumers for religiously sanctioned food: The case of halal food in India. *Young Consumers*, *21*(2), 211–232. DOI: 10.1108/YC-01-2019-0940

Hindolia, A., Arya, J., Pathak, R., & Kazmi, A. (2024). Halal B2B marketing in the metaverse: Crafting a conceptual framework to pinpoint opportunities and challenges, outlining the agenda for future research. *Journal of Islamic Marketing, ahead-of-print*. https://doi.org/DOI: 10.1108/JIMA-02-2024-0054

Iranmanesh, M., Mirzaei, M., Parvin Hosseini, S. M., & Zailani, S. (2020). Muslims' willingness to pay for certified halal food: An extension of the theory of planned behavior. *Journal of Islamic Marketing, 11*(1), 14–30. DOI: 10.1108/JIMA-03-2018-0049

Islam, M. M. (2018). Islamic marketing practice as a panacea to social marketing criticism. *International Journal of Islamic Marketing and Branding, 3*(2), 104–115. DOI: 10.1504/IJIMB.2018.094080

Islam, M. M. (2021a). Segmenting, targeting, and positioning in Islamic marketing. *Journal of Islamic Marketing, 12*(7), 1385–1404. DOI: 10.1108/JIMA-10-2018-0181

Islam, M. M. (2021b). The satisfaction of Bangladeshi pilgrims: Service gaps in spiritual tourism based on gender and expenditure. *International Journal of Religious Tourism and Pilgrimage, 9*(1). Advance online publication. DOI: 10.21427/2hw0-cd28

Islam, M. M. (2022a). Strategic perspectives of Islamic entrepreneurship and marketing. In B.A. Alserhan, V. Ramadani, J. Zeqiri, & L.P. Dana (Eds.), *Strategic Islamic marketing*. Contributions to Management Science. Springer, Cham, 183-200. https://doi.org/DOI: 10.1007/978-3-030-98160-0_13

Islam, M. M. (2022b). Evaluating negative attitudes of the students and shoppers towards halal cosmetics products. *Journal of Islamic Marketing, 13*(3), 565–585. DOI: 10.1108/JIMA-03-2020-0067

Islam, M. M. (2022c). Reaching halal and Islamic market segments: Tapping marketing opportunities beyond the borders. In Breazeale, C., Reshadi, B., & Hegeman, J. (Eds.), *Handbook of research on ethnic and intra-cultural marketing* (pp. 200–212). Edward Elgar Publishing, Inc., DOI: 10.4337/9781784717489.00017

Islam, M. M. (2023). Institutionalization of halal entrepreneurship for a sustainable economy. In Raimi, L., Adekunle, S. M., & Shabbir, M. S. (Eds.), *Contemporary discourse of halal and Islamic entrepreneurship*. Springer., DOI: 10.1007/978-981-99-6427-7_5

Islam, M. M., Ab Talib, M. S., & Muhamad, N. (2023). Challenges of halal standards and halal certification for Islamic marketing. *Muslim Business and Economic Review, 2*(1), 104–124. DOI: 10.56529/mber.v2i1.156

Islam, M. M., Ab Talib, M. S., & Muhamad, N. (2024a). Developing theoretical lenses for upstream halal businesses. *Journal of Islamic Marketing, 15*(1), 192–220. DOI: 10.1108/JIMA-05-2022-0156

Islam, M. M., Ab Talib, M. S., & Muhamad, N. (2024b). Islamic marketing and circular economy to foster sustainability of product life cycle enhancement. In A. Rafiki, V. Ramadani, L.P. Dana, & S.E. Hidayat (Eds.), *Strategic Islamic business and management*. Contributions to Management Science. Springer, Cham. https://doi.org/DOI: 10.1007/978-3-031-61778-2_7

Islam, M. M., & Hasan, M. M. (2024). *Islamic marketing of conventional banks: Bridging managers' and clients' perceived gaps*. International Journal of Islamic Accounting and Business Research., DOI: 10.1108/JIABR-11-2023-0379

Islam, M. M., Talib, M. S. A., & Muhamad, N. (2025). Could Ajka be the next frontier of halal? In *Advances in business strategy and competitive advantage book series* (pp. 69–194). IGI Global., DOI: 10.4018/979-8-3693-3980-0.ch008

Karim, A., Setiawan, M., Indrawati, N. K., & Mugiono, M. (2021). Impact of halal standards on logistic employee performance. *Acta Logistica - International Scientific Journal about. Logistics (Basel)*, *8*(3), 269–276. DOI: 10.22306/al.v8i3.237

Khan, M. I., Haleem, A., & Khan, S. (2022). Examining the link between halal supply chain management and sustainability. *International Journal of Productivity and Performance Management*, *71*(7), 2793–2819. DOI: 10.1108/IJPPM-07-2019-0354

Khan, W., Akhtar, A., Ansari, S. A., & Dhamija, A. (2020). Enablers of halal food purchase among Muslim consumers in an emerging economy: An interpretive structural modeling approach. *British Food Journal*, *122*(7), 2273–2287. DOI: 10.1108/BFJ-08-2018-0528

Lestari, F., Kurniawan, R., Arifin, J., Yasir, M., Muhammad Saleh, M., & Akbarizan, . (2023). An integrated framework for the measurement of halal good manufacturing practices on the case of SMEs in the food sector. *Journal of Islamic Marketing*, *14*(1), 82–105. DOI: 10.1108/JIMA-04-2021-0105

Liew, C. W. S., & Karia, N. (2024). Halal cosmetics: A technology-empowered systematic literature review. *Journal of Islamic Marketing*, *15*(7), 1722–1742. DOI: 10.1108/JIMA-09-2023-0295

Loussaief, A., & Lin, Y.-C. (2024, January 09). J., Phuc Dang, H., Bouslama, N., & Cheng, J.M.-S. (2023). Eating halal: A serial mediation model for the effect of religiosity on the intention to purchase halal-certified food. *Asia Pacific Journal of Marketing and Logistics*, *36*(1), 167–184. Advance online publication. DOI: 10.1108/APJML-10-2022-0868

Marmaya, N., Zakaria, Z., & Mohd Desa, M. N. (2019). Gen Y consumers' intention to purchase halal food in Malaysia: A PLS-SEM approach. *Journal of Islamic Marketing, 10*(3), 1003–1014. DOI: 10.1108/JIMA-08-2018-0136

Muflih, M., & Juliana, J. (2021). Halal labeled food shopping behavior: The role of spirituality, image, trust, and satisfaction. *Journal of Islamic Marketing, 12*(8), 1603–1618. DOI: 10.1108/JIMA-10-2019-0200

Mustapha, M. R., Ahamad, F., Hazahari, N. Y., & Samsudin, N. (2024). Ethical issues in the halal food supply chain: A systematic bibliometric review. *Journal of Islamic Marketing, 15*(12), 3804–3819. DOI: 10.1108/JIMA-07-2023-0210

Najmi, A., Ahmed, W., & Jahangir, S. (2023). Firm's readiness for halal food standard adoption: Assessing the importance of traceability system. *Journal of Islamic Accounting and Business Research, 14*(8), 1451–1473. DOI: 10.1108/JIABR-09-2020-0293

Ngah, A. H., Ramayah, T., Ali, M. H., & Khan, M. I. (2020). Halal transportation adoption among pharmaceuticals and cosmetics manufacturers. *Journal of Islamic Marketing, 11*(6), 1619–1639. DOI: 10.1108/JIMA-10-2018-0193

Ngah, A. H., Thurasamy, R., Mohd Salleh, N. H., Jeevan, J., Md Hanafiah, R., & Eneizan, B. (2021). Halal transportation adoption among food manufacturers in Malaysia: The moderated model of technology, organization, and environment (TOE) framework. *Journal of Islamic Marketing*. Advance online publication. DOI: 10.1108/JIMA-03-2020-0079

Osanlou, B., & Rezaei, E. (2025). The effect of Muslim consumers' religiosity on brand verdict. *Journal of Islamic Marketing, 16*(1), 26–64. DOI: 10.1108/JIMA-01-2023-0005

Othman, B., Shaarani, S. M., & Bahron, A. (2016). Evaluation of knowledge, halal quality assurance practices, and commitment among food industries in Malaysia. *British Food Journal, 118*(8), 2033–2052. DOI: 10.1108/BFJ-12-2015-0496

Prakoso, B. P., & Tiurma, M. R. (2023). Halal research streams: A systematic and bibliometrics review. *Cogent Social Sciences, 9*(1), 2225334. DOI: 10.1080/23311886.2023.2225334

Putera, P. B., & Rakhel, T. M. (2023). Halal research streams: A systematic and bibliometrics review. *Cogent Social Sciences, 9*(1), 2225334. DOI: 10.1080/23311886.2023.2225334

Rahman, M. H., & Chowdhury, N. M. S. I. (2024). The prospects of istijrar financing in Islamic banking: An exploratory study in Bangladesh. *Qualitative Research in Financial Markets, 16*(1), 135–158. DOI: 10.1108/QRFM-10-2022-0173

Rajendran, S. D., Kamarulzaman, N. H., & Abd Rahman, A. (2024). The mediating role of halal supply chain integrity in enhancing performance for halal herbal-based food SMEs. *Journal of Islamic Marketing, 15*(12), 3621–3648. DOI: 10.1108/JIMA-03-2022-0090

Rezai, G., Mohamed, Z., & Nasir Shamsudin, M. (2012). Non-Muslim consumers' understanding of halal principles in Malaysia. *Journal of Islamic Marketing, 3*(1), 35–46. DOI: 10.1108/17590831211206572

Robson, C. (2011). *Real world research: A resource for users of social research methods in applied settings*. Blackwell Publishing.

Saeed, M., Ahmed, Z. U., & Mukhtar, S. M. (2001). International marketing ethics from an Islamic perspective: A value-maximization approach. *Journal of Business Ethics, 32*(2), 127–142. DOI: 10.1023/A:1010718817155

Sherwani, M., Ali, A., Ali, A., & Hussain, S. (2018). Determinants of halal meat consumption in Germany. *Journal of Islamic Marketing, 9*(4), 863–883. DOI: 10.1108/JIMA-01-2018-0009

Susiang, M. I. N., Siswanti, I., Permana, D., & Wibowo, M. W. (2024). Effects of competitive intelligence and halal integrity on Halalan Tayyiban implementation strategy in Indonesian MSMEs: The mediating role of halal orientation strategy. *Journal of Islamic Marketing*. Advance online publication. DOI: 10.1108/JIMA-10-2023-0344

Usman, H., Chairy, C., & Projo, N. W. K. (2022). Impact of Muslim decision-making style and religiosity on intention to purchasing certified halal food. *Journal of Islamic Marketing, 13*(11), 2268–2289. DOI: 10.1108/JIMA-01-2021-0027

Usman, H., Chairy, C., & Projo, N. W. K. (2023). Between awareness of halal food products and awareness of halal-certified food products. *Journal of Islamic Marketing, 14*(3), 851–870. DOI: 10.1108/JIMA-07-2021-0233

Wannasupchue, W., Mohamad, S. F., Ishak, F. A. C., & Ungku Zainal Abidin, U. F. (2023). Challenges to obtain halal certification among restaurants in northeast Thailand. *Journal of Islamic Marketing, 14*(2), 607–621. DOI: 10.1108/JIMA-04-2021-0124

Woiceshyn, J., & Daellenbach, U. (2018). Evaluating inductive vs deductive research in management studies: Implications for authors, editors, and reviewers. *Qualitative Research in Organizations and Management, 13*(2), 183-195. https://doi.org/DOI: 10.1108/QROM-06-2017-1538

Zakaria, N., & Abdul-Talib, A. (2010). Applying Islamic market-oriented cultural model to sensitize strategies towards global customers, competitors, and environment. *Journal of Islamic Marketing*, *1*(1), 51–62. DOI: 10.1108/17590831011026222

Chapter 10
Does Religiosity Moderate Halal Purchase Decisions?
Examining the Role of Awareness, Certification, Marketing Mix Strategies, Socia,l and Innovation

Indah Fatmawati
https://orcid.org/0000-0003-4796-2146
Universitas Muhammadiyah Yogyakarta, Indonesia

Lieftyanna Luthfie Tiffany
Universitas Muhammadiyah Yogyakarta, Indonesia

ABSTRACT

The global halal industry is rapidly expanding, highlighting the importance of understanding consumer behavior and the role of religiosity in purchase decisions. This study explores how halal awareness, halal certification, marketing mix perception, social factors, and innovation attributes influence purchasing decisions, with religious beliefs as a moderating factor. A quantitative research approach was adopted, involving 188 respondents recruited through non-probability sampling. Data were gathered using online questionnaires distributed via Google Forms and analyzed using multiple regression and moderation regression techniques in SPSS Version 20. The results indicate that halal awareness, halal certification, and marketing mix perception significantly influence purchasing decisions, while social factors and innovation attributes do not. Religious beliefs moderate the relationship between halal awareness, halal certification, marketing mix perception, and social factors

DOI: 10.4018/979-8-3373-3917-7.ch010

but have no moderating effect on innovation attributes.

INTRODUCTION

The halal industry has become a significant driver of economic growth, particularly in countries with large Muslim populations, such as Indonesia (Randeree, 2020). As global awareness of halal principles expands, it becomes crucial to understand the factors that influence consumer behavior in this growing sector (Khan, Asad, & Mehboob, 2017). In Indonesia, the rise in halal awareness is mirrored by increasing concerns over product safety and authenticity, particularly in the cosmetics industry (Septiarini, Ratnasari, Salleh, Herianingrum, & Sedianingsih, 2023). The demand for halal-certified products has surged as consumers seek assurance that their purchases align with their religious values and meet safety standards. However, the challenge remains in identifying the factors that most significantly impact purchasing decisions in the halal industry, particularly in the context of growing religiosity among consumers.

Indonesia's cosmetics and skincare industry has experienced significant growth in recent years. Data reveals that the number of cosmetic industry enterprises increased by 21.9%, from 913 companies in 2022 to 1,010 companies by mid-2023. This growth is predominantly driven by Small and Medium Enterprises (SMEs), which account for 95% of the cosmetic industry and successfully employed approximately 59,886 workers in 2022. Furthermore, the export value of cosmetics, fragrances, and essential oils reached USD 770.8 million from January to November 2023, demonstrating the competitiveness of local products in the international market. This increase is also supported by utilising local natural resources and cultural heritage in product development, further enhancing the appeal of Indonesian cosmetics on the global stage (Coordinating Ministry for Economic Affairs of the Republic of Indonesia, 2023)

The halal cosmetics industry in Indonesia has experienced rapid growth in recent years. In 2020, halal cosmetics consumption reached USD 4.19 billion, making Indonesia the second-largest consumer in the world after India. This growth is supported by increased halal-certified products, rising from 1,913 in 2017 to 75,385 in 2021. The government has also mandated halal certification through Law No. 33 of 2014, encouraging manufacturers to ensure the halal integrity of their products. With a Muslim-majority population and growing consumer awareness, this industry has promising prospects in domestic and global markets (Coordinating Ministry for Economic Affairs of the Republic of Indonesia, 2023)

Halal awareness refers to a consumer's knowledge and understanding of the halal status of products following Islamic law (Nurhayati & Hendar, 2020). As Muslim consumers become more informed about the importance of consuming halal products, their purchasing behaviors are increasingly guided by their religiosity. Halal certification adds another layer of confidence for consumers, as it verifies that the product has undergone rigorous testing and approval by recognized Islamic authorities (Wannasupchue, Mohamad, Ishak, & Ungku Zainal Abidin, 2023). In the skincare industry, its halal certification strengthens its appeal among Muslim consumers. This idea suggests that halal awareness and certification may influence purchasing decisions within the halal industry.

Marketing efforts and social influence are important drivers of consumer behavior in the halal industry (Ali, Salman, Yaacob, & Parveen, 2019). A halal brand marketing strategy emphasizes natural ingredients and rigorous testing, positioning the brand as a safe and reliable option for consumers (Aoun & Tournois, 2015). This perception of the marketing mix, which includes product quality, price, promotion, and distribution, can significantly affect consumer purchasing decisions. Social factors, such as recommendations from peers and family members, also shape consumer choices, especially within tight-knit Muslim communities where trust and reputation hold substantial weight.

Innovation attributes are also crucial in the halal product market as they offer opportunities for differentiation and competitiveness, especially in a rapidly growing global industry. Innovative halal products can cater to evolving consumer needs, combining religious adherence with modern product development advancements, such as ingredients, packaging, and production processes. This phenomenon is particularly significant as Muslim consumers increasingly seek products that comply with Islamic law and align with their lifestyle preferences, such as sustainability, convenience, and health-consciousness (Hussain, Rahman, Zaheer, & Saleem, 2016). Moreover, product innovation in the halal sector can enhance consumer perceptions of value and quality, fostering greater trust and loyalty (Awan, Siddiquei, & Haider, 2015a). By integrating innovation with religious values, companies can appeal to a broader audience while maintaining compliance with halal standards, ultimately driving purchasing decisions in the competitive halal market.

Despite its unique position, innovation alone does not significantly impact purchasing decisions. This finding may suggest that, for halal consumers, religious and ethical considerations outweigh the appeal of new or cutting-edge products (Nurhayati & Hendar, 2020). Instead, the assurance that a product aligns with their faith and adheres to strict halal guidelines remains paramount in driving their purchasing behavior. Religiosity moderates this complex purchase decision (Muslichah, Abdullah, & Abdul Razak, 2020). Consumers with stronger religiosity will likely emphasise halal awareness and certification more when purchasing. Research has shown that the level of their religiosity often influences an individual's lifestyle, behavior, and purchasing choices (Yousaf & Malik, 2013). In this context, religiosity strengthens the relationship between halal awareness, certification, and social factors, ultimately shaping consumers' final decision to purchase halal products. This phenomenon reinforces the notion that in the halal industry, religiosity is not just a background influence but an active moderator that shapes consumer behavior.

Religiosity is a powerful moderating variable in the purchasing decisions of halal products, influencing the extent to which factors such as halal awareness, certification, marketing mix, and innovation attributes affect consumer choices. Highly religious individuals are more likely to prioritize their faith in consumption decisions, making halal compliance a non-negotiable requirement (Mukhtar & Butt, 2012). In this context, religiosity strengthens the relationship between halal awareness and purchasing decisions, as consumers with stronger religiosity are more sensitive to the authenticity of halal claims (N. J. A. Shaari & Arifin, 2010). Similarly, halal certification becomes more influential for highly religious consumers, who view it as a trusted signal of adherence to Islamic law (Tieman, 2011). The marketing mix—including product positioning, promotion, and pricing—also resonates differently with religious consumers, who are more inclined toward brands effectively communicating religious values (Shah Alam & Mohamed Sayuti, 2011). Furthermore, religious consumers perceive innovation attributes positively if they align with halal standards, enhancing product attractiveness while ensuring compliance with religious principles (Awan, Siddiquei, & Haider, 2015). Thus, religiosity intensifies the impact of these factors on purchasing decisions, making it a critical moderating influence in the halal market.

This study aims to understand the dynamics of halal awareness, certification, social influence, and innovation attributes within the context of religiosity to provide valuable insights for businesses operating in the halal skincare industry. Along with the growth of halal skincare brands, this study focused on a Malaysia-based skincare brand in Indonesia, which has grown and evolved recently by offering halal values to its consumers. The results of this study underscore the importance of halal certification and marketing strategies that resonate with consumers' faith-driven values, ultimately enhancing their purchasing decisions in the halal industry.

THEORETICAL BACKGROUND AND FRAMEWORK

One of the theoretical foundations that explain this study's conceptual framework is the Theory of Reasoned Action (TRA), which posits that an individual's behavioral intentions are determined by their attitudes toward the behavior and subjective norms, both of which are shaped by external factors such as beliefs, values, and social influences (Fishbein & Ajzen, 1975; Ajzen, 1991)The Theory of Reasoned Action suggests that consumers' decisions are influenced by their intentions, which are a function of their personal beliefs (such as halal awareness and religiosity) and the social influence they face. Social influence in our research framework represents subjective norms in the Theory of Reasoned Action. Subjective norms are individual perceptions towards their social influence toward a particular behavior.

From another point of view, our theoretical framework can also be explained using The Consumer Decision-Making Model (CDM Model) of Engel, Blackwell and Miniard (). CDM describes how consumers make purchasing decisions for products or services. This model illustrates consumers' process, from recognizing a need to purchasing and evaluating the post-purchase experience. One of the most widely used models is the Engel, Blackwell, and Miniard (EBM Model), which outlines the stages of consumer decision-making. The Consumer Decision-Making Model posits that purchasing decisions result from a series of mental and emotional processes involving need recognition, information search, alternative evaluation, purchase decision, and post-purchase evaluation. This process is influenced by various internal factors (e.g., motivation, attitudes, and perceptions) and external factors (e.g., social influence, marketing, and environmental factors). Halal awareness and religiosity beliefs represent the internal factors considered during halal purchase decisions of skincare products. In contrast, halal certification, social influence, perceived marketing mix strategies, and innovation attributes are external factors in halal skincare purchase decisions.

In the context of the halal skincare industry, consumers' attitudes toward halal-certified skincare products and their purchase decisions are influenced by external and internal influences moderated by their religiosity. Halal awareness and religiosity served as internal factors, and halal certification, marketing mix perception, social factors, and innovation attributes are key external influences that shape consumer purchase decisions. Religiosity is introduced as a moderating variable, in line with previous research showing that religiosity strengthens the relationship between consumer beliefs and purchasing decisions, particularly in faith-based markets (Mukhtar & Butt, 2012).

CONCEPTUAL DEFINITIONS

1. Halal Awareness

Halal awareness refers to the extent of knowledge and understanding consumers have regarding the concept of halal and its implications for product consumption according to Islamic law. It encompasses recognising halal standards across various product categories, including food, cosmetics, and pharmaceuticals (Shaari & Arifin, 2010). Halal awareness is critical as it influences consumer attitudes and behaviors, particularly among Muslim consumers who seek to align their purchases with their religiosity (Rezai, Mohamed, & Shamsudin, 2012). Lada, Harvey Tanakinjal, & Amin (2009) assert that higher levels of halal awareness lead to more informed purchasing decisions, as consumers with greater awareness are more likely to investigate product claims and certifications to ensure compliance with halal standards. Moreover, halal awareness has been linked to consumer trust and confidence, as consumers knowledgeable about halal processes are more inclined to trust halal-labeled products (Awan et al., 2015b). Halal awareness influences consumers' purchasing decisions as it aligns with their ethical and religious values (Shaari & Arifin, 2010). Therefore, enhancing halal awareness through education and marketing strategies is crucial for businesses targeting the growing global halal market. (Shaari & Arifin, 2010). Emphasize the significant effect of halal awareness on purchasing behavior, noting that consumers who are more aware of halal standards are more likely to make purchasing decisions that align with those standards. This leads to the formulation of our first hypothesis.

H1: Halal awareness positively affects halal purchase decisions.

2. Halal Certification

Halal certification is a formal process in which an authoritative body verifies that a product complies with Islamic law, ensuring it is permissible (halal) for consumption by Muslims. This certification thoroughly scrutinises the ingredients, production processes, and supply chain to ensure adherence to Shariah principles (Tieman, 2011). According to (Golnaz, Zainalabidin, Mad Nasir, & Eddie Chiew, 2010), Halal certification is a quality assurance mechanism that builds consumer trust, as it assures purity and adherence to religious values, which is especially important in an increasingly globalized market. Furthermore, (Fischer, 2016) notes that halal certification is significant for Muslim consumers and has also gained importance among non-Muslims due to its association with quality, hygiene, and safety standards. A halal certification label on a product can strongly influence purchasing decisions, as it is a symbol of compliance with religious obligations and a guarantee of product integrity (Marzuki, Hall, & Ballantine, 2012). In essence, halal certification has become an essential aspect of marketing for halal products, reinforcing the brand's credibility and expanding its reach in the global halal market. Halal certification is the official recognition that a product meets Islamic guidelines and standards, as verified by recognized certifying bodies such as JAKIM (Malaysia) or MUI (Indonesia). Consumers often rely on this certification as a mark of product safety and religious adherence (Tieman, 2011). Tieman (2011) found that halal certification influences consumer confidence and trust in a product, particularly within Muslim markets. Consumers often rely on certification as a sign of product authenticity and safety, directly affecting their purchasing decisions. Therefore, the authors developed the second hypothesis.

H2: Halal certification positively impacts halal purchase decisions.

3. Perceived Marketing Mix Strategies

Perceived marketing mix strategies involve the four key elements of the marketing mix—product, price, place, and promotion—and are tailored to meet customer perceptions and expectations (Kotler, Keller, & Chernev, 2022). The marketing mix has also been shown to influence consumer behavior significantly. Kotler et al. (2022) argue that a well-executed marketing mix can positively shape consumer perceptions and encourage purchases. Perceived marketing mix strategies in halal brands refer to how consumers view the combination of product, price, place, and promotion efforts specifically tailored to meet the demands of the halal market. Basir (2019) argues that halal brands must design their marketing mix to reflect Islamic values while maintaining competitiveness in the broader marketplace. This involves ensuring that products are halal-compliant and emphasizing quality and safety to attract Muslim and non-Muslim consumers (Arham, 2010). The pricing strategy is another critical element, as halal consumers often pay a premium for certified products that meet religious requirements (Shafie & Othman, 2006). Place or distribution must also consider the accessibility of halal products, ensuring they are available in regions with significant Muslim populations and through channels that reinforce their religious integrity (Wilson & Liu, 2010). Promotion strategies for halal brands often emphasize the religious aspects of products but are increasingly incorporating modern marketing tactics such as digital marketing and ethical branding to broaden their appeal (Wilson & Grant, 2013). In essence, the perceived marketing mix of halal brands is shaped by the intersection of religious adherence and contemporary marketing practices, aiming to build consumer trust and loyalty within the halal market. Based on this logical thinking, we developed the relationship between perceived marketing mix strategies and halal purchase decisions in our third hypothesis.

H3: Perceived marketing mix strategies positively affect halal purchase decisions.

4. Social Influence

Social factors are people who consider equality in status or community appreciation closely and continuously socialize formally and informally (Kotler et al., 2022). Social factors such as reference groups, family, roles, and status influence consumer behaviour. Social influence in the context of purchasing halal brands refers to society, family, peers, and broader social networks' impact on individual buying decisions, particularly within communities where religious adherence is a significant cultural factor. (Ajzen, 1991) highlights that social influence is a key determinant in shaping consumer attitudes and behaviors, especially when individuals are concerned with conforming to societal norms.

In halal markets, social pressure can come from religious communities or family members, who emphasize the importance of adhering to Islamic dietary and consumption guidelines (Mukhtar & Butt, 2012). Shaari & Arifin (2010) note that social influence is particularly strong in collectivist cultures, where individuals' purchasing behaviors are heavily influenced by their desire to maintain group harmony and follow religious expectations. Furthermore, (Bonne, Vermeir, & Verbeke, 2009) suggest that consumers are likelier to choose halal products when their social circle views halal consumption as a marker of religious commitment and ethical behavior. Social influence represents society, family, friends, and social networks' impact on individual behavior. In a religious context, social pressure may encourage individuals to purchase halal products (Ali et al., 2019). Thus, social influence plays a pivotal role in adopting halal brands, reinforcing communal values and religious identity through consumption patterns. The role of social influence on consumer behavior is well-established, particularly within religious communities where family and social networks often guide behavior. (Khraim, 2010) found that social factors significantly impact purchasing behavior. This idea leads us to develop the following hypothesis.

H4: Social influence positively affects halal purchase decisions.

5. Innovation Attributes

The concept of innovation attributes in halal brands refers to the characteristics of new or improved products that align with religious requirements and modern consumer needs, enhancing their appeal in the marketplace. Innovation attributes refer to a product's perceived novelty and technological advancements. Product innovations may influence consumers if they perceive the innovations to be beneficial or align with their needs (Rogers, 2003). Innovation attributes are often considered key drivers of consumer choice, particularly when consumers perceive the innovation to add value to their purchasing experience. Rogers (2003) identifies five key attributes of innovation—relative advantage, compatibility, complexity, trialability, and observability—that influence the adoption of new products, particularly relevant in the halal brands' context. Rogers (2003) argued how innovation attributes can influence purchasing decisions in certain contexts.

In halal markets, innovation often involves introducing products that offer unique benefits while strictly adhering to Islamic principles, such as natural ingredients, ethical sourcing, and sustainability (Wilson & Liu, 2010). Othman, Sungkar, & Sabri Wan Hussin (2009) suggest that innovation in halal brands is not limited to product features but extends to processes, packaging, and marketing strategies that resonate with religious and ethical values. Additionally, (Golnaz et al., 2010) argue that the ability of halal brands to innovate while maintaining religious integrity enhances consumer trust and brand loyalty, as Muslim consumers increasingly seek products that reflect their evolving lifestyles and values. Thus, innovation attributes in halal brands are critical in ensuring competitiveness and relevance in a dynamic market. However, in the halal industry, religious values may overshadow the impact of innovation. These discussions lead the authors to develop the following hypothesis.

H5: Innovation attributes positively impact purchasing decisions.

6. Halal Purchasing Decision

Halal purchase decisions refer to the process by which consumers choose products compliant with Islamic principles, primarily driven by religious, ethical, and health considerations. Halal purchase decisions are heavily influenced by consumers' desire to comply with religious obligations, ensuring that their products meet halal certification standards (Shafie & Othman, 2006). These decisions are motivated by the need to adhere to Islamic law and trust in the halal certification process, which signals that the product is safe, ethical, and suitable for consumption by Muslims (Bonne & Verbeke, 2008). Haque, Sarwar, Yasmin, Tarofder, & Hossain (2015) emphasize that factors, including awareness of halal principles, marketing efforts, and the availability of halal-certified products, increasingly shape halal purchase decisions. Moreover, Awan et al. (2015b) argue that the perception of halal products as being higher quality and more hygienic than their non-halal counterparts further strengthens consumers' purchase intentions. Overall, halal purchase decisions are multifaceted, influenced by religious adherence, certification credibility, marketing strategies, and perceived quality, making halal products a compelling choice for Muslim and non-Muslim consumers.

7. Religiosity as a Moderating Variable

Religiosity is the extent of an individual's beliefs, practices, and commitment, which can affect their lifestyle choices, including purchasing behavior. Religiosity moderates the influence of various factors (e.g., awareness, certification, social impact) on purchasing decisions, as individuals with strong religiosity may emphasise aligning their consumption with their religious values (Mukhtar & Butt,

2012). Religiosity can be interpreted as a person's good deeds based on faith and piety following existing religious values. Religiosity has several dimensional foundations (Ode, 2013).

Religiosity plays a central role in influencing consumer behavior, particularly in purchasing halal brands, as it reflects the degree to which religiosity and practices shape individual decision-making. Delener (1994) argues that religiosity significantly affects buying decisions, especially when products have religious connotations, as religious consumers tend to prioritize products that fulfill their spiritual and ethical needs. In the context of halal brands, religiosity drives consumer preference for products that meet Islamic dietary and lifestyle standards, reinforcing a sense of religious identity (Shah Alam & Mohamed Sayuti, 2011). Mukhtar & Butt (2012) further explain that highly religious consumers often exhibit strong loyalty toward halal brands, as they view purchasing halal products as a way of adhering to their faith. Thus, religiosity is a powerful determinant in selecting halal brands, as it aligns personal faith with consumption behavior, promoting both spiritual satisfaction and brand loyalty.

The role of religiosity in moderating consumer behavior has been explored extensively . Mukhtar & Butt (2012) demonstrated that religiosity moderates the relationship between awareness of halal principles and purchasing behavior, as consumers with higher religiosity are more likely to make faith-based consumption decisions. Therefore, the following moderating hypotheses are proposed:

Halal awareness influences consumers' purchase decisions, particularly in halal products such as cosmetics, food, and pharmaceuticals (Abdullah, R., & Abdul Razak, L. (2020) and (Rachmawati, E. & Suroso, A. (2022)). Consumers with higher halal awareness tend to seek and prefer halal-certified products, as they understand the importance of consuming products that comply with Islamic principles (Shah Alam & Sayuti, 2011). However, the strength of this relationship may vary among individuals, depending on their level of religiosity. Thus, based on the previous discussion, we have developed the following hypothesis.

H6: Religiosity moderates the influence of halal awareness on halal purchase decisions.

Halal certification is a critical factor in influencing consumers' purchase decisions, particularly for Muslim consumers who seek assurance regarding product compliance with Islamic law (Bonne & Verbeke, 2008). A halal-certified product provides credibility and trust, reducing uncertainty about whether a product meets halal requirements (Teng & Jusoh, 2013). Studies show that consumers who value halal certification tend to exhibit stronger purchase intentions toward halal products (Lada et al., 2009).

Highly religious individuals are more likely to perceive halal certification as an essential factor in their decision-making process (Mukhtar & Butt, 2012). They actively seek certified products and may reject items without proper halal labelling. Consumers with high religiosity tend to scrutinize the credibility of halal certification bodies. They may prefer certifications from well-established and government-recognized authorities over lesser-known certifications (Hanzaee & Ramezani, 2011). In contrast, some studies suggest that extremely religious consumers may rely less on formal halal certification and instead trust personal knowledge, religious scholars, or direct product sourcing (Wilson & Liu, 2010). This indicates that while religiosity generally strengthens the influence of halal certification, in certain cases, highly religious individuals may use alternative verification methods. This conception is supported by other studies by Akhtar et al. (2020). Jin, et al (2020), Abdou, et al (2024), Parvin et al (2020) and Abdullah, & Abdul (2020). Hence, based on previous studies, we propose the following hypothesis:

H7: Religiosity moderates the influence of halal certification on halal purchase decisions.

Religiosity can strengthen or weaken the relationship between the marketing mix and purchase decisions. Highly religious consumers are more attentive to how products align with religious values. They will likely scrutinize product attributes, certifications, and promotional messages to ensure compliance with their beliefs. Promotional strategies emphasising halal compliance resonate more with consumers with higher religiosity, leading to increased purchase intentions. Research indicates that religiosity significantly moderates the effect of brand awareness and habitual purchasing on halal product decisions, underscoring its role in consumer behavior (Memon et al., 2020). Studies have shown that these marketing mix elements significantly influence consumers' decisions to purchase halal products (Al-Malkawi, H. A. N., Rizwan, S., & Sarea, A. (2023)., Boon Liat, C., Nikhashemi, S. R., & Dent, M. M. (2020). Patwary, A. K., Mohammed, A. A., Hazbar, A. H., & Nor Kamal, N. S. B. (2018). According to the abovementioned discussion, the authors develop the following hypothesis:

H8 Religiosity moderates the influence of perceived marketing mix strategies on halal purchase decisions.

Religiosity can strengthen or weaken the impact of social influence on halal purchase decisions Rafiki, A., Hidayat, S.E., & Nasution, M.D.T.P. (2024). Usman, H., Chairy, C., & Projo, N.W.K. (2022). Tuhin, M.K.W., Miraz, M.H., Habib, M.M., & Alam, M.M. (2022). Purwanto, P. (2021). Individuals with strong religious convictions are likelier to internalize religious teachings, making them less susceptible to external social pressures. Their halal purchase decisions are primarily driven by personal faith and commitment rather than societal expectations. Conversely, individuals with lower levels of religiosity may rely more on social cues and external influences when making halal purchase decisions. In such cases, social influence is more substantial in shaping their purchasing behavior. Thus, the authors propose this hypothesis.

H9: Religiosity moderates social influence on halal purchase decisions.

Religiosity can influence how perceived innovation affects halal purchase decisions. Consumers with strong religious convictions may scrutinize innovations to ensure they adhere strictly to halal principles. If innovations are perceived as compliant, these consumers may be more inclined to purchase; otherwise, they may reject the product regardless of its innovative features. Consumers with lower levels of religiosity might prioritize the benefits of innovation over strict adherence to halal standards, making them more receptive to innovative products even if halal compliance is unclear. This idea is supported by the results of Boon et al. (2020).

H10: Religiosity moderates the influence of innovation attributes on halal purchase decisions.

RESEARCH FRAMEWORK

Based on the previous discussion, the research model of this study is shown in Figure 1.

Figure 1. Research model

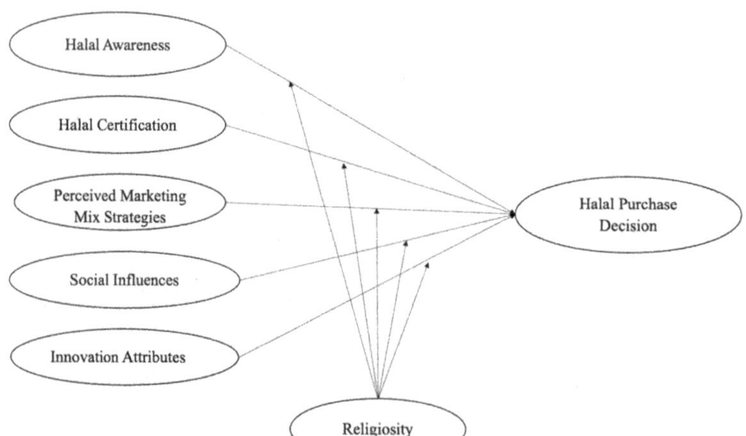

Research Methods

This study employs an explanatory research design to explore the relationships between several independent variables (halal awareness, halal certification, perceived marketing mix strategies, social influence, and innovation attributes) and their impact on halal purchase decisions. Additionally, it examines religiosity as a moderating variable which potentially strengthens or weakens these relationships. Data collection for this study was obtained from an online questionnaire distributed to respondents using Google Forms. The sample was selected based on non-probability sampling, specifically purposive sampling, with the criteria of those 17 years of age or above who have purchased the brand under investigation. Our sampling procedure resulted in 188 usable responses. The brand is Safi, a well-known Malaysia-based halal cosmetic brand, which was established as a trusted brand for Indonesian Muslim women and offers products that are not only halal-certified but also free of harmful ingredients. Holding certifications from the Malaysian Islamic Development Agency (JAKIM/Jabatan Kemajuan Islam Malaysia) and the Indonesian Ulema Council (MUI/Majelis Ulama Indonesia), this brand has distinguished itself in a competitive market.

The variables were measured using items adapted from previous research. Halal awareness was assessed using five items adapted from Awan and Shiddiquei (2015). Halal certification was measured using five items from the same source. Perceived Marketing Mix Strategies were evaluated with 19 items adapted from Yoo et al. (2000). Social Influence was measured using five items adapted from Ali et al. (2019). Innovation Attributes were assessed with six items adapted from Qader et al. (2023) and Quintane et al. (2011). Religiosity was measured using 11 items adapted from Mohd Dali et al. (2019). The purchase decision was measured with seven items adapted from Abdullah (2020).

Results

The data collection results obtained 200 responses; however, due to eligibility criteria, only 188 data were usable for further data analysis steps. Table 1 shows the demographic characteristics of the respondents.

Table 1. Respondents' demographic characteristic

Characteristic	Category	Frequency
Age	17-22	126
	23-28	52
	29-34	8
	35-40	2
Gender	Female	160
	Male	28
Education	Senior High School	103
	Diploma	22
	Undergraduate	62
	Master	1
Occupation	Student	62
	Civil/private employee	71
	Housewife	34
	Entrepreneur	21
Monthly Expenses	<2.500.000	62
	2.500.000-<5.000.000	35
	5.000.000-<7.500.000	36
	7.500.000-<10.000.000	35
	>=10.000.000	20

Table 1 shows the demographic characteristics of the respondents. Most were 17-22 years old, female, college students, with monthly expenses under 2.500.000 IDR.

INSTRUMENTS AND CLASSICAL ASSUMPTIONS TESTING

The validity test of this study was measured using the Exploratory Factor Analysis to ensure whether the item exactly measures the construct. The item was considered valid when the loading factor was greater than 0.5. At the same time, a reliability test was conducted using Cronbach's Alpha. A construct is considered reliable if Cronbach's Alpha is greater than 0.60. Table 2 shows the results of validity and reliability tests. Based on Table 2 it showed that all items have loading factors greater than 0.5. Thus, all of the items were considered valid. The reliability test results showed that each construct's Cronbach alpha is greater than 0.6; hence, all constructs are deemed reliable. Both analyses were conducted using SPSS.

Table 2. Validity test, factor analysis and reliability test

Variable	Indicators	Loading Factors	Cronbach Alpha
Halal Awareness	1. Pay attention to the halal label before buying.	0.614	0.737
	2. Always look for halal information before buying.	0.834	
	3. Avoid doubtful halal-status products	0.906	
	4. Always check the alcohol content	0.757	
	5. I feel calm when buying halal products	0.942	
Halal Certification	1. Halal certification guarantees	0.737	0.769
	2. Halal certification ensures brand safety	0.926	
	3. Halal certification consideration	0.771	
	4. Halal certification makes it easy to obtain product information	0.809	
	5. Ensuring halal certification before purchase	0.860	
Perceived Marketing Mix Strategies	1. Good product quality	0.569	0.783
	2. Popular brand.	0.650	
	3. Wide range of product variants	0.682	
	4. The use of natural ingredients.	0.699	
	5. The use of halal raw materials	0.610	
	6. Affordable price	0.508	
	7. Competitive price	0.523	
	8. Online availability	0.586	
	9. Close sales location	0.526	
	10. Widely availability in the market	0.601	
	11. The use of beauty influencers	0.559	
	12. The use of social media promotions	0.709	
	13. The use of personal selling	0.617	
	14. The use of sales promotions	0.605	
Social Influence	1. Social media review	0.795	0.739
	2. Friend review	0.813	

continued on following page

Table 2. Continued

Variable	Indicators	Loading Factors	Cronbach Alpha
	3. Friend recommendation	0.851	
	4. The family choice	0.914	
	5. Closest people choice	0.654	
Innovation Attribute	1. Innovative new product	0.806	0.724
	2. Different products to suit different skin types.	0.853	
	3. Different products to suit facial skin problems.	0.928	
	4. Latest content and is always developing	0.942	
	5. Natural ingredients in each of its products	0.818	
Religiosity	1. Believe in God in everything I do.	0.685	0.758
	2. Always do what Allah commands to do	0.632	
	3. Comply Allah forbidden	0.764	
	4. Perform the five daily prayers	0.628	
	5. Obey the rules in the Qur'an and Hadith	0.630	
	6. Perform charity	0.513	
	7. Always speak honestly	0.770	
	8. Devoted to both parents	0.612	
	9. Always keep promises	0.764	
	10. Invite people to do good	0.831	
	11. Do not repeat prohibited actions in religion	0.517	
Halal Purchase Decision	1. Choose the brand to fulfill your skincare needs.	0.865	0.775
	2. Choose the brand to fulfill cosmetic needs.	0.948	
	3. Prefer this brand over others.	0.614	
	4. Prefer this brand over others	0.593	
	5. Decided to become this brand's customer	0.563	
	6. Decided to buy this brand instead of others.	0.556	
	7. Satisfied buying this brand	0.859	

Table 2 shows the summary of validity test results through Factor Analysis. After confirming the seven factors based on the Eigen Value results, the authors found the final 52 items from the Rotated Component Matrix with loading factors greater than 0.5. These results indicated that those 52 items were considered valid. The reliability test results showed a satisfactory Cronbach Alpha coefficient value for each construct greater than 0.6, indicating that all constructs are reliable.

Using Kolmogorov Smirnov, the authors conducted a normality test to determine whether the data observations were normally distributed. Results showed an asymptotic value of 0.016, which is greater than 0.05. Thus, the data is considered normally distributed. A heteroscedasticity test was also conducted to test whether there is an inequality of variance in the regression model from the residuals of one observation to another, using the Glejser test. The results are shown in Table 3.

Table 3. Heteroscedasticity test results

Model	Unstandardized Coefficients		Sign.
	B	Std. Error	
Halal Awareness	.244	0.12	0.53
Halal Certification	.140	.079	.080
Perceived Marketing Mix Strategies	-.073	.031	.060
Social Influence	.038	.077	.627
Innovation Attribute	-.036	.079	.650

Based on Table 3, the heteroscedasticity test for the independent variables of halal awareness, halal certification, marketing mix perception, social factors and innovation attributes showed there is no heteroscedasticity as seen from the probability of significance above 5 per cent and the confidence level (significance) greater than 0.05.

The multicollinearity test is intended to see whether there is a correlation between independent variables in the regression model. A good regression model ideally does not contain correlation among its independent variables. It is indicated based on Variance Inflation Factor (VIF) and tolerance (α) values. Multicollinearity test results are shown in Table 4.

Table 4. Multicollinearity test results

Variables	Tolerance	VIF	Conclusions
Halal Awareness	.497	2.014	No multicollinearity
Halal Certification	.435	2.297	No multicollinearity
Perceived Marketing Mix Strategies	.636	1,572	No multicollinearity
Social Factor	.838	1.193	No multicollinearity

continued on following page

Table 4. Continued

Variables	Tolerance	VIF	Conclusions
Innovation Attribute	.868	1.152	No multicollinearity
Religiosity	.789	1,267	No multicollinearity
Buying Decision	.497	2.014	No multicollinearity

Based on Table 4, all variables obtained a tolerance value greater than 0.10 or a VIF value smaller than 10. Hence, all variables in this study do not have multi-collinearity.

Hypothesis testing was conducted using Moderated Regression Analysis, as shown in Table 5.

Table 5. Results of the moderated regression analysis (MRA) test.

Variables	B	Beta	t stat	Sign	Results
(Constant)	27,355		1.238	.027	
Halal Awareness (HA)	1.101	.822	1,328	.018	H1 supported
Halal Certification (HC)	.402	.338	.541	.039	H2 supported
Perceived Markt. Mix Strat (PMMS)	.744	1.326	2.650	.009	H3 supported
Social Influence (SI)	555	.347	.268	.043	H4 supported
Innovation Attribute (IA)	547	.327	.701	.485	H5 not supported
Religiosity (R)	1,027	2.025	2,090	.038	
HA * R	.026	1,603	1.262	.028	H6 supported
HC * R	.053	.204	.178	.029	H6 supported
PMMS* R	.013	2,529	2,061	.041	H6 supported
SI * R	.018	.809	1,076	.023	H6 supported
IA * R	.011	.596	.625	.133	H6 not supported
F count	3.266				
Sig F	0.000				
R Square	0.570				
Adjusted R Square	0.281				

Based on Table 5, the linear regression analysis results reveal that the significance value for halal awareness is 0.018, below 0.05, supporting the first hypothesis. This result indicates that halal awareness positively impacts purchasing halal skincare products. The effect of halal certification also shows a significance value of 0.039, below 0.05, confirming the second hypothesis, meaning halal certification positively influences purchase decisions for halal skincare products. The significance value for perceived marketing mix strategies is 0.009, also below 0.05, supporting the third hypothesis and showing a positive effect on halal skincare product purchases. For the fourth hypothesis, the significance value is 0.043, again below 0.05, indicating that social influence positively affects halal skincare product purchases. However, the fifth hypothesis is not supported, as the significance value for innovation attributes is 0.485, above 0.05, suggesting that innovation attributes do not significantly influence halal skincare purchase decisions.

The results of the moderation regression analysis show significance values of 0.028 for halal awareness, 0.29 for halal certification, 0.41 for perceived marketing mix strategies, and 0.023 for social influence. These findings indicate that religiosity significantly moderates the effects of halal awareness and social impact on halal purchase decisions. However, the insignificance of innovation attributes, with a significance value of 0.133 (greater than 0.05), suggests that religiosity does not significantly moderate the relationship between innovation attributes and halal purchase decisions.

DISCUSSION

Our statistical hypotheses testing implied the following insights. The first hypothesis testing results showed that halal awareness positively influences purchasing halal skincare products. Thus, the higher the halal awareness, the higher the consumer's probability of purchasing halal skincare products. This finding aligns with previous research findings. Research indicates a strong positive relationship between halal awareness and halal purchase decisions. Rezai, Mohamed, & Shamsudin (2012) stated that halal awareness is critical in influencing consumer attitudes and behaviours among Muslim consumers who seek to align their purchases with their religiosity. Shah Alam and Sayuti (2011) show that higher awareness fosters consumer trust, brand loyalty, and preference for halal products, particularly in Muslim-majority regions. Awareness of halal principles encourages consumers to prioritize religious compliance, enhancing perceived product quality and guiding purchase behavior. Further, Muslichah et al. (2019) stated that halal awareness influences purchasing decisions. Overall, halal awareness is critical in shaping consumer preferences and supporting purchase intentions in the halal market.

The results of the second hypothesis testing indicated that halal certification positively influences the halal purchase decision of skincare products. Therefore, halal certification branding strengthens the probability of halal skincare purchasing decisions. Research consistently shows that halal certification significantly influences halal purchase decisions by assuring consumers of product authenticity and compliance with Islamic standards. Bonne and Verbeke (2008) found that halal certification boosts consumer trust, especially among Muslims in non-Muslim countries. Ireland & Rajabzadeh (2011) found that certification builds confidence in the UAE, particularly among highly religious consumers. Studies in Malaysia by (Teng, Jamaliah, & Jusoh, 2013) and (Aziz & Chok 2013) confirmed that certification encourages purchasing and enhances perceptions of quality and safety. In Pakistan, Mukhtar and Butt (2012) concluded that certification reinforces consumer trust, aligning products with religious expectations and boosting purchase intentions. Collectively, these studies highlight halal certification as a key driver in consumer decision-making in the halal market.

Our third hypothesis testing findings revealed that perceived marketing mix strategies positively influence halal purchase decisions for halal skincare products. Thus, the better the perceived marketing mix strategies, the higher the consumer probability of purchasing halal skincare products. Several studies emphasise the significant role of marketing mix elements in influencing halal purchase decisions. (Monoarfa, Juliana, Setiawan, & Abu Karim, 2023) findings reveal that each aspect of the retail mix plays a substantial role in shaping consumer choices. Specifically, emphasising Islamic principles in product offerings and promotional strategies positively impacts consumers' purchase decisions. The research highlights how aligning retail elements with Islamic values can enhance customer loyalty and attract Muslim consumers by meeting religious expectations. This reinforces the importance of an integrated Islamic retail approach in marketing strategies. Ambali & Bakar (2014) highlighted the importance of clear halal labelling, affordable pricing, and strategic placement in enhancing purchase intentions among Muslim consumers. Lastly, Aziz & Chok (2013) highlighted that halal authenticity, affordability, and effective promotional strategies are essential for attracting price-sensitive consumers in Malaysia.

The fourth hypothesis testing results indicate that social influence positively impacts the halal purchase decision of skincare products. It means that the stronger the social influence, the higher the consumer is likely to purchase halal skincare products. Research highlights the significant impact of social influence on halal purchasing decisions among consumers. Ali et al. (2019) noted that recommendations from social networks reinforce halal purchase intentions.

Finally, the fifth hypothesis test results indicated that innovation attributes do not influence halal skin care product purchasing decisions. Thus, consumers do not consider whether the product is innovative when purchasing halal skin care products. This result is interesting since many companies have tried to attract their market with innovative products and other marketing programs. This result did not align with previous study results (Ali et al., 2019; Salim Khraim, 2011), which show that innovation influences consumer purchase decisions. Research on the impact of innovation attributes on halal purchase decisions has yielded mixed results. In contrast,

The moderating effects of religiosity yielded varying results. The moderation tests indicated that religiosity moderates the relationship between halal awareness and purchasing decisions for skincare products. Additionally, our findings revealed that religiosity moderates the impact of halal certification on halal purchase decisions for skincare products. The moderation tests further indicated that religiosity plays a role in moderating the relationship between perceived marketing mix strategies and halal purchase decisions for skincare products. Finally, this study's findings suggest that religiosity moderates the effect of social influence on halal purchase decisions. Al-hajla (2017) found a significant relationship between religiosity and attitude toward halal cosmetics. Research indicates that religiosity significantly moderates the relationship between factors influencing halal purchase decisions. These results align with those of Muslichah et al. (2019) and Sriminarti & Nora (2018), who stated that the level of religiosity belief contributes to the aspect of religiosity does not reduce the halal awareness of consumers in making decisions to purchase a product. Previous research conducted by (Ali et al., 2019; Nasution, Rossanty, & Aspan, 2017) supports and follows research which states that social factors moderated by religiosity positively impact the decision to purchase halal cosmetics.

Lastly, we found that religiosity did not moderate the effect of innovation attributes on halal purchase decisions. Research findings suggest that religiosity does not moderate the impact of innovation attributes on halal purchase decisions.

CONCLUSION

Our study revealed that halal awareness, halal certification, perceived marketing mix strategies, and social influence positively affect halal purchase decisions for skincare products. However, innovation attributes did not influence halal purchase decisions within the context of our study. Hypothesis testing demonstrated that the relationships between these independent and dependent variables were statistically significant, except for innovation attributes. Furthermore, the results highlighted that religiosity significantly moderates the relationship between halal awareness, halal certification, perceived marketing mix strategies, and social influence on halal purchase decisions. However, religiosity did not moderate the relationship between innovation attributes and halal purchase decisions for skincare products.

The findings suggest that halal product purchasing behavior is largely rational and influenced by key factors such as halal awareness, halal certification, perceived marketing mix strategies, and social influence. Religiosity emerged as an essential moderating variable, reinforcing the idea that deeply held religious values amplify the importance of these factors in shaping consumer decisions. Practically, this implies that marketers of halal skincare products should focus on aligning their strategies with the expectations of highly religious consumer segments. Specifically, businesses must ensure their products are certified halal, develop an effective marketing mix tailored to the preferences of halal-conscious consumers, and leverage social influence, such as endorsements by trusted community figures or influencers, to enhance credibility and appeal.

The insignificant impact of innovation attributes may stem from the perception that the brand examined in this study is less innovative than leading local halal brands in Indonesia. Thus, to address this limitation, future research should explore brands widely recognized for innovation to determine whether the findings differ. Additionally, increasing the sample size in future studies would enhance the generalizability and robustness of the results.

RECOMMENDATIONS

Based on the research findings, we present the following recommendations for business players to enhance their performance in the halal market effectively. Firstly, it is crucial to focus on halal certification and awareness. Halal certification is foundational in gaining consumer trust within the halal market. Marketers must ensure that their products meet all the requirements for halal certification and prominently display this certification to reassure consumers. Beyond certification, businesses should actively engage in awareness campaigns to educate consumers about the significance of halal standards and the measures the brand takes to uphold them. This can be achieved through targeted marketing efforts, such as advertisements, social media engagement, and collaborations with halal certification bodies, to emphasize the brand's commitment to halal principles.

Secondly, businesses should leverage religious values to deepen connections with their target audience. Brands can foster a stronger emotional bond by developing campaigns and crafting product positioning that aligns with their consumers' religiosity and values. For example, storytelling that highlights ethical sourcing, adherence to Islamic principles, or contributions to the community can resonate with consumers' religiosity, thus enhancing brand loyalty. This approach should also consider the cultural nuances of the target audience to ensure the messaging is authentic and impactful.

Thirdly, optimizing marketing mix strategies is essential to appeal to halal-conscious consumers. Businesses should design pricing strategies that reflect the perceived value of halal-certified products without alienating price-sensitive customers. Promotional efforts should include discounts, loyalty programs, and targeted campaigns that emphasize the unique value proposition of halal offerings. Furthermore, distribution channels should be tailored to ensure accessibility, such as partnering with Islamic stores or e-commerce platforms catering to halal consumers. By aligning the marketing mix elements with the preferences of halal-conscious customers, brands can achieve a competitive edge in the market.

Finally, enhancing social influence can bolster a brand's credibility and trustworthiness. Businesses should actively collaborate with religious leaders, influencers, and respected community figures within the halal market. These individuals can provide credible endorsements that resonate deeply with the target audience, fostering a sense of trust and authenticity. Additionally, organizing community events, sponsorships, or partnerships with mosques and religious organizations can further solidify the brand's reputation within the halal ecosystem.

We also propose several recommendations for future researchers to expand upon the current body of knowledge in the halal market domain. Firstly, there is a need to investigate alternative innovation attributes and their impact on halal purchase decisions. While the current study may have focused on specific attributes, future research could explore the influence of factors such as eco-friendliness, technological adoption, or sustainability practices. Understanding how these attributes intersect with halal principles could provide valuable insights into emerging consumer preferences and innovation strategies.

Secondly, future researchers should broaden the contexts and samples used in their studies. Conducting cross-regional studies can reveal variations in halal purchasing behavior across different geographic or cultural contexts. Similarly, including larger and more diverse samples can enhance the generalizability of the findings and provide a more comprehensive understanding of the halal market dynamics. This approach is particularly important for identifying regional or demographic differences that may influence consumer behavior.

Thirdly, exploring additional moderating variables that may affect halal purchase decisions is possible. Variables such as trust, cultural differences, or perceived risk could provide deeper insights into the complex factors that shape consumer behavior. For instance, understanding how trust in certification bodies or cultural interpretations of halal principles influence purchase decisions could offer actionable recommendations for academics and practitioners.

Lastly, researchers should consider examining longitudinal effects to capture the evolving nature of consumer behavior in the halal market. Longitudinal studies can provide insights into how changes in religiosity, market dynamics, or brand positioning impact halal purchasing decisions over time. Such studies could also shed light on the long-term effectiveness of marketing strategies and the sustainability of brand loyalty in the halal market. By addressing these recommendations, business practitioners and researchers can contribute to the continued growth and understanding of the halal market, ultimately benefiting consumers, brands, and the broader halal ecosystem.

REFERENCES

Abdou, A. H., Chan, M. P., Rehman, S. U., Albakhit, A. I. A., & Almakhayitah, M. Y. (2024). Islamic food laws: Customer satisfaction effect halal purchase intention in China. Moderating role of religiosity. *British Food Journal, 126*(8), 3088–3112. DOI: 10.1108/BFJ-10-2023-0875

Abdullah, R., & Abdul Razak, L. (2020). The effect of halal foods awareness on purchase decision with religiosity as a moderating variable: A study among university students in Brunei Darussalam. *Journal of Islamic Marketing, 11*(5), 1091–1104.

Ajzen, I. (1991). The Theory of Planned Behavior. *Organizational Behavior and Human Decision Processes, 50*(2), 179–211. DOI: 10.1016/0749-5978(91)90020-T

Akhtar, N., Jin, S., Alvi, T. H., & Siddiqi, U. I. (2020). Conflicting halal attributes at halal restaurants and consumers' responses: The moderating role of religiosity. *Journal of Hospitality and Tourism Management, 45*, 499–510. DOI: 10.1016/j.jhtm.2020.10.010

Al-hajla, A. H. (2017). Why Do People Purchase Halal Cosmetics? An Integrated Model in Saudi Arabia. *Research World, 8*(2), 22.

Al-Malkawi, H. A. N., Rizwan, S., & Sarea, A. (2023). Factors affecting buying decisions of Islamic banking products: The moderating role of religious belief. *International Journal of Emerging Markets*. Advance online publication. DOI: 10.1108/IJOEM-03-2023-0439

Ali, Q., Salman, A., Yaacob, H., & Parveen, S. (2019). Financial cost and social influence: Factors affecting the adoption of Halal cosmetics in Malaysia. *Academy of Entrepreneurship Journal, 25*(2), 1–17.

Ambali, A. R., & Bakar, A. N. (2014). People's awareness on halal foods and products: Potential issues for policy-makers. *Procedia: Social and Behavioral Sciences, 121*, 3–25. DOI: 10.1016/j.sbspro.2014.01.1104

Aoun, I., & Tournois, L. (2015). Building holistic brands: An exploratory study of halal cosmetics. *Journal of Islamic Marketing, 6*(1), 109–132. DOI: 10.1108/JIMA-05-2014-0035

Arham, M. (2010). Islamic perspectives on marketing. *Journal of Islamic Marketing, 1*(2), 149–164. DOI: 10.1108/17590831011055888

Awan, H. M., Siddiquei, A. N., & Haider, Z. (2015a). Factors affecting Halal purchase intention – evidence from Pakistan's Halal food sector. *Management Research Review*, *38*(6), 640–660. DOI: 10.1108/MRR-01-2014-0022

Awan, H. M., Siddiquci, A. N., & Haider, Z. (2015b). Management Research Review For Authors. *Management Research Review*, *38*(2). Advance online publication. DOI: 10.1108/MRR-08-2013-0185

Aziz, Y. A., & Chok, N. V. (2013). The role of Halal awareness, Halal certification, and marketing components in determining Halal purchase intention among non-Muslims in Malaysia: A structural equation modeling approach. *Journal of International Food & Agribusiness Marketing*, *25*(1), 1–23. DOI: 10.1080/08974438.2013.723997

Basir, A. (2019). Effectiveness of Halal branding as a marketing mix strategy. *Journal of Islamic Marketing*, *10*(2), 440–455.

Bonne, K., & Verbeke, W. (2008). Religious values informing halal meat production and the control and delivery of halal credence quality. *Agriculture and Human Values*, *25*(1), 35–47. DOI: 10.1007/s10460-007-9076-y

Bonne, K., Vermeir, I., & Verbeke, W. (2009). Impact of religion on halal meat consumption decision making in Belgium. *Journal of International Food & Agribusiness Marketing*, *21*(1), 5–26. DOI: 10.1080/08974430802480628

Boon Liat, C., Nikhashemi, S. R., & Dent, M. M. (2020). The chain effects of service innovation components on the building blocks of tourism destination loyalty: the moderating role of religiosity. *Journal of Islamic Marketing, 12*(9), 1887-1929. (Coordinating Ministry for Economic Affairs of the Republic of Indonesia, 2023)

Delener, N. (1994). Religious Contrasts in Consumer Decision Behaviour Patterns: Their Dimensions and Marketing Implications. *European Journal of Marketing*, *28*(5), 36–53. DOI: 10.1108/03090569410062023

Fischer, J. (2016). *Islam, Standards, and Technoscience*. Routledge.

Fishbein, M., & Ajzen, I. (1975). Belief, Attitude, Intention and Behavior: An Introduction to Theory and Research. *Contemporary Sociology*, *6*(2), 244. https://doi.org/https://dx.doi.org/10.2307/2065853

Golnaz, R., Zainalabidin, M., Mad Nasir, S., & Eddie Chiew, F. C. (2010). Non-muslims' awareness of Halal principles and related food products in Malaysia. *International Food Research Journal*, *17*(3), 667–674.

Hanzaee, K. H., & Ramezani, M. R. (2011). Intention to halal products in the world markets. *Interdisciplinary Journal of Research in Business*, *1*(5), 1–7.

Haque, A., Sarwar, A., Yasmin, F., Tarofder, A. K., & Hossain, M. A. (2015). Non-muslim consumers' perception toward purchasing halal food products in Malaysia. *Journal of Islamic Marketing*, *6*(1), 133–147. DOI: 10.1108/JIMA-04-2014-0033

Hussain, I., Rahman, S. U., Zaheer, A., & Saleem, S. (2016). Integrating factors influencing consumers' halal products purchase: Application of the theory of reasoned action. *Journal of International Food & Agribusiness Marketing*, *28*(1), 35–58. DOI: 10.1080/08974438.2015.1006973

Ireland, J., & Rajabzadeh, S. A. (2011). UAE consumer concerns about halal products. *Journal of Islamic Marketing*, *2*(3), 274–283. DOI: 10.1108/17590831111164796

Khan, M. M., Asad, H., & Mehboob, I. (2017). Investigating the consumer behavior for halal endorsed products: Case of an emerging Muslim market. *Journal of Islamic Marketing*, *8*(4), 625–641. DOI: 10.1108/JIMA-09-2015-0068

Khraim, H. (2010). Measuring religiosity in consumer research from an Islamic perspective. *Journal of Economic and Administrative Sciences*, *26*(1), 52–78. DOI: 10.1108/10264116201000003

Kotler, P., Keller, K. L., & Chernev, A. (2022). Marketing Management (16eth ed.). Pearson Education©. https://online. fliphtml5. com/xzfda/pkef

Lada, S., Harvey Tanakinjal, G., & Amin, H. (2009). Predicting intention to choose halal products using the theory of reasoned action. *International Journal of Islamic and Middle Eastern Finance and Management*, *2*(1), 66–76. DOI: 10.1108/17538390910946276

Marzuki, S. Z. S., Hall, C. M., & Ballantine, P. W. (2012). Restaurant managers' perspectives on halal certification. *Journal of Islamic Marketing*, *3*(1), 47–58. DOI: 10.1108/17590831211206581

Memon, Y. J., Azhar, S. M., Haque, R., & Bhutto, N. A. (2020). Religiosity as a moderator between the theory of planned behavior and halal purchase intention. *Journal of Islamic Marketing, 11*(6), 1821-1836.Mohd Dali, N. R. S., Yousafzai, S., & Abdul Hamid, H. (2019). Religiosity scale development. *Journal of Islamic Marketing*, *10*(1), 227–248.

Monoarfa, H., Juliana, J., Setiawan, R., & Abu Karim, R. (2023). The influences of Islamic retail mix approach on purchase decisions. *Journal of Islamic Marketing*, *14*(1), 236–249. DOI: 10.1108/JIMA-07-2020-0224

Mukhtar, A., & Butt, M. M. (2012). Intention to choose Halal products: The role of religiosity. *Journal of Islamic Marketing*, *3*(2), 108–120. DOI: 10.1108/17590831211232519

Muslichah, M., Abdullah, R., & Abdul Razak, L. (2019). The effect of halal foods awareness on purchase decision with religiosity as a moderating variable: A study among university students in Brunei Darussalam. *Journal of Islamic Marketing*, *11*(5), 1091–1104. DOI: 10.1108/JIMA-09-2017-0102

Muslichah, M., Abdullah, R., & Abdul Razak, L. (2020). The effect of halal foods awareness on purchase decision with religiosity as a moderating variable: A study among university students in Brunei Darussalam. *Journal of Islamic Marketing*, *11*(5), 1091–1104. DOI: 10.1108/JIMA-09-2017-0102

Nasution, M. D. T. P., Rossanty, Y., & Aspan, H. (2017). Towards Halal Cosmetics brand image: Mediating role of Religiosity, Evidence from Muslims women in Medan, Indonesia. *International Business Management.*

Nurhayati, T., & Hendar, H. (2020). Personal intrinsic religiosity and product knowledge on halal product purchase intention: Role of halal product awareness. *Journal of Islamic Marketing*, *11*(3), 603–620. DOI: 10.1108/JIMA-11-2018-0220

Othman, P., Sungkar, I., & Sabri Wan Hussin, W. (2009). Malaysia as an International Halal Food Hub: Competitiveness and Potential of Meat-based Industries. *ASEAN Economic Bulletin*, *26*(3), 306–320. DOI: 10.1355/AE26-3F

Parvin Hosseini, S. M., Mirzaei, M., & Iranmanesh, M. (2020). Determinants of Muslims' willingness to pay for halal-certified food: Does religious commitment act as a moderator in the relationships? *Journal of Islamic Marketing*, *11*(6), 1225–1243. DOI: 10.1108/JIMA-02-2018-0043

Patwary, A. K., Mohammed, A. A., Hazbar, A. H., & Nor Kamal, N. S. B. (2018). Factors Influencing Consumers' Intentions towards Purchasing Islamic Hotel Service: Moderating Role of Religiosity. *International Journal of Management, Accounting & Economics, 5*(7).

Purwanto, P. (2021). Society attitudes and intentions to use products in Sharia Bank of Aceh: The role of religiosity and social influence. *ABAC Journal*, *41*(2), 223–242.

Qader, G., Shahid, Z. A., Junaid, M., Shaikh, I. M., & Qureshi, M. A. (2023). The role of diffusion of innovation theory towards the adoption of halal meat supply chain. *Journal of Islamic Marketing*, *14*(5), 1211–1228. DOI: 10.1108/JIMA-01-2021-0032

Quintane, E., Mitch Casselman, R., Sebastian Reiche, B., & Nylund, P. A. (2011). Innovation as a knowledge-based outcome. *Journal of Knowledge Management*, *15*(6), 928–947. DOI: 10.1108/13673271111179299

Rachmawati, E., & Suroso, A. (2022). A moderating role of halal brand awareness to purchase decision making. *Journal of Islamic Marketing*, *13*(2), 542–563.

Rafiki, A., Hidayat, S. E., & Nasution, M. D. T. P. (2024). An extensive effect of religiosity on the purchasing decisions of halal products. *PSU Research Review*, *8*(3), 898–919. https://doi.org/10.1108/PRR-07-2022-0093

Randeree, K. (2020). Demography, demand and devotion: Driving the Islamic economy. *Journal of Islamic Marketing*, *11*(2), 301–319. DOI: 10.1108/JIMA-06-2018-0102

Rezai, G., Mohamed, Z., & Shamsudin, M. N. (2012). Non-Muslim consumers' understanding of Halal principles in Malaysia. *Journal of Islamic Marketing*, *3*(1), 35–46. DOI: 10.1108/17590831211206572

Rogers, E. M. (2003). *Diffusion of Innovations* (5th ed.). Free Press.

Salim Khraim, H. (2011). The Influence of Brand Loyalty on Cosmetics Buying Behavior of UAE Female Consumers. *International Journal of Marketing Studies*, *3*(2). Advance online publication. DOI: 10.5539/ijms.v3n2p123

Septiarini, D. F., Ratnasari, R. T., Salleh, M. C. M., Herianingrum, S., & Sedianingsih, S. (2023). Drivers of behavioral intention among non-Muslims toward halal cosmetics: Evidence from Indonesia, Malaysia, and Singapore. *Journal of Islamic Accounting and Business Research*, *14*(2), 230–248. DOI: 10.1108/JIABR-02-2021-0064

Shaari, J. A. N., & Arifin, N. S. (2010). Dimension of halal purchase intention: A preliminary study. *International Review of Business Research Papers*, *6*(4), 444–456.

Shafie, S., & Othman, M. N. (2006). Halal certification: An international marketing issue and challenge. *Proceedings of the International IFSAM VIIIth World Congress.*

Shah Alam, S., & Mohamed Sayuti, N. (2011). Applying the Theory of Planned Behavior (TPB) in halal food purchasing. *International Journal of Commerce and Management*, *21*(1), 8–20. DOI: 10.1108/10569211111111676

Sriminarti, N., & Nora, L. (2018). The Role of Product Knowledge and Attitudes toward Purchasing Intentions: The Moderating Effect of Religiosity on Halal Cosmetics. *KnE Social Sciences*, *3*(10), 518. DOI: 10.18502/kss.v3i10.3153

Teng, P. K., Jamaliah, W. W., & Jusoh, W. J. W. (2013). Investigating students' awareness and usage intention towards halal labelled cosmetics and personal care products in Malaysia. In *4th International Conference on Business and Economic Research (4th ICBER 2013), Indonesia: Bandung.*

Tieman, M. (2011). The application of Halal in supply chain management: In-depth interviews. *Journal of Islamic Marketing*, *2*(2), 186–195. DOI: 10.1108/17590831111139893

Tuhin, M. K. W., Miraz, M. H., Habib, M. M., & Alam, M. M. (2022). Strengthening consumers' halal buying behaviour: Role of attitude, religiosity and personal norm. *Journal of Islamic Marketing*, *13*(3), 671–687. DOI: 10.1108/JIMA-07-2020-0220

Usman, H., Chairy, C., & Projo, N. W. K. (2022). Impact of Muslim decision-making style and religiosity on intention to purchasing certified halal food. *Journal of Islamic Marketing*, *13*(11), 2268–2289. DOI: 10.1108/JIMA-01-2021-0027

Wannasupchue, W., Mohamad, S. F., Ishak, F. A. C., & Ungku Zainal Abidin, U. F. (2023). Challenges to obtain halal certification among restaurants in northeast Thailand. *Journal of Islamic Marketing*, *14*(2), 607–621. DOI: 10.1108/JIMA-04-2021-0124

Wilson, J. A. J., & Grant, J. (2013). Islamic marketing – a challenger to the classical marketing canon? *Journal of Islamic Marketing*, *4*(1), 7–21. DOI: 10.1108/17590831311306327

Wilson, J. A. J., & Liu, J. (2010). Shaping the Halal into a brand? *Journal of Islamic Marketing*, *1*(2), 107–123. DOI: 10.1108/17590831011055851

Yoo, B., Donthu, N., & Lee, S. (2000). An examination of selected marketing mix elements and brand equity. *Journal of the Academy of Marketing Science*, *28*(2), 195–211. DOI: 10.1177/0092070300282002

Yousaf, S., & Malik, M. S. (2013). Evaluating the influences of religiosity and product involvement level on the consumers. *Journal of Islamic Marketing*, *4*(2), 163–186. DOI: 10.1108/17590831311329296

Chapter 11
Genetic Engineering for Halal Vaccines:
Biochemical Transformation in Production and Economies of Scale

Hairrudin Hairrudin
https://orcid.org/0000-0002-1628-5376
University of Jember, Indonesia

Khairunnisa Musari
https://orcid.org/0000-0003-0525-9903
Kiai Haji Achmad Siddiq State Islamic University, Indonesia

ABSTRACT

The increasing global halal awareness also impacts the world of health. In the world of health, vaccination is one of the simplest, safest, and effective ways to protect humans from dangerous diseases. Vaccinations are still vulnerable to criticism for their halal status because the enzymes used in the past were mostly sourced from non-halal or prohibited materials. Now, through genetic engineering, enzymes sourced from non-halal or prohibited materials can be replaced. Indeed, one of the critical points of vaccine production is enzymes. As catalysts for organic chemical or biochemical reactions, enzymes are critical points in halal pharmaceuticals, including halal vaccines. Therefore, by embracing literature review and case studies, this chapter will focus on three issues as a discussion: (1) the mainstream biochemical process in vaccine production; (2) biochemical transformation of halal vaccine production through genetic engineering; (3) implications of halal vaccine production through genetic engineering for economies of scale.

DOI: 10.4018/979-8-3373-3917-7.ch011

BACKGROUND

The increasing global halal awareness has also influenced the world of health. Halal pharmaceuticals are one of the high-priority development areas in the health world which can be used to measure the progress of the halal sector. In 2022, consumer opportunity on halal pharmaceuticals was represented by US$108 billion of spending by 2 billion Muslims worldwide with the government leadership from Southeast Asian and European countries dominating this sub-sector (DinarStandard, 2023). Unfortunately, Muslims have not explored largely halal pharmaceuticals much, perhaps because the consumption of non-halal products in life-threatening situations is permitted under Islamic law (Shari'ah), so the issue of halal in terms of pharmaceuticals is often considered irrelevant (Noronha, 2020).

In the world of health, one of the issues in the halal pharmaceutical sub-sector that has been documented to have experienced polemics several times is vaccines. In the Muslim world, indeed, vaccines are polemical especially because apart from being expensive, it is also related to the status of their use in the medication, whether it is halal or not (Ahmad, 2022). In Malaysia, religious beliefs were viewed as one of the core influences for refusing vaccination (Khoo, Ghani, Navamukundan, Jahis, and Gamil, 2020). Likewise in Indonesia, the diversity of understandings regarding vaccines and their ingredients raises issues about halal and non-halal among the community, the core of which is triggered by two important elements, namely culture and theological concepts (Wiryadinata, 2023). Therefore, raising awareness of these elements may create a broader ethical consumer base for halal pharmaceuticals (Noronha, 2020).

Indeed, immunization with unclean and/or haram vaccines may be permissible under several conditions, namely when used in *al-hajat* or an emergency condition, holy and halal vaccine materials have not been found, and there is information from trusted and competent medical personnel that there is no halal vaccine (Sholeh and Helmi, 2021). This is the reason why a study by Sudarsono, Ikawati, Kurnia, Azizah, and Kholid (2024) in 32 Indonesia's provinces with 725 Muslim respondents found that religiosity, halal knowledge, and halal certification did not influence Muslims' intention to use halal vaccines at the time of COVID-19. The fatwa by the Indonesian Council of Ulama (MUI), which allowed the use of the vaccine despite containing haram ingredients, was perceived as justification for Muslims to receive non-halal vaccines.

Further, a study by Nugroho, Santoso, and Herawati (2024) of 200 respondents who had consumed the halal-labeled Flu-Bio, CoronaVac, and Vac2Bio vaccines in the Solo Raya area, Indonesia, indicated that beliefs about vaccine efficacy, awareness of halal vaccines, and the presence of a halal label directly impact purchasing behavior. Therefore, the study by Sudarsono, Ikawati, Kurnia, Azizah, and

Kholid (2024) recommended the existence of a halal vaccine, besides also avoiding the controversy over the use of non-halal vaccines. A lesson from the COVID-19 pandemic is that even though there is no definite cure, vaccines are the best way to fight the pandemic at that time, and scientific advancements played a significant role in accelerating the vaccine development process (Feizollah, Anuar, Mehdi, Firdaus, and Sulaiman, 2022).

One of the critical points of halal vaccine production is enzymes. Enzymes function as catalysts for organic chemical or biochemical reactions. In the biochemical process, a catalyst is an effort to accelerate the rate of chemical reactions at a certain temperature by lowering the activation energy of a reaction, without affecting the reaction results (products). Thus, enzymes are not only a critical point in halal pharmaceuticals, but also in halal food, halal beverage, and halal cosmetic products. Besides the vaccine manufacturers have to meet the requirements for product safety, quality, and efficacy according to World Health Organization (WHO) standards, the halalness of vaccines is an important concern for Muslims. Following applicable provisions, the submission of halal certification is mandatory for vaccine manufacturers. Through genetic engineering, enzymes sourced from non-halal or forbidden ingredients can be replaced.

Certainly, the need for such certification may have arisen due to concerns over the use of non-halal or prohibited ingredients in vaccine manufacturing. As a global leader in halal pharmaceuticals, Malaysia actually has introduced the world's first halal pharmaceutical standard, MS 2424: *Halal Pharmaceuticals – General Guidelines*, established in 2012 and revised in 2019. However, according to Ab Latiff, Zakaria, and Man (2021), Malaysia has not yet provided halal certification for vaccine products. Nevertheless, MS 2424 remains the only standard in Malaysia that serves as a general guideline. In Indonesia, the Assessment Institute for Foods, Drugs and Cosmetics Indonesian Council of Ulama (LPPOM-MUI) has certified the halalness of several vaccines, such as the influenza vaccine and the Bacillus Calmette–Guérin (BCG) vaccine (Yasni, 2021).

Most recently, as reported by Rindra (2025), as many as 64 foreign halal certification bodies from 27 countries in the world have been accredited and signed a mutual recognition agreement (MRA) regarding halal certification, including for issuing the halal status of vaccines. The growing demand for halal pharmaceuticals, including vaccines, is an emerging global issue given the increasing Muslim population and heightened awareness of halal compliance in healthcare. However, despite the potential for market expansion, practical challenges such as the availability of halal-certified raw materials, production complexities, and limited technological infrastructure in Muslim-majority countries pose significant hurdles. Existing empirical literature highlights the necessity of halal certification in pharmaceuticals

(Noronha, 2020; Ahmad, 2022), yet gaps remain in understanding the economic scalability and production feasibility of halal vaccines.

Therefore, by embracing literature review and case studies, this study conceptualizes halal vaccine production through genetic engineering as a transformative approach that enhances Shari'ah compliance while enabling economies of scale. This chapter aims to address the gaps by exploring the biochemical transformation of vaccine production through genetic engineering and its implications for economies of scale by focusing on three issues as a discussion: (1) The mainstream biochemical process in vaccine production; (2) The biochemical transformation of halal vaccine production through genetic engineering; (3) The implication of halal vaccine production through genetic engineering for economies of scale.

The remaining part of the chapter is organized into five sections. The first section presents the mainstream biochemical process. The biochemical transformation through genetic engineering is presented in the second section, while the third section explores the implication for economies of scale. The subsequent section concludes the entire chapter and provides policy recommendations as well as further research directions. In a nutshell, this chapter can be a reference to present a viable pathway for halal vaccine production, addressing ethical concerns while achieving economies of scale, for policymakers and future researcher, as well as vaccine manufacturers to meet WHO standards at once to ensure the halalness of vaccines through certification, especially when supplying them to countries with Muslim-majority populations.

THE MAINSTREAM BIOCHEMICAL PROCESS

Challenging ethical questions can arise in any vaccine research and development (R&D). In the past, indeed, some of the experiments conducted to develop vaccines would not be ethically acceptable today, however, in the history of medical inventions, more human lives have been rescued by vaccines than any other (WHO, 2022). For Christians, the concept of halal or non-halal does not bring humans closer to God; likewise, vaccination does not bring people closer to God but invites them to survive the dangers of the virus and Christian's concept of loving others can be realized by inviting them to vaccination to achieve herd immunity as a form of the importance of preserving life for others (Wiryadinata, 2023).

For Muslims, using halal products that are consumed or used in the body is a religious command, including vaccines as medical products that need to be injected into the human body to create its own antibodies against the targeted virus. Naturally, in Muslim countries, a study by Wardhana (2020) proved that vaccines and halal are intertwined with each other. In Indonesia, during the COVID-19 pandemic, concerns about the halal status of vaccines contribute to vaccine hesitancy among many Indonesian Muslims (Irfany, Nekha, Tieman, and Haq, 2024). Public demand for halal vaccination, subjective norms, and social norms can positively and significantly influence the intention to obtain a halal vaccine in Muslim community in this country (Zaid and Al Bahy, 2022).

Further, the content of a vaccine can be either the entire disease-causing microorganism that has been weakened or inactivated/killed or some of the microorganism's components, such as inactivated toxins and fragments of bacterial cellular structure. From these compositions, as shown in Table 1, vaccines can be divided into two categories, namely, live vaccines and non-live vaccines. Live vaccines consist of live-attenuated vaccines, while non-live vaccines consist of inactivated vaccines, nucleic acid, and viral vectors. Then, the inactivated vaccine consists of recombinant vaccine, toxoid vaccine, and conjugate polysaccharide-protein vaccine.

Table 1. Classification of vaccines

Type	Description	
Live vaccines		
Live-attenuated vaccine	This vaccine comprises the living microorganisms, pathogens, and in most cases viruses, that have been attenuated or weakened or modified genetically so that they can reiterate to induce an immune response, but not trigger disease, to minimize the disease-causing capability. By using live vaccines, immunity is usually very long-lived. For example: Measles, mumps, and rubella (MMR), varicella, rotavirus.	
Non-Live vaccines		
Inactivated vaccine	This vaccine comprises microorganisms that have been killed or inactivated using thermal, chemical, or other methods yet still capable to generate an immune response. **First,** killed vaccines comprise whole bacteria that have been killed. For example: whole-cell pertussis vaccine. **Second,** inactivated vaccines comprise viruses that have been inactivated in some way, so they are unable to reiterate or induce disease. For example, influenza, hepatitis A, and polio vaccines.	**Recombinant vaccine:** This type of vaccine comprises the elements of the disease-causing microorganism such as protein molecules from nucleic acid and bacteria cell walls. This vaccine is generated utilizing a gene from the disease-causing pathogen. The gene is included in a cell system for producing high quantities of the protein, where the protein can raise a protective immune response. For example: the Hepatitis B vaccine and Human papillomavirus (HPV) vaccine.
		Toxoid vaccine: This type of vaccine is produced from inactivated toxins generated by the disease-causing microorganisms, by harvesting a bacterial toxin and changing it chemically (usually with formaldehyde), to transform the toxin into a toxoid, then the toxoid vaccines raise antibodies that neutralize the dangerous toxins released by these bacteria. For example: tetanus and diphtheria.

continued on following page

Table 1. Continued

Type	Description	
		Conjugate polysaccharide-protein vaccine: This type of vaccine comprises linked polysaccharides and proteins to remedy the immune memory in infant and humoral response. Several bacteria have huge numbers of polysaccharides on their surface, such as Streptococcus pneumonia, which encapsulates the bacteria. As poorly immunogenic, Polysaccharide vaccines can only trigger a major immune response, where for future protection has no immune memory. Vaccines with polysaccharide conjugate comprise carrier proteins that are chemically attached to the polysaccharide antigens. This supplemental arises in the T-cell response activation, causing both high-affinity antibodies against the polysaccharide antigens and immune memory, and can be used in infants. For example: Pneumococcal and Haemophilus influenzae type b (Hib), Hib vaccine with polyribosylribitol phosphate (PRP), the pneumococcal conjugate vaccine (PCV13), and the meningococcal ACWY (MenACWY).
Nucleic acid	Recent vaccine technology developments have allowed messenger ribonucleic acid (mRNA) to send the genetic code to dendritic cells to generate specific viral proteins. Since mRNA is easily demolished by omnipresent ribonuclease enzymes, it is secured inside a lipid nanoparticle that also serves uptake by the dendritic cells. Inside the dendritic cell, ribosomes and vaccine mRNA produce the viral protein which is then delivered to the T and B cells in the lymph nodes. For example: Pfizer COVID-19 Vaccine (mRNA-CV).	
Viral vector	This type of vaccine uses mRNA to code for a protein to be raised in the body, however, the transportation method into cells is different. A viral vector utilizes an innocuous adenovirus to identify the protein to immune cells. Then, the immune cell produces the protein from the instructions by mRNA and triggers an immune response. For example: AstraZeneca COVID-19 vaccine (ChAd-CV).	

Source: Compiled from Soebandrio (2020); Khoo, Ghani, Navamukundan, Jahis, and Gamil (2020); Wahyudi (2021); Immunisation Advisory Centre (2022); and Author's Own.

Some of the vaccines use substances that have caused controversy regarding their halal status. These substances are gelatin and trypsin. Gelatin is a protein derivative obtained from collagen (one of the fibers that built connective tissue), while trypsin is a proteolytic enzyme produced in the pancreas. Vaccines that use gelatin and trypsin from pigs raise doubts about their halal status. The gelatin used in vaccines was obtained through hydrolysis (purification). Collagen tissue, as a material for making gelatin, is generally taken from hard bones, cartilage, tendons, and animal skin, such as pigs or cows. Some ingredients that can replace gelatin's function are pectin and carrageenan. Gelatin is colorless, transparent, tasteless, thickening, and stabilizing. Its use in vaccines is intended to provide a stabilizing effect so that the resulting vaccine is more resistant to changes in environmental conditions (Josefsberg and Buckland, 2012).

Another substance that has sparked controversy is trypsin. Trypsin is the pancreas's digestive enzyme that breaks down proteins into peptides and amino acids. This enzyme is used in the vaccine manufacturing process at the virus culture stage, especially to separate the virus from its media. Enzymes are needed because some of the vaccine production processes require enzymatic reactions. Enzymes are proteins that act as catalysts. As a catalyst, enzymes have the property of accelerating reactions and participating in reactions. At the end of the reaction, they are restored to their original form to be catalysts for the subsequent reaction. The products produced from enzymatic reactions can be separated from the enzymes. Unlike gelatin, trypsin is not found in the vaccines produced.

Some vaccines use gelatin and pork trypsin in their manufacturing process. The choice is generally based on economic and ethical considerations. Replacing these two materials (in some vaccine brands that already use them) with halal materials is not easy because it requires repeating the clinical trial procedure, which takes years. Some Muslims will tend to choose brands that are more guaranteed to have halal status. Vaccines that come into contact with materials derived from pigs will affect the perception of potential users. The parent's willingness to vaccinate their child influenced by their characteristic and perception (Utami, Hairrudin, and Suhartini, 2023).

Thus, the mainstream biochemical processes involved in halal vaccine production present ethical and religious considerations. Even though vaccines have historically saved lives, the acceptance of Muslim societies also depends on the halalness of their ingredients and production processes. The demand for halal vaccines is evident, especially in Muslim-majority countries, where public perception and religious adherence strongly influence vaccine acceptance. However, challenges remain, as most vaccine manufacturing occurs in non-Muslim countries, and halal-certified options are still very limited. Concerns about the use of porcine-derived substances such as gelatin and trypsin in vaccines highlight the need for alternative halal-compliant stabilizers and enzymes. Addressing these issues requires a concerted effort by policymakers, researchers, and industry stakeholders to develop sustainable and ethical vaccine solutions that align with religious and cultural expectations.

THE BIOCHEMICAL TRANSFORMATION THROUGH GENETIC ENGINEERING

In line with the definition of 'halal pharmaceuticals' which are products that contain ingredients permitted by the Shari'ah, namely (1) must be free of parts or derivatives of animals that are declared non-halal by Shari'ah or not slaughtered according to Shari'ah; (2) must not contain najs; and (3) must not be poisonous, intoxicating, or pose a health hazard to the users when taken according to prescription (Khoo, Ghani, Navamukundan, Jahis, and Gamil, 2020), halal vaccine can be defined similar (Soebandrio, 2020). Unfortunately, of the 57 Organization of Islamic Cooperation (OIC) member countries, there are only 16 vaccine manufacturers, and they only produce one or two vaccines, while biotechnology developers and all vaccines are in non-Muslim countries (Cochrane, 2020a; Soebandrio, 2020).

Indeed, it is hard to make a halal vaccine as the enzymes or culture media need to be changed, however, it would be easier to develop if it were done from the start, with halal certification as the goal (Cochrane, 2020b). In principle, halal vaccines adhere to the Shari'ah, they must: (1) Avoid non-halal ingredients such as gelatin from non-permissible sources; (2) Comply with halal manufacturing practices, ensuring the process avoids contamination or prohibited substances; (3) Obtain halal certification from recognized bodies to assure compliance for Muslim consumers.

Further, the methods and technologies to produce the vaccine have advanced to create safer and more immunogenic vaccines and as our understanding of biology improves. Optimizing this process while using only animal component-free (ACF) substances allows reduction of operational costs and mitigates risks of adverse effects related to animal-derived compounds. This will result in a vaccine that is free from prohibited animal components (Suarez-Zuluaga, van der Pol, van 't Oever, Bakker, and Thomassen, 2022). Certainly, genetic engineering can facilitate the rapid design of vaccines without the need for animal cells.

As a note, generating one type of vaccine until it is ready for use takes around 10-15 years. This is due to the various clinical trials that need to be carried out until finally the vaccine is considered capable of overcoming pandemic or epidemic conditions of a disease. This process is also influenced by the content of the vaccine, especially its antigen. An antigen is an active component or material designed to create an active component that triggers an immune response (Josefsberg and Buckland, 2012; Sulistyaningsih, Istinaroh, Dewi, and Hairrudin, 2022). Table 2 shows the general contents of genetic engineering in manufacturing halal vaccines.

Table 2. Genetic engineering in manufacturing halal vaccines

Substance	Description
Antigen	Antigens can be made from whole weakened microorganisms, partially, or their toxins. Based on the antigen, vaccines can be classified as follows (Josefsberg and Buckland, 2012; Cid and Bolivar, 2021): 1. Partially purified live attenuated virus, such as smallpox and rabies. 2. Inactivated purified virus, such as polio and pertussis. 3. Toxoid, such as tetanus and diphtheria. 4. Development of a purified and inactivated virus, such as Sinovac-COVID 19 and hepatitis A. 5. Development of virus-like particles, such as hepatitis B, AstraZeneca-COVID 19, and human papillomavirus. 6. Purified polysaccharides, such as pneumococcal vaccines. 7. Polysaccharide conjugated to carrier protein, such as Pneumococcal for infants, Haemophilus type B, and bacterial meningitis.
Preservative	Preservatives are used to prevent the vaccine from being easily contaminated, for example, 2-phenoxyethanol. According to FDA (2025), preservatives inhibit the growth of microorganisms, and 2-Phenoxyethanol is an organic compound commonly found in cosmetics and antiseptics. Additionally, it serves as a preservative in Ipol, an FDA-approved vaccine for polio prevention, where it is used at a concentration of 0.5%.
Stabilizer	Various factors can contribute to vaccine instability, including exposure to light, heat, radiation, environmental fluctuations, or interactions with the container or other ingredients in the formulation (Dumpa, Goel, Guo, *et al.*, 2019). Stabilizers widely used in vaccines' manufacture are magnesium sulfat (MgSO4), magnesium chloride (MgCl2), lactose-sorbitol, sorbitol-gelatin (Yasni, 2021), and glycine. Stabilizers prevent changes in the vaccine due to environmental changes or reactions between substances in it.
Surfactant	Substances amphoteric, solubilize, and produce micelles which work as nano-sized molecules in the solubilization and emulsification of vaccines such as saponin QS-21 (Das, Kumar, Begum, Bhattarai, Mondal, and Saha, 2022)
Adjuvant	They are substances that enhance or regulate the immune system's response to an antigen (Wahyudi, 2021). Essential elements that increase the efficacy of vaccine, such as aluminum phosphate, aluminum hydroxide, and amorphous aluminum hydroxy phosphate sulfate (Facciolà, Visalli, Laganà, and Di Pietro, 2022).

Source: Compiled by Author

Classical vaccines use whole pathogen antigens as live attenuated or inactivated pathogens. Some of these vaccines are produced using trypsin from pigs, such as the polio and meningitis vaccines. Now, modern vaccines use antigens obtained through genetic engineering, such as recombinant subunit vaccines. Antigen display systems such as virus-like particles or those designed with in silico rationally designed particles are able to self-assemble into nanoscale assemblies to improve antigen display (Sulistyaningsih, Istinaroh, Dewi, and Hairrudin, 2022). Nanotechnology has improved the efficacy of recombinant subunit vaccines such as the hepatitis B vaccine (Cid and Bolivar, 2021).

Religious beliefs may be one of the core influences on the refusals. Through this chapter, it is important to explain the biochemical transformation through genetic engineering to the literate public, particularly the Muslims. Certain ingredients of concern may be developed by presenting alternatives in the utilization (Khoo, Ghani,

Navamukundan, Jahis, and Gamil, 2020). The alternative materials, such as fungi, insect cells, non-animal medium, yeast, and vegetable stabilizers, can be considered to replace mainstream materials in vaccine production (Ahmad, 2022). No doubt, genetic engineering not only helps the industry achieves halal certification but also achieves economies of scale.

Although dedicated funding for the development of halal pharmaceuticals is still limited, innovation in the sector is progressing. Malaysian companies continued to drive forward such innovation, with Duopharma becoming the first in the country to receive halal certification for oncology products in 2022 and Pharmaniaga aiming to commercialize Malaysia's first halal blood anticoagulant drug by 2024 (DinarStandard, 2023). In Indonesia, the IndoVac vaccine produced and tested by Bio Farma is now one of the first halal COVID-19 vaccines for low- and middle-income Muslim-majority countries (Hotez, 2023). Further, Saudi Arabia potentially could one day become the major producer of halal vaccines for the OIC nations (Hotez, 2021).

Thus, the advancement of genetic engineering has revolutionized vaccine development, particularly in the pursuit of halal-certified vaccines that align with Islamic principles. By eliminating non-halal components and utilizing alternative substances such as fungi, insect cells, and plant-based stabilizers, the industry can enhance both compliance and accessibility for Muslim communities. Additionally, technological innovations, including nanotechnology and antigen display systems, have improved vaccine efficacy while reducing reliance on conventional animal-derived ingredients. Despite challenges such as limited funding, countries like Malaysia, Indonesia, and Saudi Arabia are making significant strides in the halal pharmaceutical sector. The growing recognition of halal vaccines not only supports religious adherence but also contributes to economies of scale, enabling broader global distribution. As demand increases, further investment and research in this field will be crucial to fostering sustainable, ethical, and effective vaccine production.

THE IMPLICATION FOR ECONOMIES OF SCALE

Society's need today for halal vaccines can be explained by the New Institutional Economics (NIE) theory. NIE takes a comprehensive view of economies, which study the structure and evolution of economies by using four aspects of analysis: culture, institutions, organizations, and markets (Ahmed, 2002, 2015; Ismal and Musari, 2009; Muazir and Musari, 2016). NIE provides an alternate institutional framework for economic analysis that combines many social disciplines to understand the existence of a halal vaccine in society and its influence on economic behavior. Through the four aspects of NIE, the evolution of society's need for halal vaccines can be understood. By adopting the Islamic Helix approach (Hidayat and Musari,

2023a; Musari, 2024b), the institutional arrangement for halal vaccines also can be developed to open the business innovation.

Additionally, the Theory of Planned Behavior (TPB) by Ajzen (1991) also helps to explain the psychological and social factors that drive demand for halal vaccines. TPB provides a useful framework for understanding why people demand halal vaccines. This study expands the TPB by indicating religious influences on consumer decision-making, where a positive attitude toward religious compliance, societal endorsement, and access to certified options enhance vaccine acceptance. No doubt, the halal industry today is recognized as a rapidly growing sector that shapes and redefines modern business practices, and it has evolved beyond its religious significance to become a global benchmark for quality, hygiene, health, and safety (Hidayat and Musari, 2022, 2023b). All of these provide a strong foundation for understanding how they shape the demand for halal vaccines globally and how this demand can create economies of scale in vaccine production.

Basic definitions of economies of scale can be narrated as: cost savings that occur when a company increases the scale of production; cost advantages realized by companies when production becomes more efficient; cost advantage experienced by a firm when it increases its level of output; cost advantages reaped by companies when production becomes efficient; average costs decrease as a firm expands, while diseconomies of scale occur when expansion leads to increasing average costs; a reduction in the average cost of a product when a company increases output; or the situation occurs when larger production volumes enable a business or industry to reduce costs through efficiencies, such as through spreading fixed costs over more units or benefiting from operational optimizations.

Thus, economies of scale in halal vaccines refer to the cost advantages that arise when the production of halal vaccines is scaled up by leading to a reduction in per-unit cost as the production volume increases. To enhance the economies of scale for the halal vaccine, genetic engineering in the biochemical process can realize it. Through innovative new forms of Shari'ah-compliant finance such as crowdsourced finance for a vaccine fund for immunizations (Osman, Hassan, Haris, and Kassim, 2018), *waqf* crowdfunding (Fauzia and Musari, 2021), the Islamic social finance partnership models (Musari and Fathorrazi, 2021; Musari and Sayah, 2023), or Islamic blended finance (Musari, 2022a, 2025), investments for halal vaccine through Islamic financial instruments can be encouraged.

Indeed, to address the performance of vaccine supply chains for future pandemics, the developing and emerging countries should prioritize practical health financing strategies, where governments, regulatory bodies, and healthcare authorities should adopt sustainable financing approaches such as advanced market commitments and co-financing policies, where large-scale expansion of vaccination efforts can also be supported by government funding or reallocating corporate social responsibility

(CSR) funds to public immunization programs by ensuring transparent financial management (Rai and Bera, 2025). In the era of climate change, a sustainable finance approach is a mandate, including for funding halal vaccines. Islamic finance already provides a taxonomy of Islamic green financing (Musari, 2022b, 2023) that offers alternatives in the form of public borrowing, charity/social finance, or joint ventures that can be embraced to enhance the economies of scale for sustainable halal vaccine.

Genetic Engineering in Generating Economies of Scale

In the halal vaccine industry, genetic engineering plays a transformative role in vaccine production by enabling cost-effective, scalable, and halal-compliant manufacturing processes. Through recombinant deoxyribonucleic acid (DNA) technology, synthetic biology, and genetic modification, so genetic engineering ensures the use of ethical materials aligned with Islamic principles while supporting the economies of scale necessary for the sustainable growth of halal vaccine production. Table 3 shows how genetic engineering can help achieve economies of scale for halal vaccine production.

Table 3. Genetic engineering in generating economies of scale for halal vaccines

Aspects	Implementation	
Recombinant DNA technology	Genetic engineering allows the replacement of non-Halal animal-derived components with recombinant proteins produced from genetically modified microorganisms.	Recombinant enzymes and adjuvants can be developed from bacteria, yeast, or insect cells, ensuring they meet halal criteria.
		Genetically modified cells can be cultured in large bioreactors, allowing high-yield production of vaccine antigens for developing Halal vaccines with minimal costs at scale.
mRNA and DNA-based vaccine	mRNA and DNA-based vaccines are modern approaches with Halal-friendly raw materials and faster production timelines.	Once the mRNA or DNA sequence is designed, large-scale production can occur quickly, reducing time-to-market and eliminating production costs.
		mRNA and DNA vaccines use synthetic nucleotides can avoid the reliance on animal products.
		Large production facilities can generate millions of doses per batch using automated platforms and lowering unit costs significantly.

continued on following page

Table 3. Continued

Aspects	Implementation	
Molecular farming or plant-based vaccine production	Genetic engineering allows the insertion of vaccine-related genes into plants, such as tobacco or algae, which can then produce vaccine components through molecular farming.	Plant-based system eliminates the risk of non-Halal contamination and has opportunity become Halal friendly source.
		Plants are inexpensive to grow and maintain, compared to traditional cell cultures, and can produce vaccines at scale with minimal infrastructure.
		Molecular farming enables massive production within short agricultural cycles to raise the economies of scale.
Gene-edited microbial cell factories	Microbial organisms, such as yeast, E. coli, or Chinese hamster ovary (CHO) cells, can be genetically edited to optimize the production of specific antigens or adjuvants for vaccines.	Gene editing can enhance microbial strains to produce higher quantities of desired proteins or compounds.
		Optimized cell factories generate fewer by-products, improving cost efficiency, and reducing waste.
		Using bioreactors, genetically engineered microbes can operate in continuous production modes, lowering operational costs over time.
Eliminating contaminants and enhancing purity	Genetic engineering enables targeted gene editing to remove unwanted elements from vaccine production processes, ensuring both Halal compliance and increased yield.	Techniques like clustered regularly interspaced short palindromic repeats (CRISPR) can modify production systems to create cleaner production by eliminating the use of fetal bovine serum (FBS) or other non-Halal growth media.
		Higher purity levels reduce the need for complex purification processes so can lower costs in purification by decreasing production costs.
		Genetically controlled production helps maintain consistent quality, meeting both Islamic and international pharmaceutical standards so this technique is regulatory compliance.
Optimizing production with synthetic biology	Synthetic biology combines engineering principles with biology to create new biological systems optimized for high-volume vaccine production.	Genetically engineered platforms can integrate with automated systems, streamlining manufacturing and lowering labor costs.
		Genetically engineered systems can be reused for multiple vaccines, making multi-product facilities feasible and supporting economies of scale.
		Synthetic biology platforms allow for rapid customization, helping meet varying demands without disrupting large-scale production.

continued on following page

Table 3. Continued

Aspects	Implementation	
International collaboration and technology transfer	Genetic engineering makes it easier to transfer vaccine production technology	OIC countries can adopt licensed technologies from international firms, using genetic engineering to modify vaccines for halal compliance.
		Genetically engineered platforms can be implemented as shared manufacturing platforms by acrossing multiple facilities, fostering cross-border cooperation and production scalability to ensure that Halal vaccine production can scale globally.
		Genetic engineering enhances workforce training programs for biotechnologists to increase production capacity.
Lower production costs through bulk manufacturing	Genetic engineering enables high-volume vaccine production in smaller, modular facilities, reducing capital and operational expenditures.	Optimized genetic systems consume fewer resources, such as media and energy, during production.
		Engineered cells or plants can yield more antigens per cycle, resulting in lower costs per dose.
		Large production capacities allow manufacturers to meet domestic demand and export surplus vaccines to other countries.

Source: Author's Own

No doubt, genetic engineering offers significant advantages for halal vaccine production, enabling the use of compliant raw materials at once reducing costs and increasing output. Considering that most vaccine production remains concentrated in non-Muslim-majority countries, Muslim countries can achieve economies of scale by leveraging technologies like recombinant DNA, molecular farming, and mRNA platforms. These innovations promote the sustainable growth of the halal pharmaceutical industry while ensuring vaccines meet both Islamic principles and international quality standards. Through strategic investments and collaboration, Halal vaccine production can scale efficiently, positioning Muslim-majority countries as leaders in sustainable halal healthcare solutions.

Further, other implications that could potentially arise from genetic engineering is social impact, particularly for increasing public willingness to be vaccinated. Referring to Utami, Hairrudin, and Suhartini (2023), perception is an essential factor influencing willingness to be vaccinated, so the existence of halal vaccines will increase Muslim trust and acceptance of the vaccination program because their perception of vaccination is better. This condition will increase immunization coverage and reduce social conflict between pro- and anti-vaccination groups. Halal vaccines are likely to impact improving public health and achieving the third target of the Sustainable Development Goals (SDGs), namely good health and well-being.

Likewise, as reported by Rindra (2025), the halal certification of vaccines plays a crucial role in shaping public trust and acceptance of immunization programs, where doubts about vaccine ingredients and manufacturing processes frequently hinder efforts to expand national vaccination coverage. Consequently, establishing a dependable halal certification system is essential for enhancing public participation and safeguarding public health. However, implementing halal certification for vaccines continues to encounter several challenges. A significant hurdle is the possible inclusion of non-halal ingredients during manufacturing.

Technologies for Sustainable Halal Vaccines Supply Chain

Producing sustainable halal vaccines requires advanced technology at various stages, from research to production and distribution. Access to halal-certified raw materials is the most difficult issue for pharmaceutical business procurement departments (Irfany, Nekha, Tieman, and Haq, 2024), and certainly, the lack of raw materials with the right halal certificates is also the main bottleneck for the halal vaccine industry. When producing vaccines that involve tissue culture, recombinant techniques, or the propagation of bacteria or viruses, it is essential to assess the materials used in the culture media (Yasni, 2021), and technologies become crucial for handling the critical point of halalness of raw materials, additives, and auxiliary materials used. Table 4 shows the alternative technologies for the sustainable halal vaccine supply chain.

Table 4. The alternative technologies for sustainable halal vaccines supply chain

Supply Chain	Technologies		
Raw material	Vaccine platform technology	A standardized approach to vaccine development that utilizes a common viral vector or carrier backbone, allowing for the incorporation of different antigens. It enables efficient vaccine production by using a shared mechanism, delivery method, or cell line to develop multiple vaccines. For examples: protein-based platforms, DNA vaccine platforms, mRNA-based platforms, replicons (self-replicating RNA), and virus and bacterial vector vaccines.	Electronic data interchange (EDI), internet, extranet, permissioned blockchain (Hyperledger Fabric), artificial intelligence (AI), big data, blockchain technology, radio frequency identification device (RFID) with hazard analysis and critical control points, RFID along with displacement loop mitochondrial deoxyribonucleic acid (mtDNA), information technology outsourcing (ITO), internet of things (IoT), Franz diffusion cell modification, liquid chromatography-high-resolution mass spectrometry (LC-HRMS), reverse transcription polymerase chain reaction (RT-PCR), Q Exactive Orbitrap mass spectrometers (MS), thermo hygrometer probe, gas chromatography-mass spectrometry (GC-MS), digital scent port for GC-MS, and olfactometer sniffer 9100.
Halal manufacturing	Cell culture modification	Modification of cell culture can be done by using cells that are guaranteed halal, such as chicken embryo cells, multiplying viruses or vaccine proteins with a closed system (bioreactor technology) by utilizing halal purification technology such as chromatography and molecular filtration or nanotechnology.	
	Plant-based fermentation technology	Technology to produce vaccine proteins using certain microbes or plants.	
	In silico analysis	In silico analysis in vaccine development is a research method that uses simulations or computer programs to analyze various things related to vaccines. The advancement of bioinformatics and biotechnology techniques can shorten the long journey of vaccine development.	
Halal distribution	Software-defined networking (SDN), time-series (TS) algorithms, blockchain, named-entity recognition (NER), global positioning system (GPS) tracking (Halaltracer technology), and optical character recognition (OCR), RFID, quick-response (QR) codes, internet of things (IoT), OCR combined with augmented reality, RFID, and multimedia messaging service (MMS) using camera phones.		

continued on following page

Table 4. Continued

Supply Chain	Technologies
Halal logistics	Shipper technology.
Halal audit process	Cloud-based mobile
Halal Certification	Blockchain.

Source: Compiled from Yasni (2021); Wahyudi (2021); Rahman, Islam, Karim, Kundu, and Kabir (2021); Sulistyaningsih, Istinaroh, Dewi, and Hairrudin (2022); Musari, Mahmudah, Hakim, and Almunawar (2025); Author's Own.

Thus, genetic engineering has a crucial role in economies of scale in halal vaccine production, which demonstrates how increased production volumes lead to cost reductions while ensuring compliance with Islamic principles. Genetic engineering, including recombinant DNA technology, mRNA-based vaccines, molecular farming, and synthetic biology, emerges as a key enabler of scalable and cost-efficient halal vaccine production. To achieve sustainable economies of scale, innovative Islamic financial instruments offer viable investment solution options. Addressing sustainable halal supply chain challenges through advanced technologies will ensure the integrity and efficiency of vaccine distribution. Ultimately, halal vaccine certification fosters greater public trust, enhancing immunization coverage and contributing to global health initiatives aligned with the SDGs.

CONCLUSION

In line with the rapid growth of the global halal industry, the NIE and TPB framework help explain why people demand halal vaccines. The NIE provides the structural foundation for the institutional of halal vaccine, while the TPB explains the psychological determinants in influencing individual decision-making related to halal vaccine consumption. Together, these two theories provide a holistic approach to understanding the need for halal-certified vaccines globally, particularly in Muslim-majority countries, where halal pharmaceuticals, including vaccines, are a crucial yet underdeveloped segment. Indeed, perceptions about halal vaccines vary across Muslim communities. Ingredients such as pork-derived gelatin and trypsin have raised concerns. Islamic jurisprudence allows the use of non-halal vaccines in emergencies. However, as halal awareness increases, demand for halal-certified vaccines has increased, especially in OIC countries.

The concept of halal vaccines stems from the need to ensure that medical care complies with Islamic ethics. The fact that most vaccine production is still concentrated in non-Muslim majority countries where halal certification is not given attention, countries with majority populations need to seriously consider how to develop a halal pharmaceutical industry, including related to halal vaccines. Although vaccines have historically been one of the most effective medical interventions, but ethical, religious, and technical concerns continue to influence their acceptance and production. The classification of vaccines demonstrates the diversity of scientific approaches used to stimulate immune responses. Despite the scientific advancements, challenges remain, particularly regarding the halal status of certain vaccines. Ingredients such as gelatin and trypsin, often derived from non-halal sources, have raised concerns among Muslim communities, affecting vaccine acceptance. Addressing these concerns through halal-certified alternatives, such as plant-based stabilizers and microbial enzymes, could enhance trust and increase vaccine uptake in Muslim-majority countries.

Overall, this study explores how genetic engineering can transform vaccine production while aligning with Islamic principles and achieving economies of scale. In the future, integrating halal principles into vaccine development will not only address religious concerns but also drive economic opportunities in the halal pharmaceutical sector. No doubt, genetic engineering for Halal vaccines can be a catalyst for economies of scale. Through genetic engineering, enzymes sourced from non-halal or forbidden ingredients can be replaced. Genetic engineering plays a transformative role in vaccine production by enabling cost-effective, scalable, and halal-compliant manufacturing processes. Through recombinant DNA technology, synthetic biology, and genetic modification, genetic engineering ensures the use of ethical materials aligned with Islamic principles while supporting the economies of scale necessary for the growth of sustainable halal vaccine production.

POLICY RECOMMENDATION

The mainstream biochemical process in vaccine production plays a critical role in shaping global public health. At least there are four challenges in achieving economies of scale for halal vaccines, namely limited demand, complex supply chains, R&D costs, regulatory barriers. Therefore, to develop an economically scalable halal vaccine industry that supports the wider halal industry, while of course also ensuring ethical compliance and technological sophistication, strategic policies are needed. The following are policy recommendations, especially for Muslim countries, to facilitate the development of the halal vaccine industry as shown by Table 5.

Table 5. Policy recommendations for the development of the halal vaccine

Policy	Description
1. Standardization, regulatory framework, and halal certification	
Harmonization of standards	Collaborating with other Muslim countries under the OIC to develop uniform halal vaccine guidelines to ease cross-border trade and approval
Unified halal standards	Harmonizing halal pharmaceutical standards across OIC countries to avoid redundancy and encourage cross-border collaboration.
Fast-track regulatory approvals	Streamlining certification and approval processes by aligning with international standards while integrating Islamic guidelines
International certification platforms	Developing centralized platforms to mutually recognize halal certifications between countries, reducing delays and duplications.
A roadmap for halal vaccines	Synergy among relevant regulators, authorities, or ministries to formulate a roadmap for halal vaccines globally or nationally.
2. R&D, innovation policies, and halal-compliant technology	
Dedicated R&D funds	Establishing government-backed grants to promote innovation in vaccine technologies using halal-compatible raw materials (e.g., recombinant proteins or plant-based materials).
Public-private partnerships (PPP)	Encouraging partnerships between academic institutions, pharmaceutical companies, and investors to accelerate the development of halal vaccines
Incentivizing universities and research centers	Offering tax breaks and funding to universities for biotechnology research to build knowledge in halal biopharmaceuticals
Scaling up production by using bioprocessing technologies	Adopting scalable technologies such as cell-culture platforms and recombinant DNA technology to produce halal-certified nationally vaccines efficiently
Plant-based and synthetic	Developing vaccines using plant-based or synthetically produced inputs, eliminating the need for non-halal animal derivatives
Automation and robotics in manufacturing	Integrating automation in production lines to reduce costs, ensure precision, and achieve large-scale production.
3. Optimizing the sustainable halal supply chain management	
Ethical sourcing policies	Implementing procurement policies ensuring supply chains comply with halal principles, avoiding components such as porcine gelatin or non-halal enzymes
Sustainable halal logistics infrastructure	Developing specialized cold chain logistics networks with halal compliance standards for vaccine transportation and storage by investing in sustainable halal-certified storage and transportation infrastructure to maintain quality and compliance throughout the supply chain and its reverse logistics and circular economy.
Regional vaccine hubs	Designating key locations within OIC member countries as vaccine production and distribution hubs to minimize logistics costs and enable economies of scale
Halal raw material sourcing networks	Developing global supply networks to source Halal-certified excipients and raw materials in bulk at reduced costs.
Demand aggregation mechanisms	Coordinating procurement among OIC countries to aggregate vaccine demand and achieve large-scale production targets.

continued on following page

Table 5. Continued

Policy	Description
4. Capacity building, workforce development, R&D collaboration and technology transfer	
Skill development programs	Offering scholarships and specialized training programs in biotechnology, bioethics, and Islamic law for students and professionals.
International collaboration	Facilitating staff exchanges and joint research initiatives with leading global vaccine developers to enhance expertise.
Technical training centres	Establishing centres of excellence focusing on biotechnology and halal pharmaceutical production to strengthen local capacities and provide specialized training programs in biotechnology and Halal pharmaceutical practices to build a skilled workforce.
Joint research programs	Fostering collaborative research between universities, pharmaceutical companies, and research centers within and beyond the OIC.
Technology transfer agreements	Technology and human capital are less developed in the pharmaceutical industry, so it is necessary to leverage partnerships with global vaccine manufacturers to acquire and localize technologies needed for halal vaccine production.
5. Investments through Islamic financial instruments and financial incentives	
Islamic financing mechanisms	Leveraging Islamic microfinance and nanofinance to encourage SMEs to participate in the vaccine ecosystem, especially in raw material production, as well as encouraging investment through Islamic public borrowing, Islamic social finance, or Islamic venture capital for halal pharmaceutical startups focusing on innovative vaccine development.
Sukuk for vaccine infrastructure development	Issuing sukuk to fund the construction of vaccine research centers, manufacturing plants, and logistics infrastructure.
Tax incentives and subsidies	Providing tax exemptions or reductions for investments in halal vaccine production, R&D, and exports, as well as providing incentives for companies investing in halal vaccine production, including tax breaks and subsidies for infrastructure.
6. Partnerships	
Collaboration and cooperation	Collaborating with international organization, such as WHO, to ensure halal vaccines meet international standards to increase acceptance and export potential, and engaging in strategic alliances with developing nations to share expertise, technology, and resources in halal vaccine production, including negotiating with leading biotechnology firms for licensing agreements to transfer essential vaccine production technologies.
Cluster development	Setting up the vaccine production clusters within OIC countries, each specializing in specific phases (e.g., R&D, raw material processing, production).
PPP	Encouraging private investments to complement government funding for infrastructure and research.
Shared manufacturing facilities	Utilizing contract manufacturing organizations (CMOs) to produce vaccines for multiple countries, achieving economies of scale.
Long-term supply contracts	Governments can pre-purchase vaccines to ensure demand stability, boosting investor confidence, and reducing production risks.

continued on following page

Table 5. Continued

Policy	Description
Market expansion to non-OIC countries	Promoting halal vaccines as ethically-produced, high-quality alternatives, expanding their appeal beyond Muslim markets, and offering incentives for exporting halal vaccines to non-OIC countries, emphasizing their ethical and quality advantages.
7. Public awareness and acceptance	
Public communication campaigns	Educating the public on the benefits of halal vaccines to ensure community trust and combat vaccine hesitancy by conducting campaigns about the importance and benefits of halal vaccines.
Transparency in production processes	Making vaccine ingredients and production processes transparent to build trust among consumers and scholars. Sharing information about ingredients and production methods to ensure community trust and compliance with halal principles.
Engage Islamic scholars and leaders	Involving religious leader, authorities, or scholars to endorse halal vaccines to support vaccine initiatives by ensuring alignment with Islamic principles.

Source: Adopted and compiled from Wahyudi (2021); Yasni (2021); Musari and Zaroni (2021); Musari (2022b, 2023, 2024a); Hidayat and Musari (2022, 2023a, 2023b); Irfany, Nekha, Tieman, and Haq (2024); Rai and Bera (2025); Musari, Mahmudah, Hakim, and Almunawar (2025); Musari and Sakti (2025); and Author's Own.

Thus, developing a robust and scalable halal vaccine industry is essential for improving global health outcomes while upholding ethical and religious values, particularly in Muslim-majority countries. Addressing the key challenges—limited demand, complex supply chains, high R&D costs, and regulatory barriers—requires comprehensive and strategic policy interventions. The recommendations outlined in this article emphasize the need for harmonized standards, investment in halal-compliant research and technology, sustainable supply chains, capacity building, and innovative financing mechanisms rooted in Islamic principles. By fostering international collaboration and public trust, Muslim countries can not only enhance self-sufficiency in vaccine production but also position sustainbhalal vaccines as a high-quality, ethical alternative in global markets.

FURTHER RESEARCH DIRECTIONS

Last but not least, this chapter also highlights future research directions regarding the biochemical transformation of vaccines through genetic engineering and its impact on economies of scale, particularly within the framework of halal pharmaceuticals. By addressing these areas, further studies can deepen the understanding of how halal vaccines can lead halal pharmaceuticals, reinforcing their role in building a halal industry, ethical, and sustainable. Here are some suggested future research directions.

First, halal certification and standardization in biopharmaceuticals. Which includes: Comparative analysis of halal certification frameworks across different OIC countries; The role of Islamic scholars and halal certification bodies in influencing public trust in halal vaccines; Integration of global good manufacturing practices and Shari'ah-compliant standards in vaccine production.
Second, Islamic finance and investment in halal vaccine production. Which includes: Feasibility of sukuk for financing halal vaccine R&D and production facilities; *Waqf* crowdfunding, Islamic blended finance, or the other Islamic social finance partnership models as alternative financing methods for halal pharmaceutical innovation; Role of Islamic Development Bank (IsDB) and other Islamic financial institutions in supporting the halal biopharmaceutical industry.
Third, supply chain and halal logistics for vaccines. Which includes: Developing a halal-compliant cold chain management system for vaccine distribution; Case studies of successful halal logistics frameworks in pharmaceuticals; Integration of blockchain technology for halal compliance traceability in vaccine distribution.
Fourth, ethical and theological perspectives on genetic engineering for halal vaccines. Which includes: Islamic bioethics on the use of genetically modified organisms (GMOs) in vaccine development; Comparative analysis of fatwas (Islamic legal rulings) on halal vaccines and GMOs; Ethical dilemmas in balancing halal integrity with global health needs.
Fifth, economic impact and market potential of halal vaccines. Which includes: Economic modeling of the potential market size for halal vaccines in Muslim-majority countries; Consumer perception and willingness to pay for halal-certified vaccines; The role of multinational pharmaceutical companies in entering the halal vaccine market.
Sixth, innovations in halal vaccine production. Which includes: Advancements in plant-based and synthetic biology-based halal vaccine production; Potential of CRISPR and gene editing technologies for halal-compliant vaccine development; AI, big data, and the other alternative technologies for sustainable halal vaccines supply chain in optimizing halal vaccine production efficiency.
Seventh, regulatory and policy frameworks for halal vaccine industry. Which includes: How OIC countries can develop a unified regulatory framework for halal vaccines; Policy interventions to encourage halal vaccine production and exports; Comparative analysis of halal vaccine regulations with global pharmaceutical standards.

REFERENCES

Ab Latiff, J., Zakaria, Z., & Man, S. (2021). The challenges in implementation of halal vaccine certification in Malaysia. *Journal of Food and Pharmaceutical Sciences*, *9*(1), 366–371. DOI: 10.22146/jfps.1147

Ahmad, M. (2022). Developing halal vaccine production in Indonesia: Challenges and future opportunities. *El-Hayah*, *9*(1), 18–30. DOI: 10.18860/elha.v9i1.18026

Ahmed, H. (Ed.). (2002). Theoretical foundation of Islamic economic. Islamic Research and Training Institute (IRTI) - Islamic Development Bank (IDB).

Ahmed, H. (2015). Knowledge, Economy and Islamic Finance: A New-Institutional Economics Perspective. Presentations for research seminar The Islamic Research and Training Institute (IRTI) Webinar, June 2nd.

Ajzen, I. (1991). The theory of planned behavior. *Organizational Behavior and Human Decision Processes*, *50*(2), 179–211. DOI: 10.1016/0749-5978(91)90020-T

Chowdhury, N. R., Ahmed, M., Mahmud, P., Paul, S. K., & Liza, S. A. (2022). Modeling a sustainable vaccine supply chain for a healthcare system. *Journal of Cleaner Production*, *370*(133423), 1–19. DOI: 10.1016/j.jclepro.2022.133423 PMID: 35975192

Cid, R., & Bolívar, J. (2021). Platforms for production of protein-based vaccines: From classical to next-generation strategies. *Biomolecules*, *11*(1072), 1–33. DOI: 10.3390/biom11081072 PMID: 34439738

Cochrane, P. (2020a, July 13). Will there be a halal covid-19 vaccine? *Salaam Gateway,* Insight, https://salaamgateway.com/story/will-there-be-a-halal-covid-19 -vaccine

Cochrane, P. (2020b, December 18). Halal but not halal certified key concerns about approved covid-19 vaccines. *Salaam Gateway,* News, https://salaamgateway.com/story/halal-but-not-halal-certified-key-concerns-about-approved-covid-19-vaccines

Das, B., Kumar, B., Begum, W., Bhattarai, A., Mondal, M. H., & Saha, B. (2022). Comprehensive review on applications of surfactants in vaccine formulation, therapeutic and cosmetic pharmacy and prevention of pulmonary failure due to covid-19. *Chemistry Africa*, *5*(3), 459–480. DOI: 10.1007/s42250-022-00345-0

DinarStandard. (2023). *State of the global Islamic economy report 2023/2024*. DinarStandard, Salam Gateway, and Dubai Economy and Tourism.

Dumpa, N., Goel, K., Guo, Y., McFall, H., Pillai, A. R., Shukla, A., Repka, M. A., & Murthy, S. N. (2019). Stability of vaccines. *AAPS PharmSciTech*, *20*(42), 42. Advance online publication. DOI: 10.1208/s12249-018-1254-2 PMID: 30610415

Facciolà, A., Visalli, G., Laganà, A., & Di Pietro, A. (2022). An overview of vaccine adjuvants: Current evidence and future perspectives. *Vaccines*, *10*(5), 819. DOI: 10.3390/vaccines10050819 PMID: 35632575

Fauzia, I. Y., & Musari, K. (2021). Waqf crowdfunding for financing the MSMEs: Evidence from ASEAN-3. In de Pablos, P. O., Zhang, X., & Almunawar, M. N. (Eds.), *Handbook of research on disruptive innovation and digital transformation in Asia* (pp. 37–49). IGI Global., DOI: 10.4018/978-1-7998-6477-6.ch003

FDA. (2025, January 15). Thimerosal and vaccines. *U.S. Food and Drug Administration (FDA),*https://www.fda.gov/vaccines-blood-biologics/safety-availability-biologics/thimerosal-and-vaccines

Feizollah, A., Anuar, N. B., Mehdi, R., Firdaus, A., & Sulaiman, A. (2022). Understanding covid-19 halal vaccination discourse on facebook and twitter using aspect-based sentiment analysis and text emotion analysis. *International Journal of Environmental Research and Public Health*, *19*(10), 6269. DOI: 10.3390/ijerph19106269 PMID: 35627806

Hidayat, S. E., & Musari, K. (2022). ASEAN towards a global halal logistics through the digitally-enabled community. [IJABIM]. *International Journal of Asian Business and Information Management*, *13*(2), 1–15. DOI: 10.4018/IJABIM.20220701.oa1

Hidayat, S. E., & Musari, K. (2023a). Towards the global halal MSMEs hub through the digitally-enabled society: An institutional arrangement with Islamic n-tuple helix. In Rafiki, A. (Ed.), *Digitalization in halal management. Contributions to Environmental Sciences & Innovative Business Technology* (pp. 15–28). Springer., DOI: 10.1007/978-981-99-5146-8_2

Hidayat, S. E., & Musari, K. (2023b). Comparative analysis of digitally-enabled community in supporting the halal industry in Muslim majority countries in the ASEAN, Central Asia, and Maghreb Region. In Rafiki, A. (Ed.), *Digitalization in halal management. Contributions to Environmental Sciences & Innovative Business Technology* (pp. 151–165). Springer., DOI: 10.1007/978-981-99-5146-8_11

Hotez, P. J. (2021). *Preventing the next pandemic: vaccine diplomacy in a time of anti-science*. Johns Hopkins University Press. DOI: 10.56021/9781421440392

Hotez, P. J. (2023). *The deadly rise of anti-science: A scientist's warning*. Johns Hopkins University Press.

Immunisation Advisory Centre. (2022). *Types of vaccines*.https://www.immune.org.nz/vaccines/vaccine-development

Irfany, M. I., Nekha, A., Tieman, M., & Haq, D. A. (2024). Halal procurement strategy for the halal pharmaceutical industry in Indonesia. *Journal of Islamic Marketing, 16*(4), 1073–1094. DOI: 10.1108/JIMA-09-2023-0274

Ismal, R., & Musari, K. (2009, January 24). New institutional economic? *Republika,* Opini.

Josefsberg, J. O., & Buckland, B. (2012). Vaccine process technology. *Biotechnology and Bioengineering, 109*(6), 1443–1460. DOI: 10.1002/bit.24493 PMID: 22407777

Khoo, Y. S. K., Ghani, A., Navamukundan, A. A., Jahis, R., & Gamil, A. (2020). Unique product quality considerations in vaccine development, registration and new program implementation in Malaysia. *Human Vaccines & Immunotherapeutics, 16*(3), 530–538. DOI: 10.1080/21645515.2019.1667206 PMID: 31652090

Musari, K., & Zaroni, Z. (2021). Reverse logistics in the age of digital transformation for circular economy and halal logistics through the leadership of Asia. In *Handbook of Research on Disruptive Innovation and Digital Transformation in Asia* (pp. 83–103). IGI Global Scientific Publishing.

Musari, K. (2022a). Integrating green sukuk and cash waqf linked sukuk, the blended Islamic finance of fiscal instrument in Indonesia: A proposed model for fighting climate change. *International Journal of Islamic Khazanah, 12*(2), 133–144. DOI: 10.15575/ijik.v12i2.17750

Musari, K. (2022b). ASEAN toward circular economy and sustainable energy in tackling the climate change: Islamic green financing taxonomy for sustainable finance. In de Pablos, P. O. (Ed.), *Handbook of research on building greener economics and adopting digital tools in the era of climate change* (pp. 210–230). IGI Global., DOI: 10.4018/978-1-6684-4610-2.ch011

Musari, K. (2023). A proposed taxonomy of Islamic green financing to address the sustainable eligible sector. A paper was presented at the 11th Islamic Economics Workshop "Islamic Economics and Environment", Istanbul - Turkiye, October 13th-15th.

Musari, K. (2024a). Driving sustainable supply chain and digital transformation in halal sectors: Evidence in ASEAN-5. In de Pablos, P. O., Almunawar, M. N., & Anshari, M. (Eds.), *Strengthening sustainable digitalization of Asian economy and society* (pp. 87–100). IGI Global., DOI: 10.4018/979-8-3693-1942-0.ch005

Musari, K. (2024b). An analysis of Islamic helix in a zero-waste soybean business of techno-savvy micro enterprises for SDGs: Case study in edamame village, jember, Indonesia. In Rafiki, A., Alserhan, B. A. A., & Bayram, K. (Eds.), *Technopreneurship in small businesses for sustainability* (pp. 21–33). IGI Global., DOI: 10.4018/979-8-3693-3530-7.ch002

Musari, K. (2025). Towards the perpetual sustainable sukuk through Islamic blended finance: Lesson from green sukuk and blue sukuk in Indonesia. In de Pablos, P. O., Lytras, M., & Malik, S. (Eds.), *Securing sustainable futures through blue and green economies* (pp. 381–402). IGI Global., DOI: 10.4018/979-8-3693-7893-9.ch015

Musari, K. Mahmudah, Hakim, Z., & Almunawar, M. N. (2025). Mapping the implementation of circular economy and reverse logistics in the sustainable halal supply chain: Evidence in ASEAN-3. In Q. M. H. Sakalayen, M. N. Almunawar, & M. Y. Ali (Eds.). *Sustainable advanced manufacturing and logistics in ASEAN* (pp. 61-78). IGI Global. DOI: 10.4018/979-8-3693-5350-9.ch004

Musari, K., & Fathorrazi, M. (2021). Islamic helix approach, the Islamic social finance partnership models for MSMEs: Lesson learned from Indonesia. In Azid, T., Mukhlisin, M., Akbar, N., & Tahir, M. (Eds.), *Monetary policy, Islamic finance, and Islamic corporate governance: An International overview* (pp. 303–322). Emerald Publishing Limited. DOI: 10.1108/978-1-80043-786-920211017

Musari, K., & Sakti, M. R. P. (2025). Recycled waste plastic for asphalt manufacturing to degrade ecological footprints in ASEAN: A policy analysis from the Islamic economics and finance approach. In Sakalayen, Q. M. H., Almunawar, M. N., & Ali, M. Y. (Eds.), *Sustainable advanced manufacturing and logistics in ASEAN* (pp. 269–288). IGI Global., DOI: 10.4018/979-8-3693-5350-9.ch015

Musari, K., & Sayah, F. (2023). Islamic quadruple helix, social finance partnership for developing digital financial inclusion in Maghreb region. In A. Rafiki, A.G. Pananjung, M.D.T.P. Nasution, *Strategies and applications of Islamic entrepreneurship* (pp. 67-82). IGI Global. DOI: 10.4018/978-1-6684-7519-5.ch005

Noronha, M. (2020, October 22). Halal for health: Scaling up halal pharmaceuticals. *Economist Impact,* https://impact.economist.com/perspectives/health/halal-health-scaling-halal-pharmaceuticals

Nugroho, A. J. S., Santoso, G. B., & Herawati, N. (2024). Development of a halal-labelled vaccine purchasing behavior model: A study on the halal lifestyle of muslim consumers and sustainable development goals (SDGs) in Indonesia. *Journal of Lifestyle and SDGs Review*, *5*(1), e03681. DOI: 10.47172/2965-730X.SDGsReview.v5.n01.pe03681

Osman, I., Hassan, F., Haris, B., & Kassim, E. S. (2018). Religion and halal consumption. In Melewar, T. C., & Alwi, S. F. S. (Eds.), *Islamic marketing and branding: Theory and practice*. Routledge.

Rahman, A., & Islam, Md. J., Karim, Md. R., Kundu, D., & Kabir, S. (2021). *An intelligent vaccine distribution process in COVID-19 pandemic through blockchain-SDN framework from Bangladesh perspective*. 2021 International Conference on Electronics, Communications and Information Technology (ICECIT), in Khulna, Bangladesh, September 14–16.

Rai, P., & Bera, S. (2025). Prioritizing performance objectives of vaccine supply chain for future pandemics. *Journal of Humanitarian Logistics and Supply Chain Management,* Vol. ahead-of-print No. ahead-of-print. DOI:.DOI: 10.1108/JHLSCM-05-2024-0072

Rindra, W. (2025, March 19). SEMOL series 1 FPH UI 2025 discusses halal vaccines from various aspects. *Faculty of Public Health, Universitas Indonesia (FKMUI) News*.https://fkm.ui.ac.id/en/semol-series-1-fph-ui-2025-discusses-halal-vaccines-from-various-aspects/

Sholeh, M. A. N., & Helmi, M. I. (2021). The covid-19 vaccination: Realization on halal vaccines for benefits. *Samarah: Jurnal Hukum Keluarga dan Hukum Islam*, 5(1), 174-190. DOI: `DOI: 10.22373/sjhk.v5i1.9769

Soebandrio, A. (2020). Webinar Series Halal Vaccine Industry: Past, Present, Future, held by PEBS UI August 29.

Suarez-Zuluaga, D. A., van der Pol, L. A., van 't Oever, A. G., Bakker, W. A. M., & Thomassen, Y. E. (2022). Development of an animal component free production process for Sabin inactivated polio vaccine. *Vaccine: X*, *12*(100223), 1–9. DOI: 10.1016/j.jvacx.2022.100223 PMID: 36217423

Sudarsono, H., Ikawati, R., Kurnia, A., Azizah, S. N., & Kholid, M. N. (2024). Effects of religiosity, halal knowledge and halal certification on the intention of Muslims to use the halal vaccine during covid-19 pandemic. *Journal of Islamic Marketing*, *15*(1), 79–100. DOI: 10.1108/JIMA-06-2021-0179

Sulistyaningsih, E., Istinaroh, N., Dewi, R., & Hairrudin, H. (2022). Expression and in silico analysis of CIDRα1 recombinant protein from plasmodium falciparum as a malaria subunit vaccine candidate. *Trends in Sciences*, *19*(23), 1621. DOI: 10.48048/tis.2022.1621

Utami, F. R., Hairrudin, H., & Suhartini, S. (2023). Lesson learned from parents' willingness to covid-19 vaccination in children aged 6-11 years (with the health belief model approach). International. *Journal of Medical Science and Clinical Research Studies*, *3*(8), 1667–1673. DOI: 10.47191/ijmscrs/v3-i8-42

Wahyudi, P. (2021, November 15). Vaccine platform technology state of the art and its critical point. *Halal MUI,*https://halalmui.org/en/technology-platform-vaccine-state-of-the-art-and-its-critical-point/

Wardhana, A. K. (2020). Should vaccine be Halal? bibliography study in scopus indexed academic paper. *Journal of Halal Product and Research*, *3*(2), 80–87. DOI: 10.20473/jhpr.vol.3-issue.2.80-87

WHO. (2022, July 22). A brief history of vaccination. *World Health Organization (WHO),* Newsroom, Spotlight, https://www.who.int/news-room/spotlight/history-of-vaccination

Wiryadinata, H. (2023). Religious education and vaccination: the concept of halal, from the slippery road to herd immunity. *PASCA: Jurnal Teologi dan Pendidikan Agama Kristen* 19(2), 141-150.

Yasni, S. (2021, December 8). Getting to know vaccine manufacturing and its halal critical point. *Halal MUI,*https://halalmui.org/en/recognize-vaccine-making-and-critical-point-halal/

Yi, Z. (2012). Analysis on the way of scale economy of Halal food and Moslem supplies industry of Ningxia. *The Fourth International Conference on Multimedia Information Networking and Security*, 761-764. DOI:DOI: 10.1109/MINES.2012.77

Zaid & Al Bahy, M. P. (2022). Examining factors influencing halal covid-19 vaccination intention among the muslim communities. [DOI:.]. *Psikis: Jurnal Psikologi Islami*, *8*(1), 40–53.DOI: 10.19109/psikis.v8i1.11913

ADDITIONAL READING

Hidayat, S. E., Musari, K., Masrohatin, S., & Smolo, E. (2024). The future of Islamic finance. In Smolo, E., & Raheem, M. M. (Eds.), *The future of Islamic finance: From shari'ah law to fintech* (pp. 221–242). Emerald Publishing Limited. DOI: 10.1108/978-1-83549-906-120241014

Morgan, P. (2022). *China's covid-19 vaccine supplies to the global south: between politics and business*. Bristol University Press.

Musari, K. (2021). Green Sukuk, Islamic Green Financing: A Lesson Learned from Indonesia. In Olarewaju, O. M., & Ganiyu, I. O. (Eds.), *Climate change and the sustainable financial sector* (pp. 1–16). IGI Global. DOI: 10.4018/978-1-7998-7967-1.ch001

Musari, K. (2021). Circular economy for plastics and digitally-enabled community towards ASEAN halal hub in Asia. In de Pablos, P. O. (Ed.), *Handbook of research on developing circular, digital, and green economies in Asia* (pp. 1–12). IGI Global. DOI: 10.4018/978-1-7998-8678-5.ch001

Musari, K. (2024). Transforming ecological footprint through circular economy innovation towards sustainable well-being in the development of (Islamic) smart cities in GCC Countries. In *The emerald handbook of smart cities in the gulf region: innovation, development, transformation, and prosperity for vision 2040* (Pp. 379-403). Emerald Publishing Limited. DOI: 10.1108/978-1-83608-292-720241026

KEY TERMS AND DEFINITIONS

Economies of Scale: Cost savings that occur when a company increases the scale of production; cost advantages realized by companies when production becomes more efficient; cost advantage experienced by a firm when it increases its level of output; cost advantages reaped by companies when production becomes efficient; average costs decrease as a firm expands, while diseconomies of scale occur when expansion leads to increasing average costs; a reduction in the average cost of a product when a company increases output; Cost reductions achieved through large-scale production.

Genetic Engineering: A process that uses laboratory-based technologies to alter the DNA makeup of an organism; manipulation and modification process to the genes of organism by using technology; direct manipulation of DNA to alter an organism's characteristics in a particular way; artificial modification, manipulation, and recombination of DNA or other nucleic acid molecules in order to modify an organism or population of organisms; methods of recombinant DNA technology.

Halal Certification: The process of inspection and testing by the halal authority on a product consumed or produced by a manufacturer has met the halal standards recognized by the authority. Official recognition from the halal authority that a product consumed or produced by a manufacturer has met the halal standards recognized by the authority.

Halal Vaccine: The modification of DNA to produce Halal-compliant vaccine components.

Vaccination: A process for making the body learn how to defend itself from disease without the dangers of a full-blown infection; a simple, safe, and effective method of safeguarding people contrary to dangerous diseases, before they contact with people.

Vaccine: A preparation that is used to stimulate the body's immune response against diseases; products that protect human against harmful diseases, by supporting human body’s natural defense - the immune system - to fight them off.

Chapter 12
Assessing the Level of Understanding of Non-Muslim Restaurant Operators Towards Halal

Lloyd David Feliciano
https://orcid.org/0009-0009-0191-6356
Don Honorio Ventura State University, Philippines

ABSTRACT

This study aimed to determine the level of understanding of non-Muslim restaurant operators in one of the 1st class city in the Philippines towards halal. 30 restaurant managers of casual dining restaurants participated in the conduct of this study. Descriptive type of research was utilized to determine the level of understanding of the restaurant operators towards halal. Results showed that overall, the respondents have high understanding towards halal. This study can serve as a reference to encourage the key players of the restaurant industries and the related government agencies to work hand-in-hand to see the potential of halal market in boosting the tourism industry of the locality.

INTRODUCTION

The rapid growth of the global Muslim population, projected to reach nearly 3 billion by 2060, has significantly influenced various industries, with the food sector experiencing one of the most profound impacts. Central to this transformation is the increasing demand for Halal-certified products, which adhere to Islamic dietary laws that dictate permissible food preparation and consumption practices. While Halal

DOI: 10.4018/979-8-3373-3917-7.ch012

food remains a religious obligation for Muslims, it has also garnered widespread appeal among non-Muslim consumers due to its associations with ethical sourcing, strict hygiene practices, and food safety. This growing demand has elevated Halal from a religious requirement to a dynamic global market force, contributing to the economic strategies of nations worldwide. Countries such as Malaysia and Indonesia have capitalized on this trend by integrating Halal certification into their national economic policies, positioning themselves as leaders in the global Halal industry. Their success has demonstrated the potential of Halal not just as a religious necessity but as a driver of trade, tourism, and economic growth.

In the Philippines, a predominantly Christian country, the Halal industry is emerging as a promising sector with untapped potential. The country is home to a significant Muslim population, particularly in regions like Mindanao and urban centers where diverse communities coexist. Additionally, the Philippines is becoming an increasingly attractive destination for Muslim tourists from Southeast Asia and the Middle East. Despite this growing demand, the availability of Halal-certified food establishments remains limited, which poses challenges for both domestic consumers and international visitors. Recognizing the economic opportunities presented by the Halal market, government agencies such as the Department of Trade and Industry (DTI) and the National Commission on Muslim Filipinos (NCMF) have launched initiatives to promote Halal certification and align local practices with international standards. These efforts aim to enhance the country's competitiveness in the global Halal economy while fostering cultural inclusivity. However, significant gaps remain in the Philippine restaurant industry's understanding and adoption of Halal practices. Many restaurant operators lack awareness of Halal certification processes and the potential business benefits associated with catering to this growing market segment. This study seeks to assess the awareness, readiness, and preparedness of restaurant operators in adapting to the increasing demand for Halal-certified food. By identifying barriers to Halal adoption and exploring opportunities for improvement, this research aims to provide insights that will support the growth of Halal-compliant businesses in the Philippines. The findings will contribute to national efforts to strengthen the Halal ecosystem, promote inclusive economic growth, and position the Philippines as a more attractive destination for both local and international Muslim consumers.

BACKGROUND

The Halal food industry is growing rapidly due to the expanding Muslim population and the increasing awareness of food safety, hygiene, and ethical sourcing among consumers. "Halal," which means "permissible" in Arabic, refers not only to dietary laws outlined in the Qur'an but also to the entire process of food preparation, handling, and certification. The global Halal market has become a multi-trillion-dollar industry that appeals to both Muslim and non-Muslim consumers who view Halal products as symbols of quality and safety. Countries such as Malaysia and Indonesia have become global leaders in the Halal industry because of strong government policies, robust certification systems, and international trade partnerships. Their success shows that Halal certification can improve food security, support local businesses, and attract foreign investments, which contribute to economic growth.

In the Philippines, the need for Halal certification has increased because the country has over 6 million Muslims who live mainly in Mindanao and the Bangsamoro Autonomous Region in Muslim Mindanao (BARMM), along with growing Muslim communities in Metro Manila, Cebu, and Davao. The Philippines also attracts a rising number of Muslim tourists from countries like Malaysia, Indonesia, and the Middle East. However, the limited availability of Halal-certified restaurants, hotels, and services affects the country's ability to compete with neighboring countries that have well-established Halal ecosystems. Although the Department of Trade and Industry (DTI) and the National Commission on Muslim Filipinos (NCMF) have promoted Halal certification, many restaurant operators do not understand its importance or the process required to obtain it. Misconceptions about the complexity and cost of certification discourage businesses from becoming Halal-compliant. This study aims to assess the knowledge, perceptions, and readiness of restaurant operators in the Philippines regarding Halal practices and certification. It seeks to identify barriers to adoption and offer insights that can help the restaurant industry align with global Halal trends, promote cultural inclusivity, and support sustainable economic growth.

MAIN FOCUS OF THE CHAPTER

This chapter focuses on the growing importance of Halal certification in the Philippines, particularly within the context of casual dining restaurants in the City of San Fernando, Pampanga. While the Philippines is predominantly Christian, it is gradually recognizing the vast economic potential of the Halal market. Government agencies such as the Department of Trade and Industry (DTI) and the National Commission on Muslim Filipinos (NCMF) have initiated efforts to promote Halal certification, aiming to enhance the country's competitiveness in the global Halal economy and address the growing needs of both domestic and international Muslim consumers (Abdulraof, 2024; Yaqub, 2024a). In January 2024, the government unveiled the Philippine Halal Industry Development Strategic Plan, aiming to increase Halal output, establish a national Halal brand, and create a centralized system for stakeholder coordination. This initiative seeks to position the Philippines as a leading

Halal-friendly hub in the Asia Pacific region (Ji, 2025). To support these objectives, the Philippines has established a National Halal Office to enhance its presence in both domestic and global markets. This office is tasked with implementing the strategic plan's goals, including doubling Halal-certified exports, generating 120,000 jobs, and attracting significant investments by 2028 (Yaqub, 2024b).

Recent studies have further emphasized the importance of Halal certification in the Philippine context. A comparative study by Sarip (2024) examined the price differences between Halal-compliant and non-Halal-compliant meat in the Lanao region, shedding light on factors influencing Halal certification and its economic implications. Another study conducted by Balah and Makakena (2024) focused on Halal food consumption, integrity, and traceability among predominantly Islamized groups in the Province of Cotabato, emphasizing the importance of robust Halal practices to maintain consumer trust. Dube et al. (2016) highlighted the role of Halal certification in facilitating firm internationalization in both the Philippines and Malaysia, while Chavez and Vicente (2025) discussed its significance for food and accommodation businesses in providing quality products, ensuring consumer trust, and expanding market reach. Moreover, Salindal et al. (2019) found that Halal certification significantly affects the business performance of Halal-certified food companies in the Philippines. Despite government efforts to promote Halal certification, challenges persist in raising awareness among business owners, addressing misconceptions about the complexity and cost of certification, and encouraging more establishments to pursue Halal compliance.

This gap is particularly evident in Pampanga, specifically in the City of San Fernando, which is rapidly gaining recognition as the soon-to-be Culinary Capital of the Philippines. Renowned for its rich culinary heritage and vibrant food culture, Pampanga has become a hub for food tourism, attracting both local and international visitors. The City of San Fernando, as the province's bustling capital, boasts a diverse array of restaurants, ranging from traditional Kapampangan eateries to modern dining concepts. Among these, casual dining restaurants play a significant role in shaping the region's food landscape. Offering a balance between affordability, comfort, and quality, casual dining establishments are popular among families, professionals, and tourists seeking enjoyable dining experiences without the formality of fine dining. Despite the city's dynamic food scene, there is a limited number of Halal-certified casual dining restaurants, restricting the ability of local businesses to fully cater to Muslim residents and tourists. This presents both a challenge and an opportunity for the local restaurant industry. By increasing awareness of Halal certification's benefits and addressing barriers to adoption, businesses can tap into the growing Halal market, attract a more diverse customer base, and contribute to the region's economic growth. This study aims to evaluate the knowledge, perceptions, and preparedness of casual dining restaurant operators in the City of San Fernando regarding Halal food practices and certification. By identifying gaps and opportunities, the research seeks to provide actionable insights that will support business growth, promote cultural inclusivity, and strengthen the Philippines' position in the global Halal industry.

Conceptual Framework

This study aims to determine the level of understanding of restaurant operators in the City of San Fernando, Philippines, regarding Halal practices. The framework is grounded in concepts from Halal certification guidelines provided by international Halal regulatory bodies and relevant literature on food safety, religious dietary practices, and cross-cultural management in the food industry. It integrates the relationship between personal and business demographic profiles and the operators' level of understanding of Halal to identify potential knowledge gaps and areas for improvement. Moreover, the study focuses on two key areas: (1) the personal demographic profile of respondents, including age, gender, nationality, religion, and educational attainment; and (2) the business demographic profile, covering the number of years in the current job, years of experience in the food service industry, prior experience in Halal-related or Halal-friendly establishments, and the type of eating establishment operated. The respondents' understanding of Halal is assessed across six dimensions: the general concept of Halal, sources of ingredients and beverages, animal slaughtering practices, food presentation and storage, food processing and cooking methods, and hygiene or sanitation standards. To explore the relationships between demographic variables and Halal understanding, the following null hypotheses were formulated:

(Ho1): There is no significant relationship between the personal demographic profile of respondents and their level of understanding of Halal.
(Ho2): There is no significant relationship between the business demographic profile of respondents and their level of understanding of Halal.

Figure 1. Conceptual framework

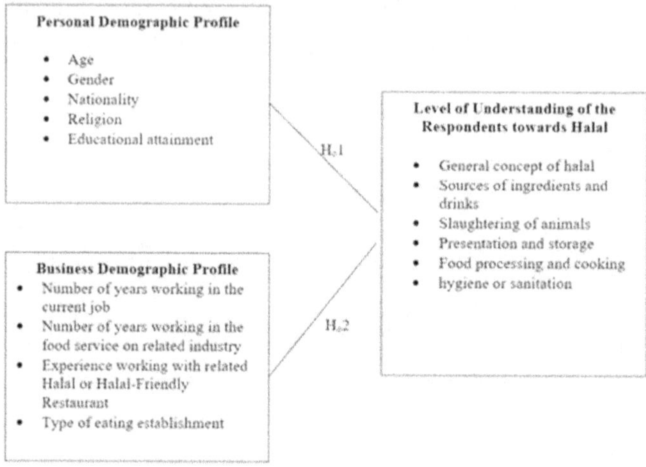

METHODS

Research Design, Instrument, Reliability, and Analysis

This study used a descriptive research design to examine the level of understanding of Halal practices among non-Muslim restaurant operators in the City of San Fernando, Philippines. The descriptive design helped identify current trends, perceptions, and practices without manipulating variables. The research focused on systematically describing respondents' knowledge of Halal concepts, food sources, slaughtering practices, food processing, and hygiene (McNabb, 2020; Wisenthige, 2023). Established Halal compliance guidelines (Azam & Abdullah, 2021; Othman & Md Nawi, 2025) served as the foundation for developing the survey instrument. The conceptual framework also drew from previous studies on Halal awareness among non-Muslim business operators (Saleh & Rajandran, 2024), which highlighted critical areas for investigation.

The data collection process involved a structured survey questionnaire distributed through Google Forms in June 2024. The study used convenience sampling to recruit non-Muslim restaurant operators through professional networks, email invitations, and social media platforms. The questionnaire had three sections. Part I gathered personal demographic information such as age, gender, nationality, religion, and educational attainment. Part II focused on business demographics, including years of experience in the food service industry, type of restaurant, and prior exposure to

Halal-related establishments. Part III measured the respondents' understanding of Halal practices. This section contained 47 items that covered general Halal concepts, sources of food and beverages, animal slaughtering practices, food presentation and storage, food processing and cooking, and hygiene and sanitation. A 4-point Likert scale was used, with options ranging from 1 (Strongly Disagree) to 4 (Strongly Agree).

The study assessed the reliability of the survey instrument through a pilot test with 30 respondents. Cronbach's Alpha measured the internal consistency of each section. The reliability coefficients were high across all categories: general understanding of Halal ($\alpha = 0.961$), sources of food ($\alpha = 0.982$), slaughtering of animals ($\alpha = 0.966$), presentation and storage ($\alpha = 0.770$), food processing and cooking ($\alpha = 0.922$), and hygiene and sanitation ($\alpha = 0.948$). The overall reliability coefficient for all 47 items was $\alpha = 0.989$, indicating excellent internal consistency. The collected data were initially organized using Microsoft Excel 2016 and then imported into IBM SPSS Statistics version 25 for analysis. Appropriate numerical codes were assigned to facilitate statistical processing. Descriptive statistics, including frequency and percentage distributions, presented respondents' personal and business demographics. Means and standard deviations described the level of understanding of Halal. Mean scores were interpreted as follows: 3.50–4.00 (Very High Understanding), 2.50–3.49 (High Understanding), 1.50–2.49 (Low Understanding), and 1.00–1.49 (Very Low Understanding). Pearson's chi-square test assessed the relationship between demographic variables and Halal knowledge, with a significance level of $p \leq 0.05$ used to determine statistical significance.

Table 1. Results of reliability testing

Sections of the Questionnaire with Ordinal Values	No. of Items	Cronbach's Alpha (α)
Understanding of Halal		
Concept of Halal	13	0.961
Sources of Halal Foods and Drinks	15	0.982
Slaughtering of Animals	7	0.966
Presentation and Storage	2	0.770
Food Processing and Cooking	4	0.922
Hygiene and Sanitation	6	0.948
Overall	47	0.989

The data collected from the 30 respondents through Google Forms were transposed into Microsoft Excel 2016 for initial organization. Appropriate numerical codes were assigned to the data, which were then imported into IBM SPSS Statistics version 25 for statistical treatment and analysis. Frequency and percentage distributions were utilized to present the personal and business demographic profiles of the respondents. To describe the respondents' level of understanding towards Halal, the mean ($\bar{x}$) and standard deviation (SD) were calculated. The levels of understanding were categorized using the following mean ranges and descriptions: 3.50–4.00 (Very High Understanding), 2.50–3.49 (High Understanding), 1.50–2.49 (Low Understanding), and 1.00–1.49 (Very Low Understanding), following the rule of rounding off numbers. To determine the significant relationship between the respondents' personal and business demographic profiles and their level of understanding of Halal, Pearson's chi-square test was applied. This test was appropriate as the variables were categorical, utilizing nominal and ordinal scales. A p-value (sig.) of less than or equal to 0.05 was considered statistically significant. The strength of the correlation was interpreted using Dancey and Reidy's (2004) guidelines for correlation coefficient values: ±1.00 indicates a perfect correlation, ±0.70 to ±0.99 represents a strong correlation, ±0.40 to ±0.69 signifies a moderate correlation, ±0.10 to ±0.39 denotes a weak correlation, and ±0.00 to ±0.09 indicates no correlation.

Respondents

The majority of respondents were between 30 and 39 years old, accounting for 46.7% (14 individuals). Other age groups represented included 40–49 years old (20% or 6 respondents), 50–59 years old (16.7% or 5 respondents), and 20–29 years old (13.3% or 4 respondents). Only one respondent (3.3%) belonged to the oldest age group of 60 years and above. Most respondents were female (56.7% or 17 individuals), while males comprised 43.3% (13 individuals). All respondents were Filipino (100%), with no representation from other nationalities. Religious affiliation was predominantly Christian (60% or 18 respondents), while the remaining 40% (12 respondents) identified as Catholic. No respondents reported following other religions, such as Islam. Regarding education, a significant majority held a bachelor's degree (73.3% or 22 respondents), followed by 20% (6 respondents) who were college-level, and 6.7% (2 respondents) who had completed a doctorate degree. Employment tenure varied among the respondents. A total of 36.7% (11 respondents) reported working in their current jobs for up to five years, with another 36.7% having been in their roles for 6–10 years. Six respondents (20%) had been in their current jobs for over 21 years, while smaller groups of 3.3% each had been employed for 11–15 years and 16–20 years. In the food service or related industries, 43.3% (13 respondents) had 6–10 years of experience, followed by 26.7% (8 respondents) with up to five years of experience. Six respondents (20%) reported over 21 years of experience in the industry. Most respondents (83.3% or 25 individuals) had no experience working in Halal or Halal-friendly establishments, while 16.7% (5 respondents) reported having such experience. Among the restaurants included in the study, 76.7% (23 establishments) were non-Halal, and 23.3% (7 establishments) were Halal-friendly. However, none of the participating establishments were Halal-certified.

RESULTS AND DISCUSSION

General Concept of Halal

The result revealed that the respondents have high understanding that the Quran requires Halal food to be cleaned and free from 'contamination,' produced with necessary measures taken to prevent any contact between Halal and non-Halal foods (SD = ±0.83, $\bar{x}$ = 3.00), which aligns with the *Maqasid Al-Shari'ah* (objectives of Islamic law) emphasizing purity (Farouk et al., 2016). They also understand that, in Islam, all food is considered Halal unless it is prohibited by the Quran (SD = ±0.83, $\bar{x}$ = 2.93), and that Halal food must be healthy (SD = ±0.91, $\bar{x}$ = 2.83), reflecting alignment with the concept of *Tayyib*, which underscores wholesomeness and health (Bonne & Verbeke, 2008). Furthermore, the respondents recognize that the consumption of Halal foods and goods is compulsory for all Muslims (SD = ±1.01, $\bar{x}$ = 2.73), and that Halal is the dietary standard prescribed in the Quran (SD = ±1.03, $\bar{x}$ = 2.67). Additionally, they acknowledge that Islamic law requires non-contact between Halal and non-Halal foods (SD = ±1.04, $\bar{x}$ = 2.60), and they understand that pork, blood, and carcasses (carrion) are considered filth and cannot be Halal (SD = ±0.90, $\bar{x}$ = 2.53). Respondents also demonstrated awareness that Halal food must be free of, and not made from, any part or substance taken or extracted from haram animals (SD = ±0.82, $\bar{x}$ = 2.53), consistent with Islamic jurisprudence (Al-Qaradawi, 2001). However, they displayed low understanding that the preparation of Halal food requires meeting international food safety standards (SD = ±1.14, $\bar{x}$ = 2.43), and that Islamic law requires Halal food to be prepared, processed, or stored in separate sections or lines within premises producing non-Halal foods (SD = ±0.93, $\bar{x}$ = 2.40). These gaps highlight challenges in ensuring compliance with modern Halal standards, such as HACCP and ISO 22000, which are vital for Halal certification and supply chain integrity (Riaz & Chaudry, 2003; Tieman, 2011). In general, the respondents have a high understanding (SD = ±0.78, $\bar{x}$ = 2.68) of the general concept of Halal, though there is a need for educational initiatives to bridge gaps in operational knowledge and ensure alignment with both religious principles and global market expectations (Regenstein et al., 2003; Zulfakar et al., 2011).

Sources of Ingredients and Drinks

The result of the analysis revealed that the respondent have high understanding that pigs and dogs are not considered Halal (SD = ±1.06, x̄ = 2.80); that water mixed with filthy water or food laced with wine and alcohol is not considered Halal (SD = ±1.04, x̄ = 2.77); that Islam forbid the intake of alcoholic and intoxicating drinks such as wines and alcoholic beers (SD = ±1.02, x̄ = 2.70); that all types of plants and their products if not poisonous, intoxicated, and harmful to human health considered Halal (SD = ±0.99, x̄ = 2.67); that *Tapai* or fermented rice is Halal to be eaten (SD = ±0.99, x̄ = 2.67); and that carbonated drinks made in the same way as the liquor production process either contained a little alcohol considered haram (SD = ±1.10, x̄ = 2.60). However, the respondents have low understanding that animals that are generally considered as repulsive e.g. lice, flies, maggots, and other similar animals are not considered Halal (SD = ±0.94, x̄ = 2.43); that birds with claws or birds that feed by snatching and tearing, are not considered Halal (SD = ±0.93, x̄ = 2.37); that Muslims are allowed to drink coffee (SD = ±0.89, x̄ = 2.37); that land animals are considered non-Halal if they are not slaughtered according to the Islamic law (SD = ±1.12, x̄ = 2.30); that animals and insects that are forbidden to be killed in Islam like ants, bees and woodpecker and any other animals are not considered Halal (SD = ±1.02, x̄ = 2.30); and that water animals that are NOT poisonous, intoxicated, and harmful to human health are considered Halal (SD = ±0.99, x̄ = 2.30). In general, the respondents have high understanding (SD = ±0.88, x̄ = 2.51) on the sources of Halal ingredients and drinks. These results resonate with broader literature emphasizing the foundational teachings of the Quran and Sunnah, particularly regarding the prohibition of haram items such as pork and alcohol (Riaz & Chaudry, 2019). Respondents' awareness of Halal plant-based foods and fermented products aligns with the *Halalan-Thoyyiban* principle, which emphasizes safety and cleanliness in food consumption (Supian & Ab Rashid, 2018). The gaps in understanding specific details, such as the prohibition of repulsive animals or the importance of proper slaughtering methods, highlight the need for more focused education on these topics (Aksamawanti, 2015). These areas reflect the complexity of Halal laws and the importance of traceability in maintaining Halal compliance from production to consumption (Wahyuni & Arfidhila, 2019).

Slaughtering of Animals

The results revealed that the respondents have high understanding that animals which are slaughtered to express respects to them and to thank Allah for providing the animals are clean and healthy food (SD = ±0.88, x̄ = 2.90); that the respiratory tract, esophagus, and jugular vein must be severed, to assure maximum removal of blood and less suffering to the animal (SD = ±0.96, $\bar{x}$ = 2.63); that the act of slaughtering must assure that the animal suffers minimal pain as possible (SD = ±0.97, $\bar{x}$ = 2.60); that slaughtering must be performed manually by Muslims of sound mind, mature and one who fully understands the fundamentals and conditions related to slaughtering (SD = ±0.86, $\bar{x}$ = 2.57); that all slaughtering devices must be sharp and are not made of bones, nails, and teeth to assure that the act of slaughtering is quick and not cruel to the animal (SD = ±0.94, $\bar{x}$ = 2.57); and that live animals living in their habitat must be healthy and not in a state of stress (SD = ±0.94, $\bar{x}$ = 2.50). The over mean that shows the high understanding of the respondents in terms of slaughtering animals for Halal food is 2.62 with standard deviation of 0.84.

Presentation and Storage

The result showed the high understanding of the respondents in the presentation and storage of Halal foods (SD = ±0.89, $\bar{x}$ = 2.70). Particularly, they have high understanding that goods coming in contact with non-Halal materials are considered as ritually unclean and Haram to be used or eaten (SD = ±0.98, $\bar{x}$ = 2.73); and that all Halal goods that are kept, displayed, and served must be isolated from goods that are non-Halal to prevent mixing or contaminating with ritually unclean (SD = ±1.09, $\bar{x}$ = 2.67).

Food Processing and Cooking

The overall result indicated a high understanding of the respondents in the food processing and cooking of Halal food (SD = ±0.94, $\bar{x}$ = 2.68). This high understanding of the respondents are expressed in terms of the Halal food must be prepared, processed or manufactured using equipment which is free from filth according to Islamic Laws, such as cutting devices, premises, containers, and other related equipment (SD = ±1.02, $\bar{x}$ = 2.83); that Halal food not come into contact or close proximity with any food which do not meet the Islamic laws (SD = ±0.96, $\bar{x}$ = 2.80); that Halal food must not be made of, or containing any parts or products from animals, which are forbidden by Islamic Laws to be consumed by Muslims or not slaughtered according to Islamic Laws (SD = ±1.14, $\bar{x}$ = 2.57); and that Halal food must not contain any products which are considered as filth according to Islamic Laws whether in little or large quantities such as pig oils, fats, lard from the carcass, types of alcohol and other items (SD = ±1.07, $\bar{x}$ = 2.53).

Hygiene and Sanitation

The result revealed that the respondents have very high understanding that regular cleaning and sanitization of the materials and premises are needed (SD = ±0.75, $\bar{x}$ = 3.70). In addition, they have high understanding that toilets and washrooms must be cleaned from time to time (SD = ±0.94, $\bar{x}$ = 3.23); that proper hand cleaning necessary after each usage of the toilet and before starting food processing (SD = ±0.99, $\bar{x}$ = 3.17); that equipment used must be clean and rinse with running water apart from using suitable cleaning agent (SD = ±0.94, $\bar{x}$ = 3.07); that the premises for the preparation and sale of food and drinks must be clean and free from any element, which can cause infestation from flies, rats, cockroaches, lizards, and other similar pests (SD = ±0.95, $\bar{x}$ = 3.00); and that the workers are required to be healthy and wear clean protective clothing to prevent food from dirt and possible contaminants (SD = ±1.02, $\bar{x}$ = 3.00). In general, the respondents have high understanding (SD = ±0.82, $\bar{x}$ = 3.19) on the hygiene and sanitation related to the preparation of Halal food. As a whole, the respondents have high level of understanding towards Halal food (SD = ±0.76, $\bar{x}$ = 2.73). In all aspects of the Halal, they have high understanding on the hygiene or sanitation (SD = ±0.76, $\bar{x}$ = 2.73), presentation and storage (SD = ±0.89, $\bar{x}$ = 2.70), general concept of Halal (SD = ±0.78, $\bar{x}$ = 2.68), food processing and cooking (SD = ±0.94, $\bar{x}$ = 2.68), slaughtering of animals (SD = ±0.84, $\bar{x}$ = 2.62), and sources of ingredients and drinks (SD = ±0.88, $\bar{x}$ = 2.51).

Relationship Between Personal Demographic Factors and Level of Understanding Towards Halal

Table 2 revealed that there is no significant relationship between the age of the respondents and their level of understanding towards Halal in terms of general concept of Halal (cc = .565, p = .295), sources of ingredients and drinks (cc = .607, p = .132), slaughtering of animals (cc = .557, p = .333), and presentation and storage (cc = .597, p = .163). Conversely, the result showed a moderate positive significant relationship between the age of the respondents and their level of understanding towards Halal in terms of food processing and cooking (cc = .665, p = .022); while a strong positive significant relationship between the age of the respondents and their level of understanding towards Halal in terms of hygiene or sanitation (cc = .735, $p < .001$). The cross-tabulation result indicated that those respondents belonged to the age brackets of 20-29 years old, 30-39 years old, 40-49 years old, and 50-59 years old have significantly higher level of understanding towards Halal in terms of food processing and cooking, and hygiene or sanitation as compared to those belong to the age bracket of 60 years old and above.

For gender, the result revealed that there is no significant relationship between the gender of the respondents and their level of understanding towards Halal in terms of general concept of Halal (cc = .329, p = .303), sources of ingredients and drinks (cc = .367, p = .197), slaughtering of animals (cc = .232, p = .635), presentation and storage (cc = .296, p = .410), food processing and cooking (cc = .345, p = .257), and hygiene or sanitation (cc = .228, p = .651). For religion, the result showed that there is no significant relationship between the religion of the respondents and their level of understanding towards Halal in terms of general concept of Halal (*cc* = .115, *p* = .940), sources of ingredients and drinks (*cc* = .081, *p* = .978), slaughtering of animals (*cc* = .152, *p* = .870), presentation and storage (*cc* = .147, *p* = .881), food processing and cooking (*cc* = .162, *p* = .847), and hygiene or sanitation (*cc* = .178, *p* = .806).

For educational attainment, the result revealed that there is a moderate positive significant relationship between the educational attainment of the respondents and their level of understanding towards Halal in terms of general concept of Halal (cc = .639, p = .002), sources of ingredients and drinks (cc = .625, p = .004), slaughtering of animals (cc = .665, p = .001), presentation and storage (cc = .546, p = .047), and food processing and cooking (cc = .607, p = .008). The cross-tabulation result indicated that those respondents who are bachelors and doctorate degree holders have significantly higher level of understanding towards Halal in terms of general concept of Halal, sources of ingredients and drinks, slaughtering of animals, presentation and storage, and food processing and cooking as compared to the respondents who only with college level of educational attainment. However, there is no significant relationship between the educational attainment of the respondents and their level of understanding towards Halal in terms of hygiene or sanitation (cc = .407, p = .427).

Table 2. Relationship between the personal demographic profile of respondents and the level of their understanding towards Halal

Level of Understanding Towards Halal	**Personal Demographic Profile**					
	Age			**Gender**		
	cc	*p*	**D**	*cc*	*p*	**D**
General concept of Halal	**.565**	**.295**	**No Correlation**	**.329**	**.303**	**No Correlation**
Sources of ingredients and drinks	.607	.132	No Correlation	.367	.197	No Correlation
Slaughtering of animals	.557	.333	No Correlation	.232	.635	No Correlation
Presentation and storage	.597	.163	No Correlation	.296	.410	No Correlation

continued on following page

Table 2. Continued

Level of Understanding Towards Halal	Personal Demographic Profile					
	Age			Gender		
	cc	*p*	**D**	*cc*	*p*	**D**
General concept of Halal	**.565**	**.295**	**No Correlation**	**.329**	**.303**	**No Correlation**
Food processing and cooking	.665*	.022	Moderate (+) Correlation	.345	.257	No Correlation
Hygiene or sanitation	.735**	<.001	Strong (+) Correlation	.228	.651	No Correlation
Level of Understanding Towards Halal	**Religion**			**Educational Attainment**		
	cc	***P***	**D**	***cc***	***p***	**D**
General concept of Halal	.115	.940	No Correlation	.639**	.002	Moderate (+) Correlation
Sources of ingredients and drinks	.081	.978	No Correlation	.625**	.004	Moderate (+) Correlation
Slaughtering of animals	.152	.870	No Correlation	.665**	.001	Moderate (+) Correlation
Presentation and storage	.147	.881	No Correlation	.546*	.047	Moderate (+) Correlation
Food processing and cooking	.162	.847	No Correlation	.607**	.008	Moderate (+) Correlation
Hygiene or sanitation	.178	.806	No Correlation	.407	.427	No Correlation

Relationship Between Business Demographic Factors and Level of Understanding Towards Halal

Table 3 result revealed that there is no significant relationship between the age of the respondents and their level of understanding towards Halal in terms of general concept of Halal (cc = .565, p = .295), sources of ingredients and drinks (cc = .607, p = .132), slaughtering of animals (cc = .557, p = .333), and presentation and storage (cc = .597, p = .163). Conversely, the result showed a moderate positive significant relationship between the age of the respondents and their level of understanding towards Halal in terms of food processing and cooking (cc = .665, p = .022); while a strong positive significant relationship between the age of the respondents and their level of understanding towards Halal in terms of hygiene or sanitation (cc = .735, p < .001). The cross-tabulation result indicated that those respondents belonged to the age brackets of 20-29 years old, 30-39 years old, 40-49 years old, and 50-59 years old have significantly higher level of understanding towards Halal in terms of food processing and cooking, and hygiene or sanitation as compared to those belong to the age bracket of 60 years old and above.

For gender, the result revealed that there is no significant relationship between the gender of the respondents and their level of understanding towards Halal in terms of general concept of Halal (cc = .329, p = .303), sources of ingredients and drinks (cc = .367, p = .197), slaughtering of animals (cc = .232, p = .635), presentation and storage (cc = .296, p = .410), food processing and cooking (cc = .345, p = .257), and hygiene or sanitation (cc = .228, p = .651). For religion, the result showed that there is no significant relationship between the religion of the respondents and their level of understanding towards Halal in terms of general concept of Halal (cc = .115, p = .940), sources of ingredients and drinks (cc = .081, p = .978), slaughtering of animals (cc = .152, p = .870), presentation and storage (cc = .147, p = .881), food processing and cooking (cc = .162, p = .847), and hygiene or sanitation (cc = .178, p = .806).

For educational attainment, the result revealed that there is a moderate positive significant relationship between the educational attainment of the respondents and their level of understanding towards Halal in terms of general concept of Halal (cc = .639, p = .002), sources of ingredients and drinks (cc = .625, p = .004), slaughtering of animals (cc = .665, p = .001), presentation and storage (cc = .546, p = .047), and food processing and cooking (cc = .607, p = .008). The cross-tabulation resultindicated that those respondents who are bachelors and doctorate degree holders have significantly higher level of understanding towards Halal in terms of general concept of Halal, sources of ingredients and drinks, slaughtering of animals, presentation and storage, and food processing and cooking as compared to the respondents who only with college level of educational attainment. However, there is no significant relationship between the educational attainment of the respondents and their level of understanding towards Halal in terms of hygiene or sanitation (cc = .407, p = .427).

Table 3. Relationship between the business demographic profile of respondents and the level of their understanding towards Halal

Level of Understanding Towards Halal	**Business Demographic Profile**					
	Number of years working in the current job			**Number of years working in the food service or related industry**		
	cc	*P*	**D**	*cc*	*p*	**D**
General concept of Halal	**.584**	**.215**	**No Correlation**	**.568**	**.285**	**No Correlation**
Sources of ingredients and drinks	.653	.055	No Correlation	.637	.059	No Correlation
Slaughtering of animals	.649	.060	No Correlation	.618	.100	No Correlation
Presentation and storage	.556	.337	No Correlation	.550	.369	No Correlation
Food processing and cooking	.671*	.017	Moderate (+) Correlation	.667*	.020	Moderate (+) Correlation
Hygiene or sanitation	.556	.337	No Correlation	.584	.212	No Correlation
Level of Understanding Towards Halal	Experience working with Halal-related or Halal-friendly restaurant			Type of eating establishment		
	cc	***p***	**D**	***cc***	***p***	**D**
General concept of Halal	.539**	.007	Moderate (+) Correlation	.279	.469	No Correlation
Sources of ingredients and drinks	.510*	.014	Moderate (+) Correlation	.457*	.048	Moderate (+) Correlation
Slaughtering of animals	.536**	.007	Moderate (+) Correlation	.336	.282	No Correlation
Presentation and storage	.518*	.012	Moderate (+) Correlation	.428	.081	No Correlation
Food processing and cooking	.393	.140	No Correlation	.316	.344	No Correlation
Hygiene or sanitation	.272	.494	No Correlation	.335	.286	No Correlation

The result further revealed that there is no significant relationship between the number of years working in the current job of the respondents and their level of understanding towards Halal in terms of general concept of Halal ($cc = .584$, $p = .215$), sources of ingredients and drinks ($cc = .653$, $p = .055$), slaughtering of animals ($cc = .649$, $p = .060$), presentation and storage ($cc = .556$, $p = .337$), and hygiene or sanitation ($cc = .556$, $p = .337$). However, the result revealed that there is a moderate positive significant relationship between the number of years working in the current job of the respondents and their level of understanding towards Halal in terms of food processing and cooking ($cc = .671$, $p = .017$). The cross-tabulation result indicated that those respondents who worked in the current job within the span of 10 years period have significantly higher level of understanding towards

Halal in terms of food processing and cooking as compared to the respondents who worked in the current job at least 11 years period.

In terms of the number of years working in the food service or related industry, the result revealed that there is no significant relationship between the number of years working in the food service or related industry of the respondents and their level of understanding towards Halal in terms of general concept of Halal ($cc = .568$, $p = .285$), sources of ingredients and drinks ($cc = .637, p = .059$), slaughtering of animals ($cc = .618, p = .100$), presentation and storage ($cc = .550, p = .369$), and hygiene or sanitation ($cc = .584, p = .212$). On the other hand, the result revealed that there is moderate positive significant relationship between the number of years working in the food service or related industry of the respondents and their level of understanding towards Halal in terms of food processing and cooking ($cc = .667, p = .020$). The cross-tabulation result indicated that those respondents who worked in the food service or related industry within the span of 10 years period have significantly higher level of understanding towards Halal in terms of food processing and cooking as compared to the respondents who worked in this industry with at least 11 years period.

In terms of experience working with Halal-related or Halal-friendly restaurant, the result revealed that there is a moderate positive significant relationship between the respondents' experience working with Halal-related or Halal-friendly restaurant and their level of understanding towards Halal in terms of general concept of Halal ($cc = .539, p = .007$), sources of ingredients and drinks ($cc = .510, p = .014$), slaughtering of animals ($cc = .536, p = .007$), and presentation and storage ($cc = .518, p = .012$). The cross-tabulation result indicated that those respondents who have experienced working in Halal-related or Halal-friendly restaurant have significantly higher level of understanding towards Halal in terms of general concept of Halal, sources of ingredients and drinks, slaughtering of animals, and presentation and storage as compared to those who do not have experienced working in this restaurant. On the other hand, there is no significant relationship between the respondents' experience working with Halal-related or Halal-friendly restaurant and their level of understanding towards Halal in terms of food processing and cooking ($cc = .393$, $p = .140$), and hygiene or sanitation ($cc = .272, p = .494$).

In terms of the type of eating establishment, the result showed that there is no significant relationship between the respondents' type of eating establishment and their level of understanding towards Halal in terms of general concept of Halal ($cc = .279, p = .469$), slaughtering of animals ($cc = .336, p = .282$), presentation and storage ($cc = .428, p = .081$), food processing and cooking ($cc = .316, p = .344$), and hygiene or sanitation ($cc = .335, p = .286$). On the other hand, the result revealed that there is a moderate positive significant relationship between the respondents' type of eating establishment and their level of understanding towards Halal in terms of sources of ingredients and drinks ($cc = .457$, $p = .048$). The cross-tabulation result indicated that the respondents from Halal-friendly restaurant have significantly higher level of understanding towards Halal in terms of sources of ingredients and drinks as compared to the respondents came from non-Halal establishment.

CONCLUSION AND FUTURE RESEARCH DIRECTIONS

There is no doubt that nowadays the concept of Halal does not just revolve within the Muslim community. It has taken its way also to the non-Muslim community. As the demand for Halal foods is increasing, the results reveal that the restaurant managers have high level of understanding on the overall concept of Halal that includes important aspects such as the sources of ingredients and drinks, slaughtering of animals, presentation and storage, hygiene/sanitation, food processing and cooking. It is seen as a positive indicator and timely response to cater the needs of the Muslim customers in a pre-dominantly non-Muslim area like San Fernando City. Knowledge on the concept of Halal by the managers can be an initial step to encourage the casual dining restaurant operators to consider the needs of Muslims in relation to food consumption. Thinking in this kind of paradigm can boost more the tourism industry of San Fernando City as it will attract more foreign and local tourists. Government agencies that are in coordination and relation with the restaurant industry like the Department of Tourism should intensify its advertisements on the growing demand for Halal food not only by the Muslims but also by the non-Muslim tourists/customers especially that San Fernando City is considered as the Capital City of Pampanga. Advertising in the national and local media the benefits or advantages of Halal foods and organizing regional and national conference, symposium and similar activities that will involve the Restaurant Management & its key players can be conducted.

REFERENCES

Abdulraof, A. (2024). The Impacts of Halal Certification Policies in the Philippines: A Literature Review. *Cognizance Journal of Multidisciplinary Studies, 4*(12), 648–667. https://doi.org/https://cognizancejournal.com/vol4issue12/V4I1266.pdf

Aksamawanti, A. (2015). Consumer Protection for Halal-Labeled Food Products: A Legal Review. Syariati: Journal of Al-Quran and Law Studies, *1*(1), 61–76. https://doi.org/https://doi.org/10.32699/syariati.v1i01.1101

Al-Qaradawi, S. Y. (2001). *The Lawful and the Prohibited in Islam.*

Azam, M. S. E., & Abdullah, M. A. (2021). Halal Standards Globally: A Comparative Study of Unities and Diversities Among the Most Popular Halal Standards Globally. *Halalsphere, 1*(1 SE-Shariah, management, marketing, and contemporary halal issue), 11–31. DOI: 10.31436/hs.v1i1.20

Balah, K. O., & Makakena, S. D. (2024). Perspectives and implications of halal food consumption among major Islamized groups in the Philippines: strengthening consumer confidence, standardization, and traceability. *Halal Research Journal, 4*(1 SE-Articles), 1–16. DOI: 10.12962/j22759970.v4i1.750

Bonne, K., & Verbeke, W. (2008). Muslim consumer trust in halal meat status and control in Belgium. *Meat Science*, *79*(1), 113–123. https://doi.org/https://doi.org/10.1016/j.meatsci.2007.08.007. DOI: 10.1016/j.meatsci.2007.08.007 PMID: 22062604

Chavez, J. V., & Vicente, M. B. (2025). Halal compliance behaviors of food and accommodation businesses in the Zamboanga Peninsula, Philippines. *Multidisciplinary Science Journal, 7*(5), e2025259. https://doi.org/https://10.31893/multiscience.2025259

Farouk, M. M., Pufpaff, K. M., & Amir, M. (2016). Industrial halal meat production and animal welfare: A review. *Meat Science*, *120*, 60–70. https://doi.org/https://doi.org/10.1016/j.meatsci.2016.04.023. DOI: 10.1016/j.meatsci.2016.04.023 PMID: 27130540

Ji, J. (2025). Philippines Enhances Halal Certification to Attract More Muslim Tourists. *ChemLinked*. https://cosmetic.chemlinked.com/news/cosmetic-news/philippines-establishes-national-halal-office-to-strengthen-domestic-and-global-market-presence

McNabb, D. E. (2020). Descriptive Research: Survey Designs. In *Research Methods for Political Science* (3rd Editio). Taylor & Francis.

Othman, B., & Md Nawi, N. H. (2025). Halal standards practices in the food industry: the impact of halal assurance and operations. *Journal of Islamic Marketing, ahead-of-p*(ahead-of-print). DOI: 10.1108/JIMA-02-2023-0051

Regenstein, J. M., Chaudry, M. M., & Regenstein, C. E. (2003). The Kosher and Halal Food Laws. *Comprehensive Reviews in Food Science and Food Safety*, *2*(3), 111–127. https://doi.org/https://doi.org/10.1111/j.1541-4337.2003.tb00018.x. DOI: 10.1111/j.1541-4337.2003.tb00018.x PMID: 33451233

Riaz, M. N., & Chaudry, M. M. (2003). *Halal Food Production*. CRC Press. https://doi.org/https://doi.org/10.1201/9780203490082

Riaz, M. N., & Chaudry, M. M. (2019). Halal Food Laws and Regulations. In M. N. Riaz & M. M. Chaudry (Eds.), *Handbook of Halal Food Production* (1st Editio). CRC Press.

Saleh, H., & Rajandran, T. (2024). Relationship between Non-Muslim consumer intention to purchase Halal Products with Halal Awareness, Halal Certification, Halal Marketing and Halal Knowledge: Systematic Review. *International Journal of Academic Research in Business & Social Sciences*, *14*(9), 416–426. https://doi .org/http://dx.doi.org/10.6007/IJARBSS/v14-i9/22495. DOI: 10.6007/IJARBSS/v14-i9/22495

Salindal, N. A. (2019). Halal certification compliance and its effects on companies' innovative and market performance. *Journal of Islamic Marketing*, *10*(2), 589–605. DOI: 10.1108/JIMA-04-2018-0080

Sarip, N. S. (2024). A Comparative Study of Halal-Compliant and Non-Halal-Compliant Meat Prices and its Influence on Halal Certification in the Lanao Region, Philippines. *Journal of Islamic Economic and Business Research, 4*(2 SE-Articles), 144–159. DOI: 10.18196/jiebr.v4i2.325

Supian, K., & Ab Rashid, N. (2018). The Role of Supplier, Top Management and Government in Halal Practices Integrity of Malaysian Food Business. *International Journal of Asian Social Science, 8*(8 SE-Articles), 549–559. DOI: 10.18488/journal.1.2018.88.549.559

Tieman, M. (2011). The application of Halal in supply chain management: In-depth interviews. *Journal of Islamic Marketing*, *2*(2), 186–195. DOI: 10.1108/17590831111139893

Wahyuni, D., & Arfidhila, N. (2019). Traceability in Halal Food Supply Chains: Literature Review. *Talenta Conference Series: Energy and Engineering (EE)*, 38–45. https://doi.org/https://doi.org/10.32734/ee.v2i4.649

Wisenthige, K. (2023). Research Design. In *Social Research Methodology and Publishing Results: A Guide to Non-Native English Speakers* (pp. 74–93). DOI: 10.4018/978-1-6684-6859-3.ch006

Yaqub, A. (2024a). Philippines Enhances Halal Certification to Attract More Muslim Tourists. *2The Halal Times*. https://www.halaltimes.com/philippines-enhances-halal-certification-to-attract-more-muslim-tourists

Yaqub, A. (2024b). Philippines Launches National Halal Office to Strengthen Global Market Presence. *The Halal Times*. https://www.halaltimes.com/philippines-launches-national-halal-office-to-strengthen-global-market-presence/

Zulfakar, M. H., Jie, F., & Chan, C. (2011). Halal supply chain integrity: From a literature review to a conceptual framework. *10th ANZAM Operatons,Supply Chain and Services Management Symposium*.

ADDITIONAL READING

Abu Bakar, I., & Ahmad, M. H. (2020). Understanding and acceptance of Halal food among non-Muslims in Malaysia: Case study in Kuantan town. *International Journal of Allied Health Sciences*, *4*(3), 1267–1276.

Ariffin, S. K., Mohsin, A. M. A., & Salamzadeh, Y. (2019). Muslim Consumers' Attitude Toward Non-Muslim's Halal Food Operators: Evidence from Malaysia. In: Bilgin, M., Danis, H., Demir, E., Can, U. (eds) *Eurasian Business Perspectives. Eurasian Studies in Business and Economics*, vol 11/2. Springer, Cham. DOI: 10.1007/978-3-030-18652-4_5

Wilkins, S., & Shams, F. (2019). The acceptance of Halal food in non-Muslim countries: Effects of religious identity, national identification, consumer ethnocentrism, and consumer cosmopolitanism. *Journal of Islamic Marketing*, *10*(4), 1308–1331. DOI: 10.1108/JIMA-11-2017-0132

Zainal, Z., Zailan, N. S., & Nasir, M. S. (2010). Non-Muslims' awareness of Halal principles and related food products in Malaysia. *International Food Research Journal*, *17*(3), 667–674.

KEY TERMS AND DEFINITIONS

Halal: Refers to permissible food and practices under Islamic law, emphasizing cleanliness, purity, and adherence to religious guidelines.

Tayyib: A concept in Islam highlighting that Halal food should also be wholesome, healthy, and free from harmful substances.

Non-Halal (Haram): Foods or practices that are explicitly forbidden by Islamic law, such as consuming pork, blood, carcasses, or alcohol.

Slaughtering Requirements: Islamic guidelines for animal slaughter, requiring specific procedures to minimize suffering and ensure cleanliness, such as severing the jugular vein, esophagus, and respiratory tract.

Separation of Foods: A critical aspect of Halal compliance requiring strict separation between Halal and non-Halal foods during processing, storage, and presentation to avoid contamination.

Hygiene and Sanitation: Emphasizes cleanliness in food preparation and storage environments, including regular cleaning, pest control, and personal hygiene of workers, as a vital part of Halal compliance.

Halalan-Thoyyiban Principle: Combines Halal (permissibility) with tayyib (wholesomeness), ensuring that food is not only religiously permissible but also safe, clean, and nutritious.

Educational Attainment and Halal Understanding: The positive correlation between higher educational qualifications (bachelor's or doctorate degrees) and a better understanding of Halal concepts and practices, indicating the role of education in Halal literacy.

Compilation of References

Ab Latiff, J., Zakaria, Z., & Man, S. (2021). The challenges in implementation of halal vaccine certification in Malaysia. *Journal of Food and Pharmaceutical Sciences*, *9*(1), 366–371. DOI: 10.22146/jfps.1147

Ab Rashid, N., & Bojei, J. (2020). The relationship between halal traceability system adoption and environmental factors on halal food supply chain integrity in Malaysia. *Journal of Islamic Marketing*, *11*(1), 117–142. DOI: 10.1108/JIMA-01-2018-0016

Ab Talib, M. S. (2017). Motivations and benefits of halal food safety certification. *Journal of Islamic Marketing*, *8*(4), 605–624. DOI: 10.1108/JIMA-08-2015-0063

Ab Talib, M. S. (2021). Identifying halal logistics constraints in Brunei Darussalam. *Journal of Islamic Marketing*, *12*(6), 1145–1158. DOI: 10.1108/JIMA-09-2019-0189

Ab Talib, M. S., Pang, L. L., & Ngah, A. H. (2020). The role of government in promoting Halal logistics: A systematic literature review. *Journal of Islamic Marketing*, *12*(9), 1682–1708. DOI: 10.1108/JIMA-05-2020-0124

Ab Talib, M. S., & Zulfakar, M. H. (2024). Sustainable halal food supply chain management in a small rentier halal market. *Arab Gulf Journal of Scientific Research*, *42*(3), 449–463. DOI: 10.1108/AGJSR-11-2022-0251

Abdallah, A., Rahem, M. A., & Pasqualone, A. (2021). The multiplicity of halal standards: a case study of application to slaughterhouses. In *Journal of Ethnic Foods* (Vol. 8, Issue 1). BioMed Central Ltd. DOI: 10.1186/s42779-021-00084-6

Abdou, A. H., Chan, M. P., Rehman, S. U., Albakhit, A. I. A., & Almakhayitah, M. Y. (2024). Islamic food laws: Customer satisfaction effect halal purchase intention in China. Moderating role of religiosity. *British Food Journal*, *126*(8), 3088–3112. DOI: 10.1108/BFJ-10-2023-0875

Abdul Mokti, H., Kamri, N. A., & Mohd Balwi, M. A. W. F. (2024). Tayyiban in halal food production: a systematic literature review. In *Journal of Islamic Marketing* (Vol. 15, Issue 2). https://doi.org/DOI: 10.1108/JIMA-03-2022-0098

Abdul Rahim, N. R., Abdullah, I., Yahya, N. A., Awang, M. N., Muhammad, S. Z., Ahmad Sabri, S., & Ahmad, N. N. (2022). Negotiation of needs towards halal talents sustainability. *Journal of Islamic Marketing*, *13*(1), 20–44. DOI: 10.1108/JIMA-11-2019-0245

Abdullah, R., & Abdul Razak, L. (2020). The effect of halal foods awareness on purchase decision with religiosity as a moderating variable: A study among university students in Brunei Darussalam. *Journal of Islamic Marketing*, *11*(5), 1091–1104.

Abdullah, R., & Rahman, M. (2022). Sustainable Practices in the Halal Industry: Opportunities and Challenges. *Journal of Cleaner Production*.

Abdulraof, A. (2024). The Impacts of Halal Certification Policies in the Philippines: A Literature Review. *Cognizance Journal of Multidisciplinary Studies, 4*(12), 648–667. https://doi.org/https://cognizancejournal.com/vol4issue12/V4I1266.pdf

Afifi, M. F., Mohsin, A., & Farouk, M. (2021). Halal hospitality goes global: Challenges of (not) serving alcohol in an Islamic tourist destination: A case study of Egypt. *Tourism Critiques*, *2*(2), 134–152. DOI: 10.1108/TRC-12-2020-0022

Agency, A. N. (n.d.). *RPH dan RPU adalah hulu strategis kehalalan suatu produk*. ANTARA News Jawa Timur. Retrieved 21 October 2022, from https://jatim.antaranews.com/berita/597201/rph-dan-rpu-adalah-hulu-strategis-kehalalan-suatu-produk

Ahmada, Z., Rahman, M. M., & Hidthiira, M. H. (2022). Corporate Social Responsibility: A Critical Analysis of Discloser and Malaysian Halal Food Industry. *Islamic Business and Covid 19 Recovery: Towards Attaining Financial And Social Wellbeing*, 11.

Ahmad, A. N., Yang, T. A., & Wan Abdullah, W. N. (2015). Perceived versus actual knowledge of alcohol and halal food among food technology undergraduate students in a Malaysian university. *Journal of Islamic Marketing*, *6*(3), 294–313. DOI: 10.1108/JIMA-10-2013-0069

Ahmad, F. N., & Nordin, N. F. H. (2023). Environmental Approach for Securing Halalan Toyyiban Concept in Food Safety-A Mini Review. *Halalsphere*, *3*(1), 27–30. DOI: 10.31436/hs.v3i1.70

Ahmad, M. (2022). Developing halal vaccine production in Indonesia: Challenges and future opportunities. *El-Hayah*, *9*(1), 18–30. DOI: 10.18860/elha.v9i1.18026

Ahmed, H. (2015). Knowledge, Economy and Islamic Finance: A New-Institutional Economics Perspective. Presentations for research seminar The Islamic Research and Training Institute (IRTI) Webinar, June 2nd.

Ahmed, H. (Ed.). (2002). Theoretical foundation of Islamic economic. Islamic Research and Training Institute (IRTI) - Islamic Development Bank (IDB).

Ahmed, H. M. (2025). Halal-Preneurship: Halal Tech Building a Digital Halal Ecosystem. Retrieved Mar 30, 2025, from The Halal Times: https://www.halaltimes.com/halal-preneurship-halal-tech-building-a-digital-halal-ecosystem/

Ahmed, H. (2021). *Islamic Finance: Principles and Practices*. Oxford University Press.

Aisyah, M., Suzanawaty, L., & Said, M. (2019). The demand for halal certified restaurants in Indonesia. *International Journal of Supply Chain Management, 8*(5). Advance online publication. DOI: 10.3390/su12030820

Ajzen, I. (1991). The Theory of Planned Behavior. *Organizational Behavior and Human Decision Processes, 50*(2), 179–211. DOI: 10.1016/0749-5978(91)90020-T

Akbar, J., Gul, M., Jahangir, M., Adnan, M., Saud, S., Hassan, S., Nawaz, T., & Fahad, S. (2023). Global Trends in Halal Food Standards: A Review. *Foods, 12*(23), 4200. DOI: 10.3390/foods12234200 PMID: 38231601

Akbar, J., Raza, A., Gul, M., & Ikramullah, M. (2022). International Halal Industry And Its Impact On Global Halal Market (A Historical Review And Future Business Prospect). *Journal of Positive School Psychology, 6*(7), 5890–5907. http://journalppw.com

Akhtar, N., Jin, S., Alvi, T. H., & Siddiqi, U. I. (2020). Conflicting halal attributes at halal restaurants and consumers' responses: The moderating role of religiosity. *Journal of Hospitality and Tourism Management, 45*, 499–510. DOI: 10.1016/j.jhtm.2020.10.010

Akmal, & Effendi, A. (2023). Business Strategy in the Halal Industry (The Use of Digital Ecosystems in Introducing Indonesia as The World's Halal Industry). *International Journal of Economics, Business and Innovation Research, 2*(4), 14-30.

Akmal, A., & Effendi, A. (2023). Business strategy in the halal industry the use of digital ecosystems in introducing Indonesia as the world's halal industry. *International Journal of Economics, Business and Innovation Research, 02*(04), pp. 14–30. Available at: https://www.e-journal.citakonsultindo.or.id/index.php/IJEBIR/article/view/320%0Ahttps://www.e-journal.citakonsultindo.or.id/index.php/IJEBIR/article/download/320/255

Aksamawanti, A. (2015). Consumer Protection for Halal-Labeled Food Products: A Legal Review. Syariati: Journal of Al-Quran and Law Studies, *1*(1), 61–76. https://doi.org/https://doi.org/10.32699/syariati.v1i01.1101

Alam, N., & Rizvi, S. (2021). *Islamic Finance: Growth and Future Prospects.* Journal of Islamic Economics.

Al-Amin, R. A. M. (2023). Food Consumption from Islamic Perspective: Evidence from Qur'an and Sunnah. *European Journal for Philosophy of Religion, 15*(3), 257–280.

Al-Ansi, A., Olya, H., & Han, H. (2023). Two decades of research on halal hospitality and tourism: A review and research agenda. *International Journal of Contemporary Hospitality Management, 35*(6), 2017–2055. DOI: 10.1108/IJCHM-12-2021-1515

Al-hajla, A. H. (2017). Why Do People Purchase Halal Cosmetics? An Integrated Model in Saudi Arabia. *Research World, 8*(2), 22.

Ali, A. (2020). Halal *Cosmetics: Trends, Opportunities, and Market Insights.* Journal of Consumer Studies.

Ali, M. H., Chung, L., Tan, K. H., Makhbul, Z. M., Zhan, Y., & Tseng, M.-L. (2023). Investigating blockchain technology adoption intention model in halal food small and medium enterprises: moderating role of supply chain integration. *International Journal of Logistics Research and Applications*, 1–25. DOI: 10.1080/13675567.2023.2217772

Ali, A. J., Al-Aali, A., & Al-Owaihan, A. (2013). Islamic perspectives on profit maximization. *Journal of Business Ethics, 117*(3), 467–475. https://www.jstor.org/stable/42001863. DOI: 10.1007/s10551-012-1530-0

Ali, A., Ali, A., Xiaoling, G., Sherwani, M., & Hussain, S. (2018). Expanding the theory of planned behaviour to predict Chinese Muslims' halal meat purchase intention. *British Food Journal, 120*(1), 2–17. DOI: 10.1108/BFJ-05-2017-0278

Ali, A., & Muda, M. (2021). Pharmaceuticals and Halal Standards: Innovations and Challenges. *Asian Journal of Pharmaceutical Sciences.*

Ali, A., Xiaoling, G., Sherwani, M., & Ali, A. (2017). Factors affecting halal meat purchase intention: Evidence from international Muslim students in China. *British Food Journal, 119*(3), 527–541. DOI: 10.1108/BFJ-10-2016-0455

Ali, H., Qazi, H. S., Hashmi, H. S., Yasin, T., & Abbas, M. H. (2025). Mapping the two decades of Islamic marketing research using bibliometric analysis and novel machine learning topic modeling. *Journal of Islamic Marketing*. Advance online publication. DOI: 10.1108/JIMA-03-2024-0127

Ali, M. H., & Suleiman, N. (2018). Eleven shades of food integrity: A halal supply chain perspective. *Trends in Food Science & Technology*, *71*, 216–224. DOI: 10.1016/j.tifs.2017.11.016

Ali, Q., Salman, A., Yaacob, H., & Parveen, S. (2019). Financial cost and social influence: Factors affecting the adoption of Halal cosmetics in Malaysia. *Academy of Entrepreneurship Journal*, *25*(2), 1–17.

Al-Mahmood, O. A., & Fraser, A. M. (2023). Perceived challenges in implementing halal standards by halal certifying bodies in the United States. PLoS ONE, *18*(8 August), 1–11. DOI: 10.1371/journal.pone.0290774

Al-Malkawi, H. A. N., Rizwan, S., & Sarea, A. (2023). Factors affecting buying decisions of Islamic banking products: The moderating role of religious belief. *International Journal of Emerging Markets*. Advance online publication. DOI: 10.1108/IJOEM-03-2023-0439

Al-Qaradawi, S. Y. (2001). *The Lawful and the Prohibited in Islam*.

Al-shami, H. A., & Abdullah, S. (2023). Halal food industry certification and operation challenges and manufacturing execution system opportunities. A review study from Malaysia. *Materials Today: Proceedings*, *80*, 3607–3614. DOI: 10.1016/j.matpr.2021.07.331

Alvarez, S., & Barney, J. (2007). Discovery and Creation: Alternative Theories of Entrepreneurial Action. *Strategic Entrepreneurship Journal*, *1*(1-2), 11–26. DOI: 10.1002/sej.4

Alzeer, J., Rieder, U., & Abou Hadeed, K. (2018). Rational and Practical Aspects of Halal and Tayyib in the Context of Food Safety. *Trends in Food Science & Technology*, *71*, 264–267. DOI: 10.1016/j.tifs.2017.10.020

Amalia, E., Rahmatullah, I., Muslim, M. B., & Fathoni, M. (2023). Enhacing halal economy ecosystem for strengthening halal business smes sector in Indonesia. *Journal of Namibian Studies*, *34*, 2197–5523.

Ambali, A. R., & Bakar, A. N. (2014). People's awareness on halal foods and products: Potential issues for policy-makers. *Procedia: Social and Behavioral Sciences*, *121*, 3–25. DOI: 10.1016/j.sbspro.2014.01.1104

Amer, M. (2023). Halal standards' implementation in Palestinian food sector: Its drivers and impact on performance. *Arab Gulf Journal of Scientific Research*. Advance online publication. DOI: 10.1108/AGJSR-09-2022-0168

Amer, M. (2024). Linkage among halal quality standard certification and SME's performance: Palestinian food halal certified SME's context. *Arab Gulf Journal of Scientific Research*, *42*(4), 1414–1425. DOI: 10.1108/AGJSR-03-2023-0109

Amrullah, A., & Abdulmalik, H. (1983). *Tafsir al-Azhar* (p. Juz VII). Pustaka Panjimas.

Anam, J., Sany Sanuri, B. M. M., & Ismail, B. L. O. (2018). Conceptualizing the relation between halal logo, perceived product quality and the role of consumer knowledge. *Journal of Islamic Marketing*, *9*(4), 727–746. DOI: 10.1108/JIMA-02-2017-0019

Annur, C. M. (2022, November 16). *Ada 1.644 Rumah Pemotongan Hewan di Indonesia pada 2022, Ini Sebaran Wilayahnya*. Katadata.co.id;Databoks. https://databoks.katadata.co.id/agroindustri/statistik/402450333383476/ada-1644-rumah-pemotongan-hewan-di-indonesia-pada-2022-ini-sebaran-wilayahnya

Aoun, I., & Tournois, L. (2015). Building holistic brands: An exploratory study of halal cosmetics. *Journal of Islamic Marketing*, *6*(1), 109–132. DOI: 10.1108/JIMA-05-2014-0035

Apriliani, F. D., Widihastuti, , Daryono, R. W., Jaya, D. J., & Rizbudiani, A. D. (2023). The Influence of Fashion Knowledge, Fashion Selection Factor, and Dress Etiquette on Dress Look. *Jurnal Pendidikan Dan Pengajaran*, *56*(1), 194–207. DOI: 10.23887/jpp.v56i1.53677

Arbak, S., Islam, R., & Al Rasyid, H. (2019a). Influence of Islamic advertising: Ethic violation on customer purchase intention of halal cosmetic products in Malaysia. *Humanities and Social Sciences Reviews*, *7*(3), 671–682. DOI: 10.18510/hssr.2019.7398

Arbak, S., Islam, R., & Al Rasyid, H. (2019b). Relationship between advertisement and purchase intention on halal cosmetic products in Malaysia. *Humanities and Social Sciences Reviews*, *7*(3), 683–694. DOI: 10.18510/hssr.2019.7399

Ardiantono, D. S., Ardyansyah, G. D., Sugihartanto, M. F., Al Mustofa, M. U., & Lisdiantini, N. (2024). Mapping the barrier and strategic solutions of halal supply chain implementation in small and medium enterprises. *Journal of Islamic Marketing*, *15*(7), 1673–1705. Advance online publication. DOI: 10.1108/JIMA-08-2022-0229

Arham, M. (2010). Islamic perspectives on marketing. *Journal of Islamic Marketing, 1*(2), 149–164. DOI: 10.1108/17590831011055888

Ariffin, A., & Zainol, F. (2016). *The* Halal *Industry in Malaysia: Market Opportunities and Challenges*. Malaysian Journal of Social Sciences and Humanities.

Arifin, E. N., Ananta, A., Musa, S. F. P. D., & Hoon, C. Y. (2024). A pioneering study on measuring poverty in the hydrocarbon-rich state of Brunei Darussalam. *Asian Population Studies, 20*(2), 222–240. DOI: 10.1080/17441730.2023.2240108

Arif, S., & Sidek, S. (2015). Application of Halalan Tayyiban in the Standard Reference for Determining Malaysian Halal Food. *Asian Social Science, 11*(17), 116. DOI: 10.5539/ass.v11n17p116

Ariska, N., Setiawan, R. A., Setiawan, A., & Zaki, K. (2023). Implementation of the self-declare halal certification process in supporting the growth of MSMEs. Journal of Community Empowerment Learning *(JP2M), 4*(4), 807-815.

Arsil, P., Tey, Y. S., Brindal, M., Phua, C. U., & Liana, D. (2018). Personal values underlying halal food consumption: Evidence from Indonesia and Malaysia. *British Food Journal, 120*(11), 2524–2538. DOI: 10.1108/BFJ-09-2017-0519

Ary, O., & Of, N. (2018). *A series published with the Society for the Anthropology of Religion*.

Aryanti, L., Rachmat, S. R., Nurniwati, E., & Kristiadi, D. (2022). Knowledge Management Strengthening Character of Entrepreneurs Students Department of Technopreneur at School of Technopreneur Nusantara. *International Journal of Information System and Technology, 6*(4), 462–468. DOI: 10.30645/ijistech.v6i4.262

Aslam, E., Asif, M., Sultan, A., Nasir, S., & Iqbal, A. (2023). The Synergy of Islamic Finance and the Halal Industry Development in Islamic Countries. *Tuijin Jishu/Journal of Propulsion Technology, 44*(3), 3849 - 3858.

Asna Annisa, A., & Indriyani, F. (2024). Understanding the digitalization of the blue economy in a global halal-hub. *Research Journal on Islamic Economics, 10*(1), 1–14.

Asy-Syirbini, S. M. bin A. (1997). *Mughni Al-Muhtaj* (1 ed.). Dar Al-Ma'rifah.

Awan, H. M., Siddiquei, A. N., & Haider, Z. (2015a). Factors affecting Halal purchase intention – evidence from Pakistan's Halal food sector. *Management Research Review, 38*(6), 640–660. DOI: 10.1108/MRR-01-2014-0022

Awan, H. M., Siddiquei, A. N., & Haider, Z. (2015b). Management Research Review For Authors. *Management Research Review, 38*(2). Advance online publication. DOI: 10.1108/MRR-08-2013-0185

Aysan, A. F., & Syarif, M. F. (2024). Shaping the halal tourism industry landscape through NFT and metaverse: New horizons for halal brand and halal booking hotel. *Journal of Islamic Marketing*. Advance online publication. DOI: 10.1108/JIMA-07-2023-0206

Azam, M. S. E., & Abdullah, M. A. (2021). Halal Standards Globally: A Comparative Study of Unities and Diversities Among the Most Popular Halal Standards Globally. *Halalsphere, 1*(1 SE-Shariah, management, marketing, and contemporary halal issue), 11–31. DOI: 10.31436/hs.v1i1.20

Aziz, F., Badshah, S. N., & Khan, B. ullah. (2021). Innovative leadership principles for peace building in society an analysis in Islamic perspective, *Acta-Islamica*, pp. 1–17. Available at: http://www.aisbbu.com/index.php/ai/article/view/43%0Ahttp://www.aisbbu.com/index.php/ai/article/download/43/39

Aziz, M., Ghofur, A., & Hidayati, N. N. (2021). Regulation on the Implementation of Halal Product Assurance in Indonesia: Statute Approaches Study. *Ulul Albab: Jurnal Studi Dan Penelitian Hukum Islam*, *4*(2), 209. Advance online publication. DOI: 10.30659/jua.v4i2.13649

Aziz, S., Md Husin, M., Gazali, S., Zameer Rahman, E., & Afaq, Z. (2025). Trends and directions of Islamic marketing: A bibliometric and scientometric analysis (2001–2023). *Journal of Islamic Marketing*. Advance online publication. DOI: 10.1108/JIMA-12-2023-0399

Aziz, Y. A., & Chok, N. V. (2013). The role of Halal awareness, Halal certification, and marketing components in determining Halal purchase intention among non-Muslims in Malaysia: A structural equation modeling approach. *Journal of International Food & Agribusiness Marketing*, *25*(1), 1–23. DOI: 10.1080/08974438.2013.723997

Bachtiar, W. F., Masruroh, N. A., Asih, A. M. S., & Sari, D. P. (2024). Halal food sustainable traceability framework for the meat processing industry. *Journal of Islamic Marketing*, *15*(11), 2759–2784. Advance online publication. DOI: 10.1108/JIMA-12-2023-0412

Badan Standarisasi Nasional. (1999). *SNI 01-6159-1999 Standar Teknis RPH*. BSN.

Badu, R., Teye, M., Bannor, R., & Awal, F. (2023). Meat consumers and Islamic scholars' understanding of humane slaughter, and effects of pre-slaughter stunning on meat purchasing decisions in Ghana. *Journal of Islamic Marketing*, *14*(2), 504–522. DOI: 10.1108/JIMA-02-2021-0041

Bagundang, E., & Gallo, M. (2024). Technological Advancements in Halal Ecosystem: Harnessing Information Technology for Certification and Traceability. *International Journal for Multidisciplinary Research*, *6*(2), 1–8.

Baharuddin, K., Kassim, N. A., Nordin, S., & Buyong, S. (2015). Understanding the Halal Concept and the Importance of Information on Halal Food Business Needed by Potential Malaysian Entrepreneurs. *International Journal of Academic Research in Business & Social Sciences*, *5*(2), 170–180. DOI: 10.6007/IJARBSS/v5-i2/1476

Bahrin, M. A. K., Othman, M. F., Azli, N. H. N., & Talib, M. F. (2016). Industry 4.0: A review on industrial automation and robotic. Jurnal Teknologi, 78(6–13), 137–143.

Bakar, M.A., Bakar, A.A., Noor, A.M., & Mohamad, N.M. (2020). Islamic Technopreneurship in the Midst of Covid-19 Pandemic: A Malaysia Review, *Palarch's Journal of Archaeology of Egypt/Egyptology, 17*(9): 3005 – 3024.

Bakhtiar, F., Prayoga, R., & Mulya, A. (2022). Analisis Literasi Keuangan Dan Financial Technology Terhadap Inklusi Keuangan Pada Pelaku UMKM Perempuan. *Akuntabel, 19*(2), 260–268. DOI: 10.30872/jakt.v19i2.11178

Balah, K. O., & Makakena, S. D. (2024). Perspectives and implications of halal food consumption among major Islamized groups in the Philippines: strengthening consumer confidence, standardization, and traceability. *Halal Research Journal, 4*(1 SE-Articles), 1–16. DOI: 10.12962/j22759970.v4i1.750

Barbe, D., Magids, S., & Thornton, K. (2003). Holistic Approach for Technology Entrepreneurship Education in Engineering. *Proceedings - Frontiers in Education Conference, FIE* (pp. T2D1 - T2D6). Institute of Electrical and Electronics Engineers Inc. DOI: 10.1109/FIE.2003.1263299

Bashir, A. M. (2019). Effect Of Halal Awareness, Halal Logo And Attitude On Foreign Consumers' Purchase Intention. *British Food Journal, 121*(9), 1998–2015. DOI: 10.1108/BFJ-01-2019-0011

Basir, A. (2019). Effectiveness of Halal branding as a marketing mix strategy. *Journal of Islamic Marketing*, *10*(2), 440–455.

Basir, K. H. (2022). Business Innovation Amid the COVID-19 Crisis in Brunei Darussalam: A Viewpoint. In Ratten, V. (Ed.), *Strategic Entrepreneurial Ecosystems and Business Model Innovation* (pp. 31–40). Emerald Publishing Limited., DOI: 10.1108/978-1-80382-137-520221003

Basir, K., Raffi, R., & Marmaya, N. (2022). Enhancing Young Graduates' Intention towards Halal Entrepreneurship Development in Brunei Darussalam: A Case of Universiti Islam Sultan Sharif Ali. *Proceedings Borneo Islamic International Conference*, 168-179.

Bayumi, M. R., Iqbal, M., & Diem, M. J., & Muhlis. (. (2022). Rekonstruksi Konsep Bisnis Halalan Thayyiban Penguatan Integrasi-Interkoneksi Ekosistem Halal Value Chain. *Al-Mashrafiyah: Jurnal Ekonomi, Keuangan. Dan Perbankan Syariah*, *6*(2). Advance online publication. DOI: 10.24252/al-mashrafiyah.v6i2.28543

Berawi, M. A. (2018). Utilizing Big Data in Industry 4.0: Managing Competitive Advantages and Business Ethics. *International Journal ofTechnology*, *3*(1), 430–433. DOI: 10.14716/ijtech.v9i3.1948

Bisri, M. A. (1977). *Moh. Adib Bisri, 'Terjemah Al Faraidul Bahiyyah Risalah Qawa-Id Fiqh* (p. 24). Menara Kudus.

Bonang, D., Fianto, B. A., & Sukmana, R. (2025). Bibliometric analysis of service quality and customer satisfaction in Islamic banking: A roadmap for future research. *Journal of Islamic Marketing*, *16*(2), 462–483. DOI: 10.1108/JIMA-06-2023-0177

Bonne, K., & Verbeke, W. (2008). Muslim consumer trust in halal meat status and control in Belgium. *Meat Science*, *79*(1), 113–123. DOI: 10.1016/j.meatsci.2007.08.007 PMID: 22062604

Bonne, K., & Verbeke, W. (2008). Religious values informing halal meat production and the control and delivery of halal credence quality. *Agriculture and Human Values*, *25*(1), 35–47. DOI: 10.1007/s10460-007-9076-y

Bonne, K., Vermeir, I., & Verbeke, W. (2009). Impact of religion on halal meat consumption decision making in Belgium. *Journal of International Food & Agribusiness Marketing*, *21*(1), 5–26. DOI: 10.1080/08974430802480628

Boon Liat, C., Nikhashemi, S. R., & Dent, M. M. (2020). The chain effects of service innovation components on the building blocks of tourism destination loyalty: the moderating role of religiosity. *Journal of Islamic Marketing, 12*(9), 1887-1929. (Coordinating Ministry for Economic Affairs of the Republic of Indonesia, 2023)

Bouzenita, A., & Boulanouar, A. (2016). Maslow's hierarchy of needs: An Islamic critique. *Intellectual Discourse, 24*(1), 59–81. https://squ.elsevierpure.com/en

Bryman, A. (2016). *Social research methods*. Oxford University Press.

Bryman, A., & Bell, E. (2011). *Business Research Methods*. Oxford University Press.

Buhalis, D., & Sinarta, Y. (2019). Real-time co-creation and nowness service: lessons from tourism and hospitality. *Real-time co-creation and nowness service: lessons from tourism and hospitality, 36*(5), 563-582. DOI: 10.1080/10548408.2019.1592059

Bujang, A., Rahman, F. A., & Omar, S. R. S. (2020). Nanotechnology in the Food Processing and Packaging: An Overview of Its Halalan Tayyiban Aspect. *Malaysian J Consum Fam Econ, 24*, 1–14.

Business, B. N. (2024). *National Definitons for Business Categories in Brunei Darusaalam*. Ministry of Finance and Economy. https://business.mofe.gov.bn/SitePages/Brunei Darussalam Micro Small & Medium Enterprise Definition.aspx

Bux, C., Varese, E., Amicarelli, V., & Lombardi, M. (2022). Halal Food Sustainability between Certification and Blockchain: A Review. *Sustainability (Basel), 14*(4), 2152. DOI: 10.3390/su14042152

Cairns, R. (2024). *Meet the woman behind Dubai's viral super-chunky chocolate bar*. CNN Travel. https://edition.cnn.com/travel/dubai-viral-chocolate-bar-fix-hnk-spc/index.html

Calder, R. (2020). Halalization: Religious Product Certification in Secular Markets. *Sociological Theory, 38*(4), 334–361. DOI: 10.1177/0735275120973248

Chan, C., Zulfakar, M. H., Chan, C., Jie, F., Pandiyan, V., & Sundram, K. (2019). Halal Accreditation And Certification In A Non- Muslim Country Setting : Insights From Australia Halal Meat Supply Chain Halal Accreditation And Certification In A Non- Muslim Country Setting. *Insights From Australia Halal Meat Supply Chain., 8*, 10–17.

Chavez, J. V., & Vicente, M. B. (2025). Halal compliance behaviors of food and accommodation businesses in the Zamboanga Peninsula, Philippines. *Multidisciplinary Science Journal, 7*(5), e2025259. https://doi.org/https://10.31893/multiscience.2025259

Chen, X., Xu, L., Ren, Z., Jia, F., & Yu, Y. (2023). Sustainable supply chain management in the leather industry: A systematic literature review. *International Journal of Logistics, 26*(12), 1663–1703. DOI: 10.1080/13675567.2022.2104233

Cheong, D., & Lawrey, R. (2009). *A Study of Unemployment Issues among Registered Job Seekers in Brunei Darussalam*. The Centre for Strategic and Policy Studies.

Choiriyah, C. (2016). Pemikiran Ekonomi Muhammad Baqir Ash-Sadr. *Islamic Banking: Jurnal Pemikiran Dan Pengembangan Perbankan Syariah, 1*(2), 49–58.

Chong, D. (2024). *Halal or not? Jakim clarifies certification issue for six popular F&B chains amid online queries*. The Malay Mail.

Chowdhury, A. J. K., Hashim, N., Marsal, C. J., & Jamaludin, M. H. (2023). Water Treatment and Aquaculture Products Towards Halal Value Chain in ASEAN Countries: A Retrospective Review on Brunei Darussalam. *Desalination and Water Treatment*, *315*, 479–491. DOI: 10.5004/dwt.2023.30014

Chowdhury, N. R., Ahmed, M., Mahmud, P., Paul, S. K., & Liza, S. A. (2022). Modeling a sustainable vaccine supply chain for a healthcare system. *Journal of Cleaner Production*, *370*(133423), 1–19. DOI: 10.1016/j.jclepro.2022.133423 PMID: 35975192

Cid, R., & Bolívar, J. (2021). Platforms for production of protein-based vaccines: From classical to next-generation strategies. *Biomolecules*, *11*(1072), 1–33. DOI: 10.3390/biom11081072 PMID: 34439738

Cochrane, P. (2020a, July 13). Will there be a halal covid-19 vaccine? *Salaam Gateway,* Insight, https://salaamgateway.com/story/will-there-be-a-halal-covid-19 -vaccine

Cochrane, P. (2020b, December 18). Halal but not halal certified key concerns about approved covid-19 vaccines. *Salaam Gateway,* News, https://salaamgateway.com/story/halal-but-not-halal-certified-key-concerns-about-approved-covid-19-vaccines

Cunningham, C. (2022). Fashion and Halal: The Emerging Trends in Muslim Consumer Markets. *Fashion Theory*.

Dahlal, N. M., & Ahmad, F. A. (2018). Beyond Halal in Food Product: Present and Future of Halalan Tayyiban. *Review of Integrative Business and Economics Research*, *7*, 276–289.

Dahlal, N. M., Saniff, S. M., & Noh, C. N. C. (2024). Harmonising Food Safety and Friendly Service through Halal and Toyyib Principles. *Halalsphere*, *4*(1), 80–87. DOI: 10.31436/hs.v4i1.89

Dakhoir, A. (2019). The fatwa authorities of National Syaria Council of Majelis Ulama Indonesia in supporting the principle if Syariah compliance. *Journal of Legal, Ethical and Regulatory Issues, 22*(1).

Darajah, M., & Kassim, U. (2019). The Factors Influence University Students Decision in Selecting Their Career as A Technopreneur in Malaysia. *International Journal of Social Science Research*, *1*(2), 76–86.

Darmalaksana, W. (2023). How is the halal certification policy implemented? Perspective analysis of small and medium enterprises (SMEs) in Indonesia. *Journal of Islamic Accounting and Business Research*. Advance online publication. DOI: 10.1108/JIABR-12-2022-0342

Darmawati, H., Hardiana, D., Mainata, D., & Nuryadin, M. B. (2023). Halal industry: A literature bibliometric analysis on halal studies. *Mazahib Jurnal Pemikiran Hukum Islam*, *22*(1), 175–211. DOI: 10.21093/mj.v22i1.5477

Darussalam Enterprise. (n.d.). Available Funding Options in Brunei. Retrieved on Mar 30, 2025 from DARe: https://www.dare.gov.bn/_files/ugd/06a3d1_456883dabef74dfa830dbf1d44100710.pdf

Das, B., Kumar, B., Begum, W., Bhattarai, A., Mondal, M. H., & Saha, B. (2022). Comprehensive review on applications of surfactants in vaccine formulation, therapeutic and cosmetic pharmacy and prevention of pulmonary failure due to covid-19. *Chemistry Africa*, *5*(3), 459–480. DOI: 10.1007/s42250-022-00345-0

Dashti, L. A. H. F., Jackson, T., West, A., & Jackson, L. (2024). Enhancing halal food traceability: A model for rebuilding trust and integrity in Muslim countries. *Journal of Islamic Marketing*, *15*(12), 3382–3408. Advance online publication. DOI: 10.1108/JIMA-06-2023-0167

De Boni, A., & Forleo, M. B. (2019). Italian halal food market development: Drivers and obstacles from experts' opinions. *Journal of Islamic Marketing*, *10*(4), 1245–1271. DOI: 10.1108/JIMA-05-2018-0087

de Pablos, P. (2003). Intellectual Capital Reporting in Spain: A Comparative View. *Journal of Intellectual Capital*, *4*(1), 61–81. DOI: 10.1108/14691930310455397

Deku, W. A., Wang, J., & Das, N. (2023). Innovations in entrepreneurial marketing dimensions: Evidence of Halal food SMEs in Ghana. *Journal of Islamic Marketing*, *14*(3), 680–713. DOI: 10.1108/JIMA-03-2021-0098

Delener, N. (1994). Religious Contrasts in Consumer Decision Behaviour Patterns: Their Dimensions and Marketing Implications. *European Journal of Marketing*, *28*(5), 36–53. DOI: 10.1108/03090569410062023

Demirci, M. N., Soon, J. M., & Wallace, C. A. (2016). Positioning Food Safety in Halal Assurance. *Food Control*, *70*, 257–270. DOI: 10.1016/j.foodcont.2016.05.059

Department of Economic Planning and Statistics. (2024a). Brunei Darussalam. *Statistical Yearbook. Annuaire Statistique*, *2023*, •••. https://deps.mofe.gov.bn/DEPD%20Documents%20Library/DOS/BDSYB/2023/RPT.pdf

Department of Economic Planning and Statistics. (2024b). *Food and Beverages Services Index: 3rd Quarter 2024.*

Department of Statistics. (2024). *Labour Force Survey 2023.* Ministry of Finance and Economy.

Deuraseh, N., Hashim, N., Raffi, R., & Rosli, N. (2022). Halal Food Producer as an Alternative Employment Job for Halal Science Graduates in Brunei Darussalam. *Journal of Halal Science and Technology, 1*(1), 55–66. DOI: 10.59202/jhst.v1i1.455

Dewar, J., & Hussain, M. (2023). *Islamic Finance Market.*

DinarStandard. (2023). *Global Islamic Economy Report 2023.* Retrieved from [DinarStandard] (https://www.dinarstandard.com)

DinarStandard. (2023). *State of the global Islamic economy report 2023/2024.* DinarStandard, Salam Gateway, and Dubai Economy and Tourism.

Djekic, I. V. (2021). Meat supply chain in the perspective of UN SDGs. *Theory and Practice of Meat Processing, 6*(3), 242–247. DOI: 10.21323/2414-438X-2021-6-3-242-247

Djunaidi, M., Oktavia, C. B. A., Fitriadi, R., & Setiawan, E. (2021). Perception and Consumer Behavior of Halal Product Toward Purchase Decision in Indonesia. *Jurnal Teknik Industri, 22*(2), 171–184. DOI: 10.22219/JTIUMM.Vol22.No2.171-184

Dumpa, N., Goel, K., Guo, Y., McFall, H., Pillai, A. R., Shukla, A., Repka, M. A., & Murthy, S. N. (2019). Stability of vaccines. *AAPS PharmSciTech, 20*(42), 42. Advance online publication. DOI: 10.1208/s12249-018-1254-2 PMID: 30610415

Eisenhardt, K. M., Graebner, M. E., & Sonenshein, S. (2016). From the editors: Grand challenges and inductive methods: Rigor without rigor mortis. *Academy of Management Journal, 59*(4), 1113–1123. https://doi.org/DOI: 10.5465/amj.2016.4004

El Daouk, M. (2022). Introducing alāl to construction supply chains in the UK's construction sector. *Journal of Islamic Marketing*. Advance online publication. DOI: 10.1108/JIMA-01-2022-0016

Elasrag, H. (2016). Halal *Industry: Key Challenges and Opportunities.*

Elias, E. M., Othman, S., Yaacob, N., & Saifudin, A. (2016). A Study of Halal Awareness and Knowledge among Entrepreneur Undergraduates. *International Journal of Supply Chain Management, 5*(3), 147–152.

Elias, E. M., Yaacob, N. S. A., & Othman, S. N. (2018). Enhancing business performance through religiosity leaderships style among the small and medium enterprises. *International Journal of Supply Chain Management*, *7*(2), 95–102.

Elkington, J. (1998). *Cannibals with Forks: The Triple Bottom Line of 21st Century Business*. New Society Publishers.

Elmelki, A., & Ben Arab, M. (2009). Ethical Investment and the Social Responsibilities of the Islamic Banks. *International Business Research*, *2*(2), 123–130. DOI: 10.5539/ibr.v2n2p123

Elseidi, R. I. (2018). Determinants of halal purchasing intentions: Evidences from the UK. *Journal of Islamic Marketing*, *9*(1), 167–190. DOI: 10.1108/JIMA-02-2016-0013

ElTayeb, T. K., Zailani, S., & Jayaraman, K. (2010). The examination on the drivers for green purchasing adoption among EMS 14001 certified companies in Malaysia. *Journal of Manufacturing Technology Management*, *21*(2), 206–225. DOI: 10.1108/17410381011014378

Euromonitor International. (2021). *Global* Halal *Food Market Report*. Retrieved from [Euromonitor] (https://www.euromonitor.com)

Facciolà, A., Visalli, G., Laganà, A., & Di Pietro, A. (2022). An overview of vaccine adjuvants: Current evidence and future perspectives. *Vaccines*, *10*(5), 819. DOI: 10.3390/vaccines10050819 PMID: 35632575

Fard, M. H., & Amiri, N. S. (2018). The effect of entrepreneurial marketing on halal food SMEs performance. *Journal of Islamic Marketing*, *9*(3), 598–620. DOI: 10.1108/JIMA-12-2016-0097

Farouk, M. M. (2019). *Introduction to Halal Food: A Practical Guide*. Wiley-Blackwell.

Farouk, M. M., Pufpaff, K. M., & Amir, M. (2016). Industrial halal meat production and animal welfare: A review. *Meat Science*, *120*, 60–70. https://doi.org/https://doi.org/10.1016/j.meatsci.2016.04.023. DOI: 10.1016/j.meatsci.2016.04.023 PMID: 27130540

Fauzan, T. R., & Syara, A. S. (2023). Enhancing Food Security through Halal System with a Logistic Regression Analysis. *Enrichment: Journal of Management*, *13*(2), 857–867.

Fauzia, I. Y., & Musari, K. (2021). Waqf crowdfunding for financing the MSMEs: Evidence from ASEAN-3. In de Pablos, P. O., Zhang, X., & Almunawar, M. N. (Eds.), *Handbook of research on disruptive innovation and digital transformation in Asia* (pp. 37–49). IGI Global., DOI: 10.4018/978-1-7998-6477-6.ch003

Fauzi, M. A., Mohd Ali, N. S., Mat Russ, N., Mohamad, F., Battour, M., & Mohd Zaki, N. N. (2024). Halal certification in food products: Science mapping of present and future trends. *Journal of Islamic Marketing*, *15*(12), 3564–3580. DOI: 10.1108/JIMA-12-2023-0407

FDA. (2025, January 15). Thimerosal and vaccines. *U.S. Food and Drug Administration (FDA),*https://www.fda.gov/vaccines-blood-biologics/safety-availability-biologics/thimerosal-and-vaccines

Febriani, R., & Sa'diyah, C. (2021, September). Febriani, rizki & Sa, C. (2021). Exploring Islamic leadership on sme performance: mediated by exploring islamic leadership on SME performance: mediated by innovative work behavior and financial technology. [JAM]. *Journal of AppliedManagement*, *19*(3), 495–506. Advance online publication. DOI: 10.21776/ub.jam.2021.019.03.04

Feizollah, A., Anuar, N. B., Mehdi, R., Firdaus, A., & Sulaiman, A. (2022). Understanding covid-19 halal vaccination discourse on facebook and twitter using aspect-based sentiment analysis and text emotion analysis. *International Journal of Environmental Research and Public Health, 19*(10), 6269. DOI: 10.3390/ijerph19106269 PMID: 35627806

Fernando, Y., Wahyuni-TD, I. S., Zainul Abideen, A., & Mergeresa, F. (2023). Traceability technology, halal logistics brand and logistics performance: Religious beliefs and beyond. *Journal of Islamic Marketing*, *14*(4), 1007–1031. DOI: 10.1108/JIMA-06-2020-0183

Fischer, J. (2016). *Islam, Standards, and Technoscience*. Routledge.

Fishbein, M., & Ajzen, I. (1975). Belief, Attitude, Intention and Behavior: An Introduction to Theory and Research. *Contemporary Sociology*, *6*(2), 244. https://doi.org/https://dx.doi.org/10.2307/2065853

Food and Agriculture Organisation. (FAO, 2006). *Food Security*. Policy Brief 2. Retrieved on 07/08/24, from https://www.fao.org/fileadmin/templates/faoitaly/documents/pdf/pdf_Food_Security_Cocept_Note.pdf

Franzoni, S., & Allali, A. (2018). Principles of Islamic Finance and Principles of Corporate Social Responsibility: What Convergence? *Sustainability (Basel)*, *10*(3), 637. DOI: 10.3390/su10030637

Fratzl, P., & Weinkamer, R. (2007). Nature's hierarchical materials. *Progress in Materials Science*, *52*(8), 1263–1334. DOI: 10.1016/j.pmatsci.2007.06.001

Fujiwara, T., & Ismail, R. M. (2018). Supplier management system in halal food supply chain: A case study approach. *International Journal of Supply Chain Management*, *7*(3), 216–220. http://dsgate.uum.edu.my/jspui/handle/123456789/4509

Fuseini, A., Wotton, S. B., Knowles, T. G., & Hadley, P. J. (2017). Halal Meat Fraud and Safety Issues in the UK: A Review in the Context of the European Union. *Food Ethics*, *1*(2), 127–142. DOI: 10.1007/s41055-017-0009-1

Gading, B. M. W. T., Respati, A. N., & Suryanto, E. (2021). Studi Kasus: Permasalahan Limbah di Tempat Pemotongan Hewan (TPH) Amessangeng, Kota Sengkang. *JURNAL TRITON*, *12*(1), 68–77. DOI: 10.47687/jt.v12i1.164

Ganefri, G. (2013). The Development of Production-Based Learning Approach to Entrepreneurial Spirit for Engineering Students. *Asian Social Science*, *9*(12), 162–167. DOI: 10.5539/ass.v9n12p162

Golnaz, R., Zainalabidin, M., Mad Nasir, S., & Eddie Chiew, F. C. (2010). Non-muslims' awareness of Halal principles and related food products in Malaysia. *International Food Research Journal*, *17*(3), 667–674.

Hafiz Zulfakar, M., Chan, C., & Jie, F. (2014). *Factors Influencing the Operations of the Halal Meat Supply Chain in Australia. March 2016*, 1–8.

Hair, J.F.Jr., Sarstedt, M., Hopkins, L., & Kuppelwieser, Volker G. (. (2014). Partial least squares structural equation modeling (PLS-SEM): An emerging tool in business research. *European Business Review*, *26*(2), 106–121. DOI: 10.1108/EBR-10-2013-0128

Haji Shahlehi, S. F., Shaya, V. N., Ismail, K., & Kawi, F. (2024). Bruneian SMEs amid the COVID-19 pandemic: Challenges for the Halal food processing industry. *Journal of Islamic Marketing*, *15*(1), 142–158. DOI: 10.1108/JIMA-11-2021-0364

Haleem, A., Khan, M. I., & Khan, S. (2019). Halal certification, the inadequacy of its adoption, modelling and strategising the efforts. *Journal of Islamic Marketing*, *11*(2), 384–404. DOI: 10.1108/JIMA-05-2017-0062

Haleem, A., Khan, M. I., & Khan, S. (2021). Conceptualising a framework linking halal supply chain management with sustainability: An India centric study. *Journal of Islamic Marketing*, *12*(8), 1535–1552. DOI: 10.1108/JIMA-07-2019-0149

Hamdan, M., & Hoon, C.-Y. (2019). Brunei Darussalam: Making Strides with a Renewed Focus on the Future. In D. Singh & M. Cook (Eds.), *Southeast Asian Affairs 2019* (Vol. 2019, pp. 85–102). ISEAS–Yusof Ishak Institute Singapore. DOI: 10.1355/9789814843164-008

Hamdan, M. N., Jalil, R. A., Ramli, M. A., Ramli, N., Ibrahim, M. N. A., Ab Rahman, M. F., & Abd Rahman, N. N. H. (2024). A Review of the Discussions on Cultivated Meat from the Islamic Perspective. *Heliyon, 10*(7), e28491. DOI: 10.1016/j.heliyon.2024.e28491 PMID: 38601623

Hamdan, N. F., & Hashim, N. (2022). The Practices of Halalan Thayyiban Aspect in Japanese Restaurants in Brunei Darussalam. *Journal of Halal Science and Technology, 1*(1), 67–73. DOI: 10.59202/jhst.v1i1.456

Hanifasari, D., Masudin, I., Zulfikarijah, F., Rumijati, A., & Restuputri, D. P. (2024). Millennial generation awareness of halal supply chain knowledge toward purchase intention for halal meat products: Empirical evidence in Indonesia. *Journal of Islamic Marketing, 15*(7), 1847–1885. DOI: 10.1108/JIMA-01-2023-0012

Hansen, G. D., & Prescott, E. C. (2002). Malthus to Solow. *The American Economic Review, 92*(4), 1205–1217. Advance online publication. DOI: 10.1257/00028280260344731

Hanzaee, K. H., & Ramezani, M. R. (2011). Intention to halal products in the world markets. *Interdisciplinary Journal of Research in Business, 1*(5), 1–7.

Haque, A., Sarwar, A., Yasmin, F., Tarofder, A. K., & Hossain, M. A. (2015). Non-muslim consumers' perception toward purchasing halal food products in Malaysia. *Journal of Islamic Marketing, 6*(1), 133–147. DOI: 10.1108/JIMA-04-2014-0033

Hariani, D., & Hanafiah, M. H. (2024). The competitiveness, challenges, and opportunities to accommodate the halal tourism market: A Sharia-law tourism destination perspectives. *Journal of Islamic Marketing, 15*(3), 919–942. DOI: 10.1108/JIMA-05-2023-0147

Harsono, A. (2013). Building Technopreneurship For Next Generation: How The Benefits Of Techno- Entrepreneurship Education Affect Career Intentions of College Students. *Jurnal Ilmiah Sistem Informasi dan Teknik Informatika, 3*(1), 31-40.

Hasanah, N. U., Safira, M. E., Kurnianingtyas Sri Agung, W., Chotib, M., Nimasari, E. P., & Lahuri, S. B. (2021). Regulation of Halal and Healthy Products for Small-Scaled Businesses as Consumer Protection. *Open Access Macedonian Journal of Medical Sciences, 9*(E), 749–753. DOI: 10.3889/oamjms.2021.6643

Hasan, Z. (2009). *Islamic Finance: Theory and Practice*. Edward Elgar Publishing.

Hashim, N. A. M. K., Aziz, R. C., & Yusoof, A. M. (2020). The success of halal supply chain management practices in Malaysia. *Journal of Advanced Research in Dynamical and Control Systems*, *12*(8), 232–236. DOI: 10.5373/JARDCS/V12I8/20202469

Hashmi, H. S., & Ali, H. (2021). Education for young generations on halal food audit and certification. In Qadri. Hussain Mohi-ud-Din & M. I. Bhatti (Eds.), *Contemporary Issues in Islamic Social Finance* (1st ed., pp. 273–292). Routledge. DOI: 10.4324/9781003050209-19

Hassan, S., Abdukadir, N., & Rashid, M. (2019). *Challenges and Opportunities in the* Halal *Market: A Global Perspective*. International Journal of Islamic Finance.

Hassan, S., Ahmed, F., & Rizvi, S. (2021). *Islamic Finance and Sustainable Development: A Collaborative Approach*. Journal of Islamic Finance.

Hassan, Y., & Pandey, J. (2020). Examining the engagement of young consumers for religiously sanctioned food: The case of halal food in India. *Young Consumers*, *21*(2), 211–232. DOI: 10.1108/YC-01-2019-0940

Heilmaier, J., & Ling, M. (2021). SMEs and HEIs: Observations from Brunei Darussalam and Germany. *Industry and Higher Education*, *35*(3), 244–251. DOI: 10.1177/0950422220944749

Henderson, J. (2021). The Global Halal Food Market: Trends and Opportunities. *International Journal of Food Sciences*.

Hernández-Espallardo, M., & Delgado-Ballester, E. (2009). Product Innovation in Small Manufacturers, Market Orientation and the Industry's Five Competitive Forces: Empirical Evidence from Spain. *European Journal of Innovation Management*, *12*(4), 470–491. DOI: 10.1108/14601060910996927

Hew, J. J., Wong, L. W., Tan, G. W. H., Ooi, K. B., & Lin, B. (2020). The blockchain-based Halal traceability systems: A hype or reality? *Supply Chain Management*, *25*(6), 863–879. DOI: 10.1108/SCM-01-2020-0044

Hidayat, H., Tamin, B., Herawati, S., Khairul, K., & Syahmaidi, E. (2019). The contribution of technopreneurship scientific learning and learning readiness towards the entrepreneurship learning outcomes in higher vocational education. *Jurnal Pendidikan Vokasi*, *9*(1), 21–32. DOI: 10.21831/jpv.v9i1.20466

Hidayati, L., Sugiatmi, S., Aini, N., & Go, R. Y. (2023). The Role of LP3H in Increasing the economic Value through Assistance with Halal Certification. *Indonesian Journal of Islamic Economics and Business*, *8*(1), 46–54.

Hidayat, R., Zulham, Z., & Ramadi, B. (2024). DEVELOPMENT STRATEGY FOR HALAL CENTER IN UNIVERSITY: A TECHNICAL RECOMMENDATION. *UMAN FALAH: Jurnal Ekonomi Dan Bisnis Islam, 11*(1), 17–35.

Hidayat, S. E., & Musari, K. (2022). ASEAN towards a global halal logistics through the digitally-enabled community. [IJABIM]. *International Journal of Asian Business and Information Management, 13*(2), 1–15. DOI: 10.4018/IJABIM.20220701.oa1

Hidayat, S. E., & Musari, K. (2023a). Towards the global halal MSMEs hub through the digitally-enabled society: An institutional arrangement with Islamic n-tuple helix. In Rafiki, A. (Ed.), *Digitalization in halal management. Contributions to Environmental Sciences & Innovative Business Technology* (pp. 15–28). Springer., DOI: 10.1007/978-981-99-5146-8_2

Hindolia, A., Arya, J., Pathak, R., & Kazmi, A. (2024). Halal B2B marketing in the metaverse: Crafting a conceptual framework to pinpoint opportunities and challenges, outlining the agenda for future research. *Journal of Islamic Marketing, ahead-of-print.* https://doi.org/DOI: 10.1108/JIMA-02-2024-0054

Hirmawan, W., & Hasanah, F. (2023). *Direktori Perusahaan Pertanian Rumah Potong Hewan (RPH) dan Tempat Pemotongan Hewan (TPH) 2023* (Vol. 9). Badan Pusat Statistik.

Ho, K. L. P. (2018). A resource-advantage theory approach on competitive advantage and financial performance of beef cattle value chain in Vietnam Central Highlands, *Dissertation*, August, *University Of Tasmania.*

Hoelman., ... M. B. (2015a). *PANDUAN SDGs Untuk Pemerintah Daerah (Kota Dan Kabupaten) Dan Pemangku Kepentingan Daerah.* International NGO Forum on Indonesian Development.

Hoelman., ... M. B. (2015b). *Panduan SDGs Untuk Pemerintah Daerah (Kota dan Kabupaten) dan Pemangku Kepentingan Daerah* (pp. 1–64). International NGO Forum on Indonesian Development.

Hole, Y., Pawar, S., & Bhaskar, M. P. (2019). Porter's five forces model: Gives you a competitive advantage. *Journal of Advanced Research in Dynamical and Control Systems, 11*(4).

Hoon, C.-Y., & Zhao, K. (2024). Emerging Chinese Foreign Direct Investment in Brunei. *East Asian Policy, 16*(03), 100–114. DOI: 10.1142/S1793930524000230

Hoque, A., Awang, Z., & Siddiqui, B. (2017). Technopreneurial Intention among University Students of Business Courses in Malaysia: A Structural Equation Modeling. *International Journal of Entrepreneurship and Small & Medium Enterprise, 4*, 1–16.

Hotez, P. J. (2021). *Preventing the next pandemic: vaccine diplomacy in a time of anti-science*. Johns Hopkins University Press. DOI: 10.56021/9781421440392

Hotez, P. J. (2023). *The deadly rise of anti-science: A scientist's warning*. Johns Hopkins University Press.

Hunt, S. D., & Morgan, R. M. (1997). Resource-advantage theory: A snake swallowing its tail or a general theory of competition? *Journal of Marketing*, *61*(4), 74–82. DOI: 10.1177/002224299706100406

Hurley, R. F., & Hult, G. T. M. (1998). Innovation, market orientation, and organizational learning: An integration and empirical examination. *Journal of Marketing*, *62*(3), 42–54. DOI: 10.1177/002224299806200303

Husin, M. M., & Haron, R. (2019). Financial Sustainability of SMEs Through Islamic Crowdfunding. In Rafay, A. (Ed.), *Handbook of Research on Theory and Practice of Global Islamic Finance* (Vol. 1, pp. 321–337). IGI Global., DOI: 10.4018/978-1-7998-0218-1.ch018

Hussain, I., Rahman, S. U., Zaheer, A., & Saleem, S. (2016). Integrating factors influencing consumers' halal products purchase: Application of the theory of reasoned action. *Journal of International Food & Agribusiness Marketing*, *28*(1), 35–58. DOI: 10.1080/08974438.2015.1006973

Husti, I., & Mahyarni, M. (2019). Islamic leadership, innovation, competitive advantages, and performance of SMEs in Indonesia. *East Asia (Piscataway, N.J.)*, *36*(4), 369–383. DOI: 10.1007/s12140-019-09325-7

Ibrahim, A. (2022). *Sustainability and Sustainable Development: An Investigation on the Role of Islamic Finance and Other Determinants in the OIC Member Countries. PhD Thesis*. University of Salford., Retrieved from https://salford-repository.worktribe.com/OutputFile/1502990

Ibrahim, M. A., Malek, J. A., & Salman, A. (2015). Evaluating the Development of Technopreneurs: A Case Study of PPR Telecenter Jalan Jelatek. *Journal of Social Sciences and Humanities*, *2*, 157–161.

Idris, P. S. R. P. H., Musa, S. F. P. D., & Sumardi, W. H. H. (2022). Halal-Tayyiban and Sustainable Development Goals: A SWOT Analysis. [IJABIM]. *International Journal of Asian Business and Information Management*, *13*(2), 1–16. DOI: 10.4018/IJABIM.20220701.oa9

Ihsan. (2023). UBD, BruIPO Sign MoU. Retrieved on 30 Mar, 2025, from UBD: https://ubd.edu.bn/2023/03/08/ubd-bruipo-sign-mou/

Ihsan. (2024). UBD Forges Stronger Industry Ties, Unveils New Entrepreneurial Initiatives at the IEED Exchange. Retrieved on Mar 30, 2025, from UBD: https://ubd.edu.bn/2024/09/05/ubd-forges-stronger-industry-ties-unveils-new-entrepreneurial-initiatives-at-the-ieed-exchange/

Ikomatussuniah, M. R. B., & Maler, M. W. (2021). Transformation of Ulama's Role in Nusantara: A Case Study of Halalan Thayyiban Food Law in Indonesia. *Journal of Academic Research in Business and Social Sciences, 11*(4), 477–462.

Immunisation Advisory Centre. (2022). *Types of vaccines.*https://www.immune.org.nz/vaccines/vaccine-development

Indung Amalia, W., & Nahidloh, S. (2023). The Indepence Of Pesantren In The Develpoment Of Halal Ecosystems Regarding The Application Of Regulations In Mta Putri Al-Amien Prenduan The Prepective Of Maslahah. *Proceeding of Annual Conference on Islamic Economy and Law, 2*(2). https://doi.org/DOI: 10.21107/aciel.v2i2.255

Insani, T. D., Al-Faizin, A. W., & Ryandono, M. N. H. (2019). the Impact of Halal At Thayyib and Consumption Ethics on Economic Growth: An Economic Tafsir of Al-Baqarah 168. *Journal of Islamic Monetary Economics and Finance, 5*(2), 459–474. DOI: 10.21098/jimf.v5i2.1071

Institute of Data. (2023). Digital Entrepreneurship: Navigating Business with Digital Platforms. Retrieved on Mar 30, 2025, from Institute of Data: https://www.institutedata.com/blog/digital-entrepreneurship-navigating-business-with-digital-platforms/

IPB University Raih Penghargaan Perguruan Tinggi SDGs Terbaik dari Bappenas—Tekno Tempo.co. (n.d.). Retrieved 7 June 2024, from https://tekno.tempo.co/read/1793738/ipb-university-raih-penghargaan-perguruan-tinggi-sdgs-terbaik-dari-bappenas

Iqbal, Z., & Mirakhor, A. (2017). *Introduction to Islamic Finance: Theory and Practice*. John Wiley & Sons.

Iranmanesh, M., Mirzaei, M., Parvin Hosseini, S. M., & Zailani, S. (2020). Muslims' willingness to pay for certified halal food: An extension of the theory of planned behavior. *Journal of Islamic Marketing, 11*(1), 14–30. DOI: 10.1108/JIMA-03-2018-0049

Ireland, J., & Rajabzadeh, S. A. (2011). UAE consumer concerns about halal products. *Journal of Islamic Marketing, 2*(3), 274–283. DOI: 10.1108/17590831111164796

Irfany, M. I., Nekha, A., Tieman, M., & Haq, D. A. (2024). Halal procurement strategy for the halal pharmaceutical industry in Indonesia. *Journal of Islamic Marketing, 16*(4), 1073–1094. DOI: 10.1108/JIMA-09-2023-0274

Isenberg, D. J. (2016). Applying the Ecosystem Metaphor to Entrepreneurship: Uses and Abuses. *Antitrust Bulletin, 61*(4), 564–573. DOI: 10.1177/0003603X16676162

Islam, M. M. (2022a). Strategic perspectives of Islamic entrepreneurship and marketing. In B.A. Alserhan, V. Ramadani, J. Zeqiri, & L.P. Dana (Eds.), *Strategic Islamic marketing*. Contributions to Management Science. Springer, Cham, 183-200. https://doi.org/DOI: 10.1007/978-3-030-98160-0_13

Islam, M. M., Ab Talib, M. S., & Muhamad, N. (2025). Could Ajka Be the Next Frontier of Halal?: Halal Food. In *Innovative Ventures and Strategies in Islamic Business* (pp. 169-194). IGI Global Scientific Publishing.

Islam, A., & Wahab, S. A. (2022). The Concerns Associated with Future Prospects of the Food Cart Business in Chittagong, Bangladesh: Is the concept of Halalan Tayyiba Missing Link? *Rajagiri Management Journal, 16*(1), 21–35. DOI: 10.1108/RAMJ-09-2020-0052

Islamic Development Bank. (2023). *Case Studies on Innovations in Islamic Finance*. United Nations Development Programme.

Islam, M. M. (2018). Islamic marketing practice as a panacea to social marketing criticism. *International Journal of Islamic Marketing and Branding, 3*(2), 104–115. DOI: 10.1504/IJIMB.2018.094080

Islam, M. M. (2021a). Segmenting, targeting, and positioning in Islamic marketing. *Journal of Islamic Marketing, 12*(7), 1385–1404. DOI: 10.1108/JIMA-10-2018-0181

Islam, M. M. (2021b). The satisfaction of Bangladeshi pilgrims: Service gaps in spiritual tourism based on gender and expenditure. *International Journal of Religious Tourism and Pilgrimage, 9*(1). Advance online publication. DOI: 10.21427/2hw0-cd28

Islam, M. M. (2022b). Evaluating negative attitudes of the students and shoppers towards halal cosmetics products. *Journal of Islamic Marketing, 13*(3), 565–585. DOI: 10.1108/JIMA-03-2020-0067

Islam, M. M. (2022c). Reaching halal and Islamic market segments: Tapping marketing opportunities beyond the borders. In Breazeale, C., Reshadi, B., & Hegeman, J. (Eds.), *Handbook of research on ethnic and intra-cultural marketing* (pp. 200–212). Edward Elgar Publishing, Inc., DOI: 10.4337/9781784717489.00017

Islam, M. M. (2023). Institutionalization of halal entrepreneurship for a sustainable economy. In Raimi, L., Adekunle, S. M., & Shabbir, M. S. (Eds.), *Contemporary discourse of halal and Islamic entrepreneurship*. Springer., DOI: 10.1007/978-981-99-6427-7_5

Islam, M. M., Ab Talib, M. S., & Muhamad, N. (2023). Challenges of Halal Standards and Halal Certification for Islamic Marketing. *Muslim Business and Economics Review*, *2*(1), 105–124. DOI: 10.56529/mber.v2i1.156

Islam, M. M., Ab Talib, M. S., & Muhamad, N. (2024a). Developing Theoretical Lenses for Upstream Halal businesses. *Journal of Islamic Marketing*, *15*(1), 192–220. DOI: 10.1108/JIMA-05-2022-0156

Islam, M. M., Ab Talib, M. S., & Muhamad, N. (2024b). Islamic Marketing and Circular Economy to Foster Sustainability of Product Life Cycle Enhancement. In *Strategic Islamic Business and Management: Solutions for Sustainability* (pp. 125–141). Springer Nature Switzerland. DOI: 10.1007/978-3-031-61778-2_7

Islam, M. M., & Hasan, M. M. (2024). *Islamic marketing of conventional banks: Bridging managers' and clients' perceived gaps*. International Journal of Islamic Accounting and Business Research., DOI: 10.1108/JIABR-11-2023-0379

Islam, M. M., Talib, M. S. A., & Muhamad, N. (2025). Could Ajka be the next frontier of halal? In *Advances in business strategy and competitive advantage book series* (pp. 69–194). IGI Global., DOI: 10.4018/979-8-3693-3980-0.ch008

Ismail, M. M., & Islam, Md. S., & Wan Bakar, W. M. M. (2013). Export Barriers to Halal Food Processing Small and Medium Enterprises (SMEs) in Malaysia. *Pertanika Journal of Social Science and Humanities, 21*(S), 31–46. http://www.pertanika.upm.edu.my/pjssh/browse/regular-issue?article=JSSH-0826-2013

Ismail, K., Shahlehi, S. F. H., & Shaya, V. N. (2024). SMEs' Perspectives on the Benefits and Challenges of Halal Certificate Application in Brunei Darussalam. *ASEAN Journal on Science and Technology for Development*, *41*(1), 3. DOI: 10.61931/2224-9028.1557

Ismal, R., & Musari, K. (2009, January 24). New institutional economic? *Republika,* Opini.

Isnawati, L. (2018). *Jual-beli Online Sesuai Syariah*. Rumah Fiqih Publishing.

Izberk-Bilgin, E., & Nakata, C. C. (2016). A new look at faith-based marketing: The global halal market. *Business Horizons*, *59*(3), 285–292. DOI: 10.1016/j.bushor.2016.01.005

Izza, N. N., Fitria, L., Arsyi, M., & Nugraha, F. (2024). Twitter Data Analysis on Halal Labeling: Insights for the Food Industry in Indonesia. *Halal Tourism and Pilgrimage*, *3*(2). Advance online publication. DOI: 10.58968/htp.v3i2.391

Jaaffar, A. H., Abd Majid, N., Kasavan, S., Isa, A., Alwi, M.N.R., & Zahari, A.R. (2024). The effect of innovative mindset and behavior on innovation performance and competitive advantage: a case of halal SMEs owner-managers from Malaysian energy-intensive industry. Journal of Innovation and Entrepreneurship, Springer, vol. 13(1), pages 1-19, December. Available at: .DOI: 10.1186/s13731-023-00359-z

Jahangir, M., Mehmood, Z., Saifullah, , Bashir, Q., Mehboob, F., & Ali, K. (2016). Halal status of ingredients after physicochemical alteration (Istihalah). *Trends in Food Science & Technology*, *47*, 78–81. DOI: 10.1016/j.tifs.2015.10.011

Jamaluddin, M. A., & Ramli, S. N. H. (2022). Smart Food for Future Sustainability: Halal and Tayyib Perspectives. *Journal of Halal Industry & Services*, *5*(1). Advance online publication. DOI: 10.36877/jhis.a0000309

Jamaluddin, M., Abdullah, M., & Has-Yun, H. (2018). The Emergence of Global Halal Industry Ecosystem. *Journal of Halal Industry & Services*, *1*(1).

Jamil, H., Wahab, A. Y. A., Razak, A. R. A., & Al-Saari, N. (2020). Exploring The Internationalization Strategy Of Higher Education Institutions And Halal Food Ecosystem in Malaysia. *Food Research*, *4*(S1), 145–150. Advance online publication. DOI: 10.26656/fr.2017.4(S1).S23

Jangcik, I., Jama, J., Rizal, F., & Rahmayati, D., & Sasmita. (2022). Categorization of Problems and Solutions in Technopreneurship Course: A Literature Study. *Journal of Positive School Psychology*, *6*(6), 6712–6711.

Jannah, S. M., & Al-Banna, H. (2021). Halal Awareness And Halal Traceability: Muslim Consumers' And Entrepreneurs' Perspectives. *Journal of Islamic Monetary Economics and Finance*, *7*(2), 285–316. Advance online publication. DOI: 10.21098/jimf.v7i2.1328

Jansen, L. (2022). Innovation in Halal Products: Trends and Developments. *Journal of Islamic Marketing*.

Javid, N. J., & Amini, M. (2023). Evaluating the effect of supply chain management practice on implementation of halal agroindustry and competitive advantage for small and medium enterprises. *International Journal of Computer Science and Information Technologies*, *15*(6), 8997–9008. https://ssrn.com/abstract=4348136

Jaya, S., & Darul Ehsan, S. (2015). Multiple halal logos and Malays' beliefs: A case of mixed signals. *International Food Research Journal*, *22*(4), 1727–1735.

Jeaheng, Y., Al-Ansi, A., & Han, H. (2019a). Halal-friendly hotels: Impact of halal-friendly attributes on guest purchase behaviors in the Thailand hotel industry. *Journal of Travel & Tourism Marketing*, *36*(6), 729–746. DOI: 10.1080/10548408.2019.1631940

Jelan, Z. A., Pratiwi, A., & Isnaeni, P. D. (2024). Halal Meat Production in the Modern Era: Concepts and Applications. *Technological Innovations in Tropical Livestock Development for Environmental Sustainability and Food Security*, 1-6.

Ji, J. (2025). Philippines Enhances Halal Certification to Attract More Muslim Tourists. *ChemLinked*. https://cosmetic.chemlinked.com/news/cosmetic-news/philippines-establishes-national-halal-office-to-strengthen-domestic-and-global-market-presence

Josefsberg, J. O., & Buckland, B. (2012). Vaccine process technology. *Biotechnology and Bioengineering*, *109*(6), 1443–1460. DOI: 10.1002/bit.24493 PMID: 22407777

Junaidi, J. (2020). Halal-Friendly Tourism And Factors Influencing Halal Tourism. *Management Science Letters*, *10*(8), 1755–1762. Advance online publication. DOI: 10.5267/j.msl.2020.1.004

Jusoh, M., & Halim, H. (n.d.). *Role of Technopreneurs in Malaysian Economic*. Retrieved November 21, 2024, from Academia.edu: https://www.academia.edu/33238691/Role_of_Technopreneurs_in_Malaysian_Economic

Kalangi, S. J. R., & Kaseke, M. M. (2017). *Macroscopic and microscopic images of the bladder in postmortem experimental animals, 5*, 3–9.

Kamarulzaman, N., Ruslan, A., & Sanny, M. (2018). Muslim Consumers' Awareness And Perception Of Halal Food Fraud. *International Food Research Journal*, •••, 25.

Kamdar, A. (2011). *Having Fun the Halal Way - Entertainment in Islam*. International Islamic Publishing House.

Kaptein, N. J. G. (2004). The Voice Of The "Ulam ": Fatwas And Religious Authority In Indonesia. *Archives de Sciences Sociales des Religions*, *125*(1), 115–130. Advance online publication. DOI: 10.4000/assr.1038

Karim, A., Setiawan, M., Indrawati, N. K., & Mugiono, M. (2021). Impact of halal standards on logistic employee performance. *Acta Logistica - International Scientific Journal about. Logistics (Basel)*, *8*(3), 269–276. DOI: 10.22306/al.v8i3.237

Kasri, R. A., Ahsan, A., Widiatmoko, D., & Hati, S. R. H. (2023). Intention to consume halal pharmaceutical products: Evidence from Indonesia. *Journal of Islamic Marketing*, *14*(3), 735–756. DOI: 10.1108/JIMA-06-2021-0192

Keputusan Menteri Agama Nomor 748 Tahun 2021. (2022, April 17). https://peraturanpedia.id/keputusan-menteri-agama-nomor-748-tahun-2021/

Khaeriyah, H. (2022). *Islam dan Transformasi Paradigma di Era Digitalisasi*. Retrieved December 2, 2024, from Kitorang News: https://kitorangnews.com/2351/islam-dan-transformasi-paradigma-di-era-digitalisasi/

Khalid, A. M., Haji Masr, M., Muhammad, N., & Pang, W. L. (2018). Brunei Darussalam: Halal Meat and Meat Products Processing. In J. Gross & P. S. Intal (Eds.), *Reducing Unnecessary Regulatory Burdens in ASEAN: Country Studies* (pp. 89–117). Economic Research Institute for ASEAN and East Asia. https://www.eria.org/uploads/media/RURB_2018_Chapter_4_Halal_meat_Brunei.pdf

Khan, M., Ahmad, M., & Shah, M. (2019). *Green Sukuk: Innovations and Future Prospects*. International Journal of Islamic Finance.

Khan, G., & Khan, F. (2019). "Is This Restaurant Halal?" Surrogate Indicators And Muslim Behaviour. *Journal of Islamic Marketing*, *11*(5), 1105–1123. Advance online publication. DOI: 10.1108/JIMA-01-2019-0008

Khan, M. I., Haleem, A., & Khan, S. (2018, April). Defining Halal Supply Chain Management. In *Supply Chain Forum* []. Taylor & Francis.]. *International Journal (Toronto, Ont.)*, *19*(2), 122–131.

Khan, M. I., Haleem, A., & Khan, S. (2022). Examining the link between halal supply chain management and sustainability. *International Journal of Productivity and Performance Management*, *71*(7), 2793–2819. DOI: 10.1108/IJPPM-07-2019-0354

Khan, M. I., Khan, S., & Haleem, A. (2022). Analysing barriers towards management of Halal supply chain: A BWM approach. *Journal of Islamic Marketing*, *13*(1), 66–80. DOI: 10.1108/JIMA-09-2018-0178

Khan, M. M., Asad, H., & Mehboob, I. (2017). Investigating the consumer behavior for halal endorsed products: Case of an emerging Muslim market. *Journal of Islamic Marketing*, *8*(4), 625–641. DOI: 10.1108/JIMA-09-2015-0068

Khan, S., Khan, M. I., & Haleem, A. (2019). Evaluation of barriers in the adoption of halal certification: A fuzzy DEMATEL approach. *Journal of Modelling in Management*, *14*(1), 153–174. DOI: 10.1108/JM2-03-2018-0031

Khan, W., Akhtar, A., Ansari, S. A., & Dhamija, A. (2020). Enablers of halal food purchase among Muslim consumers in an emerging economy: An interpretive structural modeling approach. *British Food Journal*, *122*(7), 2273–2287. DOI: 10.1108/BFJ-08-2018-0528

Khoo, Y. S. K., Ghani, A., Navamukundan, A. A., Jahis, R., & Gamil, A. (2020). Unique product quality considerations in vaccine development, registration and new program implementation in Malaysia. *Human Vaccines & Immunotherapeutics, 16*(3), 530–538. DOI: 10.1080/21645515.2019.1667206 PMID: 31652090

Khraim, H. (2010). Measuring religiosity in consumer research from an Islamic perspective. *Journal of Economic and Administrative Sciences, 26*(1), 52–78. DOI: 10.1108/10264116201000003

KiniHalal. (2023, Aug 21). *Sustaining Malaysia as the Global Leader in the* Halal *Industry*. Dipetik Mar 4, 2025, dari Halal Development Corporation Berhad: https://hdcglobal.com/news/2023/08/21/sustaining-malaysia-as-the-global-leader-in-the-halal-industry/

Koeswinarno, S. B. J., Fakhruddin, M., & Atieqoh, S. (2023). Non-Muslim Acceptance of Halal Products in the Context of Business Development. In A. Rafiki (Ed.), *Digitalization in Halal Management* (pp. 193–207). Springer. DOI: 10.1007/978-981-99-5146-8_13

Koe, W.-L., Alias, N., Marmaya, N., Majid, I., Mohamad, M., & Mohamad, M. (2020). Likelihood in Choosing Technopreneurship as Career among Undergraduate Students. *International Journal of Academic Research in Business & Social Sciences, 10*(4), 686–696. DOI: 10.6007/IJARBSS/v10-i5/7241

Kosasih, W., Ahmad, A., Salomon, L., & Utama, D. (2016). Peranan Pendidikan Technopreneurship Untuk Pembangunan Berkelanjutan: Studi Konseptual. *Jurnal Rekayasa Sistem Industri, 5*(2), 79–88. DOI: 10.26593/jrsi.v5i2.2215.79-88

Kotler, P., Keller, K. L., & Chernev, A. (2022). Marketing Management (16eth ed.). Pearson Education©. https://online. fliphtml5. com/xzfda/pkef

Kotler, P., & Keller, K. L. (2016). *Marketing Management, 15e édition. New Jersy.* Pearson Education.

KPMG. (2021). *Fintech and Islamic Finance: Innovations and Opportunities.* KPMG International.

Krishnan, S., Musa, C., Omar, C., Zahran, I., Syazwan, N., & Alyaa, S. (2017). The Awareness of Gen Z's toward Halal Food Industry. *Management, 2017*(1).

Kurniadi, M., & Frediansyah, A. (2017). Halal Perspective of Microbial Bioprocess Based-Food Products. *REAKTOR, 16*(3), 147. DOI: 10.14710/reaktor.16.3.147-160

Kusuma, N. R. (2023). Analisis Keterkaitan Produksi dengan Kelangkaan Sumberdaya Pangan dalam Perspektif Baqr Al Sadr. *ANALYSIS : Accounting, Management, Economics, and Business, 1*(2).

Lada, S., Harvey Tanakinjal, G., & Amin, H. (2009). Predicting intention to choose halal products using the theory of reasoned action. *International Journal of Islamic and Middle Eastern Finance and Management, 2*(1), 66–76. DOI: 10.1108/17538390910946276

Laldin, M. (2006). *Introduction to Shariah and Islamic Jurisprudence*. CERT Publisher.

Lateh, M. (2018). Social entrepreneurship development and poverty alleviation-A Literature review. *MAYFEB Journal of Business and Management, 2*.

Latif, I. A., Mohamed, Z., Sharifuddin, J., Abdullah, A. M., & Ismail, M. M. (2014). A comparative analysis of global Halal certification requirements. *Journal of Food Products Marketing, 20*(sup1), 85–101. DOI: 10.1080/10454446.2014.921869

Lestari, F., Kurniawan, R., Arifin, J., Yasir, M., Muhammad Saleh, M., & Akbarizan, . (2023). An integrated framework for the measurement of halal good manufacturing practices on the case of SMEs in the food sector. *Journal of Islamic Marketing, 14*(1), 82–105. DOI: 10.1108/JIMA-04-2021-0105

Lestari, F., Mawardi, M., Yola, M., Muda, Y., & Abdul Hamid, A. B. (2022). A model for assessment of Halal Good Manufacturing Practice in meat industry. *Production & Manufacturing Research, 10*(1), 666–695. DOI: 10.1080/21693277.2022.2117742

Letsoin, B., & Riorini, S. V. (2023). The Mediating Role of Attitude Toward Product Towards Halal Cosmetic Purchase Intention in Female Consumers in Indonesia. *Journal of Social Research, 2*(5), 1616–1633. Advance online publication. DOI: 10.55324/josr.v2i5.854

Lever, J., & Miele, M. (2012). The growth of halal meat markets in Europe: An exploration of the supply side theory of religion. *Journal of Rural Studies, 28*(4), 528–537. DOI: 10.1016/j.jrurstud.2012.06.004

Lia Febriati, N., & Mu'in, F. M., Santoso, R., & Latua, A. (2024). Challenges of the Halal Food Industry in Era 5.0 Perspective of Science and Islamic Law. *KnE Social Sciences*. https://doi.org/DOI: 10.18502/kss.v9i2.15024

Liew, C. W. S., & Karia, N. (2024). Halal cosmetics: A technology-empowered systematic literature review. *Journal of Islamic Marketing, 15*(7), 1722–1742. DOI: 10.1108/JIMA-09-2023-0295

Loussaief, A., Ying-Chao Lin, J., Phuc Dang, H., Bouslama, N., & Cheng, J. M. S. (2024). Eating halal: A serial mediation model for the effect of religiosity on the intention to purchase halal-certified food. *Asia Pacific Journal of Marketing and Logistics, 36*(1), 167–184. Advance online publication. DOI: 10.1108/APJML-10-2022-0868

Lubis, I., Soesilo, T. E. B., & Soemantojo, R. W. (2020). Pengelolaan Air Limbah Rumah Potong Hewan DI RPH X, Kota Bogor, Provinsi Jawa Barat (Wastewater Management of Slaughterhouse in Slaughterhouse X, Bogor City, West Java Province). *Jurnal Manusia Dan Lingkungan, 25*(1), 33. DOI: 10.22146/jml.35396

Lukita, C., Chakim, M., Supriati, R., Santoso, N., & Kamil, M. (2023). Exploration of Perceived Use of Technology Using A Digital Business Perspective. *ADI Journal on Recent Innovation, 5*(1Sp, 1SP), 87–96. DOI: 10.34306/ajri.v5i1Sp.984

Luthfi, B. A., & Salehudin, I. (2011). Marketing Impact of Halal Labeling Toward Indonesian Muslim Consumer's Behavioral Intention Based on Ajzen's Planned Behavior Theory: Policy Capturing Studies on Five Different Product Categories. *ASEAN Marketing Journal, 3*(1).

Mačiulienė, M., & Skaržauskienė, A. (2021). Conceptualizing blockchain-based value co-creation: A service science perspective. *Systems Research and Behavioral Science, 38*(3), 330–341. DOI: 10.1002/sres.2786

Manzoor, S. (2023). The Model of visionary and innovative Islamic leadership. *Society, 11*(1), 41–51. DOI: 10.33019/society.v11i1.539

Margarena, A. N., & Ikhwan Setiawan, A. (2022). The Effect Of Perceived Value Of Economic Benefits Towards Smes Halal Certification Intention Moderated By Government Policy Regulation. *International Journal of Education and Social Science Research, 05*(02), 308–320. Advance online publication. DOI: 10.37500/IJESSR.2022.5219

MarketsandMarkets. (2021). Halal *Pharmaceuticals Market Report*. Retrieved from [MarketsandMarkets] (https://www.marketsandmarkets.com)

Marmaya, N., Zakaria, Z., & Mohd Desa, M. N. (2019). Gen Y consumers' intention to purchase halal food in Malaysia: A PLS-SEM approach. *Journal of Islamic Marketing, 10*(3), 1003–1014. DOI: 10.1108/JIMA-08-2018-0136

Marti'ah, S. (2017). Kewirausahaan Berbasis Teknologi (Technopreneurship) dalam Perspektif Ilmu Pendidikan. *Jurnal Ilmiah Edutic, 3*(2), 75–82. DOI: 10.21107/edutic.v3i2.2927

Marzuki, S. Z. S., Hall, C. M., & Ballantine, P. W. (2012). Restaurant managers' perspectives on halal certification. *Journal of Islamic Marketing*, *3*(1), 47–58. DOI: 10.1108/17590831211206581

Masrianto, A., Hartoyo, H., Hubeis, A., & Hasanah, N. (2022). Digital Marketing Utilization Index for Evaluating and Improving Company Digital Marketing Capability. *Journal of Open Innovation*, *8*(3), 153. DOI: 10.3390/joitmc8030153

Masrianto, A., Hartoyo, H., Hubeis, A., & Hasanah, N. (2024). How to Boost Your Firm's Digital Marketing Capability? *International Journal of Technology*, *15*(3), 677–686. DOI: 10.14716/ijtech.v15i3.5691

Masruroh, N. (2020a). Dynamics of Identity and Religiosity in Halal Branding in Indonesia. ISLAMICA: Journal of Islamic Studies, *14*(2).

Masruroh, N. (2024). European Multidisciplinary Journal of Modern Science The Development Of Halal Lifestyle In Mashlahah Mursalah Analysis: Study Of Halal Labeling Trends In Indonesia. *European Multidisciplinary Journal of Modern Science, 26*(4), 17–28. https://journal.academicjournal.id/index.php/emjmsArticle

Masruroh, N. (2020). Dinamika Identitas dan Religiusitas pada Branding Halal di Indonesia. *ISLAMICA: Jurnal Studi Keislaman*, *14*(2), 317–338. DOI: 10.15642/islamica.2020.14.2.317-338

Masruroh, N. (2020b). The Competitiveness of Indonesian Halal Food Exports in Global Market Competition Industry. *Economica: Jurnal Ekonomi Islam*, *11*(1), 25–48. Advance online publication. DOI: 10.21580/economica.2020.11.1.3709

Masruroh, N. (2023). Pemaknaan Halal Antara Simbol Dan Bentuk Implementasi Keagamaan Oleh Pemilik Umkm Pasca Pemberlakuan UU NO. 33 TAHUN 2014. *Istinbath*, *21*(2), 351–373. Advance online publication. DOI: 10.20414/ijhi.v21i2.572

Masruroh, N., & Fadli, A. (2022). Gerak Kuasa Negara dalam Perdagangan Komoditas Bersertifikat Halal di Indonesia. *Prooceding Annual Conference on Islam, Education and Humanitites,* 1.

Masruroh, N., Fathorrazi, M., Saleh, M., & Adenan, M. (2021). The Halal Branding in International Trade of Edamame Soybean Agricultural Products. *Annals of Agri Bio Research*, *26*(2), •••.

Matnor, R. B. H., Seri, D. H. N. B. D., & Mahalle, S. H. (2024). The Contribution of Natural Foods to the Sustainability of Halalan Toyyiban Lifestyle Based on Maqasid Shari'ah in Brunei Darussalam. *Halalsphere*, *4*(2), 38–58.

Maulana, D. F., Makhrus, M., & Hasanah, H. (2022). The Urgency of MUI Halal Fatwa about Food, Beverage, Medicine and Cosmetic Products for the Consumer Protection. *Volksgeist: Jurnal Ilmu Hukum Dan Konstitusi*, *5*(2), 199–214. Advance online publication. DOI: 10.24090/volksgeist.v5i2.6421

McKinsey & Company. (2022). *The Future of E-commerce in the* Halal *Industry*. Retrieved from [McKinsey & Company] (https://www.mckinsey.com)

McKinsey & Company. (2022). *The Impact of Digitalization on the* Halal *Industry*. Retrieved from [McKinsey & Company] (https://www.mckinsey.com)

McNabb, D. E. (2020). Descriptive Research: Survey Designs. In *Research Methods for Political Science* (3rd Editio). Taylor & Francis.

Medina, C., & Rufín, R. (2009). The Mediating Effect of Innovation in the Relationship between Retailers, Strategic Orientations and Performance. *International Journal of Retail & Distribution Management*, *37*(7), 629–655. DOI: 10.1108/09590550910964639

Memon, Y. J., Azhar, S. M., Haque, R., & Bhutto, N. A. (2020). Religiosity as a moderator between the theory of planned behavior and halal purchase intention. *Journal of Islamic Marketing, 11*(6), 1821-1836.Mohd Dali, N. R. S., Yousafzai, S., & Abdul Hamid, H. (2019). Religiosity scale development. *Journal of Islamic Marketing*, *10*(1), 227–248.

Mgeni, T. O., & Nayak, P. (2015). Impact of different leadership styles of CEOs on business performance of SMEs in East Africa: A systematic review of literature. *Journal of Entrepreneurship & Management*, *4*(3). Advance online publication. DOI: 10.21863/jem/2015.4.3.012

Mickael, B. Hoelman et al. (2015). *PANDUAN SDGs Untuk Pemerintah Daerah (Kota dan Kabupaten) dan Pemangku Kepentingan Daerah*. International NGO Forum on Indonesian Development.

Millatina, A. N., Hakimi, F., Budiantoro, R. A., & Arifandi, M. R. (2022). The Impact of Halal Label in Halal Food Buying Decisions. *Journal of Islamic Economic Laws*, *5*(1), 159–176. Advance online publication. DOI: 10.23917/jisel.v5i1.17139

Ministry of Finance and Economy. (n.d.). List of fundings and financing available for businesses in Brunei Darussalam. Retrieved on Mar 30, 2025, on businessBN Portal: https://business.mofe.gov.bn/SitePages/Business%20Fundings.aspx?utm

Ministry of Transport and Infocommunications (MTIC). (2020). *Digital Economy Masterplan 2025*.

Mintel. (2022). Halal *Cosmetics Market Overview*. Retrieved from [Mintel](https://www.mintel.com)

Mohd Riza, N. S., Md Ariffin, M. F., Hamdan, M. N., & Ramli, N. (2022). Halal Food: A Social Responsibility on Cartel Meat Issue in Malaysia. *Food Research, 6*(3), 92–100. DOI: 10.26656/fr.2017.6(3).277

Monoarfa, H., Juliana, J., Setiawan, R., & Abu Karim, R. (2023). The influences of Islamic retail mix approach on purchase decisions. *Journal of Islamic Marketing, 14*(1), 236–249. DOI: 10.1108/JIMA-07-2020-0224

Mortas, M., Awad, N., & Ayvaz, H. (2022). Adulteration Detection Technologies Used For Halal/Kosher Food Products: An Overview. In *Discover Food* (Vol. 2, Issue 1). https://doi.org/DOI: 10.1007/s44187-022-00015-7

Muazu, M., & Sjahrir, E. (2023). *Halal Entrepreneurship and Its Impact on Sustainable Economy: Opportunities and Challenges. Dalam L. Raimi, S. Adekunle, & M. Shabbir (Penyunt.), Contemporary Discourse of Halal and Islamic Entrepreneurship.* Springer., DOI: 10.1007/978-981-99-6427-7_17

Mubarok, S., & Afrizal, M. (2018). ISLAM DAN. *Sustainable Development, 3*(1).

Muflih, M., & Juliana, J. (2021). Halal-labeled food shopping behavior: The role of spirituality, image, trust, and satisfaction. *Journal of Islamic Marketing, 12*(8), 1603–1618. DOI: 10.1108/JIMA-10-2019-0200

Muhamad, N., Leong, V. S., & Masri, M. (2019). Brunei Halal Tourism Outlook. In Hall, M. C., & Prayag, G. (Eds.), *The Routledge Handbook of Halal Hospitality and Islamic Tourism* (pp. 180–190). Routledge., DOI: 10.4324/9781315150604-13

Muharam, I. N., & Asutay, M. (2019). Online Disclosure Practices Of Halal-Friendly Hotels. *Journal of Islamic Marketing*. Advance online publication. DOI: 10.1108/JIMA-12-2018-0239

Muizzuddin, M., Zakiyyatul, A., Universitas, F., Abdullah, K., & Gresik, F. (2023). The Islamic Moderation (A Literature Review of the Concept Islamic Moderation according to KH. Ahmad Siddiq). *Journal of Early Childhood Islamic Education, 10.*

Mujahid, A., Tariq, M., & Ali, N. (2023). Opportunities and Challenges in Islamic Finance and Halal Industry for Green Economy. *Journal of Sustainable Development.*

Mujieb, M. A., Ismail, A., & Syafi'ah. (2009). *Ensiklopedia Tasawuf: Imam Al-Ghazali Mudah Memahami dan Menjalankan Kehidupan Spiritual* (p. 79). Hikmah.

Mukherjee, S. R. (2014). Global Halal: Meat, money, and religion. *Religions, 5*(1), 22–75. DOI: 10.3390/rel5010022

Mukhtar, A., & Butt, M. M. (2012). Intention to choose Halal products: The role of religiosity. *Journal of Islamic Marketing*, *3*(2), 108–120. DOI: 10.1108/17590831211232519

Muna, N., & Sutopo, W. (2018). Perkembangan Penelitian Halal Food Supply Chain: Studi Kasus Database Scopus. *Prosiding SNST*, *9*(1), 131–139. DOI: 10.36499/psnst.v1i1.2339

Munandar, A. (2016). The strategy development and competitive advantages of micro small medium entreprise business institution toward regional development. *AdBispreneur*, *1*(2), 103–112. DOI: 10.24198/adbispreneur.v1i2.10233

Musa, S. F. P. D. (2019). Brunei Darussalam, a Country Profile. In R. Macdonald (Ed.), *Southeast Asia and the ASEAN Economic Community* (pp. 295–311). Springer International Publishing. DOI: 10.1007/978-3-030-19722-3_8

Musari, K. (2023). A proposed taxonomy of Islamic green financing to address the sustainable eligible sector. A paper was presented at the 11th Islamic Economics Workshop "Islamic Economics and Environment", Istanbul - Turkiye, October 13th-15th.

Musari, K. Mahmudah, Hakim, Z., & Almunawar, M. N. (2025). Mapping the implementation of circular economy and reverse logistics in the sustainable halal supply chain: Evidence in ASEAN-3. In Q. M. H. Sakalayen, M. N. Almunawar, & M. Y. Ali (Eds.). *Sustainable advanced manufacturing and logistics in ASEAN* (pp. 61-78). IGI Global. DOI: 10.4018/979-8-3693-5350-9.ch004

Musari, K., & Sayah, F. (2023). Islamic quadruple helix, social finance partnership for developing digital financial inclusion in Maghreb region. In A. Rafiki, A.G. Pananjung, M.D.T.P. Nasution, *Strategies and applications of Islamic entrepreneurship* (pp. 67-82). IGI Global. DOI: 10.4018/978-1-6684-7519-5.ch005

Musari, K. (2022a). Integrating green sukuk and cash waqf linked sukuk, the blended Islamic finance of fiscal instrument in Indonesia: A proposed model for fighting climate change. *International Journal of Islamic Khazanah*, *12*(2), 133–144. DOI: 10.15575/ijik.v12i2.17750

Musari, K. (2022b). ASEAN toward circular economy and sustainable energy in tackling the climate change: Islamic green financing taxonomy for sustainable finance. In de Pablos, P. O. (Ed.), *Handbook of research on building greener economics and adopting digital tools in the era of climate change* (pp. 210–230). IGI Global., DOI: 10.4018/978-1-6684-4610-2.ch011

Musari, K. (2024a). Driving sustainable supply chain and digital transformation in halal sectors: Evidence in ASEAN-5. In de Pablos, P. O., Almunawar, M. N., & Anshari, M. (Eds.), *Strengthening sustainable digitalization of Asian economy and society* (pp. 87–100). IGI Global., DOI: 10.4018/979-8-3693-1942-0.ch005

Musari, K. (2024b). An analysis of Islamic helix in a zero-waste soybean business of techno-savvy micro enterprises for SDGs: Case study in edamame village, jember, Indonesia. In Rafiki, A., Alserhan, B. A. A., & Bayram, K. (Eds.), *Technopreneurship in small businesses for sustainability* (pp. 21–33). IGI Global., DOI: 10.4018/979-8-3693-3530-7.ch002

Musari, K. (2025). Towards the perpetual sustainable sukuk through Islamic blended finance: Lesson from green sukuk and blue sukuk in Indonesia. In de Pablos, P. O., Lytras, M., & Malik, S. (Eds.), *Securing sustainable futures through blue and green economies* (pp. 381–402). IGI Global., DOI: 10.4018/979-8-3693-7893-9.ch015

Musari, K., & Fathorrazi, M. (2021). Islamic helix approach, the Islamic social finance partnership models for MSMEs: Lesson learned from Indonesia. In Azid, T., Mukhlisin, M., Akbar, N., & Tahir, M. (Eds.), *Monetary policy, Islamic finance, and Islamic corporate governance: An International overview* (pp. 303–322). Emerald Publishing Limited. DOI: 10.1108/978-1-80043-786-920211017

Musari, K., & Sakti, M. R. P. (2025). Recycled waste plastic for asphalt manufacturing to degrade ecological footprints in ASEAN: A policy analysis from the Islamic economics and finance approach. In Sakalayen, Q. M. H., Almunawar, M. N., & Ali, M. Y. (Eds.), *Sustainable advanced manufacturing and logistics in ASEAN* (pp. 269–288). IGI Global., DOI: 10.4018/979-8-3693-5350-9.ch015

Musari, K., & Zaroni, Z. (2021). Reverse logistics in the age of digital transformation for circular economy and halal logistics through the leadership of Asia. In *Handbook of Research on Disruptive Innovation and Digital Transformation in Asia* (pp. 83–103). IGI Global Scientific Publishing.

Musa, S. P., & Idris, D. P. (2020). Addressing Issues of Unemployment in Brunei: The Mismatch between Employers Expectations and Employees Aspirations. *International Journal of Asian Business and Information Management*, *11*(2), 88–101. DOI: 10.4018/IJABIM.2020040106

Musataklima, M. (2021). Self-Declare Halal Products for Small and Micro Enterprises: Between Ease of Doing Business and Assurance of Consumer Spiritual Rights. *De Jure: Jurnal Hukum Dan Syar'iah*, *13*(1). Advance online publication. DOI: 10.18860/j-fsh.v13i1.11308

Mustaffa, K. A. (2019). Developing Halalan Tayyiban Concept In Malaysia's Food Industry. *Halal Journal, 3*.

Mustaffa, K. A. (2019). Developing Halalan Tayyiban Concept in Malaysia's Food Industry. *Halal Journal*, *3*(3), 97–108.

Mustapha, M. R., Ahamad, F., Hazahari, N. Y., & Samsudin, N. (2024). Ethical issues in the halal food supply chain: A systematic bibliometric review. *Journal of Islamic Marketing*, *15*(12), 3804–3819. DOI: 10.1108/JIMA-07-2023-0210

Mutmainah, L. (2018). The Role of Religiosity, Halal Awareness, Halal Certification, and Food Ingredients on Purchase Intention of Halal Food. *Ihtifaz: Journal of Islamic Economics, Finance, and Banking*, *1*(1), 33. Advance online publication. DOI: 10.12928/ijiefb.v1i1.284

Muttaqin, P. S., Setyawan, E. B., & Novitasari, N. (2023). Factors Influencing Readiness towards Halal Logistics among Food and Beverages Industry in the Era of E-Commerce in Indonesia. *JOIV: International Journal on Informatics Visualization*, *7*(3), 781–787. Advance online publication. DOI: 10.30630/joiv.7.3.2055

Najmi, A., Ahmed, W., & Jahangir, S. (2023). Firm's readiness for halal food standard adoption: Assessing the importance of traceability system. *Journal of Islamic Accounting and Business Research*, *14*(8), 1451–1473. DOI: 10.1108/JIABR-09-2020-0293

Nanda, Y., Salim, M. N., & Iskandar, C. D. (2017). *Yunita Nanda 1, M. Nur Salim 2, Cut Dahlia Iskandar 3 1. 01*(4), 780–787.

Nasution, A. H., Noer, B. A., & Suef, M. (2007). *Entrepreneurship: membangun spirit teknopreneurship*. ANDI.

Nasution, M. D. T. P., Rossanty, Y., & Aspan, H. (2017). Towards Halal Cosmetics brand image: Mediating role of Religiosity, Evidence from Muslims women in Medan, Indonesia. *International Business Management*.

Naudé, W. (2010). Entrepreneurship, developing countries and development economics: New approaches and insights. *Small Business Economics*, *34*(1), 1–12. DOI: 10.1007/s11187-009-9198-2

Ngah, A. H., Ramayah, T., Ali, M. H., & Khan, M. I. (2020). Halal transportation adoption among pharmaceuticals and cosmetics manufacturers. *Journal of Islamic Marketing*, *11*(6), 1619–1639. DOI: 10.1108/JIMA-10-2018-0193

Ngah, A. H., Thurasamy, R., Mohd Salleh, N. H., Jeevan, J., Md Hanafiah, R., & Eneizan, B. (2021). Halal transportation adoption among food manufacturers in Malaysia: The moderated model of technology, organization, and environment (TOE) framework. *Journal of Islamic Marketing*. Advance online publication. DOI: 10.1108/JIMA-03-2020-0079

Ngui, N. (2015, Aug 19). *M'sia halal exports hit US$2.44b*. Retrieved Jan 30, 2025, from The Jakarta Post: https://www.thejakartapost.com/news/2015/08/19/msias-halal-exports-hit-us244b.html

Nissa, E. (2023). *Profesionalisation of* Halal *Industries in Indonesia And Malaysia*. Dipetik Mar 4, 2025, dari Sinofon: https://sinofon.cz/trainee-centre/profesionalisation-of-halal-industries-in-indonesia-and-malaysia/

Nordin, F. N. M., Radzi, C. W. J. W. M., & Awang, M. D. (2022). Sustainability of Halal Food Industry: An Ethical Perspective. *Jurnal Al-Sirat*, *22*(1), 120–126.

Noronha, M. (2020, October 22). Halal for health: Scaling up halal pharmaceuticals. *Economist Impact,*https://impact.economist.com/perspectives/health/halal-health-scaling-halal-pharmaceuticals

Nugroho, A. J. S., Santoso, G. B., & Herawati, N. (2024). Development of a halal-labelled vaccine purchasing behavior model: A study on the halal lifestyle of muslim consumers and sustainable development goals (SDGs) in Indonesia. *Journal of Lifestyle and SDGs Review*, *5*(1), e03681. DOI: 10.47172/2965-730X.SDGsReview.v5.n01.pe03681

Nurainun, T., Talib, H. H. A., Jamaludin, K. R., Yusof, S. M., Putri, N. T., & Lestari, F. (2023). Identifying Factors for the Success of Halal Management Practices in Leather Industry. *Journal of Applied Engineering and Technological Science*, *4*(2), 808–824. DOI: 10.37385/jaets.v4i2.1989

Nurein, S. A. (2023). Nexus of Halal Entrepreneurship and Islamic Finance for the Creation of a Strong Halal Ecosystem. In *Contemporary Discourse of Halal and Islamic Entrepreneurship*. https://doi.org/DOI: 10.1007/978-981-99-6427-7_9

Nurhayati, T., & Hendar, H. (2020). Personal intrinsic religiosity and product knowledge on halal product purchase intention: Role of halal product awareness. *Journal of Islamic Marketing*, *11*(3), 603–620. DOI: 10.1108/JIMA-11-2018-0220

Nursita, R. D., Adelia, D., Septiani, R., & Widyaputri, P. D. (2024). The Role of Non-State Actors in Establishing the Halal Ecosystem in Indonesia. *Hasanuddin Journal of International Affairs*, *4*(01), 44–56. Advance online publication. DOI: 10.31947/hjirs.v4i01.33028

Nuryana, S., Isa, L., & Fikri, I. (2023). Studi Komparatif Terhadap Hukum Penyucian Kulit Bangkai Dengan Cara Disamak Menurut Ibnu Qudamah Al-Maqdisi dan Imam Asy-Syaukani. *Muqaranah, 7*(1), 45–54. DOI: 10.19109/muqaranah.v7i1.17199

Nusran, M., Gunawan, , Razak, M., Numba, S., & Wekke, I. S. (2018). Halal Awareness on the Socialization of Halal Certification. *IOP Conference Series. Earth and Environmental Science, 175*(1), 012217. Advance online publication. DOI: 10.1088/1755-1315/175/1/012217

Nuzula, F., & Yuni, K. K. C. (2022). Modernisasi Rumah Potong Hewan Halal RPH Krian dalam Mewujudkan Green Economy di Kabupaten Sidoarjo. *Jurnal Ilmiah Ekonomi Islam, 8*(3), 3100. DOI: 10.29040/jiei.v8i3.6796

Obaidullah, M., & Siti, H. (2022). *Integrating Islamic Finance and* Halal *Industry: Opportunities and Challenges*. Journal of Halal Studies.

Olusegun, O., Akpoviroro, K., & Adebowale, O. (2019). Impact of Technopreneurship on Business Performance. *Journal of Economics and Management Research, 8*, 55–71. DOI: 10.22364/jemr.8.03

Osanlou, B., & Rezaei, E. (2025). The effect of Muslim consumers' religiosity on brand verdict. *Journal of Islamic Marketing, 16*(1), 26–64. DOI: 10.1108/JIMA-01-2023-0005

Osman, I., Hassan, F., Haris, B., & Kassim, E. S. (2018). Religion and halal consumption. In Melewar, T. C., & Alwi, S. F. S. (Eds.), *Islamic marketing and branding: Theory and practice*. Routledge.

Othman, B., & Md Nawi, N. H. (2025). Halal standards practices in the food industry: the impact of halal assurance and operations. *Journal of Islamic Marketing, ahead-of-p*(ahead-of-print). DOI: 10.1108/JIMA-02-2023-0051

Othman, N., & Ishak, S. (2011). Kecenderungan Terhadap Pemilihan Kerjaya Keusahawanan Mengikut Persepsi Peserta Skim Usahawan Siswa. *Jurnal Teknologi (Sciences & Engineering), 56*(1), 47-63. DOI: 10.11113/jt.v56.59

Othman, B., Shaarani, S. M., & Bahron, A. (2016). Evaluation of knowledge, halal quality assurance practices, and commitment among food industries in Malaysia. *British Food Journal, 118*(8), 2033–2052. DOI: 10.1108/BFJ-12-2015-0496

Othman, B., Shaarani, S. M., & Bahron, A. (2016). The Potential of ASEAN in Halal Certification Implementation: A Review. *Pertanika Journal of Social Science & Humanities, 24*(1), 1–24.

Othman, P., Sungkar, I., & Sabri Wan Hussin, W. (2009). Malaysia as an International Halal Food Hub: Competitiveness and Potential of Meat-based Industries. *ASEAN Economic Bulletin*, *26*(3), 306–320. DOI: 10.1355/AE26-3F

Othumary Mgeni, T. (2015). Impact of entrepreneurial leadership style on business performance of SMEs in Tanzania'. *Journal of Entrepreneurship & Organization Management*, *04*(02). Advance online publication. DOI: 10.4172/2169-026X.1000142

Page, M. J., Mckenzie, J. E., Bossuyt, P. M., Boutron, I., Hoffmann, T. C., Mulrow, C. D., & Moher, D. (2021). The PRISMA 2020 Statement: An Updated Guideline for Reporting Systematic Reviews. *BMJ (Clinical Research Ed.)*, •••, 372. PMID: 33782057

Pang, L. L. (2021). Leadership and Crisis Communication During Covid-19: The Case of Brunei Darussalam. *Policy & Governance Review*, *5*(2), 97. DOI: 10.30589/pgr.v5i2.388

Parvin Hosseini, S. M., Mirzaei, M., & Iranmanesh, M. (2020). Determinants of Muslims' willingness to pay for halal-certified food: Does religious commitment act as a moderator in the relationships? *Journal of Islamic Marketing*, *11*(6), 1225–1243. DOI: 10.1108/JIMA-02-2018-0043

Patwary, A. K., Mohammed, A. A., Hazbar, A. H., & Nor Kamal, N. S. B. (2018). Factors Influencing Consumers' Intentions towards Purchasing Islamic Hotel Service: Moderating Role of Religiosity. *International Journal of Management, Accounting & Economics*, *5*(7).

Permana, A., Srihartati, R., Akbardin, J., Setiawan, A., Jatnika, D., & Rustandi, W. (2020). Technopreneur Training Model in Building an Entrepreneurship. *Journal of Architectural Research and Education*, *2*(2), 190–197. DOI: 10.17509/jare.v2i2.29258

Permentan No. 13/Permentan/OT.140/1/2010 Tahun 2010. (n.d.). Database Peraturan | JDIH BPK. Retrieved 7 June 2024, from https://peraturan.bpk.go.id/Details/161577/permentan-no-13permentanot14012010-tahun-2010

Poh, M. K. (2013). *Understanding the Halal Industry: A New Approach to Consumer Protection*. Halal Research Institute.

Polo, E. F., & Weber, W. (2010). Competitive Generic Strategies Evolution and the Importance of Michael E. Porter. *Revista de Gestão*, *17*(1), 99–117. Advance online publication. DOI: 10.5700/rege389

Poniman, D., Purchase, S., & Sneddon, J. (2015). Traceability systems in the Western Australia halal food supply chain. *Asia Pacific Journal of Marketing and Logistics*, *27*(2), 324–348. DOI: 10.1108/APJML-05-2014-0082

Porter, M. E. (1997). Michael E. Porter replies: "What Is. *Harvard Business Review*, *75*(1).

Prabowo, S., Rahman, A. A., Rahman, S. A., & Samah, A. A. (2015). Revealing factors hindering halal certification in East Kalimantan Indonesia. *Journal of Islamic Marketing*, *6*(2), 268–291. DOI: 10.1108/JIMA-05-2014-0040

Prakoso, B. P., & Tiurma, M. R. (2023). Halal research streams: A systematic and bibliometrics review. *Cogent Social Sciences*, *9*(1), 2225334. DOI: 10.1080/23311886.2023.2225334

Prayuda, D., Arby, S., Adli, I., & Al-Ayubi, S. (2023). Halal Industry: Opportunities and Challenge in the Global Market. *Jurnal Ekonomi Islam*, *14*(2), 2579–6453. DOI: 10.32507/ajei.v14i2.2376

Pujayanti, D. A. (2020). Industri Halal sebagai Paradigma bagi Sustainable Development Goals di Era Revolusi Industri 4.0. *Youth & Islamic Economic Journal*, *1*, 14.

Purnomo, S. H. (2022, April 25). *RPH dan RPU adalah hulu strategis kehalalan suatu produk*. ANTARA News Jawa Timur. https://jatim.antaranews.com/berita/597201/rph-dan-rpu-adalah-hulu-strategis-kehalalan-suatu-produk

Purwanto, P. (2021). Society attitudes and intentions to use products in Sharia Bank of Aceh: The role of religiosity and social influence. *ABAC Journal*, *41*(2), 223–242.

Puspaningtyas, M. (2021). Is halal certificate socialization effective in increasing the number of MSMEs in the food sector to register for halal certificates? In H. Pratikto, A. Taufiq, A. Voak, N. Deuraseh, H. Nur, W. Dahlan, & A. Purnomo (Eds.), *Halal Development: Trends, Opportunities and Challenges* (pp. 69-74). CRC Press. DOI: 10.1201/9781003189282-12

PWC. (2022). *Blockchain in Islamic Finance: Enhancing Transparency and Efficiency*. PricewaterhouseCoopers.

Qader, G., Shahid, Z. A., Junaid, M., Shaikh, I. M., & Qureshi, M. A. (2023). The role of diffusion of innovation theory towards the adoption of halal meat supply chain. *Journal of Islamic Marketing*, *14*(5), 1211–1228. DOI: 10.1108/JIMA-01-2021-0032

Quintane, E., Mitch Casselman, R., Sebastian Reiche, B., & Nylund, P. A. (2011). Innovation as a knowledge-based outcome. *Journal of Knowledge Management*, *15*(6), 928–947. DOI: 10.1108/13673271111179299

Qur'an Kemenag. (n.d.-a). Retrieved 30 May 2024, from https://quran.kemenag.go.id/

Qur'an Kemenag. (n.d.-b). Retrieved 14 August 2023, from https://quran.kemenag.go.id/quran/per-ayat/surah/5?from=88&to=120

Qureshi, R. U. (2020). The Relation between Hadith and Sunnah (A Research Study). *Al-Wifaq*, *3*(1), 91–102.

Rachman, M. A. (2019). Halal Industry In Indonesia: Role Of Sharia Financial Institutions In Driving Industrial And Halal Ecosystem. *Al-Iqtishad: Jurnal Ilmu Ekonomi Syariah*, *11*(1). Advance online publication. DOI: 10.15408/aiq.v11i1.10221

Rachmawati, E., & Suroso, A. (2022). A moderating role of halal brand awareness to purchase decision making. *Journal of Islamic Marketing*, *13*(2), 542–563.

Radzi, R., & Muhamed, N. (2019). Are sukuk debt or equity? A classification of sukuk by regulatory bodies and credit rating agencies. *Journal of Emerging Economies and Islamic Research*, *7*(2), 72–81. DOI: 10.24191/jeeir.v7i2.8767

Raffi, R., Deuraseh, N., Hashim, N., & Yunus, N. (2023). Determinant of Employment and Employability Attributes in the Halal Sector for Halal Science Graduates in Brunei Darussalam. *Journal of Halal Industry & Services*, *6*(1), a0000311. DOI: 10.36877/jhis.a0000311

Rafiki, A., Hidayat, S. E., & Nasution, M. D. T. P. (2023). *An extensive effect of religiosity on the purchasing decisions of halal products*. PSU Research Review., DOI: 10.1108/PRR-07-2022-0093

Rafiki, A., Hidayat, S. E., & Nasution, M. D. T. P. (2024). An extensive effect of religiosity on the purchasing decisions of halal products. *PSU Research Review*, *8*(3), 898–919. https://doi.org/10.1108/PRR-07-2022-0093

Rahim, S. I. A., Mansor, S. K. M., Ruzulan, Z., & Ismail, N. (2021). Developing Basic Criteria in Halal Food Security: An Overview from Islamic Perspectives. In *Enhancing Halal Sustainability: Selected Papers from the 4th International Halal Conference 2019* (Pp. 109-116). Springer Singapore.

Rahman, A., & Islam, Md. J., Karim, Md. R., Kundu, D., & Kabir, S. (2021). *An intelligent vaccine distribution process in COVID-19 pandemic through blockchain-SDN framework from Bangladesh perspective*. 2021 International Conference on Electronics, Communications and Information Technology (ICECIT), in Khulna, Bangladesh, September 14–16.

Rahman, M. H., & Chowdhury, N. M. S. I. (2024). The prospects of istijrar financing in Islamic banking: An exploratory study in Bangladesh. *Qualitative Research in Financial Markets*, *16*(1), 135–158. DOI: 10.1108/QRFM-10-2022-0173

Rahmayanti, I., Wardiyanta, W., & Ikawati, R. (2023). Does Islamic Entrepreneurship Aligned with Digitalization Era? *Jurnal Doktor Managemen*, *6*(2), 204–216. DOI: 10.22441/jdm.v6i2.22475

Rai, P., & Bera, S. (2025). Prioritizing performance objectives of vaccine supply chain for future pandemics. *Journal of Humanitarian Logistics and Supply Chain Management,* Vol. ahead-of-print No. ahead-of-print. DOI:.DOI: 10.1108/JHLSCM-05-2024-0072

Rajendran, S. D., Kamarulzaman, N. H., & Abd Rahman, A. (2024). The mediating role of halal supply chain integrity in enhancing performance for halal herbal-based food SMEs. *Journal of Islamic Marketing, 15*(12), 3621–3648. DOI: 10.1108/JIMA-03-2022-0090

Rajnai, Z., & Kocsis, I. (2017). Labor Market Risks of Industry 4.0, Digitization, Robots and AI. 2017 IEEE 15th International Symposium on Intelligent Systems and Informatics (SISY), 343–346.

Ramadhan, R., Ulfah, A. K., Nurzianti, R., Bunkes, P., & Kadriyani, E. (2023). Market Potential of Halal Products in Aceh: Case Study of Halal Industry Based on Halal Product Data 2014-2022. *Al-Falah: Journal of Islamic Economics, 8*(2), 171–180. DOI: 10.29240/alfalah.v8i2.7083

Ramli, M. A., Abd Razak, M. A., & Jaafar, M. H. (2023). Understanding non-Muslims' reluctance to halal food: A systematic review. *Journal of Islamic Marketing, 14*(2), 544–561. DOI: 10.1108/JIMA-05-2021-0134

Rampin, R., & Rampin, V. (2021). taguette: open source qualitative data analysis. *The Journal of Open Source Software.* https://joss.theoj.org/papers/10.21105/joss.03522.pdf

Randeree, K. (2020). Demography, demand and devotion: Driving the Islamic economy. *Journal of Islamic Marketing, 11*(2), 301–319. DOI: 10.1108/JIMA-06-2018-0102

Rashid, M. (2017). *Ethics and Compliance in the Halal Industry*. Routledge.

Regenstein, J. M., Chaudry, M. M., & Regenstein, C. E. (2003). The Kosher and Halal Food Laws. *Comprehensive Reviews in Food Science and Food Safety, 2*(3), 111–127. https://doi.org/https://doi.org/10.1111/j.1541-4337.2003.tb00018.x. DOI: 10.1111/j.1541-4337.2003.tb00018.x PMID: 33451233

Renko, M., El Tarabishy, A., Carsrud, A. L., & Brännback, M. (2013). Understanding and Measuring Entrepreneurial Leadership Style. *Journal of Small Business Management, 53*(1), 54–74. DOI: 10.1111/jsbm.12086

Rezai, G., Mohamed, Z., & Nasir Shamsudin, M. (2012). Non-Muslim consumers' understanding of halal principles in Malaysia. *Journal of Islamic Marketing, 3*(1), 35–46. DOI: 10.1108/17590831211206572

Riaz, M. N., & Chaudry, M. M. (2003). *Halal Food Production*. CRC Press. https://doi.org/https://doi.org/10.1201/9780203490082

Riaz, M. N., & Chaudry, M. M. (2003). Halal food production. *Halal Food Production*, 1–380. DOI: 10.1201/9780203490082

Riaz, M. N., & Chaudry, M. M. (2018). General Guidelines for Halal Food Production. *Handbook of Halal Food Production*, 17–28. DOI: 10.1201/9781315119564-3

Riaz, M. N., & Chaudry, M. M. (2019). Halal Food Laws and Regulations. In M. N. Riaz & M. M. Chaudry (Eds.), *Handbook of Halal Food Production* (1st Editio). CRC Press.

Riaz, M. N., & Riaz, N. M. (2023). Requirements for Halal Food Production. In *Encyclopedia of Food Safety, Second Edition, Volume 1-4* (Vols. 1–4). https://doi.org/DOI: 10.1016/B978-0-12-822521-9.00003-4

Riaz, M. N., Chaudry, M. M., Riaz, M. N., & Chaudry, M. M. (2018). Halal Food Laws and Regulations. In *Handbook of Halal Food Production*. https://doi.org/DOI: 10.1201/9781315119564-2

Rifai, M., & Thaker, M. A. M. T. (2020). *Halal Industry: Challenges and Opportunities*. International Islamic University Malaysia Press.

Rindra, W. (2025, March 19). SEMOL series 1 FPH UI 2025 discusses halal vaccines from various aspects. *Faculty of Public Health, Universitas Indonesia (FKMUI) News*. https://fkm.ui.ac.id/en/semol-series-1-fph-ui-2025-discusses-halal-vaccines-from-various-aspects/

Rizvi, S., Ali, A., & Sulaiman, N. (2022). *Certification Standards and Green Practices in the* Halal *Industry*. Asian Journal of Business and Finance.

Robson, C. (2011). *Real world research: A resource for users of social research methods in applied settings*. Blackwell Publishing.

Rogers, E. M. (2003). *Diffusion of Innovations* (5th ed.). Free Press.

Rojas-Lema, X., Alfaro-Saiz, J.-J., Rodríguez-Rodríguez, R., & Verdecho, M.-J. (2020). Performance measurement in SMEs: Systematic literature review and research directions. *Total Quality Management & Business Excellence*, •••, 1–26. DOI: 10.1080/14783363.2020.1774357

Rojko, A. (2017). Industry 4.0 Concept: Background and Overview. *International Journal of Interactive Mobile Technologies*, *11*(5), 77–90. DOI: 10.3991/ijim.v11i5.7072

Rusydiana, A. S., & Mahsyar, N. M. (2024). Developing Halal Industry in Indonesia using Interpretive Structural Modeling (ISM). *Halal Tourism and Pilgrimage*, *3*(2). Advance online publication. DOI: 10.58968/htp.v3i2.385

Ruzulan, Z., Jamaludin, M. A., & Ishak, A. H. (2021, May). Meat and Meat-Based Products: Challenges and Opportunities in Halal Food Security. [). IOP Publishing.]. *IOP Conference Series. Earth and Environmental Science*, *756*(1), 012017. DOI: 10.1088/1755-1315/756/1/012017

Saeed, M., Ahmed, Z. U., & Mukhtar, S. M. (2001). International marketing ethics from an Islamic perspective: A value-maximization approach. *Journal of Business Ethics*, *32*(2), 127–142. DOI: 10.1023/A:1010718817155

Saidi, S., & Sazali, H. (2024). Analysis of The Contention of Religious Ideology and Halal Industry in Social Media about Halal Logo Rebranding. *KOMUNIKA: Jurnal Dakwah Dan Komunikasi*, *18*(1), 1–12. Advance online publication. DOI: 10.24090/komunika.v18i1.7778

Sait, M., & Anshari, M. (2021). Industrial Revolution 4.0: A New Challenge to Brunei Darussalam's Unemployment Issue. *International Journal of Asian Business and Information Management*, *12*(4), 33–44. DOI: 10.4018/IJABIM.20211001.oa3

Sakti, R. H., Yetti, W., & Wulansari, R. E. (2020). Technopreneurship and IT-Preneurship in Vocational Education Perspective: Perspective Theory. *Jurnal Pendidikan Teknologi Kejuruan*, *3*(4), 194–198. DOI: 10.24036/jptk.v3i3.10423

Salaheldeen, M., & Battour, M. (2024). Fostering innovation capability and sustainable innovation in halal industry: The role of halal entrepreneurs' success'. *Journal of Islamic Marketing*, *15*(3), 777–799. DOI: 10.1108/JIMA-12-2022-0323

Salamon, H. B., Salbi, N. M., Rosman, A. S. B., Rosli, M. R. B., Noor, S. S. B. M., Muhamad, N. H. B. N., ... & Hussin, E. R. B. (2021). Halalan Tayyiba: An Islamic Perspective on Healthy Food. *Revista Geintec-Gestao Inovacao E Tecnologias, 11*(2), 1001-1014.

Salam, S., Mohd, H., Muflih, B., & Jaiyeoba, H. (2023). Halal industry and standardization. *Ekonomski Izazovi*, *12*(24), 20–30. DOI: 10.5937/EkoIzazov2324020S

Saleh, H., & Rajandran, T. (2024). Relationship between Non-Muslim consumer intention to purchase Halal Products with Halal Awareness, Halal Certification, Halal Marketing and Halal Knowledge: Systematic Review. *International Journal of Academic Research in Business & Social Sciences*, *14*(9), 416–426. https://doi .org/http://dx.doi.org/10.6007/IJARBSS/v14-i9/22495. DOI: 10.6007/IJARBSS/ v14-i9/22495

Salim Khraim, H. (2011). The Influence of Brand Loyalty on Cosmetics Buying Behavior of UAE Female Consumers. *International Journal of Marketing Studies, 3*(2). Advance online publication. DOI: 10.5539/ijms.v3n2p123

Salindal, N. A. (2019). Halal certification compliance and its effects on companies' innovative and market performance. *Journal of Islamic Marketing, 10*(2), 589–605. DOI: 10.1108/JIMA-04-2018-0080

Sallomi, P. (2020, March 25). *Understanding the Sector Impact of COVID-19 Technology Sector*. Retrieved November 21, 2024, from Deloitte: file:///C:/Users/offic/Downloads/COVID-19-Impact-Technology-Sector.pdf

Salman, A., Rahman, A., Sitorus, M., Wok, R., Mustapha, S., & Ghani, N. (2020). The Impact of Knowledge and Skills Acquired on Business Performance of Malaysia and Indonesia TVET Graduates. *International Journal of Technical Vocational and Engineering Technology, 2*(1), 1–14.

Santoso, L., & Rachman, A. (2023). Digitalising Halal Certification: The Dynamic of Regulations and Policies Concerning Halal Certification in Indonesia. *Jurisdictie: Jurnal Hukum Dan Syariah, 14*(2), 265–293. Advance online publication. DOI: 10.18860/j.v14i2.24115

Santoso, S., Dewandaru, G., Nugroho, L., Hidayat, S. E., Isa, S. M., Hidayat, R. N., & Marfatah, M. R. (2024). Developing an integrated innovation ecosystem to strengthen Islamic economy in Indonesia. *IQTISHODUNA: Jurnal Ekonomi Islam, 13*(2), 681–706.

Sarip, N. S. (2024). A Comparative Study of Halal-Compliant and Non-Halal-Compliant Meat Prices and its Influence on Halal Certification in the Lanao Region, Philippines. *Journal of Islamic Economic and Business Research, 4*(2 SE-Articles), 144–159. DOI: 10.18196/jiebr.v4i2.325

Saviera, L., R., Natasya Sirait, N., Mat Isa, N., Sulaiman, S., & Mohd Kamal, S. B. (2024). The Comparative Study of Muslim Friendly Homestay Programs in Indonesia and Malaysia: Social Legal Perspective. *KnE Social Sciences*. https://doi.org/ DOI: 10.18502/kss.v8i21.14760

Savitri, F. M., & Perwita, A. D. (2020). Mediating Role of Halal Technology Implementation on Halal Purchase Intention in Semarang. *International Journal Ihya' 'Ulum al-Din, 22*(1). https://doi.org/DOI: 10.21580/ihya.22.1.5574

Sayuti, M., Purnamasari, A., & Pratiwi, A. I. (2021). Penerapan Halal Logistik pada Distribusi Daging Sapi di Kabupaten Karawang. *Jurnal Integrasi Sistem industri, 8*, 11.

Selladurai, M. (2016). Conceptual Framework on Technopreneurship. *SELP Journal of Social Science*, *7*(27), 92–97.

Septiarini, D. F., Ratnasari, R. T., Salleh, M. C. M., Herianingrum, S., & Sedianingsih, S. (2023). Drivers of behavioral intention among non-Muslims toward halal cosmetics: Evidence from Indonesia, Malaysia, and Singapore. *Journal of Islamic Accounting and Business Research*, *14*(2), 230–248. DOI: 10.1108/JIABR-02-2021-0064

Setiawan, A., Riyadi, P., & Sumardianto, S. (2015). The Effect of Gambir (Uncaria Gambier) as a Tanning Agent in the Leather Tanning Process on the Physical Quality of Tilapia Fish Skin (Oreochromis Niloticus). *Journal of Fishery Products Processing and Biotechnology*, *4*(2), 124–132. https://ejournal3.undip.ac.id/index.php/jpbhp/article/view/9202/8933

Shaari, J. A. N., & Arifin, N. S. (2010). Dimension of halal purchase intention: A preliminary study. *International Review of Business Research Papers*, *6*(4), 444–456.

Shadiqe, J. (2024). *Several popular restaurant chains not halal-certified, says Jakim*. New Straits Times.

Shafiee, N. F., Karim, M., Razali, A., & Abidin, U. Z. (2017). Halalan Toiyyiban Food Handling Practices: A Review on Street Food Vendors in Malaysia. *Journal of Islamic, Social* [JISED]. *Economics and Development*, *2*, 385–394.

Shafie, S., & Othman, M. N. (2006). Halal certification: An international marketing issue and challenge. *Proceedings of the International IFSAM VIIIth World Congress.*

Shah Alam, S., & Mohamed Sayuti, N. (2011). Applying the Theory of Planned Behavior (TPB) in halal food purchasing. *International Journal of Commerce and Management*, *21*(1), 8–20. DOI: 10.1108/10569211111111676

Sharaai, A. H., Zulkifli, N. F., Mahmood, N. Z., & Sulaiman, N. M. N. (2012). *The implementation of Islamic elements in achieving best practices of sustainability concept*. DOI: 10.13140/RG.2.1.1056.7765

Sharon, A. (2018). Future-ready 'technopreneurs' important to Malaysia's transformation. Retrieved January 30, 2025 from Open Gov: https://opengovasia.com/2018/10/08/future-ready-technopreneurs-important-to-malaysias-transformation/

Shaw, D. J. (2007). World Food Summit, 1996. In *World Food Security: A History Since 1945* (pp. 347–360). Palgrave Macmillan UK. DOI: 10.1057/9780230589780_35

Sherwani, M., Ali, A., Ali, A., & Hussain, S. (2018). Determinants of halal meat consumption in Germany. *Journal of Islamic Marketing*, *9*(4), 863–883. DOI: 10.1108/JIMA-01-2018-0009

Shihab, Q. (2002). Tafsir al-Misbah Jilid 6 (yunus, hud, yusuf, ar-ra'du). *Journal of Chemical Information and Modeling*, *53*(9), •••.

Sholeh, M. A. N., & Helmi, M. I. (2021). The covid-19 vaccination: Realization on halal vaccines for benefits. *Samarah: Jurnal Hukum Keluarga dan Hukum Islam*, 5(1), 174-190. DOI: `DOI: 10.22373/sjhk.v5i1.9769

Silalahi, S. A. F., Fachrurazi, F., & Fahham, A. M. (2022). Factors affecting intention to adopt halal practices: Case study of Indonesian small and medium enterprises. *Journal of Islamic Marketing*, *13*(6), 1244–1263. DOI: 10.1108/JIMA-05-2020-0152

Simanjuntak, T., & Lestarini, R. (2022). Implementation Of The Concept Of Sustainable Development In Resolving Indigenous Law Community Conflict. *International Journal of Environmental, Sustainability, and Social Science*, *3*(3). Advance online publication. DOI: 10.38142/ijesss.v3i3.342

Siyanbola, W., Aderemi, H., Egbetokun, A., & Sanni, M. (2011). Framework for Technological Entrepreneurship Development: Key Issues and Policy Directions. *Gongshang Guanli Xuekan*, *1*(1), 10–19. DOI: 10.4236/ajibm.2011.11002

Slesman, L., & Hoon, C.-Y. (2023). Brunei Darussalam in 2022: Towards Post-COVID-19 Economic Recovery, Diversification and Sustainability. *Southeast Asian Affairs*, *2023*(1), 52–68.

Soebandrio, A. (2020). Webinar Series Halal Vaccine Industry: Past, Present, Future, held by PEBS UI August 29.

Soomro, B., & Shah, N. (2021). Technopreneurship Intention Among Nonbusiness Students: A Quantitative Assessment. *World Journal of Entrepreneurship, Management and Sustainable Development*, *17*(3), 502–514. DOI: 10.1108/WJEMSD-10-2020-0129

Soon, J. M., Chandia, M., & Mac Regenstein, J. (2017). Halal integrity in the food supply chain. *British Food Journal*, *119*(1), 39–51. DOI: 10.1108/BFJ-04-2016-0150

Spithoven, A. H. G. M. (1996). Jean-Baptiste Say (1767-1832). *International Journal of Social Economics*, *23*(7), 39–48. DOI: 10.1108/03068299610122399

Sriminarti, N., & Nora, L. (2018). The Role of Product Knowledge and Attitudes toward Purchasing Intentions: The Moderating Effect of Religiosity on Halal Cosmetics. *KnE Social Sciences*, *3*(10), 518. DOI: 10.18502/kss.v3i10.3153

Statista. (2024). *Forecast Market Revenue of Halal Food Worldwide from 2018 to 2027 (in Billion U.S. Dollars).* Retrieved on 23/08/24, from https://www.statista.com/statistics/785499/halal-food-market-revenue-global/

Suarez-Zuluaga, D. A., van der Pol, L. A., van 't Oever, A. G., Bakker, W. A. M., & Thomassen, Y. E. (2022). Development of an animal component free production process for Sabin inactivated polio vaccine. *Vaccine: X, 12*(100223), 1–9. DOI: 10.1016/j.jvacx.2022.100223 PMID: 36217423

Sudarsono, H., Ikawati, R., Kurnia, A., Azizah, S. N., & Kholid, M. N. (2024). Effects of religiosity, halal knowledge and halal certification on the intention of Muslims to use the halal vaccine during covid-19 pandemic. *Journal of Islamic Marketing, 15*(1), 79–100. DOI: 10.1108/JIMA-06-2021-0179

Sufri, N. M. H. M., Abubakar, Y. A., Masri, M. B. H., & Ab Talib, M. S. (2023). Traditional Versus Born-Global Theories and the Internationalisation of Halal Food SMEs from an SSMC: Conceptual Framework and New Propositions. *Journal of Entrepreneurship and Innovation in Emerging Economies, 9*(2), 222–237. DOI: 10.1177/23939575231186487

Suhaimi, A. R., Nur Izyana, A. R., & Nusran, M. (2023). Halal Standards and Their Contributions To the Growth of Halal Economy in Malaysia and Indonesia. [InJHSS]. *International Journal of Halal System and Sustainability, 3*(2), 2808–9154. DOI: 10.33096/injhss.v3i2.278

Suhartanto, D., Dean, D., Amin, H., Sugiama, A. G., & Amalia, F. A. (2024). Fast, Fresh, Healthy And Halal: A Mobile Food App Recipe For Muslim Millennial Loyalty. *Journal of Islamic Accounting and Business Research.* Advance online publication. DOI: 10.1108/JIABR-08-2022-0210

Suhartanto, D., Dean, D., Sarah, I. S., Hapsari, R., Amalia, F. A., & Suhaeni, T. (2021). Does religiosity matter for customer loyalty? Evidence from halal cosmetics. *Journal of Islamic Marketing, 12*(8), 1521–1534. DOI: 10.1108/JIMA-03-2020-0069

Suharti, S., Mulyawan, S., & Ridwan, A. H. (2023). Sustainability dalam Perspektif Islam dan Pengaruhnya terhadap Firm Value dan Firm Size melalui Profitabilitas sebagai Variabel Mediasi. *Nuansa Akademik: Jurnal Pembangunan Masyarakat, 8*(1), 135–150. DOI: 10.47200/jnajpm.v8i1.1582

Sukuk, M. (2023). *Green Sukuk: Financing for Sustainable Development.* International Journal of Islamic Finance.

Sulaiman, N. S., Abdullah, R., & Hashim, N. (2023). Halal Industry Development in Brunei Darussalam: Realities and Challenges, *KnE Social Sciences 5th Social and Humaniora Research Symposium,* 8(18): 1013 – 1029. DOI: DOI: 10.18502/kss/v8.18.14308

Sulaiman, N., & Yusof, N. (2020). *Green Finance and Islamic Finance: Synergies and Challenges*. Journal of Islamic Economics.

Sulaiman, N. (2022). Innovation in the Halal Industry: Digital Trends and Future Prospects. *Journal of Islamic Marketing*.

Sulaiman, N., Abdullah, R., & Hashim, N. (2023). Halal Industry Development in Brunei Darussalam: Realities and Challenges. *Social and Humaniora Research Symposium (SoRes), KnE Life Sciences*, 1013-1029. DOI: 10.18502/kss.v8i18.14308

Sulaiman, N., & Yusof, N. (2018). Pharmaceuticals and Halal Standards: A Review. *Asian Journal of Pharmaceutical Sciences*.

Sulistyaningsih, E., Istinaroh, N., Dewi, R., & Hairrudin, H. (2022). Expression and in silico analysis of CIDRα1 recombinant protein from plasmodium falciparum as a malaria subunit vaccine candidate. *Trends in Sciences*, *19*(23), 1621. DOI: 10.48048/tis.2022.1621

Sungit, F., Mohd Deni, M. I., Abdullah, M., & Syahwahid, F. (2020). Concepts and Practices of Halalan Tayyiban in the Islamic Manufacturing Practice (IMP): An Analysis from Syariah Perspective. *ESTEEM Journal of Social Sciences and Humanities*, *4*, 214–229.

Suparno, O., Covington, A. D., & Evans, C. S. (2005). New Environmentally Benign Leather Technology: Combination Tanning Using Vegetable Tannin, Naphthol and Oxazolidine. *J. Tek. Ind. Pert*, *18*(2), 79–84.

Supian, K., & Ab Rashid, N. (2018). The Role of Supplier, Top Management and Government in Halal Practices Integrity of Malaysian Food Business. *International Journal of Asian Social Science, 8*(8 SE-Articles), 549–559. DOI: 10.18488/journal.1.2018.88.549.559

Suradi, S., Yasin, M., & Rasul, M. S. (2017). Increasing Technoprencurs for a Developing a Nation: The Majlis Amanah Rakyat (MARA) Experience. *Journal of Technical Education and Training*, *9*(1), 73–86.

Surat Al-Anfal Ayat 69. (n.d.). Tafsir AlQuran Online. Retrieved 30 May 2024, from https://tafsirq.com/permalink/ayat/1229

Surat Al-Ma'idah Ayat 88 Arab, Latin, Terjemah dan Tafsir | Baca di TafsirWeb. (n.d.). Retrieved 30 May 2024, from https://tafsirweb.com/1972-surat-al-maidah -ayat-88.html

Surat An-Nahl Ayat 114. (n.d.). Tafsir AlQuran Online. Retrieved 30 May 2024, from https://tafsirq.com/permalink/ayat/2015

Suryawan, A. S., Hisano, S., & Jongerden, J. (2022). Negotiating halal: The role of non-religious concerns in shaping halal standards in Indonesia. *Journal of Rural Studies*, *92*, 482–491. DOI: 10.1016/j.jrurstud.2019.09.013

Susanty, A., Puspitasari, N. B., Caterina, A. D., & Jati, S. (2020). Mapping the barriers for implementing halal logistics in Indonesian food, beverage and ingredient companies. *Journal of Islamic Marketing, ahead-of-p*(ahead-of-print). DOI: 10.1108/JIMA-11-2019-0244

Susiang, M. I. N., Siswanti, I., Permana, D., & Wibowo, M. W. (2024). Effects of competitive intelligence and halal integrity on Halalan Tayyiban implementation strategy in Indonesian MSMEs: The mediating role of halal orientation strategy. *Journal of Islamic Marketing*. Advance online publication. DOI: 10.1108/JIMA-10-2023-0344

Sustainable Halal Food Security. (n.d.). Iofs. Retrieved 12 June 2024, from https:// iofs.org.kz/post/125

Sutyasmi, S., Widowati, T. P., & Setyadewi, N. M. (2016). The effect of mimosa on tanning vegetable tanned sheepskin jacket using the C-RFP system, reviewed from the organoleptic, physical, and morphological properties of the leather. *Leather, Rubber, and Plastic Magazine.*, *32*(1), 31. DOI: 10.20543/mkkp.v32i1.932

Suwanan, A. F., Putro, A. C., Triyanto, A., Munir, S., & Merlinda, S. (2021). Analysis of the impacts and challenges of Covid-19 on green sukuk in Indonesia. In *Halal Development*. Trends, Opportunities and Challenges., DOI: 10.1201/9781003189282-6

Svirina, A., Syurkova, S., Laizans, T., Appalonova, N., & Bazarov, R. (2017). Technopreneurial Development: Why Ecosystem Approach is Unsustainable in Case of Low Competition. *Proceedings of the 21st World Multi-Conference on Systematics, Cybernetics, and Informatics (WMSCI 2017), pp.* 31-36.

Sweeny, P. (2019). Entrepreneurial inference in the high-technology start-up: A model for optimised decision making and principled praxis. *PhD Thesis*. University of Sheffield.

Tahir, M., Burki, U., & Hayat, A. (2023). Natural resources and economic growth: Evidence from Brunei Darussalam. *International Journal of Emerging Markets*, *18*(10), 4252–4269. DOI: 10.1108/IJOEM-05-2021-0762

Talha, M., Faisal, S., & Khan, A. (2024). Shariah Law in Commercial Banking and Stock Market: Recent Development, Challenges and Practices. *International Journal of Religion*, *5*(6), 620–630. DOI: 10.61707/4brms430

Talib, M., & Hamid, A. (2015). Halal supply chain critical success factors: A literature review. *Journal of Islamic Marketing*, *6*(1), 44–71. DOI: 10.1108/JIMA-07-2013-0049

Tan, A., Gligor, D., & Ngah, A. (2020). Applying Blockchain for Halal food traceability. *International Journal of Logistics Research and Applications*. https://doi.org/DOI: 10.1080/13675567.2020.1825653

Tan, W., Egge, K., & Mohamed, O. (2010). National Venture Competition and Technopreneurship Development in Malaysia. *Journal for International Business and Entrepreneurship*, *11*(2), 69–81. https://ink.library.smu.edu.sg/lkcsb_research/2682

Tarannum, S., Jalal, M. S., & Huda, M. N. (2024). HALALCheck: A Multi-Faceted Approach for Intelligent Halal Packaged Food Recognition and Analysis. *IEEE Access : Practical Innovations, Open Solutions*, *12*, 28462–28474. Advance online publication. DOI: 10.1109/ACCESS.2024.3367983

Tarmizi, R., Septiani, N., Sunarya, P. A., & Ayu Sanjaya, Y. P. (2023). Harnessing Digital Platforms for Entrepreneurial Success: A Study of Technopreneurship Trends and Practices. [ATT]. *Aptisi Transactions on Technopreneurship*, *5*(3), 278–290. DOI: 10.34306/att.v5i3.360

Taufik, A. (2014). *TEKSTUALITAS PENAFSIRAN AL-QUR" AN (Analisis Kritis Pemahaman Nā ir al-Sa 'dī terhadap Isu Kontemporer dalam Taysīr al-Karīm al-Ra mān fī Kalām al-Mannān)* (Master's thesis, Sekolah Pascasarjana Universitas Islam Negri (UIN) Syarif Hidayatullah Jakarta). [The Textuality of the Interpretation of the Qur"an (A Critical Analysis of Nā ir al-Sa'dī's Understanding of the Contemporary Issue in Taysīr al-Karīm al-Ra mān fī Kalām al-Mannān].

Teichler, U. (1996). Research on Academic Mobility and International Cooperation in Higher Education: An agenda for the future. In Peggy, B., Goodwin, C., Smith, A., & Teichler, U. (Eds.), *Academic Mobility in a Changing World*. Jessica Kingsley Publishers.

Teng, P. K., Jamaliah, W. W., & Jusoh, W. J. W. (2013). Investigating students' awareness and usage intention towards halal labelled cosmetics and personal care products in Malaysia. In *4th International Conference on Business and Economic Research (4th ICBER 2013), Indonesia: Bandung*.

The World Bank. (2024). *What is Food Security*. Retrieved on 07/08/24, from https://www.worldbank.org/en/topic/agriculture/brief/food-security-update/what-is-food-security

Thohari, A. (2013). EpistemologiFikih Lingkungan: Revitalisasi Konsep Masalahah. *E-Journal Fakultas Syariah Dan Ilmu Hukum*, *5*(2), 146–161.

Thompson, G. (2021). *Global Islamic Economy Report 2023: Growth and Trends in the Halal Industry*. Dubai Islamic Economy Development Centre.

Thomson Reuters. (2020). *Global Islamic Economy Report 2020/21*.

Tieman, M. (2011). The application of Halal in supply chain management: In-depth interviews. *Journal of Islamic Marketing*, *2*(2), 186–195. DOI: 10.1108/17590831111139893

Tim Penyusun. (2022). *Kerangka Modernisasi Rumah Potong Hewan Halal*. Komite Nasional Ekonomi dan Keuangan Syariah.

Tuhin, M. K. W., Miraz, M. H., Habib, M. M., & Alam, M. M. (2022). Strengthening consumers' halal buying behaviour: Role of attitude, religiosity and personal norm. *Journal of Islamic Marketing*, *13*(3), 671–687. DOI: 10.1108/JIMA-07-2020-0220

Tumiwa, R. A. F., Ningsih, G. M., Romarina, A., Setyadjit, S., Slamet, B., Waruwu, E., Ie, M., & Utomo, Y. T. (2023). Investigating Halal Food Supply Chain Management, Halal Certification And Traceability On Smes Performance. *Uncertain Supply Chain Management*, *11*(4), 1889–1896. Advance online publication. DOI: 10.5267/j.uscm.2023.6.003

UBDSBE. (n.d.) Entrepreneurship Major. Retrieved on Mar 30, 2025 from UBD School of Business and Economics: https://sbe.ubd.edu.bn/new_major_entrepreneurship.aspx?val=ProStud&val2=Prospective+Students+%3E+Bachelor+of+Business+%3E+Entrepreneurship+Major&utm

Uddin, M. N. (2021). Food Controls to Build Workable Human Resource in Muslim Countries for Poverty Reduction: An Islamic View. *IIUC Studies*, *18*(1), 33–46. DOI: 10.3329/iiucs.v18i1.61273

UNISSA. (n.d.) Entrepreneurship Hub. Retrieved on Mar, 30 2025. From UNISSA: https://unissa.edu.bn/offices/entrepreneurship-hub-unissa/?utm

United Nations. (UN, 2024). *The SDGs in Action*. Retrieved on 23/08/24, from https://www.undp.org/sustainable-development-goals

ur Rahim, S. F., & Masood, M. A. B. (2023). Global view of animal feed in halal perspective. *International Journal of Halal Research, 5*(1), 45-57.

Usman, H., Chairy, C., & Projo, N. W. K. (2022). Impact Of Muslim Decision-Making Style And Religiosity On Intention To Purchasing Certified Halal Food. *Journal of Islamic Marketing*, *13*(11), 2268–2289. Advance online publication. DOI: 10.1108/JIMA-01-2021-0027

Usman, H., Chairy, C., & Projo, N. W. K. (2023). Between Awareness Of Halal Food Products And Awareness Of Halal-Certified Food Products. *Journal of Islamic Marketing*, *14*(3), 851–870. Advance online publication. DOI: 10.1108/JIMA-07-2021-0233

Usman, H., & Raharjo, N. (2012). Model Pendidikan Karakter Kewirausahaan di Sekolah Menengah Kejuruan. *Jurnal Pendidikan Teknologi Dan Kejuruan*, *21*(2), 140–147.

Usmani, M. T. (2002). *An Introduction to Islamic Finance*. Idaratul Ma'ariful.

Utami, F. R., Hairrudin, H., & Suhartini, S. (2023). Lesson learned from parents' willingness to covid-19 vaccination in children aged 6-11 years (with the health belief model approach). International. *Journal of Medical Science and Clinical Research Studies*, *3*(8), 1667–1673. DOI: 10.47191/ijmscrs/v3-i8-42

UTB. (n.d.) UTB Experiences PLUS. Retrieved on Mar 30, 2025 from UTB: https://www.utb.edu.bn/students/life-skills-development/utb-experience-plus/

Utomo, S., Sekaryuni, R., Widarjono, A., Tohirin, A., & Sudarsono, H. (2021). Promoting Islamic financial ecosystem to improve halal industry performance in Indonesia: A demand and supply analysis. *Journal of Islamic Marketing*, *12*(5), 992–1011. DOI: 10.1108/JIMA-12-2019-0259

UU No. 33 Tahun 2014. (n.d.). Database Peraturan | JDIH BPK. Retrieved 12 June 2024, from https://peraturan.bpk.go.id/Details/38709/uu-no-33-tahun-2014

Valero, A., & Reenen, J. (2019). The economic impact of universities: Evidence from across the globe. *Economics of Education Review*, *68*, 53–67. DOI: 10.1016/j.econedurev.2018.09.001

Vanany, I., Soon, J. M., Maryani, A., & Wibawa, B. M. (2019). Determinants Of Halal-Food Consumption In Indonesia. *Journal of Islamic Marketing*, *11*(2), 507–521. Advance online publication. DOI: 10.1108/JIMA-09-2018-0177

Venkataraman, S. (2004). Regional transformation through technological entrepreneurship. *Journal of Business Venturing*, *19*(1), 153–167. DOI: 10.1016/j.jbusvent.2003.04.001

Visser, H. (2019). *Islamic Finance: Principles and Practice*. Edward Elgar Publishing. DOI: 10.4337/9781786433503

Vojtovič, S., Navickas, V., & Gruzauskas, V. (2016). Strategy of Sustainable Competitiveness: Methodology of Real-Time Customers' Segmentation for Retail Shops. *Journal of Security and Sustainability Issues*, *5*(4), 489–499. DOI: 10.9770/jssi.2016.5.4(4)

Wahyudi, P. (2021, November 15). Vaccine platform technology state of the art and its critical point. *Halal MUI,* https://halalmui.org/en/technology-platform-vaccine-state-of-the-art-and-its-critical-point/

Wahyuni, D., & Arfidhila, N. (2019). Traceability in Halal Food Supply Chains: Literature Review. *Talenta Conference Series: Energy and Engineering (EE)*, 38–45. https://doi.org/https://doi.org/10.32734/ee.v2i4.649

Wannasupchue, W., Mohamad, S. F., Ishak, F. A. C., & Ungku Zainal Abidin, U. F. (2023). Challenges to obtain halal certification among restaurants in northeast Thailand. *Journal of Islamic Marketing*, *14*(2), 607–621. DOI: 10.1108/JIMA-04-2021-0124

Wardhana, A. K. (2020). Should vaccine be Halal? bibliography study in scopus indexed academic paper. *Journal of Halal Product and Research*, *3*(2), 80–87. DOI: 10.20473/jhpr.vol.3-issue.2.80-87

Weil, K. E. (1985). PORTER, Competitive advantage, creating and sustaining superior performance. *Revista de Administração de Empresas, 25*(2). https://doi.org/ DOI: 10.1590/s0034-75901985000200009

Wekke, I. S., Nusran, M., Henny, A., & Azis, St. N. (2024). Indonesia's Halal Future: Charting a Path to Global Leadership. *SSRN*: https://ssrn.com/abstract=4737469 or http://dx.doi.org/DOI: 10.2139/ssrn.4737469

Wenovita, C. A. A. (2021). Penegakan Hukum Sertifikasi Halal Rumah Potong Hewan. *Jurist-Diction*, *4*(4), 1357. DOI: 10.20473/jd.v4i4.28452

WHO. (2022, July 22). A brief history of vaccination. *World Health Organization (WHO),* Newsroom, Spotlight, https://www.who.int/news-room/spotlight/history-of-vaccination

Whyte, S. (2023). Are Fatwas Dispensable? Examining the Contemporary Relevance and Authority of Fatwas in Australia. *Oxford Journal of Law and Religion, 11*(2–3), 314–342. Advance online publication. DOI: 10.1093/ojlr/rwac015

Wibowo, A. (2021). *Bisnis digital (Algoritma Bisnis, Komputasi Awan dan Data Teknik)*. Prima Agus Teknik.

Wibowo, A. (2022). Technopreneurship Development in Indonesia: Digital Business Development. *Journal of System and Management Sciences, 12*, 87–103. DOI: 10.33168/JSMS.2022.0305

Wijayanto, G., Ayesha, I., Wibowo, T., Suparwata, D., Suroso, A., & Fathurohman, A. (2023). The Influence of Digital Literacy Mediation on the Effect of Entrepreneurship Knowledge on Technopreneurship. *International Journal of Economics. Business and Accounting Research, 7*(1), 1–10.

Wilson, J. A. J., & Grant, J. (2013). Islamic marketing – a challenger to the classical marketing canon? *Journal of Islamic Marketing, 4*(1), 7–21. DOI: 10.1108/17590831311306327

Wilson, J. A. J., & Liu, J. (2010). Shaping the *Halal* into a brand? *Journal of Islamic Marketing, 1*(2), 107–123. DOI: 10.1108/17590831011055851

Wilson, R. (2012). *Islamic Economics: A Short History*. Brill.

Winarni, D., Susilo, S., & Widiyatmoko, A. (2021). Penerapan pendekatan Socio-Scientific Issue (SSI) Menggunakan Desain Project untuk Meningkatkan Penguasaan Technopreneurship Mahasiswa. *Prosiding Seminar Nasional Pascasarjana, 4*(1), 180–184.

Wiryadinata, H. (2023). Religious education and vaccination: the concept of halal, from the slippery road to herd immunity. *PASCA: Jurnal Teologi dan Pendidikan Agama Kristen* 19(2), 141-150.

Wisdom, A. (2023, August 21). *Technopreneurship: Empowering Innovation and Business in the Digital Age.* Retrieved December 5, 2024, from LinkedIn: https://www.linkedin.com/pulse/technopreneurship-empowering-innovation-business-age-anthony

Wisenthige, K. (2023). Research Design. In *Social Research Methodology and Publishing Results: A Guide to Non-Native English Speakers* (pp. 74–93). DOI: 10.4018/978-1-6684-6859-3.ch006

Woiceshyn, J., & Daellenbach, U. (2018). Evaluating inductive vs deductive research in management studies: Implications for authors, editors, and reviewers. *Qualitative Research in Organizations and Management, 13*(2), 183-195. https://doi.org/DOI: 10.1108/QROM-06-2017-1538

World Bank Group. (2022). *Islamic Finance and the Development of Malaysia's Halal Economy*. World Bank Group.

Wulandari, S. A., Sari, R. P., & Hadining, A. F. (2023). Analysis of Customer Behavior and Attitudes (General Risk) on Satisfaction, Trust and Halal Awareness of Purchase Intentions in Food Delivery Applications. *Jurnal Dinamika Manajemen, 14*(1), 99–110. DOI: 10.15294/jdm.v14i1.38386

Yahaya, A. M., & Ruzulan, Z. (2020). Quranic Concept of Halalan Tayyiban and Its Application in Food and Beverages of Hospitality Sector in Malaysia. *Journal of Contemporary Islamic Studies*, *6*(1), 61–75. DOI: 10.24191/jcis.v6i1.4

Yahya, I., & Junaidi, A. A. (2021). Authority of Fatwa in Digital Era: Methodology and Transmission of Nahdlatul Ulama's Bahtsul Masail in Indonesia. *Webology*, *18*(2), 654–674. Advance online publication. DOI: 10.14704/WEB/V18I2/WEB18345

Yaqub, A. (2024a). Philippines Enhances Halal Certification to Attract More Muslim Tourists. *2The Halal Times*. https://www.halaltimes.com/philippines-enhances-halal-certification-to-attract-more-muslim-tourists

Yaqub, A. (2024b). Philippines Launches National Halal Office to Strengthen Global Market Presence. *The Halal Times*. https://www.halaltimes.com/philippines-launches-national-halal-office-to-strengthen-global-market-presence/

Yasni, S. (2021, December 8). Getting to know vaccine manufacturing and its halal critical point. *Halal MUI,*https://halalmui.org/en/recognize-vaccine-making-and-critical-point-halal/

Yi, L. K. (2024). *Trendspotting: Catch the chocolate pistachio 'kunafa' fever in KL with chocolate bars, croissants and even cookies*. The Malay Mail. https://www.malaymail.com/news/eat-drink/2024/11/04/trendspotting-catch-the-chocolate-pistachio-kunafa-fever-in-kl-with-chocolate-bars-croissants-and-even-cookies/155736#google_vignette

Yi, Z. (2012). Analysis on the way of scale economy of Halal food and Moslem supplies industry of Ningxia. *The Fourth International Conference on Multimedia Information Networking and Security*, 761-764. DOI:DOI: 10.1109/MINES.2012.77

Yoo, B., Donthu, N., & Lee, S. (2000). An examination of selected marketing mix elements and brand equity. *Journal of the Academy of Marketing Science*, *28*(2), 195–211. DOI: 10.1177/0092070300282002

Yousaf, S., & Malik, M. S. (2013). Evaluating the influences of religiosity and product involvement level on the consumers. *Journal of Islamic Marketing*, *4*(2), 163–186. DOI: 10.1108/17590831311329296

Yudha, P. (2010). Utilization of Human Virtual Intelligence Framework in Managing Technopreneur Knowledge. *Jurnal Generic*, *5*(1), 31–34.

Yusuf, S., Mokoagow, M., Nur, M., & Rauf, S. (2023). Islamic Financial Characteristics and the Sustainability of Islamic Banking in Indonesia: Challenges and Opportunities. *Scientific Journal of Unity Management*, *11*(2), 363–369. DOI: 10.37641/jimkes.v11i2.2036

Zaid & Al Bahy, M. P. (2022). Examining factors influencing halal covid-19 vaccination intention among the muslim communities. [DOI:.]. *Psikis: Jurnal Psikologi Islami*, *8*(1), 40–53.DOI: 10.19109/psikis.v8i1.11913

Zailani, S., Arrifin, Z., Wahid, N. A., Othman, R., & Fernando, Y. (2010). Halal Traceability and Halal Tracking Systems in Strengthening Halal Food Supply Chain for Food Industry in Malaysia (A Review). *Journal of Food Technology*, *8*(3), 74–81. DOI: 10.3923/jftech.2010.74.81

Zakaria, N., & Abdul-Talib, A. (2010). Applying Islamic market-oriented cultural model to sensitize strategies towards global customers, competitors, and environment. *Journal of Islamic Marketing*, *1*(1), 51–62. DOI: 10.1108/17590831011026222

Zakaria, Z. (2008). Tapping Into the World Halal Market : Some Discussions on Malaysian Laws and. *Shariah Journal*, *16*, 603–616.

Ziegler, Y., Uli, V., & Tatari, M. (2022). Implementing halal logistics in a non-Muslim-dominant environment: A proposal for reengineering the business processes in two stages. *Business Process Management Journal*, *28*(8), 48–65. DOI: 10.1108/BPMJ-12-2020-0593

Zuhudi, N. W. M., & Dolah, J. (2021). *An Experts' Perspective Based on Consumers' Perception of Halal-Related Issue*. Al-Risalah Journal.

Zulfakar, M. H., Anuar, M. M., & Talib, M. S. A. (2014). Conceptual Framework on Halal Food Supply Chain Integrity Enhancement. *Procedia: Social and Behavioral Sciences*, *121*(April), 58–67. DOI: 10.1016/j.sbspro.2014.01.1108

Zulfakar, M. H., Jie, F., & Chan, C. (2011). Halal supply chain integrity: From a literature review to a conceptual framework. *10th ANZAM Operatons,Supply Chain and Services Management Symposium.*

Zulkifli, M., Mohd, R., & Hassan, M. (2021). Sukuk Hijau dan Pembangunan Berkelanjutan: Tinjauan dan Implikasi. *Journal of Sustainable Finance & Investment.*

About the Contributors

Mohammad Nabil Almunawar (Scopus ID: 55308196200, Orcid: 0000-0001-5296-2576) is currently an associate professor at the School of Business and Economics, Universiti Brunei Darussalam (UBDSBE), Brunei Darussalam. He was the former dean of UBDSBE. He received his bachelor's degree in 1983 from Bogor Agricultural University, Indonesia, master's degree (MSc) from the Department of Computer Science, University of Western Ontario, London, Canada in 1991, and PhD in Computer Science/Information Systems from the University of New South Wales in 1998. Dr. Almunawar has published more than 250 papers in refereed journals, books, book chapters, and encyclopedias. He has more than 30 years of teaching experience in information systems and e-business/e-commerce. He is currently Editor-in-chief of International Journal of E-Business Research (IJEBR) (Index in Scopus and WoS) and Journal of Business and Economic Analysis. His overall research interests include applications of IT in management, e-business/commerce, digital transformation, digital marketplace/platform, digital business ecosystem, Halal business ecosystem, health informatics, information security, and cloud computing. Currently, he focuses his research on digital transformation, digital marketplace platforms, and digital business ecosystems - including healthcare business ecosystem.

Achmad Ubaedillah is a prominent academic figure at the Syarif Hidayatullah State Islamic University (UIN) Jakarta. He completed undergraduate level at the Ushuluddin Faculty of IAIN Syarif Hidayatullah Jakarta (now UIN Jakarta) in 1995 and continued his master's program with a concentration in Islamic Political Thought. In 2002 he got the opportunity to study a second master's at Ohio University, Athens, USA, in Southeast Asian Regional Studies until graduating in 2004. then continued the doctoral program in the field of Southeast Asian History at the University of Hawaii at Manoa, Honolulu, United States. He is deeply rooted in exploring Islamic Political Thought, Civic Education, ASEAN studies, and Political Movements. Professor Ubaedillah has a major contribution to the development of knowledge related to national insight. At UIN Jakarta, he focuses on developing research, and teaching programs in the field of the history of Southeast Asian Islam, the contemporary Middle East, Civic Education, and Contemporary religious movements and globalism. With his expertise, he has many publications such as journal research, and book sources that have been cited by others (Scopus ID: 564065179000).

Euis Amalia is a distinguished academic and researcher at Syarif Hidayatullah State Islamic University (UIN) Jakarta, Indonesia, where she has made significant contributions to the field of social sciences, with a particular focus on social welfare, gender studies, and Islamic economics. Her work, often interwoven with the principles of Islam, explores the dynamics of social development, poverty alleviation, and women's empowerment within Indonesian society and beyond. Holding a prominent position in UIN Jakarta's Faculty of Social and Political Sciences, Professor Amalia has been pivotal in shaping the discourse on social justice and economic inclusivity from an Islamic perspective. Her research not only provides critical insights into the challenges faced by marginalized communities but also offers practical, faith-based solutions to address these issues, thereby bridging the gap between academic theory and societal needs. Professor Amalia's contributions to academia are not limited to her research; she is also a revered educator, mentor, and advocate for social change. Through her lectures, publications, and participation in national and international forums, she inspires students, scholars, and policymakers alike to engage in meaningful dialogues and actions that promote equity and compassion in accordance with Islamic teachings. Her leadership and dedication have established her as a respected voice in her field, making a lasting impact on the community and the next generation of social scientists.

Anis Malik Thoha (ORCID: 0000-0005-7456-7880 and GND: 1235728420) is currently an Associate Professor at the Faculty of Usuluddin and the Dean of the Faculty of Islamic Development Management, UNISSA, Brunei Darussalam. He served as the Rector of Universitas Islam Sultan Agung (Unissula) from 2014 to 2018, after holding various academic and administrative positions at the International Islamic University Malaysia (IIUM) from 2001 to 2014. He earned his bachelor's degree in 1988 from the Islamic University of Medina, KSA, a master’s degree in Islamic Studies from the University of the Punjab, Pakistan, in 1992, and another master’s degree in Comparative Religion from the International Islamic University Islamabad (IIUI), Pakistan, in 1994. He completed his PhD in Comparative Religion at IIUI in 2001. He is a co-founder of the Institute for the Study of Islamic Thought and Civilizations (INSISTS) in Jakarta and the Chief Editor of the International

Journal of Umranic Studies (IJUS). With a deep commitment to the exploration of Islamic theology, philosophy, comparative religion, religious pluralism, and interfaith dialogue, Thoha's academic career is characterized by diligent study of Islamic texts and an active interest in their application to contemporary issues. He has authored numerous articles and books, illuminating the complexities of Islamic thought and advocating for a dialogue that transcends cultural and religious barriers to foster peace and understanding among diverse communities. As a professor, Thoha has mentored countless students, enriching their understanding of Islamic tradition and its significance in the modern era. His work exemplifies the vital role of education in bridging religious misunderstandings and highlights the unifying potential of faith.

***

MohamedSyazwan Ab Talib's research and teaching focus primarily on logistics and supply chain management with the inclusion of halal principles and Islamic distribution. His research also encompasses the halal management standard that centred on the association between halal standard implementation and business performance. Syazwan welcomes industry consultation, research collaboration, and academic coaching opportunities for industry professionals and fellow academics.

Tri Cahyanto earned a Bachelor of Biology Education degree from Universitas Pasundan in 2004, followed by a Master of Science degree in Biology from the Bandung Institute of Technology (ITB) in 2007 and a Doctorate in Science Education from Universitas Pendidikan Indonesia in 2014. In 2012, he joined the faculty of UIN Sunan Gunung Djati Bandung as a lecturer. He currently serves as an Associate Professor in the Biology Department, Head of the Integrated Laboratory, and Head of the Halal Center at UIN Sunan Gunung Djati Bandung. His research focuses on applying biological research to halal literacy and halal product development, which he frequently publishes and presents in academic settings. Since 2017, he has been extensively involved in various halal-related activities, including halal journal management, education, research, and serving as a resource person in the field.

Afriansyah Fadillah holds a Bachelor's degree in Biology from UIN Sunan Gunung Djati Bandung and is currently pursuing a Master's degree in Biology at the Bandung Institute of Technology (ITB). His professional experience encompasses roles as an assistant lecturer and journal editor. Currently, he works as a Halal laboratory analyst and trainer, and also serves as a sample collector and Halal supervisor, demonstrating his expertise in both laboratory analysis and Halal certification processes. His publications cover topics such as ethnobotany and phytoremediation, reflecting his research contributions. He has also participated in extensive training programs related to Halal certification and laboratory techniques.

Lloyd D. Feliciano is an Assistant Professor at Don Honorio Ventura State University and a part-time lecturer at several institutions across Central Luzon. He has over 17 years of experience in hospitality and tourism, both in academia and industry. He earned his Master of Science in Hotel and Restaurant Management from Holy Angel University, where he was awarded Outstanding Hotel and Restaurant Management Student of the Year. He also completed doctoral-level coursework in Business Administration with a focus on Hospitality and Tourism Management. He holds multiple national certifications in culinary, food service, and tourism, and is an active member of various professional organizations locally and internationally. He is known for his engaging teaching style and strong commitment to student development and hospitality education in the Philippines.

Hairrudin Hairrudin is an Assistant Professor at the Department of Biochemistry, Faculty of Medicine, University of Jember, Indonesia. He holds a medical degree and advanced degrees in medical sciences. His academic and professional expertise focuses on biochemistry, with a particular emphasis on medical and health-related research. His research interests include clinical biochemistry, molecular mechanisms in health and disease, and biomedical innovations in healthcare. He is actively involved in teaching, research, and tutoring. His research aims to contribute to the advancement of medical knowledge and biochemistry to address medical and healthcare challenges.

Syahnur Farhana Haji Shahlehi earned her PhD in Economics, specialising in the Halal food industry and the internationalisation challenges and facilitators faced by small and medium-sized enterprises (SMEs). As an active research scholar, she continuously explores the intersection of agricultural landscapes with economic development and sustainability, aiming to uncover how this sector can drive positive change. Her research interests encompass the Halal food industry, internationalisation, and both home-based and social entrepreneurship within and beyond agriculture.

Hikmatul Hasanah lecturer at the Faculty of Islamic Economics and Business, Kiai Haji Achmad Siddiq Jember State Islamic University

Norkhairiah Hashim is a Senior Assistant Professor of Halal Science at the Halalan Thayyiban Research Centre, Universiti Islam Sultan Sharif Ali, Brunei Darussalam. She obtained a PhD in Islamic education from Universiti Brunei Darussalam. Her research interests include twenty-first-century skills teaching and learning, Islamic and halal education, contemporary issues on halal products and services and maqasid syariah in the halal industry. Her publications (as coauthor) include Halal Food Producer as an alternative employment job for halal science graduates in Brunei Darussalam. Journal of Halal Science and Technology 1(1) (2022); and, The awareness of Halal Green among postgraduate students in UNISSA for a sustainable campus. Journal of Halal Science and Technology 2(2) (2023).

Afiqah Amin is an assistant lecturer in Entrepreneurship at Universiti Brunei Darussalam. Her work has appeared in journals such as Journal of Marketing Communication, Journal of Management Development, Asia Pacific Journal of Public Administration and International Journal of Asian Business and Information Management. Her main research interest is in Strategic Management, but she is also active in conducting research activities in organizational behavior and consumer behavior.

Mohammad Mominul Islam is an Assistant Professor of Marketing, College of Business Administration at IUBAT— International University of Business Agriculture and Technology. He is also a PhD Candidate at the School of Business and Economics, Universiti Brunei Darussalam (UBD), under the prestigious Graduate Scholarship. He received an MBA and BBA in Marketing from Rajshahi University Bangladesh and an MSc in Business and Economics from Sweden. His research interests focus on Islamic marketing, Islamic entrepreneurship, Halal certification, Sustainable marketing, Halal cosmetics, Halal supply chain management, Spiritual tourism, and Marketing pedagogies. His scholarly works were published in the Journal of Islamic Marketing, International Journal of Islamic Accounting and Business Research, International Journal of Islamic Marketing and Branding, International Journal of Religious Tourism and Pilgrimage, Springer, Edward Elgar Publishers, USA, and IGI Global. He presented at six international conferences and nine seminars and workshops at home and abroad. Mohammad Mominul Islam received "The Bangladesh Education Leadership Awards 2017".

Yuni Kulsum is a biologist with a strong academic background and extensive research experience. She earned her Master's degree in Biology from Institut Teknologi Bandung (ITB) and her Bachelor's degree in Biology from UIN Sunan Gunung Djati Bandung. Her research and professional experience span various areas of biology, evidenced by her publications and numerous presentations at national and international conferences. Her professional roles have included positions as a laboratory analyst, assistant lecturer, and trainer. Ms. Kulsum has received various awards and scholarships, reflecting her academic achievements. She is actively involved in several organizations, demonstrating leadership and commitment to her field.

Khairunnisa Musari is an Assistant Professor at Faculty of Islamic Economics and Business (FEBI) & Postgraduate Program, Kiai Haji Achmad Siddiq State Islamic University (UIN KHAS), Jember, Indonesia. She is a Secretary of the Indonesian Association of Islamic Economists (IAEI) for the Provincial Board of East Java since 2017. Her research interests in sukuk, waqf, esham, fiscal & monetary policies, circular economy, halal logistics, sustainable finance, climate change, and Islamic microfinance & nanofinance. She has several book chapters with international reputable publishers such as IGI Global, Emerald Publishing Limited, World Scientific Publishing, Routledge, Springer, and Palgrave Macmillan. She has experience as a Senior Specialist for Islamic Finance of United Nations Development Programme (UNDP) Indonesia and was listed as one of the Top 300 Most Influential Women in Islamic Business & Finance 2019, 2020, 2021, WOMANi Significancica 2022, and WOMANi Academica 2023 by Cambridge-IFA.

Nurhayati earned her doctorate from the Bandung Institute of Technology (ITB) in 2021, specializing in the study of electron delocalization and aromaticity in porphyrins using advanced spectroscopic techniques such as fluorescence, Raman, and scanning tunneling microscopy. Her publications demonstrate expertise in applying spectroscopic methods to analyze porphyrin properties. Prior to her doctorate, she completed both her Master's and Bachelor's degrees in Chemistry at ITB. She currently serves as Technical Manager at the Halal Testing Laboratory, UIN Sunan Gunung Djati Bandung, in addition to other academic roles. Her frequent presentations at international conferences highlight her significant contributions to spectroscopic chemistry.

Siti Fatimahwati has been an Economics Lecturer at Universiti Brunei Darussalam School of Business Economics since 2008. She has a PhD in Agricultural Economics and Rural Development from Newcastle University, United Kingdom, 2016. Her research interest revolves around the issue of youth unemployment, youth aspirations, food security and natural resource economics.

Nor Surilawana Sulaiman is an Assistant Lecturer of Halal Management at the Halalan Thayyiban Research Centre, Universiti Islam Sultan Sharif Ali (UNISSA), Brunei Darussalam. She is also appointed as Skills Workshop Coordinator (Co-curricular) at the Centre for the Promotion of Knowledge and Language (CPKL), UNISSA, for the academic year 2024/2025. She holds a Master of Muamalat Administration (Halal Products) from Universiti Sains Islam Malaysia (USIM), Malaysia, and received the Dato' Dr Abdul Halim Special Award for academic excellence in the 13th Convocation Ceremony of USIM in 2015. She also went to the Halal Product Research Institute (HPRI), Universiti Putra Malaysia (UPM), Malaysia, in 2019 for the Student Mobility Programme. She is pursuing her PhD in Halal Science (Halal Management) at the Halalan Thayyiban Research Centre, UNISSA. Her research revolves around halal, halal certification, halal management, and the halal industry. Apart from research, she also has won several medals in innovation competitions nationally and internationally. In addition, she is also active in community service activities to enhance awareness regarding halalan thayyiban and food safety to the general public and young children and youth.

Nurul Aulia Tahta earned her Bachelor of Science degree in Biology from the Faculty of Science and Technology at Universitas Islam Negeri Sunan Gunung Djati in 2024. As a fresh graduate, she is deeply passionate about biological research and the advancement of life sciences. During her academic journey, she actively participated in national seminars and community service programs, enriching her knowledge and honing her social and professional skills. Equipped with technical proficiency in software such as SPSS, ImageJ, and Matlab, as well as design tools like Adobe Photoshop, Nurul demonstrates a strong foundation in both analysis and creativity. Her achievements include a bronze medal at the 2021 National Literacy Olympiad and third place in the Indonesian Science Olympiad. Committed to lifelong learning, she aims to make a meaningful impact in the fields of biology and applied technology.

Neneng Windayani earned her Bachelor's degree in Chemistry Education from IKIP Bandung in 1997, followed by a Master's degree in Science Education in 2005. She completed her doctoral studies in Chemistry at the Bandung Institute of Technology (ITB) in 2010. Currently, she is affiliated with UIN Sunan Gunung Djati Bandung as a faculty member in the Magister Science Education Program at the Graduate School. Her research interests are focused on natural product chemistry, functional food, and halal literacy. Over the years, she has actively contributed to innovation and intellectual property, holding six Indonesian simple patents (three granted and three registered). Dr. Winda is dedicated to fostering academic excellence and interdisciplinary research while addressing the global challenges in her fields of expertise.

Muhamad Yusup is a lecturer in Islamic Economics with a concentration in Islamic Financial Management at the Faculty of Islamic Economics and Business, State Islamic University of Mataram, Indonesia. He earned his Master's degree in Islamic Studies with a concentration in Muamalah from Sunan Kalijaga State Islamic University Yogyakarta, Indonesia, in 2005, and obtained his Doctorate in

Islamic Studies with a concentration in Islamic Finance from Sunan Ampel State Islamic University Surabaya, Indonesia, in 2018. His research focuses on Islamic Economics, Islamic Banking, and Islamic Financial Management.

Index

H

I

L

M

N

P

R

S

T

V

www.ingramcontent.com/pod-product-compliance
Lightning Source LLC
LaVergne TN
LVHW080343011026
849161LV00009B/2176